Yamaha MT-125, YZF-R125 & WR125R & X

Service and Repair Manual

by Matthew Coombs

(6009-288)

Models covered

WR125R	124.7cc	2009 to 2015
WR125X	124.7cc	2009 to 2015
MT-125	124.7cc	2015
MT-125A	124.7cc	2015
YZF-R125	124.7cc	2014 to 2015
YZF-R125A	124.7cc	2015

ABCDE
FGHIJ
KLMNO
PQRST

A book in the Haynes Service and Repair Manual Series

ISBN: **978 1 78521 009 9**

British Library Cataloguing in Publication Data
A catalogue record for this book is available from the British Library.

Printed in the USA

Haynes Publishing
Sparkford, Yeovil, Somerset BA22 7JJ, England

Haynes North America, Inc
861 Lawrence Drive, Newbury Park, California 91320, USA

Haynes Publishing Nordiska AB
Box 1504, 751 45 Uppsala, Sweden

Printed using 33-lb Resolute Book 65 4.0 from Resolute Forest Products Calhoun, TN mill. Resolute is a member of World Wildlife Fund's Climate Savers programme committed to significantly reducing GHG emissions. This paper uses 50% less wood fibre than traditional offset. The Calhoun Mill is certified to the following sustainable forest management and chain of custody standards: SFI, PEFC and FSC Controlled Wood.

Contents

Contents

Yamaha
Musical instruments to motorcycles

The FS1E –
first bike of many sixteen year olds in the UK

The Yamaha Motor Company

The Yamaha name can be traced back to 1889, when Torakusu Yamaha founded the Yamaha Organ Manufacturing Company. Such was the success of the company, that in 1897 it became Nippon Gakki Limited and manufactured a wide range of reed organs and pianos.

During World War II, Nippon Gakki's manufacturing base was utilised by the Japanese authorities to produce propellers and fuel tanks for their aviation industry. The end of the war brought about a huge public demand for low cost transport and many firms decided to utilise their obsolete aircraft tooling for the production of motorcycles. Nippon Gakki's first motorcycle went on sale in February 1955 and was named the 125 YA-1 Red Dragonfly. This machine was a copy of the German DKW RT125 motorcycle, featuring a single cylinder two-stroke engine with a four-speed gearbox. Due to the outstanding success of this model the motorcycle operation was separated from Nippon Gakki in July 1955 and the Yamaha Motor Company was formed.

The YA-1 also received acclaim by winning two of Japan's biggest road races, the Mount Fuji Climbing race and the Asama Volcano race. The high level of public demand for the YA-1 led to the development of a whole series of two-stroke singles and twins.

Having made a large impact on their home market, Yamahas were exported to the USA in 1958 and to the UK in 1962. In the UK the signing of an Anglo-Japanese trade agreement during 1962 enabled the sale of Japanese lightweight motorcycles and scooters in Britain. At that time, competition between the many motorcycle producers in Japan had reduced numbers significantly and by the end of the sixties, only the big-four which are familiar with today remained.

Yamaha Europe was founded in 1968 and based in Holland. Although originally set up to market marine products, the Dutch base is now the official European Headquarters and distribution centre. Yamaha motorcycles are built at factories in Holland, Denmark, Norway, Italy, France, Spain and Portugal. Yamahas are imported into the UK by Yamaha Motor UK Ltd, formerly Mitsui Machinery Sales (UK) Ltd. Mitsui and Co. were originally a trading house, handling the shipping, distribution and marketing of Japanese products into western countries. Ultimately Mitsui Machinery Sales was formed to handle Yamaha motorcycles and outboard motors.

Based on the technology derived from its motorcycle operation, Yamaha have produced many other products, such as automobile and lightweight aircraft engines, marine engines and boats, generators, pumps, ATVs, snowmobiles, golf cars, industrial robots, lawnmowers, swimming pools and archery equipment.

Two-strokes first

Part of Yamaha's success was a whole string of innovations in the two-stroke world. Autolube engine lubrication, torque induction, multi-ported engines, reed valves and power valves kept their two-strokes at the forefront of technology. Many advances were achieved with the use of racing as a development laboratory. They went to the USA in the late 1950s with an air-cooled 250cc twin but didn't hit the GPs until the early 1960s when Fumio Ito scored a hat-trick of sixth places in the Isle of Man TT, the Dutch TT and the Belgian GP. This experiment gave rise to the idea of the over-the-counter racer, an idea that became reality in the TD1, the first in an unmatched series of two-stroke racers that were the standard issue for privateers at national and international level for years and helped Yamaha develop their road engines. While privateers raced the twins, Yamaha built the outrageously complicated vee-four 250 for Phil Read and followed it with a vee-four 125 that Bill Ivy lapped the Isle of Man on at over 100mph! When the FIM regulations were changed to limit the smaller GP classes to two cylinders, these exotic bikes died but set the scene for an unparalleled dynasty of mass-produced racers based on the same technology as the road bikes.

In the 1960s and 70s the two-stroke engined YAS3 125, YDS1 to YDS7 250 and YR5 350 formed the core of Yamaha's range. By the mid-70s they had been superseded by the RD (Race-Developed) 125, 250, and 350 range of two-stroke twins, featuring improved 7-port engines with reed valve induction. Braking was improved by the use of an hydraulic brake on the front wheel of DX models, instead of the drum arrangement used previously, and cast alloy wheels were available as an option on later RD models. The RD350 was replaced by the RD400 in 1976.

Running parallel with the RD twins was a range of single-cylinder two-strokes. Used in a variety of chassis types, the engine was used in the popular 50 cc FS1-E moped, the V50 to 90 step-thrus, RS100 and 125, YB100 and the DT trail range.

The TD racers got water-cooling in 1973 to become the TZs, the most successful and numerous over-the-counter racers ever built. That same year, Jarno Saarinen became the first rider to win a 500cc GP on a four-cylinder two-stroke on the new in-line four which was effectively a pair of TZs side-by-side. TZs won everywhere – including the Daytona 200 and 500 races when overbored to 351cc. A 700cc TZ also appeared, one year later taken out to 750cc. Steve Baker won the first Formula 750 world title – one of the precursors of Superbike – on one in 1977. The following year Kenny Roberts won Yamaha's first world 500 title and would be succeeded by Wayne Rainey and Eddie Lawson before Mick Doohan and the NSR500 took over.

The air-cooled single and twin cylinder RD road bikes were eventually replaced by the LC series in 1980, featuring liquid-cooled engines, radical new styling, spiral pattern cast wheels and cantilever rear suspension (Yamaha's Monoshock). Of all the LC models, the RD350LC, or RD350R as it was later known, has made the most impact in the market. Later models had YPVS (Yamaha Power Valve System) engines, another first for Yamaha – this was essentially a valve located in the exhaust ports which was electronically operated to alter port timing to achieve maximum power output. The RD500LC was the largest two-stroke made by Yamaha and differed from the other LCs by the use of its vee-four cylinder engine.

The Four-strokes

Yamaha concentrated solely on two-stroke models until 1970 when the XS1 was produced, their first four-stroke motorcycle. It was perhaps Yamaha's success with two-strokes that postponed an earlier move into the four-stroke motorcycle market, although their work with Toyota during the 1960s had given them a sound base in four-stroke technology.

The XS1 had a 650 cc twin-cylinder SOHC engine and was later to become known as the XS650, appearing also in the popular SE custom form. Yamaha introduced a three

The distinctive paintwork and trim of the RD models

cylinder 750 cc engine in 1976, fitted in a sport-tourer frame and called the XS750, TX750 in the USA. The XS750 established itself well in the sport tourer class and remained in production with very few changes until uprated to 850 cc in 1980.

Other four-strokes followed in 1976, with the introduction of the XS250/360/400 series twins. The XS range was strengthened in 1978 by the four-cylinder XS1100.

The 1980s saw a new family of four-strokes, the XJ550, 650, 750 and 900 Fours. Improvements over the XS range amounted to a slimmer DOHC engine unit due to the relocation of the alternator behind the cylinders, electronic ignition and uprated braking and suspension systems. Models were available mainly in standard trim, although custom-styled Maxims were produced especially for the US market. They were the basis of the XJ600S and XJ900S Diversion (Seca II) roadster models.

The FZR prefix encompasses the pure sports Yamaha models. With the exception of the 16-valve FZR400 and FZR600 models, the FZ/FZR750 and FZR1000 used 20-valve engines, two exhaust valves and three inlet valves per cylinder. This concept was called Genesis and gave improved gas flow to the combustion chambers. Other features of the new engine were the use of down-draught carburetors and the engine's inclined angle in the frame, plus the change to liquid-cooling. Lightweight Deltabox design aluminium frames and uprated suspension improved the bikes's handling. The Genesis engine concept powered the the YZF750 and 1000 models.

The Genesis concept was the basis of Yamaha's foray into four-stroke racing, first with a bike known simply as 'The Genesis', an FZ750 motor in a TT Formula 1 bike with which the factory attempted to steal the Honda RVF750's thunder at important events like the Suzuka 8 Hours and the Bol d'Or although they never fielded it for a whole World Championship season. That had to wait for the advent of the World Superbike Championship, although there was no full

The XS650 led the way for Yamaha's four-stroke range

Yamaha's XS750 was produced from 1976 to 1982 and then uprated to 850 cc

works team until 1995, instead it was left to individual importers to support teams. It was the Australian Dealer Team Yamaha which scored the factory's first World Superbike win in the series debut year of 1988. The rider? Mick Doohan. The championship had to wait until 2009 for Ben Spies and the R1.

Away from the sports bike market, the vee-twin engine has been the mainstay of the XV range of factory customs since 1981. XVs have been produced in 535, 700, 750, 920, 1000, 1100 and 1600cc engine sizes. Other uses of vee engines have been in the XZ550 of the early 1980s, the XVZ12 Venture and the mighty VMX-12 V-Max. In the mid—'90s, the company gave the custom and cruiser range their own identity under the Star name in the USA, later spinning off the brand into a standalone company althought he bikes are still sold in Yamaha showrooms.

Yamaha has always been a sporting-orientated company whose motto could be 'Racing Improves the Breed', so it's no surprise that the latest generation of lightweight sportsters are at the cutting edge of performance on and off the track. The R6 won more races than any other machine in the inaugural year of the World Supersports Championship, the R7 won a race in its debut year in World Superbike in the hands of the mercurial Noriyuki Haga, and the mighty 1000cc R1 ended Honda's domination of the Isle of Man F1 TT when David Jefferies won three races in a week in 1999. It also bought

A new family of four-strokes was released in 1980 with the introduction of the XJ range

Yamaha the World Superbike Championship. Yamaha's last two-stroke hurrah came in the 2000 250cc GPs when Olivier Jacques became world champion. When MotoGP abandoned two strokes in 2002, Yamaha fielded the first M-1, with an engine using the same principles as the original Genesis. It took two wins in the first year thanks to Max Biaggi, but the second year was a disaster in which the bike only scored one rostrum finish, and that was a third place.

Yamaha took drastic action. Valentino Rossi, unsettled at Honda, was recruited with Masao Furusawa leading for the factory.

The 2015 MT125

The 2015 YZF-125R

Back-to-back testing of several engines saw Rossi pick Furusawa's cross-plane crank, win the first GP of the year in South Africa, and go on to take the title. It was one of the most astonishing achievements of recent years, one that almost no-one gave him a chance of. Rossi and Furusawa then rubbed it in, retaining the title in 2005 and then regaining it in 2008 before winning again in '09. When Valentino was injured, Jorge Lorenzo took over then won again in '12 – six titles for Yamaha in eight years.

There was also a quiet revolution in the road bike market. Yamaha came up with a new concept in response to the recession and the shrinking of the sports bike market, the MT range; Twins and triples as affordable and fun as the old LC two strokes. Times have been tough, but Yamaha have boxed clever – not least in ensuring that as and when Valentino Rossi retires he will be remembered as a Yamaha champion.

The WR125R

The WR125X

Acknowledgements

Our thanks are due to Hayball Motorcycles of Salisbury and Bransons Motorcycles of Yeovil who supplied the machines featured in the illustrations throughout this manual. We would also like to thank NGK Spark Plugs (UK) Ltd for supplying the colour spark plug condition photographs, the Avon Rubber Company for supplying information on tyre fitting and Draper Tools Ltd for some of the workshop tools shown.

Thanks are also due to Julian Ryder who wrote the introduction 'Yamaha – musical instruments to motorcycles', and to Yamaha (UK) Ltd. who supplied model photographs.

About this Manual

The aim of this manual is to help you get the best value from your motorcycle. It can do so in several ways. It can help you decide what work must be done, even if you choose to have it done by a dealer; it provides information and procedures for routine maintenance and servicing; and it offers diagnostic and repair procedures to follow when trouble occurs.

We hope you use the manual to tackle the work yourself. For many simpler jobs, doing it yourself may be quicker than arranging an appointment to get the motorcycle into a dealer and making the trips to leave it and pick it up. More importantly, a lot of money can be saved by avoiding the expense the shop must pass on to you to cover its labour and overhead costs. An added benefit is the sense of satisfaction and accomplishment that you feel after doing the job yourself.

References to the left or right side of the motorcycle assume you are sitting on the seat, facing forward.

We take great pride in the accuracy of information given in this manual, but motorcycle manufacturers make alterations and design changes during the production run of a particular motorcycle of which they do not inform us. No liability can be accepted by the authors or publishers for loss, damage or injury caused by any errors in, or omissions from, the information given.

Frame and engine numbers

The frame serial number is stamped into the right-hand side of the steering head. The engine number is stamped into the left-hand side of the crankcase below the alternator cover. Both of these numbers should be recorded and kept in a safe place so they can be given to law enforcement officials in the event of a theft. There is also a model code label under the seat. The throttle body has an ID number stamped into its body.

The frame serial number, engine serial number, and colour code should also be kept in a handy place (such as with your driver's licence) so they are always available when purchasing or ordering parts for your machine.

The procedures in this manual use the model name, and if necessary the model year of production (which can be determined by matching the model code, marked on the label under the seat, to its year of production as listed in the table below) to identify any differences between the various models.

Model name	Model code	Production year
WR125R	22B1	2009
WR125R	22B3	2010
WR125R	22B5	2011/12
WR125R	22B7	2013
WR125R	22BB	2014
WR125X	22B2	2009
WR125X	22B4	2010
WR125X	22B6	2011/12
WR125X	22B8	2013
WR125X	22BC	2014
MT125	5D7C, 5D7L	2015
MT125A	5D7D, 5D7M	2015
YZF-R125	5D78, 5D7K	2014
YZF-R125	5D7P, 5D7R	2015
YZF-R125A	5D7E, 5D7N	2015

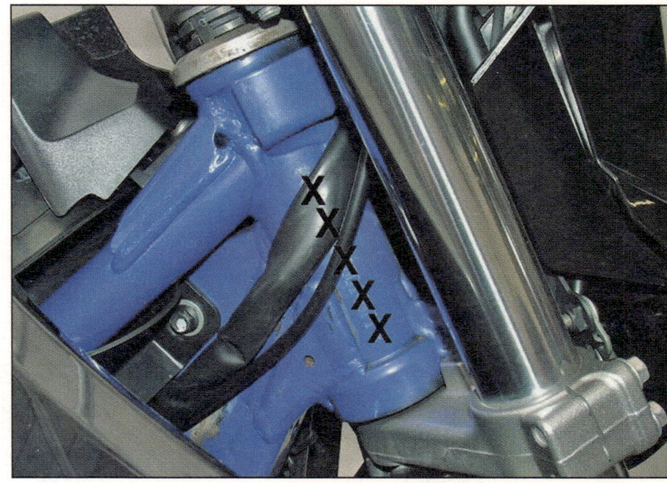

The frame number is stamped into the right-hand side of the steering head

The engine number is stamped on the left-hand side of the crankcase below the alternator cover

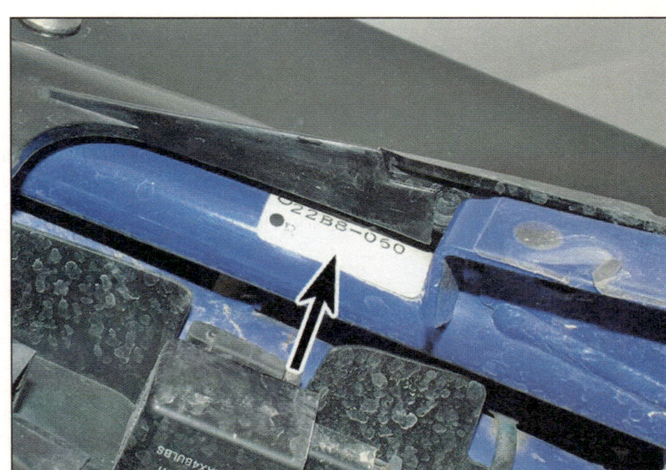

The model code label (arrowed) is under the rider's seat

Buying spare parts

Once you have found all the identification numbers, record them for reference when buying parts. Since the manufacturers change specifications, parts and vendors (companies that manufacture various components on the machine), providing the ID numbers is the only way to be reasonably sure that you are buying the correct parts.

Whenever possible, take the worn part to the dealer so direct comparison with the new component can be made. Along the path from the manufacturer to the parts shelf, there are numerous places that the part can end up with the wrong number or be listed incorrectly.

The two places to purchase new parts for your motorcycle – the franchised or main dealer and the parts/accessories store – differ in the type of parts they carry. While dealers can obtain every single genuine part for your motorcycle, the accessory store is usually limited to normal high wear items such as chains and sprockets, brake pads, spark plugs and tune-up parts.

Used parts can be obtained from breakers yards for roughly half the price of new ones, but you can't always be sure of what you're getting. Once again, take your worn part to the breaker for direct comparison, or when ordering by mail order make sure that you can return it if you are not happy.

Whether buying new, used or rebuilt parts, the best course is to deal directly with someone who specialises in your particular make.

Safety First!

Professional mechanics are trained in safe working procedures. However enthusiastic you may be about getting on with the job at hand, take the time to ensure that your safety is not put at risk. A moment's lack of attention can result in an accident, as can failure to observe simple precautions.

There will always be new ways of having accidents, and the following is not a comprehensive list of all dangers; it is intended rather to make you aware of the risks and to encourage a safe approach to all work you carry out on your bike.

Asbestos

- Certain friction, insulating, sealing and other products - such as brake pads, clutch linings, gaskets, etc. - contain asbestos. Extreme care must be taken to avoid inhalation of dust from such products since it is hazardous to health. If in doubt, assume that they do contain asbestos.

Fire

- Remember at all times that petrol is highly flammable. Never smoke or have any kind of naked flame around, when working on the vehicle. But the risk does not end there - a spark caused by an electrical short-circuit, by two metal surfaces contacting each other, by careless use of tools, or even by static electricity built up in your body under certain conditions, can ignite petrol vapour, which in a confined space is highly explosive. Never use petrol as a cleaning solvent. Use an approved safety solvent.
- Always disconnect the battery earth terminal before working on any part of the fuel or electrical system, and never risk spilling fuel on to a hot engine or exhaust.
- It is recommended that a fire extinguisher of a type suitable for fuel and electrical fires is kept handy in the garage or workplace at all times. Never try to extinguish a fuel or electrical fire with water.

Fumes

- Certain fumes are highly toxic and can quickly cause unconsciousness and even death if inhaled to any extent. Petrol vapour comes into this category, as do the vapours from certain solvents such as trichloro-ethylene. Any draining or pouring of such volatile fluids should be done in a well ventilated area.
- When using cleaning fluids and solvents, read the instructions carefully. Never use materials from unmarked containers - they may give off poisonous vapours.
- Never run the engine of a motor vehicle in an enclosed space such as a garage. Exhaust fumes contain carbon monoxide which is extremely poisonous; if you need to run the engine, always do so in the open air or at least have the rear of the vehicle outside the workplace.

The battery

- Never cause a spark, or allow a naked light near the vehicle's battery. It will normally be giving off a certain amount of hydrogen gas, which is highly explosive.
- Always disconnect the battery ground (earth) terminal before working on the fuel or electrical systems (except where noted).
- If possible, loosen the filler plugs or cover when charging the battery from an external source. Do not charge at an excessive rate or the battery may burst.
- Take care when topping up, cleaning or carrying the battery. The acid electrolyte, evenwhen diluted, is very corrosive and should not be allowed to contact the eyes or skin. Always wear rubber gloves and goggles or a face shield. If you ever need to prepare electrolyte yourself, always add the acid slowly to the water; never add the water to the acid.

Electricity

- When using an electric power tool, inspection light etc., always ensure that the appliance is correctly connected to its plug and that, where necessary, it is properly grounded (earthed). Do not use such appliances in damp conditions and, again, beware of creating a spark or applying excessive heat in the vicinity of fuel or fuel vapour. Also ensure that the appliances meet national safety standards.
- A severe electric shock can result from touching certain parts of the electrical system, such as the spark plug wires (HT leads), when the engine is running or being cranked, particularly if components are damp or the insulation is defective. Where an electronic ignition system is used, the secondary (HT) voltage is much higher and could prove fatal.

Remember...

✗ **Don't** start the engine without first ascer-taining that the transmission is in neutral.

✗ **Don't** suddenly remove the pressure cap from a hot cooling system - cover it with a cloth and release the pressure gradually first, or you may get scalded by escaping coolant.

✗ **Don't** attempt to drain oil until you are sure it has cooled sufficiently to avoid scalding you.

✗ **Don't** grasp any part of the engine or exhaust system without first ascertaining that it is cool enough not to burn you.

✗ **Don't** allow brake fluid or antifreeze to contact the machine's paintwork or plastic components.

✗ **Don't** siphon toxic liquids such as fuel, hydraulic fluid or antifreeze by mouth, or allow them to remain on your skin.

✗ **Don't** inhale dust - it may be injurious to health (see Asbestos heading).

✗ **Don't** allow any spilled oil or grease to remain on the floor - wipe it up right away, before someone slips on it.

✗ **Don't** use ill-fitting spanners or other tools which may slip and cause injury.

✗ **Don't** lift a heavy component which may be beyond your capability - get assistance.

✗ **Don't** rush to finish a job or take unverified short cuts.

✗ **Don't** allow children or animals in or around an unattended vehicle.

✗ **Don't** inflate a tyre above the recommended pressure. Apart from overstressing the carcass, in extreme cases the tyre may blow off forcibly.

✓ **Do** ensure that the machine is supported securely at all times. This is especially important when the machine is blocked up to aid wheel or fork removal.

✓ **Do** take care when attempting to loosen a stubborn nut or bolt. It is generally better to pull on a spanner, rather than push, so that if you slip, you fall away from the machine rather than onto it.

✓ **Do** wear eye protection when using power tools such as drill, sander, bench grinder etc.

✓ **Do** use a barrier cream on your hands prior to undertaking dirty jobs - it will protect your skin from infection as well as making the dirt easier to remove afterwards; but make sure your hands aren't left slippery. Note that long-term contact with used engine oil can be a health hazard.

✓ **Do** keep loose clothing (cuffs, ties etc. and long hair) well out of the way of moving mechanical parts.

✓ **Do** remove rings, wristwatch etc., before working on the vehicle - especially the electrical system.

✓ **Do** keep your work area tidy - it is only too easy to fall over articles left lying around.

✓ **Do** exercise caution when compressing springs for removal or installation. Ensure that the tension is applied and released in a controlled manner, using suitable tools which preclude the possibility of the spring escaping violently.

✓ **Do** ensure that any lifting tackle used has a safe working load rating adequate for the job.

✓ **Do** get someone to check periodically that all is well, when working alone on the vehicle.

✓ **Do** carry out work in a logical sequence and check that everything is correctly assembled and tightened afterwards.

✓ **Do** remember that your vehicle's safety affects that of yourself and others. If in doubt on any point, get professional advice.

- If in spite of following these precautions, you are unfortunate enough to injure yourself, seek medical attention as soon as possible.

Engine oil level

Before you start:

✔ Support the motorcycle upright on level ground.

✔ Start the engine and let it warm up for several minutes, then turn it off.

Caution: Do not run the engine in an enclosed space such as a garage or workshop.

✔ Allow it to stand for a few minutes for the oil level to stabilise.

Bike care:

● If you have to add oil frequently, check the engine joints, oil seals and gaskets for oil leakage. If not, the engine could be burning oil, in which case there will be white smoke coming out of the exhaust (see *Fault Finding*).

The correct oil:

● Modern, high-revving engines place great demands on their oil. It is very important that the correct oil for your bike is used.

● Always top up with a good quality motorcycle oil of the specified type and viscosity and do not overfill the engine. Do not use engine oil designed for car use.

Oil type	API grade SG or higher
Oil viscosity	SAE 10W30 or 10W40

Caution: Do not use chemical additives or oils graded CD or higher or labelled 'ENERGY CONSERVING' – such additives or oils could cause clutch slip.

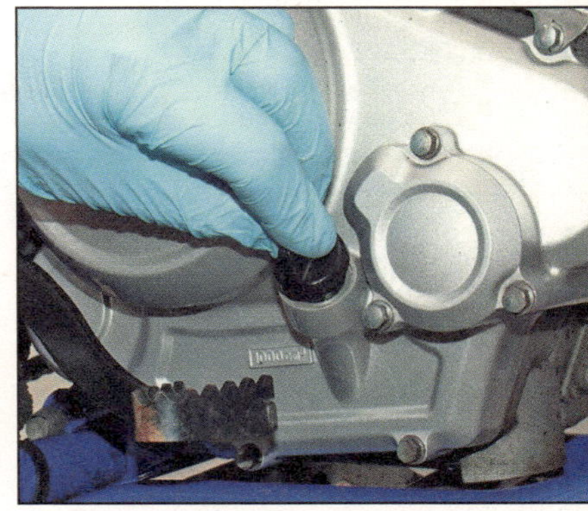

1 The oil level dipstick is incorporated with the oil filler cap, and is on the right-hand side of the engine. Unscrew the cap...

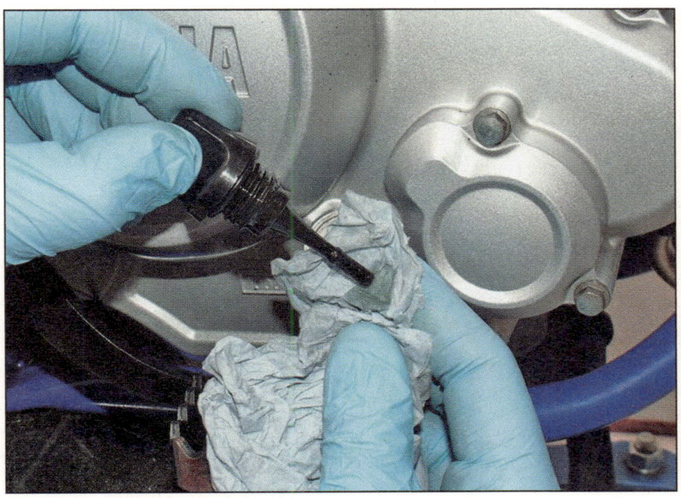

2 ... and wipe the dipstick clean.

3 Insert the dipstick so that the cap threads rest on the engine, but do not screw it in.

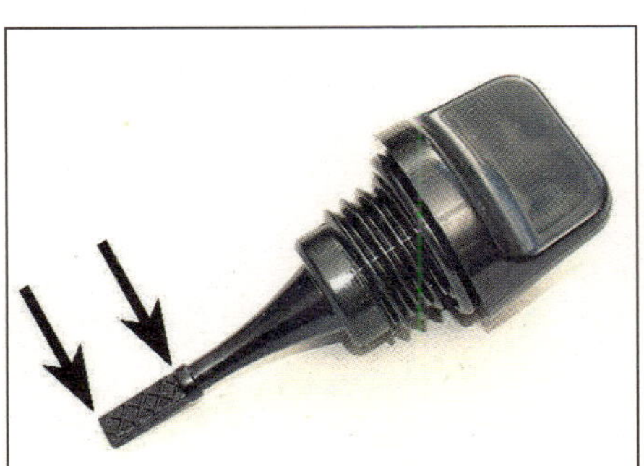

4 Remove the dipstick and check the oil mark – it should lie between the upper and lower level lines (arrowed), i.e. within the hatched area.

5 If the level is on or below the lower line, top up the engine with the recommended grade and type of oil to bring the level almost up to the upper line. Do not overfill.

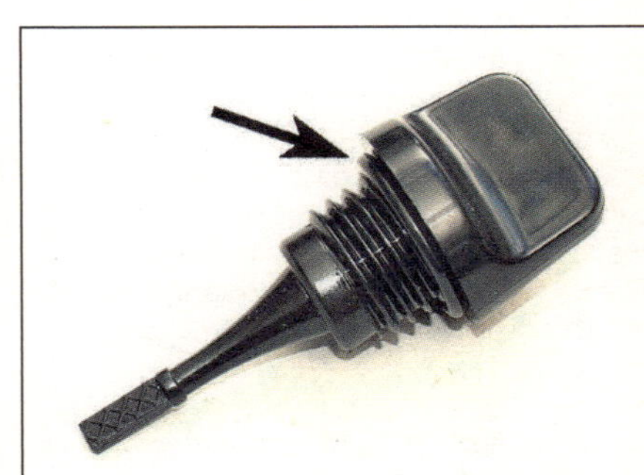

6 On completion, make sure the O-ring (arrowed) on the underside of the cap is in good condition and properly seated. Fit a new one if necessary. Wipe it clean and smear new oil onto it. Fit the cap, making sure it is secure. Run the engine for a few minutes, then turn it off and wait a few minutes, then re-check the level.

Coolant level

> ***Warning:*** ***DO NOT remove the radiator pressure cap to add coolant. Topping up is done via the coolant reservoir tank filler. DO NOT leave open containers of coolant about, as it is poisonous.***

Before you start:

✔ Make sure you have a supply of coolant available – a mixture of 50% distilled water and 50% corrosion inhibited ethylene glycol anti-freeze is needed, and is readily available pre-mixed from dealers.

✔ Always check the coolant level when the engine is cold.

✔ Support the motorcycle upright on level ground.

✔ On WR models the coolant reservoir is located behind the left-hand side cover – the level lines are visible without removing any bodywork.

✔ On MT and YZF-R models the coolant reservoir is located on the left-hand side of the engine at the front – the level lines are visible without removing any bodywork.

Bike care:

● Use only the specified coolant mixture. It is important that the correct proportion of anti-freeze is used in the system all year round, and not just in the winter. Do not top the system up using only water, as the system will become too diluted.

● Do not overfill the reservoir tank. If the coolant is significantly above the FULL level line at any time, the surplus should be siphoned or drained off to prevent the possibility of it being expelled out of the overflow hose.

● If the coolant level falls steadily, check the system for leaks (see Chapter 1). If no leaks are found and the level continues to fall, it is recommended that the machine is taken to a Yamaha dealer for a pressure test.

WR models

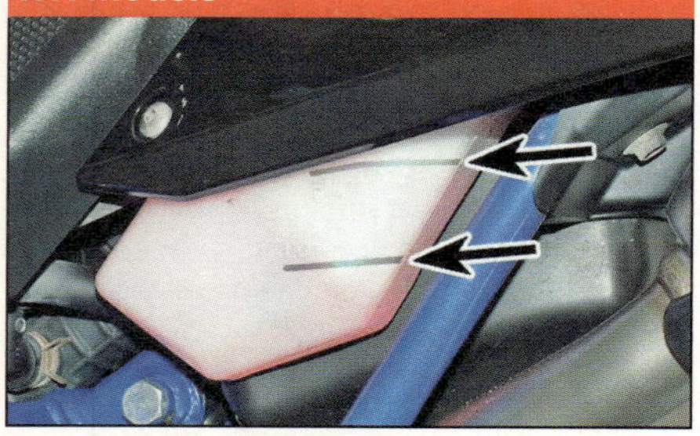

1 The coolant level should lie between the FULL and LOW level lines (arrowed) that are marked on the reservoir.

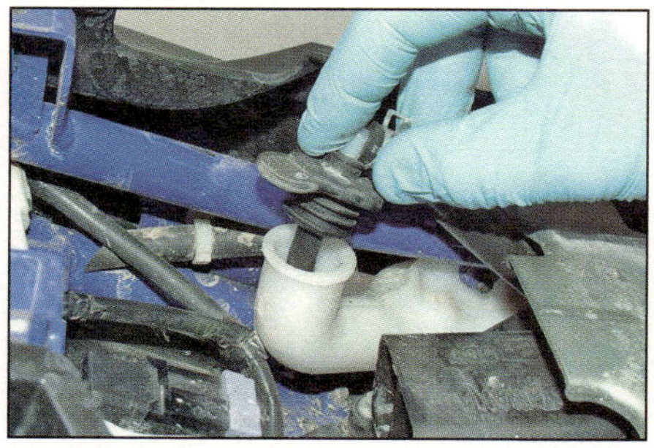

2 If the coolant level is on or below the MIN line, remove the seat (see Chapter 7). Release the reservoir filler cap and hold it aside.

3 Top the reservoir up with the recommended coolant mixture to the MAX level line, using a suitable funnel if required. Fit the cap. Install the seat

MT models

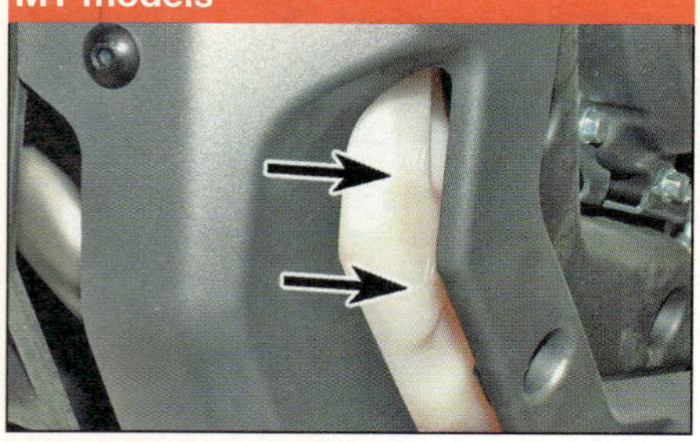

1 The coolant level should lie between the FULL and LOW level lines (arrowed) that are marked on the reservoir.

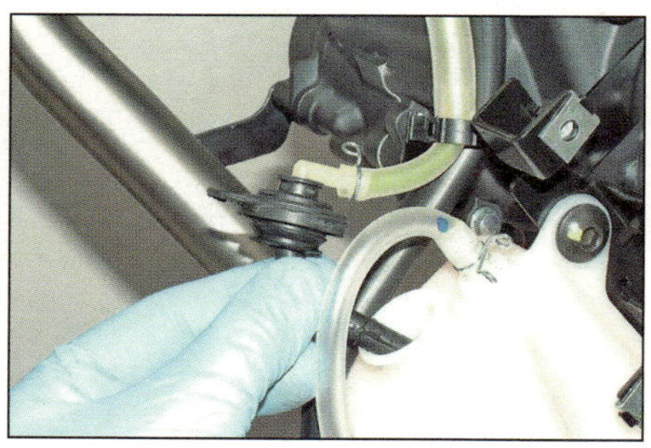

2 If the coolant level is on or below the LOW line, remove the belly-pan (see Chapter 7). Release the reservoir filler cap and hold it aside.

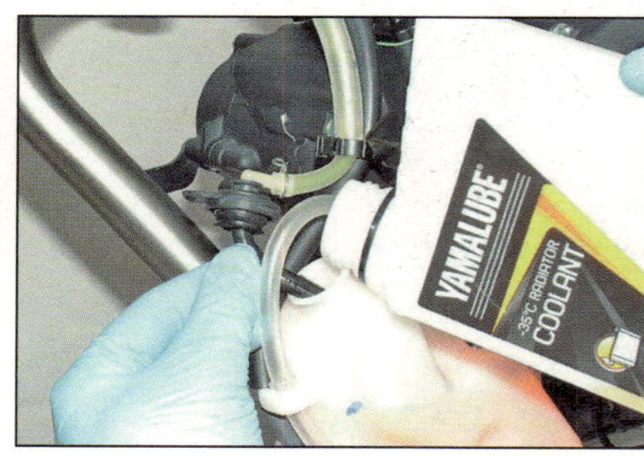

3 Top the reservoir up with the recommended coolant mixture to the FULL level line, using a suitable funnel if required. Fit the cap. Install the belly-pan.

YZF-R models

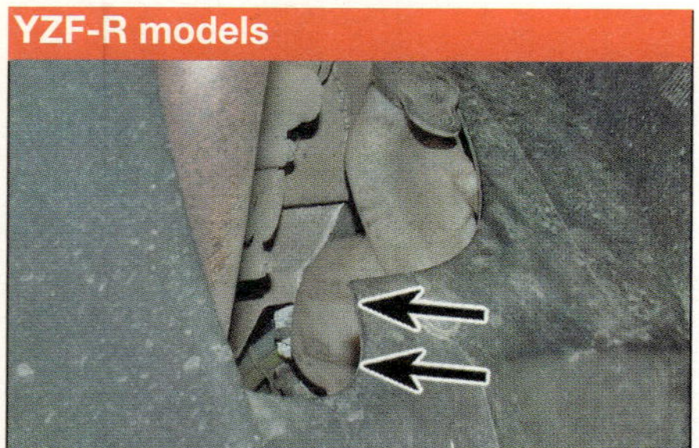

1 The coolant level should lie between the FULL and LOW level lines (arrowed) that are marked on the reservoir.

2 If the coolant level is on or below the LOW line, remove the fairing panel (see Chapter 7). Release the reservoir filler cap and hold it aside.

3 Top the reservoir up with the recommended coolant mixture to the FULL level line, using a suitable funnel if required. Fit the cap. Install the fairing panel.

Tyres

Tyre tread depth:

● At the time of writing UK law requires that tread depth must be at least 1 mm over 3/4 of the tread breadth all the way around the tyre, with no bald patches. Many riders, however, consider 2 mm tread depth minimum to be a safer limit. Yamaha recommend a minimum of 1.6 mm. Refer to the tyre tread legislation in your country.

● Many tyres now incorporate wear indicators in the tread. Identify the location marking on the tyre sidewall to locate the indicator bar and replace the tyre if the tread has worn down to the bar.

The correct pressures:

● The tyres must be checked when cold, not immediately after riding because the pressure will increase when the tyres are warm. Note that incorrect tyre pressures will cause abnormal tread wear and unsafe handling. Low tyre pressures may cause the tyre to slip on the rim or come off.

● Use an accurate pressure gauge. Many forecourt gauges are wildly inaccurate. If you buy your own, spend as much as you can justify on a quality gauge.

● Proper air pressure will increase tyre life and provide maximum stability and ride comfort.

Loading	Front	Rear
WR models		
Rider only (or total load up to 90kg /198lb)	29 psi (2.0 Bar)	29 psi (2.0 Bar)
Rider and pillion (or total load over 90kg /198lb up to max load)	29 psi (2.0 Bar)	33 psi (2.25 Bar)
MT and YZF-R models		
Rider only (or total load up to 90kg /198lb)	26.psi (1.8 Bar)	29 psi (2.0 Bar)
Rider and pillion (or total load over 90kg /198lb up to max load)	26 psi (1.8 Bar)	33 psi (2.25 Bar)

Tyre care:

● Check the tyres carefully for cuts, tears, embedded nails or other sharp objects, and excessive wear. Riding a motorcycle with excessively worn tyres is extremely hazardous, as traction and handling are directly affected.

● Check the condition of the tyre valve and ensure the dust cap is in place.

● Pick out any stones or nails which may have become embedded in the tyre tread. If left, they will eventually penetrate through the casing and cause a puncture.

● If tyre damage is apparent, or unexplained loss of pressure is experienced, seek the advice of a tyre fitting specialist without delay.

1 Remove the dust cap from the valve and do not forget to fit it after checking the pressure.

2 Check the tyre pressures when the tyres are cold.

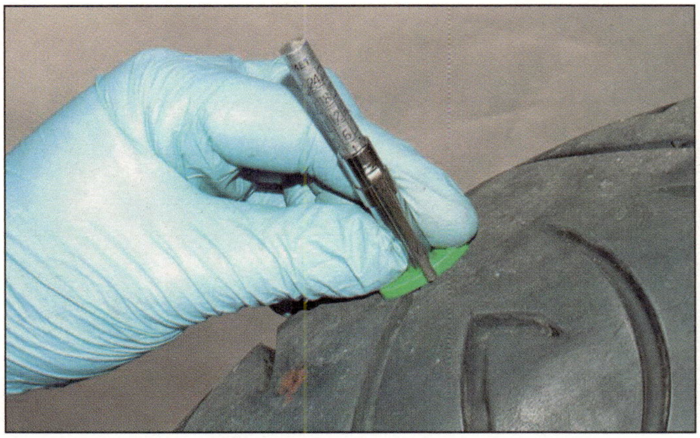

3 Measure tread depth at the centre of the tyre using a depth gauge.

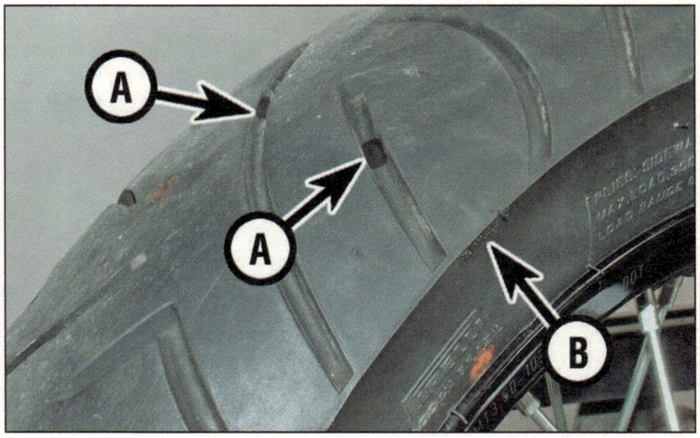

4 Tyre tread wear indicators (A) and their location marking (B) on the edge or sidewall (according to manufacturer).

Brake fluid levels

> **Warning:** ***Brake hydraulic fluid can harm your eyes and damage painted surfaces, so use extreme caution when handling and pouring it and cover surrounding surfaces with rag. Do not use fluid that has been standing open for some time, as it is hygroscopic (absorbs moisture from the air) which can cause a dangerous loss of braking effectiveness.***

Before you start:

✔ The front brake fluid reservoir is on the right-hand handlebar.

✔ The rear brake fluid reservoir is on the right-hand side.

✔ If topping up is required make sure you have the correct hydraulic fluid. DOT 4 is recommended.

✔ Wrap a rag around the reservoir to ensure that any spillage does not come into contact with painted surfaces.

Bike care:

● The fluid in each reservoir will drop as the brake pads wear down. If the fluid level is low check the brake pads for wear (see Chapter 1), and replace them with new ones if necessary (see Chapter 6). Do not top the reservoir(s) up until the new pads have been fitted, and then check to see if topping up is still necessary – when the caliper pistons are pushed back to accommodate the extra thickness of the pads some fluid will be displaced back into the reservoir.

● If either fluid reservoir requires repeated topping-up there is a leak somewhere in the system, which must be investigated immediately.

● Check for signs of fluid leakage from the hydraulic hoses and/or brake system components – if found, rectify immediately (see Chapter 6).

● Check the operation of both brakes before taking the machine on the road; if there is evidence of air in the system (spongy feel to lever or pedal), it must be bled (see Chapter 6).

FRONT BRAKE

1 Set the handlebars so the reservoir is level and check the fluid level through the window in the side of the reservoir body – it must be above the MIN level line (arrowed).

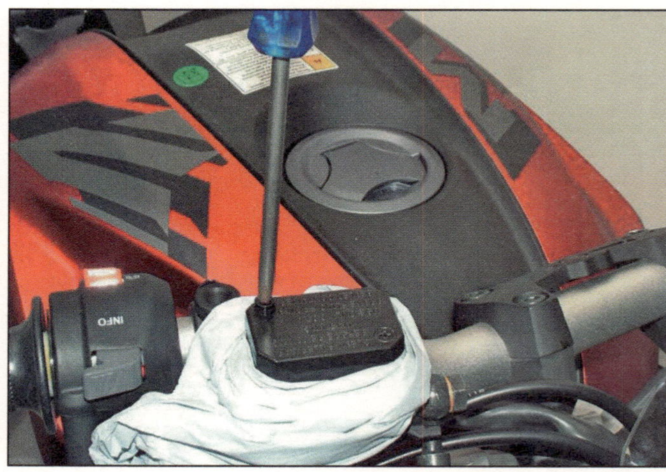

2 If the level is on or below the MIN line, undo the two reservoir cover screws and remove the cover, diaphragm plate (MT and YZF-R models only), and diaphragm.

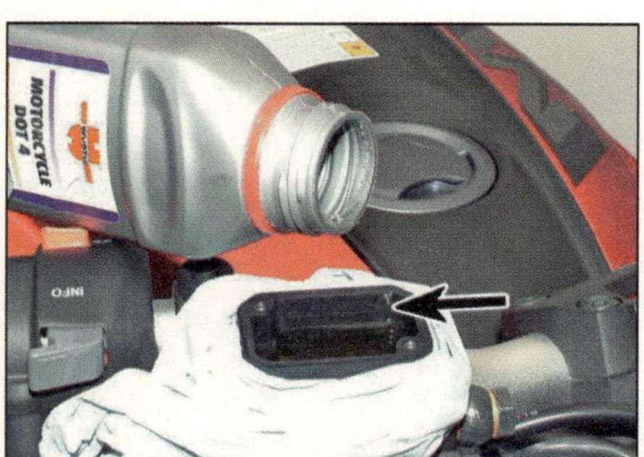

3 Top up with new clean DOT 4 hydraulic fluid, until the level is up to the line (arrowed) on the inside of the reservoir. Do not overfill and take care to avoid spills (see Warning above).

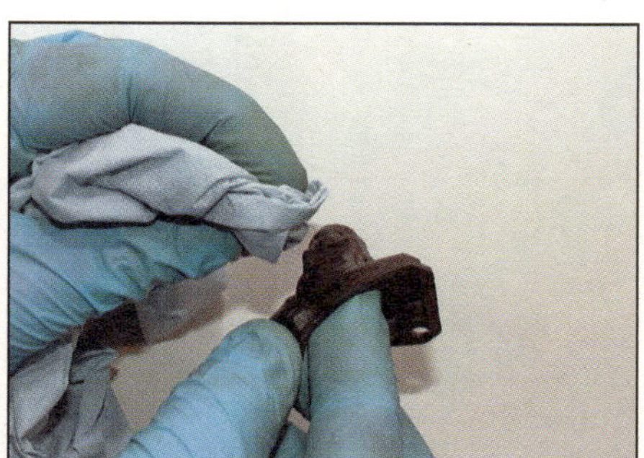

4 Wipe any moisture off the diaphragm with a tissue.

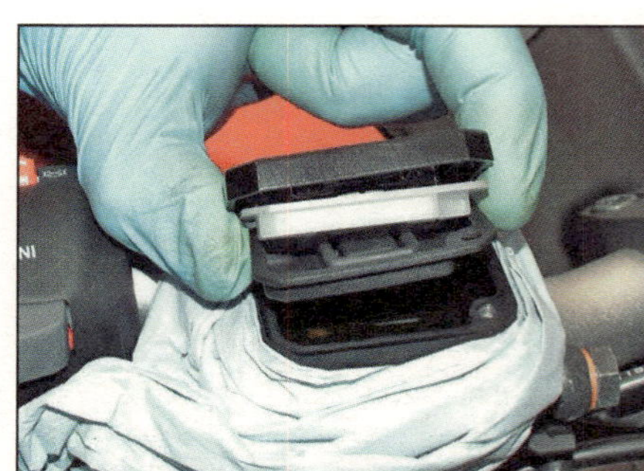

5 Make sure the diaphragm is correctly seated before fitting the diaphragm, diaphragm plate (MT and YZF-R models only), and cover. Secure the cover with its screws.

REAR BRAKE

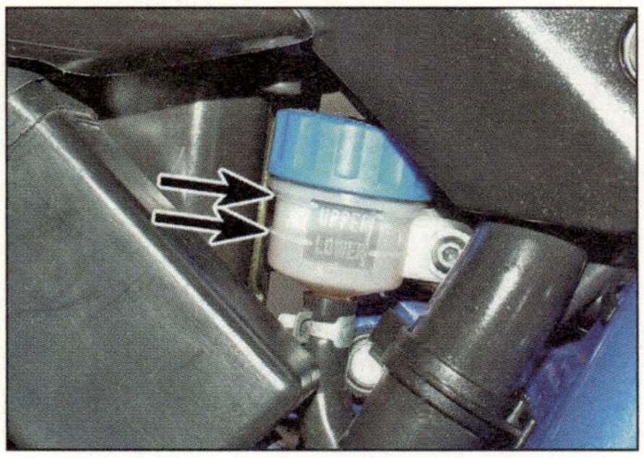

1 The rear brake fluid level is visible through the reservoir body – it must be between the UPPER and LOWER level lines (arrowed).

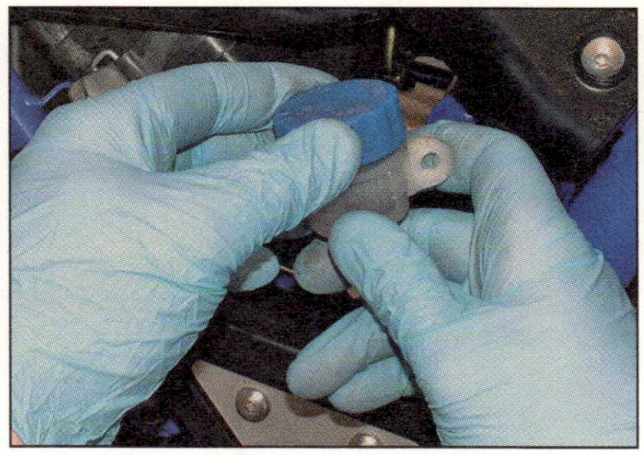

2 If the level is on or below the LOWER line on WR models unscrew the reservoir bolt and move the reservoir clear of the fuel tank cover, then unscrew the cap and remove the diaphragm plate and diaphragm.

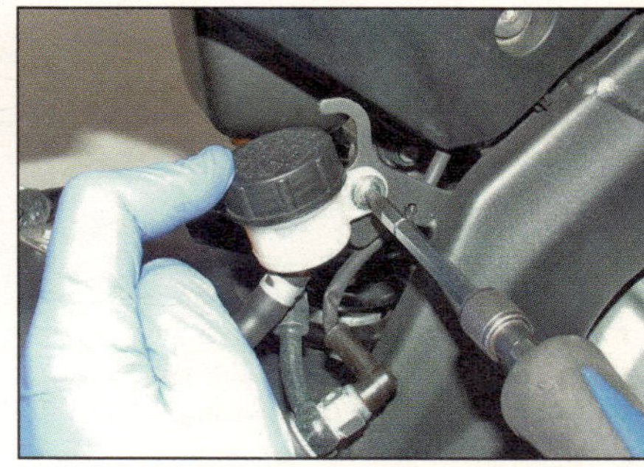

3 If the level is on or below the LOWER line on MT and YZF-R models slacken the reservoir bolt and pivot the reservoir clear of the bracket, then unscrew the cap and remove the diaphragm plate and diaphragm.

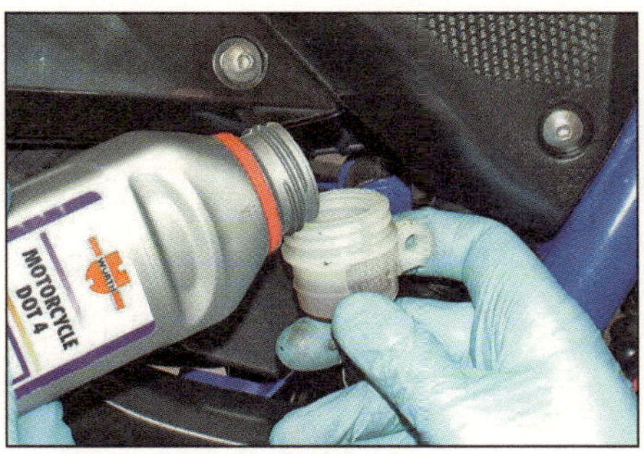

4 Top up with new clean DOT 4 hydraulic fluid, until the level is up to the UPPER line. Do not overfill and take care to avoid spills (see **Warning**).

5 Wipe any moisture off the diaphragm with a tissue.

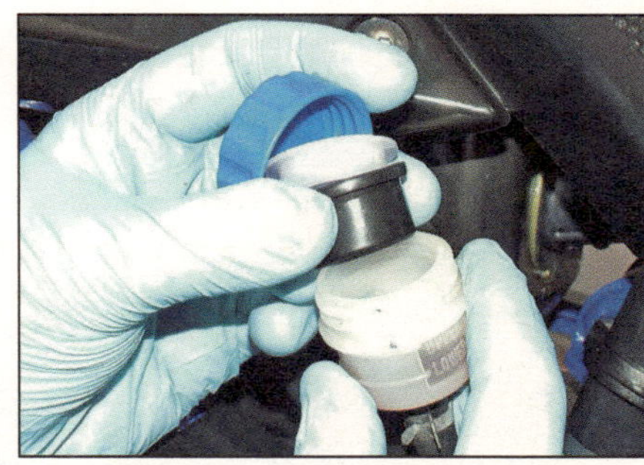

6 Make sure the diaphragm is correctly seated before fitting the plate and cap. Reposition and secure the reservoir.

Suspension, steering and drive chain

Suspension and Steering:

- Check that the front and rear suspension operates smoothly without binding (see Chapter 1).
- Check that the steering moves smoothly from lock-to-lock.

Drive chain:

- Check that the chain isn't too loose or too tight, and adjust it if necessary (see Chapter 1).
- If the chain looks dry, lubricate it (see Chapter 1).

Legal and safety

Lighting and signalling:

- Take a minute to check that the headlight, sidelight, tail light, brake light, licence plate light, instrument lights and turn signals all work correctly.
- Check that the horn sounds when the button is pressed.
- A working speedometer, graduated in mph, is a statutory requirement in the UK.

Safety:

- Check that the throttle grip rotates smoothly when opened and snaps shut when released, in all steering positions. Periodically check for the correct amount of freeplay (see Chapter 1).
- Check that the brake lever and pedal, clutch lever and gearchange lever operate smoothly. Lubricate them at the specified intervals or when necessary (see Chapter 1).
- Check that the engine shuts off when the kill switch is operated. Check the starter safety circuit (see Chapter 1).
- Check that sidestand return springs hold the stand up securely when retracted.

Fuel:

- This may seem obvious, but check that you have enough fuel to complete your journey. If you notice signs of fuel leakage – rectify the cause immediately.
- Make sure you use the correct grade unleaded fuel (min 95 RON).

Engine

All models have the same single cylinder liquid-cooled engine used in the original YZF-R125 (launched in 2008). Drive to the single overhead camshaft, which actuates the four valves via a pair of rocker arms, is by chain from the left-hand end of the crankshaft. A balancer shaft driven directly off the crankshaft keeps things smooth. It has a wet-sump lubrication system. The clutch is a conventional wet multi-plate unit and the gearbox is 6-speed constant mesh. Drive to the rear wheel is by chain and sprockets. The engine has an electric starter motor.

The fuel injection system supplies pressurised fuel from a pump housed within the tank via a single injector and throttle body. An electronic ignition system ignites the mixture via a single spark plug. The exhaust system incorporates catalytic converters.

Frame and suspension

WR models

The WR models were launched in 2009. The R model is a trail style bike, and the X model is a supermoto style bike.

The frame is a tubular steel twin cradle. Front suspension is by oil-damped telescopic forks. Rear suspension is by a single shock absorber via a three-way linkage and steel swingarm that pivots through the frame.

Wheels are steel spoked with tubed tyres.

The front and rear brake systems are hydraulic, with a twin piston sliding caliper and single disc at the front and a single piston sliding caliper and disc at the rear.

YZF-R and MT models

The YZF-R125, designed as an entry level sports bike to complement the existing R range, was launched initially in 2008, and the updated version covered in this manual was launched in 2014. The MT125, designed as an entry level naked street bike to complement the existing MT range, was launched in 2015.

The steel Deltabox frame uses the engine as a stressed member. Front suspension is by oil-damped upside-down 41 mm telescopic forks. Rear suspension is by a single shock absorber via a three-way linkage and aluminium swingarm that pivots through the frame.

Wheels are cast alloy with tubeless tyres.

The front and rear brake systems are hydraulic, with a four opposed piston caliper and single disc at the front and a single piston sliding caliper and disc at the rear. An anti-lock brake system (ABS) is available as an option.

Dimensions and weights

WR-R models

Overall length .... 2125 mm
Overall width .... 835 mm
Overall height (excluding mirrors) .... 1285 mm
Wheelbase .... 1430 mm
Seat height .... 930 mm
Ground clearance .... 265 mm
Weight (wet) .... 133 kg (293 lb)
Maximum load (rider, passenger and luggage) .... 185 kg (408 lb)

WR-X models

Overall length .... 2090 mm
Overall width .... 835 mm
Overall height (excluding mirrors)
- 2009 and 2010 models .... 1260 mm
- 2011-on models .... 1225 mm

Wheelbase
- 2009 and 2010 models .... 1430 mm
- 2011-on models .... 1415 mm

Seat height
- 2009 and 2010 models .... 920 mm
- 2011-on models .... 875 mm

Ground clearance
- 2009 and 2010 models .... 255 mm
- 2011-on models .... 227 mm

Weight (wet) .... 137 kg (302 lb)
Maximum load (rider, passenger and luggage) .... 185 kg (408 lb)

MT models

Overall length .... 1950 mm
Overall width .... 745 mm
Overall height (excluding mirrors) .... 1025 mm
Wheelbase .... 1350 mm
Seat height .... 820 mm
Ground clearance .... 140 mm
Weight (wet) .... 138 kg (304 lb)
Maximum load (rider, passenger and luggage) .... 180 kg (397 lb)

YZF-R models

Overall length .... 1955 mm
Overall width .... 680 mm
Overall height .... 1065 mm
Wheelbase .... 1355 mm
Seat height .... 825 mm
Ground clearance .... 155 mm
Weight (wet) .... 140 kg (309 lb)
Maximum load (rider, passenger and luggage) .... 180 kg (397 lb)

Engine

Type .... Four-stroke, single cylinder
Capacity .... 124.7 cc
Bore .... 52.0 mm
Stroke .... 58.6 mm
Compression ratio .... 11.2 to 1
Lubrication .... Wet sump
Cooling system .... Liquid-cooled
Clutch .... Wet multi-plate
Transmission .... Six-speed constant mesh
Final drive .... Chain and sprockets
Camshaft .... SOHC, chain-driven
Fuel system .... Single throttle body with single injector
Exhaust system .... One-into-one
Ignition system .... Fully transistorised electronic

Chassis

WR models

Frame type .... Steel cradle
Rake and Trail
- R models .... 27.00°, 107.0 mm
- X models .... 25.50°, 78.5 mm

Fuel tank
- Capacity (including reserve) .... 8.5 litres
- Reserve volume (when fuel warning light comes on) .... approx. 1.6 litres

Front suspension
- Type .... 41 mm oil-damped telescopic forks
- Wheel travel .... 240 mm (R models), 210 mm (X models)
- Adjustment .... None

Rear suspension
- Type .... Single shock absorber, rising rate linkage, box-section steel swingarm
- Wheel travel .... 230 mm
- Adjustment .... Spring pre-load

Wheels
- R models
  - Front .... 21 inch steel spoked
  - Rear .... 18 inch steel spoked
- X models .... 17 inch steel spoked

Tyres
- R models
  - Front .... 80/90-21M/C 48P/S/R tubed
  - Rear .... 110/80-18M/C 58P/S/R tubed
- X models
  - Front .... 110/70-17 M/C 54H tubed
  - Rear .... 140/70-17 M/C 66H tubed

Front brake .... Single disc with twin piston sliding caliper
Rear brake .... Single disc with single piston sliding caliper

MT and YZF-R models

Frame type .... Steel Deltabox
Rake and Trail .... 25.00°, 89.0 mm
Fuel tank
- Capacity (including reserve) .... 11.5 litres
- Reserve volume (when fuel warning light comes on) .... approx. 3.0 litres

Front suspension
- Type .... 41 mm oil-damped telescopic forks
- Wheel travel .... 130 mm
- Adjustment .... None

Rear suspension
- Type .... Single shock absorber, rising rate linkage, box-section aluminium swingarm
- Wheel travel .... 114 mm
- Adjustment .... None

Wheels .... 17 inch cast alloy
Tyres
- Front .... 100/80-17M/C 52H/S tubeless
- Rear .... 130/70-17M/C 62H/S tubeless

Front brake .... Single disc with four opposed-piston caliper
Rear brake .... Single disc with single piston sliding caliper

 Notes

Chapter 1
Routine maintenance and servicing

Contents

Degrees of difficulty

Easy, suitable for novice with little experience	**Fairly easy,** suitable for beginner with some experience	**Fairly difficult,** suitable for competent DIY mechanic	**Difficult,** suitable for experienced DIY mechanic	**Very difficult,** suitable for expert DIY or professional

Specifications

Engine

Spark plug type	
WR models	NGK CR8E
MT and YZF-R models	NGK CR9E
Spark plug electrode gap	0.7 to 0.8 mm
Engine idle speed	
WR models	1400 to 1600 rpm
MT and YZF-R models	1350 to 1550 rpm
Valve clearances (COLD engine)	
Intake valves	0.10 to 0.14 mm
Exhaust valves	0.20 to 0.24 mm

Chassis

Brake pad friction material minimum thickness	
WR models	1.0 mm
MT and YZF-R models	2.0 mm front, 1.0 mm rear
Clutch cable freeplay	10 to 15 mm
Drive chain slack	
WR models	40 to 50 mm
MT and YZF-R models	35 to 45 mm
Drive chain stretch limit (see text)	191.5 mm
Throttle cable freeplay	3 to 5 mm
Rear brake pedal height (see text)	
WR models	12.0 mm
MT and YZF-R models	46.9 mm
Tyre pressures (cold)	see *Pre-ride checks*

Lubricants and fluids

Engine oil type	SAE 10W30 or 10W40 API grade SG or higher motorcycle oil
Engine oil capacity	
Oil change	0.95 litre
Oil and filter change	1.0 litre
Following engine overhaul	1.15 litres
Coolant type	Pre-mixed coolant, or a 50% distilled water/ 50% corrosion inhibited ethylene glycol anti-freeze mix
Coolant capacity	
Radiator and engine	1.0 litre
Reservoir	0.25 litre
Brake fluid	DOT 4
Drive chain	Chain lubricant suitable for O-ring chains, or engine oil
Bearing seal lips	Lithium-based multi-purpose grease
Cables	Aerosol cable lubricant
Clutch lever pivot	Lithium-based multi-purpose grease
Front brake lever pivot and piston tip	Silicone grease
Gearchange lever/rear brake pedal/footrest pivots	Lithium-based multi-purpose grease
Sidestand pivot	Lithium-based multi-purpose grease
Steering head bearings	Lithium-based multi-purpose grease
Rear suspension linkage bearings	
WR models	Lithium-based multi-purpose grease
MT and YZF-R models	Molybdenum disulphide grease
Swingarm pivot and bearings	
2009 WR models	Lithium-based multi-purpose grease
All other models	Molybdenum disulphide grease
Throttle twistgrip	Lithium-based multi-purpose grease

Torque settings

Cooling system drain bolt	7 Nm
Engine oil drain plug	32 Nm
Engine oil filter housing cover bolts	10 Nm
Engine oil delivery check bolt	
WR models	7 Nm
MT and YZF-R models	10 Nm
Front brake master cylinder clamp bolts	9 Nm
Fork clamp bolts (top yoke)	23 Nm
Handlebar clamp bolts (YZF-R models)	23 Nm
Handlebar positioning bolts (YZF-R models)	9 Nm
Rear axle nut	
WR models	90 Nm
MT and YZF-R models	85 Nm
Spark plug	13 Nm
Steering head bearing adjuster nut	
WR models	
Initial setting	38 Nm
Final setting	
2009 and 2010 models	4 Nm
2011-on models	9 Nm
MT and YZF-R models	
Initial setting	48 Nm
Final setting	13 Nm
Steering stem nut	
WR models	140 Nm
MT and YZF-R models	110 Nm

Pre-ride

- ☐ See *Pre-ride checks* at the beginning of this manual.

After the initial 600 miles (1000 km)

- ☐ First service

Note: *The first service must be performed by a Yamaha dealer after the first 600 miles (1000 km) from new in order to comply with the terms of the warranty. Thereafter, maintenance is carried out according to the following intervals of the schedule.*

Every 300 miles (500 km) – WR models Every 600 miles (1000 km) – MT and YZF-R models

- ☐ Check, adjust, clean and lubricate the drive chain (Section 1)

1200 miles after the initial 600 mile (1000 km) service (i.e. at 1800 miles)

- ☐ Change the engine oil (Section 8)

Every 1800 miles (3000 km) thereafter

- ☐ Change the engine oil (Section 8)

Every 3500 miles (6000 km) or 12 months

- ☐ Check the spark plug (Section 2)
- ☐ Check and adjust the engine idle speed (Section 3)
- ☐ Check the fuel system and hoses (Section 4)
- ☐ Check the air induction system (Section 5) – WR models only
- ☐ Check and adjust the throttle cable (Section 6)
- ☐ Check and adjust the clutch cable (Section 7)
- ☐ Change the engine oil and fit a new oil filter (Section 8)
- ☐ Check the cooling system (Section 9)
- ☐ Check the brake system and brake light switch operation (Section 10)
- ☐ Check the brake pads for wear (Section 10)

Every 3500 miles (6000 km) or 12 months (continued)

- ☐ Check the condition of the wheels, wheel bearings and tyres (Section 11)
- ☐ Check the front and rear suspension (Section 12)
- ☐ Check and adjust the steering head bearings (Section 13)
- ☐ Lubricate the clutch and brake levers, brake pedal, sidestand pivot, and the throttle cables (Section 14)
- ☐ Check the tightness of all nuts, bolts and fasteners (Section 15)
- ☐ Check the sidestand and starter safety circuit (Section 16)
- ☐ Check the battery (Section 17)
- ☐ Clean the air filter element (Section 18)
- ☐ Check and adjust the valve clearances (Section 19)

Every 7000 miles (12,000 km)

Carry out all the items under the 3500 mile (6000 km) check, plus the following:

- ☐ Fit a new spark plug (Section 2)
- ☐ Fit a new air filter element (Section 18)
- ☐ Re-grease the suspension linkage bearings (Section 12 and Chapter 5)

Every 14,000 miles (24,000 km)

Carry out all the items under the 7000 mile (12,000 km) check, plus the following:

- ☐ Re-grease the swingarm bearings (Section 12 and Chapter 5)
- ☐ Re-grease the steering head bearings (Section 13 and Chapter 5)

Every two years

- ☐ Change the brake fluid (Section 10 and Chapter 6)

Every three years

- ☐ Change the coolant (Section 9)

Every four years

- ☐ Fit new brake hoses (Section 10 and Chapter 6)

Non-scheduled maintenance

- ☐ Fit new fuel system hoses (Section 4 and Chapter 4)
- ☐ Change the front fork oil (Section 12 and Chapter 5)

MT (and YZF) models – right side

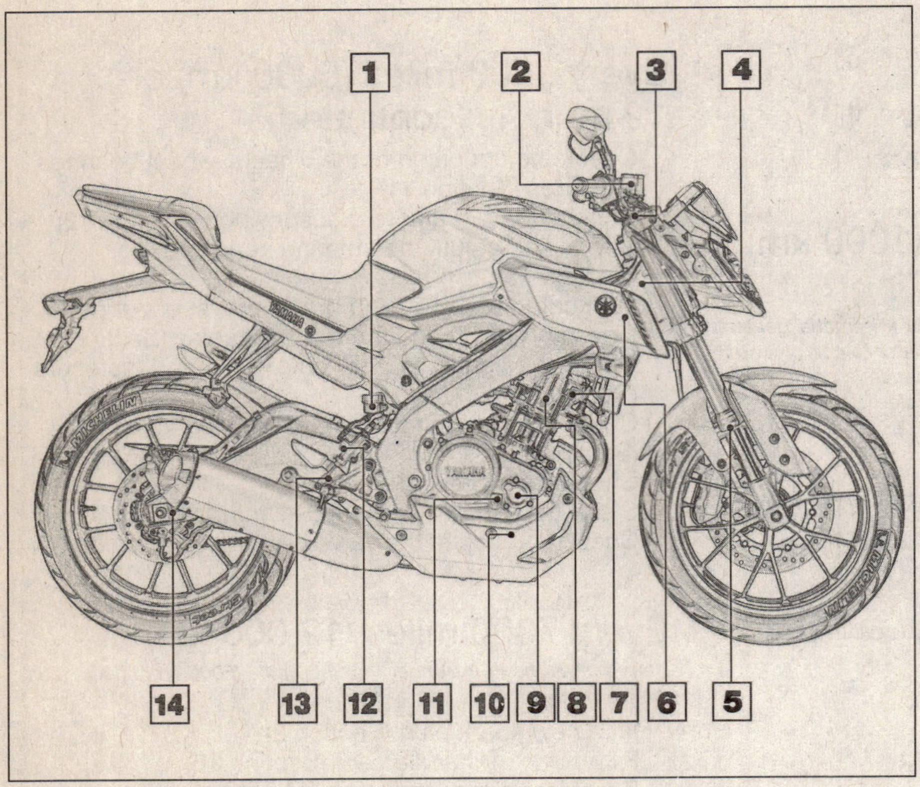

1 Rear brake fluid reservoir
2 Front brake fluid reservoir
3 Throttle cable upper adjuster
4 Frame number
5 Fork seal
6 Radiator pressure cap
7 Oil delivery check bolt
8 Spark plug
9 Oil filter element
10 Oil drain plug and strainer
11 Oil level dipstick/filler
12 Rear brake light switch (ABS models)
13 Rear brake pedal height adjuster
14 Drive chain adjuster

YZF (and MT) models – left side

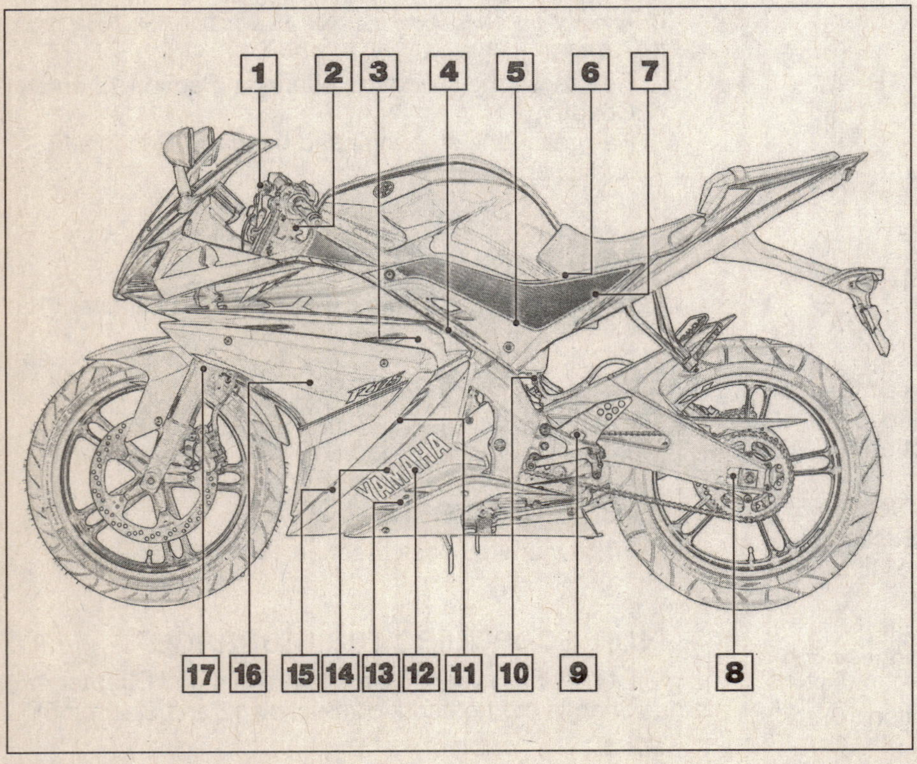

1 Clutch cable upper adjuster
2 Steering head bearing adjuster
3 Throttle cable lower adjuster
4 Idle speed adjuster
5 Air filter
6 Colour code label
7 Battery
8 Drive chain adjuster
9 Drive chain adjuster wear strip
10 Air filter housing drain
11 Clutch cable lower adjuster
12 Timing mark inspection plug
13 Engine number
14 Crankshaft turning bolt plug (for valve clearance check)
15 Coolant reservoir
16 Coolant drain bolt in cylinder block
17 Fork seal

WR models – right side

1 Rear brake fluid reservoir
2 Idle speed adjuster
3 Throttle cable lower adjuster
4 Air induction system reed valve housing
5 Front brake fluid reservoir
6 Throttle cable upper adjuster
7 Frame number
8 Fork seal
9 Battery
10 Oil delivery check bolt
11 Spark plug
12 Oil filter element
13 Oil drain plug and strainer
14 Oil level dipstick/filler
15 Rear brake pedal height adjuster
16 Drive chain adjuster

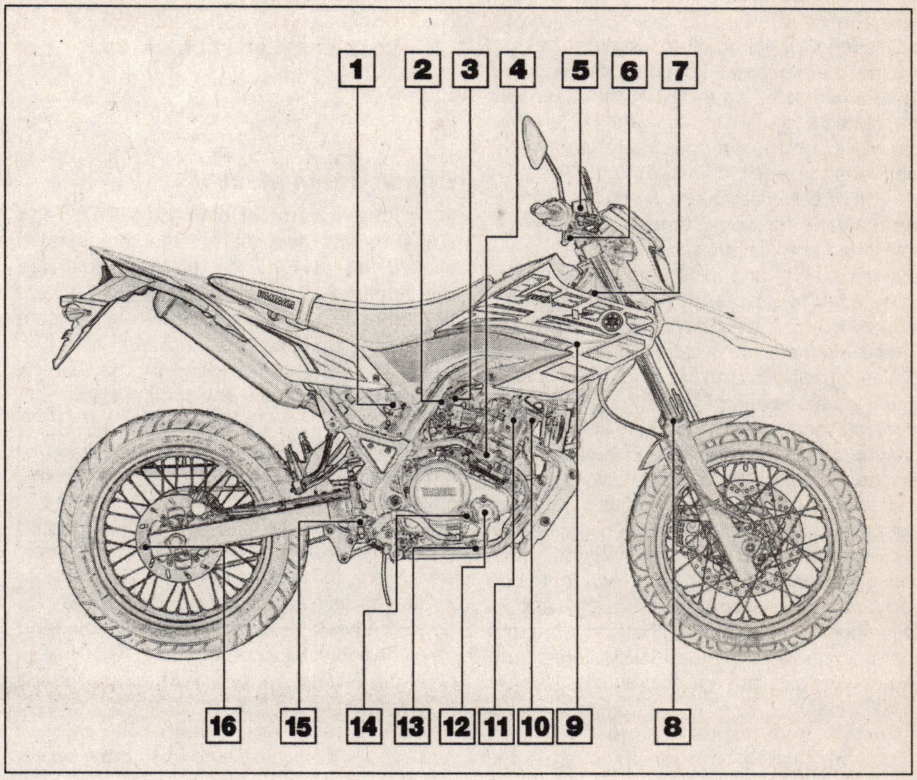

WR models – left side

1 Clutch cable upper adjuster
2 Steering head bearing adjuster
3 Air filter
4 Coolant reservoir
5 Colour code label
6 Drive chain adjuster
7 Air filter housing drain tube
8 Drive chain wear slider strip
9 Timing mark inspection plug
10 Clutch cable lower adjuster
11 Engine number
12 Crankshaft turning bolt plug (for valve clearance check)
13 Coolant drain bolt in cylinder block
14 Radiator pressure cap
15 Fork seal

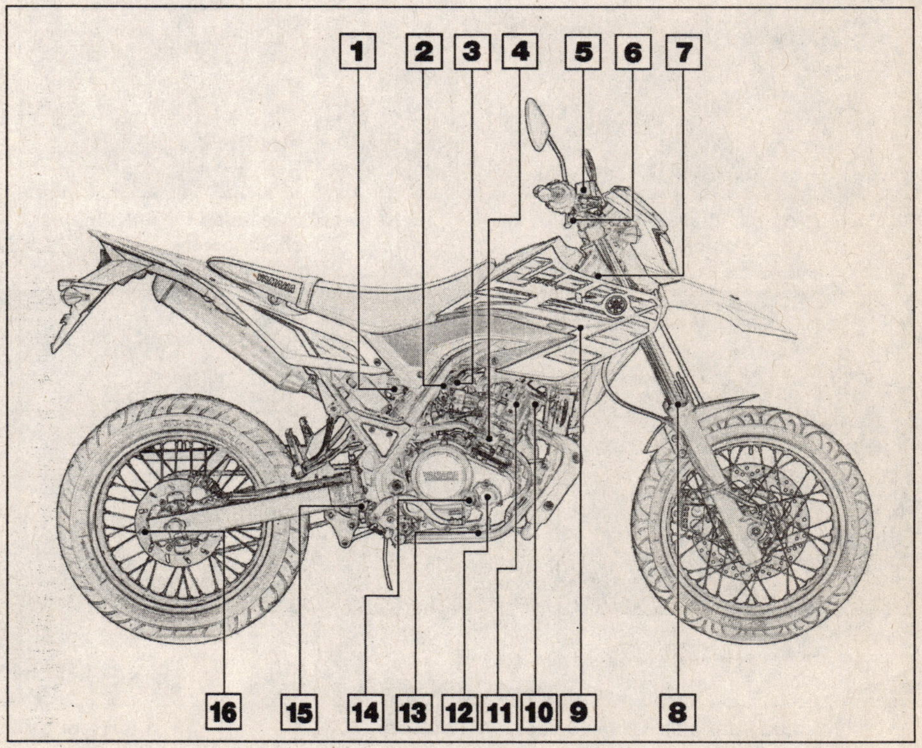

1 This Chapter is designed to help the home mechanic maintain his/her motorcycle for safety, economy, long life and peak performance.

2 Deciding where to start or plug into the routine maintenance schedule depends on several factors. If your motorcycle has been maintained according to the warranty standards and has just come out of warranty, start routine maintenance as it coincides with the next mileage or calendar interval. If you have owned the machine for some time but have never performed any maintenance on it, start at the nearest interval and include some additional procedures to ensure that nothing important is overlooked. If you have just had a major engine overhaul, then start the maintenance routine from the beginning. If you have a used machine and have no knowledge of its history or maintenance record, combine all the checks into one large service initially and then settle into the specified maintenance schedule.

3 Before beginning any maintenance or repair, clean the bike thoroughly, especially around the oil drain plug and filter housing, drive chain, suspension, wheels, etc, removing body panels as required (see Chapter 7). Cleaning will help ensure that dirt does not contaminate the engine and will allow you to detect wear and damage that could otherwise easily go unnoticed.

4 Certain maintenance information is sometimes printed on labels attached to the motorcycle. If the information on the labels differs from that included here, use the information on the label.

1 Drive chain and sprockets

Check chain slack

1 As the chain stretches with wear, adjustment is necessary. A neglected drive chain won't last long and will quickly damage the sprockets. Routine chain adjustment and lubrication isn't difficult and will ensure maximum chain and sprocket life.

2 To check the chain, place the bike on its sidestand. Make sure the transmission is in neutral. Make sure the ignition switch is OFF.

3 Measure the amount of up-and-down movement in the chain midway between the two sprockets, then compare your measurement to that specified at the beginning of the chapter **(see illustration)**. Since the chain will rarely wear evenly roll the bike forward so that another section of chain can be checked; do this several times to check the entire length of chain, and mark the tightest spot.

Caution: Riding the bike with excess slack in the chain could lead to damage.

4 In some cases where lubrication has been neglected, corrosion and dirt may cause the links to bind and kink, which effectively shortens the chain's length and makes it tight **(see illustration)**. Thoroughly clean and work free any such links, then highlight them with a marker pen or paint. Take the bike for a ride.

5 After the bike has been ridden, repeat the measurement for slack in the highlighted area. If the chain has kinked again and is still tight, replace it with a new one (see Chapter 6). A rusty, kinked or worn chain will damage the sprockets and can damage transmission bearings. If in any doubt as to the condition of a chain, it is far better to fit a new one than risk damage to other components and possibly yourself.

6 Check the entire length of the chain for damaged rollers, loose links and pins, and missing O-rings, and replace it with a new one if necessary.

7 Inspect the drive chain slider on the front of the swingarm for excessive wear and damage and replace it with a new one if necessary (see Chapter 5).

Warning: Never fit a new chain onto old sprockets, and never use the old chain if you fit new sprockets – replace the chain and sprockets as a set.

Adjust chain slack

8 Set the tightest spot of the chain at the centre of its bottom run.

9 Slacken the rear axle nut **(see illustrations)**.

10 On WR models, slacken the locknut on the adjuster on each side of the swingarm **(see illustration)**. To reduce chain slack turn the adjuster nut on each side evenly clockwise. To increase chain slack turn the adjuster on each side of the swingarm anti-clockwise then push the wheel forwards in the swingarm until it butts. Adjust the chain as required until the specified amount of freeplay is obtained at the centre of the bottom run of the chain (see Step 3). Following adjustment, make sure the wheel is pushed fully forward, then check that each chain adjustment marker is in the same position relative to the index lines on the swingarm **(see illustration)**. It is important the position is the same on each

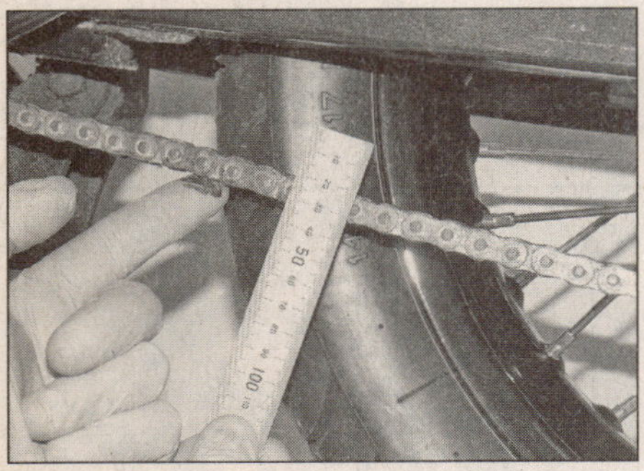

1.3 Push up on the chain and measure the slack

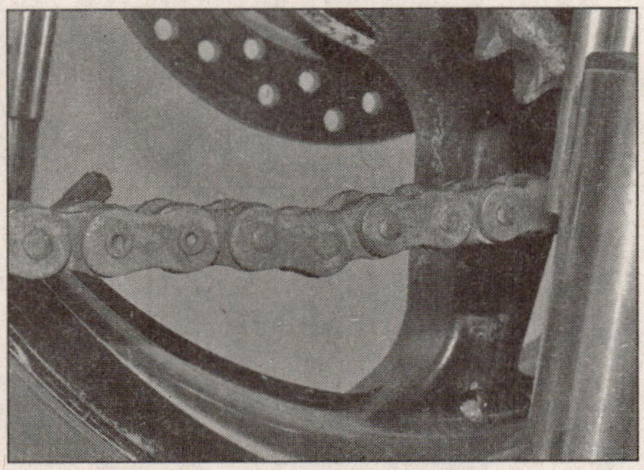

1.4 Neglect has caused the links in this chain to kink

1.9a Rear axle nut (arrowed) – WR models

1.9b Rear axle nut (arrowed) – MT and YZF-R models

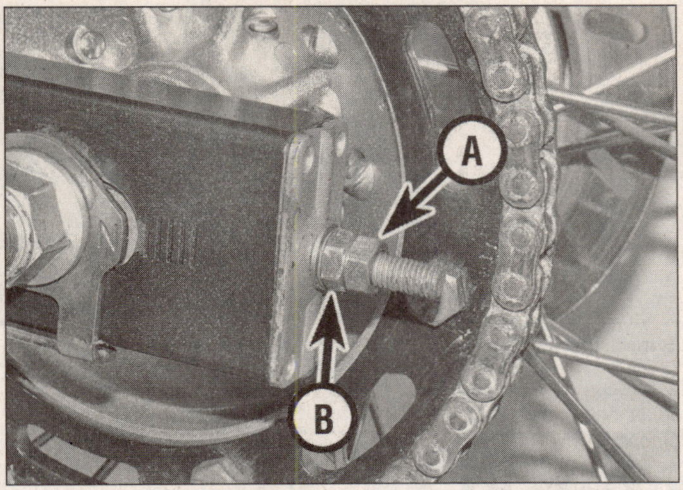

1.10a Slacken the locknut (A) on each side, then turn each adjuster nut (B) as required

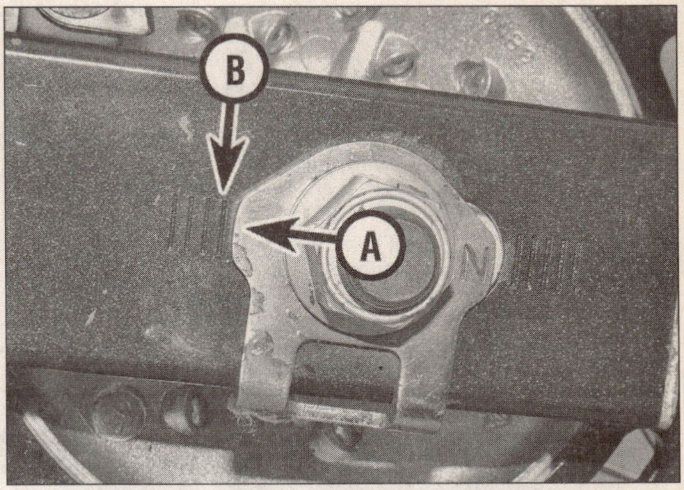

1.10b Chain adjustment marker (A) and index lines (B)

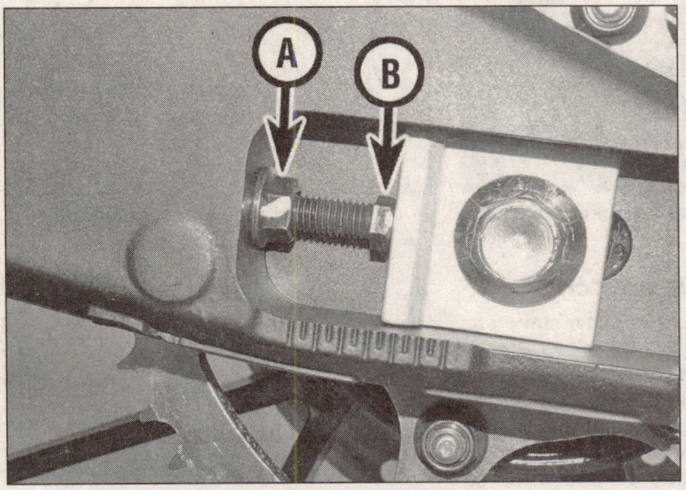

1.11a Slacken the locknut (A) on each side, then turn each adjuster bolt (B) as required

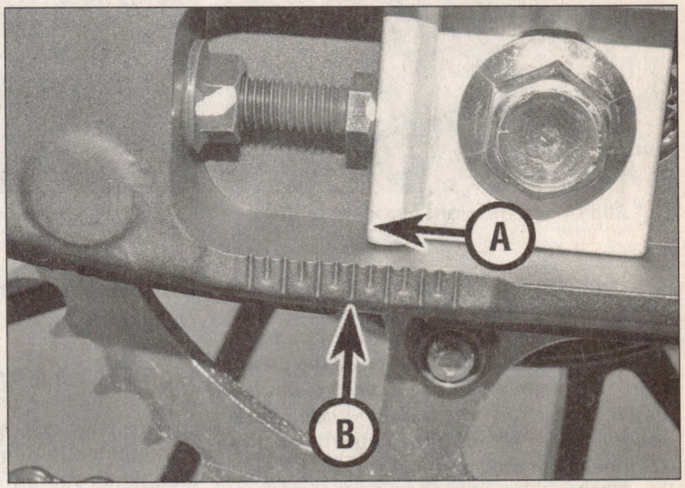

1.11b Chain adjustment marker (A) and index lines (B)

side otherwise the rear wheel will be out of alignment with the front. If there is a difference in the positions, adjust one of them so that its position is exactly the same as the other. Check the chain freeplay again and readjust if necessary.

11 On MT and YZF-R models, slacken the locknut on the adjuster bolt on each side of the swingarm **(see illustration)**. To reduce chain slack turn the adjuster bolt on each side evenly anti-clockwise. To increase chain slack turn the adjuster on each side of the swingarm clockwise then push the wheel forwards in the swingarm until it butts. Adjust the chain as required until the specified amount of freeplay is obtained at the centre of the bottom run of the chain (see Step 3). Following adjustment, make sure the wheel is pushed fully forward, then check that each chain adjustment marker is in the same position relative to the index lines on the swingarm **(see illustration)**. It is important the position is the same on each side otherwise the rear wheel will be out of alignment with the front. If there is a difference in the positions, adjust one of them so that its position is exactly the same as the other. Check the chain freeplay again and readjust if necessary.

12 From time to time check the amount of chain stretch (Steps 16 to 18).

13 When adjustment is complete, counter-hold the adjuster nuts or bolts (according to model) to prevent them turning and tighten the locknuts **(see illustration 1.10a or 1.11a)**. Push the wheel forwards and tighten the axle nut to the torque setting specified at the beginning of the chapter **(see illustration 1.9a or b)**. Recheck the adjustment as above, then make sure the wheel turns freely.

Clean and lubricate the chain

14 If required, wash the chain using a dedicated aerosol cleaner, or in paraffin (kerosene) or a suitable non-flammable or high flash-point solvent that will not damage the O-rings, using a soft brush to work any dirt out if necessary – specially shaped chain cleaning brushes are available from good suppliers **(see illustration)**. Wipe the cleaner off the chain and allow it to dry. If the chain is excessively dirty remove it from the machine and allow it to soak in the paraffin or solvent for a maximum of ten minutes (see Chapter 6).

1.14 Using a chain cleaning brush

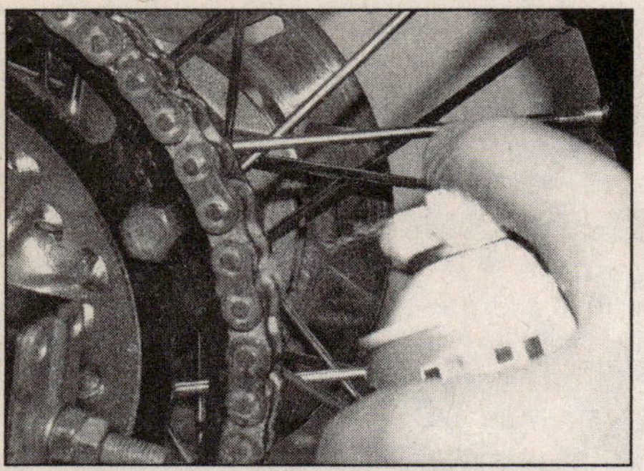

1.15 Apply the lubricant to the overlapping sections of the sideplates

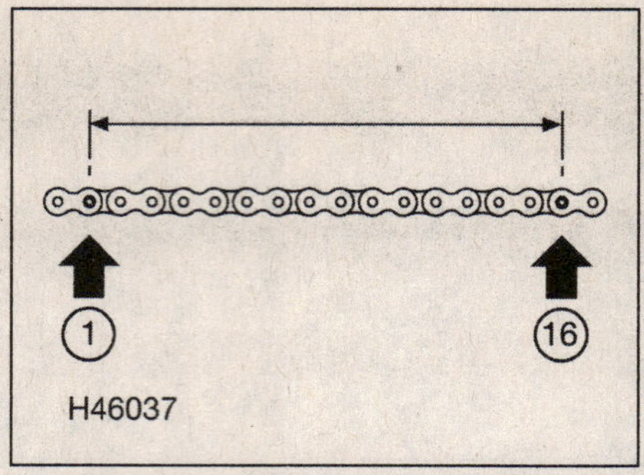

1.17 Chain stretch measurement

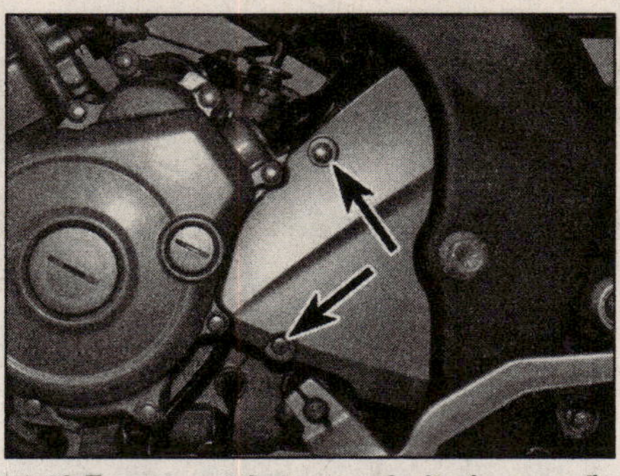

1.19 Front sprocket cover bolts (arrowed)

1.20a Check the front sprocket teeth...

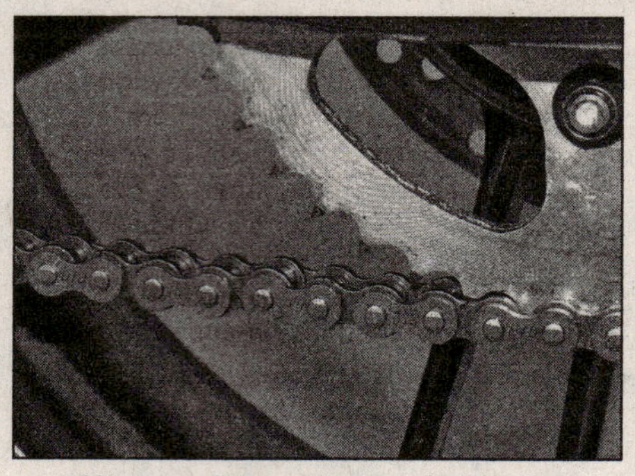

1.20b ... and the rear sprocket teeth...

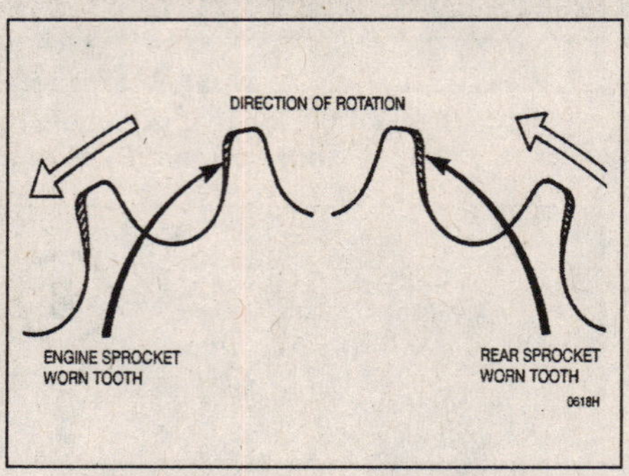

1.20c ... in the areas indicated

Caution: Don't use petrol (gasoline), an unsuitable solvent (such as benzene) or other cleaning fluids which might damage the internal sealing properties of the chain. Don't use high-pressure water to clean the chain. The entire process shouldn't take longer than ten minutes, otherwise the O-rings could be damaged.

15 The best time to lubricate the chain is after the motorcycle has been ridden. When the chain is warm, the lubricant will penetrate the joints between the sideplates better than when cold. **Note:** *Yamaha specifies engine oil or an aerosol chain lube that it is suitable for O-ring (sealed) chains; do not use any other chain lubricants – the solvents could damage the chain's sealing rings.* Apply the lubricant to the area where the sideplates overlap – not the middle of the rollers **(see illustration)**.

HAYNES HiNT ***Apply the lubricant to the top of the lower chain run, so centrifugal force will work the oil into the chain when the bike is moving. After applying the lubricant, let it soak in a few minutes before wiping off any excess.***

Warning: Take care not to get any lubricant on the tyre or brake disc. If any of the lubricant inadvertently contacts them, clean it off thoroughly using a suitable solvent or dedicated brake cleaner before riding the machine.

Check drive chain stretch

16 Measure the amount of chain stretch as follows:

17 Adjust the chain as described in Steps 9 to 11 until all slack is taken up, so the chain is fairly taut. Measure a 16 pin section along the bottom run of the chain as shown **(see illustration)**. Rotate the rear wheel so that several sections of the chain can be measured, then calculate the average and compare it to the stretch limit specified at the beginning of the chapter. If the chain stretch measurement exceeds the service limit it must be replaced with a new one (see Chapter 6).

18 If the chain is good, reset the adjusters so that there is the correct amount of freeplay (see Steps 9 to 13).

Caution: Never fit a new chain onto old sprockets, and never use the old chain if you fit new sprockets – replace the chain and sprockets as a set.

Check sprocket wear

19 On YZF-R models remove the front sprocket cover **(see illustration)**. On WR and MT models the front sprocket teeth are visible with the sprocket guard in place.

20 Check the teeth on the front sprocket and the rear sprocket for wear **(see illustrations)**. If the sprocket teeth are worn excessively, replace the chain and both sprockets with a new set. Check that the sprocket fasteners are tight (refer to Chapter 6 Specifications for torque settings).

2 Spark plug

Check and adjustment

1 Make sure your spark plug socket is the correct size (16 mm hex) before attempting to remove the plug – a suitable one is supplied in the motorcycle's tool kit, which is in the toobox on the right-hand side of the bike on WR models, and under the rider's seat on MT and YZF-R models – refer to Chapter 7 to remove the seat. On YZF-R models remove the centre section of the fairing on the right-hand side (see Chapter 7).

2 Pull the cap off the spark plug **(see illustration)**.

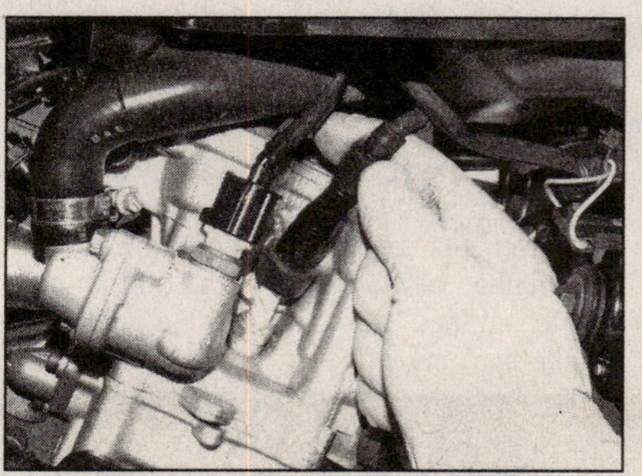

2.2 Pull the cap off the spark plug

2.4 Unscrew and remove the plug

2.6b Adjusting the gap using the fitting provided on the tool

3 Clean the area around the base of the spark plug to prevent any dirt falling into the engine.
4 Using either the plug removing tool supplied in the bike's toolkit or a deep spark plug socket, unscrew and remove the plug from the cylinder head **(see illustration)**.
5 Check the condition of the electrodes, referring to the spark plug reading chart at the end of this manual if signs of contamination are evident.
6 Clean the plug with a wire brush. Examine the tips of the electrodes; if a tip has rounded off, the plug is worn. Measure the gap between the two electrodes using a feeler gauge or a wire type gauge **(see illustration)**. The gap should be as specified at the beginning of the chapter; if necessary adjust the gap by bending the side electrode **(see illustration)**.

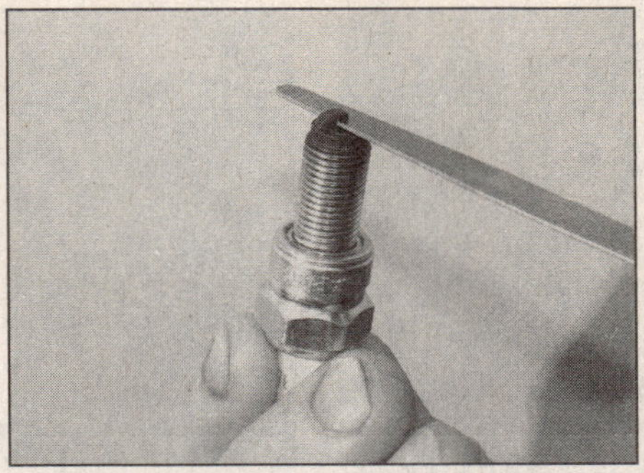

2.6a Using a feeler gauge to measure the spark plug electrode gap

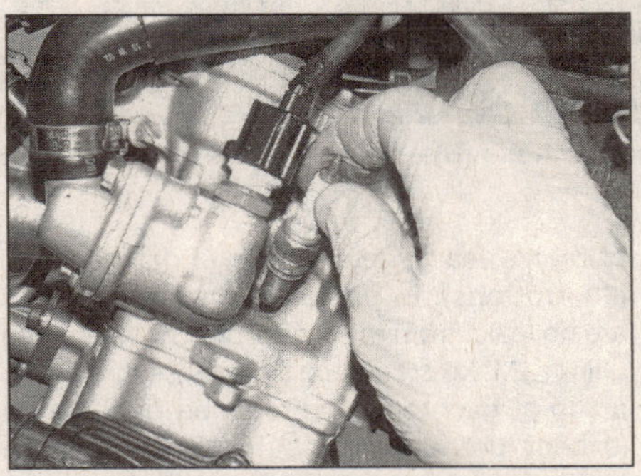

2.9 Thread the plug into the head by hand to prevent cross-threading

7 Check the threads, the washer and the ceramic insulator body for cracks and other damage.
8 If the plug is worn or damaged, or if any deposits cannot be cleaned off, replace the plug with a new one. If in any doubt as to the condition of the plug replace it with a new one – the expense is minimal.
9 Thread the plug into the cylinder head until the washer seats **(see illustration)**. Since the cylinder head is made of aluminium, which is soft and easily damaged, thread the plug as far as possible by hand. Once the plug is finger-tight, the job can be finished with a spanner on the tool supplied or a socket drive **(see illustration 2.4)**. If a new plug is being installed, tighten it by 1/2 a turn after the washer has seated. If the old plug is being reused, tighten it by 1/4 turn after the washer has seated, or if a torque wrench can be applied, tighten the spark plug to the torque setting specified at the beginning of the Chapter. Otherwise tighten it according to the instructions on the box. Do not over-tighten it.
10 Fit the spark plug cap, making sure it locates correctly onto the plug **(see illustration 2.2)**.
11 On YZF-R models install the centre section of the fairing (see Chapter 7).

HAYNES HiNT ***Stripped plug threads in the cylinder head can be repaired with a Heli-Coil insert – see 'Tools and Workshop Tips' in the Reference section***

Renewal

12 At the prescribed interval, whatever the condition of the existing spark plug, remove the plug as described above and fit a new one.

3 Idle speed

1 Before adjusting the idle speed clean or replace the spark plug and air filter according to interval, and check the valve clearances (see Sections 2, 18, 19).
2 The engine should be at normal operating temperature, which is usually reached after 10 to 15 minutes of stop-and-go riding. Make sure the transmission is in neutral.
3 On MT and YZF-R models remove the left-hand side cover (see Chapter 7).
4 The idle speed adjuster is a screw located in the right-hand side of the throttle body on WR models, and in the left-hand side on MT and YZF-R models **(see illustrations)**.

3.4a Idle speed adjuster screw (arrowed) – WR models

3.4b Idle speed adjuster screw (arrowed) – MT and YZF-R models

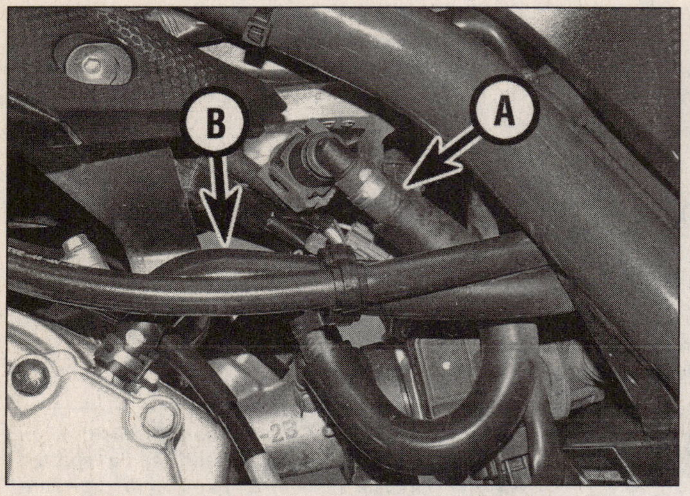

4.2a Fuel supply hose (A), crankcase breather hose (B) – WR models

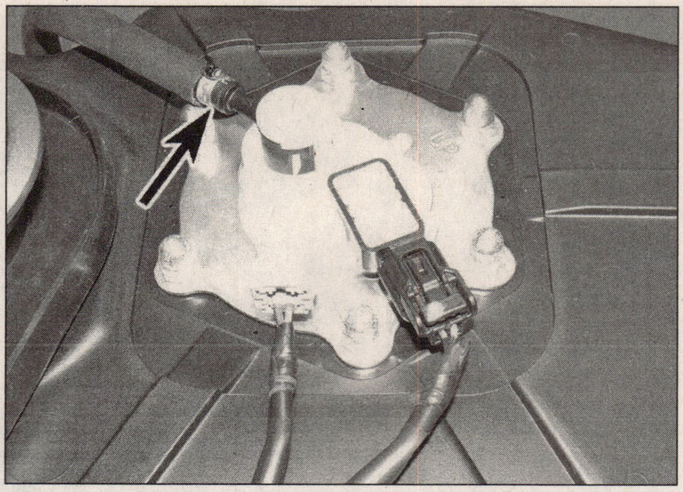
4.2b Fuel supply hose (arrowed) – MT and YZF-R models

With the engine running, turn the screw until the engine idles at the speed specified at the beginning of the chapter. Turn the screw anti-clockwise to increase idle speed, and clockwise to decrease it.

5 Snap the throttle open and shut a few times, then recheck the idle speed. If necessary, repeat the adjustment procedure. On completion check and adjust throttle cable freeplay (Section 6).

6 If the idle speed cannot be set, or if there is a problem with cold starting or fast running when warm, it is possible there is a fault with the fast idle solenoid – see Chapter 4, Section 7. Also check cylinder compression (see Chapter 2).

4 Fuel system

Warning: Petrol (gasoline) is extremely flammable, so take extra precautions when you work on any part of the fuel system. Don't smoke or allow open flames or bare light bulbs near the work area, and don't work in a garage where a natural gas-type appliance is present. If you spill any fuel on your skin, rinse it off immediately with soap and water. When you perform any kind of work on the fuel system, wear safety glasses and have a fire extinguisher suitable for a Class B type fire (flammable liquids) on hand.

1 On all models remove the fuel tank cover, on MT models remove the side covers, and on YZF-R models remove the centre and upper sections of the fairing on the left-hand side (see Chapter 7).

2 Check all the hoses to/from the fuel tank, the throttle body, the air filter housing and crankcase breather system (integral with the water pump housing), and on WR models the air induction system (see Section 5), for signs of cracks, leaks, deterioration or damage **(see illustrations)**. In particular check that there are no leaks from the fuel supply hose or hose unions. Make sure each hose is secure on its union at each end and retained by a clamp (except fuel supply hose). Replace any hose that is cracked or deteriorated with a new one.

3 Make sure the air filter housing duct clamps and intake duct clamps and bolts are tight.

4 Check the fuel tank for signs of fuel leakage. If the joint between the fuel pump and the tank is leaking, make sure the pump bolts or nuts are correctly tightened to the specified torque (see Chapter 4); if the leak persists remove the pump and fit a new seal (see Chapter 4).

5 Inspect the fuel injector assembly for signs of leakage. Remove the injector and fit new seals if necessary (see Chapter 4).

5 Air induction system (WR models only)

1 To reduce the amount of unburned hydrocarbons released in the exhaust gases, an air induction system is fitted. The system allows negative pressure pulses in the exhaust system to draw filtered air from the air filter housing, through a reed valve and into the exhaust where it mixes with the exhaust gases, causing any unburned particles of the fuel in the mixture to be burnt. This process changes a considerable amount of hydrocarbons and carbon monoxide into relatively harmless carbon dioxide and water. The reed valve prevents the flow of exhaust gases back into the air filter housing.

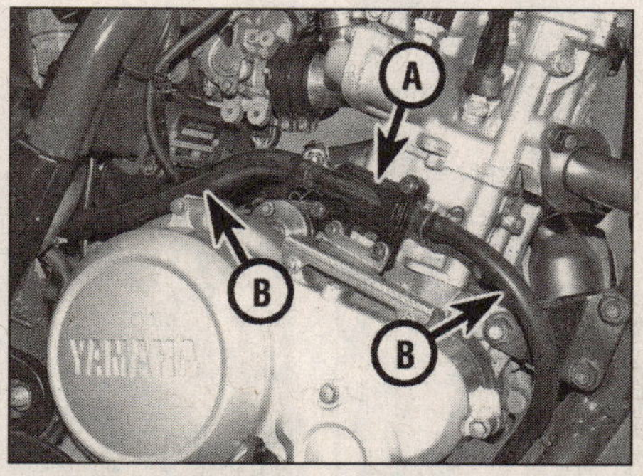

5.2 Air induction system reed valve housing (A) and hoses (B)

2 The system is not adjustable and requires little maintenance. Check that the hoses are not kinked or pinched, are in good condition and are securely connected at each end **(see illustration)**. Replace any hoses that are cracked, split or generally deteriorated with new ones.

3 Refer to Chapter 4 to check the reed valve unit if it is believed to be faulty.

6 Throttle cable(s)

1 With the engine off, make sure the throttle grip rotates smoothly and freely from fully closed to fully open with the front wheel turned at various angles, and returns without resistance from fully open to fully closed when released.

2 If the throttle sticks, this is probably due to a cable fault. Disconnect the cable(s), or remove it/them if preferred (see Chapter 4) and lubricate it/them (see Section 14). Check that the inner cable slide freely and easily in the outer cable. If not, replace the cable with a new one.

3 With the cable disconnected, make sure the twistgrip rotates freely on the handlebar – dirt combined with a lack of lubrication can cause the action to be stiff. To clean and lubricate the twistgrip, on MT and YZF-R models unscrew the handlebar end-weight. Slide the twistgrip

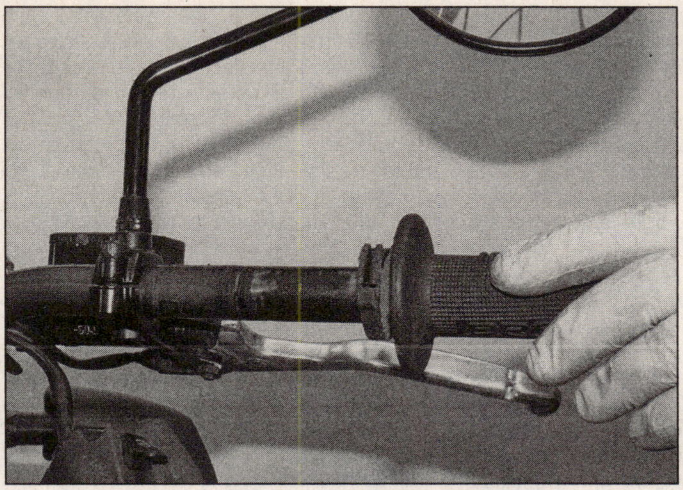

6.3 Slide the twistgrip off and clean and lubricate it

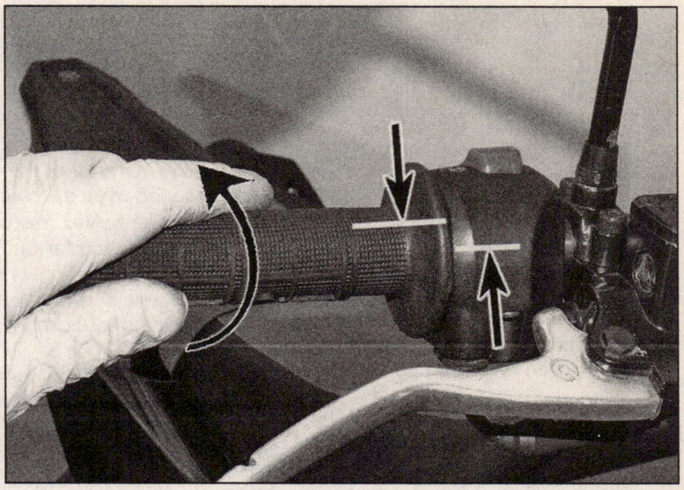

6.4 Throttle cable freeplay is measured in terms of twistgrip rotation

off the handlebar and clean any old grease from the bar and the inside of the tube **(see illustration)**. Smear some new grease of the specified type onto the bar, then refit the twistgrip. When re-fitting the end-weight make sure there is a 1 to 3 mm gap between the grip and the weight. Install the cable(s), making sure the routing is correct (see Chapter 4). If this fails to improve the operation of the throttle, the cable(s) must be replaced with a new one. Note that in very rare cases the fault could lie in the throttle body (see Chapter 4).

4 With the throttle operating smoothly, and after the idle speed has been checked and if necessary adjusted (Section 3), check for a small amount of freeplay in the cable, measured in terms of the amount of twistgrip rotation before the throttle opens, and compare the amount to that specified at the beginning of the chapter **(see illustration)**. If it's incorrect, adjust the cables to correct it as follows.

5 Initially adjust freeplay using the adjuster in the throttle cable where it leaves the throttle pulley housing on the handlebar. Pull the rubber boot off the adjuster. Loosen the locknut and turn the adjuster in or out as required until the specified amount of freeplay is obtained, then retighten the locknut **(see illustration)**.

6 If the adjuster has reached its limit of adjustment, reset it to its start point by turning it fully in, so that freeplay is at a maximum.

7 The adjuster at the throttle body end is on the right-hand side on WR models and is easily accessible, and on the left on MT and YZF-R models, and you need to remove the left-hand side cover for access (see Chapter 7). Slacken the locknut on the top of the cable bracket (the upper cable on MT and YZF-R models) until the adjuster nut below the bracket is free, then thread the adjuster nut up or down as required, until the specified amount of freeplay is obtained, then locate the adjuster nut so it is captive under the bracket and tighten the locknut **(see illustrations)**. Subsequent adjustments can be made at the throttle end when required.

8 If the cable cannot be adjusted as specified, replace it with a new one (see Chapter 4).

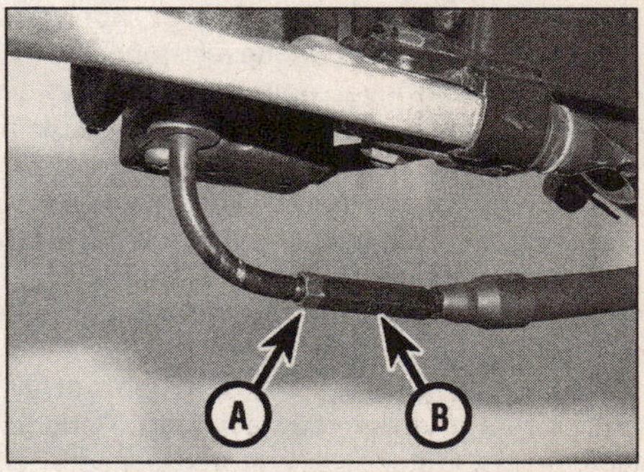

8.5 Loosen the locknut (A) and turn the adjuster (B)

Check that the throttle twistgrip operates smoothly and snaps shut quickly when released.

Warning: Turn the handlebars all the way through their travel with the engine idling. Idle speed should not change. If it does, the cable may be routed incorrectly. Correct this condition before riding the bike.

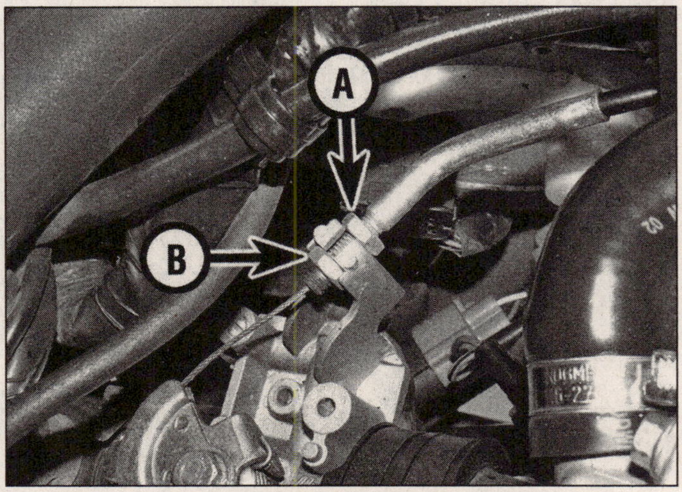

6.7a Locknut (A) and adjuster nut (B) – WR models

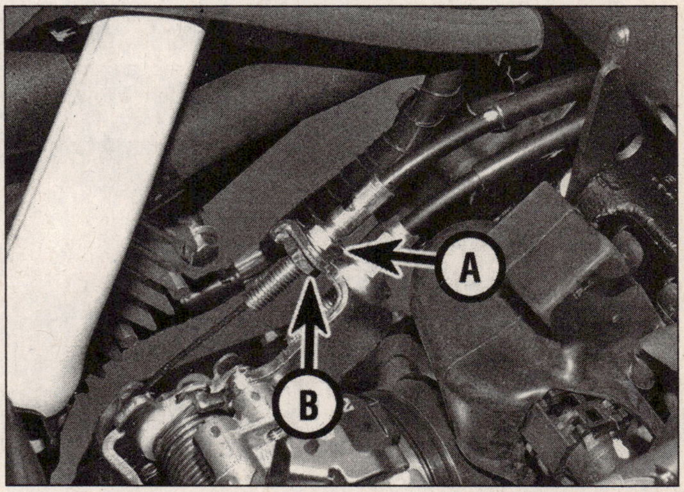

6.7b Locknut (A) and adjuster nut (B) – MT and YZF-R models

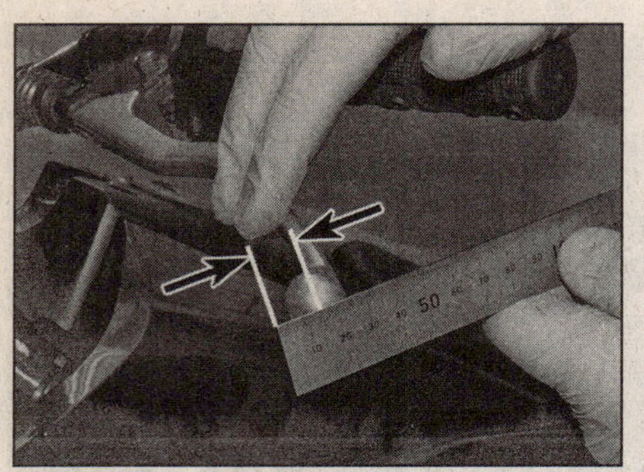

7.3 Measure the amount of freeplay at the clutch lever end as shown

7 Clutch

1 Check that the clutch lever operates smoothly and without undue resistance.

2 If the clutch lever operation is heavy or stiff, disconnect the cable, or remove it if preferred (see Chapter 2) and lubricate it (see Section 14). Check that the inner cable slides freely and easily in the outer cable. If the cable is still stiff, replace it with a new one. Connect or install the lubricated or new cable (see Chapter 2).

3 With the cable operating smoothly, check that it is correctly adjusted. Periodic adjustment is necessary to compensate for wear in the clutch plates and stretch of the cable. Check that the amount of freeplay at the clutch lever end is within the range specified at the beginning of the Chapter **(see illustration)**.

4 If adjustment is required, pull the rubber boot off the adjuster in the lever bracket. Loosen the adjuster lockring, then turn the adjuster in or out until the freeplay is as specified **(see illustration)**. To reduce freeplay, thread the adjuster out of the lever bracket. To increase freeplay, thread the adjuster into the bracket.

5 Make sure that the slots in the adjuster and the lockring are not aligned with the slot in the lever bracket – these slots are to allow removal of the cable, and if they are all aligned while the bike is in use the cable could jump out. Also make sure the adjuster is not threaded too far out of the bracket so that it is only held by a few threads – this will leave it unstable and the threads could be damaged. Tighten the lockring on completion, then refit the rubber boot.

6 If all the adjustment has been taken up at the lever, thread the adjuster all the way into the bracket to give the maximum amount of freeplay, then back it out about one turn (exactly how much will depend on the position of the slots) – this resets the adjuster to its start point. On YZF-R models remove the lower section of the fairing on the left-hand side (see Chapter 7). Set the correct amount of freeplay using the adjuster on the left-hand side of the engine **(see illustration)**. Slacken the locknut, then turn the adjuster nut as required until the freeplay at the lever end is as specified. Tighten the locknut on completion. Subsequent adjustments can now be made using the lever adjuster only.

8 Engine oil and filter

Warning: Be careful when draining the oil, as the exhaust pipe, the engine, and the oil itself can cause severe burns.

Oil change

1 Consistent routine oil changes are the single most important maintenance procedure you can perform. The oil not only lubricates the internal parts of the engine, transmission and clutch, but it also acts as a coolant, a cleaner, a sealant, and a protector. Because of these demands, the oil takes a terrific amount of abuse and should be changed at the specified intervals with new oil of the recommended grade and type (see the specifications at the beginning of the Chapter). The instruments fitted on all models incorporate an oil change reminder function – on WR models the word OIL flashes in the LCD, and on MT and YZF-R models the OIL symbol flashes and OIL SERV is displayed in the LCD. The function displays after the first 600 miles (1000 km), then after the next 1200 miles (2000 km) (i.e. at odometer reading 1800 miles or 3000 km), and every 1800 miles (3000 km) thereafter, but to maintain the correct sequence the function must be reset every time it comes on. Details on how to reset the function are given at the the end of this section. On WR models the function cannot be reset unless the display is on, so if you decide to change the oil earlier than the specified interval the function becomes ineffective. On MT and YZF-R models the function can be reset even if the display is not on, allowing you to perform an oil change earlier than specified – the reset procedure differs, and is also given at the end of this procedure.

HAYNES HiNT ***Saving a little money on the difference in cost between a good oil and a cheap oil won't pay off if the engine is damaged.***

2 Before changing the oil, warm up the engine so the oil will drain easily. Place the bike on its sidestand on level ground. On MT models remove the belly pan, and on YZF-R models remove all sections of the fairing on the right-hand side (see Chapter 7). On MT and YZF-R models also remove the seat, then

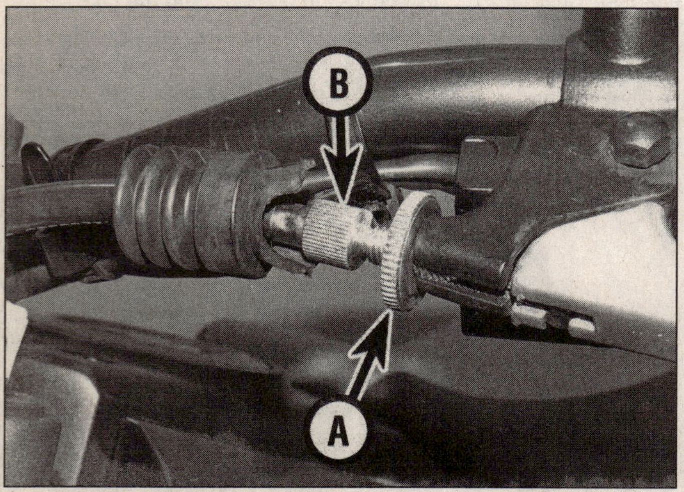

7.4 Slacken the lockring (A) and turn the adjuster (B) in or out as required

7.6 Slacken the locknut (A) and turn the adjuster nut (B) as required

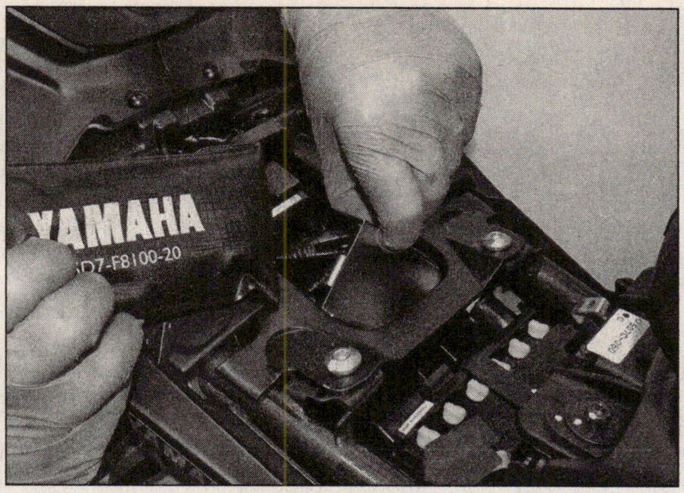

8.2a Get the chute...

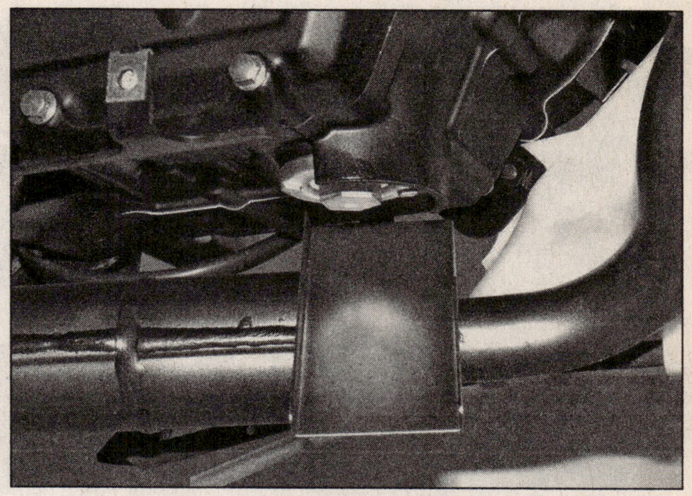

8.2b ...and locate it on the exhaust

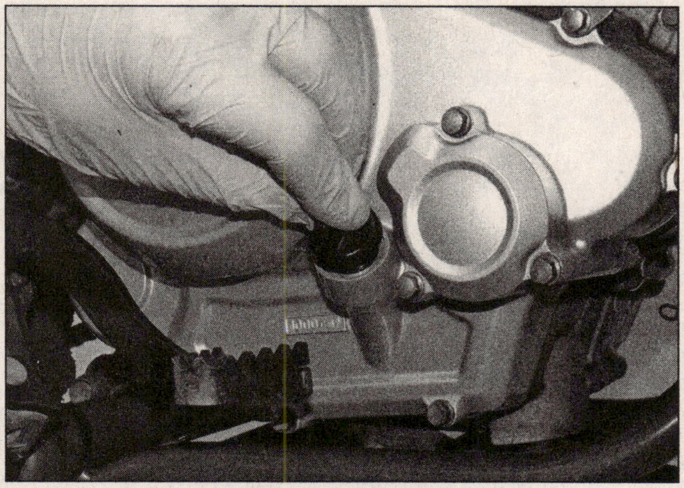

8.3a Unscrew the oil filler cap

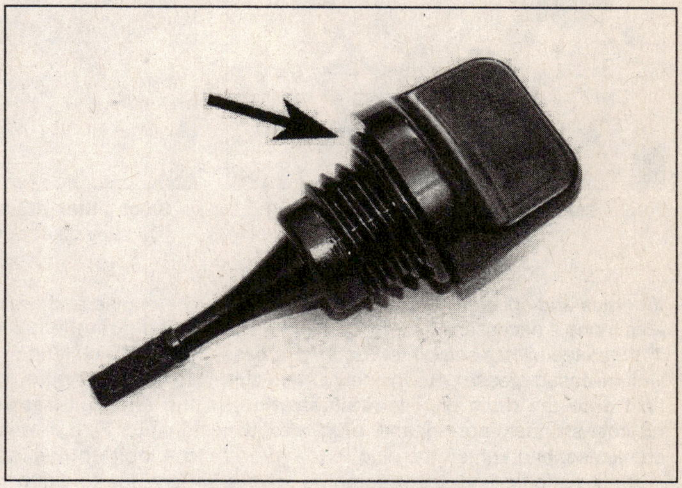

8.3b Check the O-ring (arrowed)

remove the oil drain chute (located with the toolkit) and fit it over the exhaust under the drain plug **(see illustrations)**. Prepare a clean drain tray for catching the oil.

3 Position the drain tray below the engine. Unscrew the oil filler cap to vent the crankcase and to act as a reminder that there is no oil in the engine **(see illustration)**. Check the condition of the O-ring and replace it with a new one if it is damaged or worn **(see illustration)**.

4 Unscrew the drain plug and remove the spring and strainer and allow the oil to flow into the drain tray **(see illustrations)**. Remove the O-ring from the drain plug – a new one must be fitted.

5 If you are fitting a new oil filter do so now (see Steps 12 to 16).

6 Clean the strainer, checking for any abnormal debris that could indicate internal problems **(see illustration)**. Check the gauze

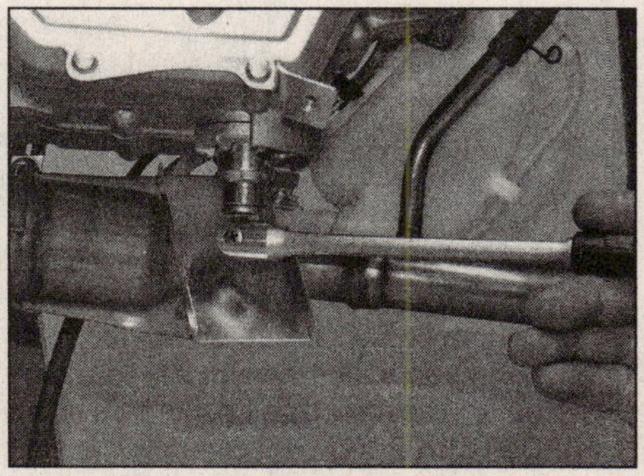

8.4a Unscrew the crankcase drain plug...

8.4b ...and allow the oil to completely drain

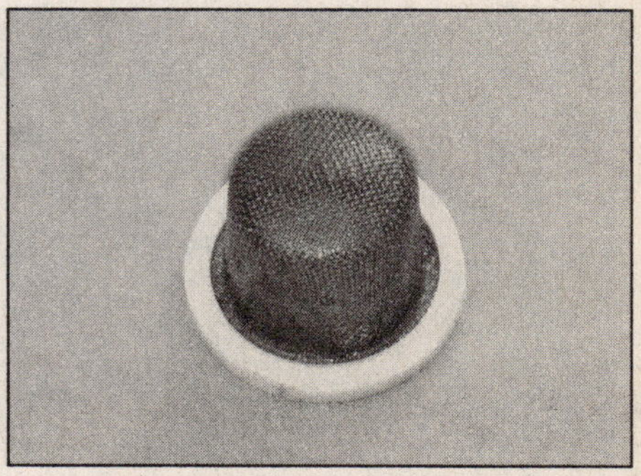

8.6 Clean and check the strainer

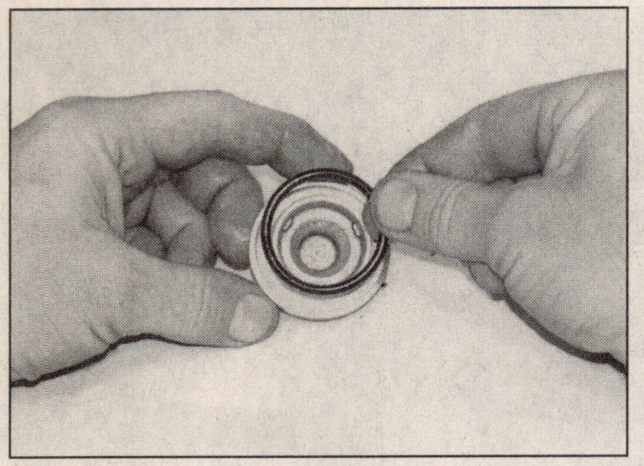

8.7a Fit a new O-ring into the groove...

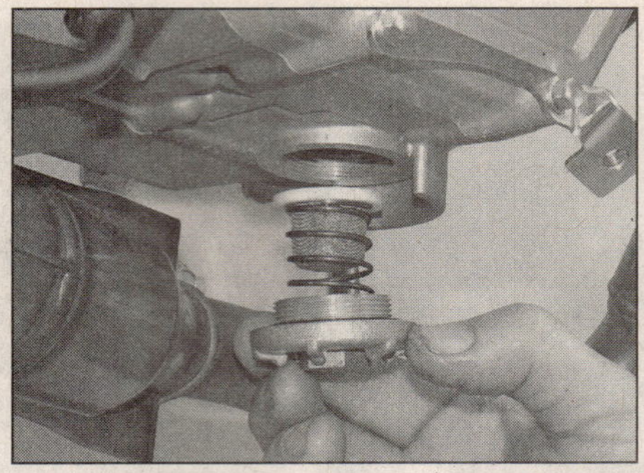

8.7b ...then fit the strainer, spring and plug as shown and tighten the plug

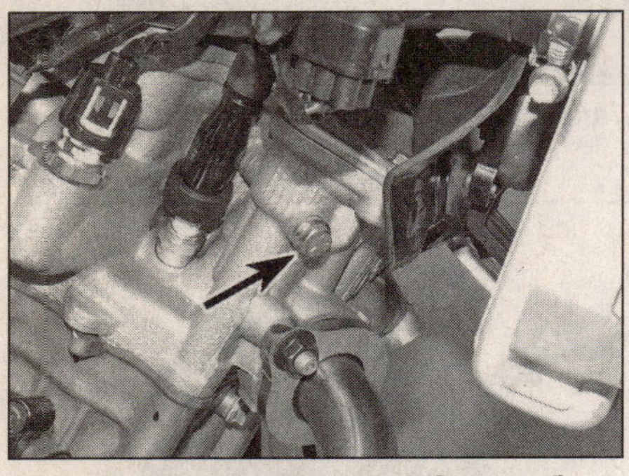

8.9a Slacken the check bolt (arrowed)...

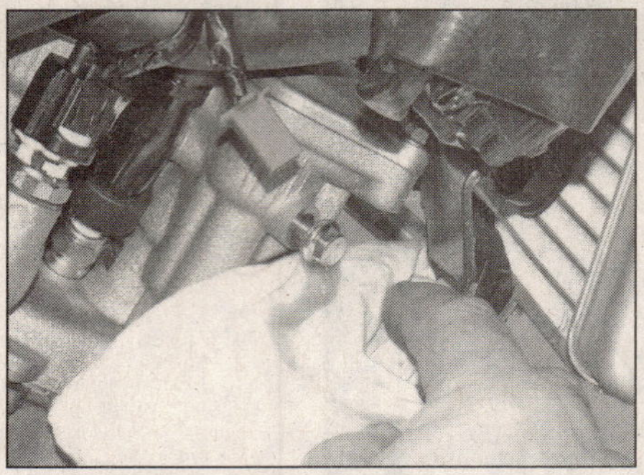

8.9b ...then start the engine and make sure oil seeps past the threads

for holes and splits – replace the strainer with a new one if necessary.

7 When the oil has completely drained, smear lithium-based grease onto the new O-ring and fit it onto the drain plug **(see illustration)**. Fit the strainer, spring and plug into the crankcase, and tighten the plug to the torque setting specified at the beginning of the Chapter **(see illustration)**.

8 Pour in the specified amount and type of new engine oil, frequently checking the level using the dipstick (see *Pre-ride checks*). Fit the filler cap **(see illustrations 8.3b and a)**.

9 Because no engine oil pressure switch and warning light are fitted, it is advisable to check that oil is flowing as it should – to do this slacken the pressure check bolt above the exhaust header pipe **(see illustration)**. Start the engine and let it idle – oil should start to weep from the bleed hole fairly quickly **(see illustration)**. If no oil appears after one minute stop the engine immediately, then check the filter, oil passages and oil pump (see Chapter 2). If oil appears as it should, tighten the bolt to the specified torque setting. Continue to warm the engine up for several minutes, then shut it off and check the level on the dipstick (see *Pre-ride checks*). Add more oil if necessary – this is likely if a new filter has been fitted.

10 Check around the drain plug and filter cover for leaks. If a leak is evident and a new O-ring was not used, you will have to drain the oil again and fit a new O-ring. If a new one was used then make sure the plug and/or cover bolts is/are tightened to the correct torque setting using a torque wrench. On MT and YZF-R models install the belly pan/fairing sections (see Chapter 7). On all models reset the oil change reminder function (see below).

11 The old oil drained from the engine cannot be re-used and should be disposed of properly. Check with your local refuse disposal company, disposal facility or environmental agency to see whether they will accept the used oil for recycling. Don't pour used oil into drains or onto the ground.

HAYNES HiNT ***Check the old oil carefully – if it is very metallic coloured, then the engine is experiencing wear from break-in (new engine) or from insufficient lubrication. If there are flakes or chips of metal in the oil, then something is drastically wrong internally and the engine will have to be disassembled for inspection and repair. If there are pieces of fibre-like material in the oil, the clutch is experiencing excessive wear and should be checked.***

OIL CARE – FOLLOW THE CODE

Note: It is illegal and anti-social to dump oil down the drain. To find the location of your local oil recycling bank in the UK, call 03708 506 506 or visit www.oilbankline.org.uk

Oil and filter change

12 The filter must be changed at every second oil change. Drain the oil as described in Steps 2 to 4.

13 Unscrew the filter housing cover bolts and remove the cover, and allow any oil to drain **(see illustrations)**. Withdraw the filter, noting which way round it fits **(see illustration)**. Clean the cover and housing using a clean lint-free cloth.

14 Remove the O-ring from the cover – a new one must be fitted **(see illustration 8.15)**.

15 Smear lithium-based grease onto the new O-ring and fit it into the groove in the

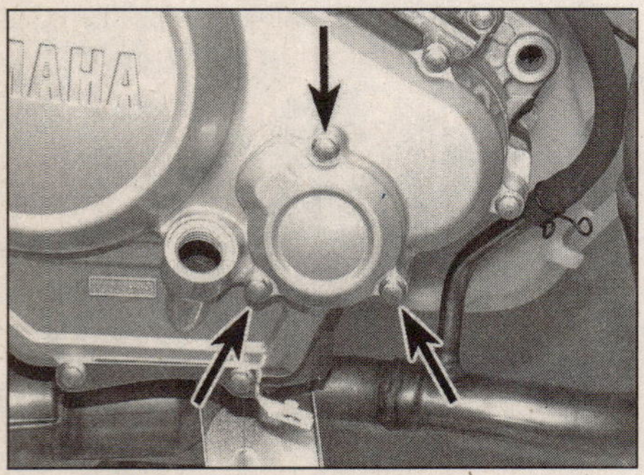

8.13a Unscrew the bolts (arrowed)...

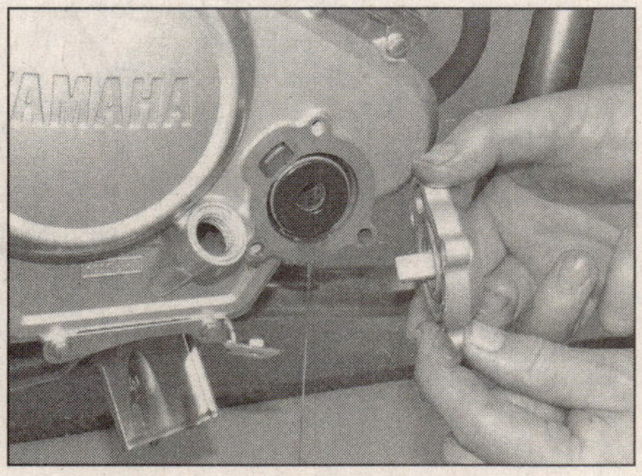

8.13b ...allow the oil to drain...

8.13c ...then remove the filter

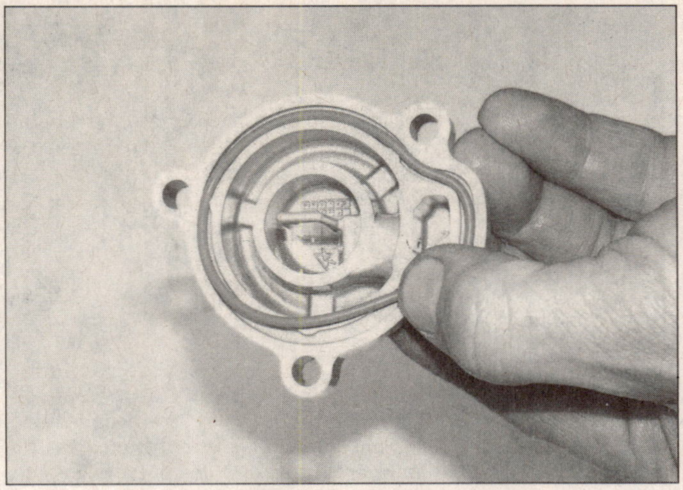

8.15 Fit a new O-ring into the groove

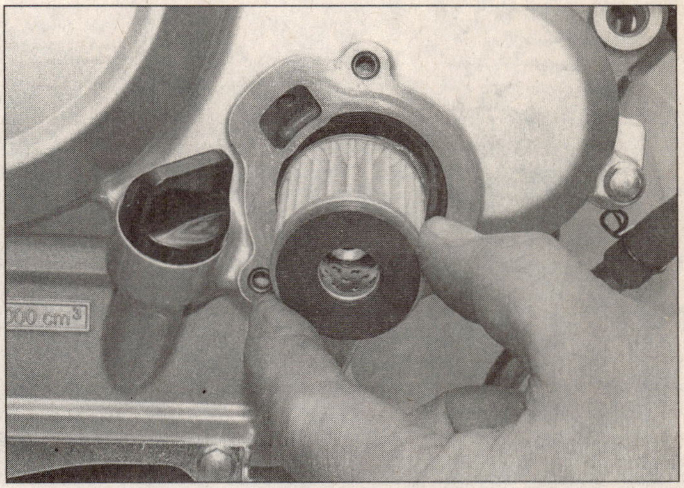

8.16a Fit the new filter...

8.16b ...then fit the cover

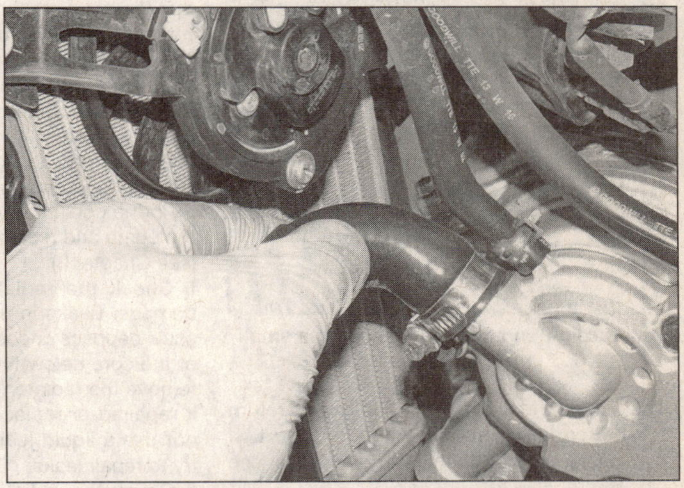

9.2 Check the hoses for cracks and hardening

cover, making sure it is correctly seated **(see illustration)**.

16 Fit the new filter into the housing **(see illustration)**. Fit the cover and tighten the bolts evenly in a few stages to the torque setting specified at the beginning of the chapter **(see illustration)**.

17 Refill the engine with the correct type and quantity of oil (see Steps 6 to 11).

Oil change reminder function reset

WR models

18 To reset the oil change reminder press the RESET/SELECT button briefly, then press it again for at least five seconds. When the OIL display stops flashing and stays on release the RESET/SELECT button within three seconds, and the OIL display should go off. If the display continues to flash repeat the reset procedure.

MT and YZF-R models

19 To reset the oil change reminder after a scheduled oil change (i.e. after an 1800 mile interval), make sure the instruments are in ODO mode, then press the RESET button for two seconds until the OIL SERV display flashes, then press the RESET button for at least fifteen seconds. Note that when the OIL SERV function is reset the DIST SERV function (that shows the distance covered since the last reset) will also be reset.

20 To reset the oil change reminder after a non-scheduled (i.e early) oil change, make sure the instruments are in ODO mode, then press the INFO button to select DIST SERV, then press the RESET button for two seconds until the DIST SERV display flashes, then press the RESET button for at least fifteen seconds. Note that when the DIST SERV function is reset the OIL SERV function will also be reset.

9 Cooling system

Check

⚠ ***Warning: The engine must be cool before beginning this procedure.***

1 On WR models remove the fuel tank cover, on MT models remove the air scoops, and on YZF-R models remove the centre and upper sections of the fairing on each side (see Chapter 7). Check the coolant level in the reservoir (see *Pre-ride checks*).

2 Check the entire cooling system for evidence of leaks. Examine each rubber coolant hose along its entire length. Look for cracks, abrasions and other damage. Squeeze each hose at various points to see whether they are dried out or hard **(see illustration)**.

9.3a Check around the pump (arrowed)...

9.3b ...and the thermostat housing (arrowed)

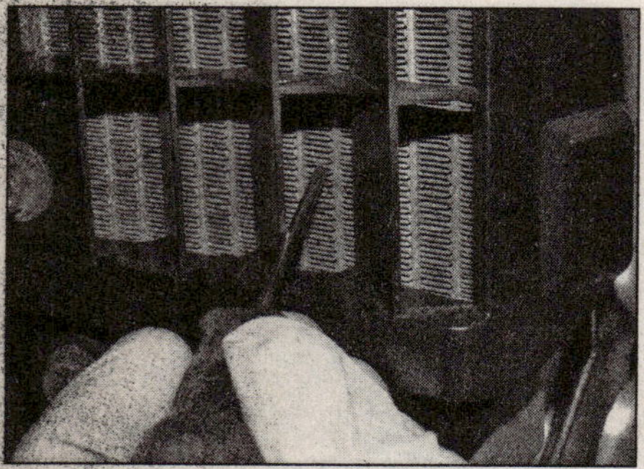

9.6 Straighten any bent fins using a small screwdriver

They should feel firm, yet pliable, and return to their original shape when released. If necessary, replace them with new ones (see Chapter 3).

3 Check for evidence of leaks at each cooling system hose connection, and around the water pump and the thermostat housing **(see illustrations)**. If the pump cover, pump body or thermostat housing cover is leaking, check that the bolts are tight. If they are, remove the pump cover or complete pump or thermostat cover as required and fit a new gasket or O-ring(s) as required (see Chapter 3).

4 To prevent leakage of coolant from the cooling system to the lubrication system and vice versa, a double-lipped seal is fitted around the pump shaft. If there is evidence of oil in the coolant or coolant in the oil, remove the pump and replace the seal with a new one (see Chapter 3).

5 Check the radiator for leaks and other damage. Leaks in the radiator leave tell-tale scale deposits or coolant stains on the outside of the core below the leak. If leaks are noted, remove the radiator (see Chapter 3) and have it repaired or replace it with a new one – do not use a liquid leak stopping compound to try to repair leaks.

6 Check the radiator fins for mud, dirt and insects, which may impede the flow of air through it. If the fins are dirty, remove the radiator (see Chapter 3) and clean it using water or low pressure compressed air directed through the fins from the back of the radiator. If the fins are bent or distorted, straighten them carefully with a screwdriver **(see illustration)**. If the air flow is restricted by bent or damaged fins over more than 20% of the radiator's surface area, replace the radiator with a new one.

Warning: Do not remove the pressure cap when the engine is hot. It is good practice to cover the cap with a heavy cloth and turn the cap slowly anti-clockwise. If you hear a hissing sound (indicating that there is still pressure in the system), wait until it stops, then continue turning the cap until it can be removed.

7 On WR models undo the locking screw on the radiator pressure cap **(see illustration)**. On all models remove the pressure cap from the radiator filler neck by turning it anti-clockwise until it reaches the stop. If you hear a hissing sound (indicating there is still pressure in the system), wait until it stops. Now press down on the cap and continue turning it until it can be removed **(see illustration)**.

8 Check the condition of the coolant

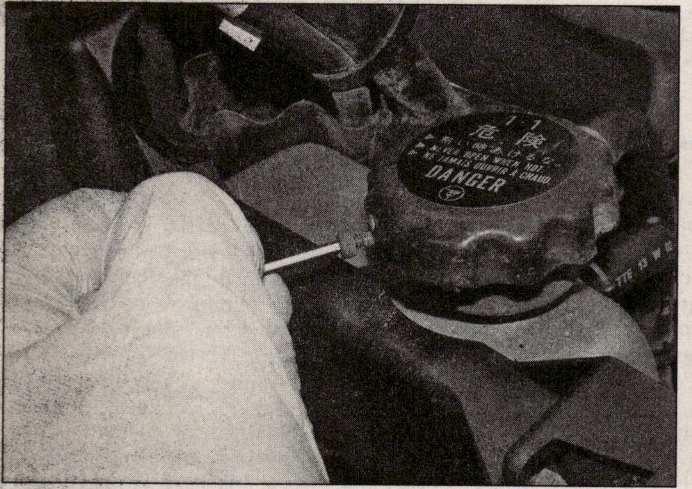

9.7a Undo the locking screw on WR models

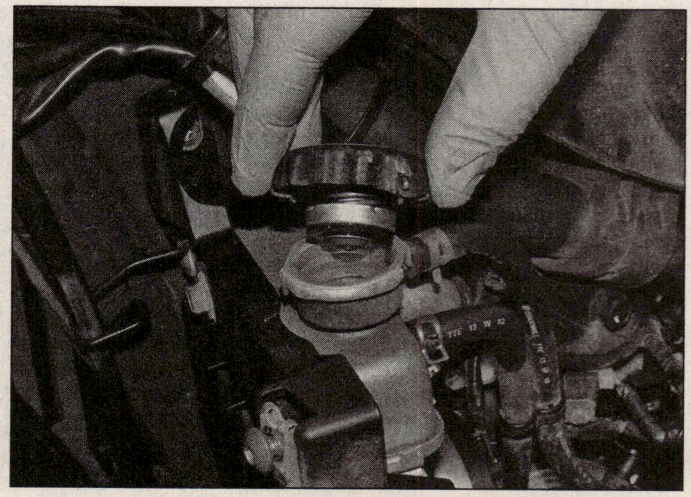

9.7b Remove the pressure cap as described

9.14a Unscrew the drain bolt...

9.14b ...and allow the coolant to drain

in the system. If it is rust-coloured or if accumulations of scale are visible, drain, flush and refill the system with new coolant (see below). If available check the antifreeze content of the coolant with an antifreeze hydrometer. The system must have the correct coolant mixture, as specified at the beginning of the chapter – if the coolant is too weak (too little anti-freeze) there will not be adequate protection against freezing and corrosion, and if it is too strong the ability to cool the engine is reduced. If the hydrometer indicates an incorrect mixture, drain, flush and refill the system (see below).

9 Check the cap seal for cracks and other damage. If in doubt about the pressure cap's condition, or if problems such as overheating or a loss of coolant occur (and there are no signs of leakage), have it tested by a Yamaha dealer or fit a new one.

10 Fit the cap by turning it clockwise until it reaches the first stop then push down on it and continue turning until it can turn no further. Start the engine and let it reach normal operating temperature, then check for leaks again. As the coolant temperature increases, the electric fan mounted on the back of the radiator should come on automatically and the temperature should begin to drop. If it does not, check the fan and fan circuit (see Chapter 3).

11 If the coolant level is consistently low, and no evidence of leaks can be found, have the entire system pressure checked by a Yamaha dealer.

Change the coolant

⚠ ***Warning: Allow the engine to cool completely before performing this maintenance operation. Also, don't allow anti-freeze to come into contact with your skin or the painted surfaces of the motorcycle. Rinse off spills immediately with plenty of water. Anti-freeze is highly toxic if ingested. Never leave anti-freeze lying around in an open container or in puddles on the floor; children and pets are attracted by its sweet smell and may drink it. Check with local authorities (councils) about disposing of anti-freeze. Many communities have collection centres which will see that anti-freeze is disposed of safely. Anti-freeze is also combustible, so don't store it near open flames.***

Draining

12 On WR models remove the fuel tank cover, on MT models remove the air scoops and belly-pan, and on YZF-R models remove the centre and upper sections of the fairing on the right-hand side, and all sections on the left-hand side (see Chapter 7).

13 On WR models undo the locking screw on the radiator pressure cap **(see illustration 9.7a)**. On all models remove the pressure cap from the top of the radiator by turning it anti-clockwise until it reaches a stop. If you hear a hissing sound (indicating there is still pressure in the system), wait until it stops. Now press down on the cap and continue turning the cap until it can be removed **(see illustration 9.7b)**.

14 Position a suitable container below the front of the engine. Unscrew the drain bolt from the cylinder and allow the coolant to completely drain **(see illustrations)**. Keep the sealing washer for use during flushing, but note that a new washer must be fitted before refilling the system with coolant.

15 On WR models remove the reservoir and drain it (see Chapter 3). On MT and YZF-R models detach the hose from the bottom of the reservoir and allow it to drain **(see illustration)**.

Flushing

16 Flush the system with clean tap water by inserting a hose in the radiator filler neck. Allow the water to run through the system until it is clear and flows out cleanly. If the radiator is extremely corroded, remove it (see Chapter 3) and have it cleaned by a specialist. Also flush the reservoir, then on WR models refit it, and on MT and YZF-R models fit the hose back onto its union.

Refilling

17 Fit the cooling system drain bolt using a new sealing washer and tighten it to the torque setting specified at the beginning of the Chapter.

18 Fill the system to the base of the radiator filler neck with the specified coolant mixture **(see illustration)**. Note: Pour the coolant in slowly to minimise the amount of air entering the system, and when full carefully waggle the bike from

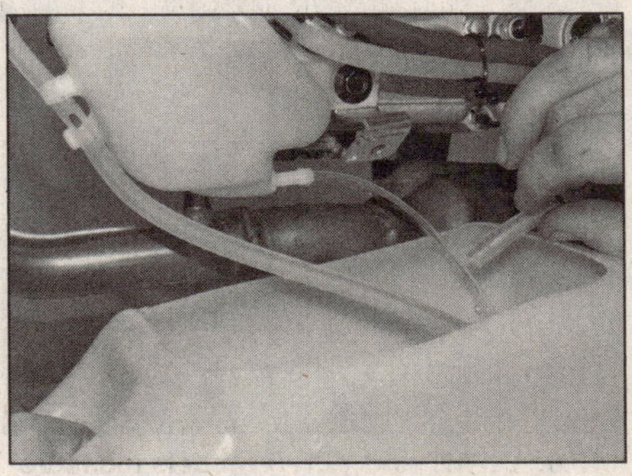

9.15 Detach the hose and drain the reservoir

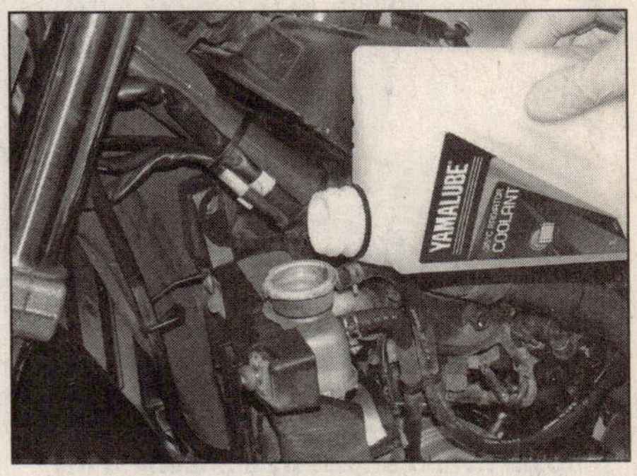

9.18 Fill the cooling system as described using the specified coolant

side to side to dislodge any trapped air. Fill the reservoir to the FULL line (see *Pre-ride checks*). Fit the radiator cap and the reservoir cap.

19 Start the engine and allow it to reach normal operating temperature, then shut it off. Let the engine cool then remove the pressure cap as described in Step 10. Check that the coolant level is still up to the base of the upper radiator filler neck. If it's low, add the specified mixture until it reaches the base of the filler neck. Refit the cap.

20 Check the coolant level in the reservoir and top up if necessary.

21 Check the system for leaks. Install the body panels (see Chapter 7).

22 Do not dispose of the old coolant by pouring it down the drain. Instead pour it into a heavy plastic container, cap it tightly and take it into an authorised disposal site or service station – see Warning.

Hose renewal

23 The hoses will deteriorate with age and should be replaced with new ones regardless of their apparent condition (see Chapter 3).

10 Brake system

Brake system check

1 A routine general check of the brake system will ensure that any problems are discovered and remedied before the rider's safety is jeopardised. Check the brake pads for wear (see below), and make sure the fluid level in each reservoir is correct (see *Pre-ride checks*).

2 Make sure all brake component fasteners are tight. Check the brake lever and pedal for improper or rough action, excessive play, bends, and other damage. Replace any damaged parts with new ones (see Chapter 6). Clean and lubricate the lever and pedal pivots if their action is stiff or rough (see Section 14). If the lever or pedal is spongy, bleed the brakes (see Chapter 6).

3 Twist and flex the hoses while looking for cracks, bulges and seeping hydraulic fluid. Check extra carefully around the areas where the hoses connect with the banjo fittings, as these are common areas for hose failure **(see illustration)**. Inspect the banjo fittings connected to the brake hoses, and on MT and YZF-R models check the section of pipe under the bottom yoke and where it joins with the hoses. If the fittings are rusted, scratched or cracked, fit new hoses. On MT-A and YZF-RA (ABS) models also check the brake pipes and hose/pipe joints all the way to the ABS modulator under the rider's seat.

4 Make sure the brake light comes on when the front brake lever is applied, then repeat the check for the rear brake pedal. If the light does not come on with the front brake lever applied check the switch (see Chapter 8). If the light does not come on with the rear brake pedal applied on models without ABS check the switch (see Chapter 8). On models with ABS refer to the following Step and first check the adjustment of the switch. If the switches are good check the tail light (see Chapter 8).

5 Models with ABS have a conventional and adjustable spring actuated switch (rather than a hydraulically actuated switch as on non-ABS models). Make sure the brake light comes on just before the rear brake takes effect. The switch is mounted behind the rider's right-hand footrest bracket. If the brake light comes on too soon or too late, or is permanently on or does not come on at all, adjustment is necessary – hold the switch and turn the adjuster nut on the switch body until the brake light is activated when required **(see illustration)**. If the brake light comes on too late or not at all, turn the nut clockwise. If the brake light comes on too soon or is permanently on, turn the nut anti-clockwise. If the brake light still does not come on following adjustment, first check the switch, then check the tail light (see Chapter 8).

6 The height of the rear brake pedal in relation to the footrest should be as specified at the beginning of the Chapter, or to suit the rider's preference if required **(see illustration)**. To adjust the height, slacken the clevis locknut on the master cylinder pushrod, then turn the pushrod until the pedal is at the desired height **(see illustration)**. On completion tighten the locknut.

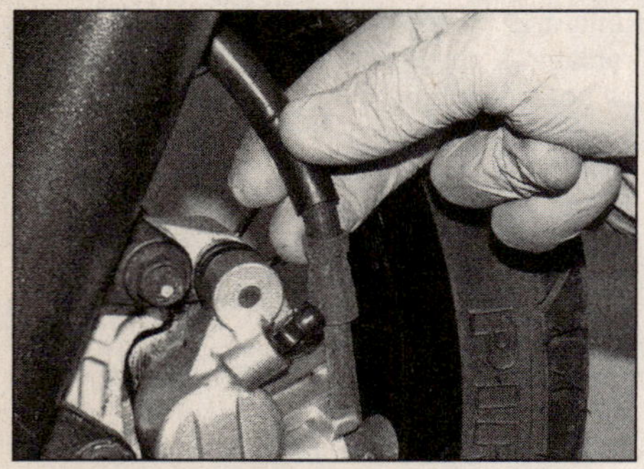

10.3 Twist and flex the hoses to check for cracks and deterioration

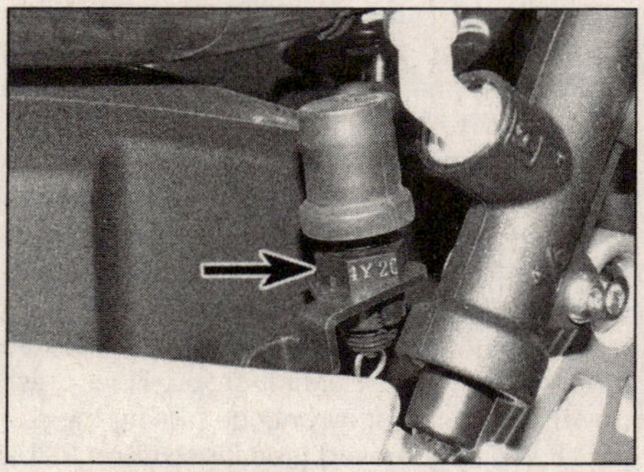

10.5 Hold the switch and turn the nut (arrowed) as required

10.6a On WR models measure the height of the top of the footrest above the top of the pedal...

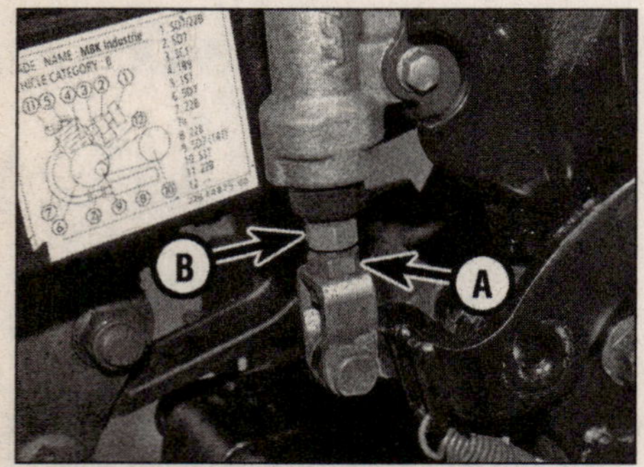

10.6b ...and adjust by slackening the locknut (A) and turning the pushrod nut (B)

10.6c On MT and YZF-R models measure the height of the middle of the footrest above the middle of the pedal...

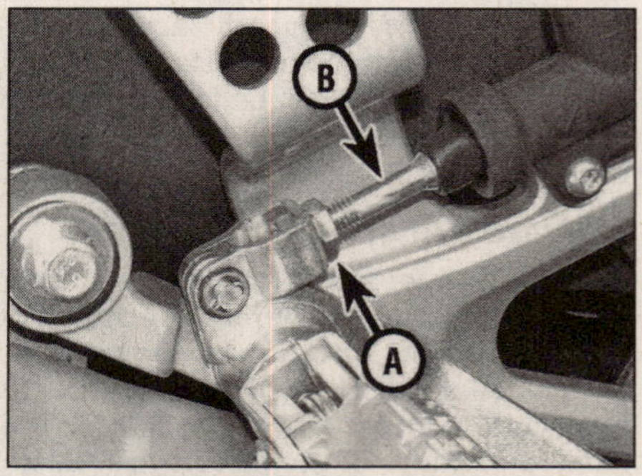

10.6d ...and adjust by slackening the locknut (A) and turning the pushrod (B)

10.7a Front brake pad wear limit lines (arrowed) – WR models

10.7b Rear brake pad wear limit lines (arrowed) – WR models

10.7c Front brake pad wear indicator grooves (arrowed) – MT and YZF-R models

10.7d Rear brake pad wear indicator groove (arrowed) – MT and YZF-R models

Brake pad wear check

7 Each brake pad has wear indicators in the form of wear limit lines or grooves in the friction material, but note that an accumulation of road dirt and brake dust could make the indicators difficult to see **(see illustrations)**. If either pad has worn to the limit line or to the bottom of the groove(s) new pads must be fitted (see Chapter 6).

8 If the wear indicators aren't visible, then visually check the amount of friction material remaining. Yamaha specify a minimum thickness of 1 mm for all pads on WR models, and of 2 mm for the front pads and 1 mm for the rear pads on MT and YZF-R models. Replace the pads with new ones when they are approaching the minimum thickness (see Chapter 6). On the front caliper also check that the pads are wearing evenly – uneven wear is indicative of a sticking piston, in which case the caliper should be overhauled (see Chapter 6).

9 If the pads are dirty or if you are in doubt as to the amount of friction material remaining, remove them for inspection (see Chapter 6). If the pads are excessively worn, check the brake discs (see Chapter 6).

Brake fluid change

10 The brake fluid should be changed every two years. Refer to Chapter 6, Section 11 for details. Ensure that all the old fluid is pumped from the hydraulic system and that the level in the fluid reservoir is checked and the brakes tested before riding the motorcycle.

Brake hoses

11 The hoses will deteriorate with age and should be replaced with new ones every four years regardless of their apparent condition, or sooner if necessary (see Chapter 6).

12 Always replace the banjo union sealing washers with new ones when fitting new hoses. Refill the system with new brake fluid and bleed the system as described in Chapter 6.

11 Wheels, tyres and wheel bearings

Wheels

WR models

1 Check the spokes for damage and corrosion. A broken or bent spoke must be replaced with a new one immediately because the load taken by it will be transferred to the other spokes, which in turn may fail. Check the tension in each spoke by tapping it with a screwdriver – each spoke should emit the same sharp pinging sound. An overtight spoke will emit a ping with a higher pitch than the rest, and a loose spoke will emit a dull sounding low pitch ping. If a spoke needs adjustment turn the adjuster on the rim end using a spoke adjustment tool or suitable spanner until the pitch is correct and the same as the rest **(see illustration)**.

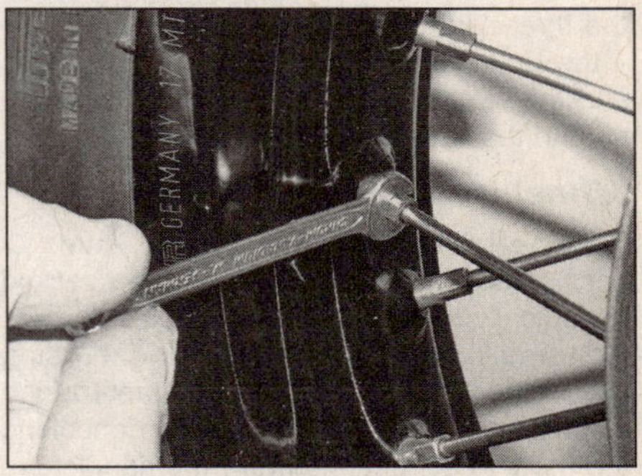

11.1 Adjusting spoke tension

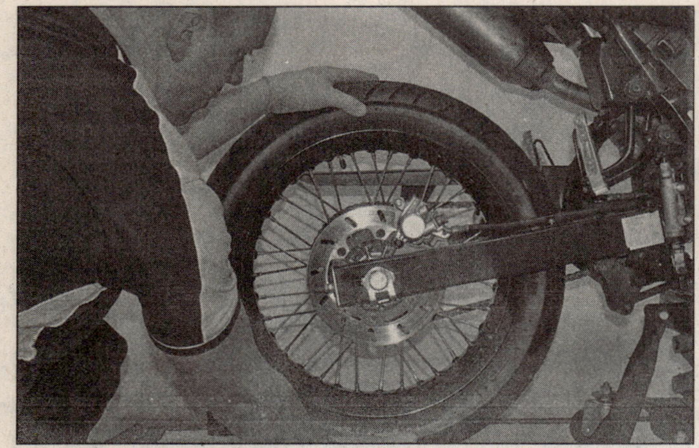

11.8 Checking for play in the rear wheel bearings

12.2 Compress and release the front suspension

2 If unevenly tensioned spokes have been found check wheel runout and alignment as described in Chapter 6. Seek the advice of a dealer or wheel specialist if the rim is misaligned.

MT and YZF-R models

3 Cast wheels are virtually maintenance free, but they should be kept clean and checked periodically for cracks and other damage. Also check the wheel runout and alignment (see Chapter 6). Never attempt to repair damaged cast wheels; they must be replaced with new ones if damaged.

All models

4 Check that any wheel balance weights are firmly in place on the rim. If you think a weight has fallen off, or the wheel is unbalanced, have it balanced by a dealer or tyre fitting centre.

Tyres

5 Check the tyre condition and tread depth thoroughly – see *Pre-ride checks*.
6 Make sure the valve cap is in place and tight. Check the valve for signs of damage. If tyre deflation occurs and it is not due to a slow puncture the valve core may be loose or it could be leaking past the seal – remove the cap and make sure the core is tight; if it is tight then it could be leaking – unscrew the core from the valve housing using a core removal tool and thread a new one in its place. A tool can be made quite easily by cutting a slot into the threaded end of a bolt using a hacksaw – the bolt must fit inside the valve housing and the slot must be deep enough to locate around the flat sides of the core and grip it.

Wheel bearings

7 Wheel bearings will wear over a considerable mileage and should be checked periodically to avoid handling problems.
8 Support the motorcycle upright using an auxiliary stand so that the wheel being examined is off the ground. When checking the front wheel bearings turn the handlebars to full lock on one side so you have something to push against. Check for any play in the bearings by pushing and pulling the wheel against the hub **(see illustration)**. Also spin the wheel and check that it turns smoothly and without any grating noises – take into account any brake drag and noise, and if in doubt displace the brake caliper (see Chapter 6) and repeat the check. When checking the rear wheel also take into account drive chain drag and noise.
9 If any play is detected in the hub, or if the wheel does not rotate smoothly and freely, remove the wheel and inspect the bearings for wear or damage (see Chapter 6).

12 Suspension

1 The suspension components must be maintained in top operating condition to ensure rider safety. Loose, worn or damaged suspension parts decrease the motorcycle's stability and control.

Front suspension check

2 While standing alongside the motorcycle, apply the front brake and push on the handlebars to compress the forks several times **(see illustration)**. See if they move up-and-down smoothly without binding. If binding is felt, the forks should be disassembled and inspected (see Chapter 5).
3 Inspect the fork inner tubes for scratches, corrosion and pitting – if there is any on the section that passes through the seal with the movement of the fork this will cause premature seal failure. If necessary, disassemble the fork (see Chapter 5), and either fit new tubes, or have the tubes re-chromed by a specialist (they must be hard chromed, bright chrome is no good).
4 Inspect the inner tube just above (WR models) or below (MT and YZF-R models) the dust seal for signs of oil leakage, then carefully lever the seal off using a flat-bladed screwdriver and inspect the area around the fork seal **(see illustration)**. If leakage is evident, the seals must be replaced with new ones (see Chapter 5). If there is evidence of corrosion between the seal retaining ring and its groove in the fork outer tube, spray the area with a penetrative lubricant, otherwise the ring will be difficult to remove if needed. Press the dust seal back into the top of the fork outer tube on completion.
5 Check the tightness of the fork clamp bolts in the yokes, referring to the illustrations and torque settings specified in Chapter 5.

Rear suspension check

6 Inspect the rear shock absorber for fluid leakage and tightness of the mountings **(see illustration)**. If leakage is found, the shock must be replaced with a new one (see Chapter 5).

12.4 Check for oil leakage and corrosion on the inner tube – WR shown

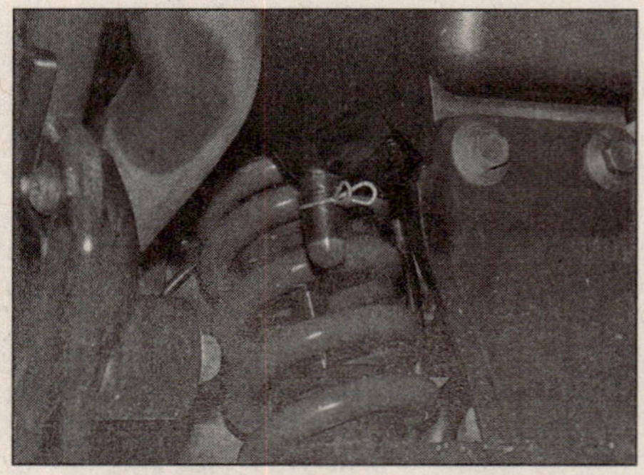

12.6 Check for signs of oil leakage on the rod

12.7 Compress and release the rear suspension

12.8 Checking for play in the swingarm bushes

7 With the aid of an assistant to support the bike, compress the rear suspension several times **(see illustration)**. It should move up-and-down freely without binding and grating. If any binding is felt or grating is heard, the worn or faulty component must be identified and checked (see Chapter 5). The problem could be due to either the shock absorber, the suspension linkage, or the swingarm pivot.

8 Support the motorcycle so that the rear wheel is off the ground and so no weight is taken through the rear suspension. Grab the swingarm and rock it from side-to-side – there should be no discernible movement at the rear **(see illustration)**. If there's a little movement or a slight clicking can be heard, inspect the tightness of the swingarm, shock absorber and suspension linkage bolts and nuts, referring to the torque settings specified at the beginning of Chapter 5, then re-check for movement.

9 Grasp the swingarm ends or the top of the rear wheel and attempt to pull upwards – there should be no discernible freeplay before the shock absorber compresses **(see illustration)**. Any freeplay felt in either check indicates worn bushes or bearings in the shock absorber, swingarm or suspension linkage. The worn components must be identified and replaced with new ones (see Chapter 5).

10 To make an accurate assessment of the swingarm bearings, remove the rear wheel (see Chapter 6) and the bolt securing the suspension linkage to the swingarm (see Chapter 5). Grasp the rear of the swingarm with one hand and place your other hand at the junction of the swingarm and the frame. Try to move the rear of the swingarm from side-to-side. Any wear (play) in the bushes should be felt as movement between the swingarm and the frame at the front. If there is any play the swingarm will be felt to move forward and backward at the front (not from side-to-side). If there is any play in the swingarm, remove it for inspection (see Chapter 5).

Front fork oil change

11 Although there is no set interval for changing the fork oil, note that the oil will degrade over a period of time and lose its damping qualities. Refer to Chapter 5 for details of fork removal, oil draining and refilling. The forks do not need to be completely disassembled to change the oil.

Rear suspension lubrication

12 At the prescribed intervals remove the suspension linkage and swingarm, and clean and re-grease all the components, replacing grease seals and bearings with new ones as required (see Chapter 5).

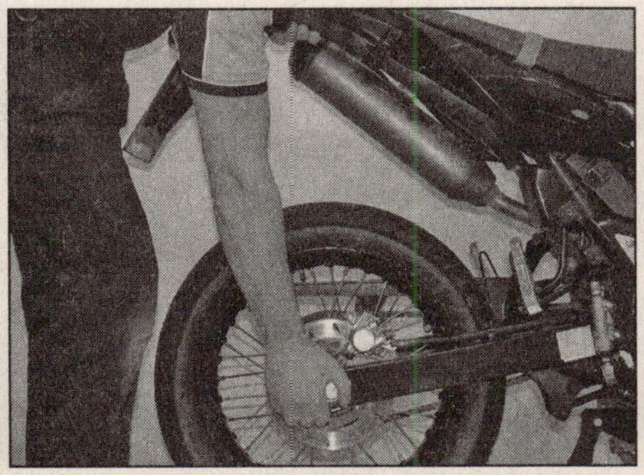

12.9 Checking for play in the rear shock mountings and suspension linkage

13.4 Checking for play in the steering head bearings

13 Steering head bearings

Freeplay check and adjustment

1 Steering head bearings can become dented, rough or loose during normal use of the machine. In extreme cases, worn or loose steering head bearings can cause steering wobble – a condition that is potentially dangerous.

Check

2 On MT models remove the belly-pan, and on YZF-R models remove the lower sections of the fairing on each side (see Chapter 7). On all models raise the front wheel off the ground using an auxiliary stand placed under the engine – do not take the weight of the bike through the exhaust pipe. Always make sure that the bike is properly supported and secure.

3 Point the front wheel straight-ahead and slowly move the handlebars from lock to lock – the movement should feel smooth and free. Any dents or roughness in the bearing races will be felt and if the bearings are too tight the bars will not move smoothly and freely. Again point the wheel straight-ahead, and tap the front of the wheel to one side. The wheel should 'fall' under its own weight to the limit of its lock, indicating that the bearings are not too tight (take into account the restriction that the brake hose, cables and wiring may have). Check for similar movement to the other side. If the bearings feel tight, adjust them, but if they feel rough and/or notchy remove the steering stem and check the bearings (see Chapter 5), and either replace them with new ones, or clean and re-grease them, as required.

4 Next, grasp the bottom of the forks and gently pull and push them forward and backward **(see illustration)**. Any looseness or freeplay in the steering head bearings will be felt as front-to-rear movement of the forks. If

13.6 Unscrew the bolt (arrowed)

13.7 Unscrew the bolt (arrowed) on each side and pitch the assembly forwards

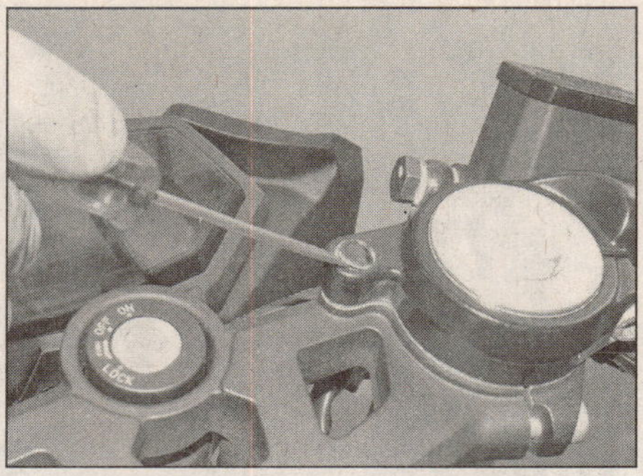
13.8a Remove the blanking caps

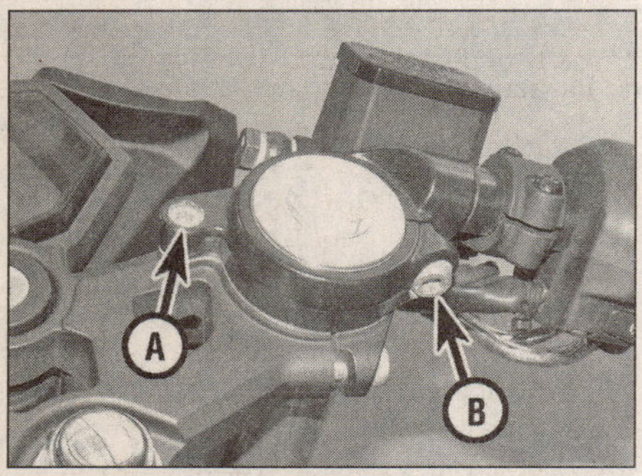

13.8b Handlebar positioning bolt (A) and clamp bolt (B)

13.9a On WR models slacken the clamp bolts (arrowed) on each side

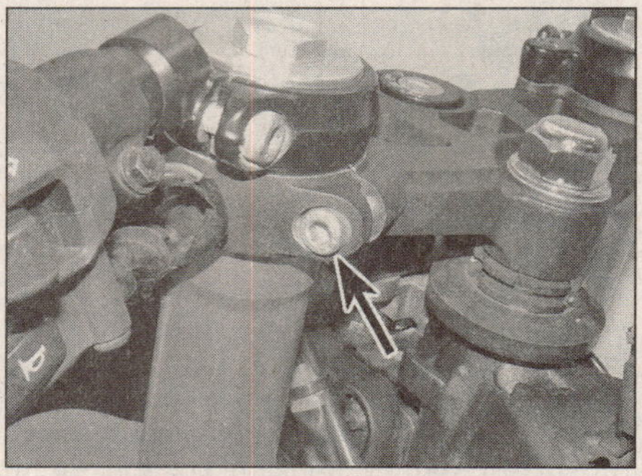
13.9b On MT and YZF-R models slacken the clamp bolt (arrowed) on each side – YZF-R shown, on MT models the bolt is in the front

play is felt, adjust the bearings as described below.

> **HAYNES HiNT** ***Make sure you are not mistaking any movement between the bike and stand, or between the stand and the ground, for freeplay in the bearings. Do not pull and push the forks too hard – a gentle movement is all that is needed. Freeplay between the fork tubes due to worn bushes can also be misinterpreted as steering head bearing play – do not confuse the two.***

Adjustment

5 To prevent the possibility of damage should a tool slip, on all models remove the fuel tank cover, and on YZF-R models remove the centre and upper sections of the fairing on each side, and the front fairing (see Chapter 7). If you do not want to remove them cover them in plenty of rag.

6 On WR models remove the headlight (see Chapter 8). Undo the bracket bolt below the instruments **(see illustration)**.

7 On MT models disconnect the front brake light switch wiring connectors from the switch on the underside of the master cylinder. Displace the master cylinder from the handlebar, wrap it in some rag and support it clear. Undo the headlight bracket bolt on each side and tip the headlight assembly forwards a bit, then tie it to the fork(s) so it remains clear of the yoke but can't fall forwards **(see illustration)**.

8 On YZF-R models ease the cap from each handlebar positioning bolt **(see illustration)**. Slacken the positioning bolts and the handlebar clamp bolts **(see illustration)**.

9 Slacken the fork clamp bolt(s) in each side of the top yoke **(see illustrations)**.

10 Unscrew the steering stem nut and remove the washer.

11 Ease the top yoke/handlebar assembly up the forks until there is enough space to lift the tabbed lockwasher clear of the nuts.

12 Lift the tabbed lock washer, noting how it locates, and when the tabs are clear of the locknut turn it to offset the tabs from the notches and rest it on top of the nut **(see illustration)**. Slacken the locknut, using a C-spanner or a peg spanner if necessary, though it should only be finger-tight **(see illustration)**.

13 Using either a C-spanner or a drift located in one of the notches, slacken the adjuster nut slightly until pressure is just released,

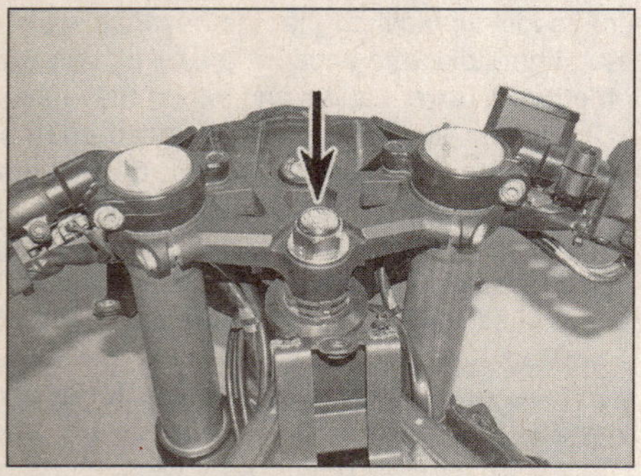
13.10 Steering stem nut (arrowed) – YZF-R shown

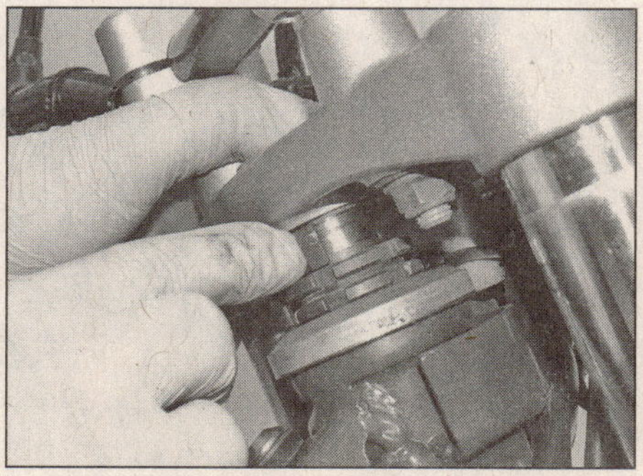
13.12a Lift and turn the lockwasher...

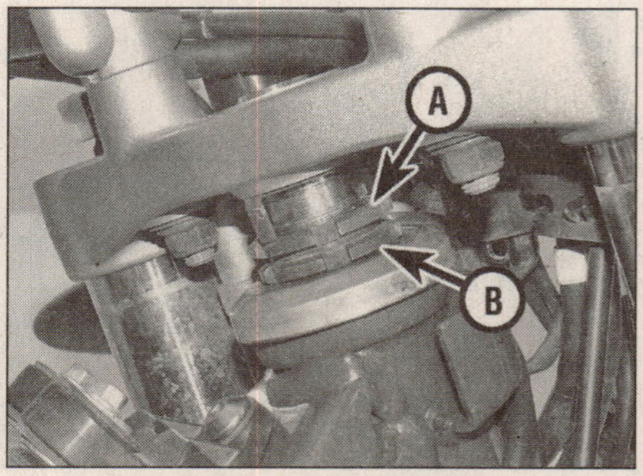

13.12b ... then slacken the locknut (A). Adjuster nut (B)

then tighten it until all freeplay is removed, then tighten it a little more **(see illustration 13.12b)**. This pre-loads the bearings. Now slacken the nut, then tighten it again, setting it so that all freeplay is just removed, yet the steering is able to move freely from side to side. To do this tighten the nut only a little at a time, and after each tightening repeat the checks outlined above (Steps 3 to 4) until the bearings are correctly set. The object is to set the adjuster nut so that the bearings are under a very light loading, just enough to remove any freeplay. The torque setting at the beginning of this Chapter can be applied if you have access to the Yamaha tool (see Chapter 5 Section 9).

Caution: Take great care not to apply excessive pressure because this will cause premature failure of the bearings.

14 With the bearings correctly adjusted, tighten the locknut finger-tight, then tighten it a little further until its notches align with those in the adjuster nut. If necessary, counter-hold the adjuster nut and use a C-spanner to turn the locknut until the notches align, but make sure the adjuster nut does not turn as well, and note that the locknut should not be any tighter than necessary for alignment of the notches or the rubber washer will be damaged. Fit the tabbed lock washer so that the tabs fit into the notches in both the locknut and adjuster nut **(see illustration 13.12a)**.

15 Slide the top yoke down the forks. Fit the washer and steering stem nut and tighten the nut to the torque setting specified at the beginning of the Chapter. Now tighten the fork clamp bolt(s) to the specified torque setting **(see illustration 13.9a or b)**.

16 Re-check the bearing adjustment as described above and re-adjust if necessary.

17 On WR models fit the bracket bolt then install the headlight **(see illustration 13.6)**.

18 On MT models align the headlight bracket and fit the bolts **(see illustration 13.7)**. Mount the master cylinder on the handlebar, fitting the clamp with the arrow pointing forwards and aligning the clamp mating surfaces with the punch mark on the back of the handlebar, then tighten the front bolt first, then the rear bolt, to the specified torque. Connect the brake light switch wiring.

19 On YZF-R models tighten the handlebar positioning bolts to the specified torque and fit the caps, then tighten the clamp bolts to the specified torque **(see illustrations 13.8b and a)**.

20 Install the fuel tank cover, and on YZF-R models the fairing sections if removed (see Chapter 7).

Lubrication

21 Over time the grease in the bearings will be dispersed or will harden allowing the ingress of dirt and water.

22 At the specified interval disassemble the steering head and clean and re-grease the bearings (see Chapter 5).

14 General lubrication

1 The cables, footrest pivots, clutch and brake lever pivots, brake pedal pivot and sidestand pivots are exposed to the elements, and so need to be checked and lubricated periodically to ensure safe and trouble-free operation.

Pivot points

2 In order for the lubricant to be applied where it will do the most good, the component should be disassembled (see Chapters 5 and 6). The lubricant recommended by Yamaha for each application is listed at the beginning of the Chapter. If aerosol lubricant is being used, it can be applied to the pivot joint gaps and will usually work its way into the areas where friction occurs, so less disassembly of the component is needed (however it is always better to do so and clean off all corrosion, dirt and old lubricant first). If motor oil or light grease is being used, apply it sparingly as it may attract dirt (which could cause the controls to bind or wear at an accelerated rate).

Cables

3 To lubricate the cables, disconnect the relevant cable at its upper end, then lubricate it with a pressure adapter and aerosol lubricant **(see illustrations)**. See Chapter 4 for the throttle cable removal procedure, and Chapter 2 for the clutch cable.

15 Nuts and bolts

1 Since vibration of the machine tends to loosen fasteners, all nuts, bolts, screws, etc. should be periodically checked for proper tightness.

2 Pay particular attention to the following, referring to the relevant Chapter:

a) Spark plug
b) Engine oil drain plug
c) Lever and pedal bolts
d) Footrest bracket bolts
e) Sidestand pivot bolt and nut
f) Engine mounting bolts/nuts
g) Shock absorber and suspension linkage bolts/nuts; swingarm pivot bolt/nut
h) Handlebar bolts
i) Front fork clamp bolts (top and bottom yoke)
j) Steering stem nut
k) Front axle clamp bolt and axle
l) Rear axle nut
m) Front sprocket retainer bolts and rear sprocket nuts
n) Brake caliper and master cylinder mounting bolts
o) Brake hose banjo bolts and caliper bleed valves
p) Brake disc bolts
q) Exhaust system bolts/nuts

3 If a torque wrench is available, use it along with the torque settings given at the beginning of this and other Chapters.

16 Sidestand and starter safety circuit

1 Check the stand springs for damage and distortion. The springs must be capable of retracting the stand fully and holding it retracted when the motorcycle is in use. If a spring is sagged or broken it must be replaced with a new one.

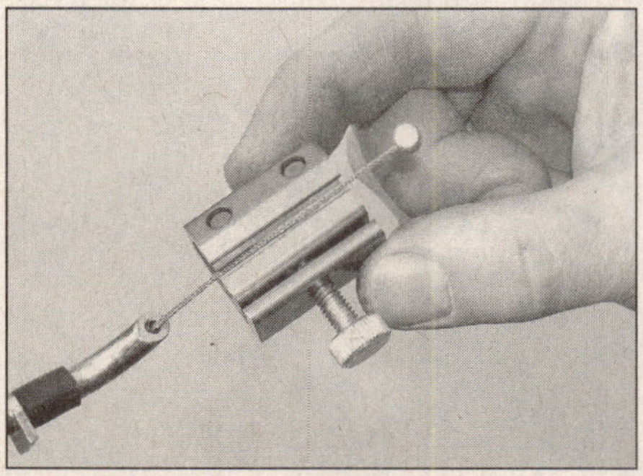

14.3a Fit the cable into the adapter...

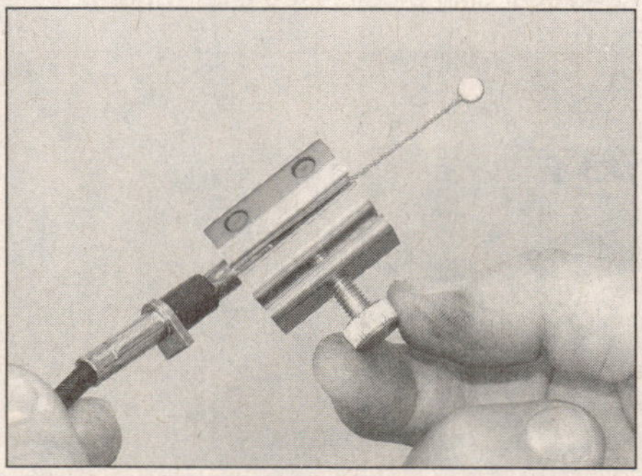

14.3b ...and tighten the screw to seal it in...

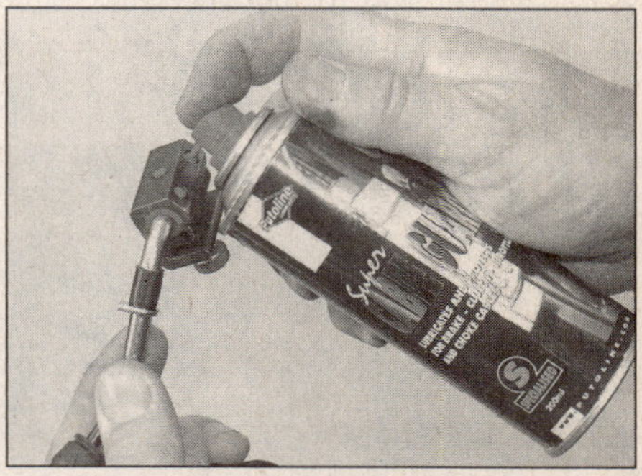

14.3c ...then apply the lubricant using the nozzle provided inserted in the hole in the adapter

2 Lubricate the stand pivot regularly (see Section 16).

3 Check the stand and its mount for bends and cracks. Stands can often be repaired by welding.

4 The starter safety circuit, comprising the neutral switch, the clutch switch and the sidestand switch, prevents the engine from being started unless it is in neutral, or if it is in gear unless the sidestand is up and the clutch lever is pulled in. It also stops the engine if the sidestand is moved down when in gear. Check the circuit is working correctly.

5 If the circuit does not operate as described, check the neutral switch, the clutch switch, the sidestand switch, the starter circuit cut-off relay and diodes, and the wiring between them (see Chapter 8).

17 Battery

Note: *A standard battery is factory fitted on all models, but a maintenance free (MF) battery may have been fitted as a replacement at some point. The different types are easy to distinguish – standard ones have removable caps across the top and electrolyte level lines (marked UPPER and LOWER or MAX and MIN), while MF batteries do not, and are usually marked MF on the front. Access the battery (see Chapter 8) and identify the type before proceeding.*

Caution: Do not attempt to remove the battery caps to check the electrolyte level or battery specific gravity on MF batteries. Removal will damage the caps, resulting in electrolyte leakage and battery damage.

Caution: Be extremely careful when handling or working around the battery. The electrolyte is very caustic and an explosive gas (hydrogen) is given off when the battery is charging.

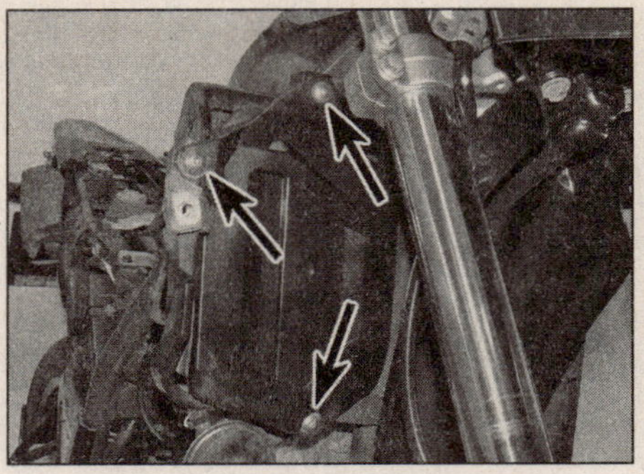

17.1 Undo the screws (arrowed) and remove the cover on WR models

1 On WR models remove the fuel tank cover (see Chapter 7), then remove the battery cover **(see illustration)**. On MT and YZF-R models remove the battery (see Chapter 8).

2 The electrolyte level should be visible through the translucent battery case and should be between the UPPER and LOWER or MAX and MIN level marks **(see illustration)**.

3 If the electrolyte is low, on WR models remove the battery (see Chapter 8). On all models remove the relevant cell cap or caps and fill each cell to the upper level mark with distilled water **(see illustrations)**. Do not use tap water (except in an emergency), and do not overfill. The cell holes are quite small, so use a small funnel or a clean plastic squeeze bottle with a small spout to add the water. Fit the cell caps.

4 Keep the battery case clean to prevent current leakage, which can discharge the battery over a period of time (especially when it sits unused). Wash the outside of the case with a solution of baking soda and water. Rinse the battery thoroughly, then dry it.

5 Look for cracks in the case and replace the battery if any are found. If acid has been spilled on the frame or battery box, neutralise it with a baking soda and water solution, dry it thoroughly, then touch up any damaged paint.

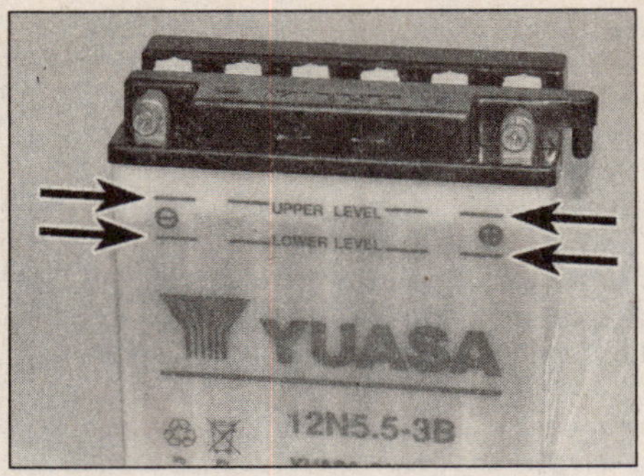

17.2 The electrolyte must lie between the lines (arrowed)

HAYNES HiNT ***Battery corrosion can be kept to a minimum by applying a layer of battery terminal grease or petroleum jelly (Vaseline) to the terminals after the leads have been connected. DO NOT use a mineral based grease.***

6 If the motorcycle sits unused for long periods of time, refer to Chapter 8 and charge the battery once every month to six weeks.

7 The condition of the battery can be assessed by measuring its specific gravity and open-circuit voltage (see Chapter 8).

8 Check the battery terminals and leads are free of corrosion. If corrosion is evident, clean the terminals and lead ends with a wire brush or knife and emery paper.

9 Install the battery (see Chapter 8).

18 Air filter

Caution: If the machine is continually ridden in wet or dusty conditions, the

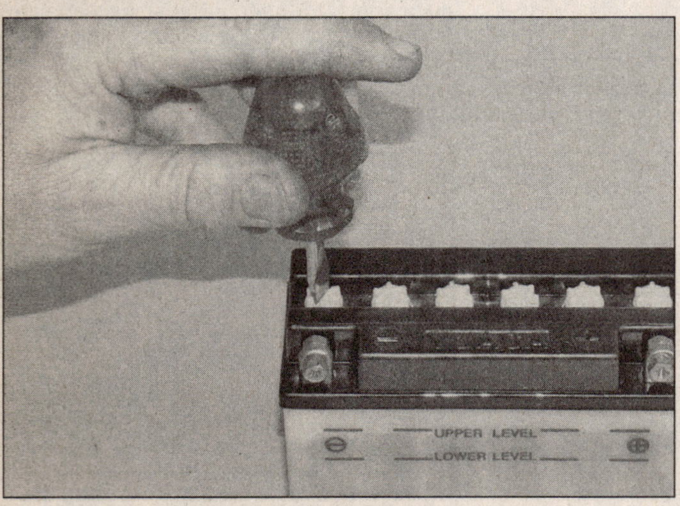

17.3a Unscrew the cap(s) ...

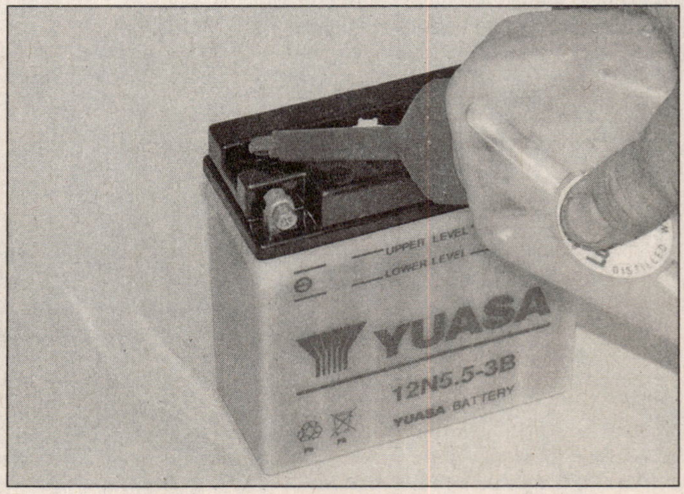

17.3b ... and top the cell(s) up as required

18.1 Unscrew the bolts (arrowed) and remove the bracket

18.3 Undo the screws (arrowed) and remove the cover

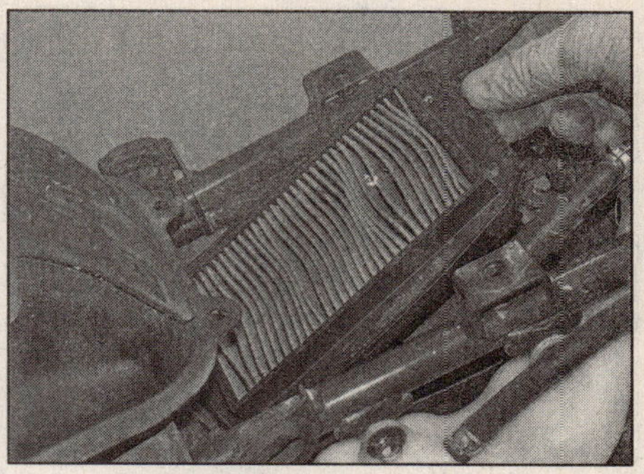

18.4 Remove the filter

18.5a Remove debris caught in the folds

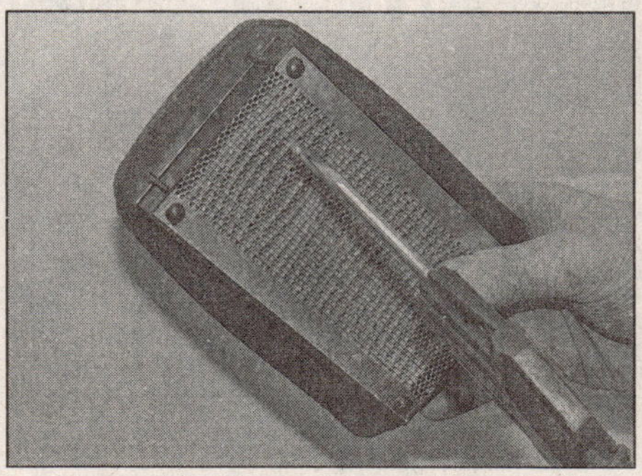

18.5b Direct the air in the opposite direction to normal flow as shown

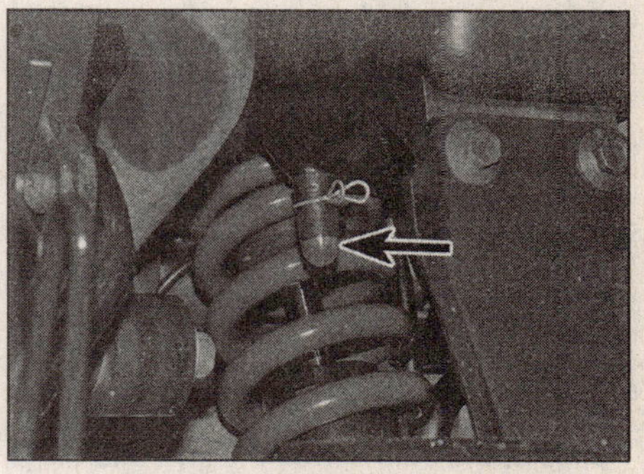

18.7 Check the drain collector (arrowed) for residue

filter should be cleaned between service intervals, or replaced with a new one more often than specified.

Caution: If the machine is continually ridden in wet conditions or at full throttle, the air filter housing drain should be checked more frequently.

Caution: Never run the engine without an air filter.

1 On WR models remove the seat (see Chapter 7). Remove the seat bracket **(see illustration)**.

2 On MT and YZF-R models remove the fuel tank (see Chapter 4).

3 Undo the air filter cover screws and remove the cover **(see illustration)**.

4 Remove the filter, noting how it fits **(see illustration)**.

5 To clean the filter tap it on a hard surface to dislodge any dirt, then check between the folds of the filter for any trapped debris **(see illustration)**. If available use compressed air to blow through the filter, directing the air in the opposite way to normal flow, i.e. from the underside **(see illustration)**. If the filter cannot be cleaned or is in any way torn or damaged replace it with a new one.

6 At the specified interval fit a new filter even if the existing one looks clean and in good condition.

7 Check the drain on the underside of the filter housing for residue **(see illustration)**. If necessary place some rag under the drain, then release the clamp and remove the collector. Allow any residue to drain from the housing, and clean out the collector and the inside of the housing.

8 Make sure the cover and housing rim seals are in good condition and properly seated – fit new ones if necessary. Fit the new filter, then fit the cover and secure it with its screws.

9 On WR models fit the seat bracket, then fit the seat.

10 On MT and YZF-R models install the fuel tank (see Chapter 4).

19 Valve clearances

1 The engine must be completely cool for this maintenance procedure, so let the bike stand overnight before beginning.

2 On YZF-R models remove all sections of the fairing on the left-hand side (see Chapter 7). Remove the centre and upper sections of the fairing on the right-hand side (see Chapter 7).

3 Remove the fuel tank (see Chapter 4).

4 Remove the spark plug (see Section 2).

5 Remove the valve cover (see Chapter 2).

6 Unscrew the timing inspection cap and the crankshaft end cap from the alternator cover on the left-hand side of the engine **(see illustration)**. Check the condition of the cap O-rings and replace them with new ones if necessary.

7 To check the valve clearances the engine must be turned so the piston is at top dead centre (TDC) on its compression stroke so that all valves are closed.

8 Turn the engine anti-clockwise using a suitable socket on the alternator rotor nut until the index line on the rotor aligns with the pointer in the inspection hole, and the camshaft lobes are facing down **(see**

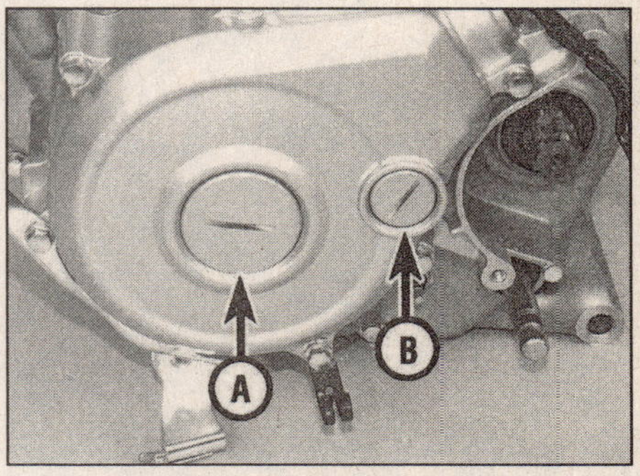

19.6 Remove the crankshaft end cap (A) and the timing inspection cap (B)

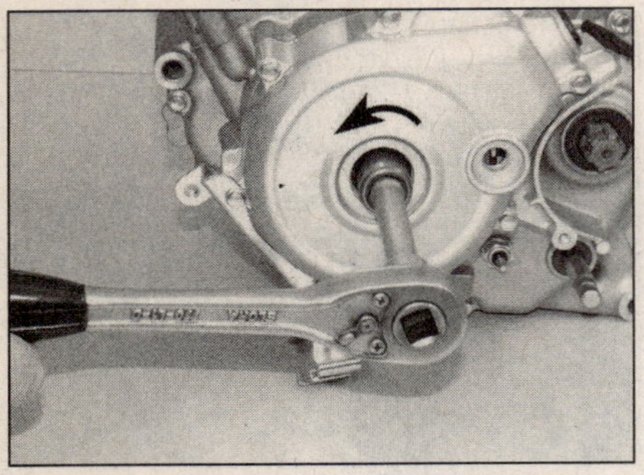

19.8a Turn the engine anti-clockwise using the nut...

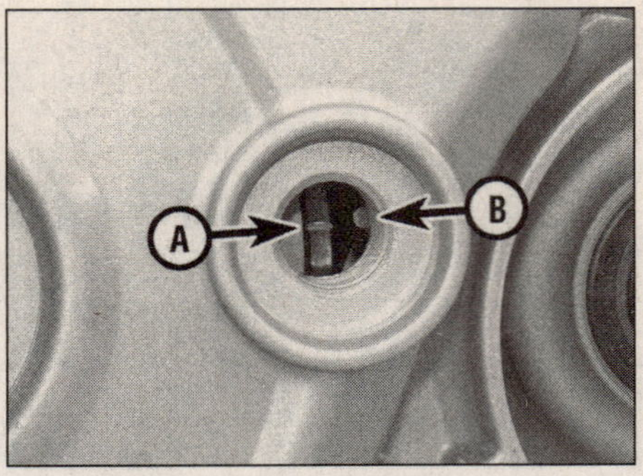

19.8b ... until the line (A) on the rotor aligns with the pointer (B)...

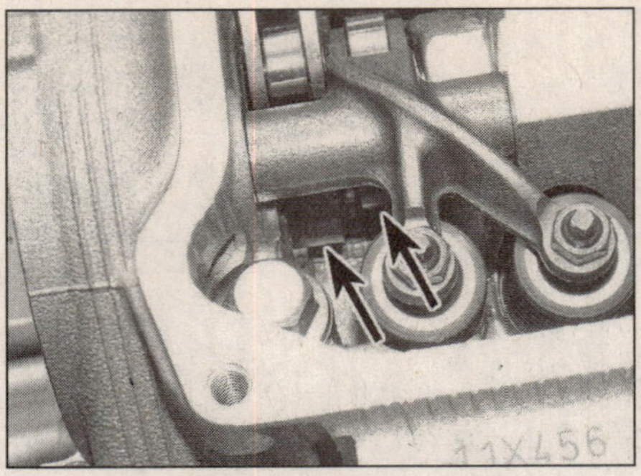

19.8c ... and the camshaft lobes (arrowed) point down

19.9 Insert the feeler gauge between the base of the adjuster on the arm and the top of the valve stem as shown

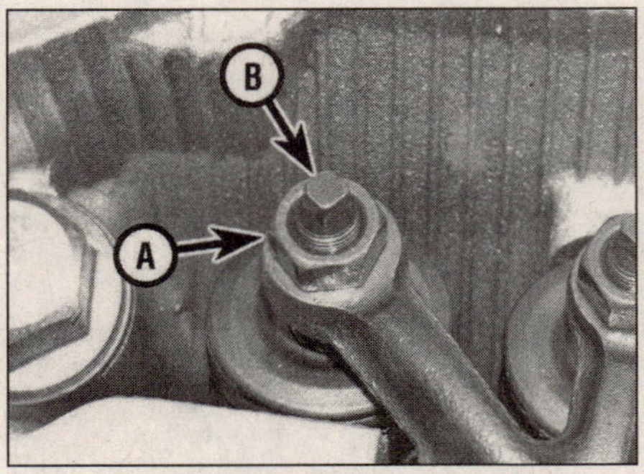

19.10a Locknut (A) and adjuster (B)...

19.10b ... turn the adjuster until the gap is correct, then hold the adjuster while tightening the locknut

illustrations). Note: *Do not confuse the TDC index line on the rotor with one of the upright lines on the ignition timing H mark that comes just before it as you turn the engine*. If the index line aligns but the lobes are facing up rotate the engine anti-clockwise one full turn (360°) until the index line on the rotor again aligns with the pointer inside the inspection hole – the lobes will now be facing down. There should now be some freeplay in each rocker arm, i.e. they are not contacting the valve stem.

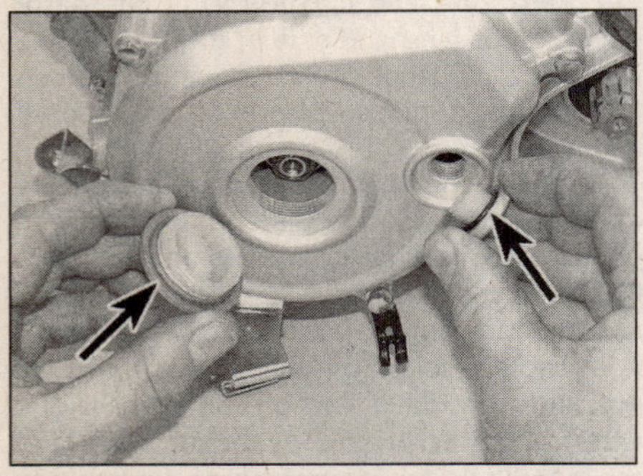

19.12 Fit the caps using new O-rings (arrowed) if required and smear them with grease

9 With the engine in this position, check the clearance of each valve by inserting a feeler gauge of the same thickness as the correct valve clearance (see Specifications) in the gap between the rocker arm and the valve stem **(see illustration)**. The intake valves are on the back of the cylinder head and the exhaust valves are on the front. The gauge should be a firm sliding fit – you should feel a slight drag when you pull the gauge out.

10 If the gap (clearance) is either too wide or too narrow, slacken the locknut on the adjuster in the rocker arm **(see illustration)**. Turn the adjuster as required using a pair of pliers, until the gap is as specified and the feeler gauge is a sliding fit **(see illustration)**. Hold the adjuster still and tighten the locknut. Recheck the clearance after tightening the locknut.

11 When all clearances have been checked install the valve cover (see Chapter 2).

12 Fit the timing inspection cap and crankshaft end cap using new O-rings if required, and smear the O-rings with grease **(see illustration)**.

13 Install the spark plug (Section 2) and the fuel tank (Chapter 4).

14 Check and adjust the idle speed (see Section 3).

15 On YZF-R models install the fairing sections (see Chapter 7).

Chapter 2
Engine, clutch and transmission

Contents

Degrees of difficulty

Easy, suitable for novice with little experience	**Fairly easy,** suitable for beginner with some experience	**Fairly difficult,** suitable for competent DIY mechanic	**Difficult,** suitable for experienced DIY mechanic	**Very difficult,** suitable for expert DIY or professional

Specifications

General

Type	Four-stroke, single cylinder
Capacity	124.7 cc
Bore	52.0 mm
Stroke	58.6 mm
Compression ratio	11.2 to 1
Lubrication	Wet sump
Cooling system	Liquid-cooled
Clutch	Wet multi-plate
Transmission	Six-speed constant mesh
Final drive	Chain and sprockets
Camshaft	SOHC, chain-driven

Camshafts and rockers

Intake lobe height	
Standard	30.225 to 30.325 mm
Service limit (min)	30.125 mm
Exhaust lobe height	
WR models	
Standard	30.232 to 30.332 mm
Service limit (min)	30.132 mm
MT and YZF-R models	
Standard	30.261 to 30.361 mm
Service limit (min)	30.161 mm
Runout (max)	0.03 mm
Rocker arm bore diameter	
Standard	9.985 to 10.000 mm
Service limit (max)	10.015 mm
Rocker arm shaft diameter	
Standard	9.966 to 9.976 mm
Service limit (min)	9.941 mm
Rocker arm-to-shaft clearance	
Standard	0.009 to 0.034 mm
Service limit (max)	0.074 mm

Cylinder head

Warpage (max)	0.03 mm

Valves, guides and springs

Valve clearances	see Chapter 1
Seat width	
Standard	0.90 to 1.10 mm
Service limit (max)	1.6 mm
Stem diameter	
Intake valve	
Standard	4.475 to 4.490 mm
Service limit (min)	4.445 mm
Exhaust valve	
Standard	4.460 to 4.475 mm
Service limit (min)	4.430 mm
Guide bore diameter – intake and exhaust valves	
Standard	4.500 to 4.512 mm
Service limit (max)	4.550 mm
Stem-to-guide clearance	
Intake valve	
Standard	0.010 to 0.037 mm
Service limit	0.08 mm
Exhaust valve	
Standard	0.025 to 0.052 mm
Service limit	0.10 mm
Valve stem runout (max)	0.010 mm
Valve spring free length – intake and exhaust valves	
Standard	41.71 mm
Service limit (min)	39.62 mm
Valve spring tilt (max)	1.8 mm

Cylinder bore

Standard	52.000 to 52.010 mm
Service limit (max)	52.110 mm
Ovality (out-of-round) (max)	0.005 mm
Taper (max)	0.05 mm

Cylinder compression

Standard	78.2 psi (5.5 Bar) @ 600 rpm
Maximum	88.2 psi (6.2 Bar) @ 600 rpm
Minimum	68.2 psi (4.8 Bar) @ 600 rpm

Piston

Piston diameter	51.962 to 51.985 mm (measured 5 mm up from skirt, at 90° to piston pin axis)
Piston-to-bore clearance	0.015 to 0.048 mm
Piston pin diameter	
Standard	13.995 to 14.000 mm
Service limit (min)	13.975 mm
Piston pin bore diameter in piston	
Standard	14.002 to 14.013 mm
Service limit (max)	14.043 mm
Piston pin-to-piston pin bore clearance	
Standard	0.002 to 0.018 mm
Service limit (max)	0.068 mm

Piston rings

Ring type	
Top ring	Barrel
Second ring	Taper
Ring size	
Top ring	0.80 x 1.90 mm
Second ring	0.80 x 2.10 mm
Oil ring	1.50 x 1.95 mm
Ring end gap (installed)	
Top ring	
Standard	0.10 to 0.25 mm
Service limit (max)	0.50 mm
Second ring	
Standard	0.10 to 0.25 mm
Service limit (max)	0.60 mm
Oil ring side-rail	0.20 to 0.70 mm
Ring-to-groove clearance	
Top ring	
Standard	0.030 to 0.065 mm
Service limit (max)	0.10 mm
Second ring	
Standard	0.020 to 0.055 mm
Service limit (max)	0.10 mm
Oil ring side-rail	0.040 to 0.160 mm

Clutch

Friction plates	
WR models	
Type 1	1
Type 2 (wide ID)	1
Type 3 (marked green)	3
MT and YZF-R models	
Type 1	4
Type 2 (marked yellow)	1
Friction plate thickness	
Standard	2.90 to 3.10 mm
Service limit (min)	2.80 mm
Plain plates	4
Plain plate thickness	
WR models	1.45 to 1.75 mm
MT and YZF-R models	1.90 to 2.10 mm
Plain plate warpage (max)	0.20 mm
Springs	4
Spring free length	
WR models	
Standard	38.71 mm
Service limit (min)	36.77 mm
MT and YZF-R models	
Standard	40.48 mm
Service limit	36.80 mm
Long pushrod bend limit	0.50 mm

Oil pump

	Standard	Service limit
Inner rotor tip-to-outer rotor clearance	0.15 mm	0.23 mm
Outer rotor-to-housing clearance	0.13 to 0.18 mm	0.25 mm
Rotor end-float	0.06 to 0.11 mm	0.18 mm

Crankshaft and connecting rod

Crankshaft runout (max)	0.03 mm
Crankshaft width (see text)	47.95 to 48.00 mm
Connecting rod big-end side clearance	0.110 to 0.410 mm
Connecting rod big-end radial clearance	0.004 to 0.014mm

Transmission

Gear ratios (no. of teeth)	
Primary reduction	3.042 to 1 (73/24)
Final reduction	
WR models	3.786 to 1 (53/14)
MT and YZF-R models	3.429 to 1 (48/14)
1st gear	2.833 to 1 (34/12)
2nd gear	1.875 to 1 (30/16)
3rd gear	1.364 to 1 (30/22)
4th gear	1.143 to 1 (24/21)
5th gear	0.957 to 1 (22/23)
6th gear	0.840 to 1 (21/25)
Shaft runout (max)	0.08 mm

Selector drum and forks

Selector fork end thickness	
Input shaft fork (C)	5.76 to 5.89 mm
Output shaft forks (R and L)	4.76 to 4.89 mm

Torque settings

Balancer shaft nut (securing balancer driven gear)	50 Nm
Cam chain tensioner blade bolt	10 Nm
Cam chain tensioner cap bolt (MT and YZF-R models)	8 Nm
Cam chain tensioner mounting bolts	10 Nm
Camshaft/rocker shaft retainer bolts	7 Nm
Camshaft sprocket bolt	30 Nm
Clutch cover bolts	10 Nm
Clutch nut	70 Nm
Clutch short pushrod locknut	8 Nm
Clutch spring bolts	12 Nm
Crankcase bolts	10 Nm
Crankshaft nut (securing drive gears)	60 Nm
Cylinder head bolts	
Top bolts	22 Nm
Side bolts	10 Nm
Engine mounting bolts/nuts	
WR models	
Lower rear mounting bolt nut	67 Nm
Middle mounting bracket bolts	46 Nm
Middle mounting bolt nut	67 Nm
Rear mounting bracket bolts	33 Nm
Upper rear mounting bolt nut	67 Nm
Front mounting bracket bolt nuts	67 Nm
Front mounting bolt nut	67 Nm
MT and YZF-R models	53 Nm
Gearchange lever pinch bolt	10 Nm
Gearchange mechanism stopper arm pivot bolt	10 Nm
Intake duct bolts	10 Nm
Oil pressure delivery check bolt	7 Nm
Oil baffle plate bolts	10 Nm
Oil pump screws	4 Nm
Rider's footrest bracket bolts (WR models)	62 Nm
Starter clutch bolts	14 Nm
Transmission input shaft bearing retainer bolts	7 Nm
Valve cover bolts	10 Nm

1 General Information

1 The engine/transmission unit is a liquid-cooled single cylinder of unit construction. The four valves are operated by rocker arms actuated by a single overhead camshaft which is chain driven off the left-hand end of the crankshaft. The crankshaft drives a single balancer shaft. The crankcase divides vertically.

2 The crankcase incorporates a wet sump, pressure-fed lubrication system which uses a trochoidal oil pump that is gear-driven off the crankshaft. Oil is filtered by a standard cartridge filter and by a strainer in the sump.

3 The water pump is mounted on the left-hand side of the cylinder head and is driven off the camshaft.

4 The alternator is on the left-hand end of the crankshaft. The crankshaft position sensor triggers for the ignition timing are on the outside of the alternator rotor, and the sensor is mounted in the alternator cover along with the stator.

5 Power from the crankshaft is routed to the transmission via the clutch. The clutch is of the wet, multi-plate type and is gear-driven off the crankshaft. The clutch is operated by cable. The transmission is a six-speed constant-mesh unit. Final drive to the rear wheel is by chain and sprockets.

2 Component access

Operations possible with the engine in the frame

1 The components and assemblies listed below can be removed without having to remove the engine from the frame. If however, a number of areas require attention at the same time, removal of the engine is recommended.

a) Valve cover
b) Camshaft and rockers
c) Water pump
d) Cylinder head
e) Cylinder block and piston
f) Clutch
g) Primary drive, balancer drive and oil pump drive shaft gears
h) Oil pump and filter
i) Gearchange mechanism
j) Alternator
k) Starter clutch
l) Cam chain, tensioner and blades
m) Starter motor
n) Transmission output shaft oil seal

Operations requiring engine removal

2 It is necessary to remove the engine from the frame to gain access to the following components.

a) Crankshaft, connecting rod and bearings
b) Transmission shafts and bearings
c) Selector drum and forks
d) Balancer shaft

3 Engine wear assessment

Cylinder compression check

Note: *Special tool: A compression gauge is required to perform this test. Yamaha tools are available – ask your dealer.*

1 Poor engine performance may be caused by leaking valves, incorrect valve clearances, a leaking head gasket, or a worn piston, piston rings or cylinder. A cylinder compression check will highlight these conditions and can also indicate the presence of excessive carbon deposits in the cylinder head.

2 The only tools required are a compression gauge (there are two types, one with a threaded adapter to fit the spark plug hole in the cylinder head, the other has a rubber seal which is pressed into the spark plug hole to create a seal – the threaded adapter type is preferable), and a spark plug socket. Depending on the outcome of the initial test, a squirt-type oil can may also be needed.

3 Make sure the valve clearances are correctly set (see Chapter 1).

4 Run the engine until it is at normal operating temperature.

5 Remove the spark plug (see Chapter 1). Fit the plug back into the plug cap and earth the plug against the engine – if the plug is not earthed the ignition system could be damaged.

6 Fit the gauge along with any necessary adapter into the spark plug hole **(see illustrations)** – if the rubber cone type is used keep the gauge pressed onto the hole throughout the test to maintain a good seal.

7 With the ignition switch ON, the throttle held fully open and the spark plug earthed, turn the engine over on the starter motor until the gauge reading has built up and stabilised **(see illustration)**.

8 Compare the reading on the gauge to the cylinder compression figures listed at the beginning of the Chapter.

9 If the reading is low, it could be due to a worn cylinder bore, piston or rings, failure of the head gasket, loose cylinder head bolts, or worn valve seats. To determine which is the cause, pour a small quantity of engine oil into the spark plug hole to seal the rings, then repeat the compression test. If the figures are noticeably higher the cause is worn cylinder, piston or rings. If there is no change the cause is probably a leaking head gasket or worn valve seats, but could also be due to a holed piston or broken ring(s).

10 If the reading is high there could be a build-up of carbon deposits in the combustion chamber. Remove the cylinder head and scrape all deposits off the piston and the cylinder head.

11 Install the spark plug (see Chapter 1).

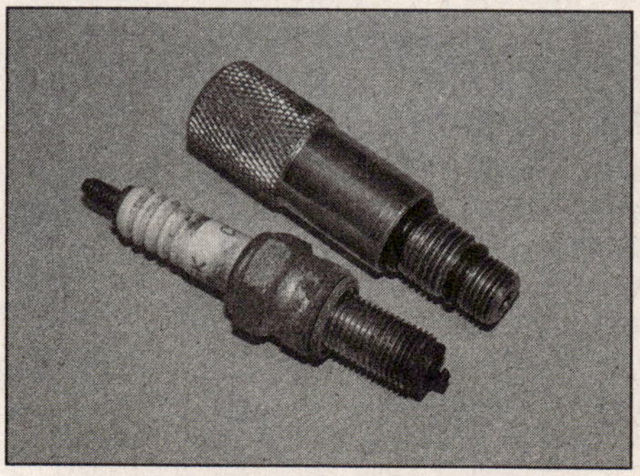

3.6a Select the correct adapter to match the spark plug threads...

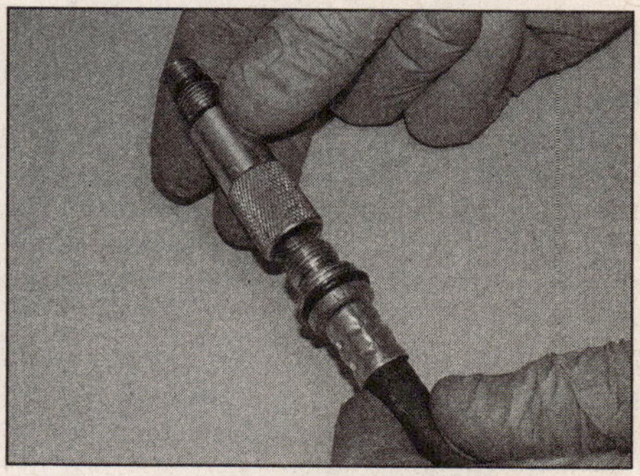

3.6b ...and fit it onto the gauge hose...

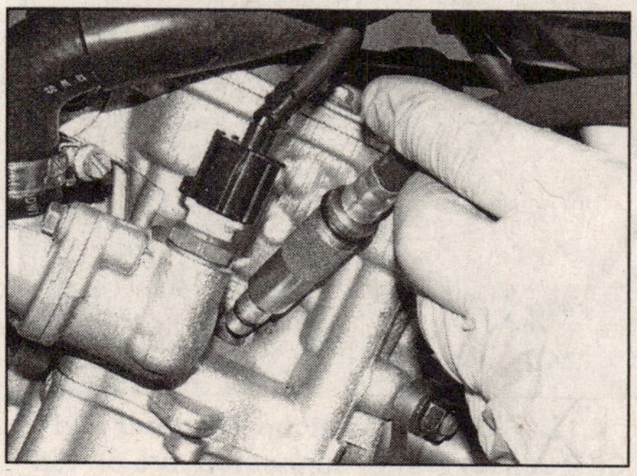

3.6c ...then thread the gauge into the plug hole

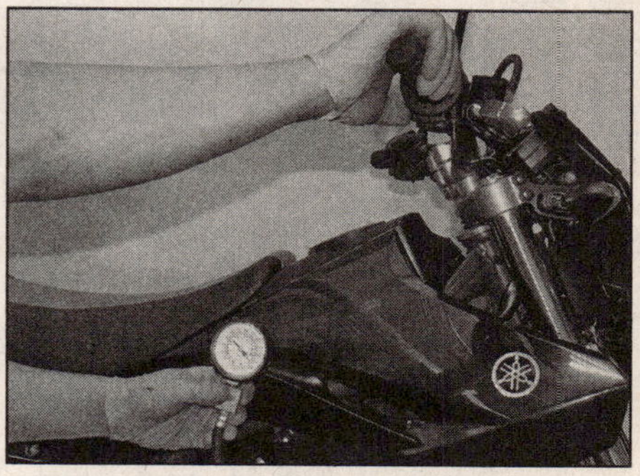

3.7 Hold the throttle open and turn the engine over

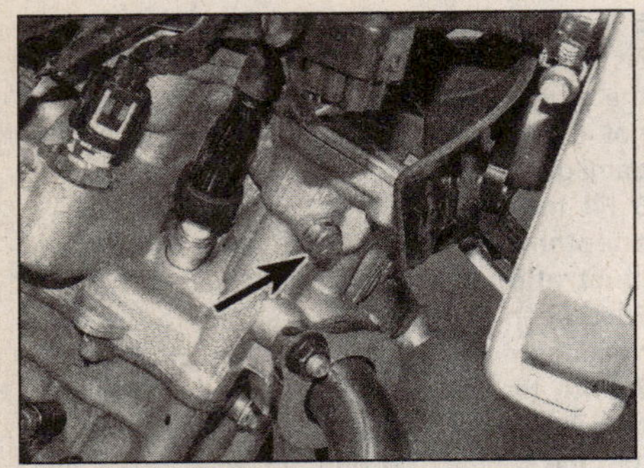

3.15 Slacken the check bolt (arrowed)...

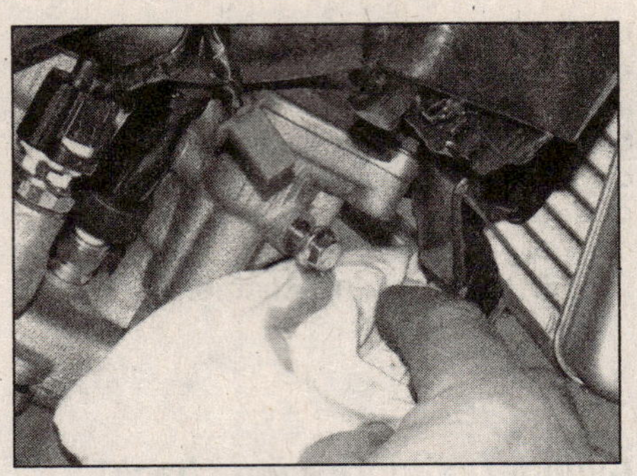

3.16 ...and make sure oil seeps past the threads

Engine oil delivery check

12 If there is any doubt about the performance of the engine lubrication system an oil delivery check must be carried out. The check provides useful information about the state of wear of the engine.

13 There is no oil pressure switch or level sensor, and therefore no oil pressure or level warning light in the instrument cluster.

14 Check the engine oil level and make sure it is correct, and make sure the correct grade oil is being used (see *Pre-ride checks*). On YZF-R models remove the fairing centre section on the right-hand side (see Chapter 7). Make sure there is no obvious oil leakage from anywhere around the engine, and that the drain plug is tight (see Chapter 1).

15 Loosen the oil delivery bolt above the exhaust header pipe **(see illustration)**. Have some rag to hand to catch the oil that will come out of the hole.

16 Start the engine and allow it idle, and watch the pressure check hole – oil should seep out around the bolt threads quite soon after starting the engine **(see illustration)**. When the oil appears stop the engine. If no oil appears after one minute stop the engine immediately.

17 If no oil comes out, the pressure is significantly lower than it should be or non-existent. Either the oil pump or its drive mechanism is faulty, the filter is blocked, an oil passage is blocked, or there is other engine damage. Begin diagnosis by checking the oil filter and strainer, then the oil pump (see Section 19). If those items check out okay, the engine needs to be overhauled to clean out all oil passages.

18 Tighten the oil delivery check bolt to the torque setting specified at the beginning of the Chapter. On YZF-R models install the fairing section (see Chapter 7).

4 Engine removal and installation

Caution: The engine is heavy. Engine removal and installation should be carried out with the aid of an assistant; personal injury or damage could occur if the engine falls or is dropped.

Removal

1 On WR models remove the fuel tank cover, frame covers and left-hand side cover (see Chapter 7). On MT models remove the air scoops, side covers, fuel tank cover and belly-pan (see Chapter 7). On YZF-R models remove all sections of the fairing on each side (see Chapter 7).

2 Support the bike upright on level ground using a rear paddock stand or other auxiliary stand **(see illustration 4.21)**, axle stands or blocks of wood under the bottom of the frame or passenger footrest brackets, or tie the rear of the bike up using a hoist or support frame. Work can be made easier by raising the machine to a suitable working height on an hydraulic ramp or a suitable platform. Make sure the motorcycle is secure and will not topple over. Tie the front brake lever to the handlebar to prevent it rolling forwards.

3 If the engine is dirty, particularly around its mountings, wash it thoroughly. This will make work much easier and rule out the possibility of caked on lumps of dirt falling into some vital component.

4 Drain the engine oil and coolant (see Chapter 1).

5 Disconnect the leads from the battery (see Chapter 8).

6 Remove the fuel tank and the throttle body (see Chapter 4). Plug the intake on the engine with clean rag. Detach the crankcase breather hose from its union on the water pump housing and remove it.

7 Remove the radiator along with its hoses (i.e. detach them from the water pump and thermostat cover), noting their routing (see Chapter 3). On MT and YZF-R models remove the coolant reservoir along with its hoses, again noting their routing (see Chapter 3).

8 Remove the exhaust system (see Chapter 4).

9 On WR models remove the air induction system (AIS) reed valve and hoses, and the ignition coil (see Chapter 4).

10 Pull the spark plug cap off the plug and secure it clear **(see illustration)**.

11 Remove the front sprocket (see Chapter 6).

12 Disconnect the sidestand switch, alternator and crankshaft position (CKP) sensor wiring connectors, releasing any cable-ties as required **(see illustrations)**. Feed the wiring to its source, again releasing any ties, and noting its routing.

13 Disconnect the wiring connector from the

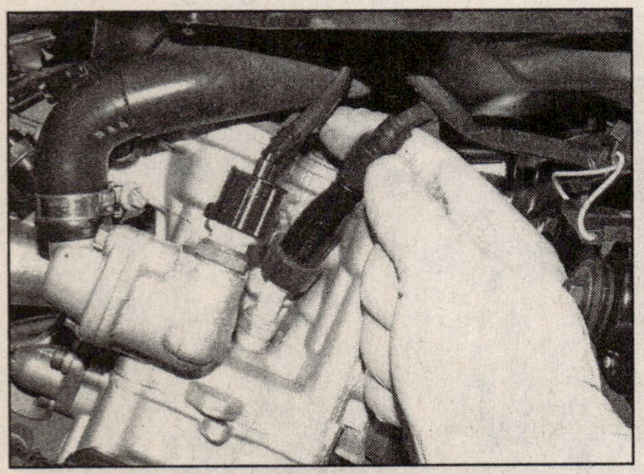

4.10 Pull the cap off the spark plug

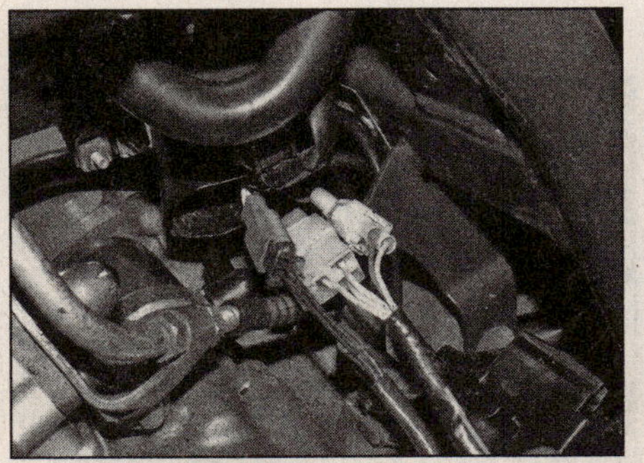

4.12a Sidestand switch, alternator and CKP sensor wiring connectors are on top of crankcase on WR models

4.12b Sidestand switch, alternator and CKP sensor wiring connectors are inside the boot (arrowed) between the frame and air filter housing on MT and YZF-R models

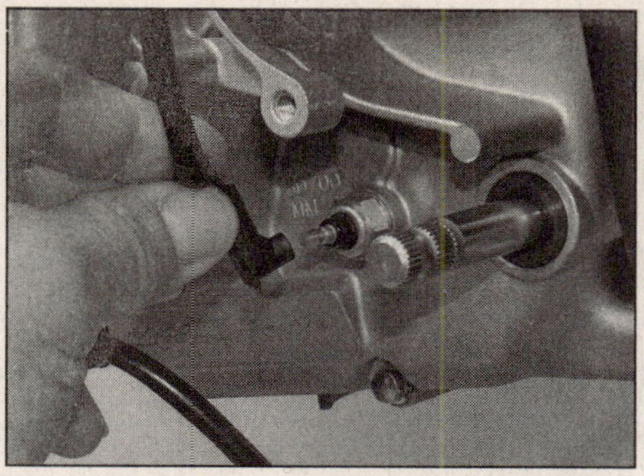
4.13 Pull the connector off the neutral switch

4.14 Disconnect the ECT sensor wiring connector (arrowed)

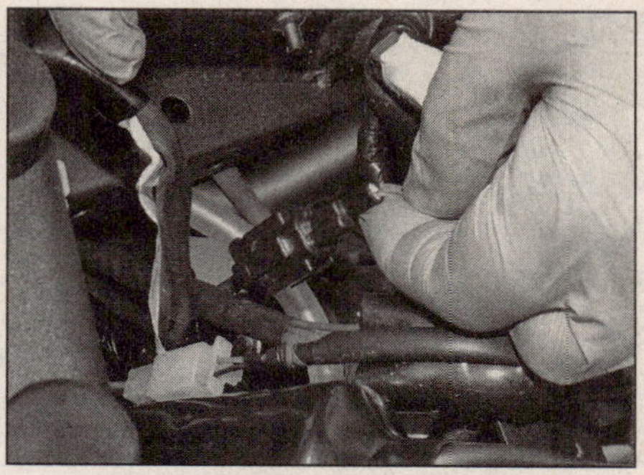
4.15a Disconnect the oxygen sensor connector...

neutral switch **(see illustration)**. Release the wiring from any ties securing it to the engine and position the wire clear, noting its routing.
14 Disconnect the wiring connector from the engine coolant temperature (ECT) sensor **(see illustration)**.
15 On MT and YZF-R models disconnect the oxygen sensor wiring connector, and on models without ABS the speed sensor wiring connector **(see illustrations)**. Undo the battery breather hose guide screw **(see illustration)**.
16 Detach the clutch cable from the engine (see Section 17). Position the cable clear.
17 Make an alignment mark where the slit in the gearchange lever clamp aligns with the shaft **(see illustration)**. Unscrew the pinch bolt and slide the lever off.
18 Remove the starter motor (see Chapter 8).
19 Unscrew the earth lead bolt **(see illustration)**. Secure the lead clear of the engine.
20 On WR models undo the rider's left-hand footrest bracket bolts and remove the footrest bracket/sidestand assembly **(see illustration)**. Remove the circlip from the inner end of the rear brake master cylinder pushrod clevis pin, withdraw the pin and detach the pushrod from the pedal **(see illustration)**. Unscrew the right-hand footrest bracket bolts and remove the footrest bracket/rear brake pedal assembly.
21 Position an hydraulic or mechanical jack under the engine with a block of wood between them **(see illustration)**. Make sure

4.15b ... and the speed sensor connector (arrowed)

4.15c Undo the screw (arrowed)

4.17 Note the alignment of the lever on the shaft, then unscrew the bolt (arrowed) and slide the lever off – WR model shown

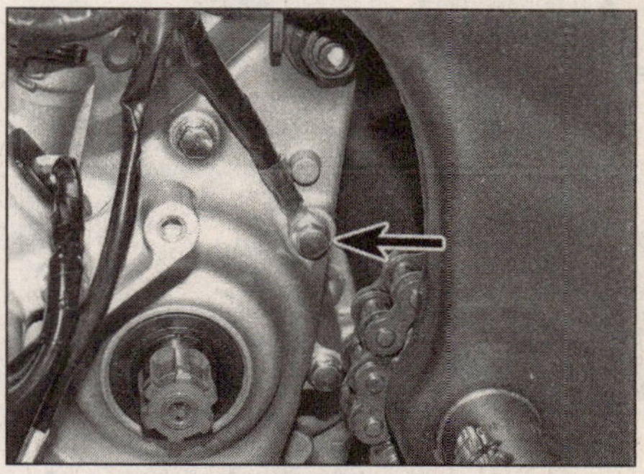
4.19 Unscrew the bolt (arrowed) and detach the earth lead

4.20a Footrest bracket/sidestand assembly bolts (arrowed)

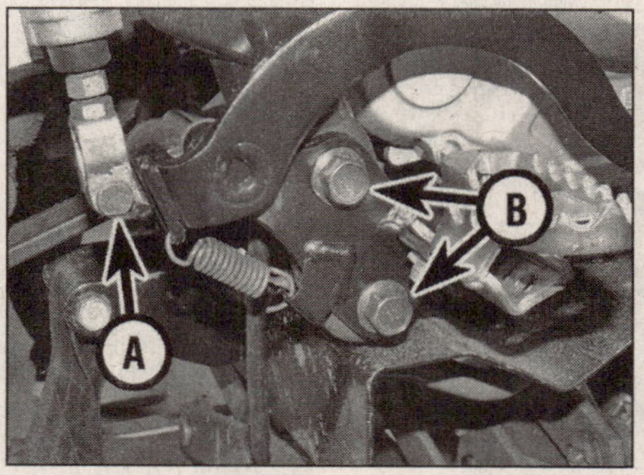

4.20b Remove the clevis (A) as described then unscrew the bolts (B)

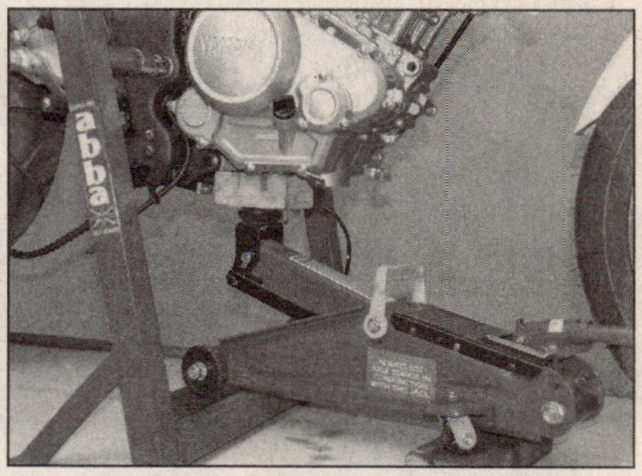
4.21 Support the engine on a jack

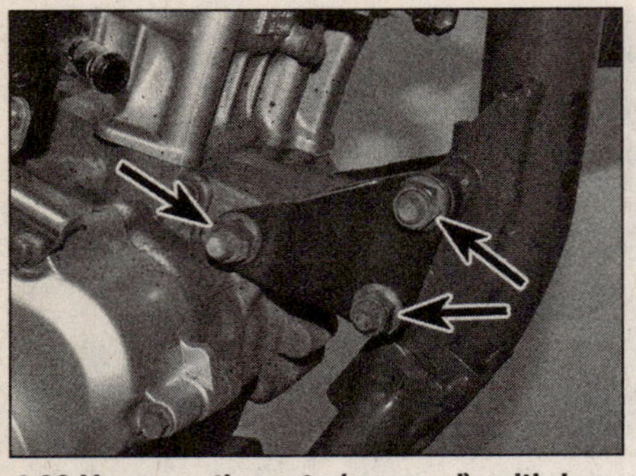

4.22 Unscrew the nuts (arrowed), withdraw the bolts and remove the brackets

4.23a Middle engine mounting bolt nut (arrowed)

4.23b Unscrew the bolts (arrowed) on each side and remove the brackets

the jack is centrally positioned so the engine will not topple in any direction when the last mounting bolt is removed. Raise the jack to take the weight of the engine, but make sure it is not lifting the bike and taking the weight of that as well. The idea is to support the engine so that there is no pressure on any of the mounting bolts once they have been slackened, so they can be easily withdrawn. Note that it may be necessary to alter the position of the jack as some of the bolts are removed to relieve the stress transferred to the other bolts.

WR models

22 Unscrew the front engine mounting bolt nut and the front mounting bracket bolt nuts, then withdraw the bolts and remove the brackets **(see illustration)**.

23 Unscrew the nut on the right-hand end of the middle engine mounting bolt, then withdraw the bolt **(see illustration)**. Unscrew the middle mounting bracket bolts and remove the brackets **(see illustration)**.

24 Check that the engine is properly supported by the jack. Check that all wiring, cables and hoses are free from and clear of the engine.

25 Unscrew the nut on the right-hand end of the upper rear engine mounting bolt, then withdraw the bolt **(see illustration)**. Unscrew the rear mounting bracket bolts and remove the bracket **(see illustration)**.

26 Unscrew the nut on the right-hand end of the lower rear mounting bolt **(see illustration)**. Have an assistant hold the engine, then withdraw the lower rear mounting bolt. Carefully lift the engine off the jack and out to the right-hand side, keeping it clear of the frame (see Caution above).

MT and YZF-R models

27 Unscrew the nut on the right-hand end of the upper engine mounting bolt, then withdraw the bolt **(see illustration)**.

28 Unscrew the nuts on the left-hand ends of the middle and lower mounting bolts **(see illustration)**.

29 Check that the engine is properly

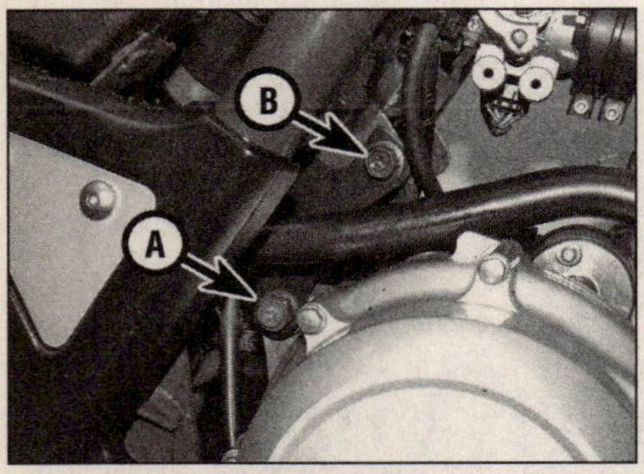

4.25a Unscrew the nut (A) and withdraw the bolt, then unscrew the bracket front bolt (B)...

4.25b ... and rear bolt (arrowed)

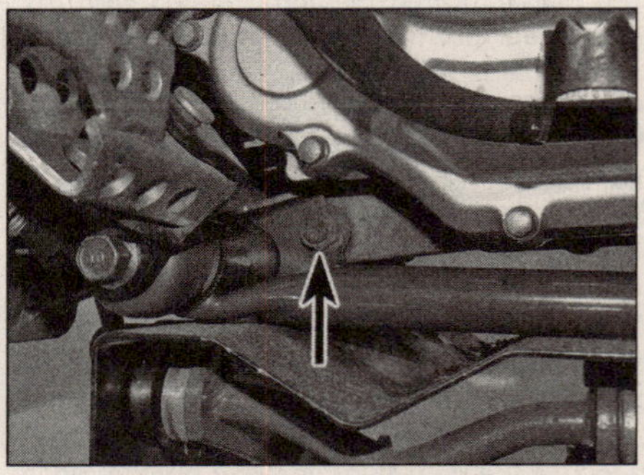

4.26 Lower rear mounting bolt nut (arrowed)

4.27 Unscrew the nut (arrowed) and withdraw the bolt

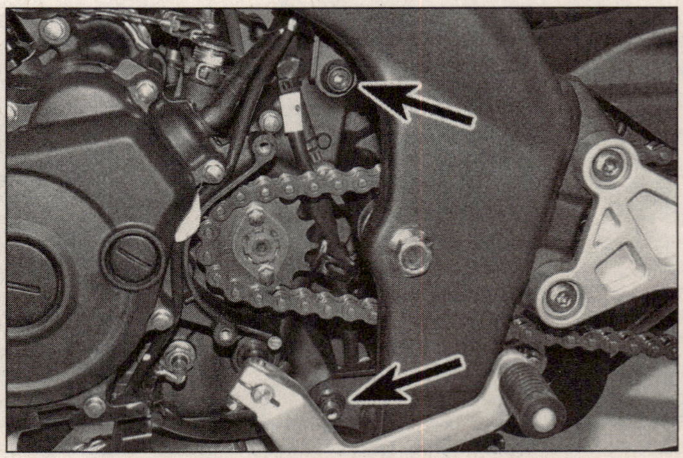

4.28 Unscrew the nuts (arrowed)

supported by the jack. Check that all wiring, cables and hoses are free from and clear of the engine.

30 Have an assistant hold the engine, then withdraw the middle and lower mounting bolts, noting the washers. Carefully lower the jack, then lift the engine off the jack and out to the right-hand side, keeping it clear of the frame (see Caution above).

Installation

31 Manoeuvre the engine into position in the frame and support it with a jack **(see illustration 4.21)**. Align all the mounting bolt holes, making sure that all cables and wiring are correctly routed and do not get trapped. Note that it may be necessary to adjust the jack as some of the bolts are installed to realign the other bolt holes.

WR models

32 Insert the upper and lower rear mounting bolts from the left-hand side **(see illustrations 4.26 and 4.25b and a)**. Fit the rear engine bracket and tighten the bolts finger-tight. Fit the nuts onto the upper and lower rear mounting bolts and tighten them finger-tight.

33 Fit the middle mounting brackets and tighten the bolts finger-tight **(see illustration 4.23b)**. Insert the middle mounting bolt from the left-hand side, then fit the nut and tighten it finger-tight **(see illustration 4.23a)**.

34 Fit the front mounting brackets, inserting the bolts from the left-hand side, then fit the nuts and tighten them finger-tight **(see illustration 4.22)**. Insert the front mounting bolt from the left-hand side, then fit the nut and tighten it finger-tight.

35 Remove the jack.

36 Tighten the lower rear mounting bolt nut to the torque setting specified at the beginning of the Chapter.

37 Tighten the middle mounting bracket bolts to the specified torque, then tighten the middle mounting bolt nut to the specified torque.

38 Tighten the rear mounting bracket bolts to the specified torque, then tighten the upper rear mounting bolt nut to the specified torque.

39 Tighten the front mounting bracket bolts to the specified torque, then tighten the front mounting bolt nut to the specified torque.

MT and YZF-R models

40 Insert the middle and lower mounting bolts with their washers from the right-hand side, and the upper bolt from the left. Fit the nuts and tighten them finger-tight **(see illustrations 4.28 and 4.27)**.

41 Remove the jack.

42 Counter-hold the head of the lower mounting bolt and tighten the nut to the torque setting specified at the beginning of the Chapter.

43 Next tighten the nut on the middle bolt to the specified torque.

44 Finally tighten the nut on the upper mounting bolt to the specified torque.

All models

45 The remainder of the installation procedure is the reverse of removal, noting the following points, and referring to the relevant illustrations in the removal procedure, and to the relevant Chapters where directed:

- On WR models tighten the rider's footrest bracket bolts to the specified torque.
- Use a new gasket on the exhaust header pipe (see Chapter 4).
- Make sure all wires, cables and hoses are correctly routed and connected, and secured by any clips or ties.
- Align the slit in the gearchange lever clamp with the mark on the shaft **(see illustration 4.17)**. Fit the pinch bolt with its washer and tighten to the specified torque.
- Refill the engine with the specified oil and coolant to the correct level (see Chapter 1 and *Pre-ride checks*).
- Adjust throttle and clutch cable freeplay.
- Adjust the drive chain (see Chapter 1).
- Start the engine and check that there are no oil or coolant leaks. Adjust the idle speed (see Chapter 1).

5 Engine disassembly and reassembly general information

1 Before beginning the engine overhaul, read through the related procedures to familiarise yourself with the scope and requirements of the job. Overhauling an engine is not all that difficult, but it is time consuming, and worth taking time over. Check on the availability of parts and make sure that any necessary special tools are obtained in advance.

2 Most work can be done with a decent set of typical workshop hand tools, although a number of precision measuring tools are required for inspecting parts to determine if they are worn.

3 To ensure maximum life and minimum trouble from a rebuilt engine, everything must be assembled with care in a spotlessly clean environment.

Disassembly

4 Before disassembling the engine, thoroughly clean its external surfaces. This will prevent contamination of the engine internals, and will also make the job a lot easier and cleaner. A high flash-point solvent, such as paraffin (kerosene) can be used, or better still, a proprietary engine degreaser such as Gunk. Use old paintbrushes and toothbrushes to work the solvent into the various recesses of the casings. Take care to exclude solvent or water from the electrical components and intake and exhaust ports.

Warning: The use of petrol (gasoline) as a cleaning agent should be avoided because of the risk of fire.

5 When clean and dry, position the engine on the workbench, leaving suitable clear area for working. Gather a selection of small containers, plastic bags and some labels so that parts can be grouped together in an easily identifiable manner. Also get some paper and a pen so that notes can be taken. You will also need a supply of clean rag, which should be as absorbent as possible.

6 Before commencing work, read through the appropriate sectionso that some idea of the necessary procedure can be gained. When removing components note that great force is seldom required, unless specified (checking the specified torque setting of the particular bolt being removed will indicate how tight it is, and therefore how much force should be needed). In many cases, a component's reluctance to be removed is indicative of an incorrect approach or removal method – if in any doubt, re-check with the text.

7 When disassembling the engine, keep 'mated' parts together (including gears, valves, etc, that have been in contact with each other during engine operation). These 'mated' parts must be reused or replaced as an assembly.

8 A complete engine strip should be done in the following general order with reference to the appropriate Sections.

a) Remove the water pump (Chapter 3)
b) Remove the cylinder head
c) Remove the cylinder block and piston
d) Remove the clutch
e) Remove the primary drive, balancer shaft and oil pump drive gears
f) Remove the oil pump
g) Remove the gearchange mechanism
h) Remove the alternator and starter clutch (see Chapter 8)
i) Remove the cam chain and tensioner blade
j) Separate the crankcase halves
k) Remove the transmission shafts and selector drum and forks
l) Remove the crankshaft and balancer shaft

Reassembly

9 Reassembly is accomplished by reversing the general disassembly sequence.

6 Valve cover

Note: *The valve cover can be removed with the engine in the frame. If the engine has been removed, ignore the steps which do not apply.*

Removal

1 On YZF-R models remove the upper section of the fairing on each side (see Chapter 7).

2 Remove the fuel tank (see Chapter 4).

3 On MT and YZF-R models remove the ignition coil (see Chapter 4). Release the wiring ties, disconnect the wiring connectors and move the wiring and connectors clear of

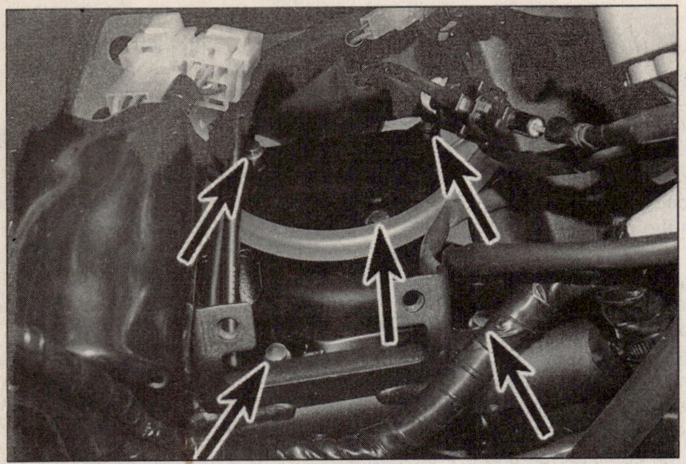

6.3 Disconnect and/or move aside the various wiring connectors above the valve cover as required to access the bolts (arrowed)

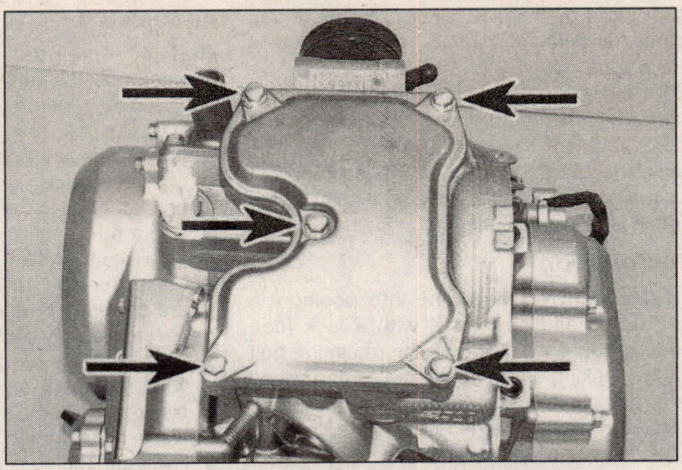

6.4 Unscrew the bolts (arrowed) and remove the cover

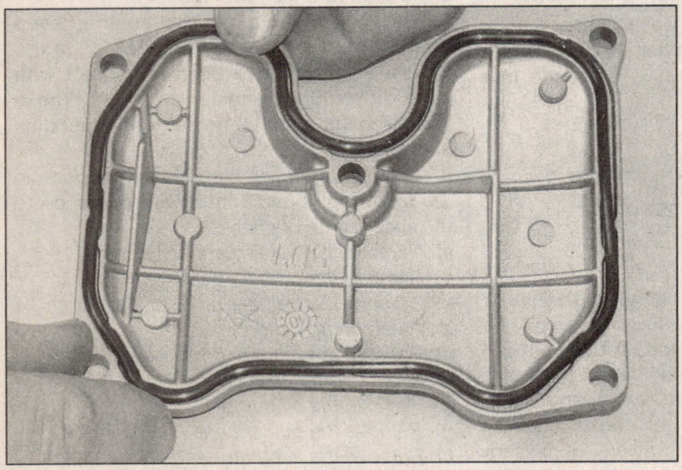

6.7 Fit the new greased seal into the groove

6.8a Make sure the seal stays in place when fitting the cover...

the cover as required **(see illustration)**. Push the rubber cover to the front of the valve cover so it is out of the way.

4 Unscrew the valve cover bolts and remove the cover **(see illustration)**. Note the bolt with the sealing washer – a new washer should be used **(see illustration 6.8b)**.

5 Remove the seal and discard it **(see illustration 6.7)** – a new one must be used.

6 Remove all traces of old glue or grease from the groove in the cover.

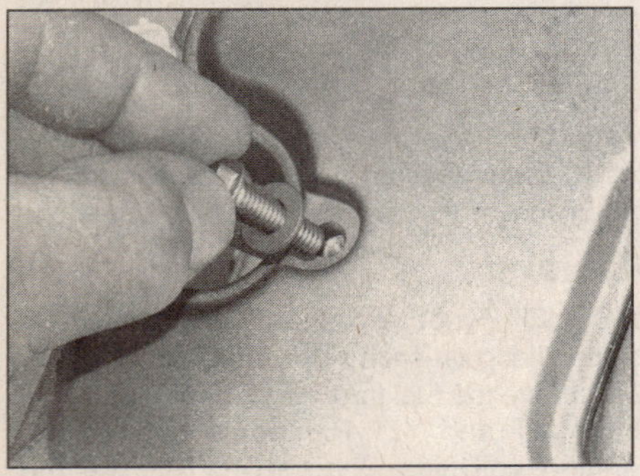

6.8b ... and use a new sealing washer on the middle bolt

Installation

7 Make sure the seal groove in the cover is clean and dry. Smear the new seal with grease and fit it into the groove **(see illustration)**.

8 Fit the cover onto the head, making sure the seal stays in place **(see illustration)**. Fit the bolts, using a new sealing washer on the centre bolt, and tighten them evenly in a criss-cross pattern to the torque setting specified at the beginning of the Chapter **(see illustration)**.

7.3 Unscrew the bolts (arrowed) and remove the tensioner

9 On MT and YZF-R models reposition the rubber cover, connect the wiring and secure it using new cable-ties. Install the ignition coil (see Chapter 4).

10 Install the fuel tank (see Chapter 4).

7 Cam chain tensioner

Note: *The cam chain tensioner can be removed with the engine in the frame. If the engine has been removed, ignore the steps which do not apply.*

Removal

1 Refer to Section 19 in Chapter 1 and set the piston at TDC on the compression stroke.

2 On MT and YZF-R models unscrew the tensioner cap bolt and remove the spring. Remove the O-ring.

3 Unscrew the tensioner mounting bolts and displace the clutch cable guide **(see illustration)**. Withdraw the tensioner from the engine.

4 Remove the gasket and discard it – a new one must be used on installation.

5 Remove all traces of old gasket from the tensioner and cylinder block mating surfaces.

Inspection

6 On WR models remove the rubber blanking plug from the tensioner. Insert a small flat-bladed screwdriver in the end of the tensioner so that it engages the slot **(see illustration)**. Turn the screwdriver clockwise until the plunger is fully retracted. Release the screwdriver – the plunger will spring back out. The plunger should move smoothly when wound into the tensioner and spring back out freely when released. If not, replace the tensioner with a new one.

7 On MT and YZF-R models lift the ratchet off the plunger and push the plunger all the way into the body, checking it moves smoothly and freely. Release the ratchet onto the plunger, then insert the spring and push it into the body – the plunger should extend easily under the ratchet. Remove the spring. Try to push the plunger into the body against the ratchet lock – you should not be able to. If the tensioner is worn or damaged in any way replace it with a new one.

Installation

8 Ensure the tensioner and cylinder block mating surfaces are clean and dry. Clean any old sealant off the tensioner bolt threads, then apply some fresh sealant (such as Yamaha bond 1215). Fit a new gasket onto the tensioner body **(see illustration)**.

9 On WR models remove the rubber blanking plug from the tensioner. Insert a small flat-bladed screwdriver in the end of the tensioner so that it engages the slotted plunger **(see illustration 7.6)**. Turn the screwdriver clockwise until the plunger is fully retracted, and hold it in this position while fitting the tensioner. Install the tensioner with its mounting bolts and the clutch cable guide and tighten the bolts enough so the tensioner is securely held **(see illustration)**. Release the screwdriver – as you release it, it should turn as the plunger extends. Tighten the tensioner bolts to the torque setting specified at the beginning of the Chapter. Fit the tensioner blanking plug **(see illustration)**.

10 On MT and YZF-R models lift the ratchet off the plunger and push the plunger all the way into the body, then release the ratchet. Install the tensioner with its mounting bolts and the clutch cable guide and tighten the bolts to the torque setting specified at the beginning of the Chapter. Grease the O-ring and fit it onto the tensioner. Insert the spring and fit the cap bolt – as you do the plunger should be heard to extend under the ratchet. Tighten the cap bolt to the specified torque.

11 Refer to Section 19 in Chapter 1 and turn the engine anti-clockwise through two full turns and check that all the timing marks still align, then refit all components.

8 Camshaft and rocker arms

Note: *The camshaft and rockers can be removed with the engine in the frame.*

Removal

1 Drain the cooling system (see Chapter 1). Remove the water pump (see Chapter 3).

2 Remove the valve cover (see Section 6).

3 Remove the spark plug (see Chapter 1).

4 Unscrew the timing inspection cap and the crankshaft end cap from the alternator cover on the left-hand side of the engine **(see illustration)**. Check the condition of the cap O-rings and replace them with new ones if necessary.

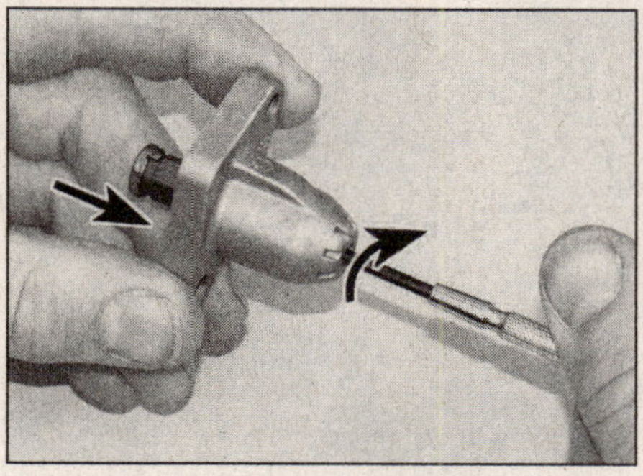

7.6 Insert a screwdriver and turn it to retract the plunger

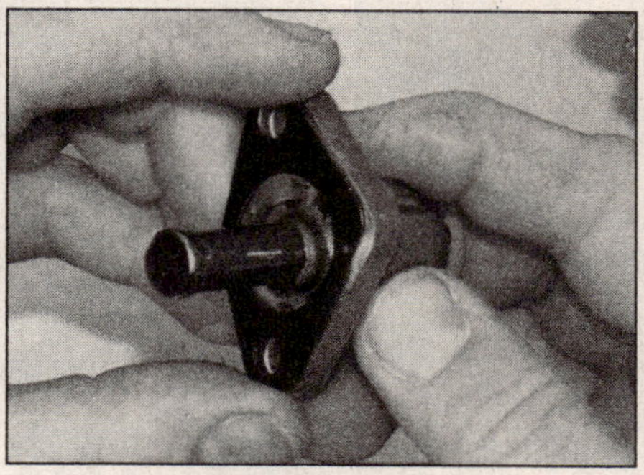

7.8 Fit a new gasket

7.9a Keep the screwdriver held while fitting the tensioner

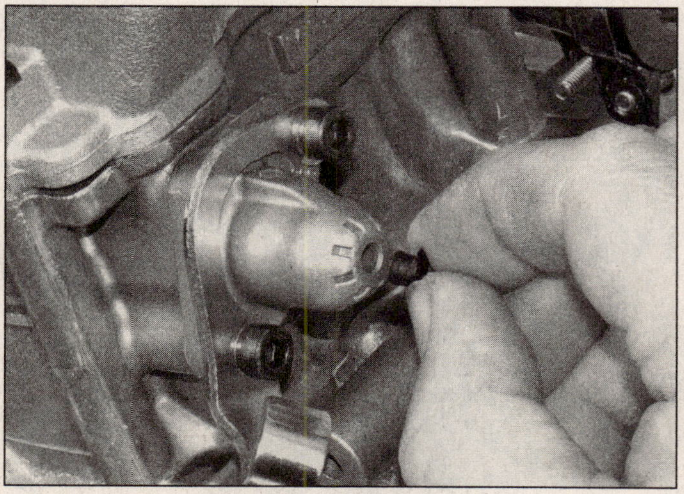

7.9b Fit the blanking plug

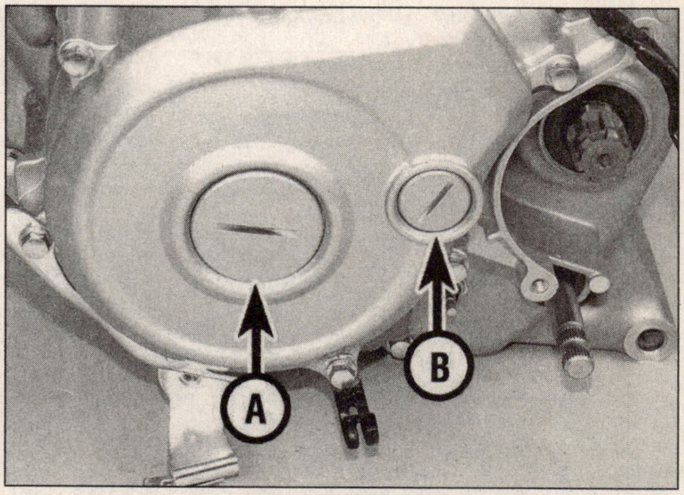

8.4 Remove the crankshaft end cap (A) and the timing inspection cap (B)

8.5a Turn the engine anti-clockwise using the nut...

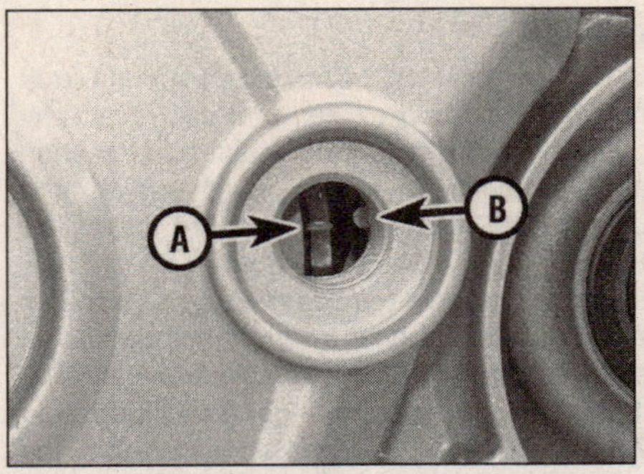

8.5b ... until the line (A) on the rotor aligns with the pointer (B)...

8.5c ... and the line (A) on the camshaft sprocket aligns with the notch (B)

5 The engine must be turned so the piston is at top dead centre (TDC) on its compression stroke with all valves closed. Turn the engine anti-clockwise using a suitable socket on the alternator rotor nut until the index line on the rotor aligns with the pointer in the inspection hole, and the index line on the camshaft sprocket aligns with the notch on the top of the cylinder head **(see illustrations)**. **Note:** *Do not confuse the TDC index line on the rotor with one of the upright lines on the ignition timing H mark that comes just before it as you turn the engine.* There should now be some freeplay in each rocker arm (i.e. they are not contacting the valve stem). If the index line on the sprocket is at the bottom, rotate the engine anti-clockwise one full turn (360°) until the index line on the rotor again aligns with the pointer inside the inspection hole – the index line on the sprocket will now be at the top.

6 Remove the cam chain tensioner (see Section 7).

7 Counter-hold the alternator rotor nut and unscrew the cam chain sprocket/decompression mechanism assembly bolt **(see illustrations)**. Slip the assembly off the end of the camshaft, noting how it locates, and disengage it from the chain **(see illustration)**. Secure the chain with a piece of wire to prevent it dropping down the tunnel. Withdraw the decompression cam from the camshaft **(see illustration)**.

8.7a Unscrew the bolt (arrowed)...

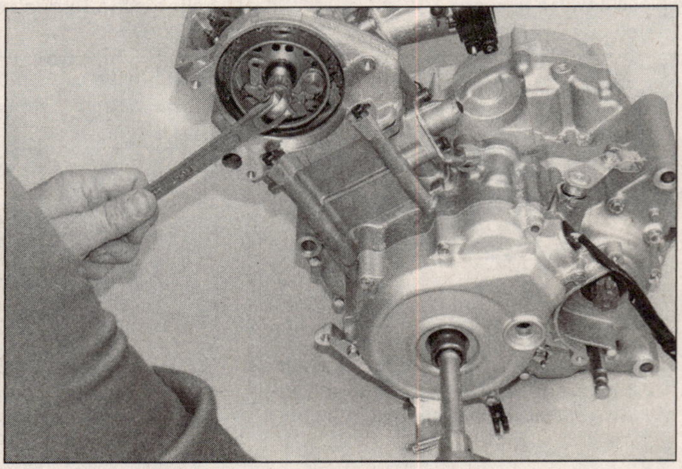

8.7b ... counter-holding the rotor nut...

8.7c ... then slip the assembly off and disengage the chain

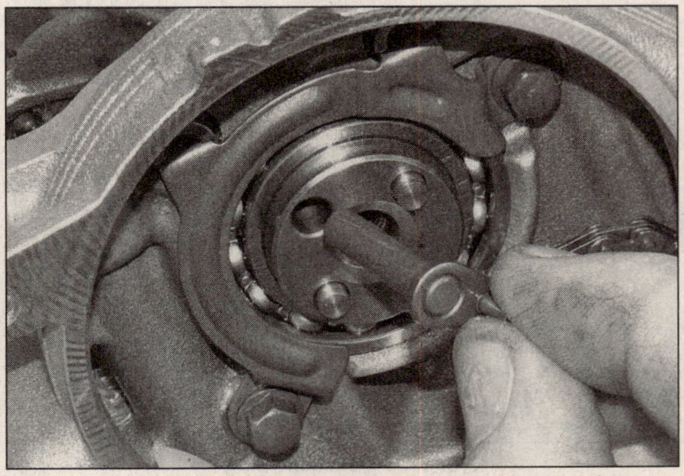

8.7d Withdraw the decompression cam

8.8 Unscrew the bolts (arrowed) and remove the retainer

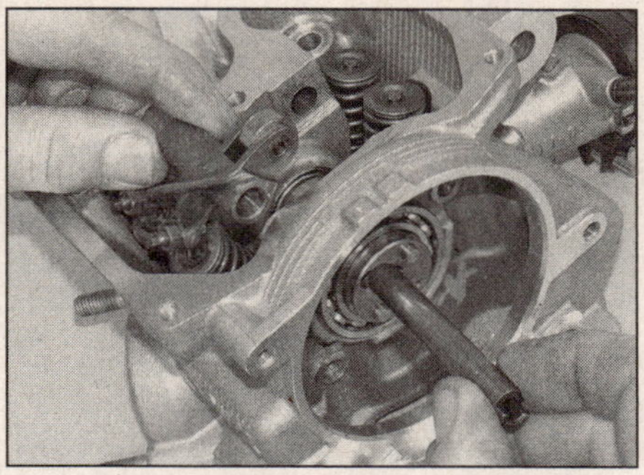

8.9 Withdraw the shafts and remove the arms

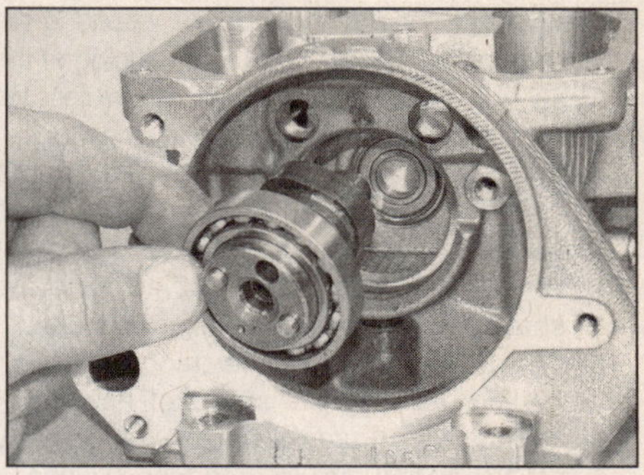

8.10 Withdraw the camshaft

8 Unscrew the camshaft/rocker shaft retainer bolts and remove the retainer, noting how its tabs locate against the cut-out in the end of each rocker shaft **(see illustration)**.

9 Mark each rocker arm according to its location in the holder. Withdraw each rocker shaft and remove the arm, then slide the rocker back onto its shaft to keep mated parts together **(see illustration)** – both shafts are the same, but the arms are different. Repeat the procedure for the other rocker arm and shaft.

10 Withdraw the camshaft from the cylinder head **(see illustration)**. If necessary carefully tap the camshaft out using a screwdriver located on the recessed section between the lobes so you are tapping against the edge of the outer lobe. On WR models remove the O-ring from the inner end of the shaft **(see illustration 8.20)** – a new O-ring must be used.

11 While the camshaft is out do not rotate the crankshaft – the chain may bind. Place a rag over the cylinder head.

Inspection

12 Clean the camshaft, rockers and shafts. Blow the oil passages through with compressed air.

13 Check the camshaft bearings, one on the shaft and one in the cylinder head – they must run smoothly, quietly and freely, and there should be no excessive play between the inner and outer races, or between the inner race and the camshaft, or between the outer race and the cylinder head **(see illustration)**. Replace the bearings with new ones if necessary as follows. To remove the outer bearing from the camshaft, support the camshaft, bearing facing down, on a suitable socket that does not contact the bearing inner race and tap the bearing off using a suitable drift located on the inner race where it is exposed by the cut-outs provided in the bearing seat **(see illustration)**. To fit the new outer bearing support the bearing inner race on a suitable socket, with its marked side facing down, and drive the camshaft into the bearing using another socket that fits over the shaft end and seats on the inner lobe **(see illustration)**. To remove the inner bearing from the head you need an internal expanding puller with slide-hammer attachment, which you may be able to hire. Locate the correct adapter in the bearing and expand it so the knife edges locate behind the inner race, then fit the slide-hammer attachment and jar the bearing out – if the engine or cylinder head has been removed you will need an assistant to hold it **(see illustrations)**. Drive the new bearing in using a socket that bears on the outer race and an extension piece.

14 Check the camshaft lobes for heat discoloration (blue appearance), score marks, chipped areas, flat spots and pitting. Measure the height of each lobe with a micrometer

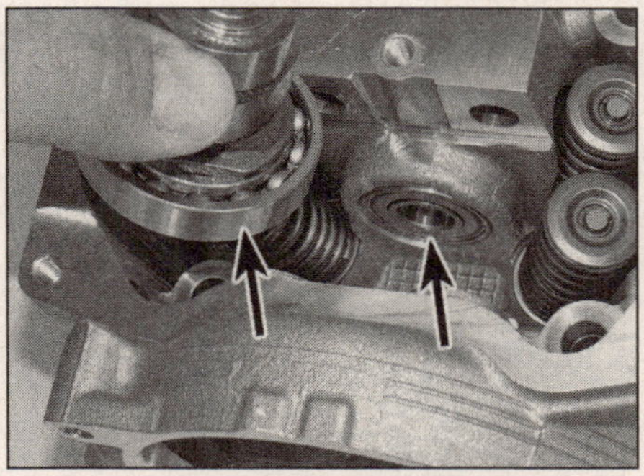

8.13a Check the bearings (arrowed)

8.13b Support the camshaft as described and drive the bearing off, locating the drift on the inner race

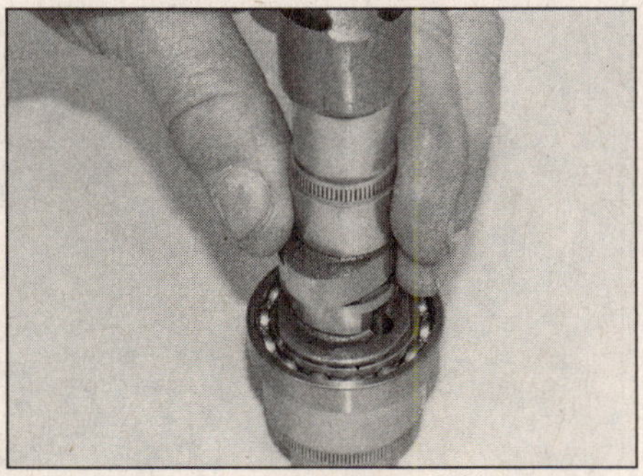

8.13c Support the bearing as described and drive the camshaft into it

8.13d Fit the adapter (arrowed) into the bearing…

8.13e …and jar the bearing out using the slide-hammer

(see illustration) and compare the results to the minimum height specified at the beginning of the chapter. If damage is noted or wear is excessive, the camshaft must be replaced with a new one.

15 Check the amount of camshaft runout by supporting each end on V-blocks, and measuring any runout using a dial gauge. If the runout exceeds the specified limit the camshaft must be replaced with a new one.

16 Check the action of the decompression mechanism lever in the sprocket assembly, making sure it moves smoothly and freely against the spring and returns when released **(see illustration)**. Also check all contacting surfaces between the lever and the cam.

> **HAYNES HiNT** ***Refer to Tools and Workshop Tips in the Reference section for details of how to read a micrometer and dial gauge.***

17 Check the rocker arm rollers for heat discoloration (blue appearance), score marks, chipped areas, flat spots and pitting where they contact the camshaft lobes, and make sure they turn freely **(see illustration)**. Similarly check the bottom of each clearance adjuster and the top of each valve stem **(see illustration)**. If damage is noted or wear is excessive, the rocker arms, camshaft and valves must be replaced with new ones as required.

18 Check for freeplay between each rocker arm and its shaft **(see illustration)**. The arms should move freely with a light fit but no appreciable freeplay. If necessary measure the internal diameter of the arm bores and the corresponding diameter of the shaft and calculate the difference (clearance) to determine the extent of wear **(see illustration)**. Replace the arms and/or shafts with new ones if they are worn beyond their specifications. Check that the fork shaft holes in the cylinder head are neither worn nor damaged.

19 Except in cases of oil starvation, the cam chain should wear very little. If the chain has stretched excessively, which makes it difficult to maintain proper tension, or if it is stiff or the links are binding or kinking, replace it with a new one. Refer to Section 9 for replacement. Check the sprocket for wear, cracks and other damage, and replace it with a new one if necessary. If the sprocket teeth are worn, the cam chain is also worn, and so probably is the sprocket on the crankshaft. If severe wear is apparent, the entire engine should be disassembled for inspection.

Installation

20 On WR models fit a new O-ring smeared with molybdenum disulphide grease onto the inner end of the camshaft **(see illustration)**. On all models lubricate the camshaft bearings with clean engine oil and the camshaft lobes with molybdenum disulphide oil (a 50/50 mixture of molybdenum disulphide grease and engine oil). Slide the camshaft fully into the head and locate the shaft end in the inner bearing **(see illustration 8.10)** – if necessary use a drift to tap it home.

21 Lubricate the exhaust side rocker shaft and its rocker arm bore with molybdenum disulphide oil (a 50/50 mixture of molybdenum disulphide grease and engine oil). Position the rocker arm in the front of the head, with the adjusters on the outside and the contact roller located against the left-hand camshaft lobe, then slide the shaft all the way through **(see illustration 8.9)**. Repeat for the other arm and shaft **(see illustration)**. Position the cut-out section on each shaft end facing down.

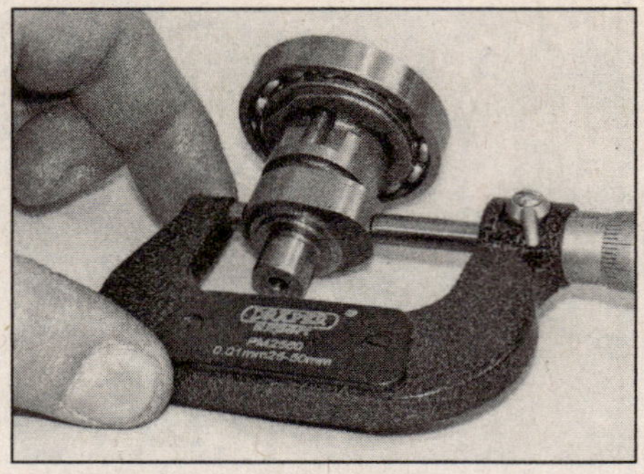

8.14 Measure the height of the camshaft lobes with a micrometer

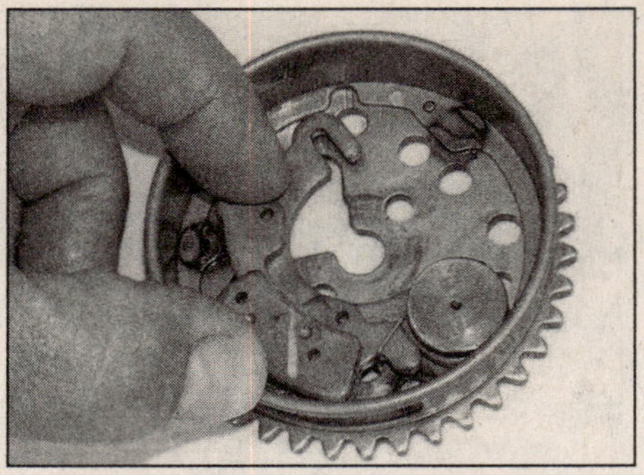

8.16 Check the action of the mechanism and look for wear and damage

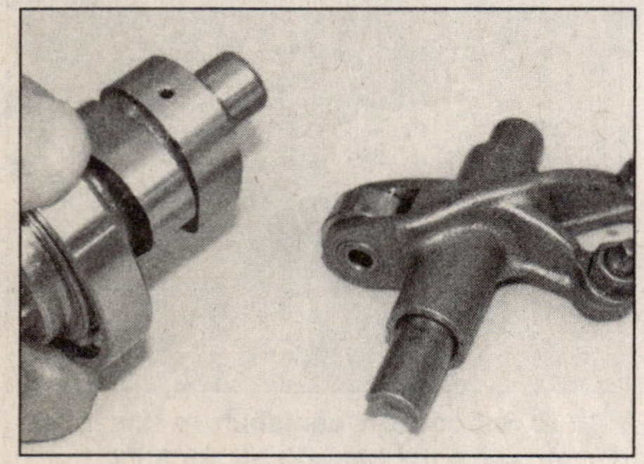

8.17a Check the contacting surfaces of the rocker arm rollers and camshafts...

8.17b ...and of the adjusters and valve stems

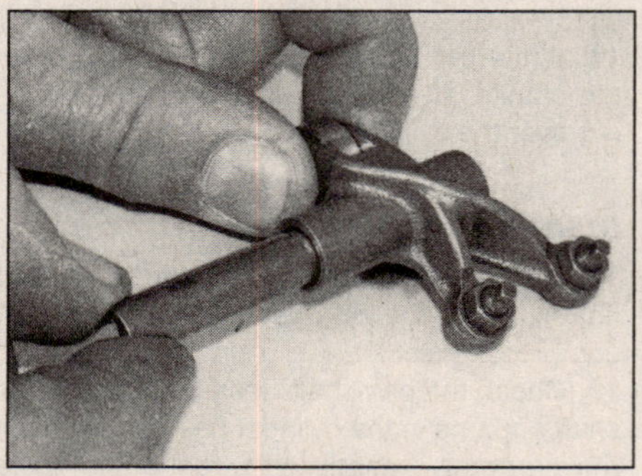

8.18a Check for freeplay between the arm and the shaft...

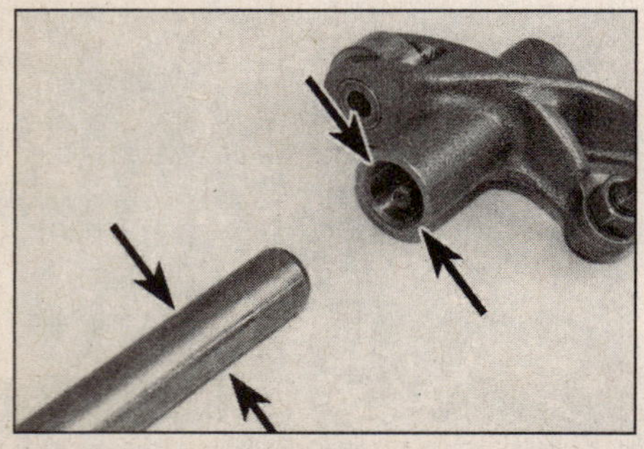

8.18b ...and measure the internal diameter of the bore and the external diameter of the shaft

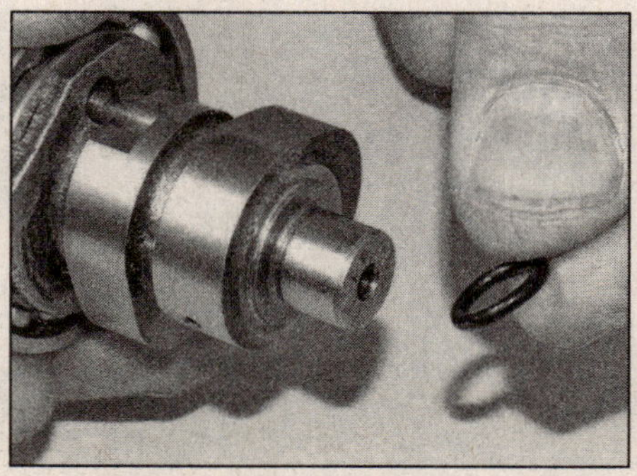

8.20 Fit a new O-ring smeared with molybdenum grease into the groove

8.21 Installing the intake side rocker arm and shaft

8.22 Fit the retainer plate, applying threadlock to the bolts

8.24 Make sure the three pins (arrowed) locate correctly

8.25 Fit and lightly tighten the bolt

22 Make sure both rocker shafts and the camshaft are fully inserted in the head. Clean the threads of the retainer bolts then apply a suitable non-permanent thread locking compound, then fit the retainer and tighten the bolts to the torque setting specified at the beginning of the Chapter **(see illustration)**.
23 Check that the index line on the alternator rotor aligns with the pointer in the inspection hole **(see illustration 8.5b)**. Turn the camshaft so the pins and hole in the camshaft are positioned as shown **(see illustration 8.8)**. Smear the decompression cam with oil and fit it into the camshaft **(see illustration 8.7d)**.
24 Engage the cam chain sprocket with the chain **(see illustration 8.7c)**, making sure the index line on the camshaft sprocket is aligned with the notch on the top of the cylinder head **(see illustration 8.5c)**, the crankshaft does not rotate, the front run of the chain between the sprockets is tight and that any slack is in the rear run so it will be taken up by the tensioner, then fit the sprocket onto the camshaft, locating the pins on the camshaft in the holes and the decompression mechanism cam pin in the slot in the arm **(see illustration)**.
25 Fit the cam chain sprocket bolt and lightly tighten it **(see illustration)**.
26 Use a piece of wooden dowel or other suitable tool to press on the back of the cam chain tensioner blade via the tensioner bore in the cylinder block to ensure that any slack in the cam chain is taken up and transferred to the rear run of the chain. At this point check that the timing marks are still in exact alignment as described in Step 5 **(see illustrations 8.5b and c)**. Note that it is easy to be slightly out (one tooth on the sprocket) without the marks appearing drastically out of alignment. If the marks are out unscrew the sprocket bolt and slide the sprocket off the camshaft, then reposition the sprocket in the chain and move the camshaft as required, fit the sprocket back into the chain and onto the camshaft, and check the marks again.
Caution: If the marks are not aligned exactly as described, the valve timing will be incorrect and the valves may strike the piston, causing extensive damage to the engine.
27 Install the cam chain tensioner (see Section 7).
28 Turn the engine anti-clockwise through two full turns and check again that all the timing marks still align (see Step 5) **(see illustrations 8.5a, b and c)**.
29 Counter-hold the alternator rotor nut and tighten the camshaft sprocket bolt to the specified torque setting **(see illustration)**.
30 Check the valve clearances and adjust them if necessary (see Chapter 1).
31 When the clearances are correct install the valve cover (see Section 6).
32 Fit the timing inspection cap and crankshaft end cap using new O-rings if required, and smear the O-rings with grease **(see illustration)**.
33 Install the spark plug (Chapter 1).
34 Install the water pump (Chapter 3). Refill the cooling system (see Chapter 1).
35 Run the engine and check and adjust the idle speed (see Chapter 1).

9 Cam chain, tensioner blade and guide blade

Note: *The cam chain and its blades can be removed with the engine in the frame.*

Removal

Cam chain

1 Remove the camshaft sprocket/ decompression mechanism assembly (see Section 8).

8.29 Counter-hold the rotor nut and tighten the sprocket bolt to the specified torque

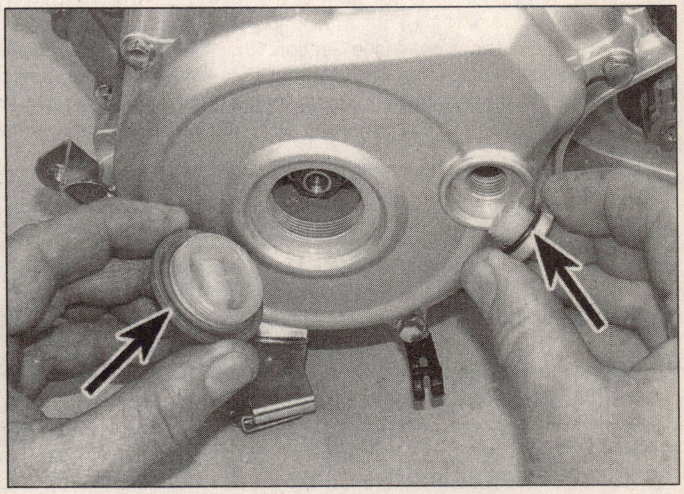

8.32 Fit the caps using new O-rings (arrowed) if required and smear them with grease

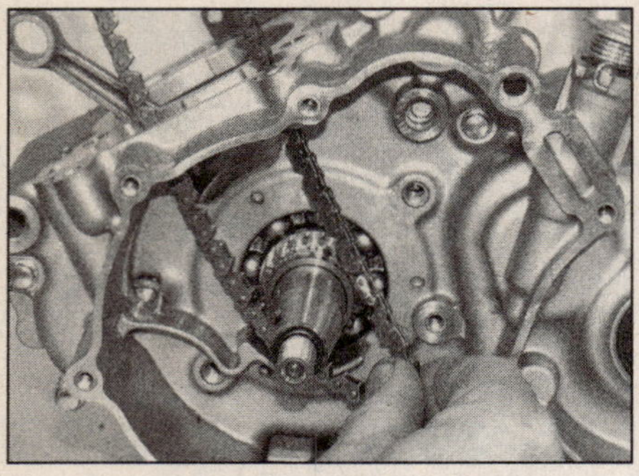

9.3 Removing the cam chain

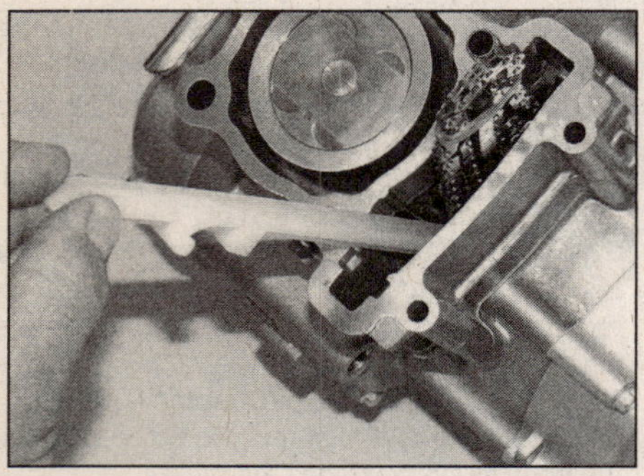

9.8 Draw the guide blade out, noting how it locates

2 Remove the tensioner blade (Steps 4 to 6).
3 Draw the cam chain off the crankshaft sprocket and out of the engine **(see illustration)**.

Tensioner blade

4 Remove the cylinder head (see Section 10).
5 Remove the alternator rotor and starter clutch (see Chapter 8).
6 Unscrew the tensioner blade bolt, then draw the blade out of the top of the cylinder block, collecting the chain guide **(see illustration)**. Note the collar in the blade pivot **(see illustration)**.

Guide blade

7 Remove the cylinder head (see Section 10).
8 Draw the guide blade out of the top of the cylinder block, noting how it locates **(see illustration)**.

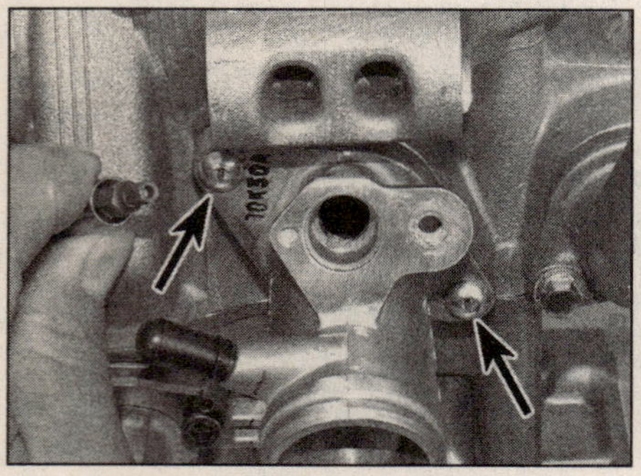

10.2 Unscrew the bolts (arrowed)

9.6a Unscrew the bolt (A) and remove the blade and chain guide (B)

9.11 Make sure the bottom locates in its seat and the lugs locate in the cut-outs

Inspection

Cam chain

9 Check the chain for binding, kinks and any obvious damage and replace it with a new one if necessary. Check the camshaft and crankshaft sprocket teeth for wear and replace the cam chain, camshaft sprocket/ decompression mechanism assembly and crankshaft with a new set if necessary – the drive sprocket on the crankshaft is part of the crankshaft and is not available separately.

Tensioner and guide blades

10 Check the sliding surface and edges of the blades for excessive wear, deep grooves, cracking and other obvious damage, and replace them with new ones if necessary.

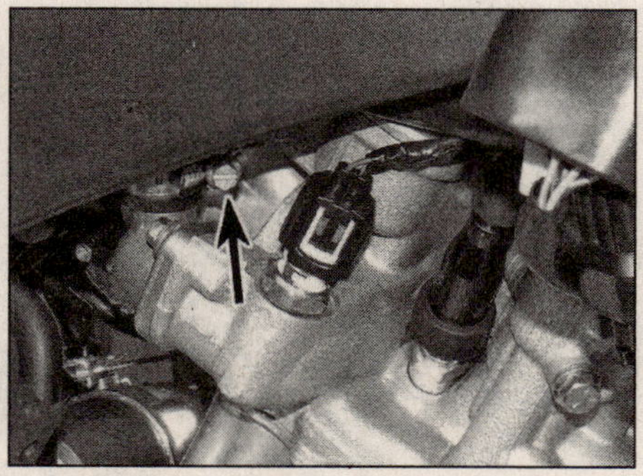

10.3 Slacken the clamp (arrowed) and detach the hose

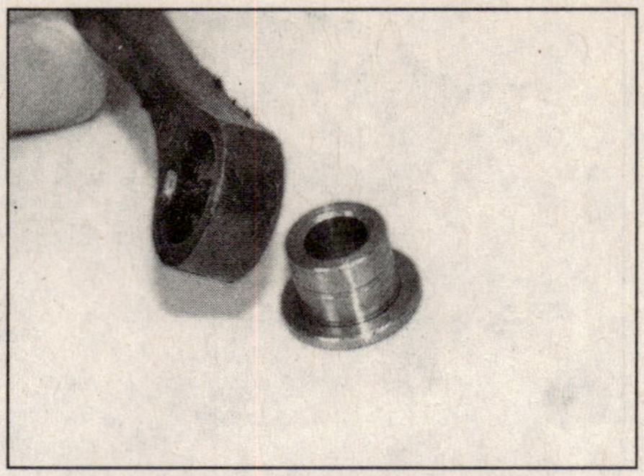

9.6b Note the collar fitted in the back of the blade

Installation

11 Installation of the chain and blades is the reverse of removal. Note that the cam chain locates around the outer set of teeth on the crankshaft **(see illustration 9.6a)** – the inner set is not a sprocket. Make sure the bottom of the guide blade sits in its seat and the lugs near its top locate in the cut-outs in the cylinder block **(see illustration)**. Make sure the collar is fitted in the tensioner from the inner side **(see illustration 9.6b)** – do not forget to fit the chain guide, and tighten the tensioner blade bolt to the torque setting specified at the beginning of the Chapter **(see illustration 9.6a)**.

10 Cylinder head

Note: *The cylinder head can be removed with the engine in the frame.*

Removal

1 Remove the exhaust system (see Chapter 4).
2 Remove the throttle body and the injector assembly (see Chapter 4). Unscrew the intake duct bolts and detach it from the cylinder head **(see illustration)** – on WR models security Torx bolts are used, for which a special bit (readily available from good tool suppliers) is required. Remove the O-ring – a new one must be used.
3 Drain the cooling system (see Chapter 1). Slacken the clamp securing the coolant outlet hose on the thermostat cover and detach the hose **(see illustration)**. If required remove the thermostat and ECT sensor (see Chapter 3). For best access remove the radiator (see Chapter 3).
4 Remove the camshaft sprocket/ decompression mechanism assembly (see Section 8, Steps 1 to 7). If required also remove the camshaft and rocker arms, but note that you can do this after removing the head.
5 Unscrew the nut on the right-hand end of the engine mounting bolt, then withdraw the bolt **(see illustration 4.23a or 4.27)**.
6 The cylinder head is secured by six bolts –

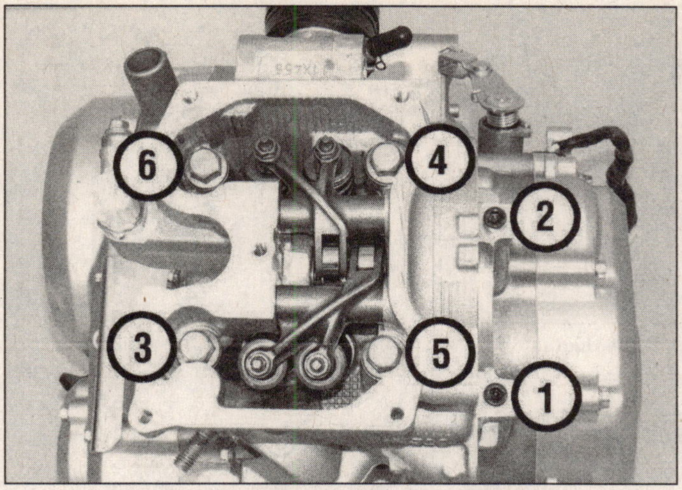

10.6 Unscrew the bolts in the sequence shown

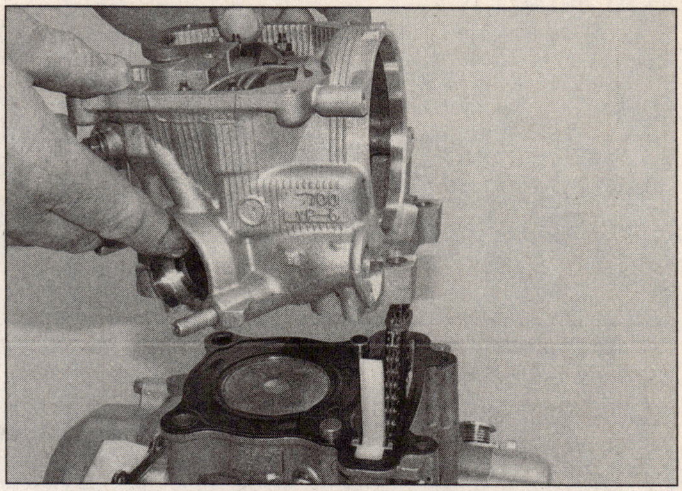

10.7 Carefully lift the head up off the block

two on the side of the cam chain tunnel, and four on the top. Unscrew the bolts 1/4 a turn at a time in the sequence shown until they are all loose, then remove them (except bolts 3 and 5 on MT and YZF-R models if the engine is in the frame), noting the washers with the four top bolts **(see illustration)**. Discard the washers as new ones must be used.

7 Pull the cylinder head up off the block, feeding the cam chain down and laying it over the front of the block **(see illustration)**. If the head is stuck, tap around the joint faces with a soft-faced mallet. Do not attempt to free it by inserting a screwdriver between the head and block mating surfaces – you'll damage them. On MT and YZF-R models, if the engine is in the frame now remove bolts 3 and 5 from the head along with their washers.

8 Remove the cylinder head gasket – a new one must be used **(see illustration 10.12)**. If they are loose, remove the dowels from the cylinder block or the underside of the cylinder head.

9 Check the cylinder head gasket and the mating surfaces on the cylinder head and cylinder block for signs of leakage, which could indicate warpage. Refer to Section 11 and check the cylinder head gasket surface for warpage.

10 Clean all traces of old gasket material from the cylinder head and cylinder block. Also clean off any carbon deposits from the combustion chamber. If a scraper is used, take care not to scratch or gouge the soft aluminium. Be careful not to let any of the gasket material fall into the cylinder bore or the oil passages.

Installation

11 If removed, fit the dowels into the cylinder block **(see illustration 10.12)**. Make sure the cam chain guide blade is correctly seated (see Section 9).

12 Check the cylinder head and cylinder block mating surfaces are clean. Lay the new head gasket onto the block, locating it over the dowels and making sure all the holes are correctly aligned **(see illustration)**. Never reuse the old gasket. On MT and YZF-R models, if the engine is in the frame, refer to Step 14 and illustration 10.6 and fit bolts 3 and 5 into the head.

13 Carefully fit the cylinder head over the cam chain blades, passing the chain up through the tunnel, and onto the block, making sure it locates correctly onto the dowels **(see illustration 10.7)**.

14 Apply engine oil to the threads, under the heads and onto both sides of the new sealing washers on the top bolts. Fit the washers onto the bolts with their rounded side facing the underside of the bolt head. Fit the bolts into the head **(see illustration)**. Lubricate the threads and under the heads of the side bolts and fit them into the head **(see illustration)**. Tighten all six bolts finger-tight.

15 Now tighten all bolts evenly and a little at a time in reverse order of the numerical sequence shown for loosening the bolts **(see illustration 10.6)**, tightening them to the torque settings specified at the beginning of the Chapter **(see illustration)**.

16 Insert the engine mounting bolt from the left, then fit the nut and tighten it to the

10.12 Fit the dowels (arrowed) then lay the new gasket on the block

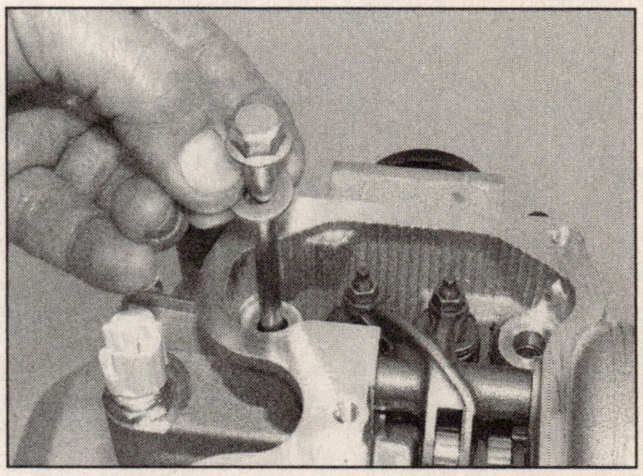

10.14a Fit the top bolts with new sealing washers, lubricated as described...

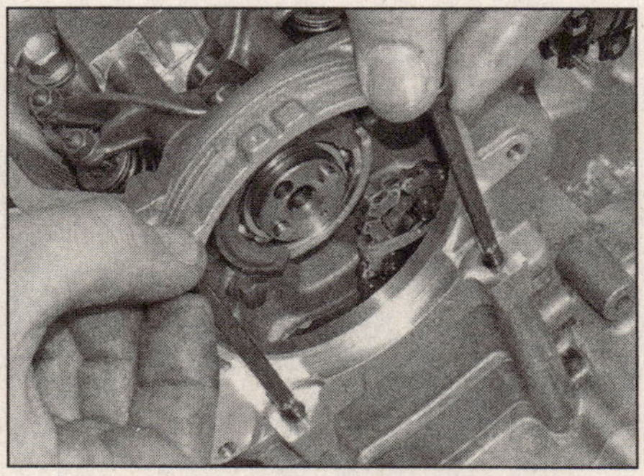

10.14b ...then fit the lubricated side bolts

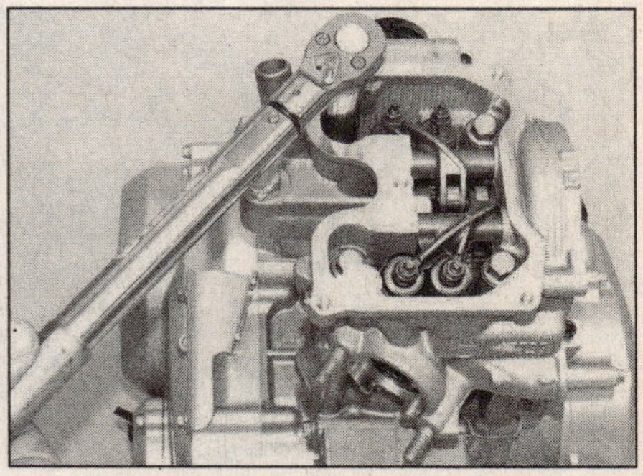

10.15 Tighten the bolts as described to the specified torque settings

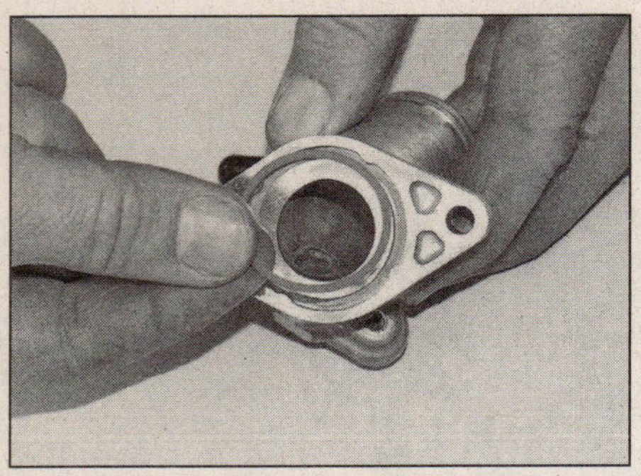

10.19a Fit a new O-ring into the groove...

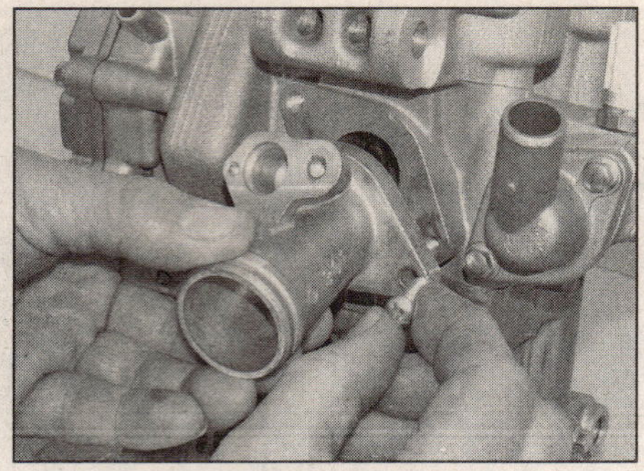

10.19b ...then fit the duct

specified torque (67 Nm on WR models, and 53 Nm on MT and YZF-R models), counter-holding the bolt head **(see illustration 4.23a or 4.27)**.

17 Install the camshaft and rocker arms if removed and not already done, then the camshaft sprocket/decompression mechanism assembly (see Section 8).

18 Fit the radiator, thermostat and ECT sensor if removed (see Chapter 3). Connect the coolant hose and tighten the clamp **(see illustration 10.3)**. Refill the cooling system (see Chapter 1).

19 Fit the intake duct using a new O-ring smeared with grease and tighten the bolts to the torque setting specified at the beginning of the Chapter **(see illustrations)**. Install the fuel injector and throttle body (see Chapter 4).

20 Install the exhaust system (see Chapter 4).

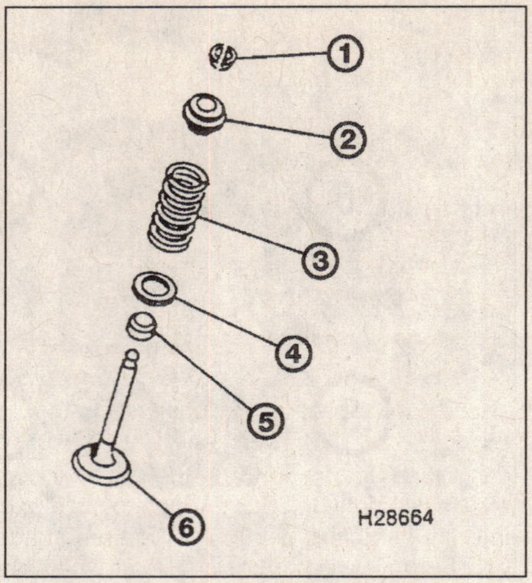

11.5 Valve components

1 Collets	*4 Spring seat*
2 Spring retainer	*5 Valve stem oil seal*
3 Valve spring	*6 Valve*

11 Cylinder head and valve overhaul

1 Because of the complex nature of this job and the special tools and equipment required, most owners leave servicing of the valves, valve seats and valve guides to a professional. However, you can make an initial assessment of whether the valves are seating correctly, and therefore sealing, by tilting the head and pouring a small amount of solvent into each of the valve ports in turn. If the solvent leaks past either valve into the combustion chamber area the valve is not seating correctly and sealing.

2 With the correct tools (a valve spring compressor is essential – make sure it is suitable for motorcycle work), you can also remove the valves and associated components from the cylinder head, clean them and check them for wear to assess the extent of the work needed, and, unless seat cutting or guide replacement is required, grind in the valves and reassemble them in the head.

3 A dealer service department or specialist can replace the guides and re-cut the valve seats.

4 After the valve service has been performed, be sure to clean the head very thoroughly before installation to remove any metal particles or abrasive grit that may still be present from the valve service operations. Use compressed air, if available, to blow out all the holes and passages.

Disassembly

5 Before proceeding, arrange to label and store the valves along with their related components in such a way that they can be returned to their original locations without getting mixed up **(see illustration)**. Labelled plastic bags or a plastic container with four compartments are ideal.

6 Compress the valve spring on the first valve with a spring compressor, making sure it is correctly located onto each end of the valve assembly **(see illustration)** – on the top of the valve the adaptor needs to be about the same size as the spring retainer – if it is too small it will be difficult to remove and install the collets **(see illustration)**. On the underside of the head make sure the plate on the compressor only contacts the valve and not the soft aluminium of the head **(see illustration)** – if the plate is too big for the valve, use a spacer between them. Do not compress the spring any more than is absolutely necessary.

7 Remove the collets, using a magnet or a screwdriver with a dab of grease on it **(see illustration)**. Carefully release the valve spring compressor and remove the spring retainer, noting which way up it fits, the spring and the

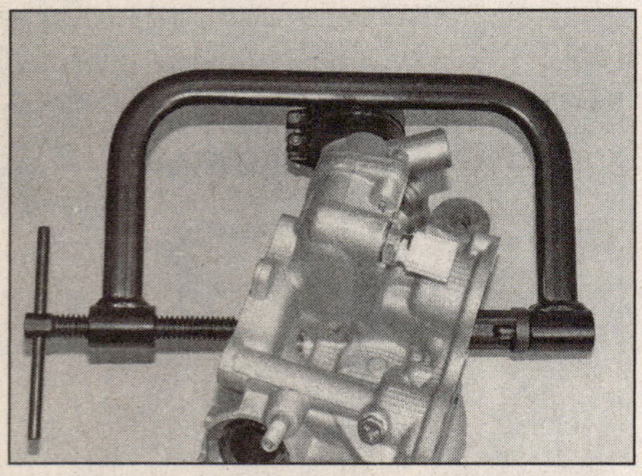

11.6a Fit the valve spring compressor as shown...

11.6b ...making sure it locates correctly both on the top of the spring retainer...

11.6c ...and on the bottom of the valve

11.7a Remove the collets...

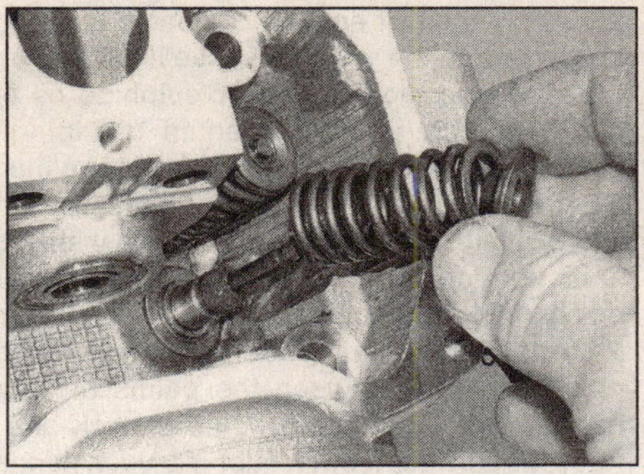

11.7b ...the spring retainer and spring...

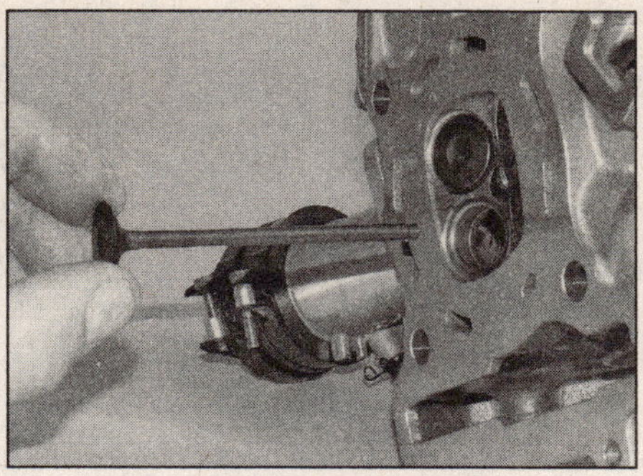

11.7c ...and the valve

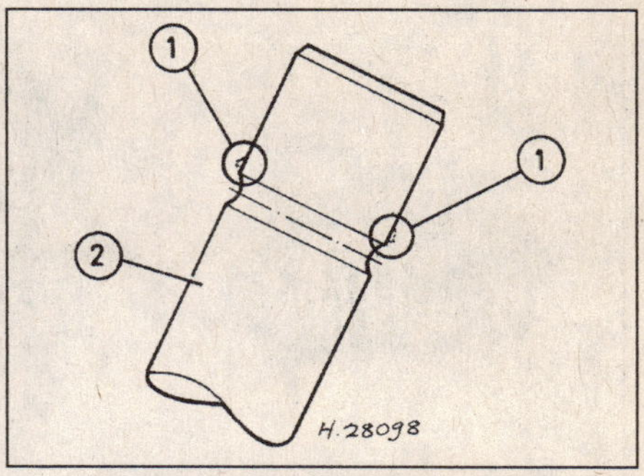

11.7d If the valve stem (2) won't pull through the guide, deburr the area (1) above the collet groove

valve **(see illustrations)**. If the valve binds in the guide and won't pull through, push it back into the head and deburr the area around the collet groove with a very fine file or whetstone **(see illustration)**.

8 Pull the valve stem seal off the top of the valve guide with pliers and discard it (the old seals should never be reused) **(see illustration)**. Remove the spring seat noting which way up it fits **(see illustration)**.

9 Repeat the procedure for the other valves. Remember to keep the parts for each valve together so they can be reinstalled in the same location.

10 Clean the cylinder head with solvent and dry it thoroughly. Compressed air will speed the drying process and ensure that all holes and recessed areas are clean. Note: Do not use a wire brush mounted in a drill motor to clean the combustion chamber as the head material is soft and may be scratched or eroded away by the wire brush.

11 Clean all of the valve springs, collets, retainers and spring seats with solvent and dry them thoroughly. Do the parts from one valve at a time so that no mixing of parts occurs.

12 Scrape and clean off any deposits that may have formed on the valves.

Inspection

13 Inspect the head very carefully for cracks and other damage. If cracks are found, a new head is required.

14 Using a precision straight-edge and a feeler gauge set to the warpage limit listed in the specifications at the beginning of the Chapter, check the head gasket mating surface for warpage. Take six measurements, one along each side and two diagonally across. If the head is warped beyond the limit specified at the beginning of this Chapter, consult a Yamaha dealer or take it to a specialist repair shop for an opinion, though be prepared to have to buy a new one.

15 Examine the valve seats in the combustion chamber. If they are pitted, cracked or burned, the head will require work beyond the scope of the home mechanic. Measure the valve seat width and compare it to that given in the specifications at the beginning of the chapter **(see illustration)**. If it exceeds the service limit, or if it varies around its circumference, overhaul is required. Similarly check the seating surface on the valve.

16 Working on one valve and guide at a time, measure the valve stem diameter **(see illustration)**. Clean the valve's guide using a guide reamer to remove any carbon build-up. Now measure the inside diameter of the guide (at both ends and in the centre of the guide) with a small bore gauge, then measure the gauge with a micrometer **(see illustration)**. Measure the guide at the ends and at the centre to determine if it is worn in a bell-mouth pattern (more wear at the ends). Subtract the stem diameter from the valve guide diameter to obtain the valve stem-to-guide clearance. If the stem-to-guide clearance is greater than that given in the specifications, replace whichever component is beyond its specifiied limits with a new one – take the head to a specialist for valve guide replacement. If the valve guide is within specifications, but is worn unevenly, it should be replaced with a new one. Repeat for the other valves.

17 Carefully inspect each valve face, stem and collet groove area for cracks, pits and burned spots.

18 Rotate the valve and check for any obvious indication that it is bent, in which

11.8a Pull the seal off the valve stem...

11.8b ...then remove the spring seat

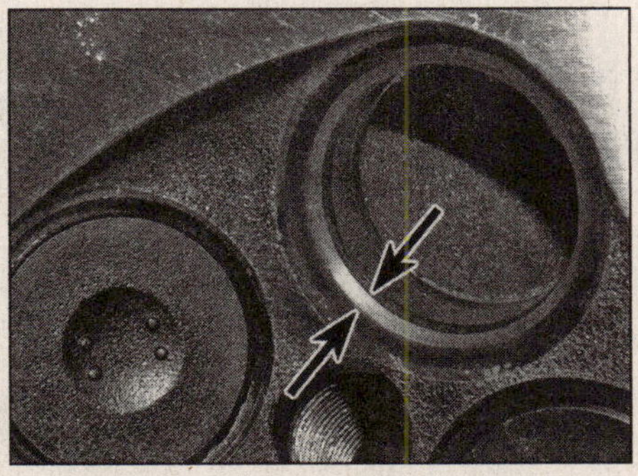

11.15 Measure the valve seat width

11.16a Measure the valve stem diameter with a micrometer

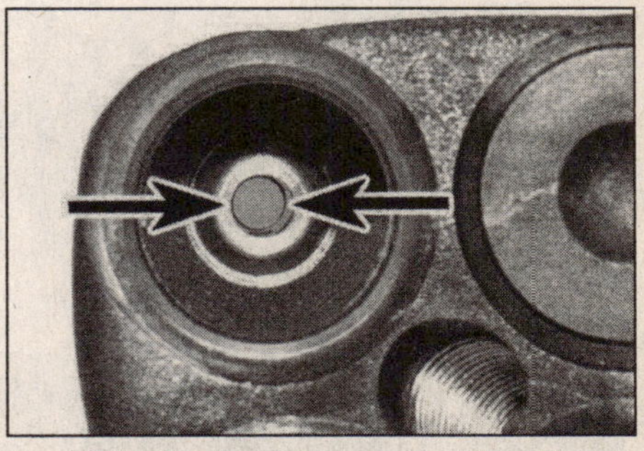

11.16b Measure the valve guide with a small bore gauge, then measure the bore gauge with a micrometer

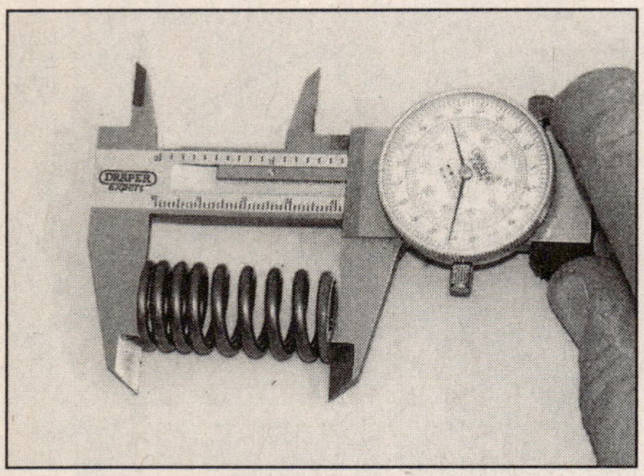

11.19 Measure the free length of the valve springs and check them for bend

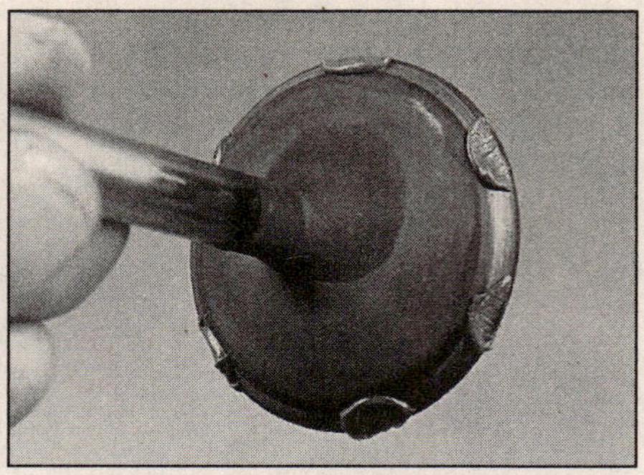

11.23 Apply small dabs of the paste around the circumference of the valve

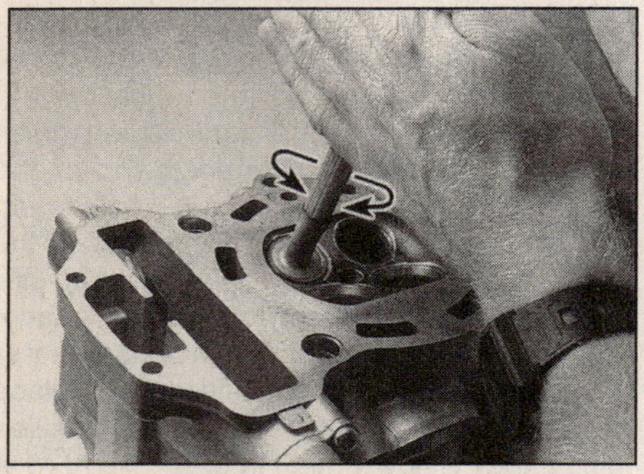

11.24a Using a valve lapping tool

11.24b Make sure the contact areas are as described

case it must be replaced with a new one – if you are not sure place the valve stem in V-blocks and check for runout using a dial gauge, comparing your findings with the runout limit in the Specifications. Check the end of the stem for pitting and excessive wear. The presence of any of the above conditions indicates the need for valve servicing.

19 Check the end of the valve spring for wear and pitting. Measure the spring free length and compare it to the specifications **(see illustration)**. If any spring is shorter than specified it has sagged and must be replaced with a new one. Also place the spring upright on a flat surface and check it for bend by placing a ruler against it, or alternatively lay it against a set square. If the bend in any spring exceeds the specified limit, it must be replaced with a new one.

20 Check the spring seats, retainers and collets for obvious wear and cracks. Any questionable parts should not be reused, as extensive damage will occur in the event of failure during engine operation.

21 If the inspection indicates that no overhaul work is required, the valve components can be reinstalled in the head.

Reassembly

22 Unless a valve service has been performed, before installing the valves in the head they should be ground in (lapped) to ensure a positive seal between the valves and seats. This procedure requires coarse and fine valve grinding compound and a valve grinding tool (either hand-held or drill driven – note that some drill-driven tools specify using only a fine grinding compound). If a grinding tool is not available, a piece of rubber or plastic hose can be slipped over the valve stem (after the valve has been installed in the guide) and used to turn the valve.

23 Apply a small amount of coarse grinding compound to the valve face **(see illustration)**. Smear some molybdenum disulphide oil (a 50/50 mixture of molybdenum disulphide grease and engine oil) to the valve stem, then slip the valve into the guide **(see illustration 11.28)**. Note: Make sure each valve is installed in its correct guide and be careful not to get any grinding compound on the valve stem.

24 Attach the grinding tool to the valve and rotate the tool between the palms of your hands **(see illustration)**. Use a back-and-forth motion (as though rubbing your hands together) rather than a circular motion (i.e. so that the valve rotates alternately clockwise and anti-clockwise rather than in one direction only). If a motorised tool is being used, take note of the correct drive speed for it – if your drill runs too fast and is not variable, use a hand tool instead. Lift the valve off the seat and turn it at regular intervals to distribute the grinding compound properly. Continue the grinding procedure until the valve face and seat contact area is of uniform width, and unbroken around the entire circumference **(see illustration and 11.15)**.

25 Carefully remove the valve and wipe off all traces of grinding compound, making sure none gets in the guide. Use solvent to clean the valve and wipe the seat area thoroughly with a solvent soaked cloth.

26 Repeat the procedure with fine valve grinding compound, then use solvent to clean the valve and flush the guide, and wipe the seat area thoroughly with a solvent soaked cloth. Repeat the entire procedure for the other valves. On completion thoroughly clean the entire head again, then blow through all passages with compressed air. Make sure all traces of the grinding compound have been removed before assembling the head.

27 Working on one valve at a time, fit a new valve stem seal onto the guide, using finger pressure, a stem seal fitting tool or an appropriate size deep socket, to push the seal squarely onto the top of the valve guide until it is felt to clip into place **(see illustrations)**.

28 Coat the valve stem with molybdenum disulphide oil (a 50/50 mixture of molybdenum disulphide grease and engine oil), then slide it into its guide **(see illustration)**. Check that the valve moves up-and-down freely in the guide.

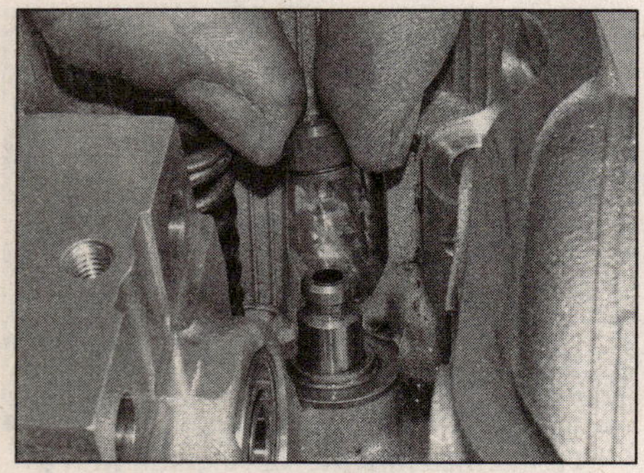

11.27a Fit a new valve stem seal...

11.27b ...and press it squarely into place using a deep socket of the appropriate size

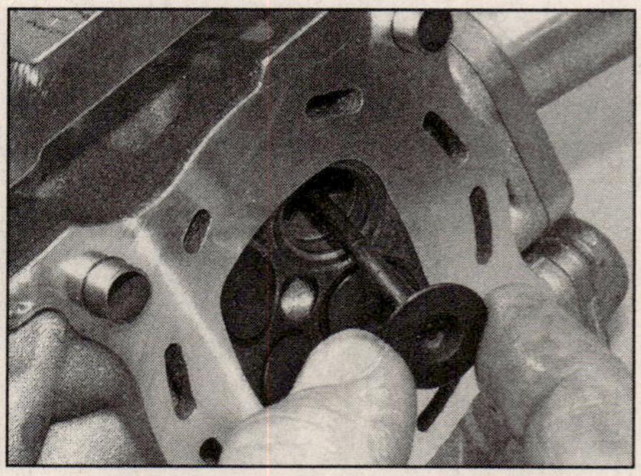

11.28 Lubricate the valve stem and fit it into the guide

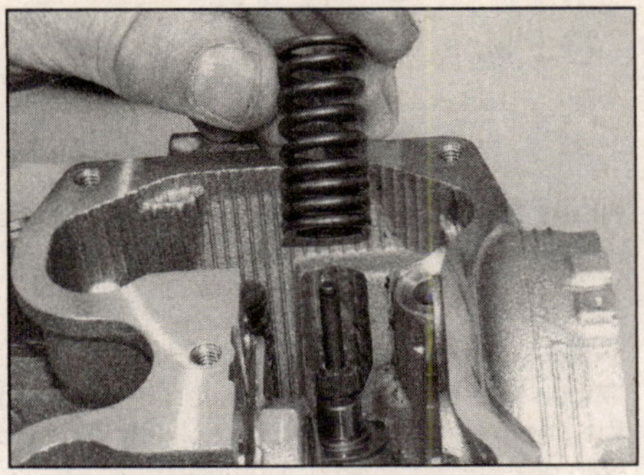

11.30a Fit the spring...

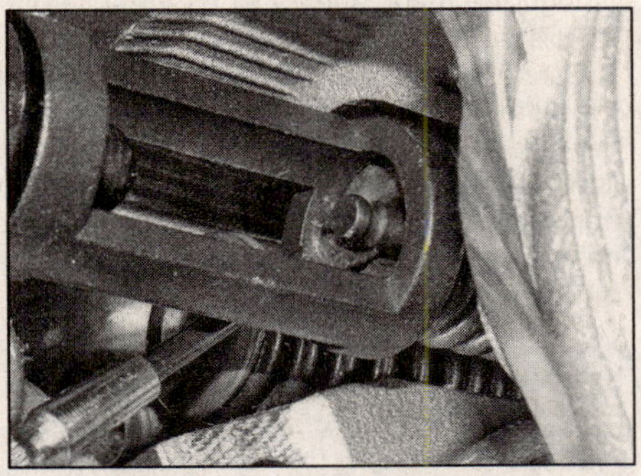

11.31 Use grease to stick each collet in place

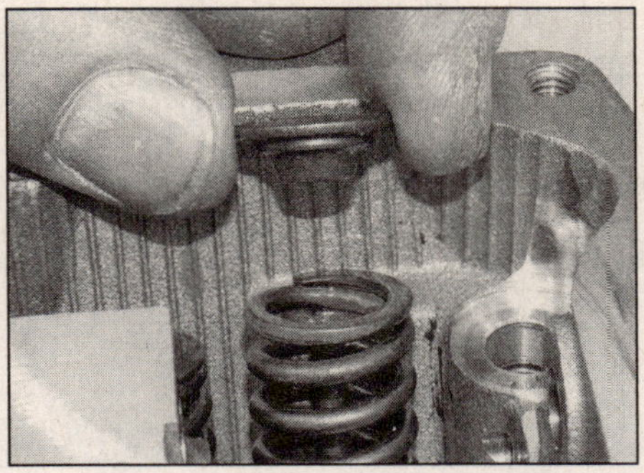

11.30b ...then fit the retainer shouldered side down

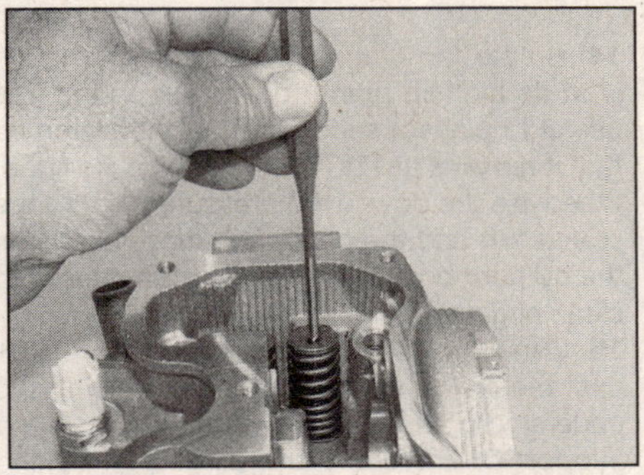

11.33 Tap the top of each valve stem to test the collets

29 Lay the spring seat in place in the cylinder head with its shouldered side facing up **(see illustration 11.8b)**.

30 Next fit the spring, with the painted end up so the closer-wound coils face down into the cylinder head **(see illustration)**. Fit the spring retainer, with its shouldered side facing down so that it fits into the top of the spring **(see illustration)**.

31 Apply a small amount of grease to the collets to help hold them in place. Compress the valve spring with a spring compressor, making sure it is correctly located onto each end of the valve assembly (see Step 6) **(see illustrations 11.6a, b and c)**. Do not compress the spring any more than is necessary to slip the collets into place. Locate each collet in turn into the groove in the valve stem using a screwdriver with a dab of grease on it **(see illustration)**. Carefully release the compressor, making sure the collets seat and lock in the retaining groove.

32 Repeat the procedure for the other valves.

33 Support the cylinder head on blocks so the valves can't contact the work surface, then tap the end of each valve stem lightly to make sure the collets have seated in their grooves **(see illustration)**.

34 After the cylinder head and camshaft have been installed, check the valve clearances and adjust as required (see Chapter 1).

HAYNES HiNT ***Check for proper sealing of the valves by pouring a small amount of solvent into each of the valve ports. If the solvent leaks past any valve into the combustion chamber the valve grinding operation on that valve should be repeated.***

12 Cylinder block

Note: *The cylinder block can be removed with the engine in the frame.*

Removal

1 Remove the cylinder head (see Section 10).

2 Draw the cam chain guide blade out of the top of the block, noting how it locates **(see illustration 9.8)**.

3 Pull the cylinder block up off the crankcase, supporting the piston so the connecting rod does not knock against the crankcase, and feeding the cam chain down and laying it over the front **(see illustration)**. If the block is stuck, tap around the joint faces with a soft-faced mallet. Do not attempt to free it by inserting a screwdriver between the block and crankcase mating surfaces – you'll damage them.

4 Remove the base gasket – a new one must be used. If they are loose, remove the dowels from the crankcase or the underside of the cylinder block **(see illustration 12.12)**.

5 Stuff some clean rag into the cam chain tunnel and around the connecting rod to protect and support it and the piston and to prevent anything falling into the engine.

6 Clean all traces of old gasket material from the cylinder block and crankcase. If a scraper is used, take care not to scratch or gouge the soft aluminium. Be careful not to let any of the gasket material fall into the engine.

Inspection

Note: *Do not attempt to separate the cylinder liner from the cylinder block. The liner is made of aluminium and so great care must be taken not to scratch or gouge it.*

7 Check the cylinder wall carefully for scratches and score marks.

8 Using a telescoping bore gauge and a micrometer, check the dimensions of the cylinder to assess the amount of wear, taper and ovality. Measure near the top (but below the level of the top piston ring at TDC), centre and bottom (but above the level of the oil ring at BDC) of the bore, both parallel to and across the crankshaft axis **(see illustrations)**.

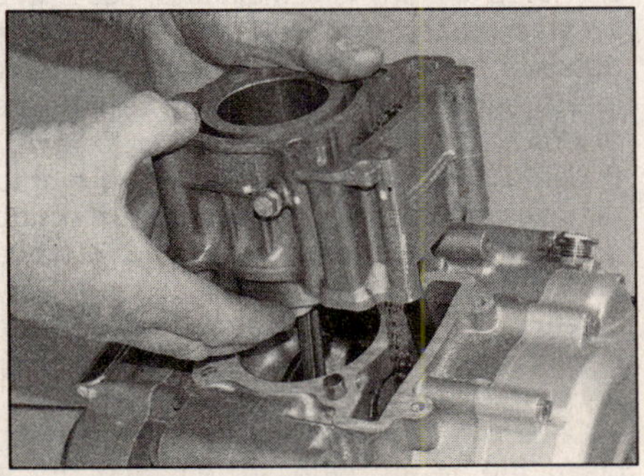

12.3 Carefully lift the block up off the crankcase

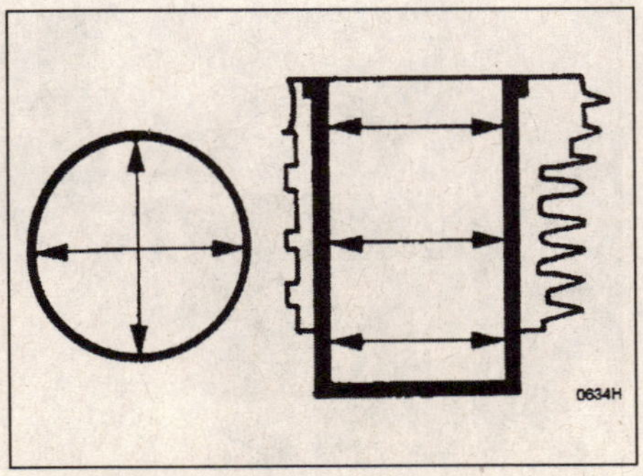

12.8a Measure the cylinder bore in the directions shown...

12.8b ...using a telescoping gauge, then measure the gauge with a micrometer

12.12 Lay the new gasket over the dowels (arrowed) and onto the crankcase

Compare the results to the specifications at the beginning of the Chapter. If the cylinder is worn, oval or tapered beyond the service limit it must be replaced with a new one – do not re-bore the cylinder as oversize sets of pistons and rings are not available from Yamaha. If a new cylinder block is fitted also fit a new piston and rings.

9 If the precision measuring tools are not available, take the cylinder block to a Yamaha dealer or specialist motorcycle repair shop for assessment and advice.

Installation

10 Check that the mating surfaces of the cylinder block and crankcase are free from oil or pieces of old gasket.

11 If removed, fit the dowels into the crankcase and push them firmly home **(see illustration 12.12)**.

12 Remove the rags from around the piston and the cam chain tunnel, taking care not to let the connecting rod fall against the rim of the crankcase. Lay the new base gasket in place, locating it over the dowels **(see illustration)**. The gasket can only fit one way, so if all the holes do not line up properly it is the wrong way round. Never re-use the old gasket.

13 Ensure the piston ring end gaps are positioned correctly before fitting the cylinder block (see Section 14) **(see illustration 14.10)**. If possible, have an assistant to support the cylinder block while the piston rings are fed into the bore.

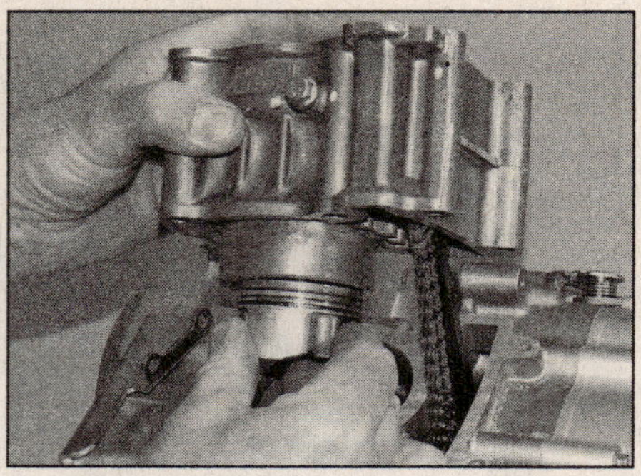

12.15 Carefully fit the piston into the bore and feed each ring in as you lower the block

14 Rotate the crankshaft so that the piston is at its highest point (top dead centre). It is useful to place a support under the piston so that it remains at TDC while the block is fitted, otherwise the downward pressure will turn the crankshaft and the piston will drop. Lubricate the cylinder bore, piston and piston rings with clean engine oil.

15 Carefully lower the block onto the piston until the crown fits into the bore, holding the underside of the piston if you are not using a support to prevent it dropping, and making sure it enters the bore squarely and does not get cocked sideways **(see illustration)**.

16 Carefully compress and feed each ring into the bore as the cylinder is lowered. If necessary, use a soft mallet to gently tap the cylinder down, but do not use force if it appears to be stuck as the piston and/or rings will be damaged.

17 When the piston and rings are correctly located in the bore, feed the cam chain up through the tunnel and lay it over the front of the block, then remove the support if used and press the cylinder block down onto the base gasket, making sure the dowels locate.

18 Hold the block down and turn the crankshaft to check that everything moves as it should.

19 Install the cam chain guide blade, making sure the bottom of the blade sits in its seat and the lugs near its top locate in the cut-outs in the cylinder block **(see illustrations 9.8 and 9.11)**.

20 Install the cylinder head (see Section 10).

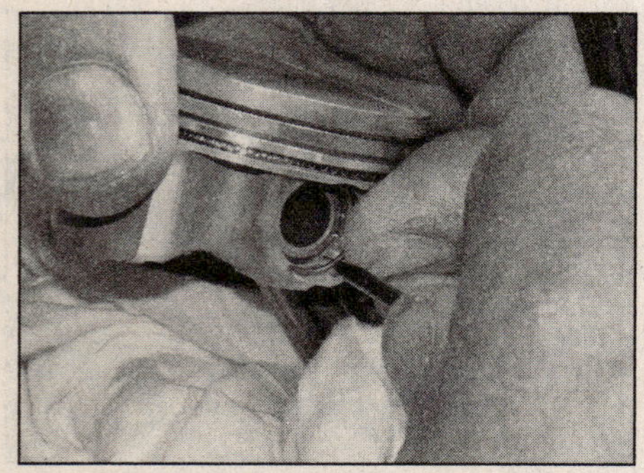

13.3a Prise out the circlip using a suitable tool in the notch...

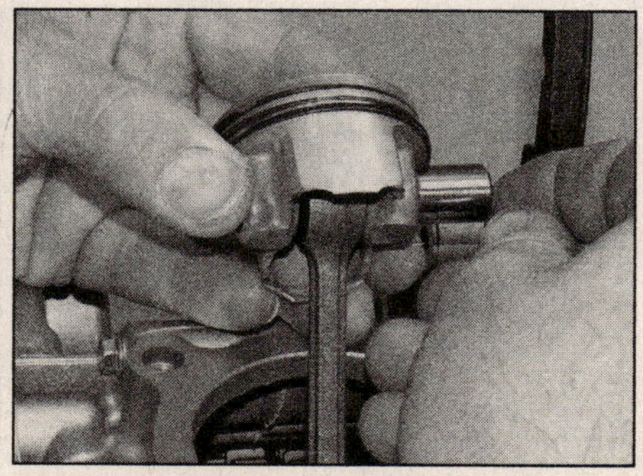

13.3b ...then push out the pin and separate the piston from the rod

13 Piston

Note: *The piston can be removed with the engine in the frame.*

Removal

1 Remove the cylinder block (see Section 12). Check that the holes into the crankcase and the cam chain tunnel are completely blocked with rag.

2 Note that the piston crown has a circular mark or arrow on its front (exhaust) side, though the mark is likely to be invisible until the piston is cleaned.

3 Carefully prise out the circlip on one side of the piston using needle-nose pliers or a small flat-bladed screwdriver inserted into the notch **(see illustration)**. Push the piston pin out from the other side to free the piston from the connecting rod **(see illustration)**. Remove the other circlip – new ones must be used.

HAYNES HiNT ***If the piston pin is a tight fit in the piston bosses, heat the piston using a hot air gun – this will expand the piston sufficiently to release its grip on the pin. If the piston pin is particularly stubborn, extract it using a drawbolt tool, but be careful not to mark the pin's bearing surfaces in the piston. Do not drive the pin out with a hammer.***

4 Using your thumbs or a piston ring removal and installation tool, carefully remove the rings from the piston **(see illustrations 14.9, 14.8b, 14.6c, b and a)**. Do not nick or gouge the piston in the process. Carefully note which way up each ring fits and in which groove as they must be installed in their original positions if being re-used. The upper surface of the top and second ring should have a manufacturer's mark so they cannot be fitted upside down **(see illustration 14.8a)**.

5 Scrape all traces of carbon from the top of the piston. A hand-held wire brush or a piece of fine emery cloth can be used once most of the deposits have been scraped away. Do not, under any circumstances, use a wire brush mounted in a drill motor to remove deposits from the piston; the piston material is soft and will be eroded away by the wire brush.

6 Use a piston ring groove cleaning tool to remove any carbon deposits from the ring grooves. If a tool is not available, a piece broken off an old ring will do the job. Be very careful to remove only the carbon deposits. Do not remove any metal and do not nick or gouge the sides of the ring grooves.

7 Once the deposits have been removed, clean the piston with solvent and dry it thoroughly. Make sure the oil return holes below the oil ring groove are clear.

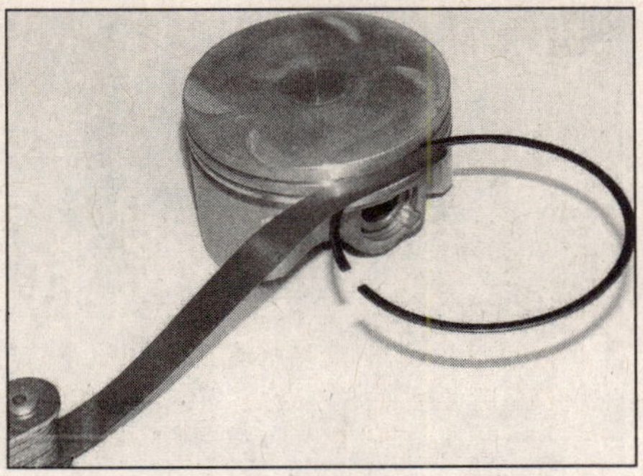

13.10 Measure the piston ring-to-groove clearance with a feeler gauge

Inspection

8 Carefully inspect the piston for cracks around the skirt, at the pin bosses and at the ring lands. Normal piston wear appears as even, vertical wear on the thrust surfaces. If the skirt is scored or scuffed, the engine may have been suffering from overheating and/or abnormal combustion, which caused excessively high operating temperatures. Also check that the circlip grooves are not damaged.

9 A hole in the top of the piston, in one extreme, or burned areas around the edge of the piston crown, indicate that pre-ignition or knocking under load have occurred. If you find evidence of any problems the cause must be corrected or the damage will occur again (see Fault Finding9,6 in the Reference section).

10 Measure the piston ring-to-groove clearance by laying each piston ring in its groove and slipping a feeler gauge in beside it **(see illustration)**. Make sure you have the correct ring for the groove (see Step 4). Check the clearance at three or four locations around the groove. If the clearance is greater than that specified at the beginning of the chapter, replace both the piston and rings as a set. If new rings are being used, measure the clearance using the new rings. If the clearance is greater than that specified, the piston is worn and must be replaced with a new one.

11 Check the piston-to-bore clearance by measuring the bore (see Section 12), then measure the piston 5 mm up from the bottom of the skirt and at 90° to the piston pin axis **(see illustration)**. Refer to the Specifications and subtract the piston diameter from the bore diameter to obtain the clearance. If it is greater than the specified figure, the piston must be replaced with a new one (assuming the bore itself is within limits).

12 Apply clean engine oil to the piston pin, insert it into the piston and check for any freeplay between the two **(see illustration)**. Measure the pin external diameter at each end, and the pin bore in the piston **(see illustration)**. Calculate the difference to obtain the piston pin-to-piston pin bore clearance. Compare the result to the specifications. If the clearance is greater than specified, replace the components that are worn beyond their specified limits with new ones. Feel for excessive freeplay between the middle of the pin and the connecting rod small-end **(see illustration)**.

13.16a Fit the piston with the circular mark or arrow to the front of the engine

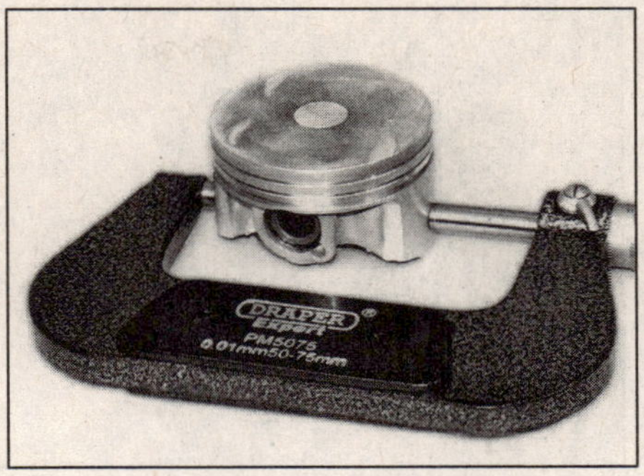

13.11 Measure the piston diameter with a micrometer at the specified distance from the bottom of the skirt

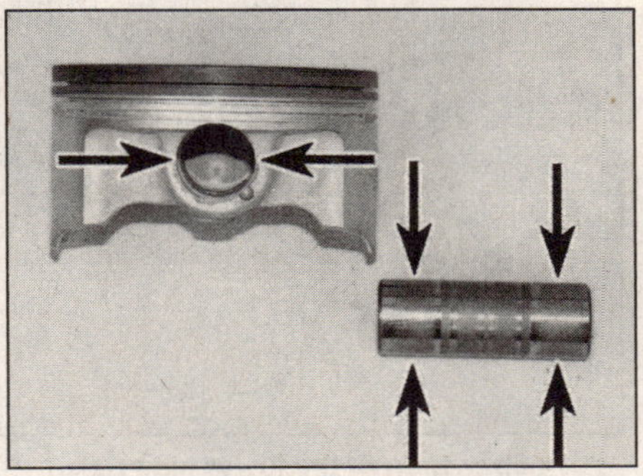

13.12b Measure the external diameter of each end of the pin and the internal diameter of the bore in the piston on each side

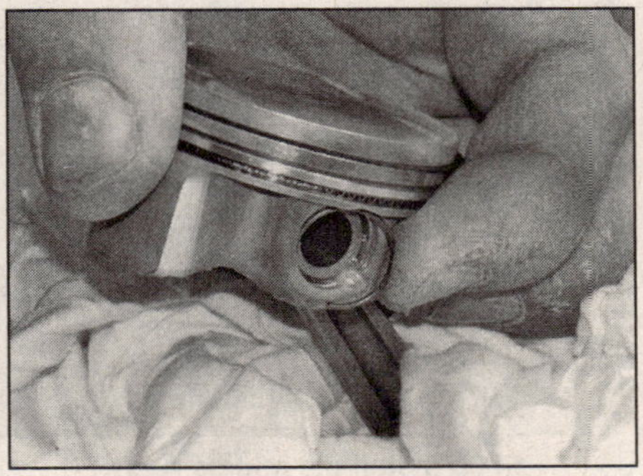

13.16b Use new circlips and make sure they locate correctly

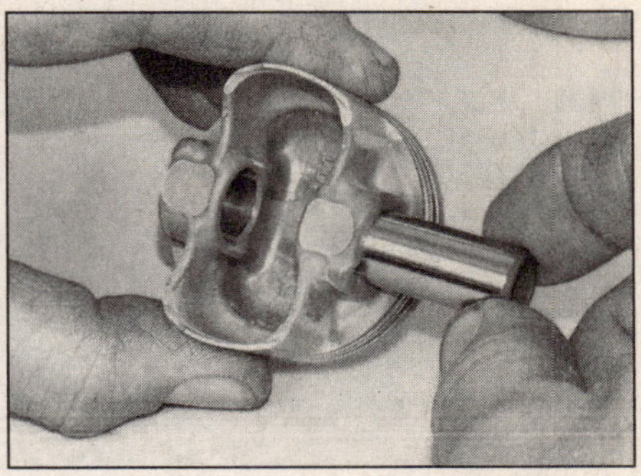

13.12a Fit the pin into the piston and check for any freeplay

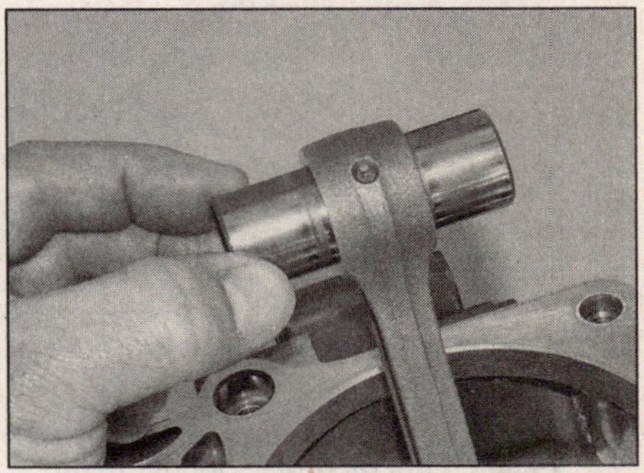

13.12c Fit the pin into the connecting rod and check for any freeplay

Installation

13 Inspect and install the piston rings (see Section 14).

14 Lubricate the piston pin, the piston pin bore and the connecting rod small-end bore with clean engine oil.

15 Fit a new circlip into one side of the piston (do not reuse old circlips). When fitting the circlip, compress it only just enough to fit it in the piston, and make sure it is properly seated in the groove with the open end away from the removal notch.

16 Line up the piston on the connecting rod with the circular mark or arrow at the front and insert the piston pin from the opposite side to the fitted circlip **(see illustration)**. Secure the pin with the other new circlip **(see illustration)**.

17 Install the cylinder block (see Section 12).

14 Piston rings

Inspection

1 It is good practice to replace the piston rings with a new set when an engine is being overhauled. Before fitting the new rings, check the end gaps with the rings in the bore, as follows.

2 Insert the top ring into the bottom of the bore and square it up with the bore walls by

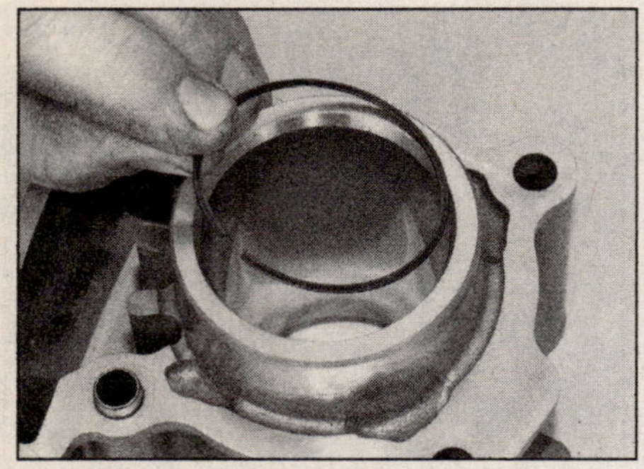

14.2a Fit the ring in the bore...

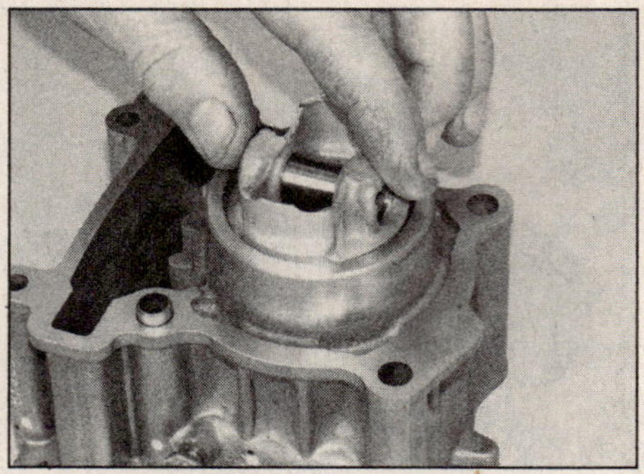

14.2b ...and set it square using the piston...

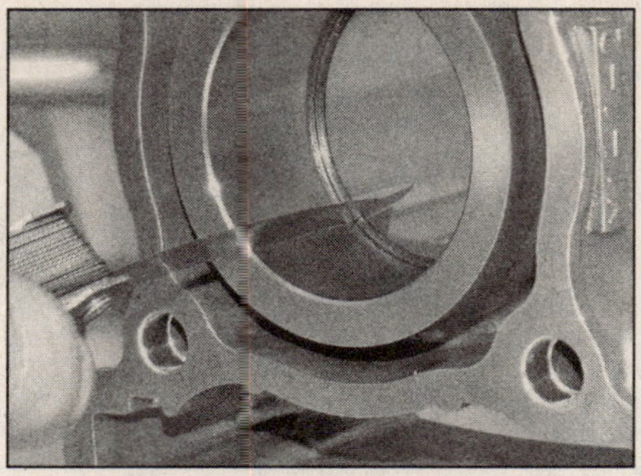

14.2c ...then measure the end gap using a feeler gauge

14.6a Fit the oil ring expander in its groove...

14.6b ...then fit the lower side rail...

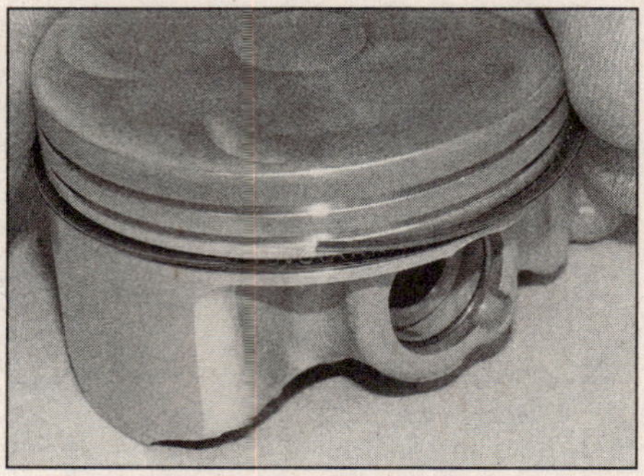

14.6c ...and the upper side rail on each side of it

pushing it in with the top of the piston **(see illustrations)**. The ring should be about 40 mm below the top edge of the bore. Slip a feeler gauge between the ends of the ring and compare the measurement to the specifications at the beginning of the Chapter **(see illustration)**.

3 If the gap is larger or smaller than specified, double check to make sure that you have the correct ring before proceeding; excess end gap is not critical unless it exceeds the service limit. If the gap is too small, the ring ends may come in contact with each other during engine operation, which can cause serious damage.

4 Repeat the procedure for the second (middle) ring and oil control ring side-rails but not the expander ring.

5 If the service limit is exceeded with new rings, check the bore for wear (see Section 12).

Installation

6 Fit the oil control ring (lowest on the piston) first. It is composed of three separate components, namely the expander and the upper and lower side-rails. Slip the expander into the groove, making sure the ends don't overlap, then fit the lower side-rail **(see illustrations)**. Do not use a piston ring installation tool on the side-rails as they may be damaged. Instead, place one end of the side-rail into the groove between the expander and the ring land. Hold it firmly in place and slide a finger around the piston while pushing the rail into the groove. Next, fit the upper side-rail in the same manner **(see illustration)**. Check that the ends of the expander have not overlapped.

7 After the three oil ring components have been installed, check to make sure that both the upper and lower side-rails can be turned smoothly in the ring groove.

8 Fit the second (middle) ring next. Make sure that the identification mark near the end gap is facing up **(see illustration)**. Fit the ring into the middle groove in the piston **(see illustration)**. Do not expand the ring any more than is necessary to slide it into place. To avoid breaking the ring, use a piston ring installation tool.

9 Finally, fit the top ring in the same manner into the top groove in the piston **(see illustration)**.

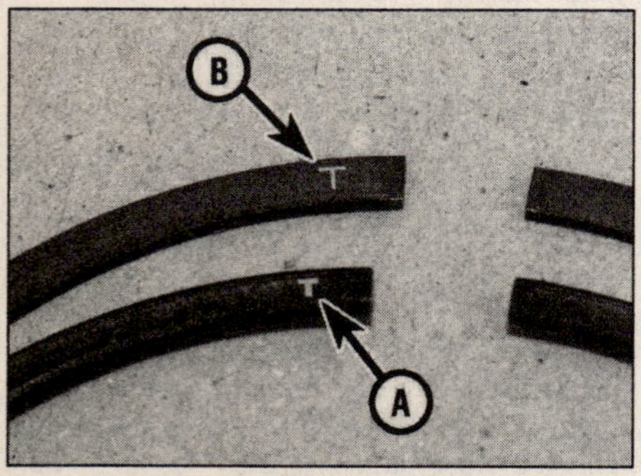

14.8a Note the mark on the middle and upper rings which must face up – upper ring (A), middle ring (B)

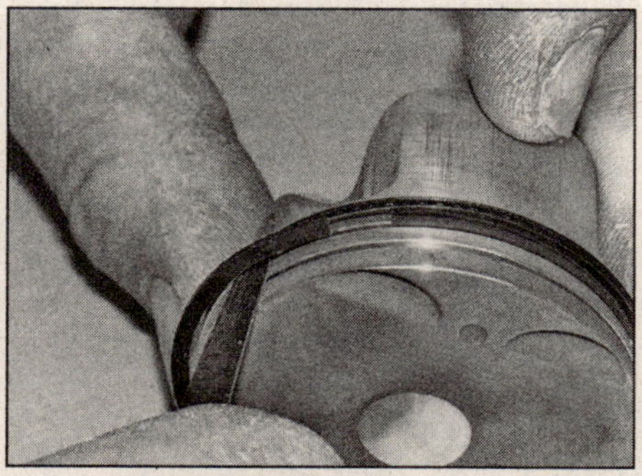

14.8b Install the middle ring...

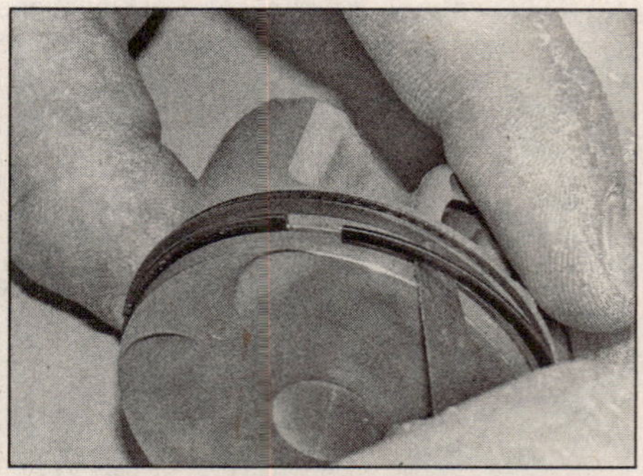

14.9 ...and the top ring as described

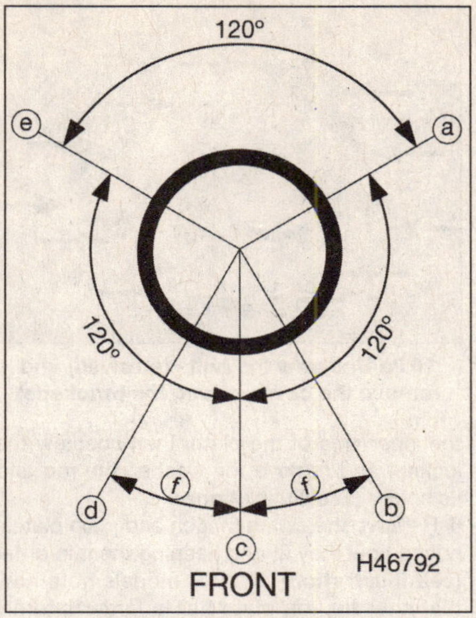

14.10 Piston ring installation details – stagger the ring end gaps as shown

a Top ring
b Upper side rail
c Oil ring expander
d Lower side rail
e Second (middle) ring
f 20 mm at piston edge

10 Once the rings are correctly installed, check they move freely without snagging and stagger their end gaps as shown **(see illustration)**.

15 Starter clutch and gears

Note: *The starter clutch can be removed with the engine in the frame.*

Check

1 The operation of the starter clutch can be checked while it is in situ. Remove the starter motor (see Chapter 8). Check that the starter idle/reduction gear is able to rotate freely clockwise as you look at it via the starter motor aperture, but locks when rotated anti-clockwise. If not, the starter clutch is faulty and should be removed for inspection.

Removal

2 Remove the alternator rotor and starter driven gear (see Chapter 8) – the starter clutch is bolted to the back of the rotor.

3 Withdraw the idle/reduction gear shaft and remove the gear, noting the thrust washer **(see illustration)**.

Inspection, disassembly and reassembly

4 With the rotor face down on a workbench, check that the starter driven gear rotates freely anti-clockwise and locks against the rotor clockwise **(see illustration)**. If it doesn't, remove the starter driven gear, rotating it anti-clockwise as you do **(see illustration)**.

5 Check the condition of the rollers and the corresponding surface on the driven gear hub. If the rollers are damaged, marked or flattened at any point, remove them along with the plungers and springs, noting how they fit, and replace them with new ones **(see illustrations)**.

6 To remove the starter clutch from the back of the alternator rotor hold the rotor using a holding strap and unscrew the three bolts **(see illustration)**. Note that Yamaha specify that new bolts should be used, but if they are not available, on installation clean the threads of the bolts and apply a suitable non-permanent thread locking compound, and tighten them to the torque setting specified at the beginning of the Chapter.

7 Check the needle bearing and its bearing surfaces in the starter driven gear hub and on the crankshaft **(see illustration 15.4b)**. Replace the bearing with a new one if necessary.

8 Check the teeth of the idle/reduction gear and the corresponding teeth of the starter driven gear and starter motor drive shaft. Replace the gears and/or starter motor if worn or chipped teeth are discovered on related gears. Also check the gear shaft for damage, and check that the gear is not a loose fit on it. Check the shaft ends and the bores they run in for wear.

Installation

9 If removed fit a new circlip into the groove in the idle/reduction gear shaft. Lubricate the shaft with molybdenum disulphide oil (a 50/50 mixture of molybdenum disulphide grease and

15.3 Withdraw the shaft and remove the gear

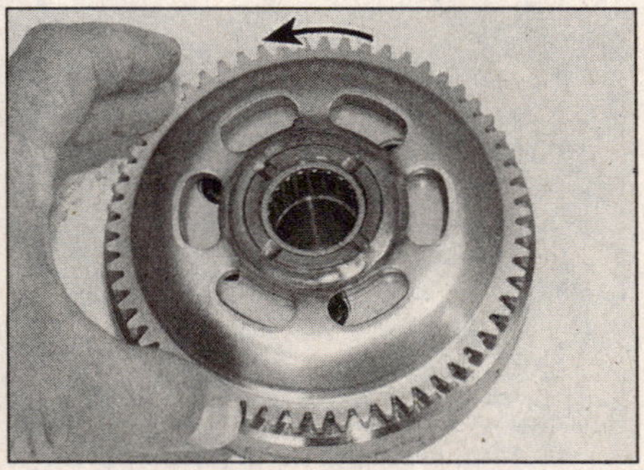

15.4a Check the operation of the clutch as described

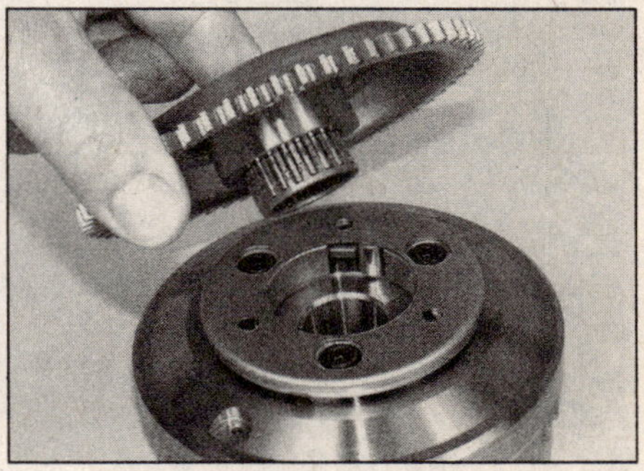

15.4b Withdraw the driven gear and check all components as described

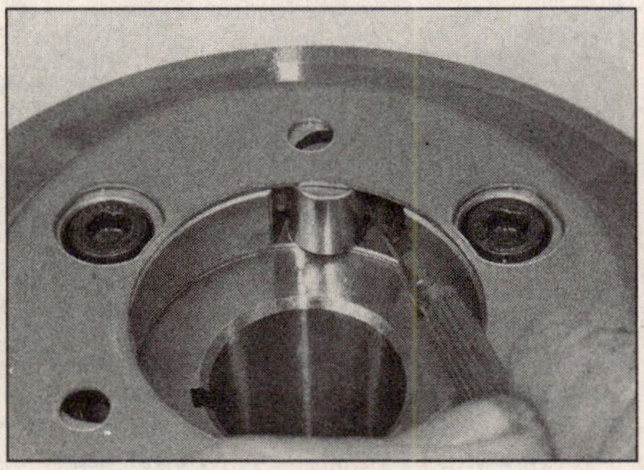

15.5a Ease the rollers out...

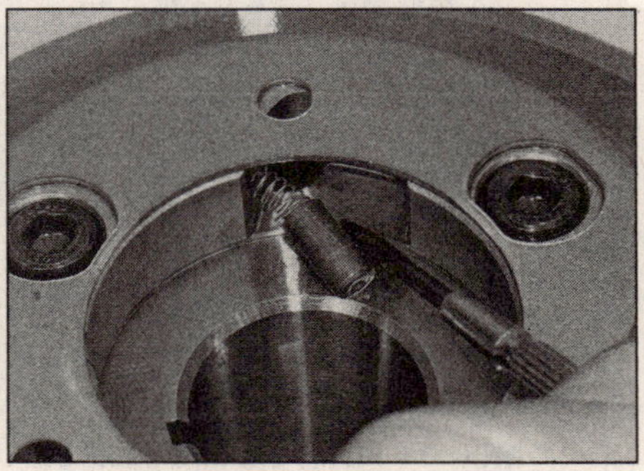

15.5b ...and remove the plungers and springs

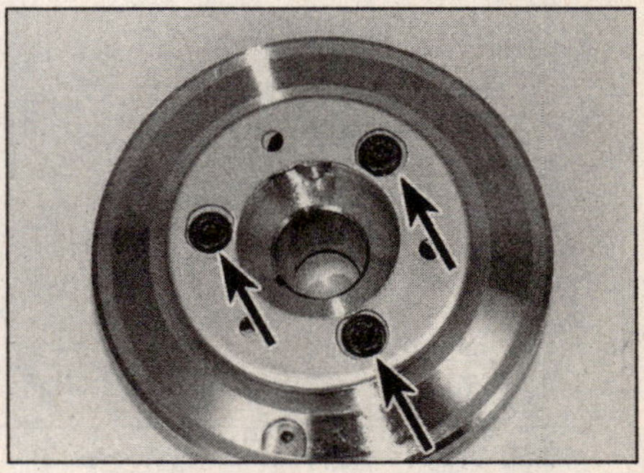

15.6 Starter clutch bolts (arrowed)

engine oil), then slide the washer on and then the gear with the smaller pinion facing the circlip **(see illustration 15.3)**. Fit the shaft into the crankcase with the circlip end facing out.

10 Install the starter driven gear components and alternator rotor (see Chapter 8).

16 Clutch

Note: *The clutch can be removed with the engine in the frame.*

Removal

1 Drain the engine oil and remove the filter (see Chapter 1).

2 On YZF-R models remove the lower section of the fairing on the left-hand side (see Chapter 7). Detach the clutch cable (see Section 17, Step 2). On WR models displace the AIS reed valve housing **(see illustration)**.

3 Working evenly in a criss-cross pattern, slacken then unscrew and remove the clutch cover bolts, noting how the reed valve (WR models), belly-pan (MT models) or fairing (YZF-R models) bracket(s) fit(s) **(see illustration)**. Remove the cover, being prepared to catch any residual oil. Remove the gasket **(see illustration 16.31a)** – a new one must be used. Remove the two dowels from either the cover or the crankcase if they are loose. Lever the oil seal out of the cover using a screwdriver or seal hook **(see illustration)** – a new seal must be fitted.

16.2 Unscrew the bolts (arrowed) to release the housing from the bracket

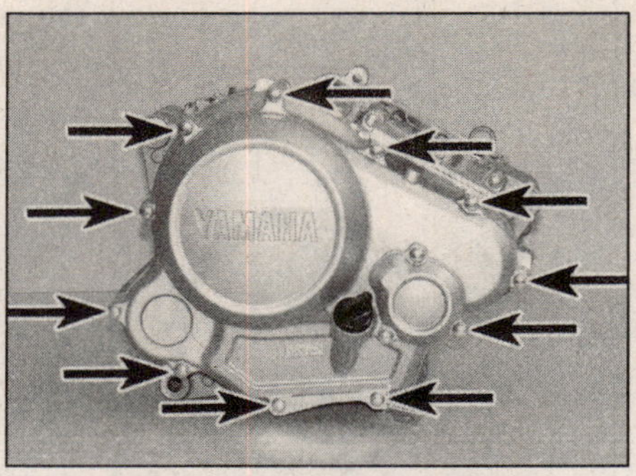

16.3a Unscrew the bolts (arrowed) and remove the cover, noting the bracket(s)

4 Working in a criss-cross pattern, gradually slacken the clutch spring bolts until pressure is released **(see illustration)**. To prevent the clutch from turning, cover it with a rag and hold it securely – the bolts are not very tight. If available, have an assistant hold the clutch while you unscrew the bolts. Remove the bolts, springs and the pressure plate, noting the short pushrod fitted in it **(see illustrations 16.28 and 16.27)**.

5 There is a bearing ball that sits between the inner ends of the short and long pushrods – if the engine has been removed you can tip it out (though oil stiction may hold it in), otherwise it can stay inside the shaft **(see illustration)**. Do not remove the short pushrod from the pressure plate unless necessary as clutch release mechanism adjustment will be affected – if you do need to remove it mark the setting of the pushrod in its holder on the inner side of the plate, then unscrew the locknut and remove the washer, the rod and its holder **(see illustration)**.

6 Remove the clutch friction and plain plates, noting how they fit and keeping them in order **(see illustration)**. On WR models note how the inner friction plate has a larger internal diameter so it seats around the anti-judder spring and spring seat. If you are replacing the plates with new ones and no further disassembly of the clutch is intended, refer to Steps 11 to 14 and follow the relevant inspection procedures, then refer to Steps 24-on to fit the new plates.

7 On WR models remove the anti-judder spring and spring seat, noting which way round they fit **(see illustrations 16.23b and a)**.

8 Bend the clutch nut lockwasher raised tab(s) off the nut **(see illustration)**. To unscrew the clutch nut, the input shaft must be locked

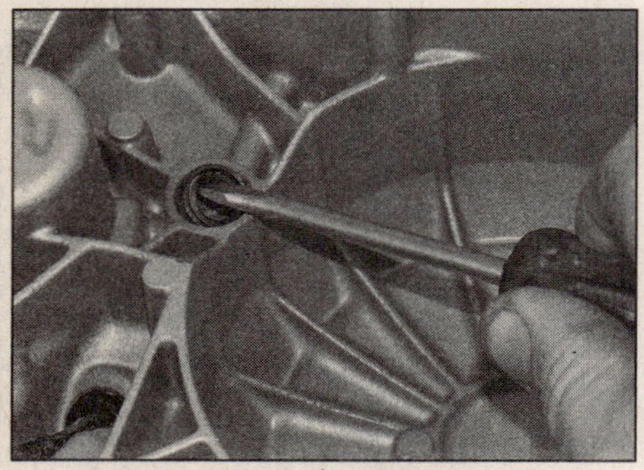

16.3b Lever the oil seal out

16.4 Unscrew the bolts (arrowed) as described

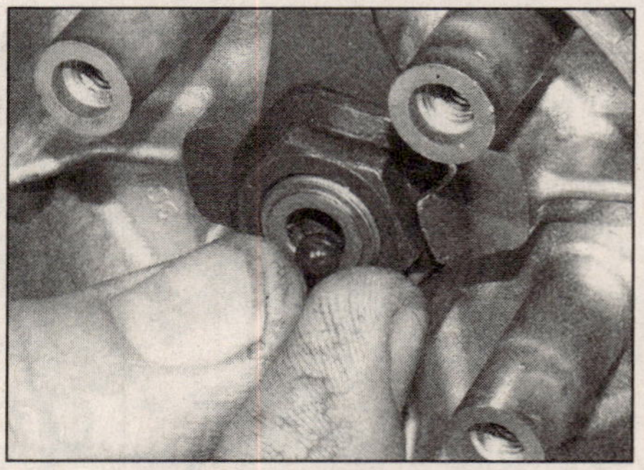

16.5a Remove the bearing ball if required

16.5b Unscrew the locknut (arrowed) to release the short pushrod from the pressure plate

16.6 Draw the plates out as a pack and keep them in order

16.8a Bend back the lockwasher tabs...

16.8b ... then lock or hold the clutch and unscrew the nut – this shows a commercially available holding tool

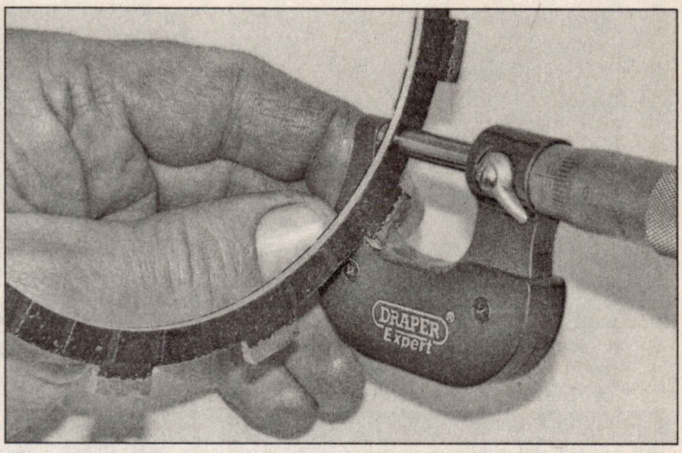

16.11 Measuring clutch friction plate thickness

– if the engine is in the frame, engage 6th gear and have an assistant hold the rear brake on hard with the rear tyre in firm contact with the ground; alternatively, and if the engine has been removed, the Yamaha service tool (Pt. No. 90890-04086) or a commercially available clutch holding tool (as shown) can be used to stop the clutch centre from turning **(see illustration)**. Unscrew the nut and remove the washer **(see illustrations 16.22b and a)**. Check the condition of the washer and replace it with a new one if necessary – Yamaha specify to use a new one.

9 Slide the clutch centre off the shaft, followed by the thrust washer **(see illustrations 16.21b and a)**.

10 Slide the clutch housing off the shaft, followed by the spring washer, noting which way round it fits **(see illustrations 16.20b and a)**.

Inspection

11 After an extended period of service the clutch friction plates will wear and promote clutch slip. Measure the thickness of each friction plate **(see illustration)**. If any plate has worn to or beyond the service limit given in the Specifications at the beginning of the Chapter, or if any of the plates smell burnt or are glazed, the friction plates must be replaced with a new set.

12 The plain plates should not show any signs of excess heating (bluing). Check for warpage using a flat surface and feeler gauges **(see illustration)**. If any plate exceeds the maximum permissible amount of warpage, or shows signs of bluing, all plain plates must be replaced with a new set.

16.12 Check the plain plates for warpage

13 Measure the free length of each clutch spring **(see illustration)**. Place each spring upright on a flat surface and check it for bend by placing a ruler against it, or alternatively lay it against a set square. If any spring is below the minimum free length specified or if the bend in any spring is excessive, replace all the springs as a set.

14 Inspect the friction plate tabs and the clutch housing slots for burrs and indentations on the edges **(see illustration)**. Similarly check for wear between the inner teeth of the plain plates and the slots in the clutch centre **(see illustration)**. Wear of this nature will cause clutch drag and slow disengagement during gear changes as the plates will snag when the pressure plate is lifted. With care a small amount of wear can be corrected by dressing with a fine file, but if this is excessive the worn components should be replaced with new ones.

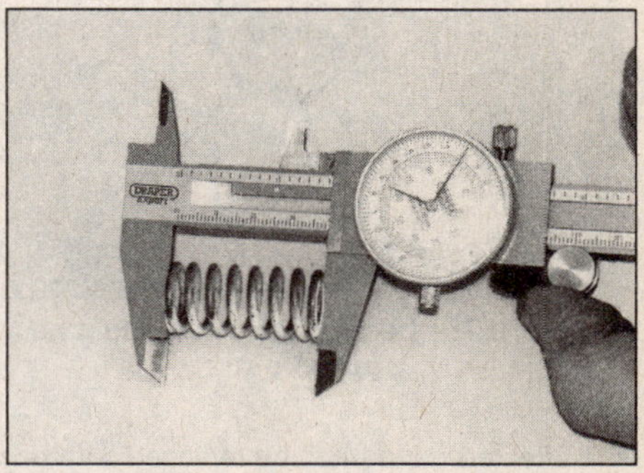

16.13 Measure the free length of the clutch springs and check them for bend

15 Inspect the bearing surfaces of the clutch housing bush and the input shaft **(see illustration)**. If there are any signs of excessive wear (the oil retention dimples should be visible), pitting or other damage,

16.14a Check the friction plate tabs and housing slots...

16.14b ... and the plain plate teeth and centre slots as described

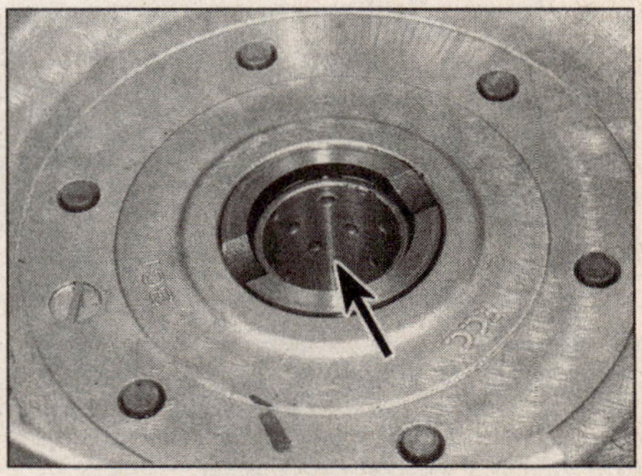

16.15 Check the bearing surfaces on the bush (arrowed) and the shaft

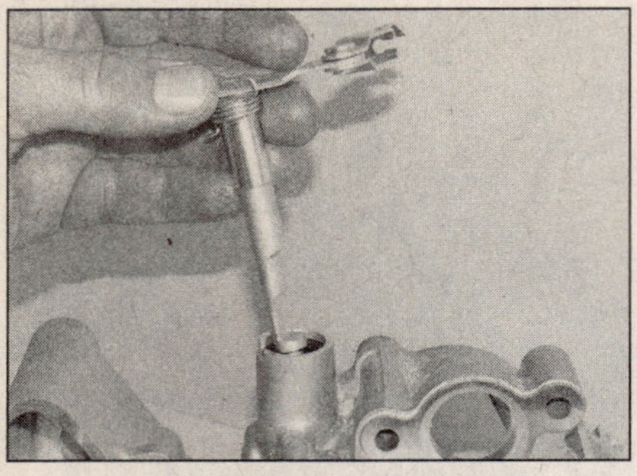
16.17a Withdraw the shaft

16.17b Release the circlip...

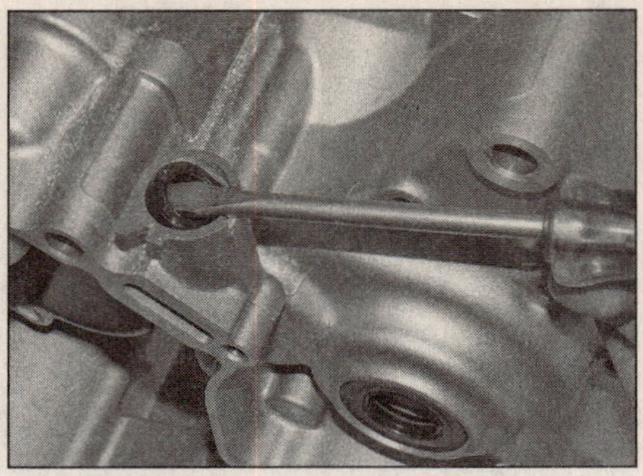
16.17c ...then lever the seal out

16.17d The bearing (arrowed) must be pulled out

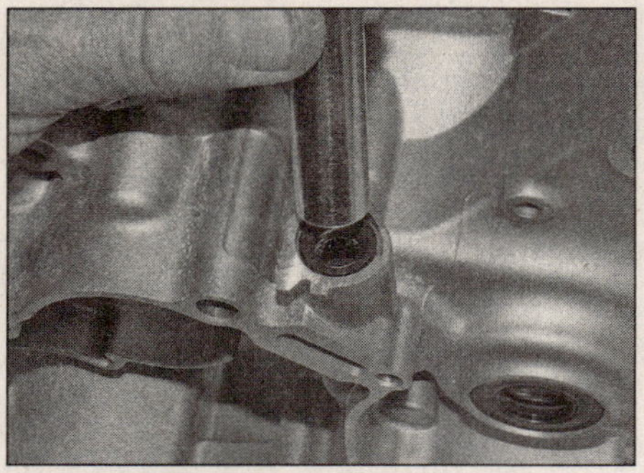
16.17e Use a socket to drive the new bearing and seal in

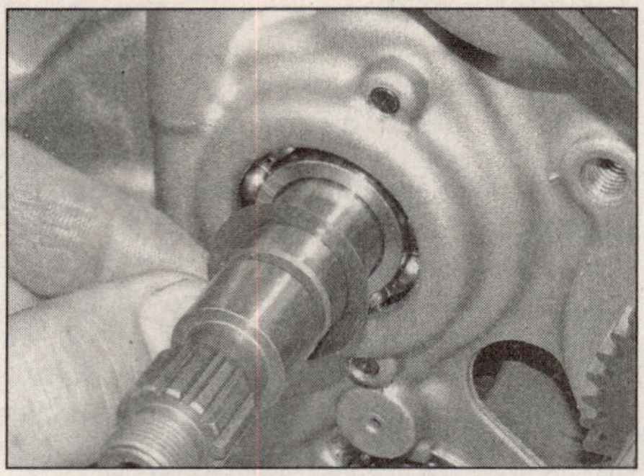
16.20a Slide the spring washer on...

the affected parts must be replaced with new ones.

16 Check the pressure plate and short pushrod for signs of wear or damage. Replace any parts necessary with new ones (see Step 5).

17 Check the release mechanism shaft in the left side of the crankcase for a smooth action. If the action is stiff or rough, withdraw the shaft, noting how the spring ends locate **(see illustration)**. Clean and check the oil seal and the bearing in the crankcase, and the bearing surfaces on the shaft. The seal can be replaced by removing the circlip, then levering it out with a seal hook or screwdriver **(see illustrations)**. The bearing cannot be removed with the engine in the frame, and must be pulled out using an expanding puller with slide-hammer attachment **(see illustration)** – refer to Tools and Workshop Tips9,1 in the reference section for more information. Fit the new bearing and seal, using a suitable socket to drive them in if necessary **(see illustration)**. Lubricate the bearing with molybdenum disulphide oil (a 50/50 mixture of molybdenum disulphide grease and engine oil) and the seal lips with grease before fitting a new circlip and installing the shaft. Make sure the return spring ends locate correctly.

18 Check the teeth of the primary driven gear on the back of the clutch housing and the corresponding teeth of the primary drive gear on the crankshaft. Replace the clutch housing and/or primary drive gear with a new one if worn or chipped teeth are discovered – refer to Section 18 for the primary drive gear. Check for any rotational play between the primary driven gear and the clutch housing and replace the housing with a new one if any is evident.

Installation

19 Remove all traces of old gasket from the crankcase and clutch cover surfaces.

20 Slide the spring washer onto the shaft so the outer rim is raised away from the crankcase **(see illustration)**. Smear the bush in the centre of the clutch housing with clean engine oil **(see illustration 16.15)**. Slide the housing onto the shaft making sure that the teeth of the primary driven gear on the back of the housing engage with those of the primary drive gear **(see illustration)**.

21 Slide the thrust washer onto the shaft with its sharp-edged side facing in, followed by the clutch centre **(see illustrations)**.

22 Fit the lockwasher, preferably using a new

16.20b ...then fit the clutch housing

16.21a Fit the thrust washer onto the splines...

16.21b ...then slide the clutch centre on

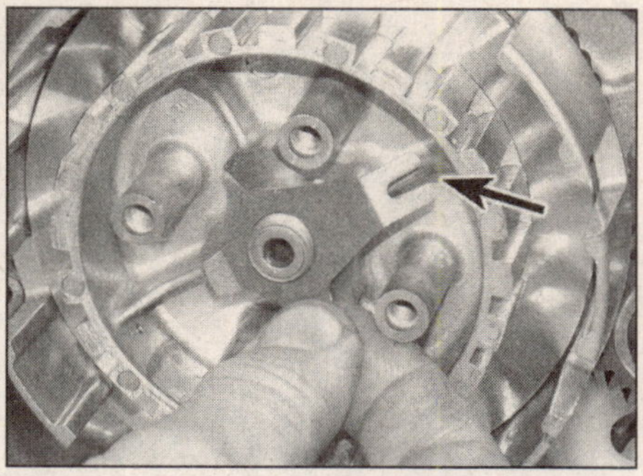

16.22a Locate the washer slit over the rib (arrowed)

16.22b Thread the nut on…

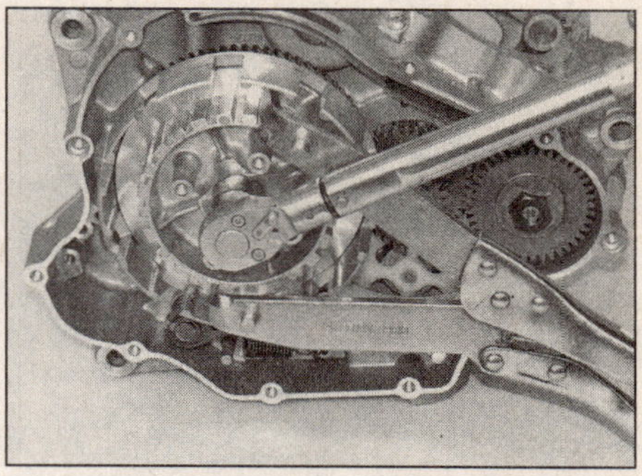

16.22c …and tighten it to the specified torque

16.22d Bend the tabs up against the nut

16.23a Fit the spring seat…

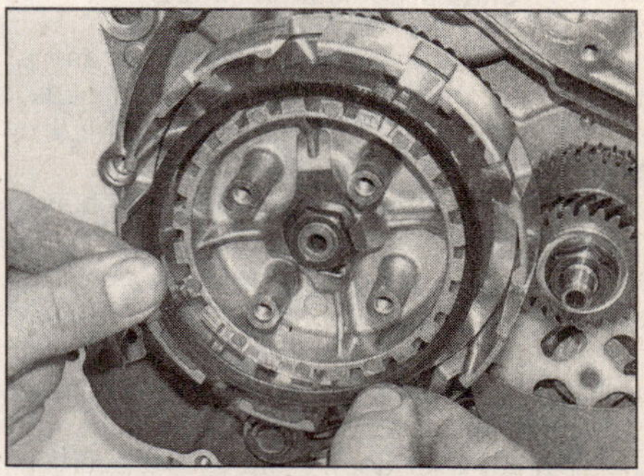

16.23b …and the spring with its outer edge raised off the seat

one, and locating the slit in its large tab over a rib in the clutch centre **(see illustration)**. Lubricate the threads and seating surface of the clutch nut with clean oil. Thread the nut on **(see illustration)**. Using the method employed on removal to lock the input shaft, tighten the nut to the torque setting specified at the beginning of the Chapter **(see illustration)**. Bend one of the small tabs of the washer up against a flat on the nut to lock it **(see illustration)**.

23 On WR models fit the anti-judder spring seat into the clutch centre, then fit the spring so that its outer edge is raised off the seat and facing outwards **(see illustrations)**.

24 On WR models there are three different types of friction plate and they must be installed in the correct order. There is one Type 1 plate, one Type 2 plate, and three Type 3 plates. The Type 3 plates are distinguishable by their lighter colour and the green mark on one of the tabs. The Type 2 plate has a larger internal diameter. The plain plates are all identical, and there must be a plain plate between each pair of friction plates. Coat each plate with engine oil prior to installation, then build up the plates as follows. First fit the Type 2 friction plate with the larger internal diameter, seating it around the anti-judder spring and spring seat **(see illustration)**, then fit a plain plate **(see illustration)**, then fit the Type 3 friction plates, alternating them with plain plates **(see illustration)**, then fit the final Type 1 friction plate **(see illustration)**.

25 On MT and YZF-R models there are two different types of friction plate and they must be installed in the correct order. There are four Type 1 plates and one Type 2 plate. The Type 2 plate is distinguishable by the yellow mark on one of the tabs. The plain plates are all identical, and there must be a plain plate between each pair of friction plates. Coat each plate with engine oil prior to installation, then build up the plates as follows. First fit a Type 1 friction plate, then fit a plain plate, then fit another Type 1 friction plate and a plain

16.24a Fit the Type 2 friction plate with the larger internal diameter first…

16.24b …then a plain plate

16.24c …then the lighter and colour-coded Type 3 plates…

16.24d …and finally the Type 1 friction plate

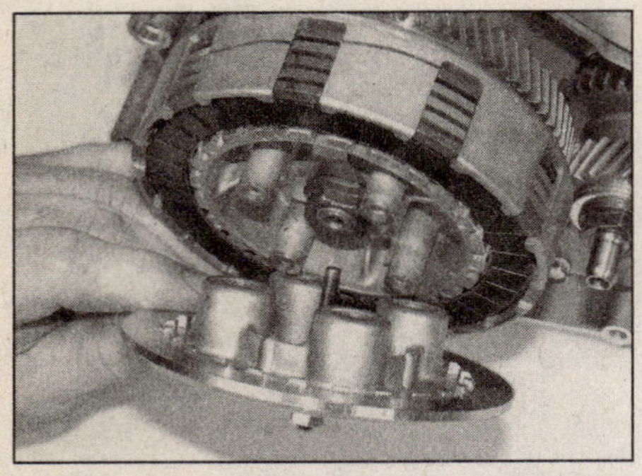

16.27 Fit the pressure plate engaging the castellations on the inner face with the slots of the clutch centre

16.28 Fit the springs and tighten the bolts as described

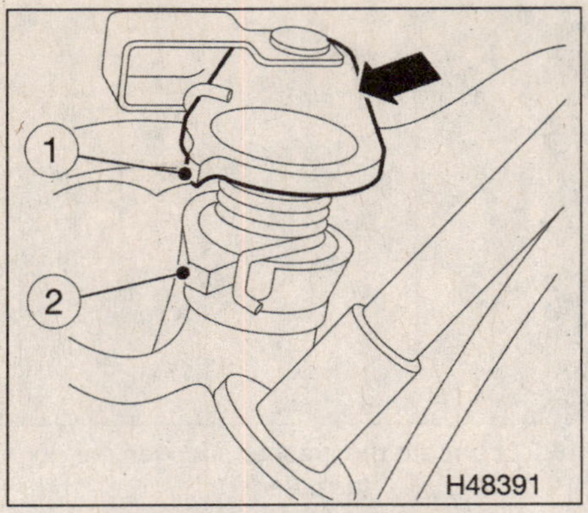

16.29 Push the arm forwards in the direction of the arrow and check the alignment

1 Pointer on release mechanism arm
2 Crankcase mark

plate, then fit the Type 2 friction plate and a plain plate, then fit a Type 1 friction plate, a plain plate, then fit the final Type 1 friction plate.

26 If the bearing ball was removed fit it into the shaft bore **(see illustration 16.5a)**. If the short pushrod was removed from the pressure plate, fit the holder and rod into the pressure plate so the threaded end is on the outside, and seat the holder, setting the position of the rod as noted on removal. Fit the washer and the locknut, then double check the position of the rod relative to the holder before holding the rod and tightening the locknut **(see illustration 16.5b)**.

27 Fit the pressure plate, making sure the castellations locate in the clutch centre **(see illustrations)**. Hold the pressure plate and check for any gaps between the clutch plates – there should be none; if there are, it means the pressure plate has not located properly.

28 Fit the clutch springs and bolts and tighten the bolts evenly and a little at a time in a criss-cross sequence to the specified torque **(see illustration)**.

29 Push the release mechanism arm forwards until it stops – the pointer should align with the mark on the crankcase **(see illustration)**. If not slacken the short pushrod locknut and adjust the position of the rod in the pressure plate by turning it with a screwdriver until the pointer and mark align, then hold the pushrod and tighten the locknut **(see illustration 16.5b)**.

30 Fit a new oil seal into the cover with its marked side facing in and set it so the ridge on its outside seats in the groove **(see illustration)**. If there is no ridge set the seal so its outer face is 1.4 to 1.9 mm below the rim of the bore.

31 Fit the two dowels into the crankcase if removed, then fit a new gasket, locating it over the dowels **(see illustration)**. Fit the cover onto the dowels **(see illustration)**. Fit all the bolts finger-tight, not forgetting the bracket(s), then tighten them evenly and a little at a time in a criss-cross sequence to the specified torque **(see illustrations)**.

32 On WR models fit the AIS reed valve housing onto its bracket **(see illustration 16.2)**. On all models connect the clutch cable (see Section 17).

33 Fit the oil filter then fill the engine with the correct amount and type of oil (see Chapter 1).

34 Run the engine and check the operation of the clutch. On MT models install the belly-pan, and on YZF-R models install the fairing panels (see Chapter 7).

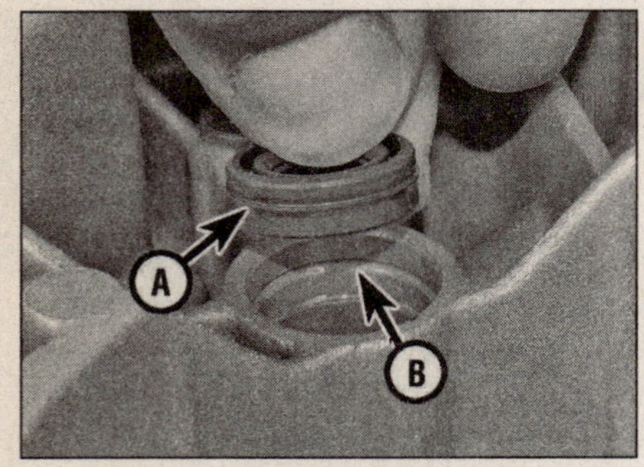

16.30 Set the seal so the ridge (A) seats in the groove (B)

16.31a Locate the new gasket over the dowels (arrowed)...

17 Clutch cable

1 On YZF-R models remove the lower section of the fairing on the left-hand side (see Chapter 7).

16.31b ... then fit the cover

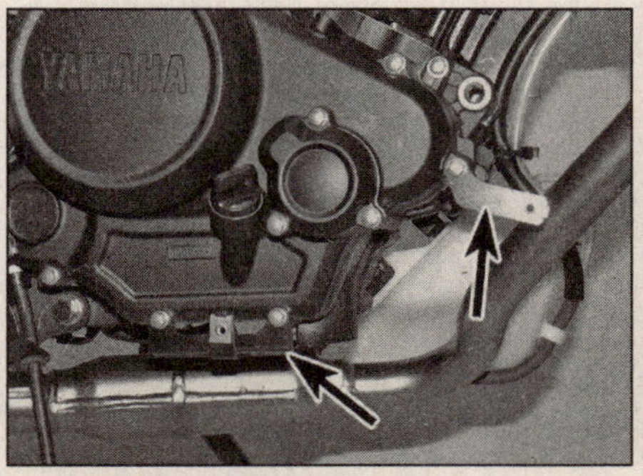

16.31c Belly-pan brackets (arrowed) – MT models

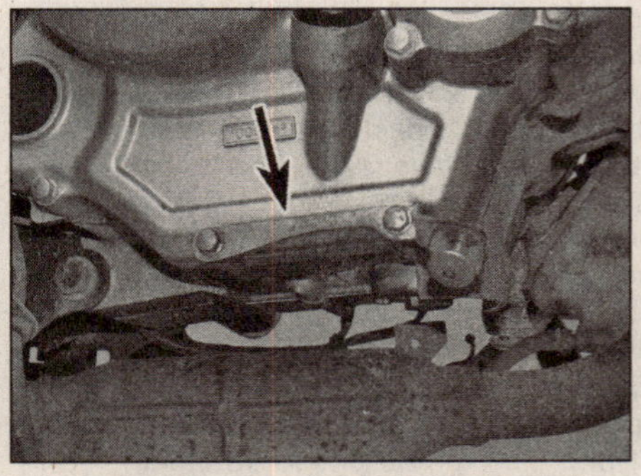

16.31d Fairing panel bracket (arrowed) – YZF-R models

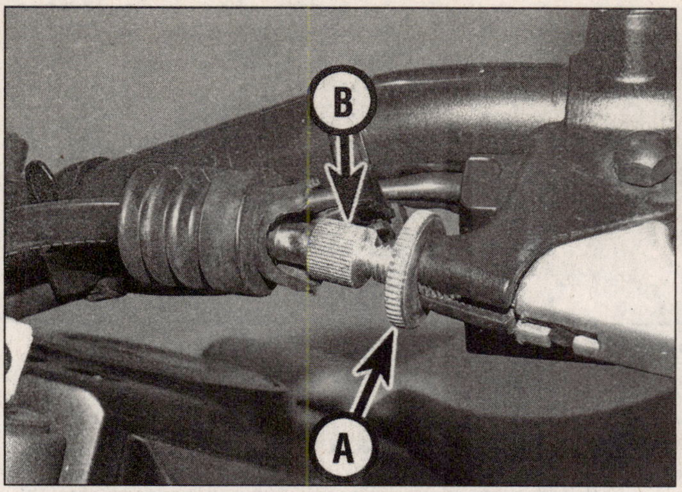

17.2 Pull back the boot, slacken the lockring (A) and turn the adjuster (B) in

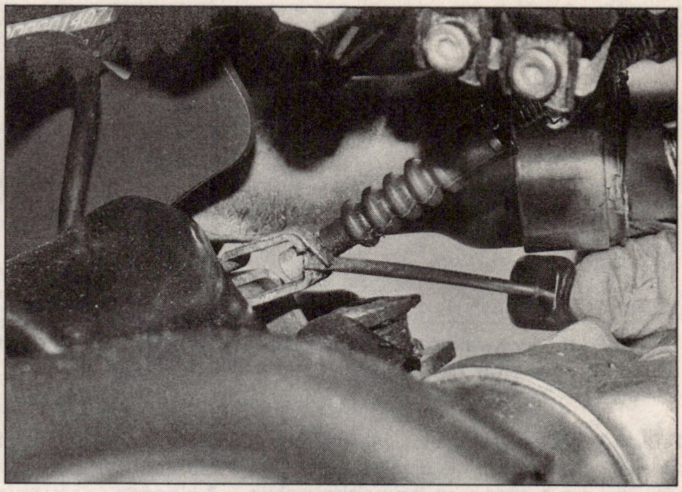

17.3a Bend the retaining tab up

17.3b Slacken the nuts (arrowed)...

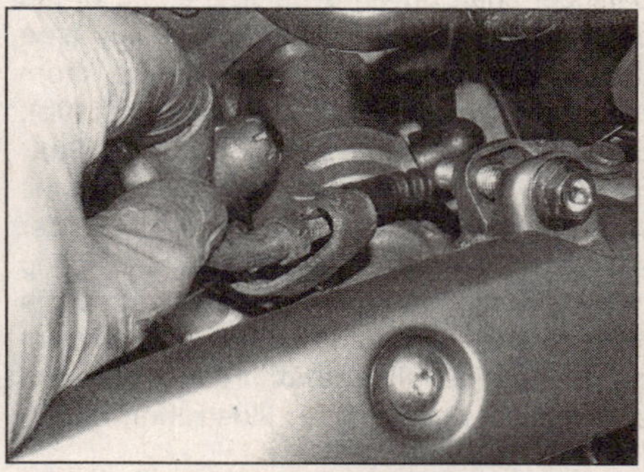

17.3c ...then slip the cable out of the bracket...

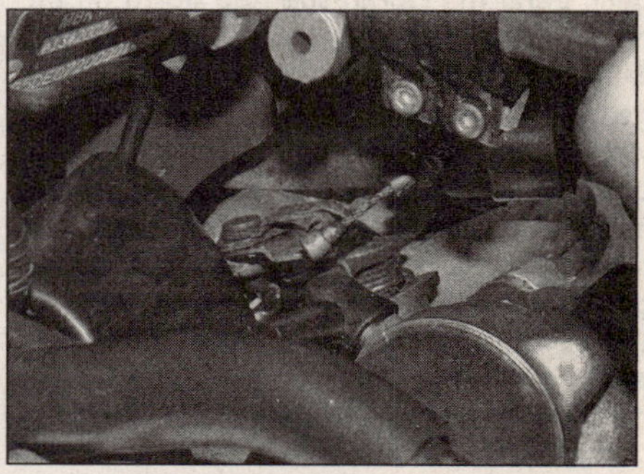

17.3d ...and detach the end from the arm

2 Pull the rubber boot off the adjuster at the handlebar end of the cable. Fully slacken the lockring, then thread the adjuster fully in **(see illustration)**. This provides freeplay in the cable and resets the adjuster to the beginning of its span.

3 Bend the retaining tab on the release arm up **(see illustration)**. Slacken the nuts securing the clutch cable in the bracket on the crankcase, slip the cable out of the bracket and free the end from the release arm **(see illustrations)**.

4 Align the slots in the adjuster and lockring at the handlebar end of the cable with that in the lever bracket, then pull the outer cable end from the socket in the adjuster and release the inner cable from the lever **(see illustrations)**. Remove the cable from the machine, noting its routing.

5 Installation is the reverse of removal. Apply grease to the cable ends. Make sure the cable is correctly routed. Adjust the amount of clutch lever freeplay (see Chapter 1). Do not forget to bend the tab on the release arm down.

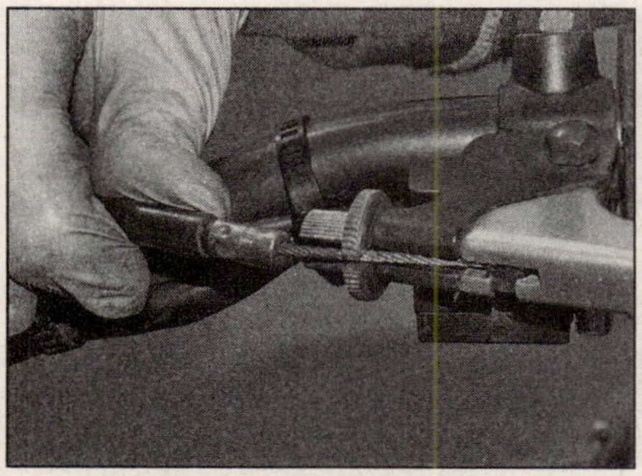

17.4a Free the outer cable from the adjuster...

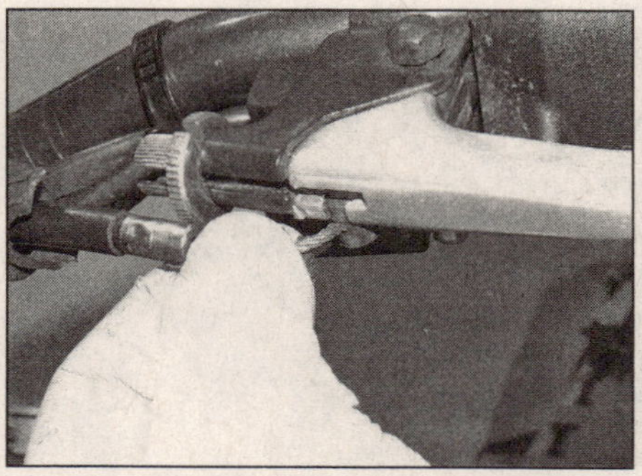

17.4b ...and the inner cable from the lever

HAYNES HiNT ***Before removing the cable from the bike, tape the lower end of the new cable to the upper end of the old cable. Slowly pull the lower end of the old cable out, guiding the new cable down into position. Using this method will ensure the cable is routed correctly.***

18 Primary drive gear, balancer shaft gears and oil pump gear

Note: *These gears can be removed with the engine in the frame.*

Removal

1 Remove the spark plug (see Chapter 1).

2 Remove the clutch (see Section 16).

3 The primary drive, balancer shaft and oil pump drive gears are secured by a nut on the end of the crankshaft and the balancer shaft driven gear is secured by a nut on the end of the balancer shaft. The balancer shaft nut has a lockwasher behind it – note that a new lockwasher should be used on installation.

18.5 Bend the lockwasher tab back to free the nut

18.6a Lock the gears at the bottom ...

18.6b ... or at the top as required and described when unscrewing the nuts

4 Turn the crankshaft clockwise using a spanner or socket on the crankshaft nut and align the punch marks on the balancer shaft drive and driven gears **(see illustration 18.10c)**.

5 If you are removing the balancer driven gear, bend the lockwasher tab down off the nut **(see illustration)**.

6 To unscrew the nuts you need to lock the gears to prevent them turning – to do this wedge a stout piece of rag or rolled up strap, or if available a piece of aluminium plate as shown (DO NOT use steel), between the teeth of the balancer shaft drive and driven gears where they mesh at the bottom when unscrewing the nut on the crankshaft, and at the top when unscrewing the nut on the balancer shaft **(see illustrations)**. With the gears locked slacken the nut(s). Remove the rag, strap or plate.

7 Unscrew the balancer shaft nut and remove the lockwasher, noting how it locates **(see illustrations 18.10e and d)**. Slide the balancer shaft driven gear off the end of the shaft, noting how it locates on the key **(see illustrations 18.10c)**. Remove the key from the slot in the shaft **(see illustration 18.10b)**. Slide the spacer off **(see illustration 18.10a)**.

8 Unscrew the crankshaft nut and remove the washer, then slide the primary and balancer shaft drive gears off the end of the shaft, noting how they locate on the key **(see illustrations 18.9e, d and c)**. Remove the key from the slot in the shaft **(see illustration 18.9b)**. Slide the oil pump drive gear off **(see illustration 18.9a)**.

Installation

9 Slide the oil pump drive gear onto the shaft, and engage it with the driven gear **(see illustration)**. Fit the long key into the slot in the crankshaft **(see illustration)**. Slide the balancer drive gear onto the shaft with the punch mark facing out **(see illustration)**, seating the slot in the gear over the key **(see illustration)**. Slide the primary drive gear on with its shouldered side facing in, seating the slot in the gear over the key **(see illustration)**. Slide the washer on with its sharp-edged side facing the gear **(see illustration)**. Tighten the nut finger-tight.

10 Slide the spacer onto the balancer shaft **(see illustration)**. Fit the short key into the

18.9a Slide the oil pump drive gear on

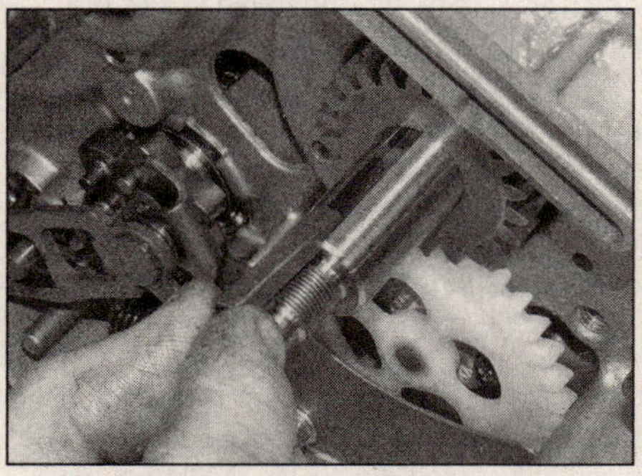

18.9b Fit the key into the slot ...

18.9c ... then fit the balancer drive gear ...

18.9d ... and the primary drive gear ...

18.9e ... and the washer and nut, tightening it finger-tight

18.10a Slide the spacer on ...

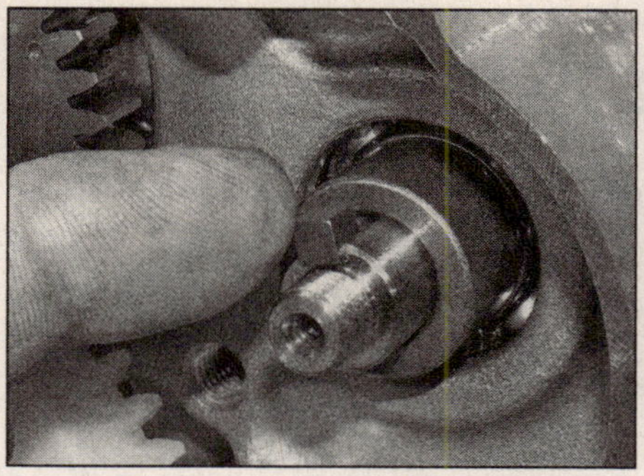

18.10b ... then fit the key into the slot

18.10c Slide the balancer driven gear on, aligning the punch marks

18.10d Fit the lockwasher, locating the tab in the slot...

18.10e ... then fit the nut and tighten finger-tight

18.11 Bend the lockwasher tab up to secure the nut

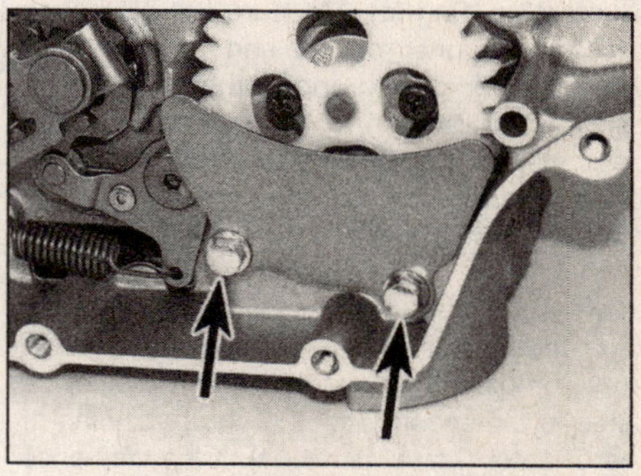

19.3 Unscrew the bolts (arrowed) and remove the plate

slot in the shaft **(see illustration)**. Slide the balancer driven gear onto the shaft with the punch mark facing out, aligning the mark with that on the drive gear, turning the shaft(s) as required, and seating the slot in the gear over the key **(see illustration)**. Fit a new lockwasher, locating the inward facing tab in the slot in the gear **(see illustration)**. Tighten the nut finger-tight **(see illustration)**.

11 Wedge the stout piece of rag, strap or aluminium plate where the balancer drive and driven gear teeth mesh at the top to tighten the nut on the crankshaft and at the bottom to tighten the nut on the balancer shaft **(see illustrations 18.6b and a)** – tighten both nuts to the torque settings specified at the beginning of the Chapter. Bend the lockwasher tab up against the nut on the balancer shaft **(see illustration)**.

12 Install the clutch (see Section 16) and the spark plug (see Chapter 1).

19 Oil pump

Note: *The oil pump can be removed with the engine in the frame.*

Removal

1 Remove the clutch (see Section 16).

2 Remove the primary, balancer and oil pump drive gears (see Section 18).

3 Unscrew the oil baffle plate bolts and remove the plate **(see illustration)**.

4 Undo the oil pump screws and remove the pump **(see illustration)**.

Inspection

Note: *Individual components are not available for the oil pump – it comes as an assembly.*

5 Undo the screw on the back of the pump and remove the cover **(see illustration)**. Slide the rotor housing towards the gear to expose the drive pin and withdraw it **(see illustration 19.13d)**. Slide the rotor housing off the pump shaft and remove the rotors, noting which way round they fit **(see illustrations 19.13c, b and a)**.

6 Clean all the components in solvent.

7 Inspect the pump body and rotors for scoring and wear. If any damage, scoring or uneven or excessive wear is evident, replace the pump with a new one.

8 Fit the inner and outer rotors into the housing **(see illustrations 19.13a and b)**. Slide the housing onto the shaft **(see**

19.4 Undo the screws (arrowed) and remove the pump

19.5 Undo the screw (arrowed) and remove the cover

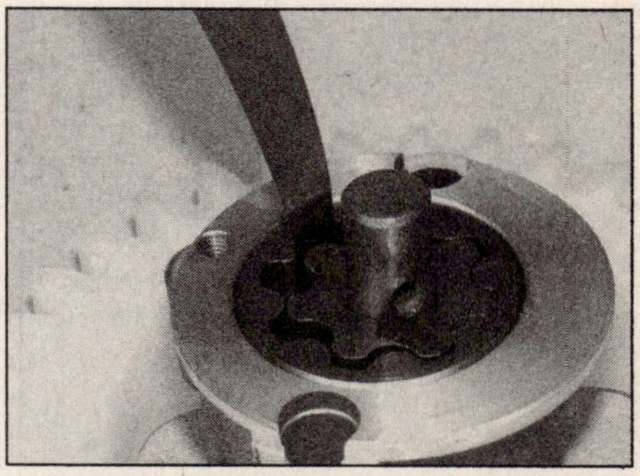

19.8 Measure the inner rotor tip-to-outer rotor clearance as shown

19.9 Measure the outer rotor-to-body clearance as shown

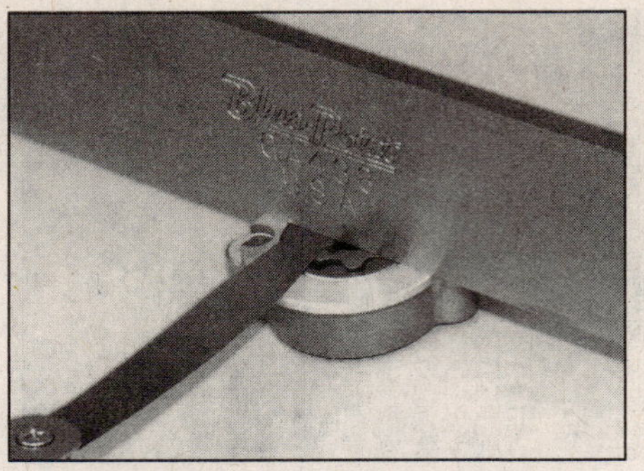

19.10 Measure rotor end-float as shown

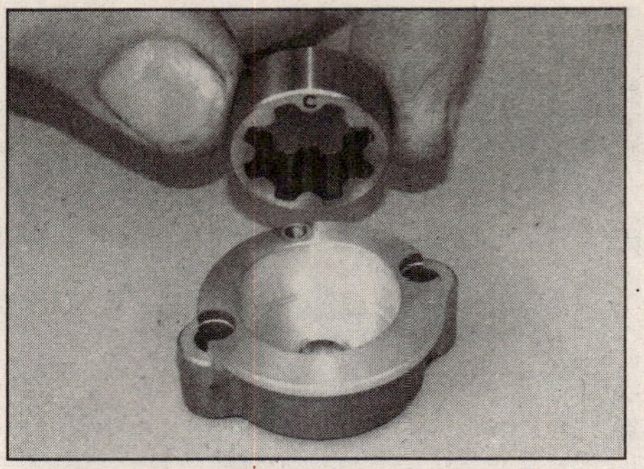

19.13a Fit the outer rotor with the C mark facing in...

illustration 19.13c). Measure the clearance between the inner rotor tip and the outer rotor with a feeler gauge and compare it to the service limit listed in the specifications at the beginning of the Chapter **(see illustration)**. If the clearance measured is greater than the maximum listed, replace the pump with a new one.

9 Measure the clearance between the outer rotor and the pump housing with a feeler gauge and compare it to the maximum clearance listed in the specifications at the beginning of the Chapter **(see illustration)**. If the clearance measured is greater than the maximum listed, replace the pump with a new one.

10 Lay a straight-edge across the rotors and the pump housing and, using a feeler gauge, measure the rotor end-float (the gap between the rotors and the straight-edge **(see illustration)**. If the clearance measured is greater than the maximum listed, replace the pump with a new one.

11 Check the pump drive and driven gears, shaft and drive pin for wear and damage, and replace the pump with a new one if necessary.

12 If the pump is good, make sure all the components are clean, then lubricate them with new engine oil.

13 Fit the outer rotor into the housing with the C mark facing in **(see illustration)**. Fit the inner rotor into the outer rotor with the drive pin slots facing out **(see illustration)**. Slide the housing onto the shaft **(see illustration)**. Fit the drive pin into its hole, then draw the housing up the shaft so the drive pin ends seat in the cut-outs in the face of the inner rotor. Fit the cover and tighten the screw **(see illustration)**.

14 Rotate the pump gear and check the rotors turn smoothly and freely. Prime the pump with clean engine oil via the holes **(see illustration)**.

Installation

15 Fit the pump with the cover screw at the bottom and tighten the mounting screws to the torque setting specified at the beginning of the Chapter **(see illustration)**. Make sure the pump gear turns smoothly.

16 Clean the threads of the oil baffle plate bolts. Apply a suitable non-permanent thread locking compound to the threads, then fit the plate and tighten the bolts to the specified torque setting **(see illustration 19.3)**.

17 Install the oil pump, balancer and primary drive gears (see Section 18).

18 Install the clutch (see Section 16).

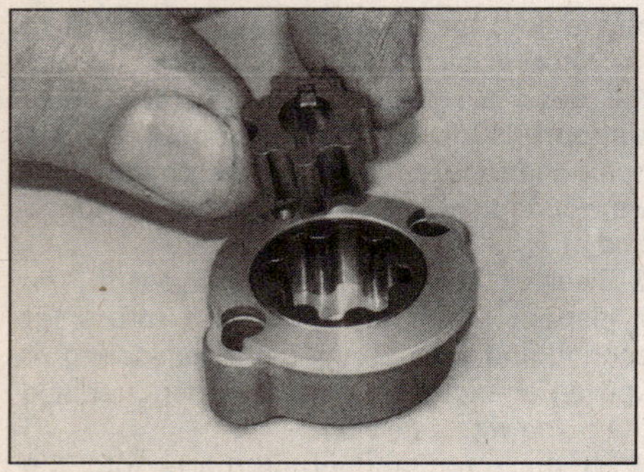

19.13b ... and the inner rotor with the drive pin slot facing out

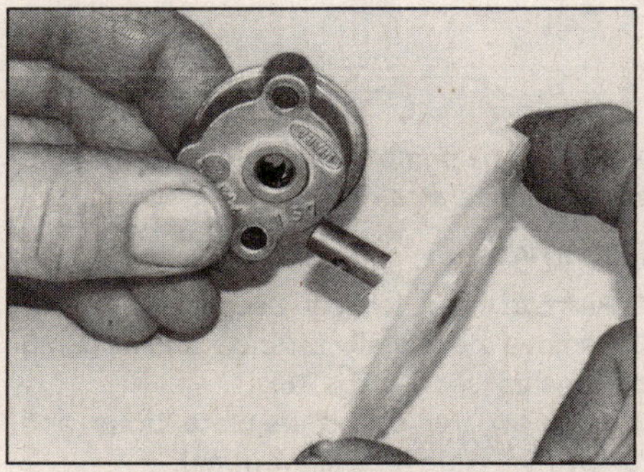

19.13c Fit the housing onto the shaft...

19.13d ... then fit the drive pin...

19.13e ... and the cover

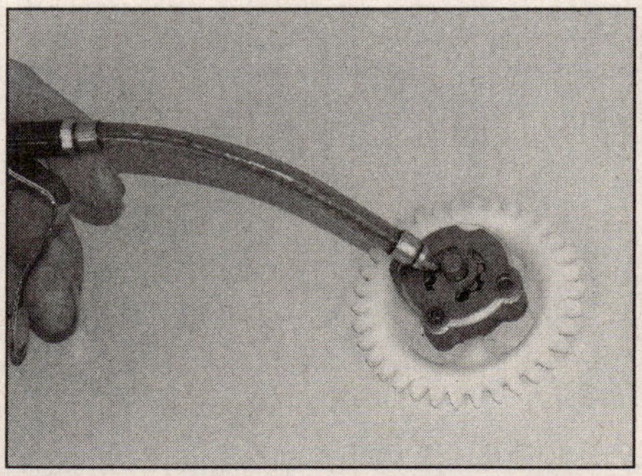

19.14 Prime the pump with oil via the inlet and outlet holes

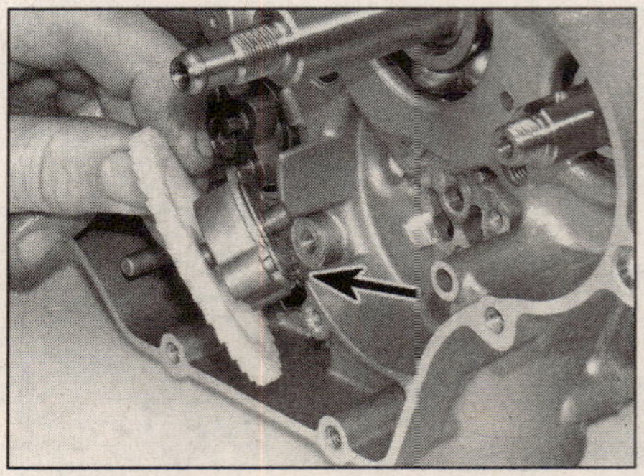

19.15 Fit the pump with the cover screw (arrowed) at the bottom

20 Gearchange mechanism

Note: *The gearchange mechanism can be removed with the engine in the frame.*

Removal

1 Remove the clutch (see Section 16).

2 Make sure the transmission is in neutral. Unscrew the oil baffle plate bolts and remove the plate **(see illustration 19.3)**.

3 Note the alignment of the gearchange lever on the shaft – if no mark is evident, make one where the shaft aligns with the slit in the lever clamp **(see illustration 4.17)**. Unscrew the pinch bolt, noting the washer, and slide the arm off.

4 Note how the gearchange shaft centralising spring ends fit on each side of the locating pin in the casing, how the pawls on the selector arm locate onto the pins on the selector drum cam plate, and how the stopper arm roller locates in the neutral detent in the cam.

5 Grasp the shaft/selector arm assembly and withdraw it from the crankcase **(see illustration)**.

6 Unhook the stopper arm spring **(see illustration)**. Unscrew the pivot bolt and remove the arm.

Inspection

7 Check the selector arm for cracks, distortion and wear of its pawls, and check for any corresponding wear on the pins on the selector drum cam plate **(see illustration)**. Also check the stopper arm roller and the detents in the cam plate for any wear or damage, and make sure the roller turns freely **(see illustration)**. Replace any components that are worn or damaged with new ones – the selector drum cam is an integral part of the drum (see Section 27).

8 Inspect the shaft centralising spring and the stopper arm spring for fatigue, wear or damage **(see illustration)**. To remove the centralising spring remove the E-clip from its groove and slide the spring off the shaft. Also check the movement of the pawl plate – make sure it is smooth and returns to centre from the pressure of its spring **(see illustration)**. The pawl plate and its spring are part of the shaft and are not available separately.

20.5 Withdraw the shaft/arm assembly, noting how it fits

20.6 Unhook the spring, then unscrew the bolt (arrowed) and remove the arm

9 Check the gearchange shaft is straight and look for damage to the splines. If the shaft is bent you can attempt to straighten it, but if the splines are damaged the shaft must be replaced with a new one.

10 Check the condition of the shaft oil seal in the left side of the crankcase. If it is damaged, deteriorated or shows signs of leakage it must be replaced with a new one, though it is advisable to fit a new one whatever the apparent condition. Lever out the old seal with a seal hook or screwdriver **(see illustration)**. Press the new seal in using your thumbs, a driver or socket **(see illustration)**.

Installation

11 Apply some grease to the lips of the gearchange shaft oil seal in the left side of the crankcase **(see illustration 20.10b)**.

12 Clean the threads of the stopper arm

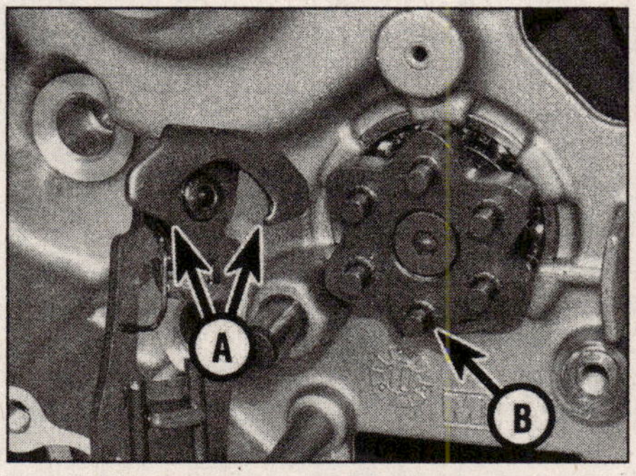

20.7a Check the selector arm pawls (A) and cam plate pins (B)

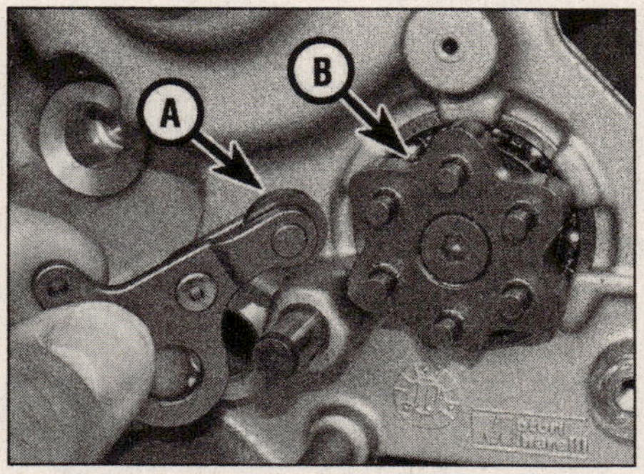

20.7b Check the stopper arm roller (A) and cam plate detents (B)

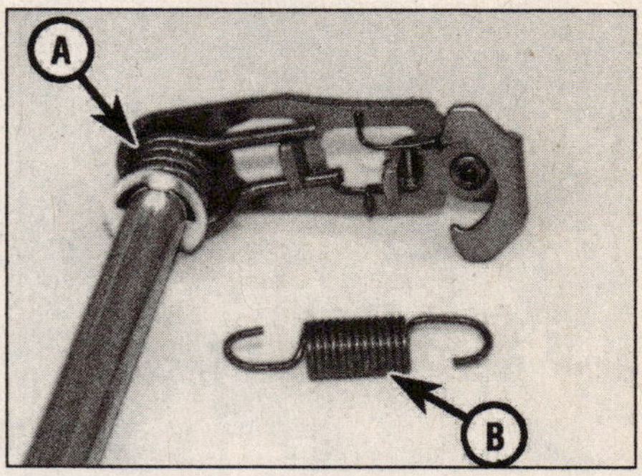

20.8a Check the centralising spring (A) and stopper arm spring (B)

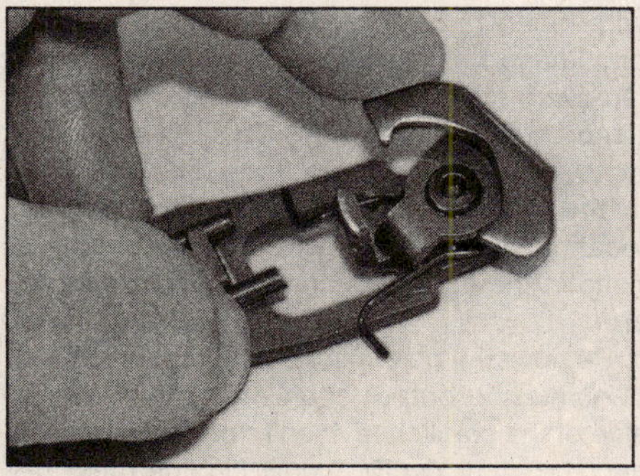

20.8b Make sure the pawl plate moves smoothly and centres correctly

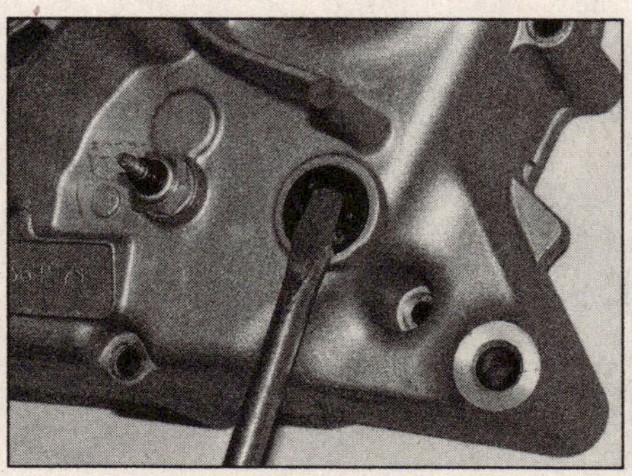

20.10a Lever the seal out

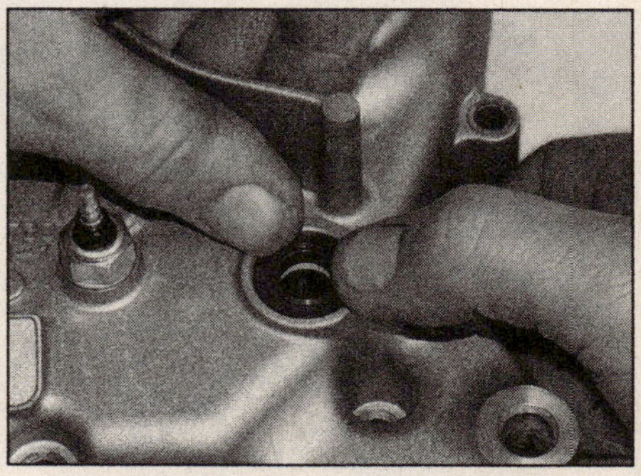

20.10b Press the new seal in with your thumbs

20.12 Hook the spring on, then fit the arm

20.14 The installed assembly should be as shown

pivot bolt. Fit the spring onto the arm if removed **(see illustration)**. Apply a suitable non-permanent thread locking compound to the pivot bolt threads. Fit the arm, locating the roller into the neutral detent on the cam and tighten the pivot bolt to the torque setting specified at the beginning of the chapter. Fit the spring onto its post **(see illustration 20.6)**.

13 Check that the shaft centralising spring is properly positioned and the E-clip is seated in its groove in the shaft **(see illustration 20.8a)**. Smear some clean oil onto the shaft. Slide the shaft into place, locating the selector arm pawls onto the pins and the centralising spring ends onto each side of the locating pin in the crankcase **(see illustration 20.5)**.

14 Check that all components are correctly positioned **(see illustration)**.

15 Clean the threads of the oil baffle plate bolts. Apply a suitable non-permanent thread locking compound to the threads, then fit the plate and tighten the bolts to the specified torque setting **(see illustration 19.3)**.

16 Align the slit in the gearchange lever clamp with the mark on the shaft **(see illustration 4.17)**. Fit the pinch bolt with its washer and tighten to the specified torque.

17 Check the function of the gearchange mechanism.

18 Install the clutch (see Section 16).

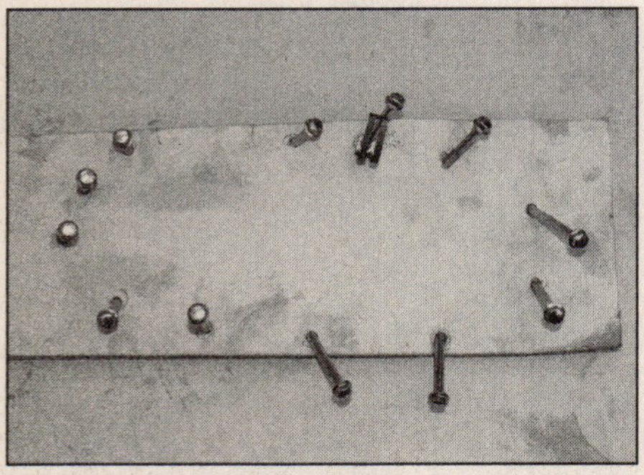

21.3 Make a cardboard template like the one shown to store the bolts

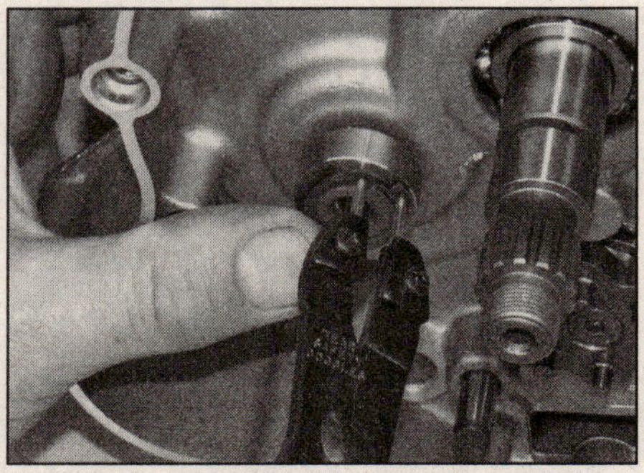

21.4a Remove the outer circlip ...

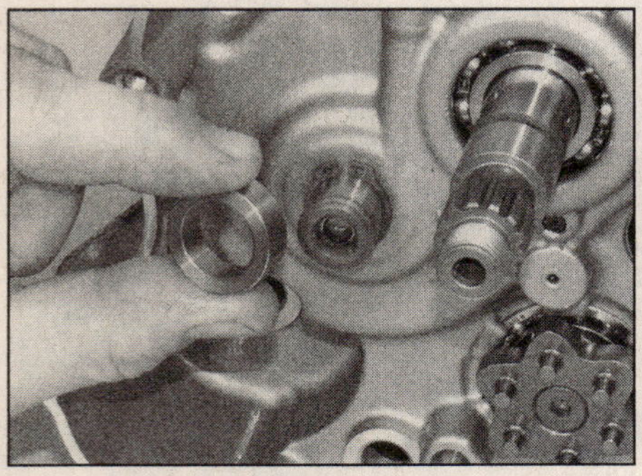

21.4b ... the spacer ...

21.4c ... and the inner circlip

21 Crankcase separation and reassembly

Note: *To separate the crankcase halves, the engine must be removed from the frame.*

Separation

1 To access the crankshaft and connecting rod assembly, balancer shaft, transmission shafts, selector drum and forks, and their bearings, the engine must be removed from the frame (see Section 4), then the crankcase must be split into its two halves.

2 Before the crankcases can be separated the following components must be removed:

a) Alternator rotor and starter driven gear (Chapter 8)
b) Cylinder head (Section 10)
c) Cam chain and blades (Section 9)
d) Cylinder block (Section 12)
e) Piston (Section 13)
f) Clutch (Section 16)
g) Primary drive, balancer shaft and oil pump drive gears, and balancer shaft driven gear (section 18)
h) Oil pump (Section 19)
i) Gearchange mechanism (Section 20)

3 Make a cardboard template punched with holes to match all the bolts in the left crankcase half – as each crankcase bolt is removed, store it in its relative position in the template **(see illustration)**. This will ensure all bolts, of which there are three different sizes in the left half, are installed in the correct location on reassembly. There are only two bolts in the right half, and they are the same size.

4 Remove the outer circlip from the end of the transmission output shaft on the right-hand side of the crankcase, then remove the spacer and the inner circlip – new circlips must be used on reassembly **(see illustrations)**.

5 Turn the selector drum cam by hand to

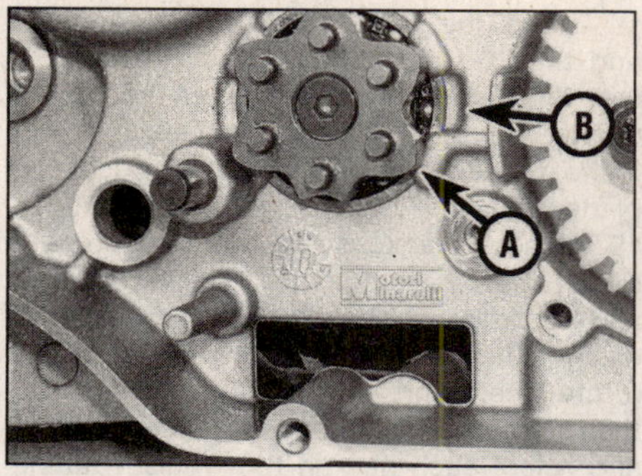

21.5 Turn the drum to align the cam peaks (A) with the cut-outs (B)

21.7 Carefully separate the crankcase halves

21.12 Make sure the spring (A) and thrust washer (B) are in place

align the cam peaks with the cut-outs in the crankcase **(see illustration)**.

6 With the engine upright unscrew the crankcase bolts on each side evenly, a little at a time and in a reverse of the tightening sequence shown in illustration 21.18 – there are two bolts in the right side and eleven in the left.

7 Holding both halves of the crankcase place the engine on its left side, laying it on wooden blocks so the shaft ends are clear of the bench. Carefully lift the right crankcase half off the left half **(see illustration)** – if necessary use a soft-faced mallet to tap around the joint to break the seal, and on the right-hand ends of the crankshaft, balancer shaft and transmission input shaft when lifting the right half to ensure they remain in the left-hand crankcase. Note: If the halves do not separate easily, make sure all fasteners have been removed. Do not try and separate the halves by levering against the crankcase mating surfaces as they are easily scored and will leak oil in the future if damaged. The right crankcase half will come away leaving the crankshaft, balancer shaft, transmission shafts and selector drum and forks in the left half. Note there is a spring in each end of the selector fork shaft – make sure the right-hand one is still in place, or if it has stuck to the crankcase retrieve it and keep it safe **(see illustration 21.12)**. If the thrust washer on the end of the output shaft has stuck to the bearing in the right crankcase retrieve it and fit it back onto the shaft **(see illustration 21.12)**.

8 Remove the two locating dowels from the crankcase if they are loose – they could be in either half **(see illustration 21.13)**.

9 Refer to Sections 22 to 27 for the removal of the main components housed within the crankcases. On 2009 to 2013 WR models, note that if the balancer shaft is not being removed a new O-ring must be fitted on its right-hand end anyway (see Section 24).

Reassembly

10 Remove all traces of sealant from the crankcase mating surfaces. Clean the threads of all the crankcase bolts.

11 Double check that all components and their bearings, and the transmission output shaft oil seal, are in place in the left crankcase half, and that all bearings and the bearing retainer are in the right half.

12 Refer to Sections 22 to 27 for the installation of the main components housed within the crankcases. On 2009 to 2013 WR models, if the balancer shaft has not been removed fit a new O-ring on its right end (see Section 24). Make sure the spring is in the right-hand end of the selector fork shaft, and the thrust washer is on the right end of the transmission output shaft **(see illustration)**. Make sure the selector drum is positioned as on separation.

13 If removed, fit the two locating dowels into the left crankcase half **(see illustration)**.

14 Generously lubricate the crankshaft and transmission shaft bearings and gears and the selector fork shafts and fork ends and the tracks in the selector drum with clean engine oil, then use a rag soaked in high flash-point solvent to wipe over the mating surfaces of both crankcase halves to remove all traces of oil.

15 Apply a small amount of suitable sealant (Yamaha-Bond 1215 or equivalent RTV sealant – ask your dealer) to the mating surface of the right-hand crankcase half as shown, avoiding the oil gallery **(see illustration)**.

Caution: Apply the sealant only to the mating surfaces. Do not apply an excessive amount as it will ooze out when the case halves are assembled and may obstruct oil passages. Do not apply the sealant close to any of the oil passages.

16 Check again that all components are in

21.13 Make sure the locating dowels (arrowed) are fitted

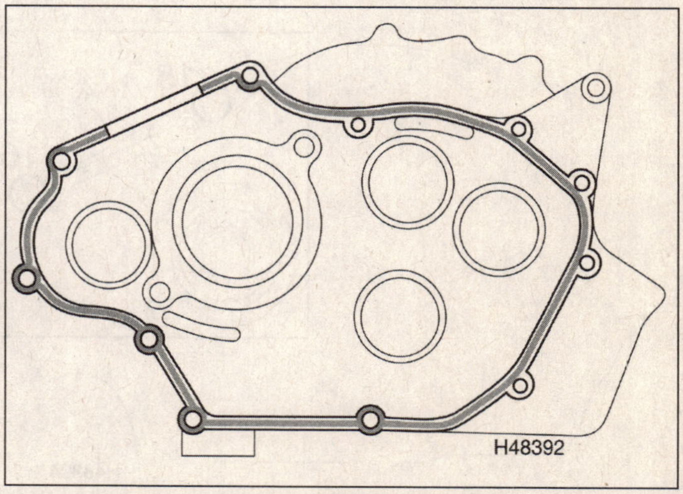

21.15 Apply the sealant to the shaded area, making sure none blocks the oil passages

21.16 Make sure the connecting rod is correctly positioned

21.17 Fit and secure the two right-hand bolts finger-tight

position. Carefully fit the right-hand crankcase half down onto the left-hand half, making sure the shaft ends and dowels all locate correctly **(see illustration 21.7)**, and that the connecting rod is aligned with the cylinder aperture **(see illustration)**.

17 Check that the right-hand crankcase half is correctly seated. Fit the two bolts into the right crankcase and tighten them finger-tight **(see illustration)**. Grasp both halves of the crankcase and position the engine upright.

Caution: The crankcase halves should fit together without being forced. If the casings are not correctly seated, remove the right-hand crankcase half and investigate the problem. Do not attempt to pull them together using the crankcase bolts as the casing will crack and be ruined.

18 Fit the eleven left crankcase bolts, and tighten them finger-tight. In case you didn't make a template, the 45 mm long bolts are numbers 1 to 6 and 11 in the tightening sequence, the 55 mm bolts are 15 and 16, and the 70 mm bolts are 8 to 10 and 12 **(see illustration)**. Now tighten all the bolts a quarter turn at a time in the sequence shown to the torque setting specified at the beginning of the Chapter.

19 With all crankcase fasteners tightened, check that the crankshaft, balancer shaft and transmission shafts rotate smoothly and easily. Check that the transmission shafts rotate freely and independently in neutral, then rotate the selector drum cam by hand and select each gear in turn whilst rotating the input shaft. If there are any signs of undue stiffness, tight or rough spots, poor or incorrect gear selection, or of any other problem, the fault must be rectified before proceeding further.

20 Fit a new circlip into the inner groove in the right-hand end of the transmission output shaft, then fit the spacer and a new outer circlip **(see illustrations 21.4c, b and a)** – double check the circlips are correctly seated.

21 Install all other removed components and assemblies.

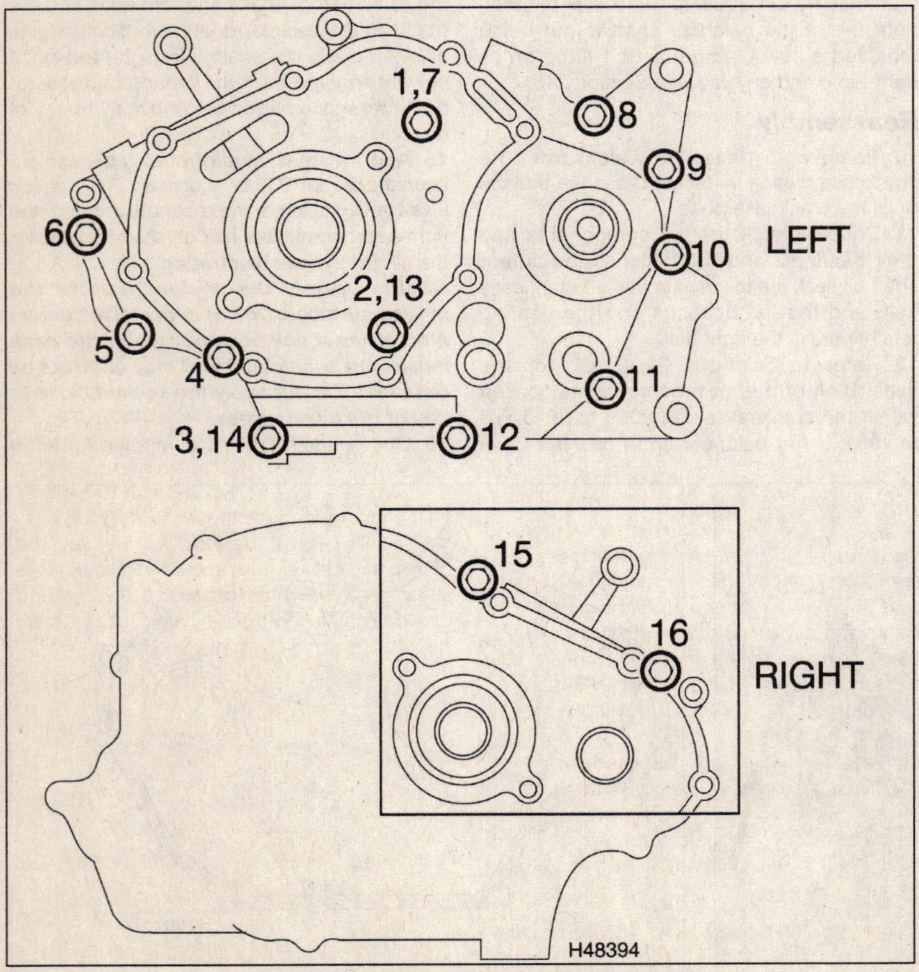

21.18 Crankcase bolt tightening sequence

See text for screw identification

22 Crankcases and bearings

Crankcases

1 After the crankcases have been separated, remove the crankshaft and balancer shaft, the selector drum and forks and the transmission shafts, referring to the following Sections of this Chapter. Also remove the neutral switch (see Chapter 8), and on MT and YZF-R models without ABS the speed sensor (see Chapter 4 Section 7), if required.

2 Clean the crankcases thoroughly with new solvent and dry them with compressed air. Blow out all oil passages with compressed air.

3 Remove all traces of old gasket sealant from the mating surfaces. Clean up minor damage to the surfaces with a fine sharpening stone or grindstone.

Caution: Be very careful not to nick or gouge the crankcase mating surfaces or oil leaks will result. Check both crankcase halves very carefully for cracks and other damage.

4 Small cracks or holes in aluminium castings can be repaired with an epoxy resin adhesive as a temporary measure or with one of the low temperature welding kits. Permanent repairs can only be done by TIG (tungsten inert gas or heli-arc) welding, and only a specialist in this process is in a position to advise on the economy or practical aspect of such a repair. If any damage is found that can't be repaired, replace the crankcase halves as a set.

5 Damaged threads can be economically reclaimed using a diamond section wire insert, for example of the Heli-Coil type (though there are other makes), which are easily fitted after drilling and re-tapping the affected thread.

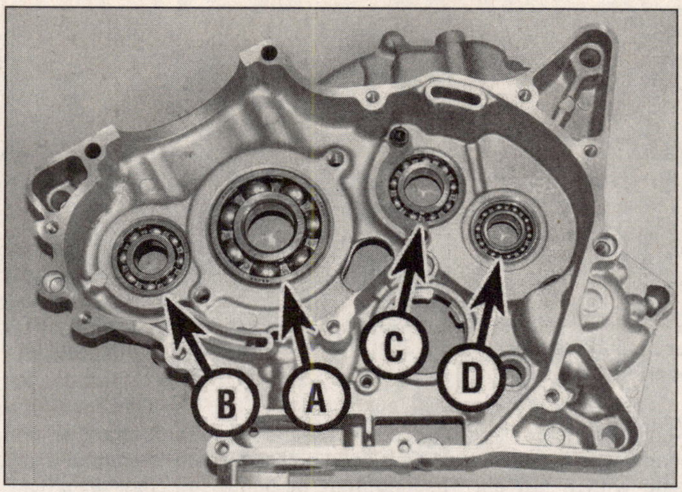

22.8a Crankshaft bearing (A), balancer shaft bearing (B), transmission input shaft bearing (C) and output shaft bearing (D) – right-hand crankcase half

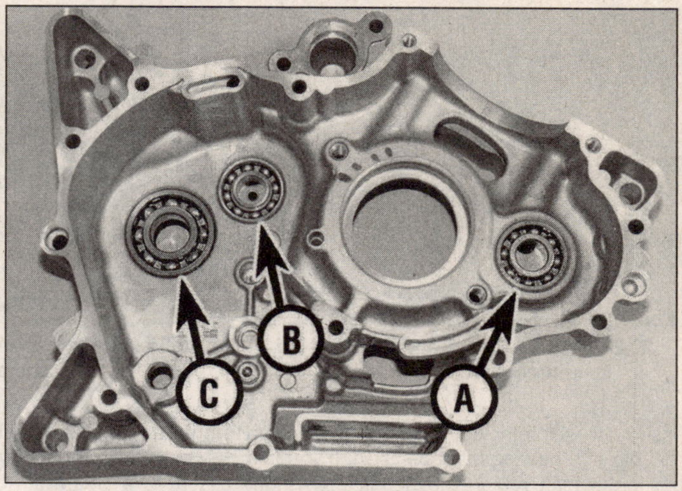

22.8b Balancer shaft bearing (A), transmission input shaft bearing (B) and output shaft bearing (C) – left-hand crankcase half

6 If a bolt or screw has sheared above its bore line, it can be removed using a conventional stud extractor. Bolts or screws that have sheared below their bore can sometimes be removed with extractors, which consist of a tapered, left-hand thread screw of very hard (but brittle) steel. These are threaded anti-clockwise into a pre-drilled hole in the stud, and the theory is that they tighten into the hole and by continuing to turn them anti-clockwise they thread the sheared stud out of its hole. If that doesn't work the stud must be drilled out and then the hole must be tapped with a new thread.

7 Install all components and assemblies, referring to the relevant Sections of this and the other Chapters, before reassembling the crankcase halves.

HAYNES HiNT *Refer to Tools and Workshop Tips in the Reference Section for details of installing a thread insert and using screw extractors.*

Bearing information

8 The crankshaft, balancer shaft, and transmission shaft bearings should all be replaced with new ones as part of a complete engine overhaul, or individually as required due to wear or failure **(see illustrations)**.

9 Bearing failure occurs mainly because of lack of lubrication, the presence of dirt or other foreign particles, overloading the engine, break-up of one or more of the bearing components due to fatigue, or corrosion. Regardless of the cause of bearing failure, it must be corrected before the engine is reassembled to prevent it from happening again.

10 The bearings should rotate smoothly, freely and quietly, there should be no rough spots, and there should be no excessive play between the inner and outer races, or between the inner race and the shaft it fits on, or between the outer race and its housing in the crankcase.

11 Dirt and other foreign particles get into the engine in a variety of ways. They may be left in the engine during assembly or they may pass through filters or breathers, then get into the oil and from there into the bearings. Metal chips from machining operations and normal engine wear are often present. Abrasives are sometimes left in engine components after reconditioning operations, especially when parts are not thoroughly cleaned using the proper cleaning methods. The best prevention for this cause of bearing failure is to clean all parts thoroughly and keep everything spotlessly clean during engine reassembly. Regular oil changes in accordance with the specified schedule are also essential.

12 Lack of lubrication or lubrication breakdown has a number of interrelated causes. Excessive heat (which thins the oil), overloading and oil leakage all contribute to lubrication breakdown. Blocked oil passages will starve a bearing of lubrication and destroy it.

13 Riding habits can have a definite effect on bearing life. Full throttle low speed operation, or labouring the engine, puts very high loads on bearings. Short trip riding leads to corrosion of bearings, as insufficient engine heat is produced to drive off the condensed water and corrosive gases produced. These products collect in the engine oil, forming acid and sludge. As the oil is carried to the engine bearings, the acid attacks and corrodes the bearing material.

14 Incorrect bearing installation during engine assembly will lead to bearing failure as well. To avoid bearing problems, clean all parts thoroughly before reassembly, and lubricate the new bearings with clean engine oil during installation.

Bearing removal and installation

Note: *If the correct bearing removal and installation tools are not available take the crankcases and crankshaft to a Yamaha dealer for removal and installation of the bearings – do not risk damaging either the cases or the crankshaft.*

Crankshaft (main) bearings

15 If the crankshaft (main) bearings have failed, excessive rumbling and vibration will be felt when the engine is running. If only one bearing has failed, it is best to replace both with new ones.

16 Separate the crankcase halves (Section 21) and remove the crankshaft (Section 23).

17 The right-hand main bearing is in the crankcase **(see illustration 22.8a)**. To remove the bearing heat the housing with a hot air gun, then tap the bearing out of the crankcase using a bearing driver or a suitable socket located on the outer side of the bearing **(see illustration 22.24)**.

18 Smear the outside of the new bearing with clean oil and fit it with its marked side towards the inside of the engine, then heat the housing again and drive the bearing squarely in until it seats using a driver or socket that bears only on the outer race **(see illustration 22.26)**.

19 The left-hand bearing is part of the crankshaft assembly and is not available separately **(see illustration)**. If the bearing has failed a complete new crankshaft

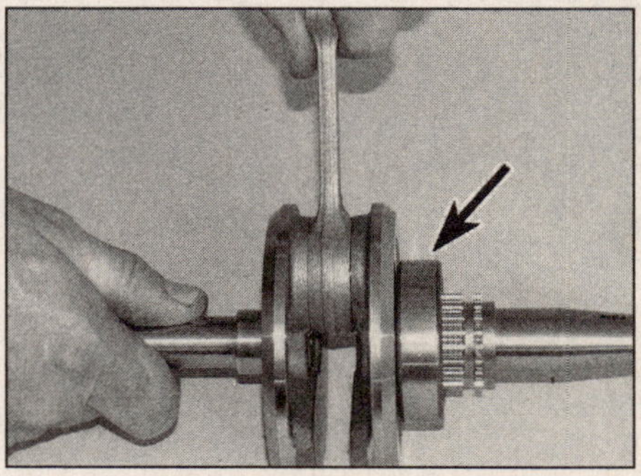

22.19 Left-hand main bearing (arrowed)

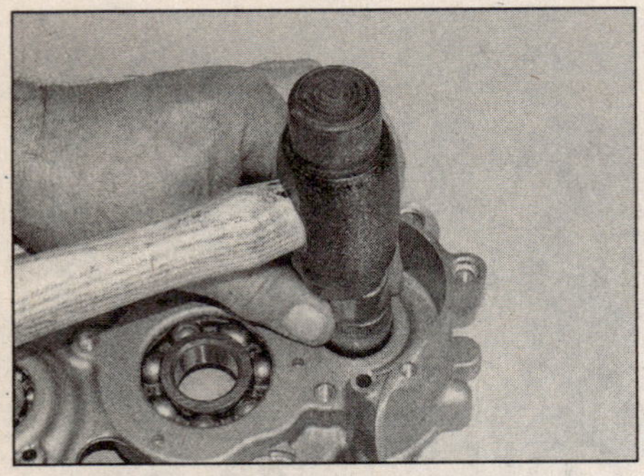

22.24 Heat the housing then drive the bearing out from the outside

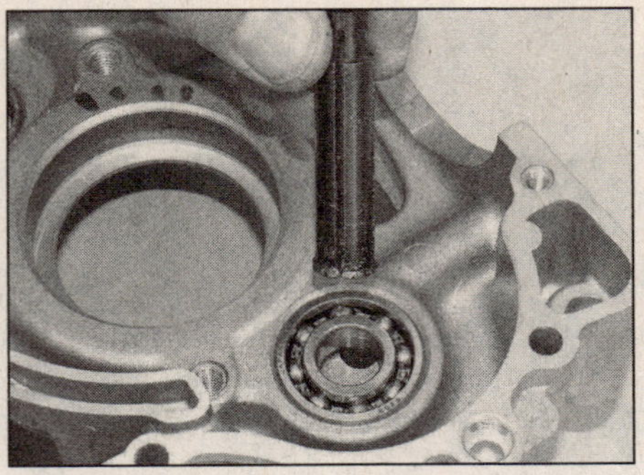

22.25a Fit the expander behind the inner race of the bearing...

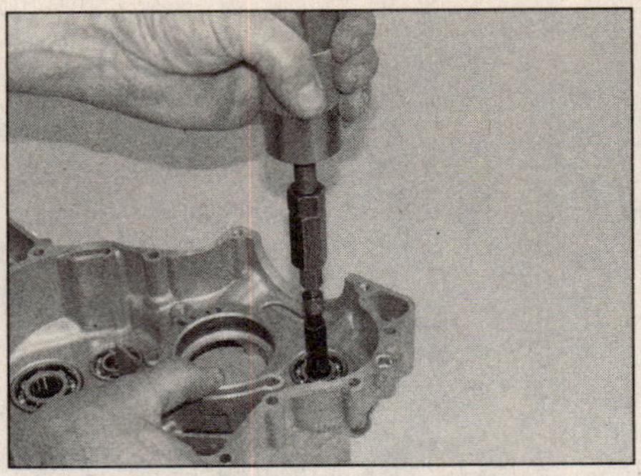

22.25b ...then fit the slide-hammer and jar the bearing out

assembly, which includes the connecting rod and big-end bearing must be fitted. If you fit a new crankshaft you should also fit a new right main bearing.

Connecting rod (big-end) bearing

20 If the connecting rod (big-end) bearing has failed, there will be a pronounced knocking noise when the engine is running, particularly under load and increasing with engine speed. Refer to Section 23, Step 7 for checks that can be made.

21 The bearing is part of the complete assembled crankshaft. If it fails fit a new crankshaft, and also fit a new right-hand main bearing (Steps 17 and 18).

Balancer shaft bearings

22 If the balancer bearings have failed, excessive rumbling and vibration will be felt when the engine is running.

23 Separate the crankcase halves (Section 21) and remove the balancer shaft (Section 24).

24 To remove the right-hand bearing from the crankcase, heat the bearing housing from the outside of the crankcase with a hot air gun, then tap the bearing out of the crankcase using a bearing driver or a suitable socket located on the outer side of the bearing **(see illustration)**.

25 To remove the left-hand bearing from the crankcase, heat the bearing housing with a hot air gun and tap the casing face down on a wood surface until the bearing drops out **(see illustration 22.8b)**. If it doesn't come out, an expanding knife-edge bearing puller with slide-hammer attachment is required. Heat the bearing housing with a hot air gun, then fit the expanding end of the puller behind the bearing, then turn the puller to expand it and lock it **(see illustration)**. Attach the slide-hammer to the puller, then hold the crankcase firmly down and operate the slide-hammer to jar the bearing out **(see illustration)**.

26 Smear the outside of the bearing with clean oil and fit it with its marked side towards the inside of the engine, then heat the housing again and drive the bearing squarely in until it seats using a driver or socket that bears only on the outer race **(see illustration)**.

Transmission shaft bearings

27 If the transmission bearings have failed, excessive rumbling and vibration will be felt when the engine is running.

28 Separate the crankcase halves (Section 21) and remove the transmission shafts and the output shaft oil seal (Section 25).

29 Unscrew the input shaft right-hand bearing retainer bolts and remove the retainer **(see illustration)**.

30 To remove the input shaft bearing from the right-hand crankcase and the output shaft bearing from the left-hand crankcase, heat the bearing housing with a hot air gun, then tap the bearing out of the crankcase using a bearing driver or a suitable socket located on the outer side of the bearing **(see illustration 22.24)**.

31 To remove the input shaft bearing from the left-hand crankcase and the output shaft bearing from the right-hand crankcase, heat the bearing housing with a hot air gun and tap the casing face down on a wood surface until the bearing drops out. If it doesn't come out, an expanding knife-edge bearing puller with slide-hammer attachment is required. Heat the bearing housing with a hot air gun, then fit the expanding end of the puller behind the bearing, then turn the puller to expand it and lock it **(see illustration 22.25a)**. Attach the slide-hammer to the puller, then hold the crankcase firmly down and operate the slide-hammer to jar the bearing out **(see illustration 22.25b)**.

32 Smear the outside of each new bearing with clean oil and fit it with its marked side towards the inside of the engine, then heat the housing again and drive the bearing squarely in until it seats using a driver or socket that bears only on the outer race **(see illustration 22.26)**.

33 Clean the threads of the bearing retainer bolts. Apply a suitable non-permanent thread locking compound to the threads, then fit the retainer with the OUT mark facing out and tighten the bolts to the torque setting specified at the beginning of the Chapter **(see illustration 22.29)**.

23 Crankshaft and connecting rod

Note: *To remove the crankshaft the engine must be removed from the frame and the crankcase halves separated.*

Removal

1 Remove the engine from the frame (see Section 4) and separate the crankcase halves (see Section 21).

2 Remove the balancer shaft (see Section 24).

3 The crankshaft needs to be pressed out of the left crankcase – do not attempt to drive it out by hitting on the end of the shaft. You could use either the Yamaha tool part No. 90890-01135 or a suitable equivalent set-up

22.26 Drive the new bearing in using a socket or driver on the outer race

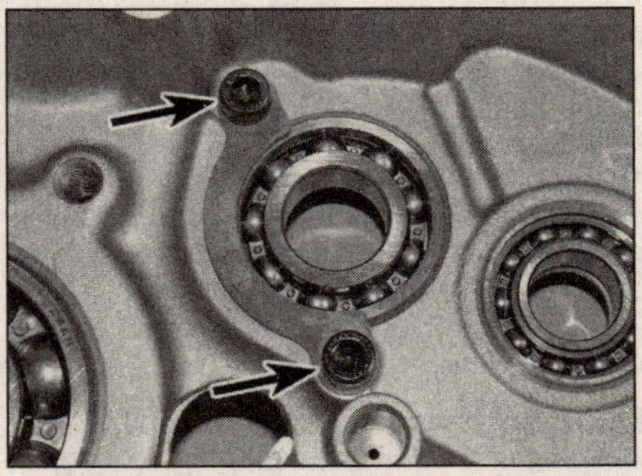

22.29 Unscrew the bolts (arrowed) and remove the retainer

23.3a This set-up uses old bearing races and a socket seating against the sprocket...

23.3b ...to take the force of the puller bolt which pushes the crankshaft out of the case

as shown **(see illustrations)** – the studs thread into the holes in the crankcase, the socket and spacers (or a piece of steel tube can be used) locate against the cam chain sprocket flange (avoid the teeth), and the piece of steel plate across the end of the crankshaft bears on the socket or tube, and turning the centre bolt pushes the crankshaft out. Heat the bearing housing with a hot air gun after setting the tool up and before applying pressure. If you do not have the tools or experience required, or if the set-up you use fails to shift the bearing/crankshaft an hydraulic press could be required; take the crankcase to a dealer or specialist.

Inspection

4 Clean the crankshaft with solvent. If available, blow the crank dry with compressed air. Check the cam chain sprocket for wear or damage. If any of the teeth are excessively worn, chipped or broken, the crankshaft must be replaced with a new one.

5 Place the crankshaft on V-blocks and check for runout using a dial gauge **(see illustration)**. Compare the reading to the maximum specified at the beginning of the Chapter. If the runout exceeds the limit, the crankshaft must be replaced with a new one.

6 Measure the connecting rod side clearance (the gap between the connecting rod big-end and the crankshaft web) with a feeler gauge **(see illustration)**. If the clearance is greater than the service limit specified, replace the crankshaft with a new one.

7 Hold the crankshaft still and check for any radial (up and down) play in the big-end bearing by pushing and pulling the rod against the crank **(see illustration)**. If a dial gauge is available measure the amount of radial play and compare the reading to the maximum specified at the beginning of the Chapter. If the play exceeds the limit, the crankshaft must be replaced with a new one.

8 Refer to Section 13, Step 12 and check the connecting rod small-end and piston pin for wear.

9 Have the rod checked for twist and bend by a Yamaha dealer if you are in doubt about its straightness.

10 Refer to Section 22 and check the crankshaft (main) bearings.

11 Measure the width of the crankshaft from between the outer edge of each web **(see illustration)**. Replace the crankshaft assembly with a new one if it is not within the specified limits.

Installation

12 The crankshaft can be drawn into the left-hand crankcase using the Yamaha tools part Nos. 90890-01274, 01275, 01278, and 04081, or an equivalent set-up using a puller. If using the Yamaha tools set them up as shown, making sure it is central to the shaft

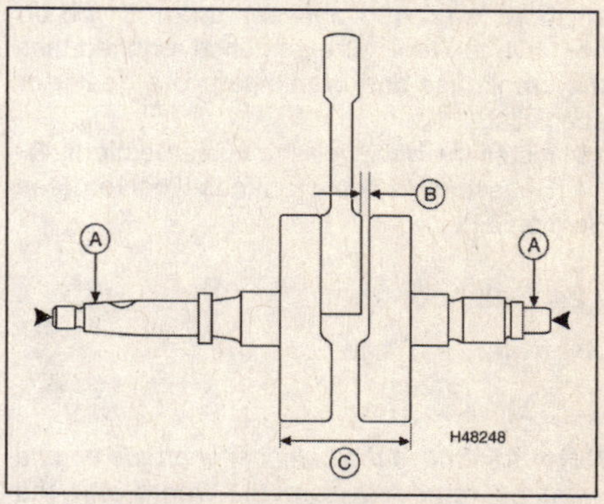

23.5 Crankshaft measurement points

A Runout
B Connecting rod side clearance
C Width across webs

23.6 Measuring the connecting rod side clearance

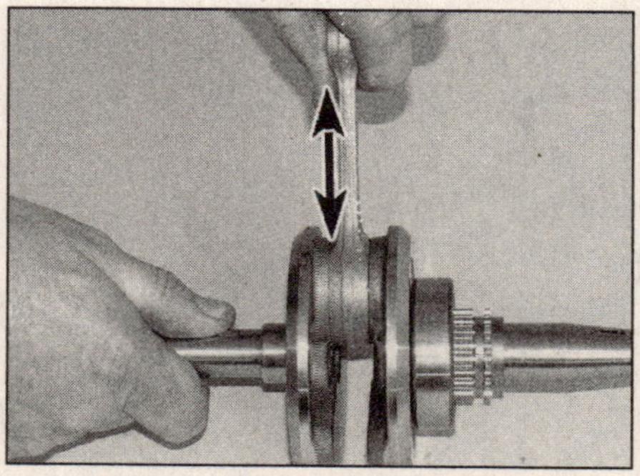

23.7 Check for any radial play in the big-end bearing

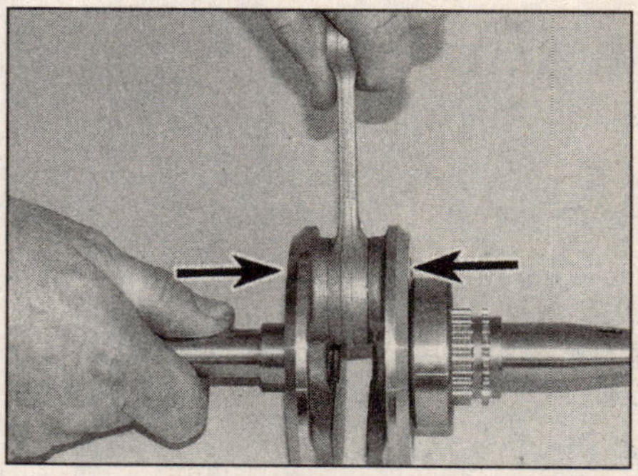

23.11 Measure the width of the crankshaft across the webs

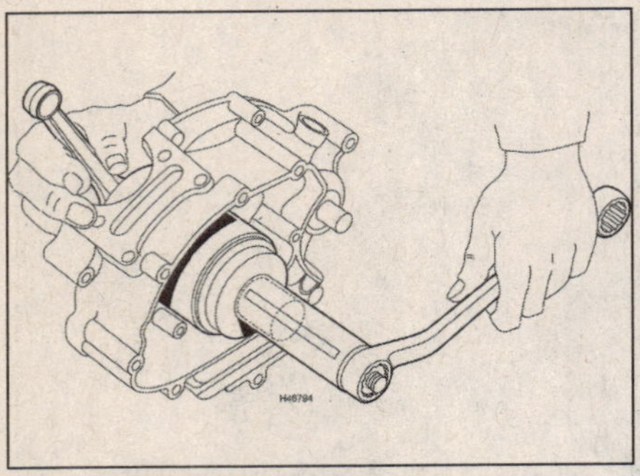

23.12a Installing the crankshaft using the Yamaha special tool

23.12b Set-up used to draw the crankshaft in

23.12c Heat the bearing housing ...

23.12d ... and turn the nut to draw the bearing in ...

23.12e ... until it seats

axis, and draw the crankshaft in until it seats **(see illustration)**. Alternatively thread an M12 x 1.25 nut onto the end of the crankshaft, leaving half its threads clear, then thread some rod into the nut and braise it **(see illustration)**. Now fit the rod through the puller cross-piece and thread another nut onto it and against the cross-piece **(see illustration)**. Heat the area around the bearing housing with a hot air gun to ease installation, and turn the nut until the crankshaft is drawn in so the bearing seats **(see illustrations)**. Whichever method you use, make sure the connecting rod is positioned so it sits in the opening for the cylinder bore, and make sure the outer race of the bearing is seated against the crankcase so there is no gap between them. If you do not have the tools or experience required take the crankcase and crankshaft to a dealer or specialist.

13 Install the balancer shaft (see Section 24).

14 Reassemble the crankcase halves (see Section 21).

24 Balancer shaft

Note: *To remove the balancer shaft the engine must be removed from the frame and the crankcases separated.*

Removal

1 Remove the engine from the frame (see Section 4) and separate the crankcase halves (see Section 21).

2 Lift balancer shaft out of the crankcase **(see illustration)**.

3 On 2009 to 2013 WR models remove the O-ring from each end of the shaft, noting which fits where **(see illustration 24.6)** – new ones must be used, and they are different sizes.

24.2 Removing the balancer shaft

Inspection

4 Clean the balancer shaft with solvent. If available, blow it dry with compressed air. Check the balancer drive and driven gears for wear or damage. If any of the gear teeth are excessively worn, chipped or broken, the gears must be replaced with a new set.

5 Refer to Section 22 and check the balancer shaft bearings.

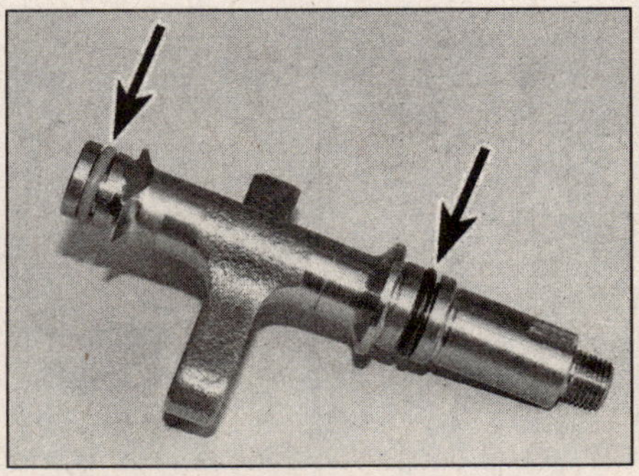

24.6 Fit new O-rings (arrowed) into the grooves

Installation

6 On 2009 to 2013 WR models fit a new O-ring smeared with grease into the groove in each end of the shaft – make sure the correct O-ring is fitted in the correct end as they are different sizes **(see illustration)**.

7 Carefully fit the balancer shaft into its bearing in the left crankcase **(see illustrations 24.2)**.

8 Reassemble the crankcase halves (see Section 21).

25 Transmission shaft and oil seal removal and installation

Note: *To remove the transmission assembly the engine must be removed from the frame and the crankcases separated.*

Transmission shafts

Removal

1 Remove the engine from the frame (see Section 4) and separate the crankcase halves (see Section 21).

2 Remove the selector drum and forks (Section 27).

3 Lift the shafts out of the crankcase together, holding the bottom pinions on the output shaft to prevent them dropping off, and noting that the long clutch pushrod and steel ball are inside the input shaft and could drop out if not

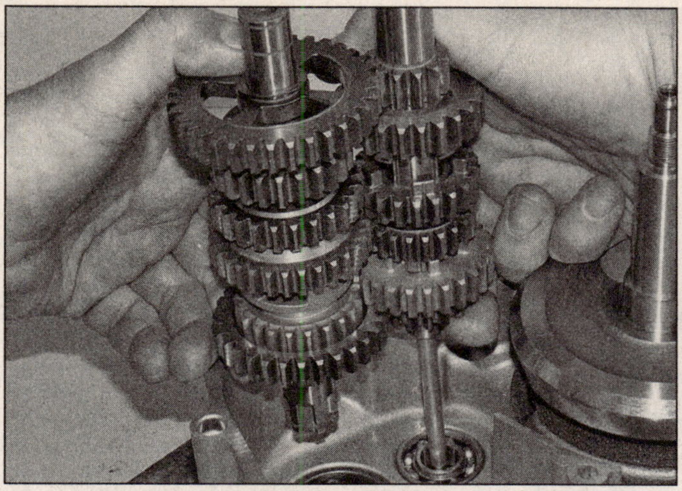

25.3a Lift the transmission shafts out together, noting the clutch pushrod inside the input shaft

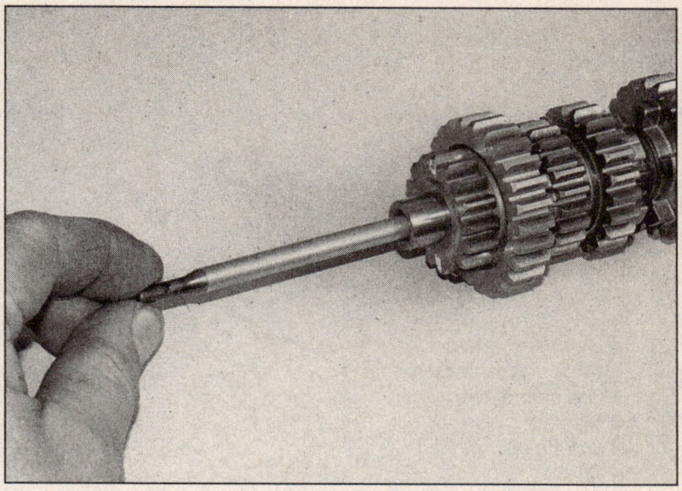

25.3b Withdraw the ball and rod from the shaft

held **(see illustration)**. If the shafts are stuck, use a soft-faced hammer and gently tap on their ends. Lay the shafts flat then push the ball out using the pushrod and withdraw the rod **(see illustration)**.

4 If the thrust washer on the end of the output shaft has fallen off or stuck to the bearing in the left crankcase retrieve it and fit it back onto the shaft **(see illustration 25.9)**.

5 Prise the output shaft oil seal out of the left crankcase using a seal hook or screwdriver **(see illustration)** – a new one must be fitted.

6 If required remove the clutch release mechanism shaft from the crankcase, noting how the spring ends locate **(see illustration)**.

7 Refer to Section 22 and check the transmission shaft bearings. Refer to Section 26 and check the transmission shafts – if necessary, the shafts can be disassembled and new components fitted.

Installation

8 Grease the lips of the new seal. Press or drive the seal into its housing until its outer face is flush with the housing rim **(see illustration)** – using a piece of wood across the seal is a good way to achieve this.

9 Smear some grease over the thrust washer on the left end of the output shaft to prevent it dropping off **(see illustration)**. If removed fit the clutch release mechanism shaft into the crankcase, making sure the spring ends locate correctly **(see illustration 25.6)**.

10 Join the shafts together on the bench so their related gears are engaged.

11 Grasp the shafts, holding the pinions on the left end to prevent them dropping off, and fit the shaft ends into their bearings in the left crankcase **(see illustration 25.3a)**.

12 Make sure the transmission shafts are correctly seated and engaged.

13 Install the selector drum and forks (Section 27).

14 Position the gears in the neutral position and check the shafts are free to rotate easily and independently (i.e. the input shaft can turn whilst the output shaft is held stationary) before proceeding further.

15 Lubricate each end of the long clutch pushrod with molybdenum grease and fit it into the input shaft **(see illustration 25.3b)**. Fit the steel ball into the shaft now if preferred, or alternatively fit it later when installing the clutch **(see illustration 16.5a)**.

16 Reassemble the crankcase halves (see Section 21).

25.5 Remove and discard the oil seal

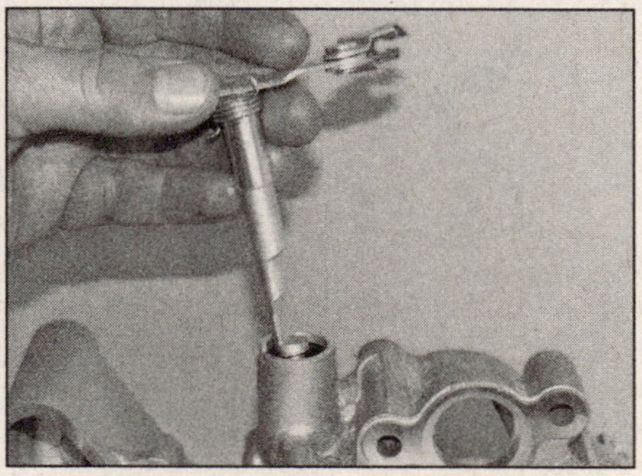

25.6 Withdraw the release shaft

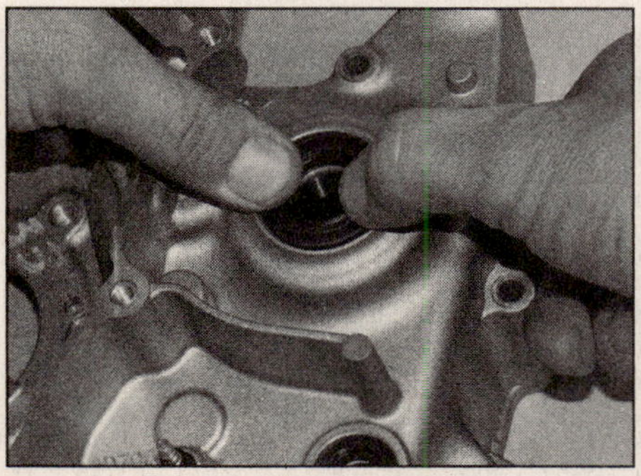

25.8 Drive the seal in, setting it flush with the rim

25.9 Smear some grease onto the thrust washer (arrowed) to keep it in place

Output shaft oil seal

17 If there is evidence of leakage from the oil seal in normal use it can be replaced with a new one without having to remove the transmission assembly.

18 Remove the front sprocket (see Chapter 6).

19 Push one side of the seal in so it tilts then prise out the other side.

20 Wrap some insulating tape around the end of the shaft. Grease the lips of the new seal. Slide the seal over the shaft and press it into its housing. Press or drive the seal in until its outer face is flush with its housing. Remove the tape.

21 Install the front sprocket (see Chapter 6).

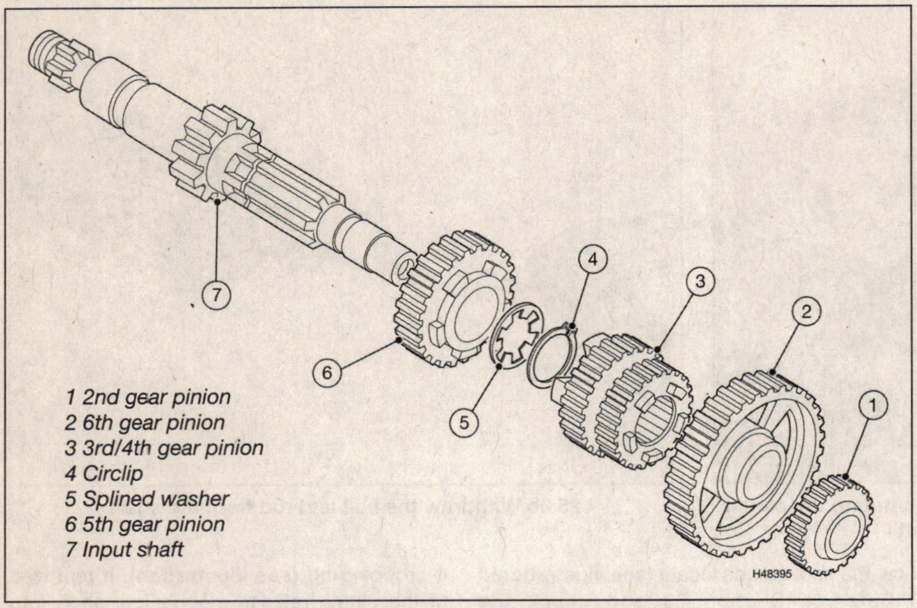

26.2a Transmission input shaft components

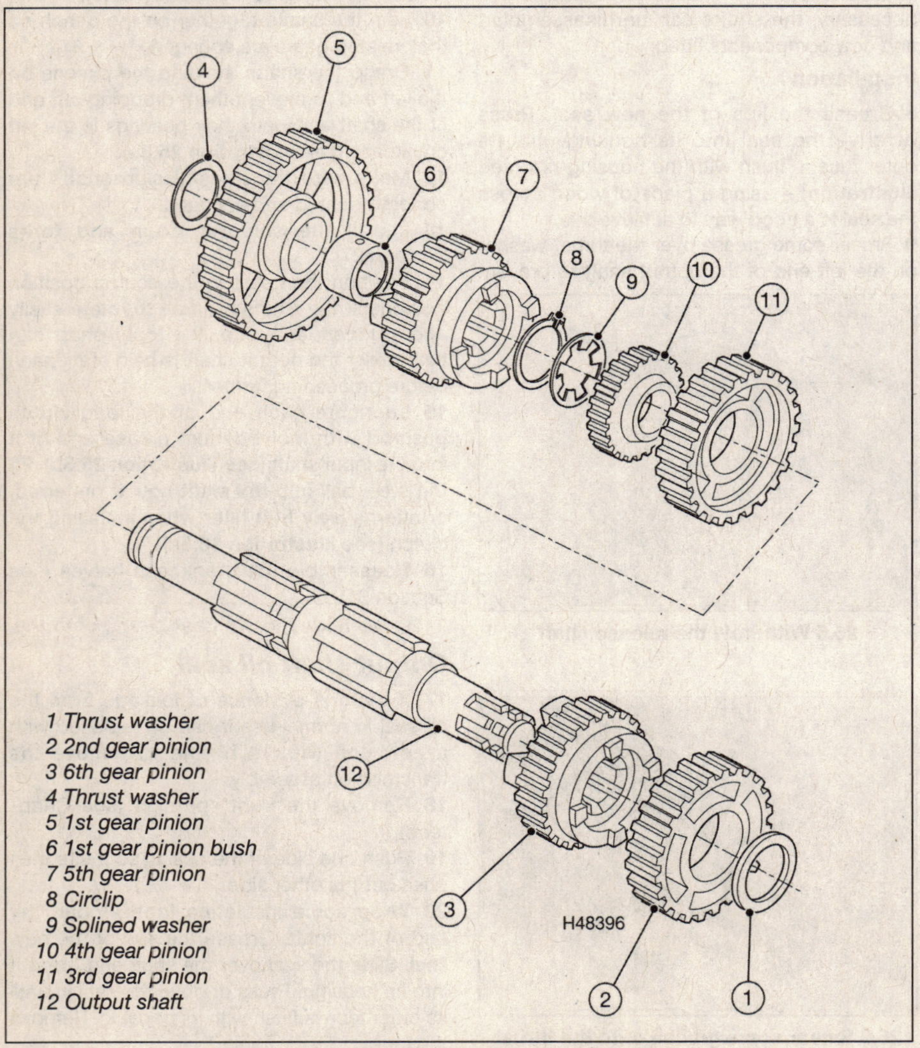

26.2b Transmission output shaft components

26 Transmission shaft overhaul

1 Remove the transmission assembly from the crankcase (see Section 25).

2 Always disassemble the transmission shafts separately to avoid mixing up the components **(see illustrations)**.

Input shaft

Disassembly

3 The 2nd gear pinion is an interference fit on the left end of the shaft and must be removed using a puller or press. Use a soft metal interface between the puller or press head to protect the shaft, or fit an 8 mm bolt inside the shaft with the head resting on its end **(see illustration)**. Because the gear is much smaller than the 6th gear pinion behind it seat the puller legs or press base against the back of the 6th pinion **(see illustration)**. Mark the outer face of the 2nd gear pinion to avoid getting it the wrong way round as it is the same on both sides.

4 Slide the combined 3rd/4th gear pinion off the shaft **(see illustration 26.16)**.

> **HAYNES HiNT** ***When disassembling the transmission shafts, place the parts on a long rod or thread a wire through them to keep them in order and facing the proper direction.***

26.3a An 8 mm bolt can be used to protect the shaft

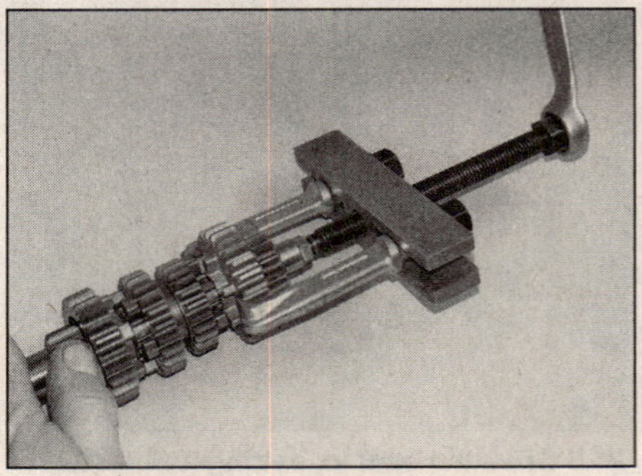

26.3b Set the puller up as shown

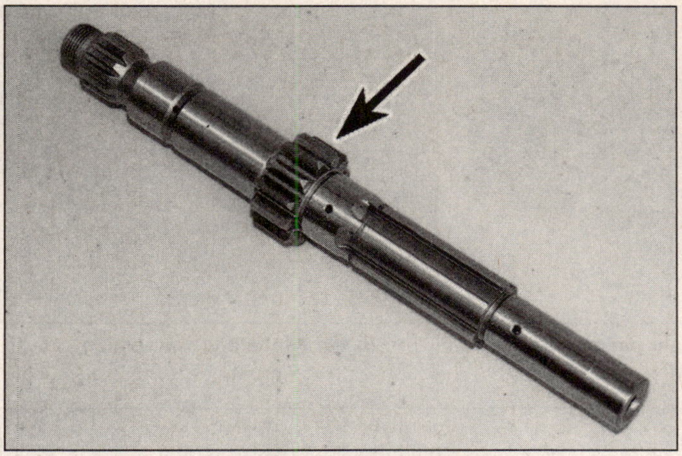

26.6 1st gear pinion (arrowed) is part of the shaft

26.8 Check the dogs and dog holes for rounding and wear

5 Remove the circlip securing the 5th gear pinion, then slide the splined washer and the pinion off the shaft **(see illustrations 26.15c, b and a)**.

6 The 1st gear pinion is integral with the shaft **(see illustration)**.

Inspection

7 Check the gear teeth for cracking, chipping, pitting and other obvious wear or damage. Any pinion that is damaged as such must be replaced with a new one.

8 Inspect the dogs and the dog holes in the gears for cracks, chips, and excessive wear especially in the form of rounded edges **(see illustration)**. Make sure mating gears engage properly. Replace the paired gears as a set if necessary.

9 Check for signs of scoring or bluing on the pinions, bush and shaft **(see illustration)**. This could be caused by overheating due to inadequate lubrication. Replace any damaged pinions with new ones.

10 Check that each pinion moves freely on the shaft or bush but without undue freeplay.

11 The shaft is unlikely to sustain damage unless the engine has seized, placing an unusually high loading on the transmission, or the machine has covered a very high mileage. Check the surface of the shaft, especially where a pinion turns on it, and replace the shaft if it has scored or picked up, or if there are any cracks. Damage of any kind can only be cured by replacement. Using V-blocks and a dial gauge check the shaft for runout – replace the shaft with a new one if it exceeds the specified limit. Also check the long clutch pushrod is straight by rolling it on a flat surface such as piece of glass – any bend must not exceed 0.5 mm.

12 Check the washers and circlips and replace any that are bent or appear weakened or worn. Use new ones if in any doubt. Note that it is good practice, and specified by Yamaha, to use new circlips when overhauling the transmission shafts.

Reassembly

13 Wash all of the components in clean solvent and dry them off. Check that all the oil holes and passages are clear.

14 During reassembly, apply molybdenum disulphide oil (a 50/50 mixture of molybdenum disulphide grease and clean engine oil) to the mating surfaces of the shaft and pinions. When fitting circlips, do not expand their ends any further than is necessary, and position them between the raised splines as shown in illustration 26.15d. Fit the circlip so that its chamfered side faces away from the thrust side, i.e. towards the pinion it secures.

15 Slide the 5th gear pinion onto the shaft with its dogs facing away from the integral 1st gear **(see illustration)**. Slide the splined washer onto the shaft, then fit the circlip, making sure that it locates correctly in the groove in the shaft **(see illustrations)**.

26.9 Check the pinion bushes (arrowed) for wear

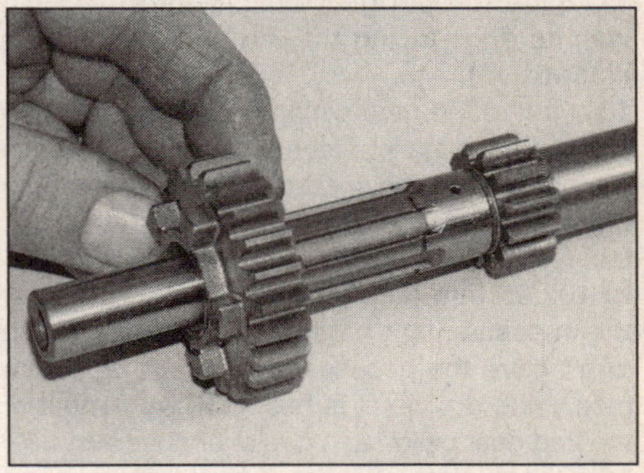

26.15a Slide the 5th gear pinion onto the shaft...

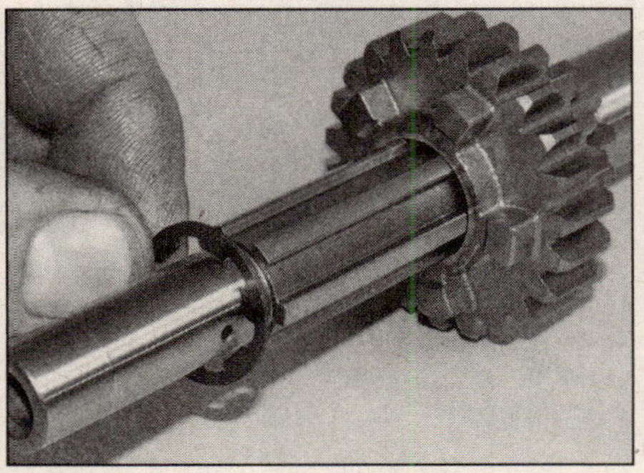

26.15b ...followed by the splined washer...

26.15c ...then fit the circlip...

26.15d ...making sure it locates properly in its groove

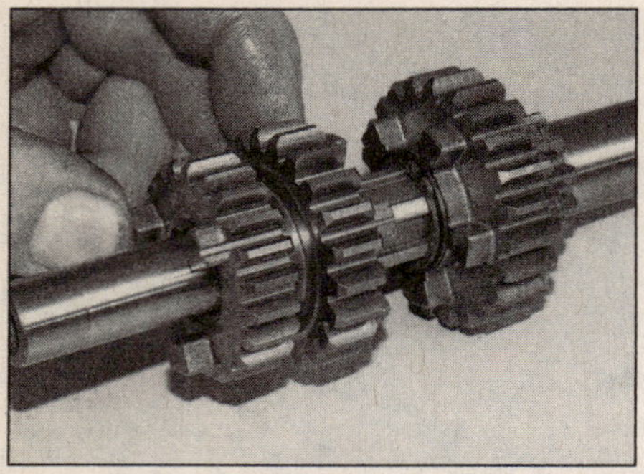

26.16 Slide the 3rd/4th gear pinion onto the shaft

26.17 Slide the 6th gear pinion onto the shaft

26.18a Fit the 2nd gear pinion...

26.18b ...and press or drive it on...

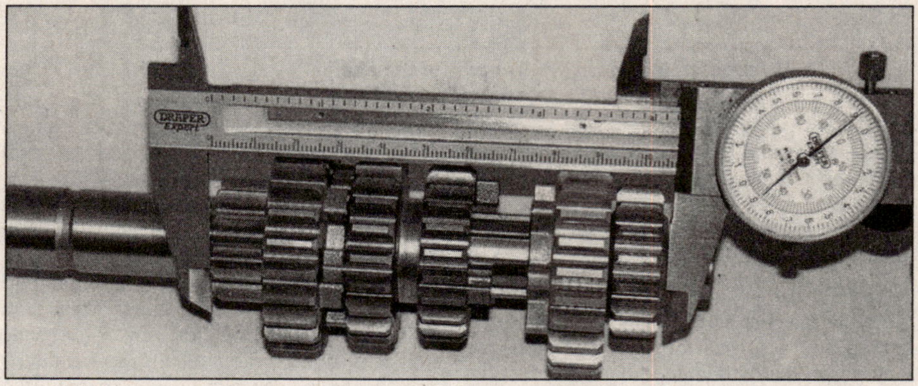

26.18c ...setting it so the length of the assembled shaft is as specified when measured as shown

16 Slide the combined 3rd/4th gear pinion onto the shaft with the larger 4th gear pinion facing the 5th **(see illustration)**.

17 Slide the 6th gear pinion onto the shaft with its dogs facing the 3rd gear pinion **(see illustration)**.

18 Fit the 2nd gear pinion onto the end of the shaft with the marked face outermost, then drive the pinion onto the shaft or press the shaft into the pinion until the distance between the outer faces of the 2nd and 1st gear pinions is 106.85 to 107.05 mm **(see illustrations)** – note that this measurement must be correct, so if you don't have the necessary tools and accurate measuring devices it is best to leave fitment of the 2nd gear pinion to a dealer or specialist.

19 Check that all components have been correctly installed **(see illustration)**.

Output shaft

Disassembly

20 Slide the thrust washer off the left end of the shaft, followed by the 2nd gear pinion and the 6th gear pinion **(see illustrations 26.30c, b and a)**.

21 Slide the thrust washer off the right end of the shaft, followed by the 1st gear pinion, its bush and the 5th gear pinion **(see illustrations 26.29c, b and a, and 26.28)**.

22 Remove the circlip, then slide the splined washer, the 4th gear pinion and the 3rd gear pinion off the shaft **(see illustrations 26.27c, b and a, and 26.26)**.

Inspection

23 See Steps 7 to 12.

Reassembly

24 Wash all of the components in clean solvent and dry them off. Check that all the oil holes and passages are clear.

25 During reassembly, apply molybdenum disulphide oil (a 50/50 mixture of molybdenum disulphide grease and clean engine oil) to the mating surfaces of the shaft, pinions and bushes. When installing the circlips, do not expand their ends any further than is necessary, and position them between the raised splines as shown in illustration 26.26d.

26 Slide the 3rd gear pinion onto the right end of the shaft with its recessed side facing the middle of the shaft **(see illustration)**.

27 Slide the 4th gear pinion onto shaft with its raised centre section facing the 3rd gear

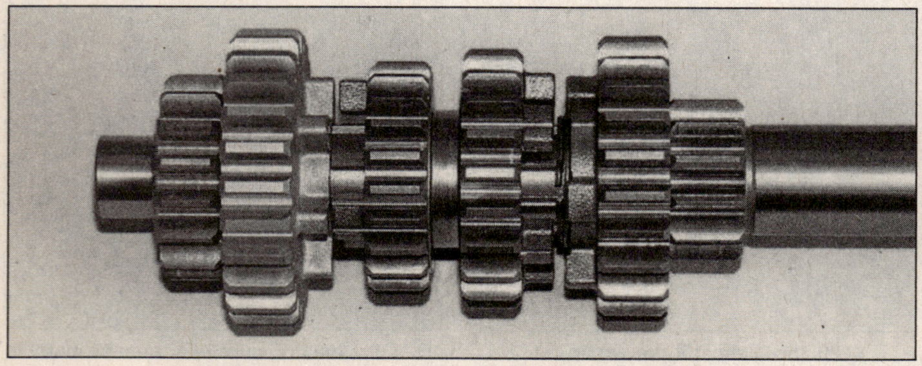

26.19 The complete input shaft should be as shown

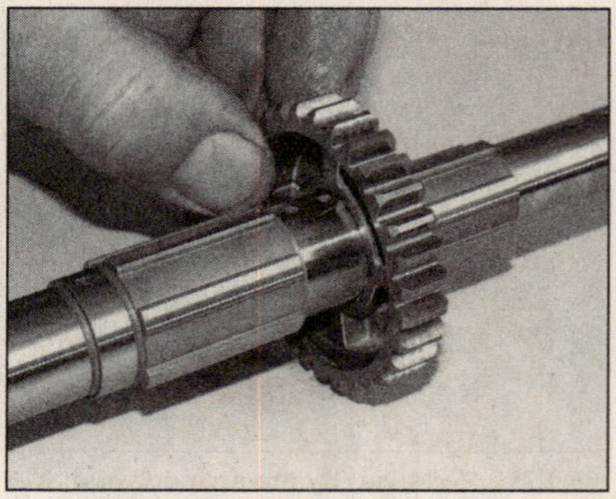

26.26 Slide the 3rd gear pinion onto the shaft

26.27a Slide the 4th gear pinion onto the shaft...

26.27b ...followed by the splined washer...

26.27c ...and secure them with the circlip...

pinion **(see illustration)**. Slide the splined washer on, then fit the circlip, making sure it is locates correctly in its groove in the shaft **(see illustrations)**.

28 Slide the 5th gear pinion onto shaft with its selector fork groove facing the 4th gear pinion **(see illustration)**.

29 Slide the 1st gear pinion bush onto the shaft, then fit the pinion onto the bush with its recessed face and raised centre section facing the 5th gear pinion **(see illustrations)**. Slide the thrust washer onto the shaft **(see illustration)**.

30 Slide the 6th gear pinion onto the left end of the shaft with its selector fork groove facing the 3rd gear pinion **(see illustration)**. Slide the 2nd gear pinion on with its recessed side facing the 6th, then fit the thrust washer **(see illustrations)**.

26.27d ...making sure it locates in the groove

26.28 Slide the 5th gear pinion onto the shaft

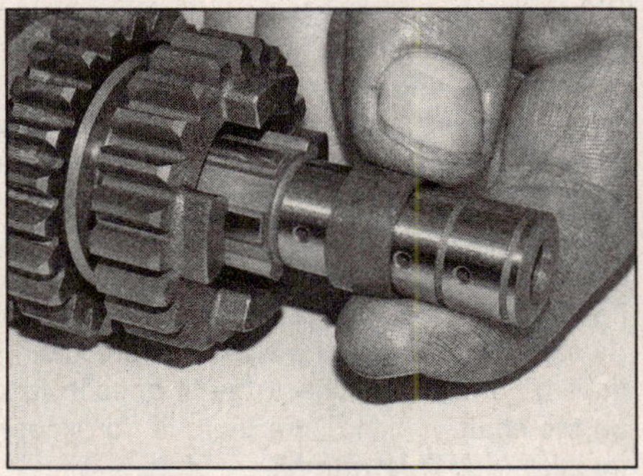
26.29a Slide the 1st gear pinion bush onto the shaft...

26.29b ...then slide the pinion onto the bush

26.29c Slide the washer onto the shaft

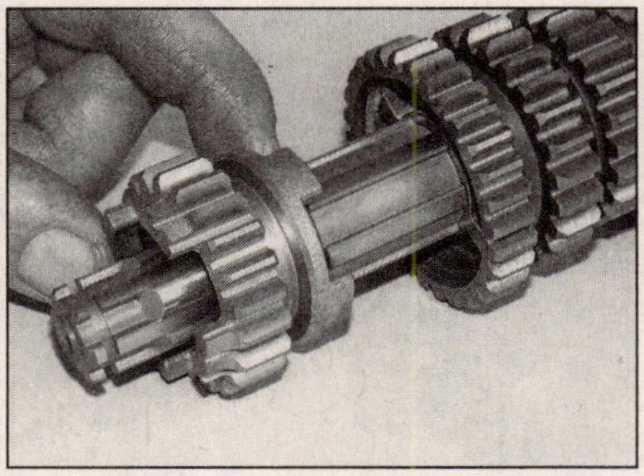
26.30a Slide the 6th gear pinion onto the shaft

26.30b Slide the 2nd gear pinion onto the shaft

26.30c Slide the washer onto the shaft

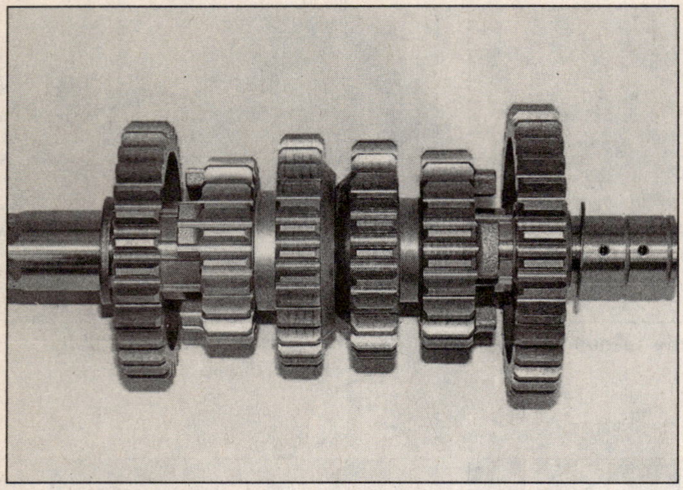

26.31 The assembled output shaft should be as shown

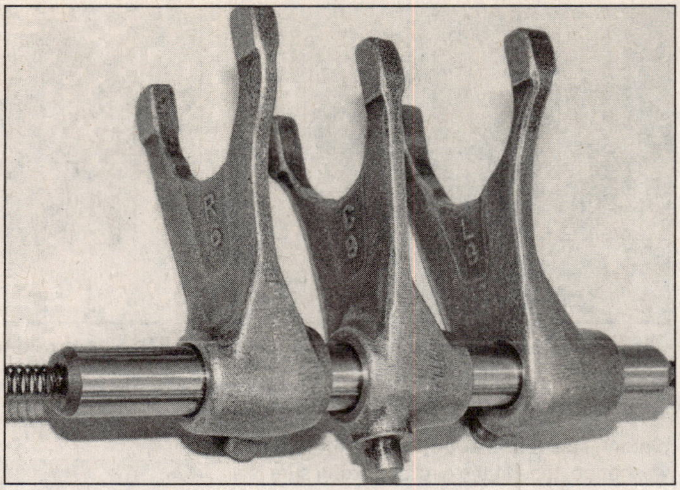

27.2 Each fork is marked with an identification letter

31 Check that all components have been correctly installed **(see illustration)**.

27 Selector drum and forks

Note: *To remove the selector drum and forks the engine must be removed from the frame and the crankcases separated.*

Removal

1 Remove the engine (see Section 4) and separate the crankcase halves (see Section 21).

27.3 Withdraw the shaft...

2 Before removing the selector drum and forks, note that each fork carries an identification letter **(see illustration)**. The right-hand fork has R, the centre fork C, and the left-hand fork L, with all marks facing the right-hand side of the engine. If no letters are visible, mark them yourself using a felt pen. The R and L forks fit into the output shaft, and the C fork fits into the input shaft.

3 Withdraw the selector fork shaft, taking care to retrieve the spring from each end, noting the one in the left end could fall out **(see illustration)**.

27.4 ... then move the forks aside and remove the drum, noting its alignment with the neutral switch (arrowed)

4 Pivot each selector fork out of its track in the selector drum, then remove the drum **(see illustration)**.

5 Remove each fork from its pinion **(see illustrations 27.15, 14 and 13)**. Slide the forks back onto the shaft in the correct order and way round.

Inspection

6 Inspect the selector forks for any signs of wear or damage, especially around the fork ends where they engage with the groove in the pinion. Check that each fork fits correctly in its pinion groove **(see illustration)**. Measure the thickness of each fork end and replace them with new ones if worn below the specified thickness **(see illustration)**. Check closely to see if the forks are bent. If the forks are in any way damaged they must be replaced with new ones.

7 Check that the fork shaft ends and their holes in the casings are neither worn nor damaged and the shafts are a smooth sliding fit with no freeplay. Check the fit of each fork on the shaft, making sure there is no excess freeplay **(see illustration)**.

8 Check the selector fork shaft is straight. A bent rod will cause difficulty in selecting gears and make the gearchange action heavy.

27.6a Check the fit of each fork in its pinion...

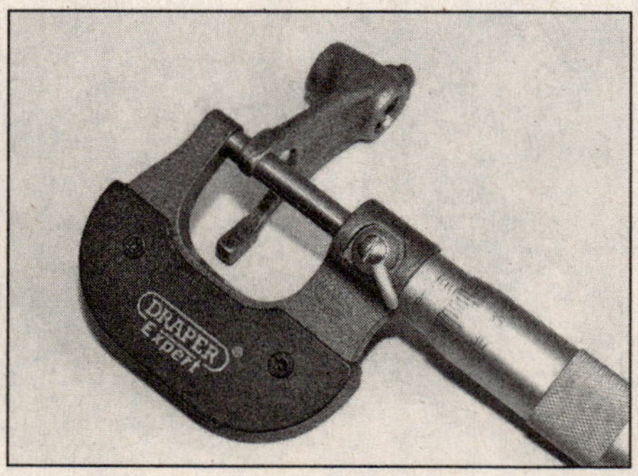

27.6b ... and measure the thickness of each end

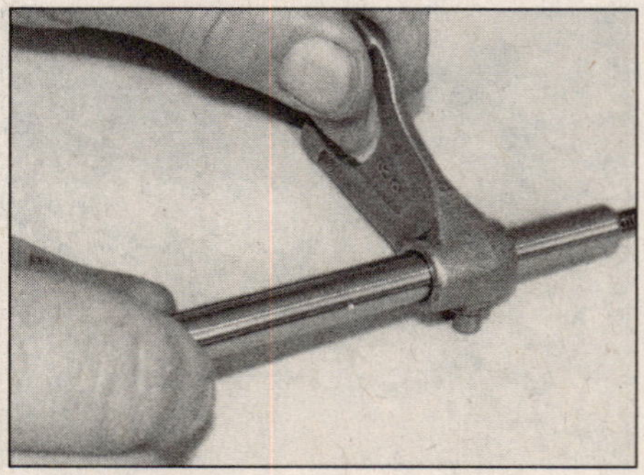

27.7 Check the fit and feel of each fork on the shaft

Replace the shaft with a new one if it is bent. Check the springs for distortion.

9 Inspect the selector drum grooves and selector fork guide pins for signs of wear or damage **(see illustration)**. If either component shows signs of wear or damage the fork(s) and drum must be replaced with new ones.

10 Check that the selector drum bearing rotates smoothly and freely, and check the fit of the plain end in its bore in the crankcase **(see illustrations)**. Replace the drum and/ or crankcases with new ones if they are worn.

11 Check the neutral switch contact, and also check the plunger on the switch **(see illustration 27.4)**. Make sure the plunger moves in and out freely. Replace any damaged or worn parts with new ones.

Installation

12 Lubricate the ends of each selector fork and fork shaft and the guide pins with molybdenum disulphide oil (a 50/50 mixture

27.9 Check the guide pins and their grooves in the drum

of molybdenum disulphide grease and clean engine oil).

13 Locate the selector fork marked L in its pinion groove in the output shaft with the letter facing away from the left crankcase **(see illustration)**.

14 Locate the selector fork marked C in its

27.10a Check the drum bearing (arrowed)...

pinion groove in the input shaft with the letter facing away from the left crankcase **(see illustration)**.

15 Locate the selector fork marked R in its pinion groove in the output shaft with the letter facing away from the left crankcase **(see illustration)**.

27.10b ...and the fit of the shaft in its bore

27.13 Fit the L fork...

27.14 ...then C fork...

27.15 ...and the R fork

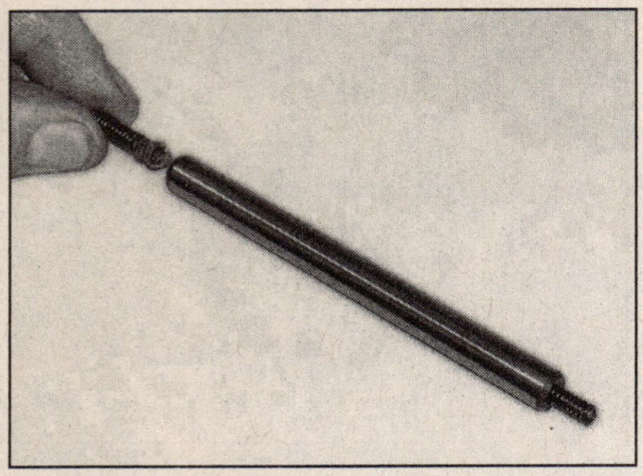

27.17 Fit a spring into each end of the shaft using grease to hold them in

16 Fit the selector drum, aligning the neutral contact with the switch hole **(see illustration 27.4)**. Pivot each fork around and seat its guide pin in its track.

17 Make sure the springs are fitted into each end of the fork shaft – use some grease to stick the spring in the left-hand end to prevent it dropping out **(see illustration)**. Align the bores of the forks and slide the shaft through each in turn and its hole in the crankcase **(see illustration 27.3)**.

18 Check that all components have been correctly installed.

19 Reassemble the crankcase halves (see Section 21).

28 Running-in procedure

1 Make sure the engine oil and coolant levels are correct (see *Pre-ride checks*). Make sure there is fuel in the tank.

2 Turn the engine kill switch to the ON position and shift the gearbox into neutral. Turn the ignition ON.

3 Start the engine and allow it to run with no throttle until it reaches operating temperature.

4 Refer to Section 3 and loosen the oil delivery check bolt, following the procedure to check oil is circulating. If a lubrication failure is suspected, stop the engine immediately and try to find the cause. If an engine is run without oil, even for a short period of time, severe damage will occur.

5 Check carefully that there are no oil or coolant leaks and make sure the transmission and controls, especially the brakes, function properly before road testing the machine.

6 Treat the machine gently for the first few miles to make sure oil has circulated throughout the engine and any new parts installed have started to seat.

7 Upon completion of the initial road test, and after the engine has cooled down completely, recheck the valve clearances (see Chapter 1) and check the engine oil level (see *Pre-ride checks*).

8 After a complete engine rebuild, or if a new piston and rings and/or a new cylinder has been fitted, the engine should be run in as if it were new according to Yamaha's guidelines as follows – for the first 300 miles (500 km) avoid prolonged use above 6000 rpm and do not use too much throttle, and after every hour of use stop the engine and allow it cool for five or ten minutes. There's no point in keeping to any set speed limit – the main idea is to keep from labouring the engine, but making sure you vary engine speed and load within those limits. From 300 to 600 miles (500 to 1000 km) avoid prolonged use above 8000 rpm and full throttle opening. Gradually increase performance, and again do not run the engine for more than an hour without letting it cool down for five to ten minutes. Experience is the best guide, since it's easy to tell when an engine is running freely. After 600 miles (1000 km) change the oil and fit a new filter (see Chapter 1). The engine can now be run normally.

Chapter 3
Cooling system

Contents

Degrees of difficulty

Easy, suitable for novice with little experience	**Fairly easy,** suitable for beginner with some experience	**Fairly difficult,** suitable for competent DIY mechanic	**Difficult,** suitable for experienced DIY mechanic	**Very difficult,** suitable for expert DIY or professional

Specifications

Coolant

Mixture type and capacity	see Chapter 1

ECT sensor

WR models	
Resistance @ 20°C	2.32 to 2.59 K-ohms
Resistance @ 80°C	310 to 326 ohms
MT and YZF-R models	
Resistance @ 20°C	2.51 to 2.78 K-ohms
Resistance @ 100°C	210 to 221 ohms

Thermostat

Opening temperature	80.5 to 83.5°C
Fully open	95°C
Valve lift	3 mm (min)

Radiator

Cap valve opening pressure	15.6 to 20 psi (1.08 to 1.4 Bar)

Torque settings

Cooling fan bolts	8 Nm
ECT sensor	
WR models	18 Nm
MT and YZF-R models	14 Nm
Thermostat cover bolts	10 Nm
Water pump mounting bolts and cover bolts	10 Nm
Water pump impeller shaft retainer bolts	10 Nm

1 General Information

1 The cooling system uses a water/ anti-freeze coolant to carry away excess heat from the engine and maintain as constant a temperature as possible. The cylinder is surrounded by a water jacket from which the heated coolant is circulated by thermo-syphonic action in conjunction with a water pump, which is on the left side of the cylinder head and driven off the camshaft. The hot coolant passes through the thermostat and to the radiator. The coolant then flows across the core of the radiator, then to the water pump and back to the engine.

2 A thermostat is fitted in the cylinder head to prevent the coolant flowing when the engine is cold, therefore accelerating the speed at which the engine reaches normal operating temperature. The ECT (engine coolant temperature) sensor mounted in the cylinder head transmits information to the ECU (electronic control unit). If the engine gets too hot the ECU actuates the cooling fan on the back of the radiator via a relay to draw extra air through, and if necessary turns on the temperature warning light in the instrument cluster.

3 The complete cooling system is partially sealed and pressurised, the pressure being controlled by a valve contained in the spring-loaded radiator cap. By pressurising the coolant the boiling point is raised, preventing premature boiling in adverse conditions. The overflow pipe from the system is connected to a reservoir into which excess coolant is expelled under pressure. The discharged coolant automatically returns to the radiator by the vacuum created when the engine cools.

Warning: Do not remove the pressure cap from the radiator when the engine is hot. Scalding hot coolant and steam may be blown out under pressure, which could cause serious injury. When the engine has cooled, place a thick rag, like a towel, over the pressure cap; slowly rotate the cap anti-clockwise to the first stop. This procedure allows any residual pressure to escape. When the steam has stopped escaping, press down on the cap while turning it anti-clockwise and remove it.

Caution: Do not allow anti-freeze to come in contact with your skin or painted surfaces of the motorcycle. Rinse off any spills immediately with plenty of water. Anti-freeze is highly toxic if ingested. Never leave anti-freeze lying around in an open container or in puddles on the floor; children and pets are attracted by its sweet smell and may drink it. Check with the local authorities about disposing of used anti-freeze. Many communities will have collection centres which will see that anti-freeze is disposed of safely.

Caution: If preparing a mix of anti-freeze and distilled water, take care to mix it in the correct proportion. The anti-freeze contains corrosion inhibitors which are essential to avoid damage to the cooling system. A lack of these inhibitors could lead to a build-up of corrosion which would block the coolant passages, resulting in overheating and severe engine damage. Distilled water must be used as opposed to tap water to avoid a build-up of scale which would also block the passages.

2 Cooling fan and relay

1 If the engine is overheating and the cooling fan does not come on, first check the fan fuse (see Chapter 8). If the fuse is good, check the relay (see Steps 2 to 5). If the fuse and relay are good check the fan motor (Steps 10 and 11).

Cooling fan relay

Check

2 Remove the relay (see Steps 7 and 8).

3 Set a multimeter to the ohms x 1 scale and connect it across the red/white and blue wire terminals on the relay **(see illustration)**. There should be no continuity (infinite resistance). Using a fully-charged 12 volt battery and two insulated jumper wires, connect the positive (+) terminal of the battery to the red/black wire terminal on the relay, and the negative (–) terminal to the green/black (WR models) or green/yellow (MT and YZF-R models) wire terminal on the relay. At this point the relay should be heard to click and the multimeter read 0 ohms (continuity). If this is the case the relay is proved good. If the relay does not click when battery voltage is applied and still indicates no continuity (infinite resistance) across its terminals, it is faulty and must be replaced with a new one.

4 If the relay is good, check for battery voltage at the red/white wire in the wiring connector with the ignition switch OFF, and at the red/black wire in the wiring connector with the ignition switch ON. If there is no voltage, check the wiring in the relevant circuit to the connector for continuity, referring to Electrical System Fault Finding at the beginning of Chapter 8 and the relevant wiring diagram at the end of it. If voltage is present, check that there is continuity in the green/black wire (WR) or green/yellow wire (MT/YZF) to the ECU wiring connector, and in the blue wire to the fan motor connector. There should be continuity in all wires.

5 If the fan is on the whole time, pull the relay off its connector. The fan should stop. If it does, the relay is defective and must be replaced with a new one.

6 If the fan works but is suspected of cutting in at the wrong temperature, check the ECT sensor (see Section 3).

Removal and installation

7 On WR models remove the seat (see Chapter 7), then remove the plastic cover **(see illustration)**. On MT and YZF-R models remove the passenger seat (see Chapter 7).

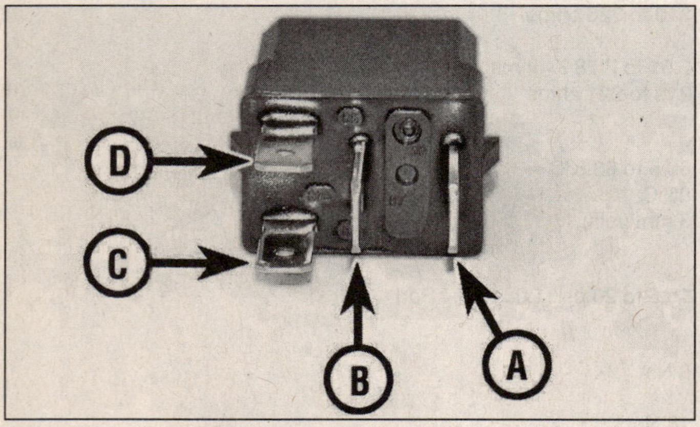

2.3 Relay terminal test connections

A Red/white terminal
B Blue terminal
C Red/black terminal
D Green/black (WR) or Green/yellow (MT/YZF) terminal

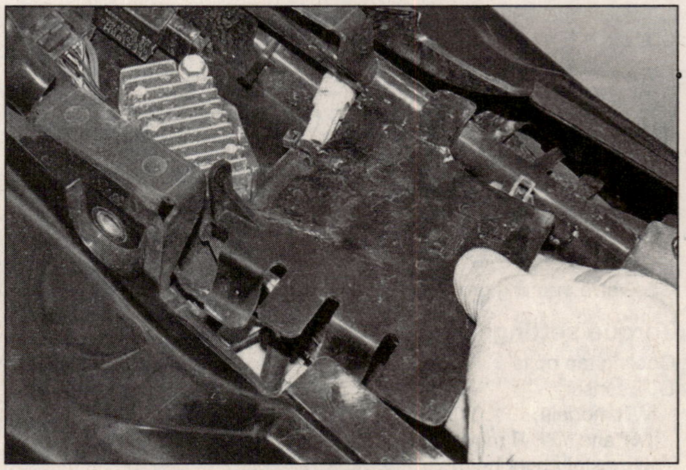

2.7 Remove the relay cover

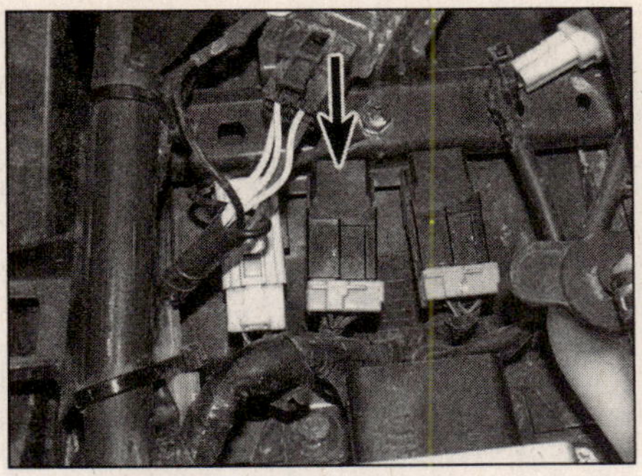
2.8a Cooling fan relay (arrowed) – WR models

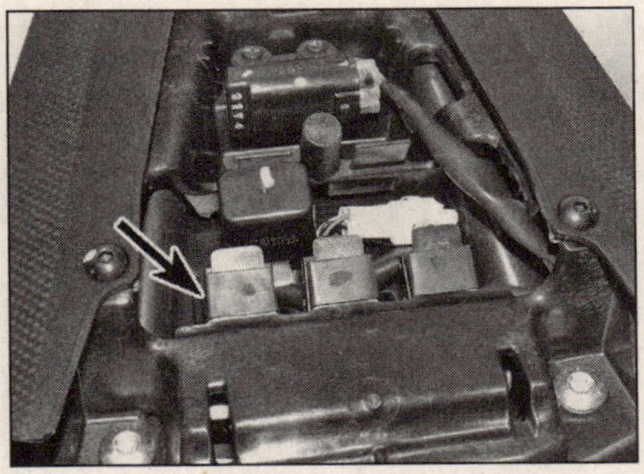
2.8b Cooling fan relay (arrowed) – MT and YZF-R models

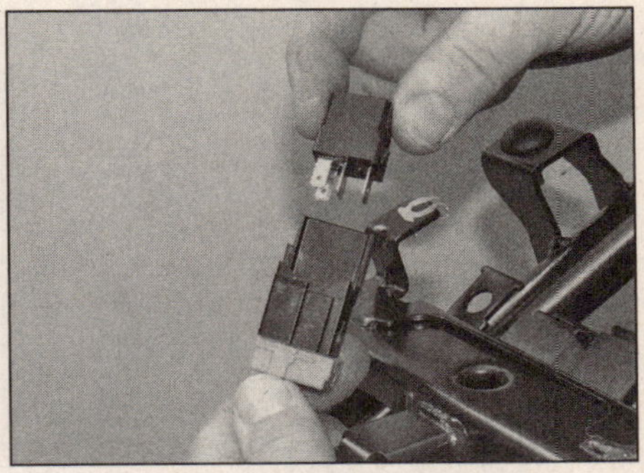
2.8c Release the relay from its holder, leaving the holder clipped to the wiring connector

8 Locate the relay and displace it from its mount **(see illustrations)**. Release the relay from its holder **(see illustration)**.
9 Installation is the reverse of removal.

Cooling fan

Check

10 The cooling fan is on the back of the radiator. On WR models remove the fuel tank cover (see Chapter 7). On MT and YZF-R models remove the fuel tank (see Chapter 4). Trace the wiring from the fan and disconnect the connector **(see illustrations)**.
11 Using a 12 volt battery and two jumper wires with suitable connectors, connect the battery positive (+) lead to the blue wire terminal on the fan side of the wiring connector, and the battery negative (–) lead to the black wire terminal on the connector. Once connected the fan should operate. If it does not, and the connector and the wiring between it and the motor are good, then the fan motor is faulty. Individual components are not available – replace the fan assembly with a new one.

Removal and installation

Warning: The engine must be completely cool before carrying out this procedure.

WR models

12 Remove the fuel tank cover (see Chapter 7).
13 Disconnect the fan wiring connector **(see illustration 2.10a)**.
14 Unscrew the bolts and remove the fan **(see illustration)** – remove the fuel tank for better access to the inner bolt if required (see Chapter 4).
15 Installation is the reverse of removal. Tighten the fan bolts to the torque setting specified at the beginning of the Chapter.

MT and YZF-R models

16 Remove the radiator (see Section 5).
17 Unscrew the bolts and remove the fan **(see illustration)**.
18 Installation is the reverse of removal. Tighten the fan bolts to the torque setting specified at the beginning of the Chapter.

2.10a Cooling fan wiring connector (arrowed) – WR models. Cut the cable-tie if required.

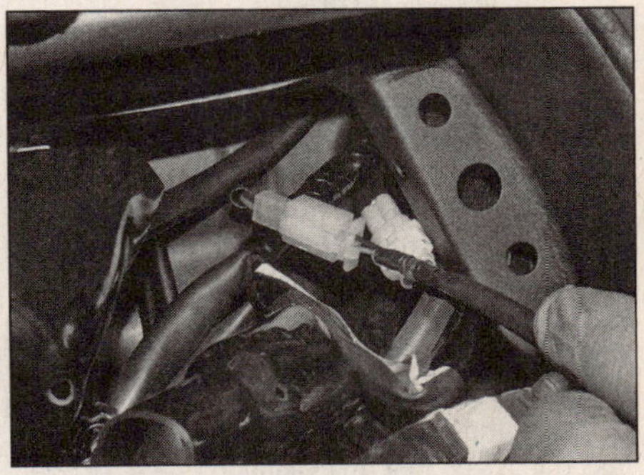
2.10b Cooling fan wiring connector – MT and YZF-R models

3 Temperature display and ECT sensor

Temperature display

Caution: If the high temperature warning display comes on during normal use, stop the engine and check the coolant level in the reservoir (see Pre-ride checks).

1 The circuit consists of the ECT sensor mounted in the cylinder head on the right-hand side and the display in the instrument cluster. On WR models the display consists of a high temperature warning symbol that illuminates if the coolant temperature is too high. On MT and YZF-R models the display consists of a segmented temperature gauge, with the segments coming on as the coolant temperature rises, and if the coolant temperature is too high the second segment from top will start to flash, and if it gets higher still the top segment will also flash and a high temperature warning symbol will flash and HIGH TEMP is displayed. When the ignition is first switched on the display should come on for a few seconds then go out – if it doesn't, check the instrument cluster wiring connectors (see Chapter 8), then check the wiring and connectors between the instrument cluster, the ECU and the ECT sensor, referring to the wiring diagrams at the end of Chapter 8.
2 If the wiring is good the circuit in the instrument cluster could be faulty – refer to Chapter 8.

ECT sensor

Check

3 The resistance of the sensor changes with changes in temperature – see the Specifications at the beginning of the chapter.

2.14 Cooling fan bolts (arrowed)

2.17 Cooling fan bolts (arrowed)

3.5 ECT sensor wiring connector (arrowed)

4.3 Release the clamp (arrowed) and detach the hose

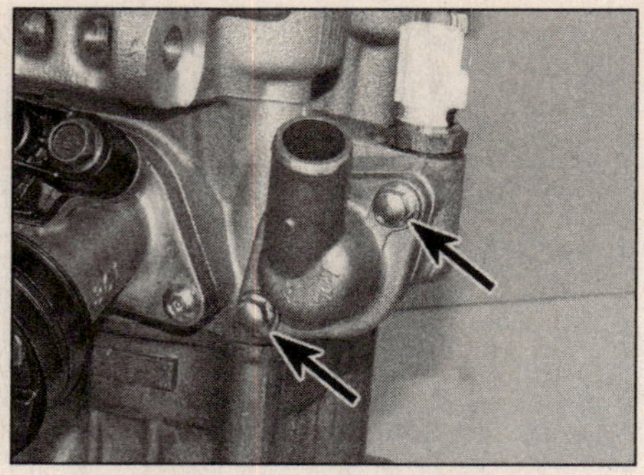

4.4 Unscrew the bolts (arrowed) and detach the cover...

While in theory it is possible to bench test the sensor at those temperatures, in practice the test is difficult to set up and perform. However you can test the resistance of the sensor with the engine cold, and as it warms up.

4 On YZF-R models remove the centre and upper sections of the fairing on the right-hand side (see Chapter 7).

5 Disconnect the sensor wiring connector **(see illustration)**. Connect the probes of a multimeter set to read resistance to the sensor terminals and compare the reading to that specified for 20°C, taking into account any variation due to ambient temperature. Reconnect the connector, then run the engine until it is at normal temperature. Stop the engine and repeat the test, comparing the reading to that specified for 80°C or 100°C (according to model). If the readings obtained are roughly as specified then the sensor is probably functioning correctly. If the sensor fails it is most likely to give a zero, constant, or infinite resistance reading at all temperatures.

Removal and installation

Warning: The engine must be completely cool before carrying out this procedure.

Caution: The ECT sensor is fragile and could be damaged if dropped or struck.

6 Drain the cooling system (see Chapter 1). The sensor is mounted in the cylinder head on the right-hand side **(see illustration 3.5)**.

7 Disconnect the sensor wiring connector. Unscrew and remove the sensor, and discard the sealing washer.

8 Fit a new sealing washer onto the sensor. Fit the sensor and tighten it to the torque setting specified at the beginning of the Chapter for your model. Connect the wiring.

9 Refill the cooling system (see Chapter 1) and check the coolant level (see *Pre-ride checks*).

4 Thermostat

1 The thermostat is automatic in operation and should give many years service without requiring attention. In the event of a failure, the valve will probably jam open, in which case the engine will take much longer than normal to warm up. Conversely, if the valve jams shut, the coolant will be unable to circulate and the engine will overheat. Neither condition is acceptable, and the fault must be investigated promptly.

Removal

Warning: The engine must be completely cool before carrying out this procedure.

2 Drain the cooling system (see Chapter 1). The thermostat housing is in the back of the cylinder head on the right-hand side.

3 If required release the hose clamp and detach the hose **(see illustration)**.

4 Unscrew the cover bolts and detach it from the cylinder head **(see illustration)**.

5 Withdraw the thermostat, noting how it fits **(see illustration)**.

Check

6 Examine the thermostat visually before carrying out the test. If it remains in the open position at room temperature, it should be replaced with a new one.

7 Suspend the thermostat by a piece of wire in a container of cold water. Suspend a thermometer capable of reading temperatures up to 110°C in the water so that the bulb is close to the thermostat **(see illustration)**. Make sure neither the thermostat nor thermometer touches the container. Heat the water, noting the temperature when the thermostat opens, and compare the result with the specifications given at the beginning of the Chapter. Also check the amount the valve opens after it has been heated for a few minutes and compare the measurement to the specifications. If the readings obtained differ from those given, the thermostat is faulty and must be replaced with a new one.

8 In the event of thermostat failure, if the thermostat is permanently closed, as an emergency measure only it can be removed and the machine used without it (this is better than leaving it in as the engine will overheat). If it is permanently open you are better to leave it in. In both cases take care when starting the engine from cold as it will take much longer than usual to warm up. Ensure that a new unit is installed as soon as possible.

Installation

9 Make sure the thermostat seal is in good condition – if not fit a new thermostat.

10 Fit the thermostat into the housing with the hole at the top **(see illustration)**.

11 Fit the cover and tighten the bolts to the

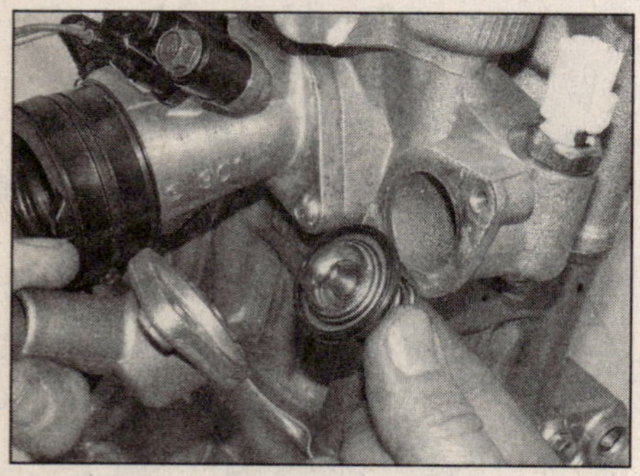

4.5 ... then withdraw the thermostat from the housing

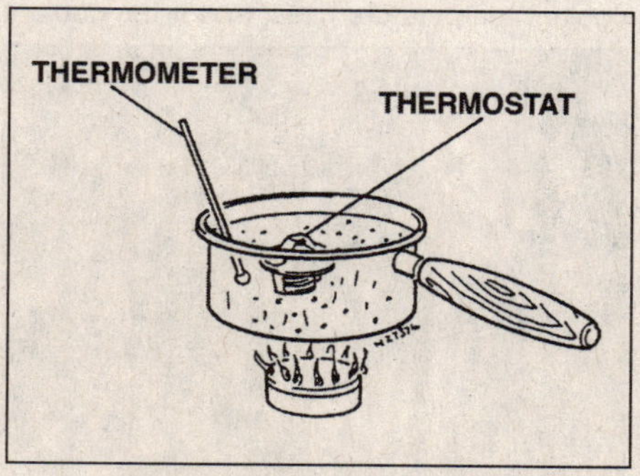

4.7 Thermostat testing set-up

4.10 Fit the thermostat with the hole (arrowed) at the top

5.4a On WR models detach the hoses (arrowed)

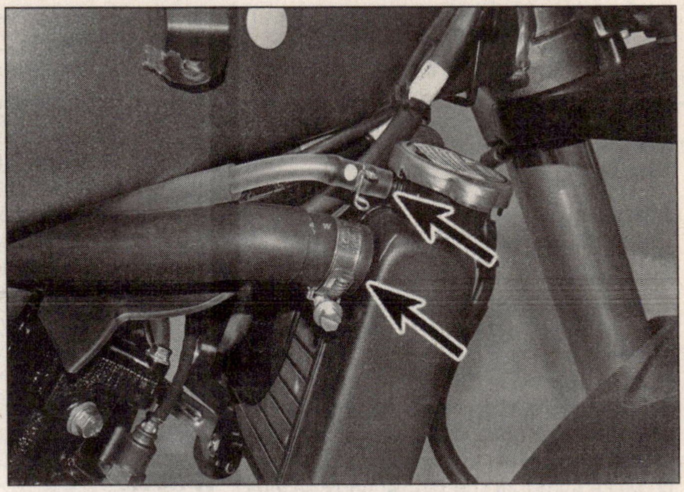

5.4b On MT and YZF-R models detach the hoses (arrowed) from the right-hand side of the radiator...

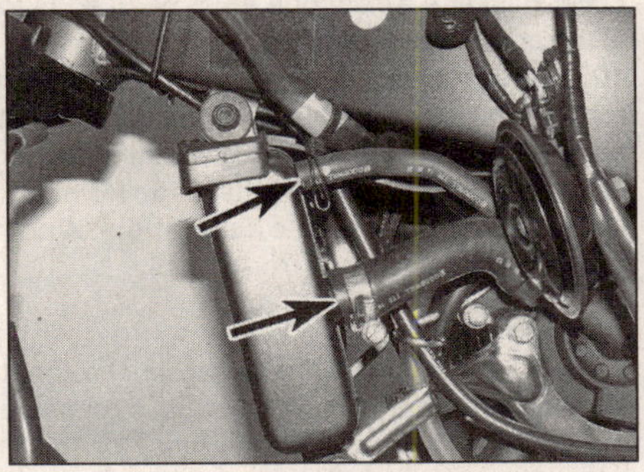

5.4c ... and from the left-hand side

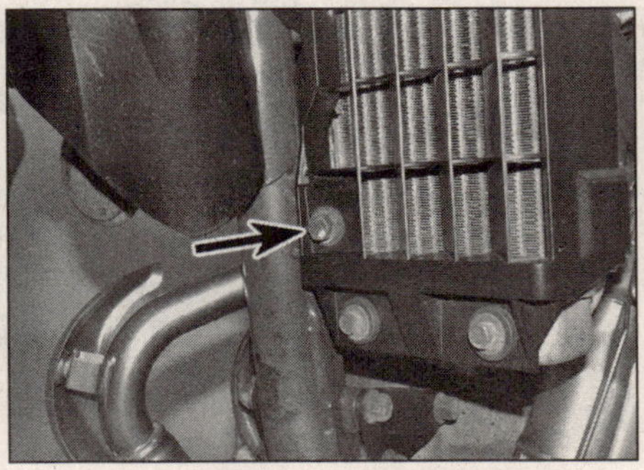

5.5a Unscrew the lower bolt (arrowed)...

5.5b ... then the upper bolt (arrowed)

torque setting specified at the beginning of the Chapter **(see illustration 4.4)**.

12 If detached fit the hose and tighten the clamp **(see illustration 4.3)**. Refill the cooling system (see Chapter 1) and check the coolant level (see *Pre-ride checks*).

5 Radiator

Note: *If the radiator is being removed as part of the engine removal procedure, detach the hoses from their unions on the engine rather than on the radiator and remove the radiator complete with its hoses. Note the routing of the hoses.*

Removal

⚠ ***Warning: The engine must be completely cool before carrying out this procedure.***

1 Drain the cooling system (see Chapter 1).

2 On MT and YZF-R models remove the fuel tank (see Chapter 4).

3 Disconnect the cooling fan wiring connector **(see illustration 2.10a or b)**.

4 Release the clamps securing the hoses to the radiator and detach them **(see illustrations)**.

5 On WR models unscrew the two bolts and remove the radiator **(see illustration)**. On 2009 and 2010 models remove the guard and mounting bracket from the radiator if required, and on 2011-on models remove the guard if required. Note the mounting bolt collars on 2011-on models, and the arrangement of the washers, collars and grommets in the bracket or guard mounts, according to model. Replace the grommets with new ones if they are damaged, deformed or deteriorated.

6 On MT and YZF-R models unscrew the two bolts on the left-hand side and the bolt on the right-hand side, noting the washers, and on models with ABS how the upper bolts secure the brake hose bracket, and remove the radiator, bringing the rubber cover with it or releasing it from the mounts and leaving it behind, as required **(see illustrations)**. Note the arrangement of the sleeves (left-hand mounts only) and rubber grommets in the radiator mounts. Replace the grommets with new ones if they are damaged, deformed or deteriorated.

5.6a Unscrew the bolts (arrowed)...

5.6b ... and the bolt (arrowed)

7 Check the radiator for signs of damage and clear any dirt or debris that might obstruct air flow and inhibit cooling. If the radiator fins are badly damaged or broken the radiator must be replaced with a new one. To enable full examination and cleaning, remove the cooling fan from the radiator (see Section 2).

Installation

8 Installation is the reverse of removal, noting the following.

- Make sure the coolant hoses are in good condition (see Chapter 1), and are securely retained by their clamps, using new ones if necessary.
- Make sure the rubber grommets and collars, sleeves and washers are correctly fitted, according to model.
- Make sure that the fan wiring is securely connected.
- On completion refill the cooling system as described in Chapter 1 and check the coolant level (see *Pre-ride checks*).

Pressure cap check

9 If problems such as overheating or unexplained loss of coolant occur, check the entire system as described in Chapter 1. The radiator cap opening pressure should be checked by a Yamaha dealer with the special tester required to do the job. If the cap is defective, replace it with a new one.

6 Water pump

Check

1 Refer to Chapter 1, Section 9.

Removal

2 Drain the coolant (see Chapter 1).
3 On MT and YZF-R models remove the fuel tank to improve access, if required (see Chapter 4).
4 Release the clamps securing the hoses to the unions on the pump and detach the hoses **(see illustrations)**.
5 On MT and YZF-R models unscrew the lower mounting bolt for the radiator **(see illustration 5.6a)**.
6 Unscrew the bolts and remove the pump assembly **(see illustrations)**.
7 Remove the O-rings – new ones must be used **(see illustration 6.25)**.

Disassembly

8 Remove the pump (see Steps 2 to 7).
9 Unscrew the cover bolts and remove the radiator bracket (MT and YZF-R models) and the cover **(see illustration)**. Remove the cover gasket – a new one must be used **(see illustrations 6.23b and a)**.
10 Undo the impeller retainer bolts and remove the retainer, the plate and the gasket **(see illustrations)** – note how the retainer locates in the groove in the impeller shaft. Draw the impeller out **(see illustration)**. A new gasket must be used on reassembly.

Inspection

11 Check the impeller bearing in the inner side of the pump. If there is excessive movement, or the bearing is noisy or rough when turned, the bearing must be replaced with a new one.

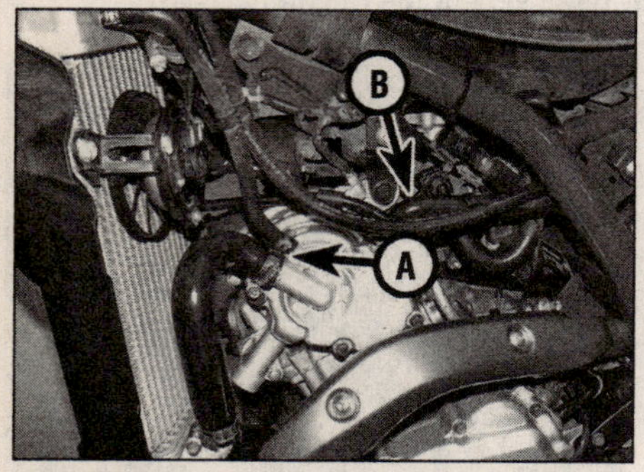

6.4 Release the clamps and detach the coolant hoses (A) and crankcase breather hose (B)

6.6a Unscrew the bolts (arrowed)...

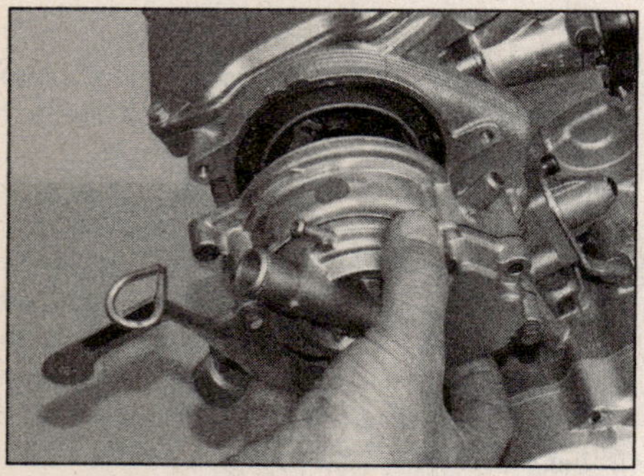

6.6b ...and remove the pump assembly

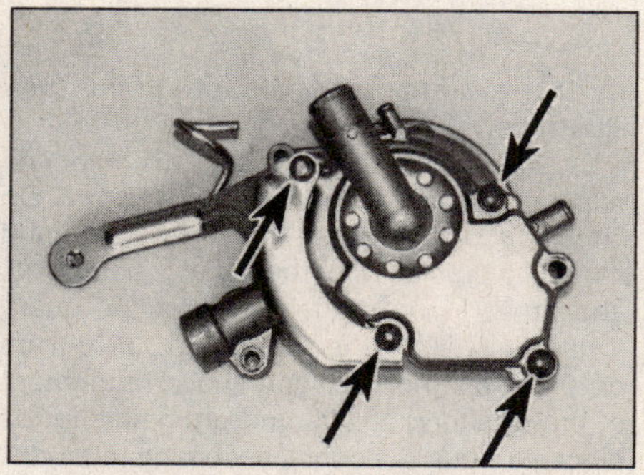

6.9 Unscrew the bolts (arrowed) and remove the cover

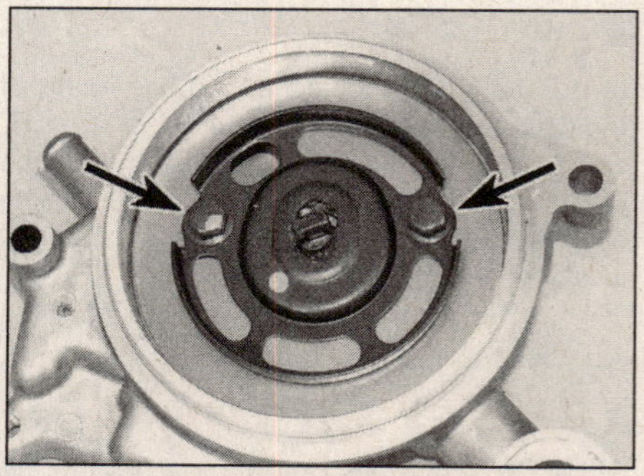

6.10a Undo the bolts (arrowed) and remove the retainer...

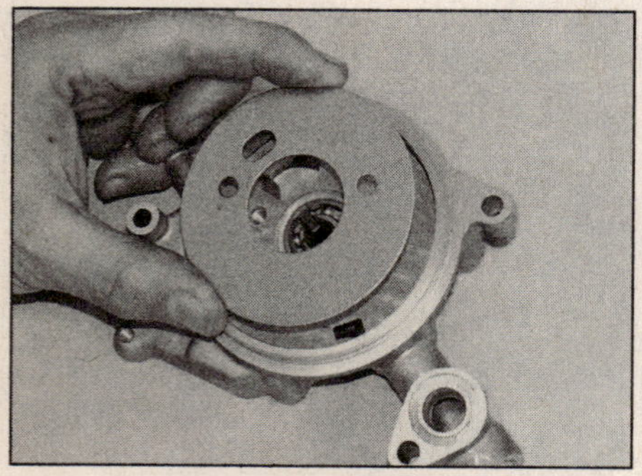

6.10b ...the plate...

6.10c ...and the gasket...

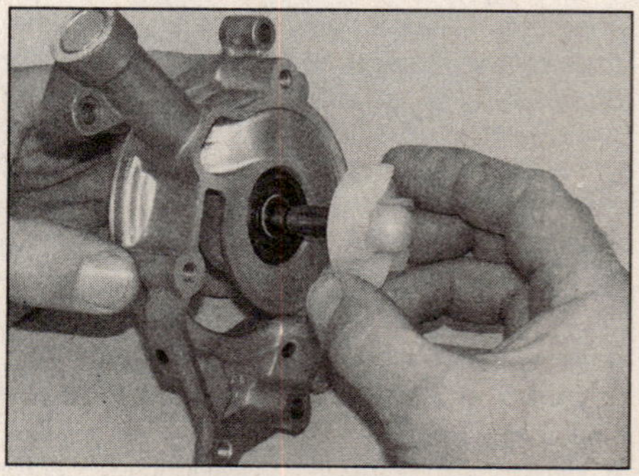

6.10d ...then draw the impeller out

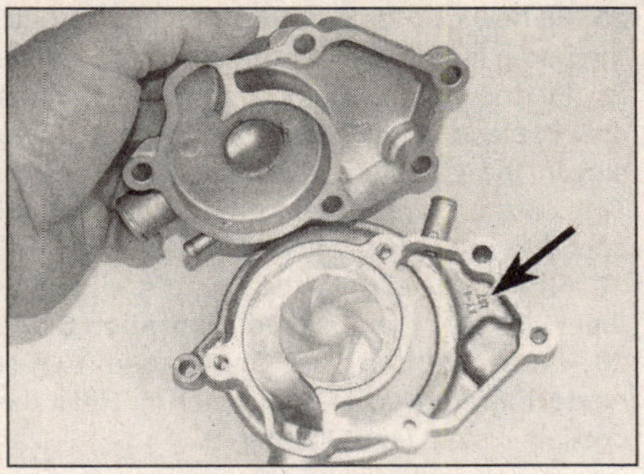

6.14 **The chamber (arrowed) next to the pump is for the crankcase breathing system**

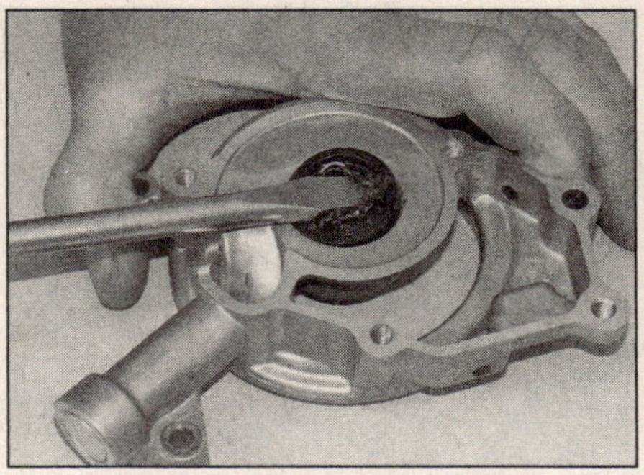

6.16 Lever the seal out...

6.17 ...then drive the bearing out from the outer side

12 Check the condition of the impeller and shaft. If there are signs of wear or other damage, the impeller must be replaced with a new one.

13 Check the condition of the pump mechanical seal. If there is evidence of oil in the coolant or vice versa the seal has failed.

14 Inspect the pump body and cover for corrosion or a build-up of scale and clean with steel wool as necessary, then rinse the pump body in running clean water. Also clean out the crankcase breather chamber of any oil mist **(see illustration)**.

Seal and bearing replacement

15 Remove and disassemble the pump (see Steps 2 to 10).

16 Carefully lever the seal out using a suitable screwdriver or seal hook **(see illustration)**.

17 Drive the bearing out using a socket from the outer side of the pump **(see illustration)**.

18 Clean any traces of sealant from around the mechanical seal seat with a suitable solvent.

19 Drive the new bearing into the pump using a suitable driver or socket located on the outer race until it is seated **(see illustration)**.

20 Press the new seal, with the WATER SIDE mark facing out, into the pump body using either the Yamaha tools (part nos. 90890-04145 and 04058) or the set-up shown or a suitable equivalent **(see illustrations)**. The seal must be set to the correct depth as shown rather than until it seats, so there is an advantage in using the Yamaha tools as they are designed to do this. If using an alternative method make sure the seal rim sits no deeper than 0.5 mm below the rim of its bore, but also does not protrude above it, though it can be flush **(see illustration)**.

Reassembly

21 Lubricate the seal lips and impeller shaft with lithium grease. Slide the impeller shaft into the pump body and through the seal and bearing **(see illustration 6.10d)**.

22 Fit a new gasket, then fit the plate, aligning them as shown **(see illustrations 6.10c and b)**. Fit the retainer over the shaft, then slide it across so it locates in the groove

6.19 Drive the new bearing in from the inner side

6.20a The side marked WATER SIDE...

6.20b ...must face out

6.20c Press or carefully drive the seal in using a socket and piece of wood...

6.20d ...until the rim is set...

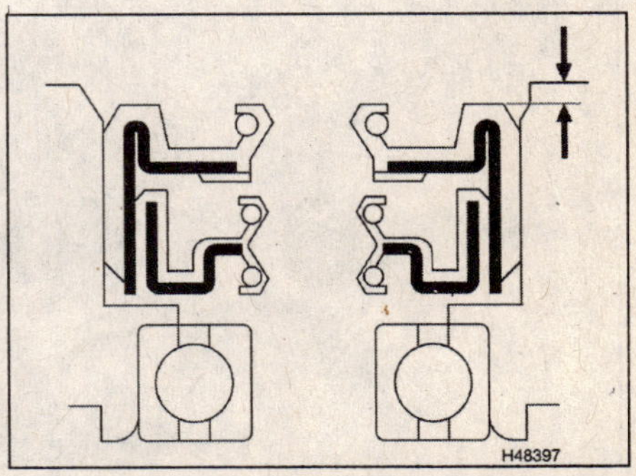

6.20e ...between 0 and 0.5 mm below the rim of the bore

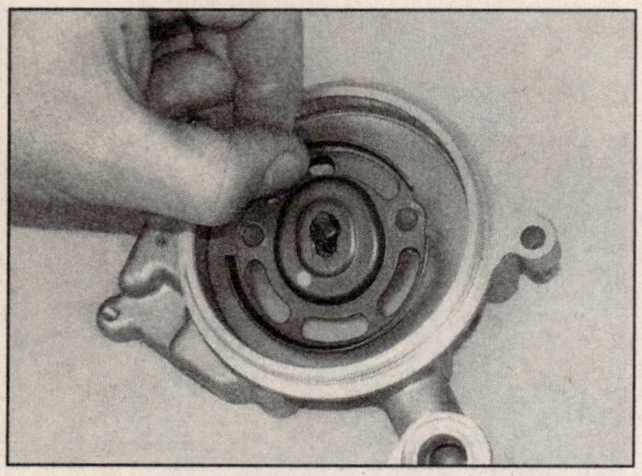

6.22a Fit the retainer over the shaft...

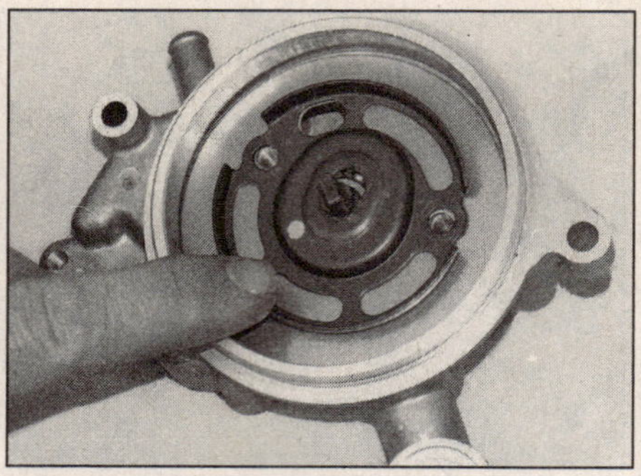

6.22b ... then slide it across to align the bolt holes

(see illustrations). Clean the threads of the retainer bolts, then apply fresh threadlock and tighten them to the torque setting specified at the beginning of the chapter. Turn the impeller by hand and check it turns as it should.

23 Fit a new cover gasket, the cover, and on MT and YZF-R models the radiator bracket, and tighten the cover bolts to the specified torque **(see illustrations)**.

Installation

24 Clean the pump and cylinder head mating surfaces.

25 Fit new O-rings smeared with grease onto the pump **(see illustration)**.

26 Fit the pump, making sure the O-rings stay in place, and locating the drive tab in the slot in the camshaft bolt **(see illustration)**. Tighten the pump bolts to the torque setting specified at the beginning of the Chapter.

27 Fit the hoses onto the pump and secure them with their clamps **(see illustration 6.4)**.

28 Install the fuel tank on MT and YZF-R models if removed (see Chapter 4). Refill the cooling system (see Chapter 1).

7 Coolant reservoir

Removal

1 On WR models the reservoir is behind the left-hand side cover. Remove the side cover

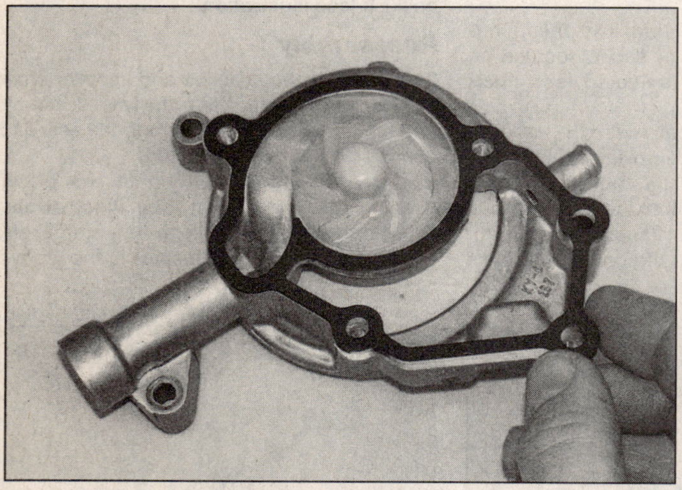

6.23a Fit a new gasket...

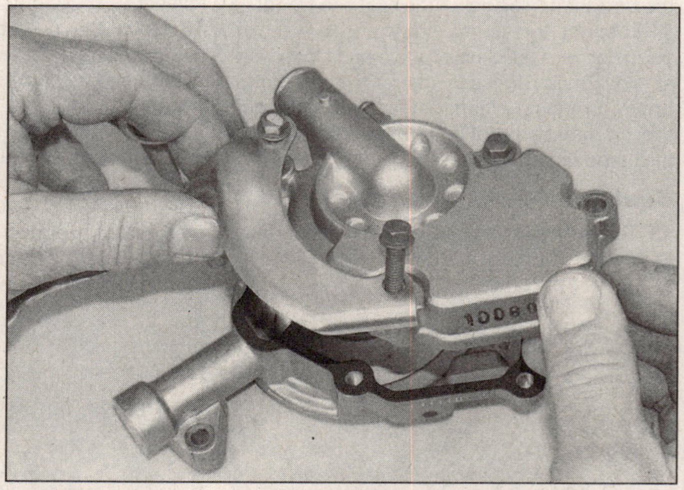

6.23b ... then fit the cover, and bracket on MT and YZF models

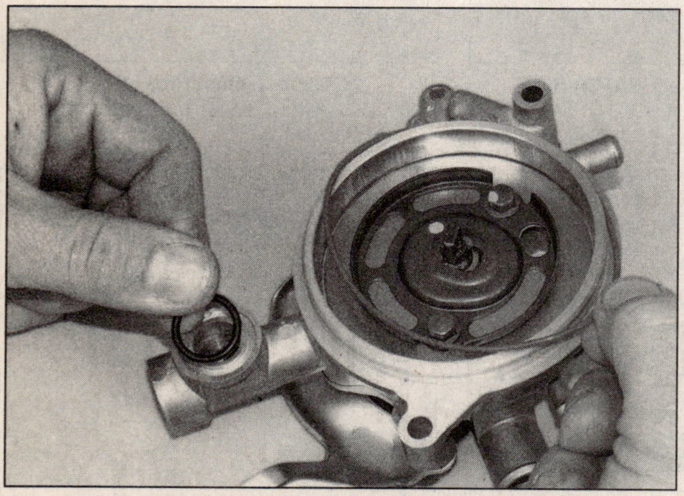

6.25 Fit new O-rings and smear them with grease

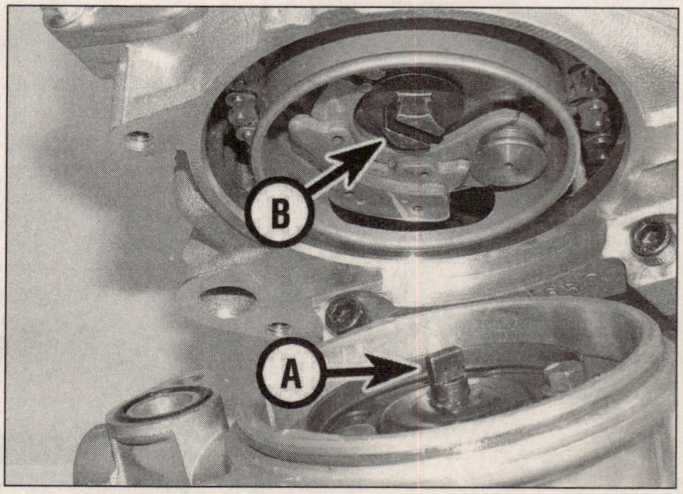

6.26 Locate the drive tab (A) in the slot in the bolt (B)

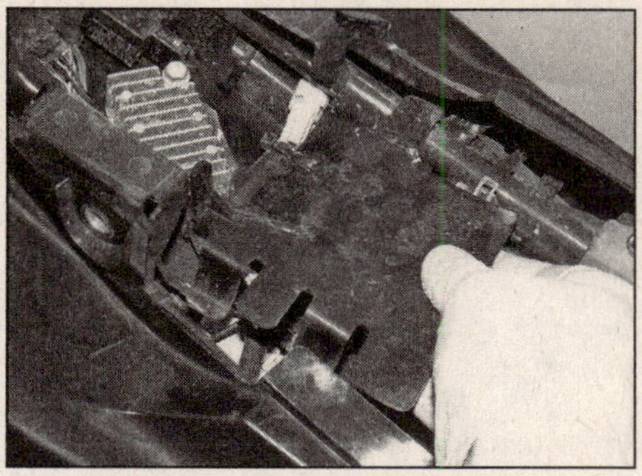

7.1a Remove the frame cover

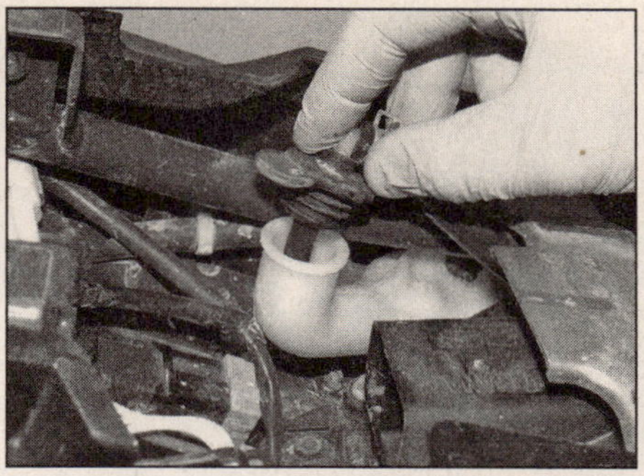

7.1b Release the cap and draw out the hose

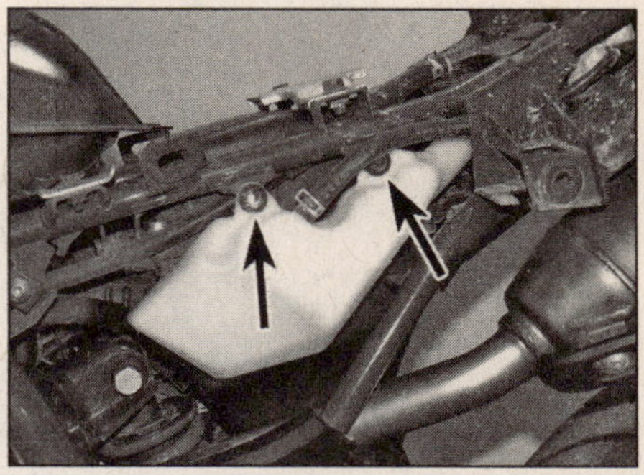

7.1c Reservoir mounting bolts (arrowed)

(see Chapter 7). Get a suitable container to drain the coolant into. Remove the plastic frame cover, then release the reservoir cap and draw the hose out **(see illustrations)**. Unscrew the bolts and remove the reservoir, then tip the coolant into the container **(see illustration)**.

2 On MT models the coolant reservoir is located at the front of the engine on the left side. Get a suitable container to drain the coolant into. Remove the belly-pan (see Chapter 7). Release the reservoir cap and draw the hose out **(see illustration)**. Unscrew the bolts and remove the reservoir, then tip the coolant into the container **(see illustration)**.

3 On YZF-R models the coolant reservoir is located at the front of the engine on the left side. Get a suitable container to drain the coolant into. Remove all sections of fairing on the left-hand side (see Chapter 7). Detach the bottom hose and drain the reservoir **(see illustration)**. Unscrew the bolts and remove the reservoir **(see illustration)**.

Installation

4 Installation is the reverse of removal. Refill the reservoir to the FULL level line with the specified coolant mixture (see *Pre-ride checks*).

8 Coolant hoses

Removal

1 Before removing a hose, drain the coolant (see Chapter 1).

2 Use a screwdriver to release or slacken the larger-bore hose clamps, then slide them back along the hose and clear of the union spigot. The smaller-bore hoses are secured by spring clamps, which can be expanded by squeezing their ears together with pliers.

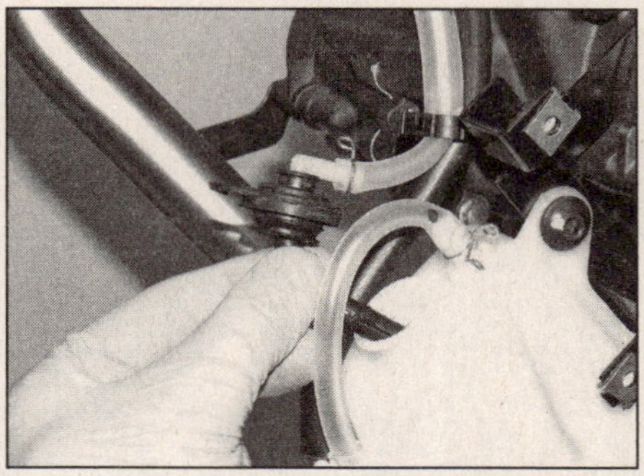

7.2a Release the cap and draw out the hose

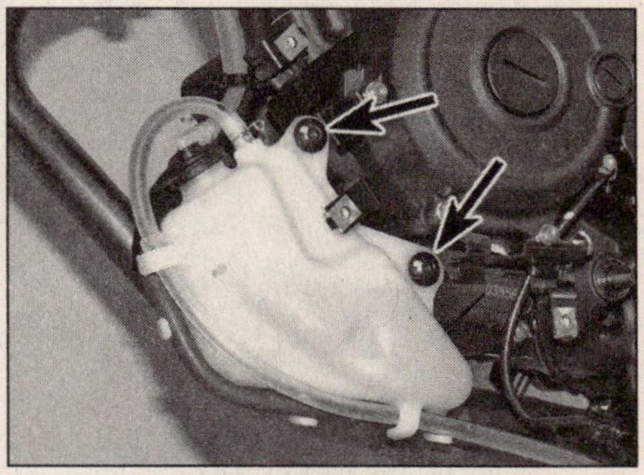

7.2b Reservoir mounting bolts (arrowed)

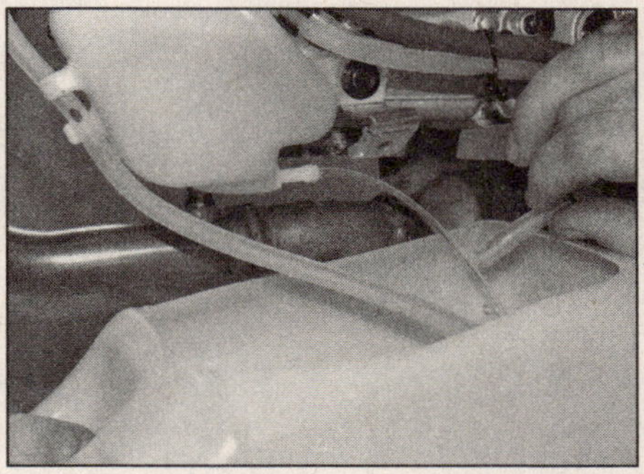

7.3a Detach the bottom hose and drain the reservoir...

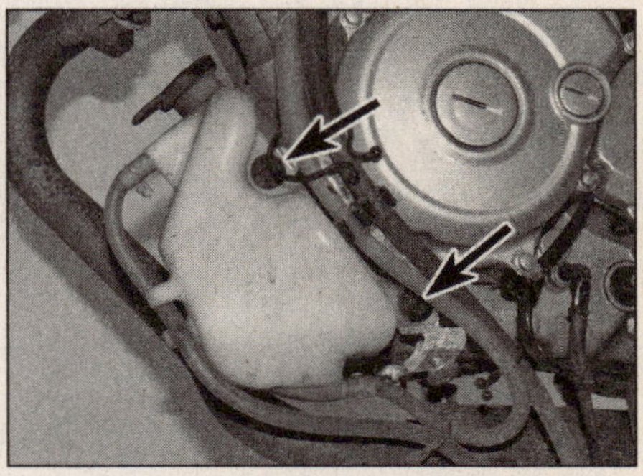

7.3b ...then unscrew the mounting bolts (arrowed)

Caution: The radiator unions are fragile. Do not use excessive force when attempting to remove the hoses.

3 If a hose proves stubborn, release it by rotating it on its union before working it off. If all else fails, cut the hose with a sharp knife. Whilst this means replacing the hose with a new one – it is preferable to buying a new radiator.

Installation

4 Slide the clamps onto the hose and then work the hose on to its union as far as the spigot where present.

HAYNES HiNT ***If the hose is difficult to push on its union, soften it by soaking it in very hot water,or alternatively a little soapy water on the union can be used as a lubricant.***

5 Rotate the hose on its unions to settle it in position with no twist before sliding the clamps into place and tightening them securely.

6 Refill the cooling system with fresh coolant (see Chapter 1) and check the coolant level (see *Pre-ride checks*).

Notes

Chapter 4
Engine management system

Contents

Degrees of difficulty

Easy, suitable for novice with little experience	**Fairly easy,** suitable for beginner with some experience	**Fairly difficult,** suitable for competent DIY mechanic	**Difficult,** suitable for experienced DIY mechanic	**Very difficult,** suitable for expert DIY or professional

Specifications

Fuel

Grade	Unleaded. Minimum 95 RON
Fuel tank	
WR models	
Capacity (including reserve)	8.5 litres
Reserve volume (when bottom segment of gauge flashes)	1.6 litres
MT and YZF-R models	
Capacity (including reserve)	11.5 litres
Reserve volume (when bottom segment flashes and warning symbols come on)	3.0 litres

Ignition system

Spark plug	see Chapter 1
Primary winding resistance	2.16 to 2.64 ohms @ 20°C
Secondary winding resistance (without cap)	8.64 to 12.96 K-ohms @ 20°C
Spark plug cap resistance	approx 5 K-ohms @ 20°C

Fuel injection system

Throttle body	
WR models	
Type	Mikuni SE AC28-2/1
ID mark	5D71 00
MT and YZF-R models	
Type	Mikuni SE AC28-12/1
ID mark	5D78 10
Idle speed	
WR models	1400 to 1600 rpm
MT and YZF-R models	1350 to 1550 rpm
Crankshaft position (CKP) sensor resistance	248 to 372 ohms @ 20°C
Engine coolant temperature (ECT) sensor resistance	
WR models	
Resistance @ 20°C	2.32 to 2.59 K-ohms
Resistance @ 80°C	310 to 326 ohms
MT and YZF-R models	
Resistance @ 20°C	2.51 to 2.78 K-ohms
Resistance @ 100°C	210 to 221 ohms
Fuel pressure (at idle speed)	36.3 psi (2.5 Bar)
Intake air pressure (IAP) sensor output voltage	4.7 to 5.2 volts
Intake air temperature (IAT) sensor resistance	5.7 to 6.3 K-ohms
Speed sensor voltage	0.6 to 4.8 V fluctuating
Throttle position sensor	
Input voltage	5 V
Output voltage (throttle closed)	0.63 to 0.73 V
Tip-over (TO) sensor output voltage	
Sensor upright	0.4 to 1.4 V
Sensor tilted more than 65°	3.7 to 4.4 V
Fuel injector resistance	approx. 12.5 ohms
Fast idle solenoid resistance	31.5 to 38.5 ohms

Torque settings

Air induction system reed valve housing bolts	10 Nm
Exhaust system	
WR models	
Header pipe nuts	20 Nm
Middle mounting bolt	27 Nm
Silencer mounting bolt	27 Nm
Silencer clamp bolt	18 Nm
MT and YZF-R models	
Header pipe nuts	15 Nm
Middle mounting bolt	32 Nm
Silencer mounting bolt	20 Nm
Fuel pump bolts (WR models)	4 Nm
Fuel pump nuts (MT and YZF-R models)	10 Nm
Fuel tank mounting bolts	10 Nm
Intake duct bolts	10 Nm
Oxygen sensor (MT and YZF-R models)	25 Nm

1 General information and precautions

Fuel system

1 The fuel supply system consists of the fuel tank, an internal and integrated fuel pump, strainer, filter, pressure regulator and level sensor, the fuel hose, fuel injector, throttle body, and throttle cable(s). The injection system supplies fuel and air to the engine via a single throttle body. The injector is operated by the Electronic Control Unit (ECU) using the information obtained from the sensors it monitors (refer to Section 5 for more information on the operation of the fuel injection system). Cold start idle speed is controlled by the fast idle unit that is controlled by the ECU.

2 Air is drawn into the throttle body via an air filter fitted in a housing behind the throttle body.

3 The exhaust system contains twin catalytic converters.

4 There is a digital fuel gauge in the instrument cluster, actuated by a level sensor inside the fuel tank – when the bottom segment starts to flash there is approximately 1.6 litres of fuel left on WR models, and 3.0 litres on MT and YZF-R models.

Ignition system

5 All models are fitted with a fully transistorised electronic ignition system which, due to its lack of mechanical parts, is totally maintenance-free. The system comprises a set of triggers, a crankshaft position (CKP) sensor, electronic control unit (ECU), and ignition coil (refer to Wiring Diagrams for details).

6 The ignition triggers, which are on the generator rotor on the left-hand end of the crankshaft, magnetically operate the crankshaft position sensor as the crankshaft rotates. The sensor sends a signal to the electronic control unit, which then supplies the ignition coil with the power necessary to produce a spark at the plug.

7 The ECU incorporates an electronic advance system.

8 The system has a starter safety circuit, comprising the neutral switch, the clutch switch, and the sidestand switch, that prevents the engine from being started unless it is in neutral, or if it is in gear unless the clutch lever is pulled in and the sidestand is up.

9 Because of their nature, the individual ignition system components can be checked but not repaired. If ignition system troubles occur, and the faulty component can be isolated, the only cure for the problem is to replace the part with a new one. Keep in mind that most electrical parts, once purchased, cannot be returned. To avoid unnecessary expense, make very sure the faulty component has been positively identified before buying a replacement part.

10 Note that there is no provision for adjusting the ignition timing.

Precautions

Warning: Petrol (gasoline) is extremely flammable, so take extra precautions when you work on any part of the fuel system. Always remove the battery (see Chapter 8). Don't smoke or allow open flames or bare light bulbs near the work area, and don't work in a garage where a natural gas-type appliance is present. If you spill any fuel on your skin, rinse it off immediately with soap and water. When you perform any kind of work on the fuel system, wear safety glasses and have a fire extinguisher suitable for a class B type fire (flammable liquids) on hand.

11 Residual pressure will remain in the fuel supply hose and fuel injector after the motorcycle has been used. Before disconnecting any fuel hose, ensure the ignition is switched OFF and have some rag handy to catch any fuel. It is vital that no dirt or debris is allowed to enter the fuel system. Any foreign matter could result in injector damage or malfunction. Ensure the ignition is switched OFF before disconnecting or reconnecting any fuel injection system wiring connector. If a connector is disconnected or reconnected with the ignition switched ON, the electronic control unit (ECU) may be damaged.

12 Always perform service procedures in a well-ventilated area to prevent a build-up of fumes.

13 Never work in a building containing a gas appliance with a pilot light, or any other form of naked flame. Ensure that there are no naked light bulbs or any sources of flame or sparks nearby.

14 Do not smoke (or allow anyone else to smoke) while in the vicinity of petrol (gasoline) or of components containing it. Remember the possible presence of vapour from these sources and move well clear before smoking.

15 Check all electrical equipment belonging to the house, garage or workshop where work is being undertaken (see the Safety first! section of this manual). Remember that certain electrical appliances such as drills, cutters etc, create sparks in the normal course of operation and must not be used near petrol (gasoline) or any component containing it. Again, remember the possible presence of fumes before using electrical equipment.

16 Always mop up any spilt fuel and safely dispose of the rag used.

17 Any stored fuel that is drained off during servicing work must be kept in sealed containers that are suitable for holding petrol (gasoline), and clearly marked as such; the containers themselves should be kept in a safe place. Note that this last point applies equally to the fuel tank if it is removed from the machine; also remember to keep its filler cap closed at all times.

18 Read the Safety first! section of this manual carefully before starting work.

2 Fuel tank

Warning: Refer to the precautions given in Section 1 before starting work.

Draining

1 The best way to drain the tank is to use a pump, cheaply available at any good parts shop.

2 Remove the filler cap, insert the suction end of the pump in the tank and the expulsion end into a container suitable and large enough for storing the fuel, then pump away, moving the suction nozzle around all the extremities of the tank, until empty. Refit the filler cap.

Removal

WR models

3 Remove the fuel tank cover (see Chapter 7).

4 Slide the fuel hose connector security clip down **(see illustration)**. Have a rag ready to catch any residual fuel. Press the release tabs in and pull the hose off its union **(see illustration)**.

5 Make sure the fuel filler cap is secure. Unscrew the rear bolts **(see illustration)**.

6 Unscrew the front bolt, noting the collar **(see illustration)**.

7 Carefully lift and support the rear of the tank, and disconnect the fuel pump wiring connector **(see illustration)**. Remove the tank.

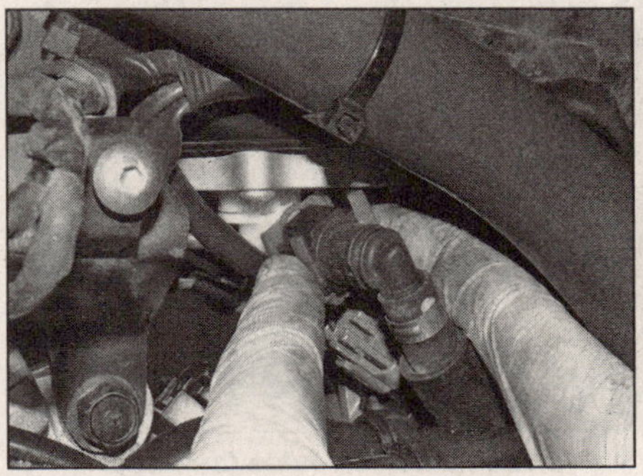

2.4a Slide the security clip down...

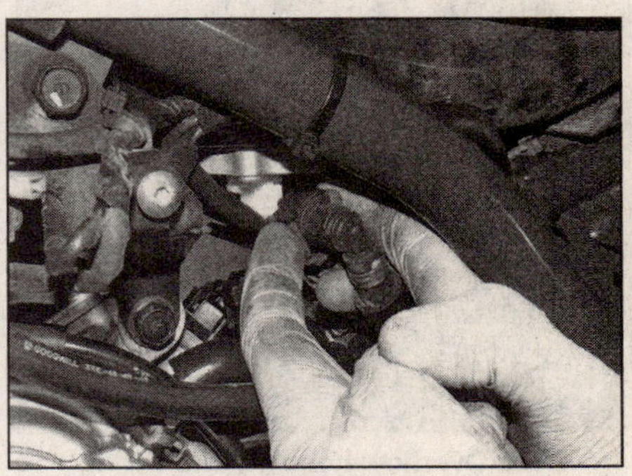

2.4b ...then press the tabs in and pull the hose off

2.5 Unscrew the bolt (arrowed) on each side

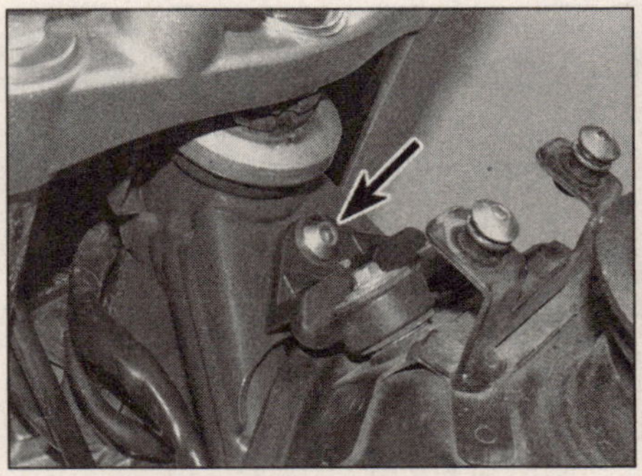

2.6 Unscrew the bolt (arrowed)

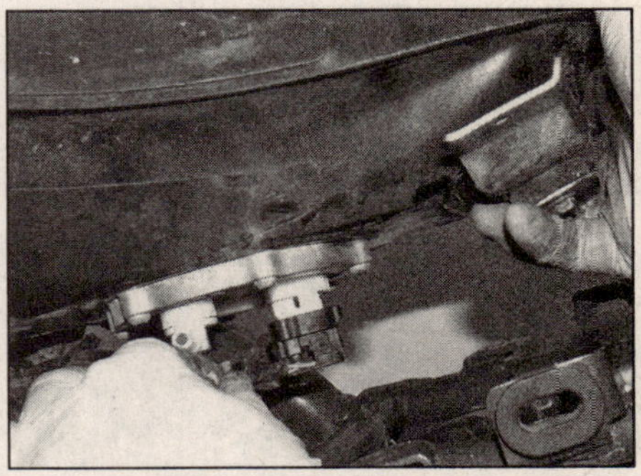

2.7 Lift the tank and disconnect the wiring

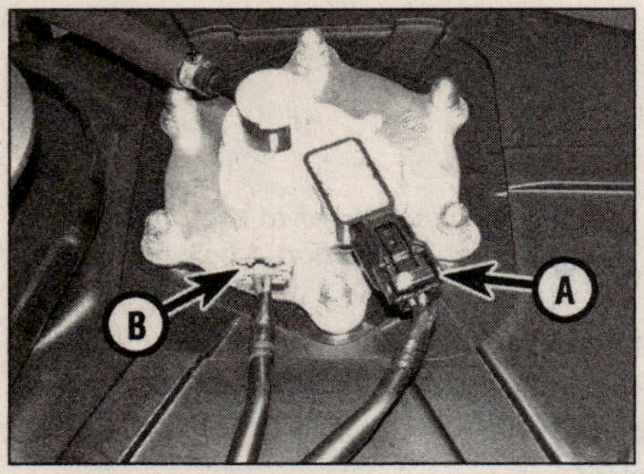

2.10 Fuel pump wiring connector (A), fuel level sender wiring connector (B)

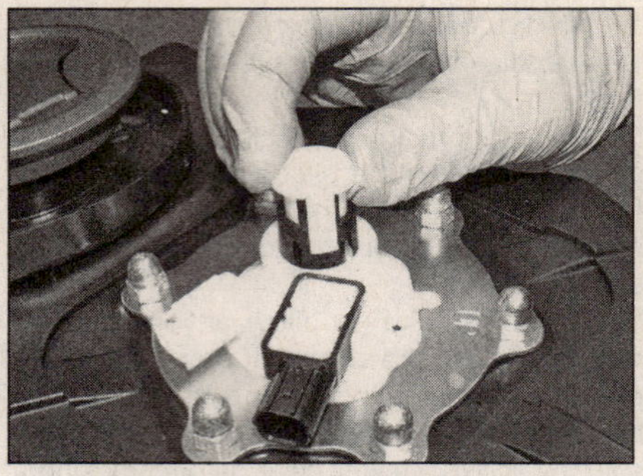

2.11a Press the clip in and remove the cover

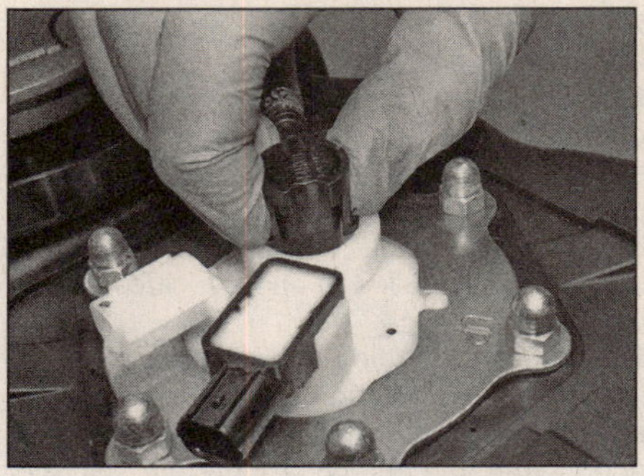

2.11b Press the tabs in and pull the connector off

8 Inspect the tank mounting rubbers for signs of damage or deterioration and replace them with new ones if necessary.

MT and YZF-R models

9 Remove the fuel tank cover (see Chapter 7).
10 Disconnect the fuel pump and level sender wiring connectors **(see illustration)**.
11 Remove the fuel hose connector cover **(see illustration)**. Have a rag ready to catch any residual fuel. Press the release tabs in and pull the hose off its union **(see illustrations)**
12 Detach the overflow hose and release it and the wiring from the guides **(see illustration)**. Release the fuel hose from its guide **(see illustration)**.
13 Make sure the fuel filler cap is secure. Unscrew the rear bolts, noting the washers **(see illustration)**
14 Unscrew the front bolt, noting the washer **(see illustration)**.
15 Carefully lift the tank and remove it.
16 Remove the collar from the underside of the front mount for safekeeping **(see illustration)**.
17 Inspect the tank mounting rubbers for signs of damage or deterioration and replace them with new ones if necessary.

Installation

18 Installation is the reverse of removal, noting the following:

- Make sure the tank rubbers and mounting parts are correctly fitted.
- Tighten the tank mounting bolts to the torque setting specified at the beginning of the Chapter.
- Make sure the fuel hose is fully pushed onto the union until it clicks into place, then make sure you cannot pull it off again. On WR models push the security clip back up *(see illustration 2.4a)*. On MT and YZF-R models fit the connector cover (see illustration 2.11a).
- Make sure the wiring connector(s) is/are securely connected.
- On MT and YZF models make sure the overflow hose is correctly fitted. Make sure the hoses and wiring are secured in the guides (see illustrations 2.12a and b).
- Start the engine and check that there is no sign of fuel leakage, then turn it off.

Fuel tank storage, cleaning and repair

19 If the fuel tank is removed from the bike, it should not be placed in an area where sparks or open flames could ignite the fumes coming out of the tank. Be especially careful inside garages where a natural gas-type appliance is located, because the pilot light could cause an explosion.
20 Any repairs to the fuel tank should be carried out by a professional who has experience in this critical and potentially dangerous work.

3 Fuel pressure check

Note: *Special Tool: A fuel pressure gauge is required for this procedure.*

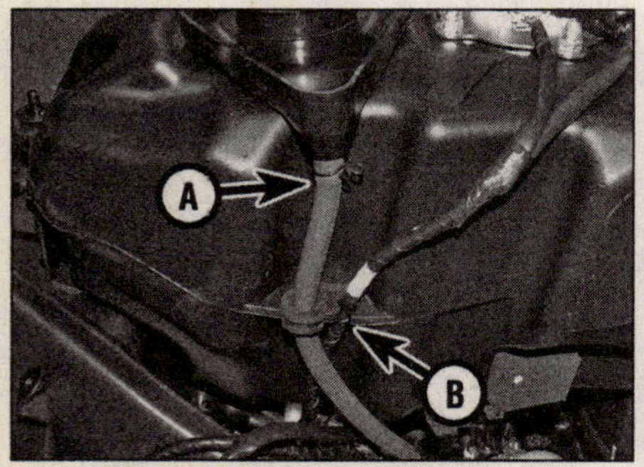

2.12a Overflow hose (A) and wiring guide (B)

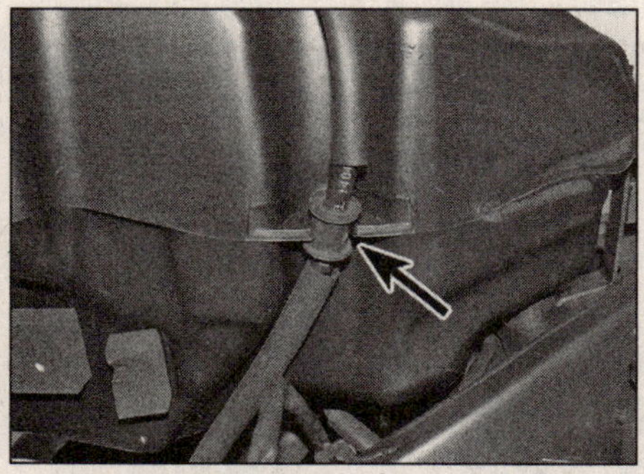

2.12b Fuel hose guide (arrowed)

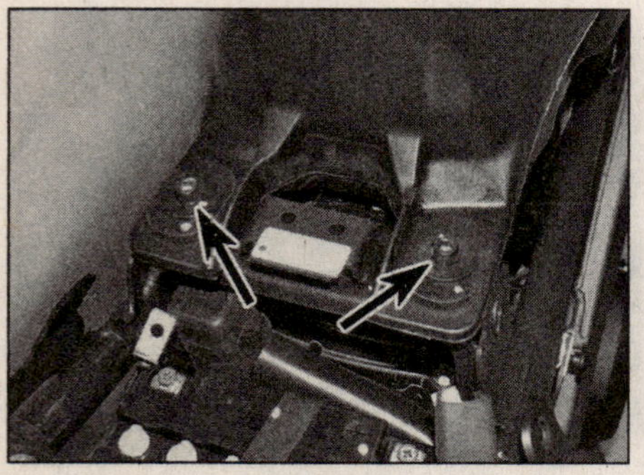

2.13 Unscrew the bolts (arrowed)

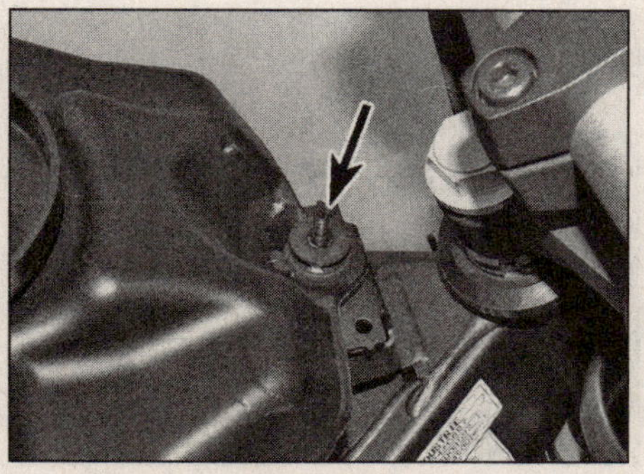

2.14 Unscrew the bolt and remove the washer

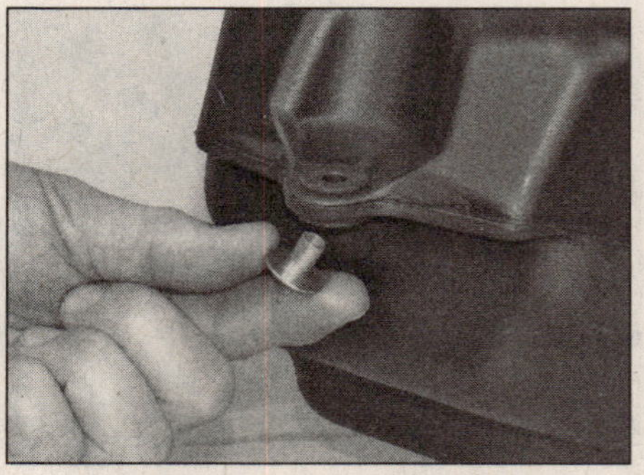

2.16 Remove the collar from the front mount

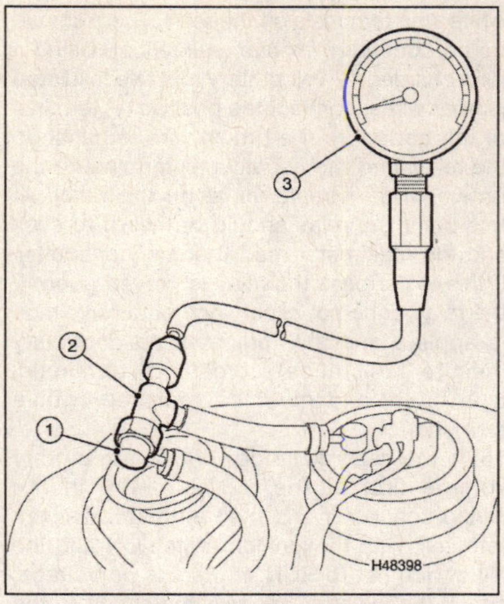

3.3 Fuel pressure test set-up

1 Fuel hose 2 Adapter 3 Pressure gauge

1 To check the fuel pressure, a suitable gauge and adapter hose (Yamaha part. Nos. 90890-03153, and 90890-03186 on WR models, and 90890-03181 on MT and YZF-R models) are needed. Remove the fuel tank cover (see Chapter 7).

2 Disconnect the fuel hose from the pump (see Section 2).

3 Connect the adapter and gauge between the hose and the pump as shown **(see illustration)**.

4 Start the engine and check the pressure with the engine idling. It should be as specified at the beginning of this Chapter.

5 Turn the ignition OFF and remove the gauge assembly, using a rag to catch any residual fuel.

6 Reconnect the fuel hose (see Section 2).

7 If the pressure is too low, check for a leak in the fuel supply system from the tank to the injector – any leak should be obvious. If there is no leak the pressure regulator could be faulty, the pick-up in the pump could be blocked, or the pump could be faulty. The pressure regulator is part of the pump. Refer to Section 4 to check the pump.

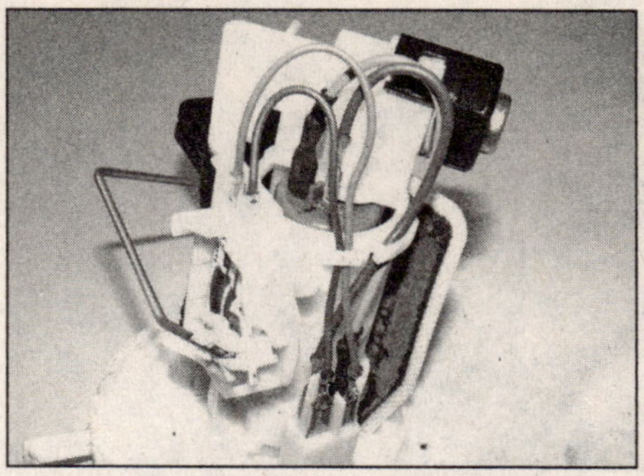

4.3 Make sure all the internal wiring is secure – WR model pump shown

8 If the pressure is too high, either the pressure regulator or the fuel pump check valve is faulty or the injector could be clogged. Check the pump and injector.

4 Fuel pump

Check

1 The fuel pump is inside the fuel tank. With the kill switch in the RUN position, when the ignition is switched ON it should be possible to hear the pump run for a few seconds until the system is up to pressure. If you can't hear anything, first make sure the battery is charged and the ignition fuse is good (see Chapter 8).

2 Next remove the fuel tank cover (see Chapter 7). Disconnect the wiring connector from the pump (see Section 2). With the ignition switch ON and the kill switch set to RUN check for battery voltage at the red/white wire terminal in the connector using a multimeter. If there is no voltage check the circuit back to the ignition switch via the kill switch for continuity, then check the switch itself – refer to *Electrical System Fault Finding* at the beginning of Chapter 8 and the wiring diagram at the end of it. If that side of the circuit is good check the yellow/black (WR models) or yellow (MT and YZF-R models) wire from the connector to the ECU.

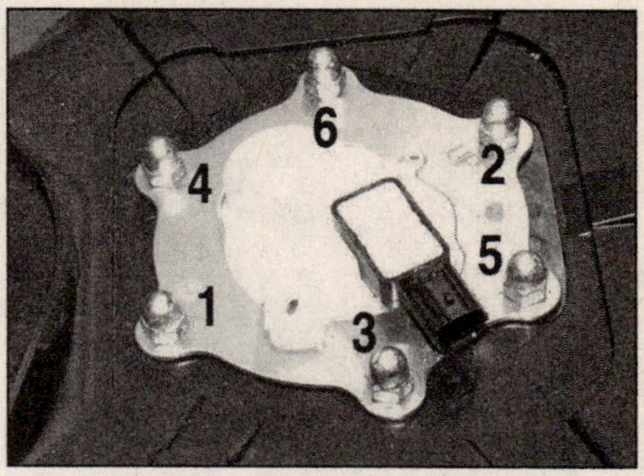

4.6 Fuel pump nuts (MT/YZF-R type shown) – numbers denote tightening sequence

3 To confirm the pump is faulty connect the positive (+) terminal of a fully charged 12V battery to the red/white wire terminal in the pump socket using an auxiliary lead, and connect the negative (-) terminal to the yellow/black or yellow wire terminal – the pump should operate. If it doesn't, remove the pump (see below) and check the internal wiring connectors **(see illustration)**. If they are all good replace the pump with a new one.

4 If the pump is working check all the other components in the circuit, including the starter circuit relay and diodes (see Chapter 8), and the fuel pump relay on MT and YZF-R models with ABS (see below).

Removal

5 On WR models remove the fuel tank (see Section 2). On MT and YZF-R models remove the fuel tank cover (see Chapter 7).

6 Unscrew the pump bolts or nuts and remove the retaining ring **(see illustration)**.

7 Carefully lift the pump out of the tank **(see illustrations)**.

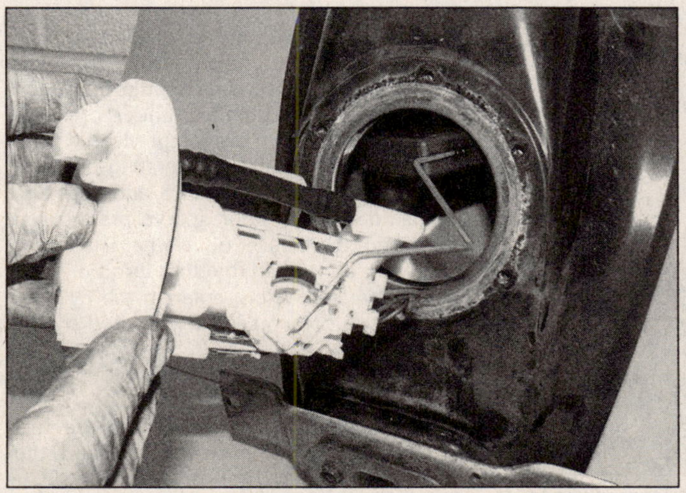

4.7a Removing the pump on WR models – take care not to snag the float arm

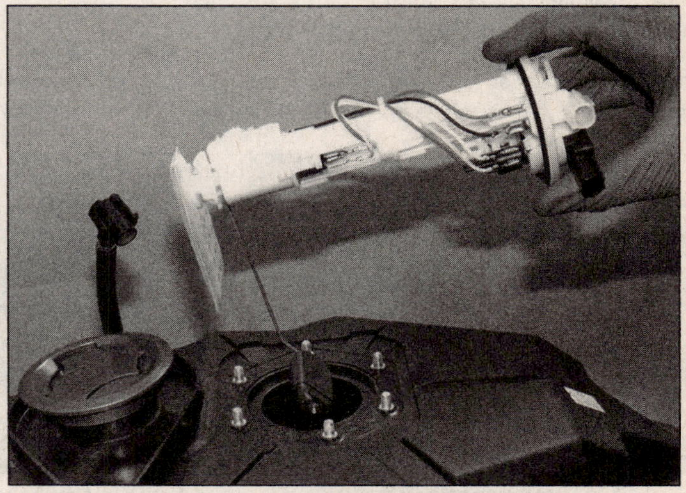

4.7b Removing the pump on MT and YZF-R models – take care not to snag the float arm

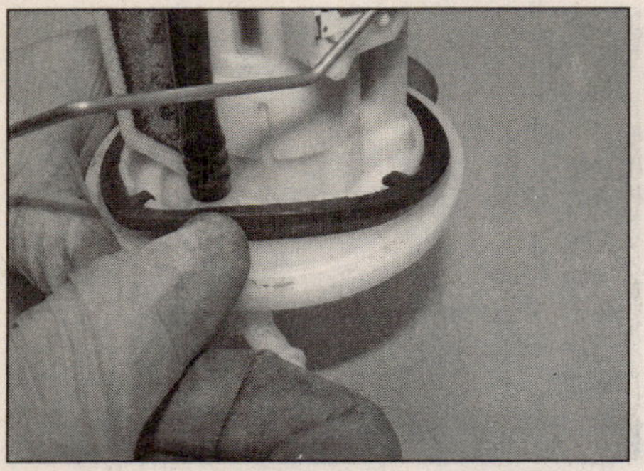

4.9a On WR models fit the sealing ring with the flat side facing up and locate the tabs in the cut-outs

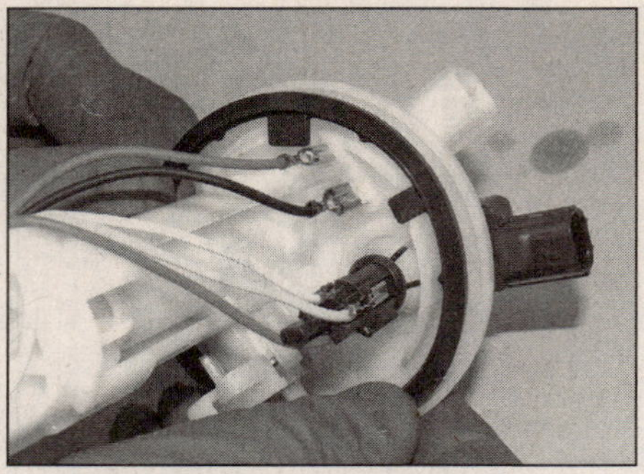

4.9b On MT and YZF-R models fit the sealing ring with the flat side seating against the pump base and locate the tabs in the cut-outs

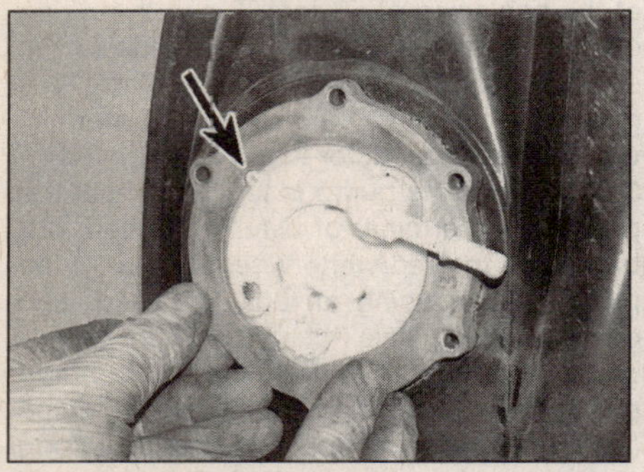

4.10a On WR models position the pump as shown and locate the cut-out in the ring (arrowed) around the peg

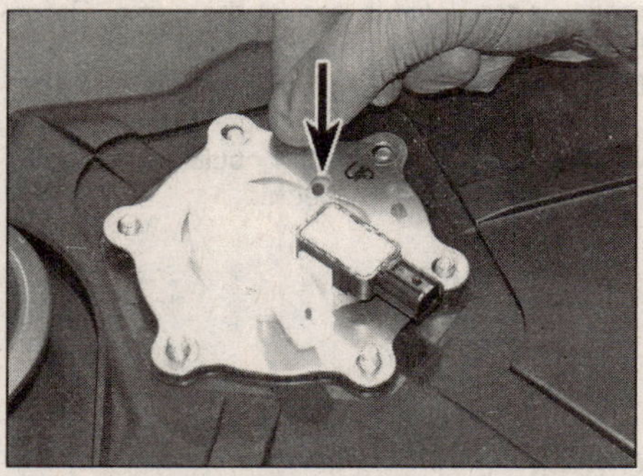

4.10b On MT and YZF-R models position the pump as shown, fit the ring with the UP mark facing up and locate the cut-out (arrowed) around the peg

8 Remove the sealing ring, noting which way round it fits **(see illustration 4.9a or b)** – a new one must be used.

Installation

9 Fit a new sealing ring onto the pump **(see illustrations)**.

10 Carefully manoeuvre the pump into the tank **(see illustration 4.7a or b)** – when seated make sure it is orientated as shown, then fit the retaining ring, locating the cut-out around the peg on the pump base **(see illustrations)**.

11 Fit the bolts or nuts and tighten them evenly and a little at a time in the sequence shown **(see illustration 4.6)** and to the torque setting specified at the beginning of the Chapter for your model.

12 On WR models install the tank, and on all models install the tank cover. Check for leaks around the pump base, particularly on WR models.

Fuel pump relay (MT and YZF-R models with ABS)

Check

13 Remove the relay (see below).

14 Set a multimeter to the ohms x 1 scale and connect it across the red/blue and red/white wire terminals on the relay. There should be no continuity (infinite resistance). Using a fully-charged 12 volt battery and two insulated jumper wires, connect the positive (+) terminal of the battery to the brown wire terminal on the relay, and the negative (–) terminal to the brown/white wire terminal on the relay. At this point the relay should be heard to click and the multimeter read 0 ohms (continuity). If this is the case the relay is proved good. If the relay does not click when battery voltage is applied and still indicates no continuity (infinite resistance) across its terminals, it is faulty and must be replaced with a new one.

15 If the relay is good, check for battery voltage first at the red/blue wire in the wiring connector and then at the brown wire terminal, with the ignition switch ON and the kill switch set to RUN. If there is no voltage, check the wiring in the relevant circuit to the connector for continuity, referring to *Electrical System Fault Finding* at the beginning of Chapter 8 and the relevant wiring diagram at the end of it. If voltage is present, check that there is continuity in the red/white wire to the pump and in the brown/white wire to earth. There should be continuity in all wires.

Removal and installation

16 Remove the passenger seat (see Chapter 7).

17 Locate the relay and displace it from its mount, then disconnect the wiring connector **(see illustrations)**. If required remove the relay from its holder.

18 Installation is the reverse of removal.

4.17a Fuel pump relay (arrowed) – MT models shown

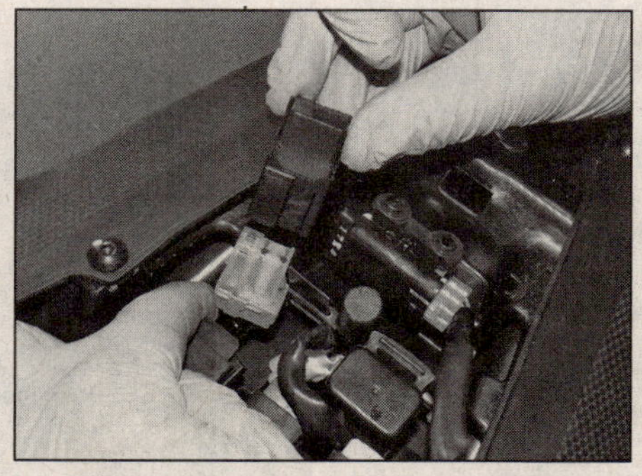

4.17b Displace the relay then disconnect the wiring connector

5 Engine management system description

1 The management system consists of the fuel injection circuit and the electronic control circuit.

2 The fuel circuit consists of the tank with internal integrated pump/pressure regulator/filter, the fuel hose, the throttle body and injector. Fuel is pumped under pressure from the tank to the injector via the filter and pressure regulator. Operating pressure is maintained by the pump and pressure regulator. The injector sprays pressurised fuel into the intake duct where it mixes with air controlled by the throttle body and vaporises before entering the cylinder where it is compressed and ignited by the spark plug.

3 The electronic control circuit consists of the electronic control unit (ECU), which operates and co-ordinates both the fuel injection and ignition systems, and the various sensors that provide the ECU with information on engine operating conditions.

4 The electronic control unit (ECU) monitors signals from the following sensors:
- Intake air temperature (IAT) sensor
- Intake air pressure (IAP) sensor
- Throttle position (TP) sensor
- Crankshaft position (CKP) sensor
- Engine coolant temperature (ECT) sensor
- Tip-over (TO) sensor

5 Based on the information it receives, the ECU calculates the appropriate ignition and fuel requirements of the engine. By varying the length of the electronic pulse it sends to the injector, the ECU controls the length of time the injector is held open and thereby the amount of fuel that is supplied to the engine. Fuel supply varies according to the engine's needs for starting, warming-up, idling, cruising and acceleration. In the event of the machine falling over, the tip-over sensor cuts power to the fuel and ignition systems.

6 The engine trouble warning light should come on for 2 to 3 seconds when the ignition is switched ON, then go out – this serves as a check that the circuit is working correctly. If not, check the instrument cluster (see Chapter 8).

7 The fuel injection system has its own fault diagnosis function (Section 6). In the event of a problem the engine trouble warning light in the instrument cluster comes on or flashes and any fault codes are stored in the ECU. The ECU will determine whether the engine can still be run safely. If it can, a back-up mode substitutes the sensor signal with a fixed signal, restricting performance but allowing the bike to be ridden home or to a dealer. When this occurs, the engine trouble warning light in the instrument cluster will come on and stay on. In some cases the engine will continue to run after the fault has been registered, but once stopped the engine will not be able to be restarted. If the fault is serious, the fuel injection system will be shut down and the engine will not run. When this occurs, the engine trouble warning light will flash while the start switch is being pressed.

8 After the engine has been stopped the fault code is displayed, as a series of timed flashes of the warning light on WR models (see Section 6, Step 2), and as the code itself in the bottom right-hand corner of the instrument display on MT and YZF-R models. The code is also stored in the ECU memory. Yamaha produce a diagnostic tool (part No. 90890-03182 for WR models, and 90890-03231 for MT and YZF-R models) that, among other things, can be used to assess the function of the sensor or actuator related to the fault code displayed – see Section 6, Step 3.

6 Engine management system fault diagnosis

Note: *The engine trouble warning light comes on for a short time when the ignition is turned ON. If the light does not come on, check the LED (see Chapter 8).*

1 The system incorporates a self-diagnostic function whereby most faults, when they occur, are identified by a two digit fault code, which on WR models is displayed as a series of flashes of the engine trouble warning light in the instrument cluster after the engine has been stopped (see Step 2), and on MT and YZF-R models is displayed in the bottom right-hand corner of the instrument display. The code(s) is/are stored in the ECU memory. In the case of a minor fault in the system, the warning light will come on and stay on and the engine will continue to run, and can be restarted, enabling the machine to be ridden, although performance will be affected. In the case of a major fault the warning light will flash while the start switch is being pressed, or if already running the engine will stop and not be able to be restarted – this applies to fault codes 12, 19, 30, 33, 39, 41 and 50 (refer to the accompanying table). If a fault code is displayed refer to the table to identify the faulty component and the appropriate diagnostic code (where given). If a diagnostic code is given and if the diagnostic tool is available you can use the tool to assess the function of the sensor or actuator concerned (see Step 3). If a diagnostic code is not given for a particular fault code (e.g. 12), refer to Section 7 and check the component as described. Certain faults will not activate the warning light and are not subject to a fault code, but have a related diagnostic code. If the engine does not run correctly but no warning light and fault code are shown, check the diagnostic code and details given in the table that relate to the fault, then use the diagnostic mode of the tool to assess the function of the sensor or actuator concerned. If the diagnostic tool is not available just use the details given in the table and the relevant procedure(s) in Section 7, or if necessary take the bike to a Yamaha dealer equipped with the tool. If the system as a whole rather than just an individual component does not seem to function, refer to Chapter 8 and check the fuses and the starter circuit cut-off relay.

2 On WR models all fault codes are displayed as a series of flashes of the engine trouble warning light. The first number of any code is indicated by long (1 second) flashes with 1.5 second intervals, the number of flashes representing the number of the code. The second number of any code is indicated by short (0.5 second) flashes with 0.5 second intervals, the number of flashes representing the number of the code. For example fault code 15 comprises one long flash and five short flashes, and fault code 43 comprises four long flashes and three short flashes. If there is more than one code the lowest number is indicated first, with a 3 second gap between numbers. Make a note of the number displayed, then use Table 1 to identify the faulty component and the appropriate diagnostic code (where given). If a diagnostic code is not given for a particular fault code (i.e. 12 and 46), refer to Section 7 and check the component as described.

3 If a diagnostic code is given, and you have the Yamaha diagnostic tool (part No. 90890-03182 for WR models, and 90890-03231 for MT and YZF-R models), connect the tool and set it to diagnostic mode as follows: make sure the ignition switch is OFF and set the kill switch to RUN. Remove the seat (rider's seat on MT and YZF-R models) (see Chapter 7). Disconnect the self-diagnosis wiring connector – it is a 3-pin connector containing a yellow/green wire on WR models, and a single bullet connector with a yellow/green wire on MT and YZF-R models **(see illustrations)**. Connect and use the diagnostic tool according to the instructions supplied. To cancel the diagnostic mode, turn the ignition switch OFF. Disconnect the tool and reconnect the self-diagnosis wiring connector.

4 Once the fault has been corrected, confirm that the fault code is no longer displayed by turning the ignition switch OFF and then ON again. If the code is no longer displayed the repair is complete.

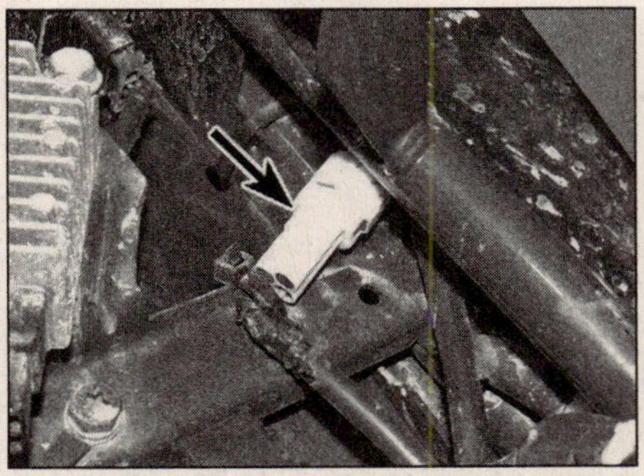

6.3a Diagnostic tool wiring connector (arrowed) – WR models

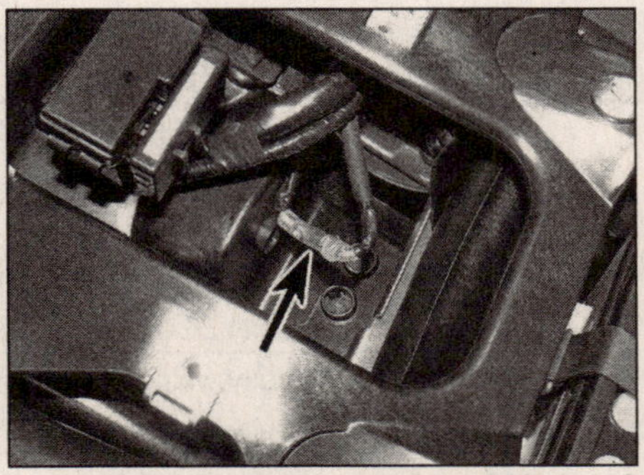

6.3b Diagnostic tool wiring connector (arrowed) – MT and YZF-R models

Table 1 Engine management system fault codes

Fault code	Faulty component – symptoms	Possible causes	Diagnostic code (according to model)
12	Crankshaft position sensor – engine will stop and will not restart	Faulty wiring or wiring connector Damaged or improperly installed sensor or timing rotor Faulty ECU	-
13	Intake air pressure sensor – engine will run, air pressure signal fixed	Faulty wiring or wiring connector Damaged or faulty sensor Faulty ECU	D03
14	Intake air pressure sensor air hole – engine will run, air pressure signal fixed	Air hole blocked Faulty ECU	D03
15	Throttle position sensor – engine will run, sensor signal fixed fully open	Faulty wiring or wiring connector Damaged or improperly installed sensor Faulty ECU	D01
16	Throttle position sensor – engine will run, sensor signal fixed fully open	Throttle position sensor stuck Faulty ECU	D01
19	ECU power input (blue/yellow wire) – engine will stop and will not restart	Faulty blue/yellow wire or wiring connector, faulty sidestand switch Faulty ECU	D20
21	Coolant temperature sensor – engine will run, coolant temperature fixed	Faulty wiring or wiring connector Damaged or improperly installed sensor Faulty ECU	D06
22	Intake air temperature sensor – engine will run, intake temperature fixed at 20°C	Faulty wiring or wiring connector Damaged or improperly installed sensor Faulty ECU	D05
24	Oxygen sensor – engine will run	Damaged sensor, faulty wiring or connector	
30	Tip-over sensor – engine stops and will not restart	Machine overturned Faulty ECU	D08
33	Ignition coil – engine stops and will not restart	Faulty wiring or wiring connector Damaged ignition coil Faulty ignition cut-off circuit Faulty ECU	D30
39	Fuel injector – engine stops and will not restart	Faulty wiring or wiring connector Damaged injector Faulty ECU	D36
41	Tip-over sensor – engine will stop and will not restart	Faulty wiring or wiring connector Damaged sensor Faulty ECU	D08
42	Speed sensor – engine will run	Damaged speed sensor Faulty wiring or wiring connector Faulty ECU	D07
44	Carbon monoxide density in exhaust gas incorrect – engine will run	Error writing CO to EPROM Faulty ECU	D60
46	Abnormal power supply to system – engine will run	Faulty wiring or wiring connector Faulty charging system	
50	ECU malfunction – fault code may not be displayed, engine stops and will not restart	Faulty wiring or wiring connector Damaged ECU	-

Table 2 Fuel system diagnostic codes and data – WR models

Diagnostic code	Issue	Action required	Data displayed
D01	Throttle angle	Check angle data displayed with throttle fully closed	Fully closed – 14 to 20
		Check angle data displayed with throttle fully open	Fully open – 97 to 107
D03	Intake air pressure	Turn the engine stop switch ON and crank the engine using the starter motor to generate a pressure difference.	Intake air pressure – if the value changes when turning, the throttle the sensor is working
D05	Intake air temperature	Check the temperature next to the throttle body and compare with data displayed	Intake air temperature
D06	Coolant temperature	Check the temperature of the engine coolant and compare with data displayed	Engine coolant temperature
D07	Vehicle speed sensor pulse	Turn the front wheel in the normal direction of rotation and check pulses are generated and displayed	0 to 999 (number of recorded pulses, returns to 0 on reaching 999)
D08	Tip-over sensor	Check the operation of the tip-over sensor	Machine or sensor upright – 0.4 to 1.4V Machine or sensor tilted more than 65° – 3.7 to 4.4V
D09	Voltage supply to fuel system	Check battery voltage (see Chapter 8)	Normally around 12V
D20	Sidestand switch	Move stand up and down	Stand up – ON Stand down – OFF In gear – OFF
D30	Ignition coil	Check the operation of the ignition coil – pressing the MODE button will generate five sparks in the coil and the engine trouble warning light comes on. Check for the sparks by removing the plug and checking as described in Section 15	-
D36	Fuel injector	Check the operation of the fuel injector – pressing the MODE button will generate five pulses in the injector and the engine trouble warning light comes on.	-
D51	Cooling fan relay	Check the operation of the radiator cooling fan relay – pressing the MODE button will actuate the relay five times and the engine trouble warning light comes on. You should be able to hear the relay – refer to Chapter 3 for access and further checks	-
D52	Headlight relay	Check the operation of the headlight relay – pressing the MODE button will actuate the relay five times and the engine trouble warning light comes on. You should be able to hear the relay and the light should come on – refer to Chapter 8 for access and further checks	-
D54	Fast idle solenoid	Check the operation of the solenoid – pressing the MODE button will actuate the solenoid five times and the engine trouble warning light comes on. You should be able to hear the solenoid – refer to Section 7 for more checks	
D60	EEPROM		01 00 when no fault
D61	Fault code history		12 to 50 00 when no fault
D62	Fault code history erasure		00 to 16
D70	Control number	Programme control number displayed	00 to 254

Table 3 Fuel system diagnostic codes and data – MT and YZF-R models

Diagnostic code	Issue	Action required	Data displayed
D01	Throttle angle	Check angle data displayed with throttle fully closed	Fully closed – 14 to 20
		Check angle data displayed with throttle fully open	Fully open – 92 to 102
D03	Intake air pressure	Operate the throttle with the front brake lever pulled in and the start button pressed.	Intake air pressure – if the value changes when turning the throttle, the throttle the sensor is working
D05	Intake air temperature	Check the temperature next to the throttle body and compare with data displayed	Intake air temperature
D06	Coolant temperature	Check the temperature of the engine coolant and compare with data displayed	Engine coolant temperature
D07	Vehicle speed sensor pulse	Turn the front wheel in the normal direction of rotation and check pulses are generated and displayed	0 to 999 (number of recorded pulses, returns to 0 on reaching 999)
D08	Tip-over sensor	Check the operation of the tip-over sensor	Machine or sensor upright – 0.4 to 1.4V Machine or sensor tilted more than 65° – 3.7 to 4.4V
D09	Voltage supply to fuel system	Check battery voltage (see Chapter 8)	Normally around 12V
D20	Sidestand switch	Move stand up and down	Stand up – ON Stand down – OFF In gear – OFF
D30	Ignition coil	Check the operation of the ignition coil – pressing the MODE button will generate five sparks in the coil and the engine trouble warning light comes on. Check for the sparks by removing the plug and checking as described in Section 15	-
D36	Fuel injector	Check the operation of the fuel injector – pressing the MODE button will generate five pulses in the injector and the engine trouble warning light comes on.	-
D51	Cooling fan relay	Check the operation of the radiator cooling fan relay – pressing the MODE button will actuate the relay five times and the engine trouble warning light comes on. You should be able to hear the relay – refer to Chapter 3 for access and further checks	-
D52	Headlight relay	Check the operation of the headlight relay – pressing the MODE button will actuate the relay five times and the engine trouble warning light comes on. You should be able to hear the relay and the light should come on – refer to Chapter 8 for access and further checks	-
D54	Fast idle solenoid	Check the operation of the solenoid – pressing the MODE button will actuate the solenoid five times and the engine trouble warning light comes on. You should be able to hear the solenoid – refer to Section 7 for more checks	
D60	EEPROM		01 00 when no fault
D61	Fault code history		12 to 50 00 when no fault
D62	Fault code history erasure		00 to 16
D70	Control number	Programme control number displayed	00 to 254

7 Engine management system components

1 If a fault is indicated in any of the system components, first check the wiring and connectors between the appropriate component and the ECU (refer to Electrical System Fault Finding at the beginning of Chapter 8, and to the Wiring diagram at the end of it). A continuity test of all wires will locate a break or short in any circuit. Inspect the terminals inside the wiring connectors and ensure they are not loose, bent, broken or corroded. Spray the inside of the connectors with a proprietary electrical terminal cleaner or protector before reconnection. If the system as a whole rather than just an individual component does not seem to function refer to Chapter 8 and check the fuses and starter circuit cut-off relay.

2 It is possible to undertake most checks on system components using a multimeter and comparing the results with the specifications at the beginning of the Chapter. Note: Different meters may give slightly different results to those specified even though the component being tested is not faulty – do not consign a component to the bin before having it double-checked. However, some faults will only become evident when a component is tested with specialised equipment, in which

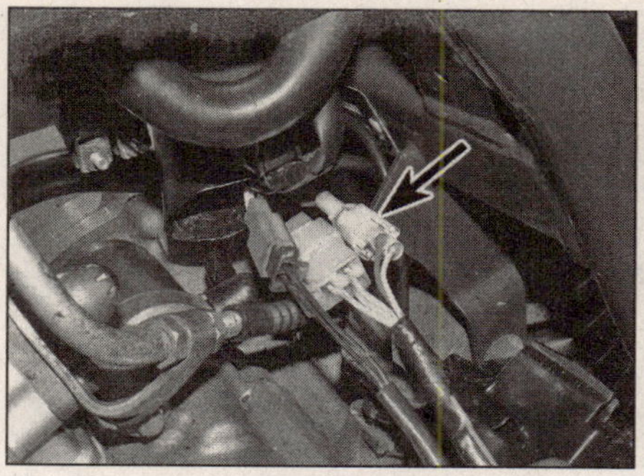

7.5a CKP sensor wiring connector (arrowed) – WR models

7.5b CKP sensor connector is inside the boot (arrowed) on MT and YZF-R models

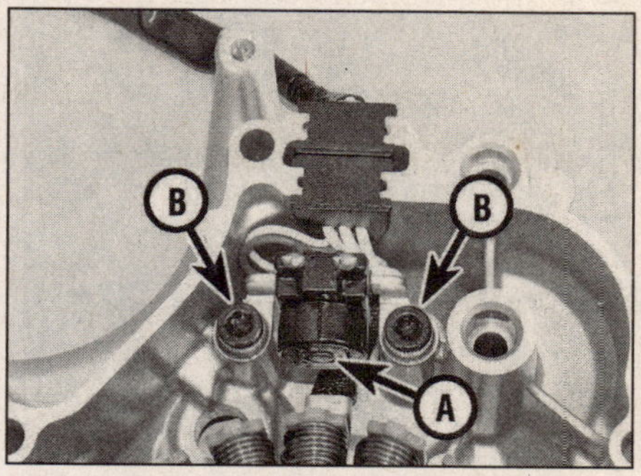

7.6 Check the sensor head (A) and bolts (B)

case the checks should be undertaken by a Yamaha dealer.

3 If after a thorough check the source of a fault has not been identified, it is possible that the ECU itself is faulty. Yamaha provides no test specifications for the ECU. In order to determine conclusively that the unit is defective, it should be substituted with a known good one. If the problem is rectified, the original unit is faulty.

Crankshaft position (CKP) sensor

Check

4 Make sure the ignition is OFF. On MT and YZF-R models remove the left-hand side cover (see Chapter 7).

5 The crankshaft position sensor is in the alternator cover on the left-hand side of the engine. Trace the wiring from the cover and disconnect it at the 2-pin connector housed in the rubber boot **(see illustrations)**. Using an ohmmeter or multimeter set to the ohms x 100 scale, measure the resistance between the terminals on the sensor side of the connector. If the result is not as specified at the beginning of the chapter, replace the sensor with a new one (Step 7).

6 If the result is good, and you have checked the wiring and connectors as described in Step 1, remove the alternator cover (see Chapter 8) and check whether the sensor head is fouled or the sensor has come loose on its mounts **(see illustration)**.

Removal and installation

7 Make sure the ignition is OFF. Remove the alternator cover, then remove the stator and CKP sensor from it (see Chapter 8) – the stator and CKP sensor come as an integrated assembly.

8 After installing the new sensor, turn the engine over on the starter motor to reinstate the system, then check the fault code has been erased by turning the ignition switch OFF and then ON again. If the code is no longer displayed the repair is complete.

Intake air pressure sensor

9 Make sure the ignition is OFF. Remove the fuel tank (see Section 2).

10 The sensor is part of the sensor unit, containing the intake air pressure and temperature sensors and the throttle position sensor, and is on the side of the throttle body **(see illustration)**.

11 For fault code 13, first check the wiring and connectors as in Step 1. Next, using a voltmeter or multimeter set to the volts (DC) scale, insert the positive (+) probe of the meter into the pink/white wire terminal in the back of the connector, with the connector still connected, and insert the negative (-) probe into the grey/black (WR models) or black/blue (MT and YZF-R models) wire terminal. Turn the ignition ON and measure the sensor output voltage. Turn the ignition OFF.

12 If the voltage is not as specified at the beginning of the chapter, replace the throttle body with a new one (see Section 9) – the sensor assembly is part of it and is not available separately.

13 For fault code 14, make sure the throttle body and sensor assembly are clean and the aperture to the sensor is not blocked.

14 After installing the new throttle body, for fault code 13 turn the ignition switch ON, and for fault code 14 run the engine at idle speed, to reinstate the system, then check the fault code has been erased by turning the ignition switch OFF and then ON again. If the code is no longer displayed the repair is complete.

Intake air temperature sensor

15 Make sure the ignition is OFF. Remove the fuel tank (see Section 2).

16 The sensor is part of the sensor unit, containing the intake air pressure and temperature sensors and the throttle position sensor, and is on the side of the throttle body **(see illustration 7.10)**.

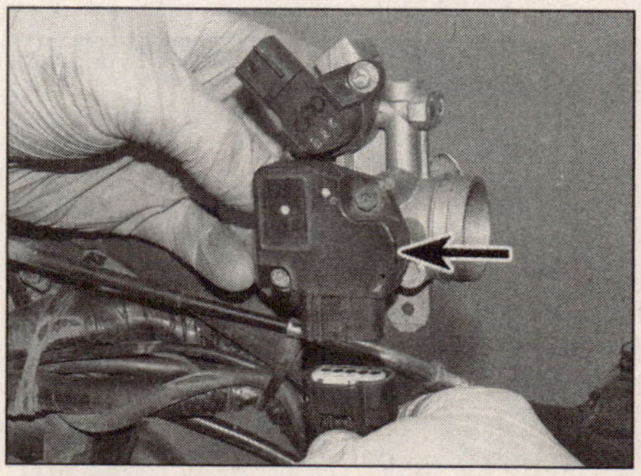

7.10 IAP, IAT and TP sensor unit (arrowed) and its wiring connector – WR model shown, throttle body displaced for clarity

17 First check the wiring and connectors as in Step 1. Next, disconnect the wiring connector from the sensor assembly. Using an ohmmeter or multimeter set to the K-ohms scale, connect the positive (+) probe to the brown/white wire terminal in the sensor socket and the negative (-) probe to the grey/black (WR models) or black/blue (MT and YZF-R models) wire terminal and measure the resistance.

18 If the resistance is not as specified at the beginning of the chapter, replace the throttle body with a new one – the sensor assembly is part of it and is not available separately.

19 After installing the new throttle body, turn the ignition switch ON to reinstate the system, then check the fault code has been erased by turning the ignition switch OFF and then ON again. If the code is no longer displayed the repair is complete.

Throttle position sensor

20 Make sure the ignition is OFF. Remove the fuel tank (see Section 2).

21 The sensor is part of the sensor unit, containing the intake air pressure and temperature sensors and the throttle position sensor, and is on the side of the throttle body **(see illustration 7.10)**.

22 First check the wiring and connectors as in Step 1. Also make sure the sensor assembly is not loose on the throttle body, and that the throttle twistgrip turns smoothly and freely from fully closed to fully open.

23 Next, using a voltmeter or multimeter set to the volts (DC) scale, insert the positive (+) probe of the meter into the grey/red (WR models) or blue (MT and YZF-R models) wire terminal in the back of the connector, with the connector still connected, and insert the negative (-) probe into the grey/black (WR models) or blue/black (MT and YZF models) wire terminal. Turn the ignition ON and measure the sensor input voltage. If the voltage is not as specified at the beginning of the chapter, and the grey/red or blue wire between the sensor and the ECU is OK, the ECU could be faulty. Turn the ignition OFF.

24 To check the output voltage, insert the

7.26 ECT sensor (arrowed)

7.28a Tip-over sensor (arrowed) – WR models

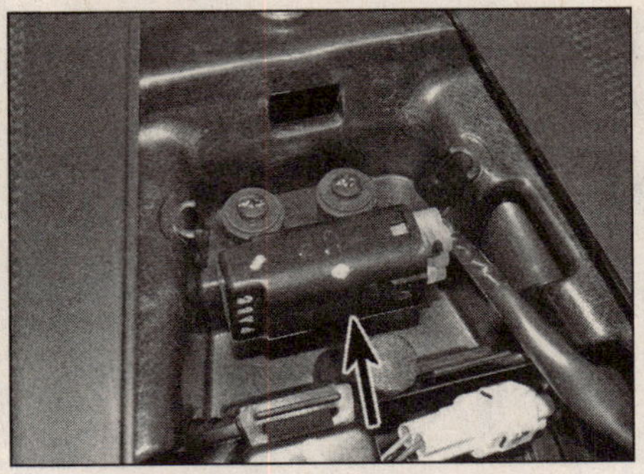

7.28b Tip-over sensor (arrowed) – MT and YZF-R models

positive (+) probe of the meter into the yellow (WR models) or yellow/blue (MT and YZF-R models) wire terminal in the back of the connector, with the connector still connected, and insert the negative (-) probe into the grey/black (WR models) or black/blue (MT and YZF-R models) wire terminal. Turn the ignition ON and measure the sensor output voltage. Now slowly open the throttle and check that the voltage increases steadily. If the voltage in the closed position is not as specified, or if it does not rise or rises abruptly when opened, replace the throttle body with a new one – the sensor assembly is part of it and is not available separately.

25 After installing the new throttle body, for fault code 15 turn the ignition switch ON, and for fault code 16, on WR models run the engine first at idle speed and then quickly open and close the throttle so the engine races but does not exceed the red line, and on MT and YZF-R models turn the ignition on then fully open and close the throttle, to reinstate the system, then check the fault code has been erased by turning the ignition switch OFF and then ON again. If the code is no longer displayed the repair is complete.

Engine coolant temperature sensor

26 The sensor is in the back of the cylinder head on the right side **(see illustration)**. First check the wiring and connectors as in Step 1.

27 Refer to Chapter 3 for checks and removal/installation details.

Tip-over sensor

Check

28 On WR models remove the seat and the tail cover, and on MT and YZF-R models remove the passenger seat (see Chapter 7) **(see illustrations)**.

29 Make sure the ignition is OFF. First check the wiring and connectors as in Step 1. Also make sure the sensor is not loose on its mounts.

30 Displace the sensor (see Step 35) leaving the wiring connected.

31 Using a voltmeter or multimeter set to the volts (DC) scale, insert the positive (+) probe of the meter into the yellow/green wire terminal in the back of the connector, with the connector still connected, and insert the negative (-) probe into the grey/black (WR models) or black/blue (MT and YZF-R models) wire terminal. Turn the ignition ON. Hold the sensor in its normal position when the bike is upright with the UP mark facing up, then tilt it 65° to one side and then the other, in each case noting the voltage reading on the meter. Turn the ignition OFF.

32 If the voltage is not as specified at the beginning of the chapter when the sensor is upright and tilted over, replace the sensor with a new one. Note the top surface of the sensor is marked UP.

33 After fitting the new sensor, turn the ignition switch ON, then OFF then back ON to reinstate the system, then check the fault code has been erased by turning the ignition switch OFF and then ON again. If the code is no longer displayed the repair is complete.

Removal and installation

34 On WR models remove the seat and the tail cover, and on MT and YZF-R models remove the passenger seat (see Chapter 7).

35 Make sure the ignition is OFF. Undo the screws securing the sensor, noting the washers **(see illustration 7.28a or b)**. Displace the sensor and disconnect the wiring connector. Note the top surface of the sensor is marked UP – make sure this mark is on top when installing the sensor.

Speed sensor

Check

36 On WR models the sensor is on the front wheel. On MT and YZF-R models without ABS the sensor is in the top of the crankcase – on MT and YZF-R models with ABS the speed sensor function is carried out by the wheel speed sensors for the ABS system (see Chapter 6). Make sure the ignition is OFF. On WR models remove the headlight (see Chapter 8) to access the wiring connector, which is inside the rubber boot – release the cable-tie and draw the connector out **(see illustration)**. On YZF-R models remove all the sections of the fairing on the left-hand side (see Chapter 7) to access the wiring connector. On MT and YZF-R models disconnect the connector from the sensor **(see illustration)**. Check the wiring and connectors as in Step 1.

37 Support the machine on an auxiliary stand so the front wheel on WR models and the rear wheel on MT and YZF models is off the ground.

38 Using a voltmeter or multimeter set to the volts (DC) scale, insert the positive (+) probe of the meter into the grey wire terminal in the back of the connector, with the connector still connected, and insert the negative (-) probe into the grey/black terminal. Turn the ignition switch ON and rotate the front (WR models) or rear (MT and YZF-R models) wheel by hand in its normal direction of rotation. As the engine turns, the output voltage should fluctuate between the two levels given in the

7.36a Speed sensor wiring connector (arrowed) – WR models

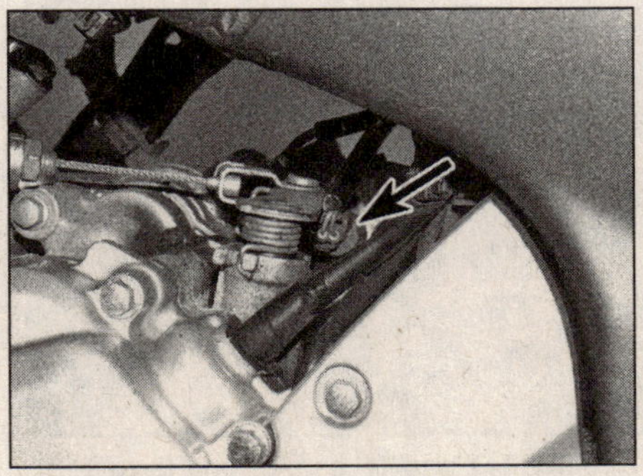

7.36b Speed sensor wiring connector (arrowed) – MT and YZF-R models

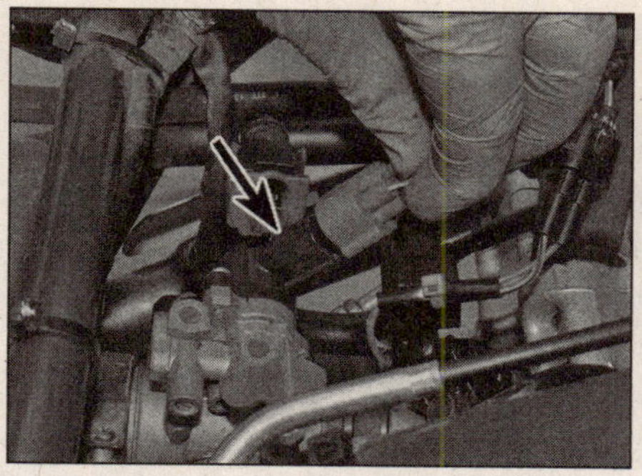
7.50a Fast idle solenoid (arrowed) and its wiring connector – WR models

7.50b Fast idle solenoid (arrowed) and its wiring connector – MT and YZF-R models

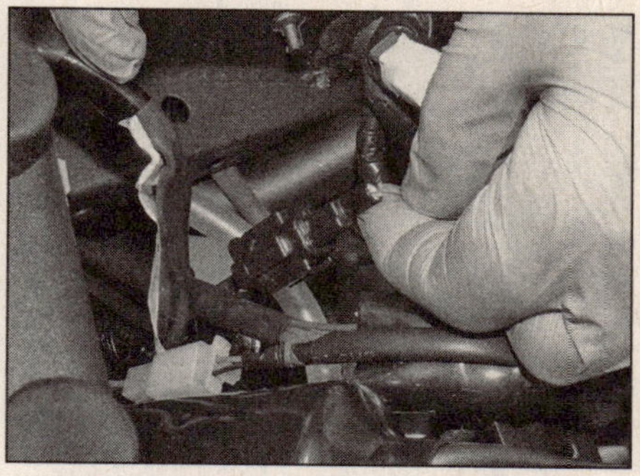
7.56 Disconnect the wiring connector

specifications at the beginning of the Chapter. Turn the ignition OFF.

39 If the voltage is not as specified, replace the sensor with a new one.

40 After installing the new sensor, take the bike for a ride making sure you exceed 20 mph (30 kph) to reinstate the system, then check the fault code has been erased by turning the ignition switch OFF and then ON again. If the code is no longer displayed the repair is complete.

Removal and installation

WR models

41 The sensor is on the front wheel. Make sure the ignition is OFF.

42 Remove the headlight. Release the cable-tie around the rubber boot and disconnect the sensor wiring connector **(see illustration 7.36a)**. Remove the front mudguard (see Chapter 7). Undo the wiring clamp screw. Feed the wire back to the sensor, releasing it from any ties and guides, noting its routing.

43 Refer to Chapter 6 and remove the front wheel to free the sensor.

44 On installation, apply grease to the rotor, and make sure the wiring is correctly routed and the connector terminals are clean and the pins are not damaged.

MT and YZF-R models

45 On YZF-R models remove all sections of the fairing on the left-hand side (see Chapter 7).

46 Disconnect the wiring connector from the sensor **(see illustration 7.36b)**.

47 Unscrew the bolt and remove the sensor.

48 Installation is the reverse of removal.

Fast idle solenoid

Check

49 Make sure the ignition is OFF. Remove the fuel tank (see Section 2).

50 The fast idle solenoid is on the throttle body. Disconnect the wiring connector **(see illustrations)**. Using an ohmmeter or multimeter set to the ohms x 10 scale, measure the resistance between the terminals on the solenoid. If the result is not as specified at the beginning of the chapter, remove the solenoid (see below) and replace it with a new one.

Removal and installation

51 Make sure the ignition is OFF. Remove the fuel tank (see Section 2).

52 The solenoid is on the top of the throttle body. Disconnect the wiring connector **(see illustration 7.50a or b)**.

53 Undo the screws and remove the solenoid.

54 Installation is the reverse of removal.

Oxygen sensor (MT and YZF-R models)

Removal and installation

55 Remove the fuel tank (see Section 2).

56 Disconnect the sensor wiring connector and feed it out to the sensor **(see illustration)**.

57 Unscrew and remove the sensor **(see illustration)**.

58 Installation is the reverse of removal – tighten the sensor to the torque setting specified at the beginning of the Chapter. Start the engine and warm it up, then race the engine briefly (not beyond the red line) to reinstate the system. Check the fault code is no longer displayed.

Fuel injector

59 Refer to Section 10.

Ignition coil

60 Refer to Section 16.

8 Air filter housing

Removal

1 Remove the fuel tank (see Section 2). Remove the air filter (see Chapter 1).

2 Detach the crankcase breather and noise suppression hoses, and on WR models the AIS system hose, noting which fits where **(see illustrations)**.

3 On WR models remove the mudguard from the rear of the housing **(see illustration 8.2b)**.

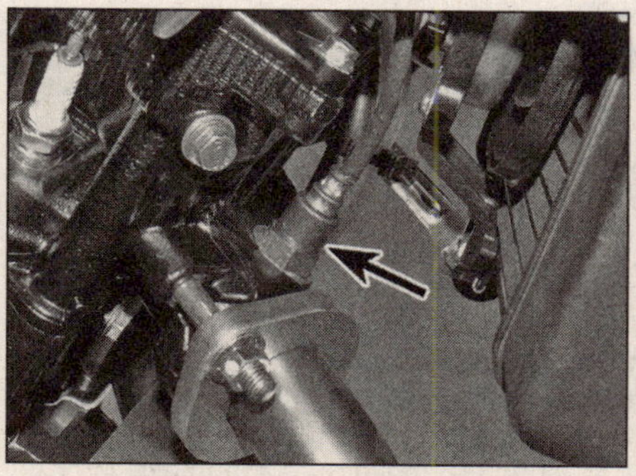
7.57 Oxygen sensor (arrowed)

8.2a Detach the crankcase breather and noise suppression hoses (arrowed)...

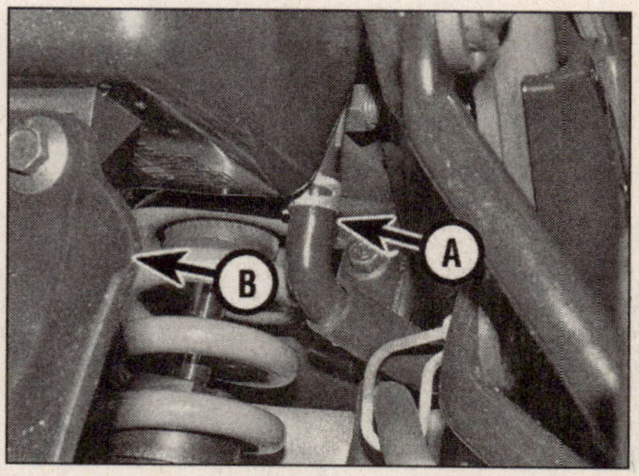

8.2b ...and on WR models the AIS hose (A). Mudguard (B)

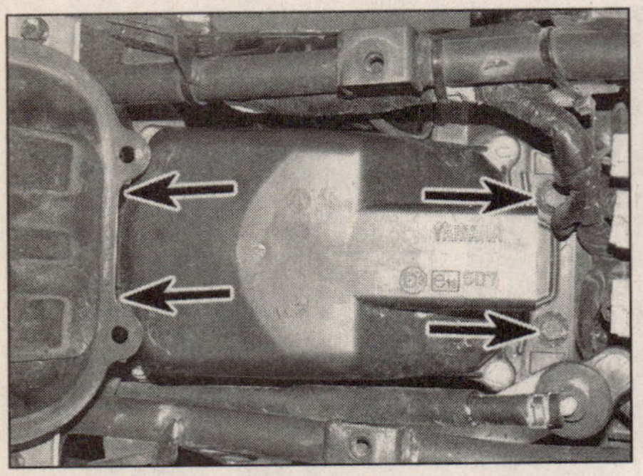

8.4a Air filter housing bolts (arrowed, front ones hidden by fuel tank) – WR models

8.4b On MT and YZF-R models unscrew the bolt (arrowed) on each side

8.5 Air duct clamp screw (arrowed) – WR model shown

4 Unscrew the air filter housing bolts **(see illustrations)**.

5 Slacken the air duct clamp screw, noting the orientation of the clamp and how it locates **(see illustration)**. Carefully lift the housing out.

Installation

6 Installation is the reverse of removal. Make sure the air duct clamp indent is located over the rib on the duct. Make sure all hoses are securely and correctly connected.

9 Throttle body

Warning: Refer to the precautions given in Section 1 before starting work.

9.4 Slacken the clamp screw (arrowed)...

9.5a ...displace the throttle body...

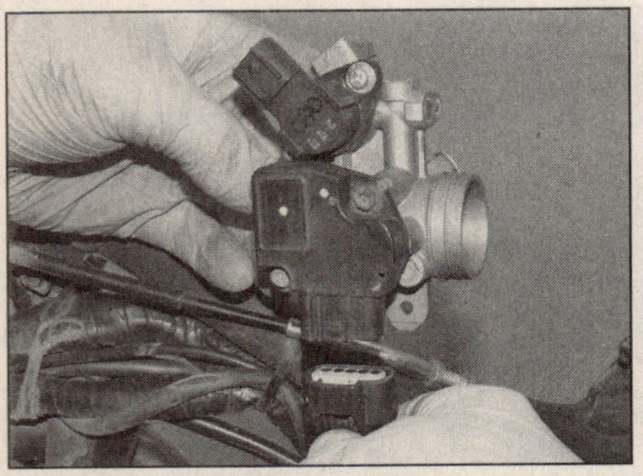

9.5b ...and disconnect the wiring

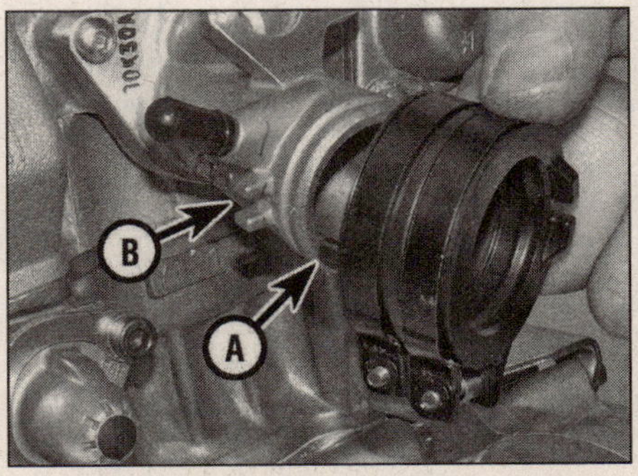

9.6 Tab (A) seats between the ribs (B)

Removal

1 Remove the fuel tank (see Section 2). On MT and YZF-R models remove the air filter housing (see Section 8).

2 Disconnect the fast idle solenoid wiring connector **(see illustration 7.50a or b)**.

3 Detach the throttle cable(s) (Section 11).

4 Fully slacken the clamp screw securing the throttle body to the intake joint – note the orientation of the clamp and how it locates **(see illustration)**. On WR models also slacken the clamp screw securing the throttle body to the air duct **(see illustration 8.5)**.

5 Ease the throttle body out of the intake joint, and then on WR models out of the air duct, then disconnect the sensor unit wiring connector and remove the throttle body **(see illustrations)**.

6 If required slacken the intake joint clamp screw and detach it from the intake duct – note the orientation of the clamp and how it locates, and how the joint locates on the duct **(see illustration)**.

Caution: Do not snap the throttle valve from fully open to fully closed once the cable has been disconnected because this can lead to engine idle speed problems.

Caution: Tape over or stuff clean rag into the intake joint, duct or cylinder head (according to what has been removed) to prevent anything from falling in.

7 Remove the fast idle solenoid from the throttle body if required (see Section 7). Do not remove the sensor unit from the throttle body – it as integral part and is not available separately, and should not be disturbed.

Cleaning

Caution: Use only a dedicated cleaner or petroleum-based solvent for cleaning. Do not use caustic cleaners.

8 Clean the throttle body using a petrol (gasoline) based cleaner – do not use a caustic cleaner.

9 Loosen and remove any varnish and other deposits using a nylon-bristle brush – do not use any metallic or pointed tool to clean passages. Rinse, then dry with compressed air, blowing out all of the passages.

Inspection

10 Check the air duct and intake joint for signs of cracking or deterioration and replace with new ones if necessary.

11 Check the throttle body and intake duct for cracks, distorted sealing surfaces and other damage. If any defects are found, replace the faulty component with a new one.

12 Make sure the butterfly valve moves smoothly and returns under spring pressure. Make sure the valve is not distorted or loose on its shaft.

Installation

13 Installation is the reverse of removal, noting the following:

- Remove the tape/plug from the intake joint or duct.
- If removed, make sure the intake joint is correctly located with the tab between the ribs on the side of the intake duct, and

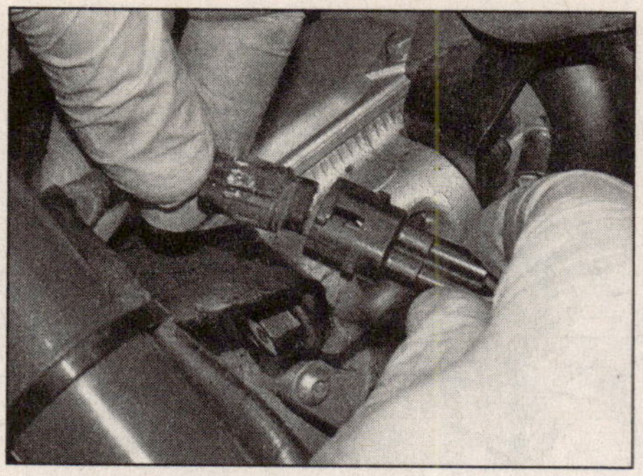

10.2 Disconnect the wiring connector

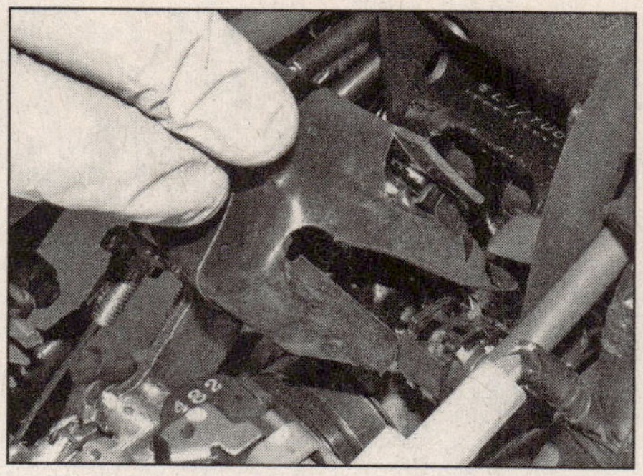

10.3a Remove the rubber cover

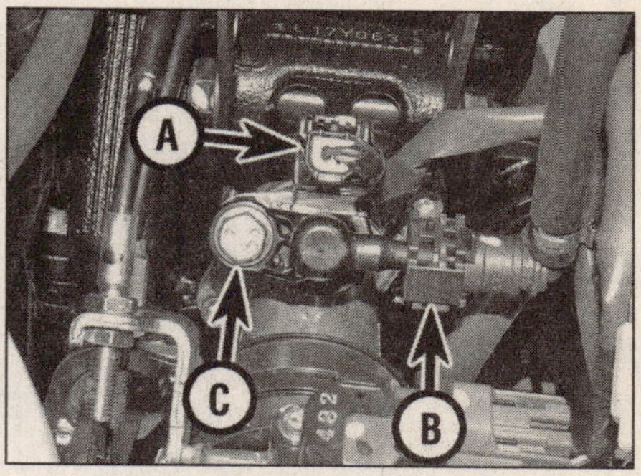

10.3b Injector wiring connector (A), fuel hose connector (B) and injector bolt (C)

locate the indent in the clamp over the rib on the bottom *(see illustration 9.6)*.

- Make sure the throttle body is pushed all the way into the joint and located with its tab seated between the ribs on the joint (see illustration 9.4).
- Make sure the wiring connectors are securely connected.
- Check the operation of the throttle and adjust the cable(s) as necessary (see Chapter 1).
- Run the engine and check that the fuel system is working correctly before taking the machine out on the road. Check the idle speed and adjust if necessary (see Chapter 1).

10 Fuel injector

Warning: *Refer to the precautions given in Section 1 before starting work.*

Check

1 Remove the fuel tank (see Section 2).

2 On WR models disconnect the injector wiring connector **(see illustration)**.

3 On MT and YZF-R models remove the injector cover **(see illustration)**. Disconnect the injector wiring connector **(see illustration)**.

4 Connect an ohmmeter or multimeter set to the ohms x 1 scale between the terminals on the injector and check the resistance – it should be as specified at the beginning of the Chapter **(see illustration)**. If not the injector is probably faulty.

Removal

5 Remove the fuel tank (see Section 2). On MT and YZF-R models remove the injector cover **(see illustration 10.3a)**.

6 Have a rag ready to catch any residual fuel. On WR models slide the fuel hose connector security clip up, then press the release tabs in and pull the hose off its union **(see illustration)**. On MT and YZF-R models, pull the connector lock up or down (according to the orientation of the connector – two types have been fitted) while simultaneously pulling the locking tabs towards the fuel hose end, and pull the connector off its union **(see illustration 10.3b)**.

7 Disconnect the fuel injector wiring connector **(see illustration 10.2 or 10.3b)**.

8 Unscrew the bolt and lift the injector and its plate off the intake duct, noting how the plate locates **(see illustration)**.

9 On WR models remove the seal from the injector seat, or from the injector if not in the seat, and on all models remove the O-ring from the injector **(see illustration 10.8)**. New ones must be used.

Installation

10 Installation is the reverse of removal, noting the following:

- Fit a new O-ring onto the injector **(see illustration 10.8)**.
- On WR models fit a new seal onto the injector **(see illustration 10.8)**

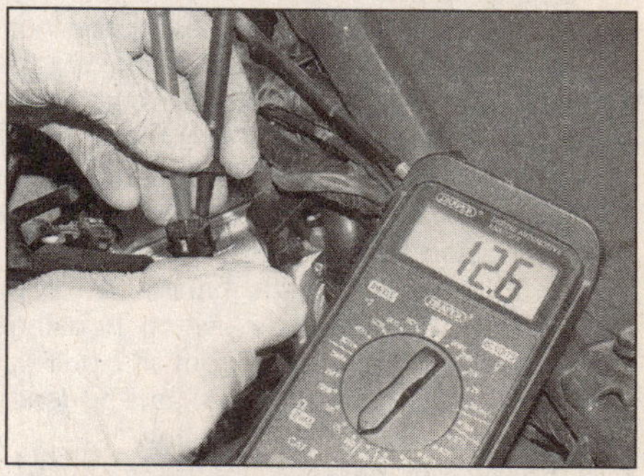

10.4 Checking injector resistance on WR models

- When fitting the plate onto the injector, there is a hole in the upper side of the plate that locates over a pin on the injector, and a pin on the lower side that fits into the hole in the intake duct **(see illustration 10.10)**. Carefully push the injector into the duct, making sure the O-ring does not dislodge and the injector seats correctly.
- Make sure the wiring connector is securely connected **(see illustration 10.2 or 10.3b)**.
- Push the fuel hose connector fully onto the union on the fuel injector until it is heard to click into place, then push the security clip or lock (according to model) across **(see illustration 10.6 or 10.3b)**.
- Run the engine and check that the fuel system is working correctly, with no leaks, before taking the machine out on the road.

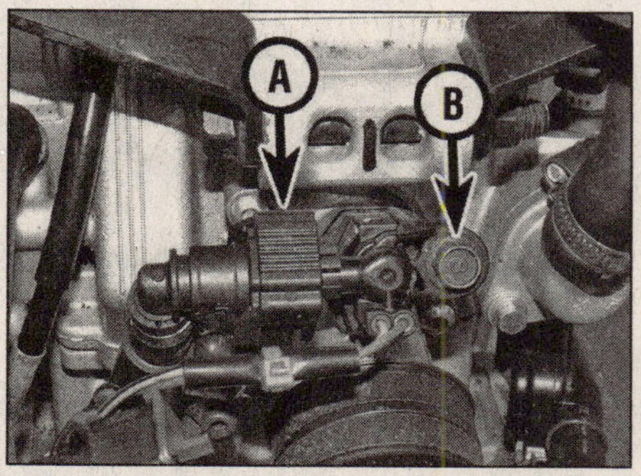

10.6 Fuel hose connector (A) and injector bolt (B) – WR models

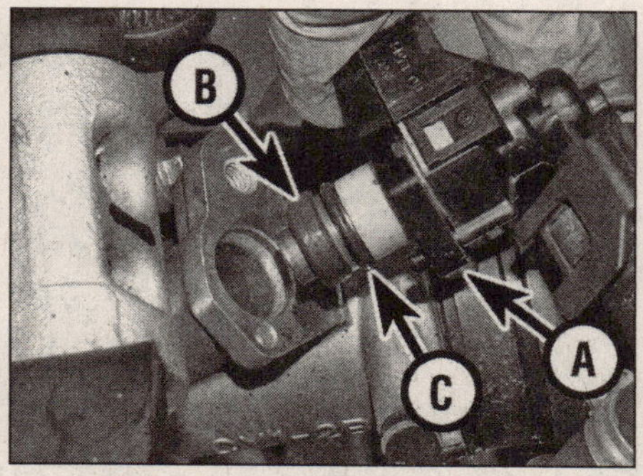

10.8 Removing the injector assembly – injector plate (A), seal (B – WR models), and O-ring (C)

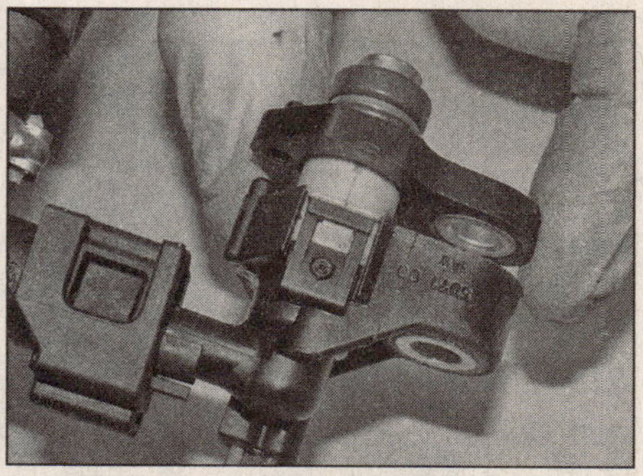

10.10 Fit the plate, locating the pins in the holes as described

11 Throttle cable(s)

Warning: *Refer to the precautions given in Section 1 before proceeding.*

WR models

Removal

1 Remove the fuel tank cover (see Chapter 7), and for best access remove the fuel tank (see Section 2).

2 Working at the throttle body end, fully slacken the cable locknut so the adjuster nut is free, then thread the adjuster nut off, lift the cable and slip the inner cable out of the bracket **(see illustrations)**. Detach the cable end from the throttle pulley **(see illustration)**.

3 Undo the cable retainer screw and the switch housing screws on the underside of the switch housing on the handlebar **(see illustration)**. Displace the switch housing and detach the cable end from the pulley, then draw the cable out of the housing **(see illustrations)**.

4 Withdraw the cable from the machine, carefully noting the correct routing – you can tie string to the end which can be drawn through with the cable and then used as a guide to draw the new cable in.

Installation

5 Feed the cable through from the handlebar to the throttle body, making sure it is correctly routed – if used on removal tie the string to the end and pull it through. The cable must not interfere with any other component and should not be kinked or bent sharply.

6 Fit the cable into the switch housing **(see illustration 11.3c)**. Lubricate the cable end with multi-purpose grease and fit it into the throttle pulley **(see illustration 11.3b)**. Fit the housing halves onto the handlebar, locating the peg in the top half in the hole in the handlebar and making sure the washer is between the housing and the twistgrip, not inside the housing **(see illustration 11.16)**. Fit and tighten the housing screws **(see illustration 11.3a)**. Make sure the cable elbow is correctly positioned. Fit the retainer and tighten the screw. Pull the rubber boot off the adjuster and check its position – if there is thread exposed between the locknut and the elbow, fully slacken the locknut and turn the adjuster fully in to reset it at its start point, then tighten the locknut and fit the boot.

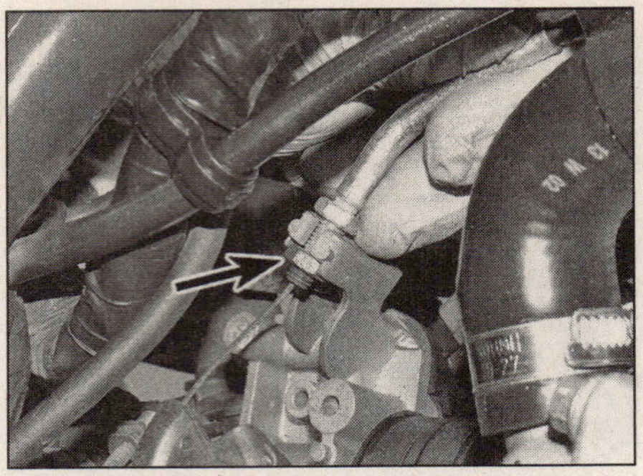

11.2a Fully slacken the locknut (arrowed)...

11.2b ...and thread the adjuster nut off...

11.2c ...then lift the threaded section out of the bracket and slip the inner cable out the side...

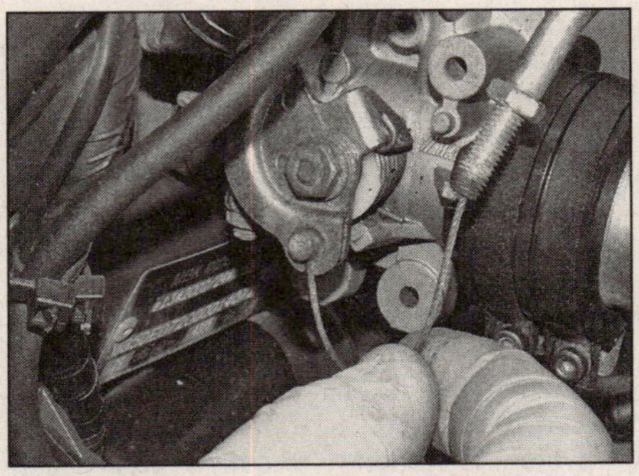

11.2d ...and detach the cable end

7 Fit the cable end into its socket on the throttle body pulley, then locate the cable in the bracket **(see illustrations 11.2d and c)**. Thread the adjuster nut up under the bracket, then pull the cable up to seat the adjuster nut captive under the bracket and tighten the locknut down **(see illustrations 11.2b and a)** – adjust the position of the adjuster nut as required so there is the specified amount of freeplay in the cable at the throttle twistgrip (see Chapter 1).

8 Operate the throttle to check that it opens and closes freely. Turn the handlebars back and forth to make sure the cable doesn't cause the steering to bind.

9 Start the engine and check that the idle speed does not increase as the handlebars are turned. If it does, the throttle cable is routed incorrectly. Correct the problem before riding the motorcycle.

10 Install the fuel tank if removed (see Section 2) and the fuel tank cover (see Chapter 7).

MT and YZF-R models

Removal

11 Remove the fuel tank (see Section 2). On YZF-R models remove the centre and upper sections of the fairing on the left-hand side (see Chapter 7).

12 Working at the throttle body end, fully slacken the locknut on the upper (opening)

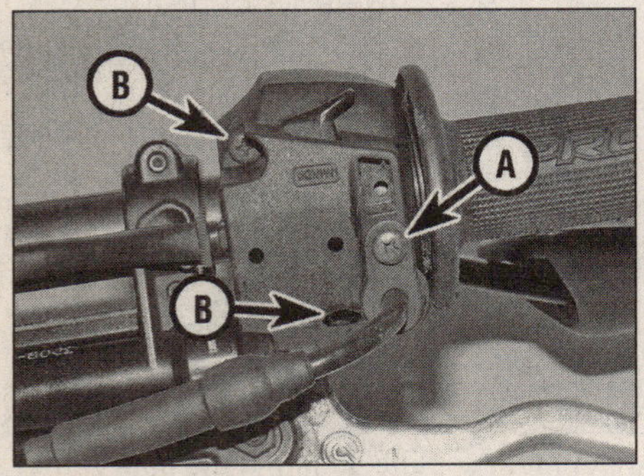

11.3a Undo the cable retainer screw (A), then the housing screws (B)...

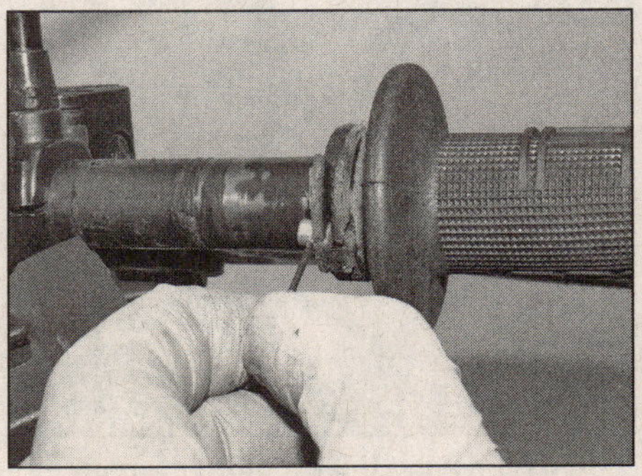

11.3b ...split the housing and detach the cable end...

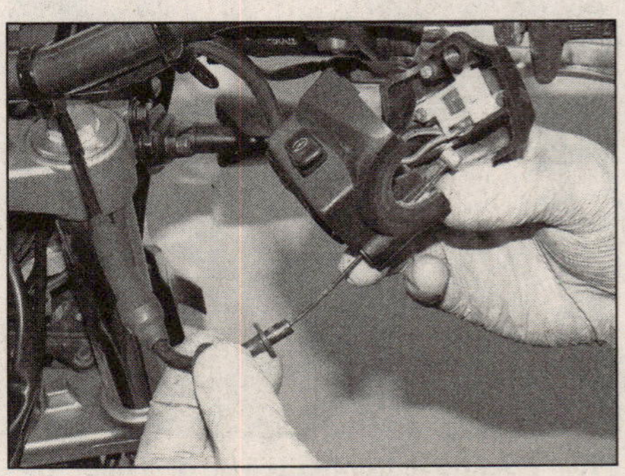

11.3c ...and draw the cable out

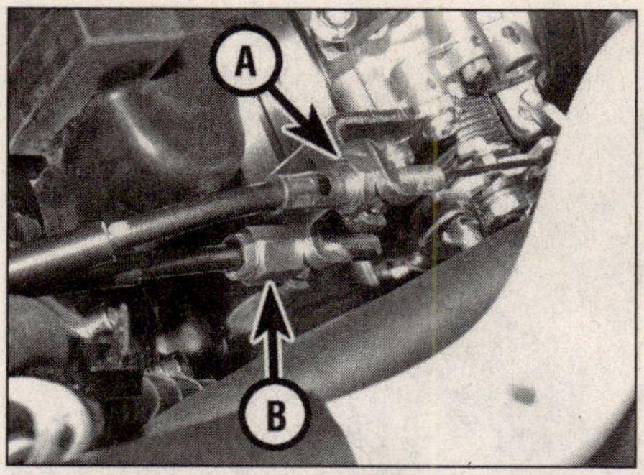

11.12 Opening cable locknut (A), closing cable hex (B)

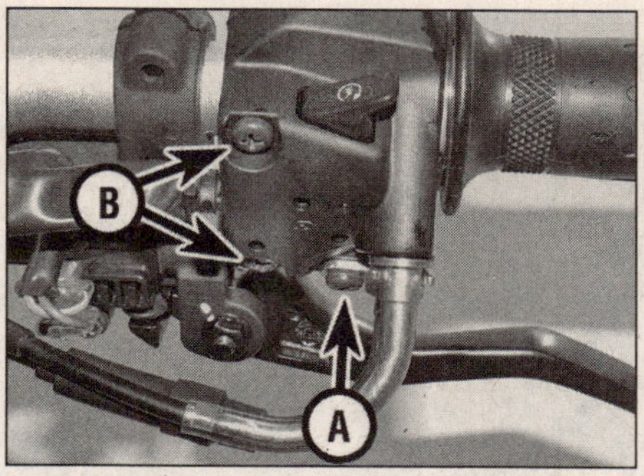

11.13a Undo the cable retainer screw (A), then the housing screws (B) ...

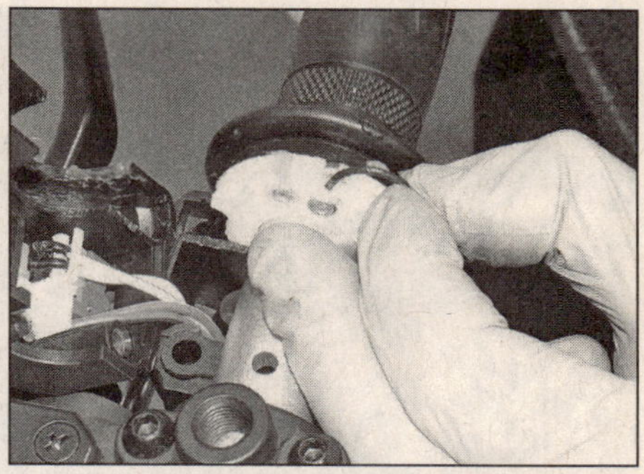

11.13b ... split the housing and detach the cable ends ...

cable so the adjuster nut is free, then slip the cable out of the bracket **(see illustration)**. Slacken the hex on the lower (closing) cable until the lower nut is free and slip the cable out of the bracket. Detach the cable ends from the throttle pulley.

13 Undo the cable retainer screw and the switch housing screws on the underside of the switch housing on the handlebar **(see illustration)**. Displace the switch housing and detach the cable ends from the pulley, then draw the cables out of the housing **(see illustrations)**.

14 Withdraw the cables from the machine, carefully noting the correct routing – you can tie string to the ends which can be drawn through with the cable and then used as a guide to draw the new cables in.

Installation

15 Feed the cables through from the handlebar to the throttle body, making sure they are correctly routed – if used on removal tie the string to the ends and pull them through. The cables must not interfere with any other component and should not be kinked or bent sharply.

16 Fit the opening cable (with the adjuster) into the front of the switch housing, and the closing cable into the rear **(see illustration 11.13c)**. Lubricate the cable ends with multi-purpose grease and fit them into the throttle pulley **(see illustration 11.13b)**. Fit the housing halves onto the handlebar, locating the peg in the top half in the hole in the handlebar, and making sure the washer is between the housing and the twistgrip, not inside the housing **(see illustration)**. Fit and tighten the housing screws **(see illustration 11.13a)**. Make sure the cable elbows are correctly positioned. Fit the retainer, seating the open forked end around the closing cable shoulder, and tighten the screw. Pull the rubber boot off the adjuster and check its position – if there is thread exposed between the locknut and the elbow, fully slacken the locknut and turn the adjuster fully in to reset it at its start point, then tighten the locknut and fit the boot.

17 Fit the closing cable end into the lower socket in the throttle pulley, then fit the cable in the bracket and tighten the hex onto it **(see illustrations 11.12)**. Fit the opening cable end into the upper socket in the pulley and fit the cable in the bracket, then thread the adjuster nut up to the bracket, pull the cable up to seat the adjuster nut captive under the bracket and tighten the locknut onto it – adjust the position of the adjuster nut as required so there is the specified amount of freeplay in the cable at the throttle twistgrip (see Chapter 1).

18 Operate the throttle to check that it opens and closes freely. Turn the handlebars back and forth to make sure the cable doesn't cause the steering to bind.

19 Start the engine and check that the idle speed does not increase as the handlebars are turned. If it does, the throttle cable is routed incorrectly. Correct the problem before riding the motorcycle.

20 Install the fuel tank (see Section 2).

12 Exhaust system

Warning: If the engine has been running the exhaust system will be very hot. Allow the system to cool before carrying out any work.

HAYNES HiNT ***Before starting work on the exhaust system spray the header pipe nuts and mounting bolts with penetrating fluid – they are prone to corrosion.***

11.13c ... and draw the cables out

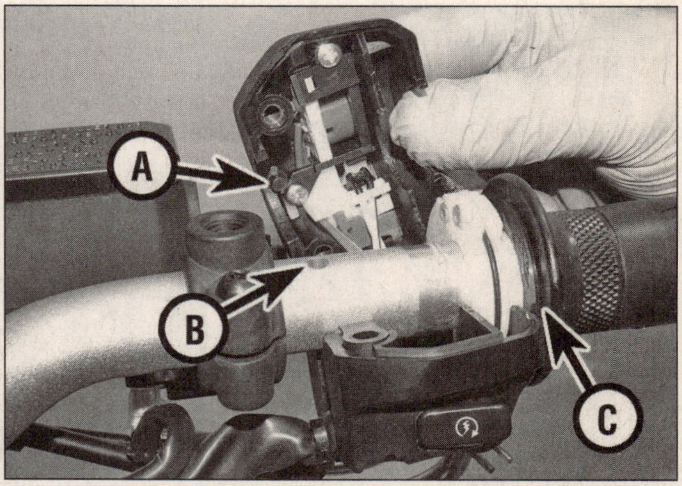

11.16 Locate the peg (A) in the hole (B) and make sure the washer (C) is on the outside

12.2a Silencer clamp bolt (arrowed)

12.2b Unscrew the mounting bolts (arrowed) ...

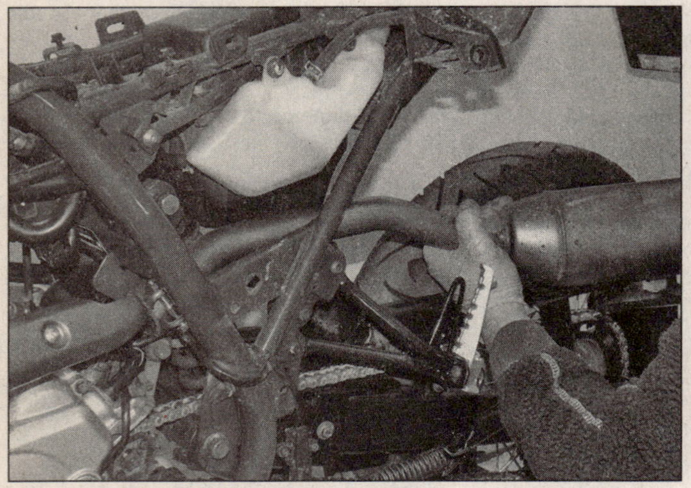

12.2c ... and remove the silencer as described

12.3 Release the clamp and detach the hose

Removal

WR models

1 Remove the left-hand frame cover and side cover (see Chapter 7).

2 Slacken the silencer clamp bolt **(see illustration)**. Support the silencer and unscrew the mounting bolts, then draw the silencer out of the downpipe, twisting it as shown for clearance, and remove it **(see illustrations)**.

3 Detach the AIS hose from the downpipe **(see illustration)**.

4 Unscrew the nuts securing the header pipe to the cylinder head **(see illustration)**. Draw the flange off the studs and remove the pipe **(see illustration)**.

5 Remove the sealing ring from the port in the cylinder head – a new one must be used **(see illustration)**. Check the condition of the sealing ring in the silencer pipe and replace it

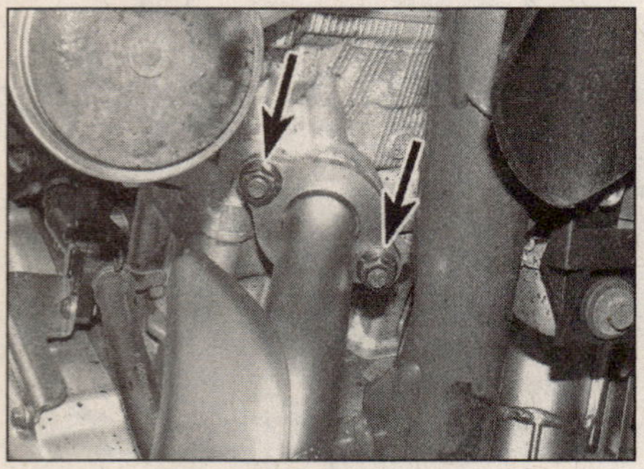

12.4a Unscrew the nuts (arrowed) ...

12.4b ... draw the flange off and pull the pipe out of the head

12.5a Remove the header pipe sealing ring

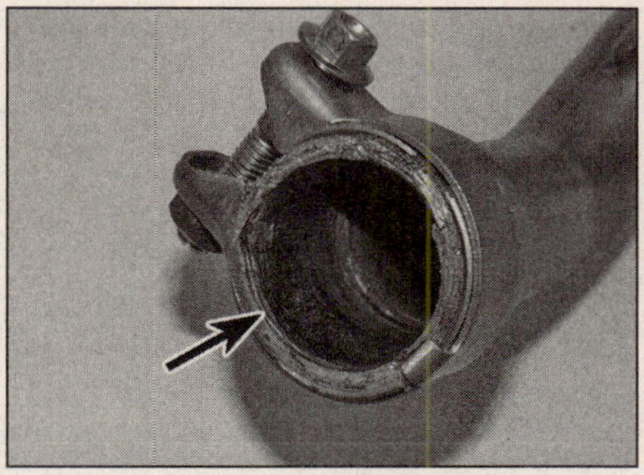

12.5b Remove the silencer sealing ring (arrowed) if necessary

12.7 Unscrew the nuts (arrowed) and draw the flange off

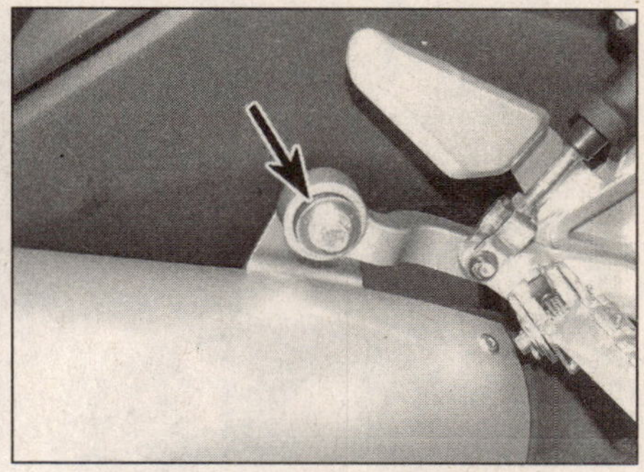

12.8a Unscrew the silencer bolt (arrowed)...

12.8b ...then the middle bolt (arrowed)

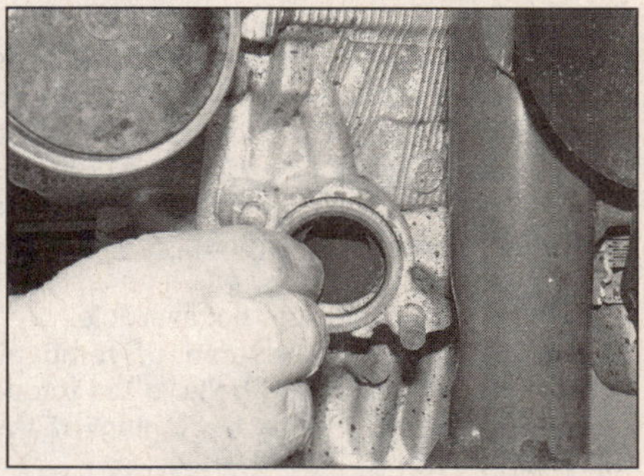

12.10 Always use a new sealing ring

with a new one if necessary **(see illustration)** – you will have to dig the old one out using a suitable tool, and take great care when fitting the new one as they are easily damaged.

MT and YZF-R models

6 On MT models remove the belly-panel, and on YZF-R models remove all sections of the fairing on the right-hand side (see Chapter 7).

7 Unscrew the nuts securing the header pipe to the cylinder head **(see illustration)**. Draw the flange off the studs.

8 Unscrew the silencer mounting bolt **(see illustration)**. Support the system and unscrew the middle bolt, then manoeuvre the exhaust off the head and remove it **(see illustrations)**.

9 Remove the sealing ring from the port in the cylinder head – a new one must be used **(see illustration 12.5a)**. Note the collar fitted into the inner side of the rubber bush in the silencer mount.

Installation

10 Installation is the reverse of removal, noting the following:

- Replace any damaged, deformed or deteriorated mounting bolts, nuts, washers, collar or rubber with new ones. On MT and YZF-R models make sure the collar is fitted in the rubber from the inner side of the silencer mount.
- Use a new sealing ring in the cylinder head port, and dab it with grease to stick it in place **(see illustration)**.
- Apply a smear of copper grease to all nuts and bolts to prevent them from seizing up.
- Fit all nuts/bolts finger-tight first, then tighten the header nuts, then the middle bolt, then the silencer bolt to the torque settings specified at the beginning of the Chapter for your model.
- On WR models tighten the silencer clamp bolt to the specified torque, and do not forget to connect the AIS hose **(see illustrations 12.2a and 12.3)**.
- Run the engine and check that there are no leaks.

13 Air induction system (WR models)

Function

1 The air induction system (AIS) uses exhaust gas pulses to suck fresh air into the exhaust pipe, where it mixes with hot combustion gases. The extra oxygen causes continued combustion, allowing unburnt hydrocarbons to burn off, thereby reducing emissions. The system comprises the reed valve housing, and the hoses linking it to the air filter housing and the exhaust pipe **(see illustration)**. The reed valve allows the flow of air in one direction only, opening when there is negative pressure on the exhaust side, and otherwise closing to prevent exhaust gases flowing into the air filter housing.

Testing

2 Detach the hose from the exhaust downpipe and clean its end thoroughly **(see illustration 12.3)**.

3 Check the operation of the system by sucking on the hose – air should be drawn freely through the reed valves.

4 Now try to blow up the hose – you should not be able to, indicating the reed valve is closing and sealing correctly. If you can blow air through, remove and disassemble the valve housing for cleaning (see Steps 7 to 9), then test it again. Replace the valve assembly with a new one if necessary.

Removal and installation

5 Release the hose clamps and detach the hoses from the air filter, exhaust pipe and reed valve housing as required **(see illustrations 8.2b, 12.3 and 13.1)**.

6 Unscrew the reed valve housing mounting bolts and remove the housing **(see illustration)**.

7 To check the reed valve undo the housing

13.1 AIS reed valve housing (arrowed)

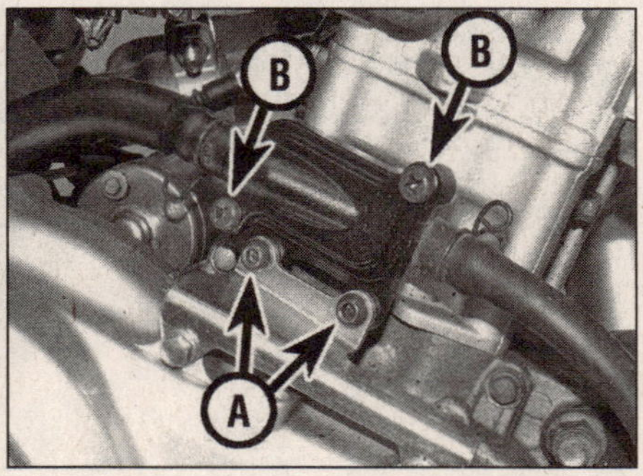

13.6 Reed valve housing mounting bolts (A) and cover screws (B)

13.7a Remove the reed valve

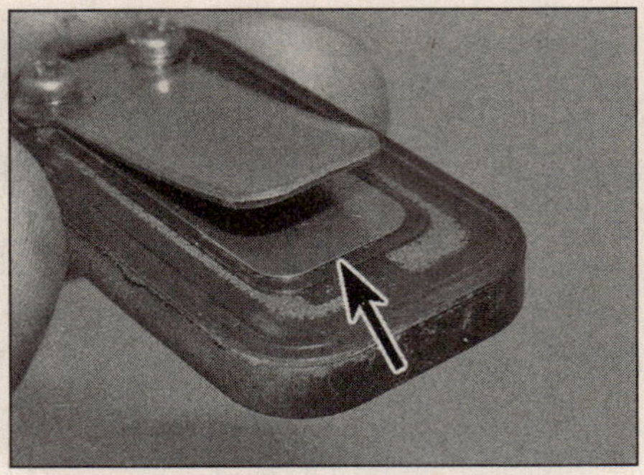

13.7b Check there is no gap between the reed (arrowed) and its seat

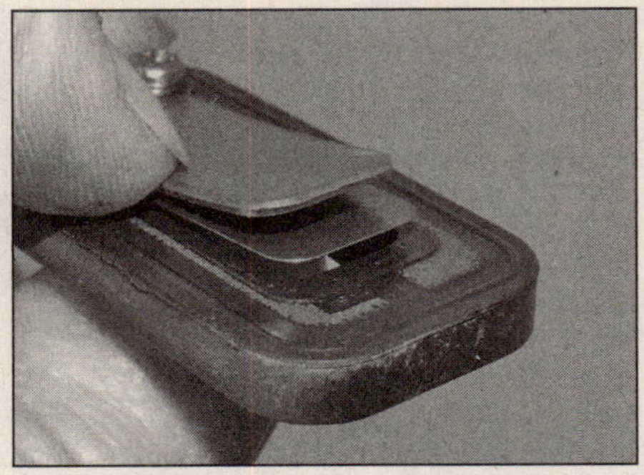

13.7c Gently lift the reed off its seat to check it is not stuck

cover screws and remove the cover **(see illustration 13.6)**. Remove the reed valve, noting which way round it fits **(see illustration)**. Clean off all carbon deposits. Check the reed is seated and sealing correctly, then carefully lift it off the seat to check it is not stuck **(see illustrations)**. Replace the valve assembly with a new one if necessary – individual components are not available.

8 Installation is the reverse of removal. Tighten the valve housing bolts to the torque setting specified at the beginning of the chapter.

14 Catalytic converters

General information

1 Two catalytic converters are incorporated in the exhaust system to minimise the level of exhaust pollutants released into the atmosphere. On WR models it is an open-loop system with no feedback to the ECU. On MT and YZF-R models it is a closed-loop system with an oxygen sensor mounted in the exhaust port on the cylinder head feeding back information on exhaust gas content to the ECU.

2 A catalytic converter consists of a canister containing a fine mesh impregnated with a catalyst material, over which the hot exhaust gases pass. The catalyst speeds up the oxidation of harmful carbon monoxide, unburned hydrocarbons and soot, effectively reducing the quantity of harmful products released into the atmosphere via the exhaust gases.

Precautions

3 A catalytic converter is a reliable and simple device that needs no maintenance in itself, but there are some facts to be aware of if the converter is to function properly for its full service life.

- DO NOT use leaded or lead replacement petrol (gasoline) – the additives will coat the precious metals, reducing their converting efficiency and will eventually destroy the catalytic converter.
- Always keep the ignition and fuel systems well-maintained in accordance with the manufacturer's schedule – if the fuel/air mixture is suspected of being incorrect have it checked on an exhaust gas analyser.
- If the engine develops a misfire, do not ride the bike at all (or at least as little as possible) until the fault is cured.
- DO NOT use fuel or engine oil additives – these may contain substances harmful to the catalytic converter.
- DO NOT continue to use the bike if the engine burns oil to the extent of leaving a visible trail of blue smoke.
- Avoid bump-starting the bike unless absolutely necessary.

15 Ignition system check

Warning: The energy levels in electronic systems can be very high. On no account should the ignition be switched on whilst the plug or plug cap is being held. Shocks from the HT circuit can be most unpleasant. Secondly, it is vital that the engine is not turned over with the plug cap removed, and that the plug is soundly earthed (grounded) when the system is checked for sparking. The ignition system components can be seriously damaged if the HT circuit becomes isolated.

1 As no means of adjustment is available, any failure of the system can be traced to failure of a system component or a simple wiring fault. Of the two possibilities, the latter is by far the most likely. In the event of failure, check the system in a logical fashion, as described. First make sure the battery is fully charged and a related fuse has not blown (see Chapter 8).

2 On YZF-R models remove the centre section of the fairing on the right-hand side (see Chapter 7).

3 Pull the cap off the spark plug **(see illustration)**. Fit a spare spark plug that is known to be good into the cap and lay the plug against the cylinder head with the threads contacting it. If necessary, hold the spark plug with an insulated tool.

Warning: Do not remove the spark plug from the engine to perform this check – atomised fuel being pumped out of the open spark plug hole could ignite, causing severe injury! Make sure the plug is securely held against the engine – if it is not earthed when the engine is turned over, the ECU could be damaged.

4 Check that the transmission is in neutral, then turn the ignition switch ON, set the kill switch to RUN, and turn the engine over on the starter motor. If the system is in good condition a regular, fat blue spark should be evident at the plug electrodes. If the spark appears thin or yellowish, or is non-existent, further investigation will be necessary. Turn the ignition off.

5 The ignition system must be able to produce a spark which is capable of jumping at least a 6 mm gap. Simple ignition spark gap testing tools are commercially available – follow the manufacturer's instructions **(see illustration)**.

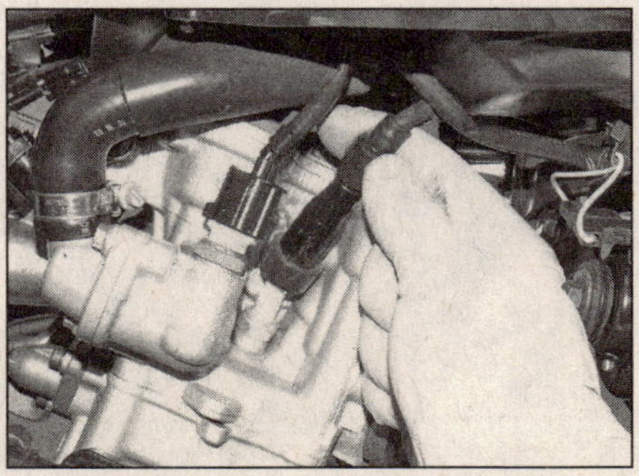

15.3 Pull the cap off the spark plug

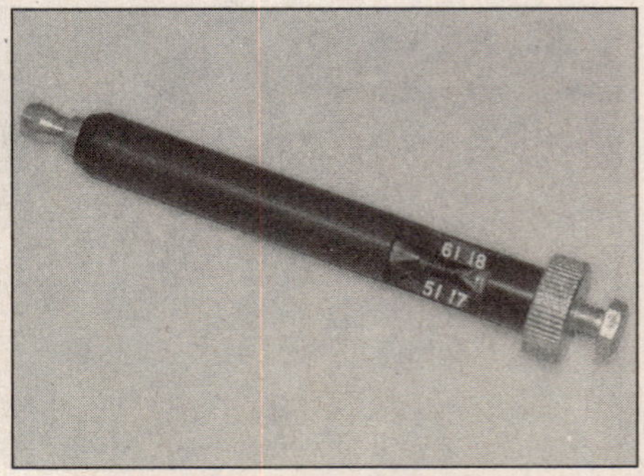

15.5 A typical spark gap testing tool

6 If the test results are good the entire ignition system can be considered good.

7 Ignition faults are listed below, starting with the most probable source of failure. Work through the list systematically, referring to the subsequent sections for full details of the necessary checks and tests, and to the Wiring Diagram at the end of Chapter 8. Note: Before checking the following items ensure that the battery is fully charged and that all fuses are in good condition.

- Loose, corroded or damaged wiring connections, broken or shorted wiring between any of the component parts of the ignition system (see Chapter 8).
- Faulty HT lead or spark plug cap, faulty spark plug, dirty, worn or corroded plug electrodes, or incorrect gap between electrodes (See Section 16 and Chapter 1).
- Faulty neutral, clutch or sidestand switch, or safety circuit diodes (see Chapter 8).
- Faulty engine kill switch (see Chapter 8).
- Faulty tip-over sensor (see Section 7).
- Faulty crankshaft position sensor (see Section 7) or damaged trigger.
- Faulty ignition coil (see Section 16).
- Faulty ignition switch (see Chapter 8).
- Faulty starter circuit cut-off relay or diodes (see Chapter 8).
- Faulty ECU (see Section 17).

8 If the above checks don't reveal the cause of the problem, have the ignition system tested by a Yamaha dealer.

16 Ignition coil and spark plug cap

Check

1 On WR models remove the fuel tank cover, and on YZF-R models remove the centre section of the fairing on the right-hand side (see Chapter 7). On MT and YZF-R models remove the fuel tank (see Section 2). Check the coil visually for loose or damaged connectors and terminals, loose mountings, cracks and other damage (see illustration 16.3a or b).

2 Make sure the ignition is off.

3 Disconnect the primary wiring connectors

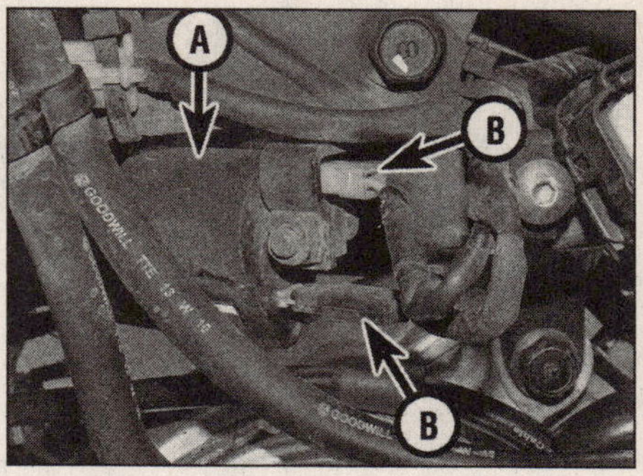

16.3a Ignition coil (A) and its primary wiring connectors (B) – WR models

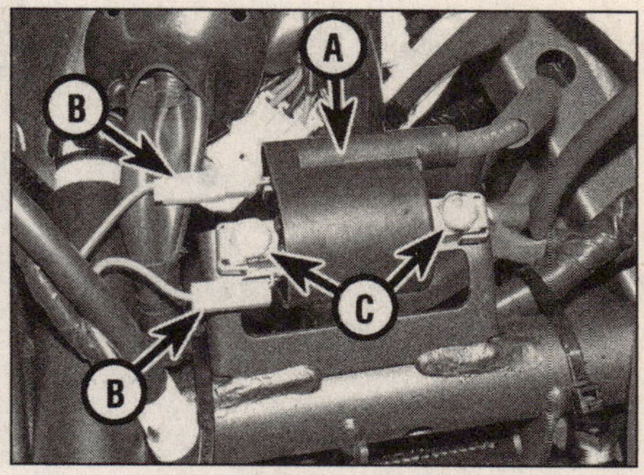

16.3b Ignition coil (A) and its primary wiring connectors (B) and mounting bolts (C) – MT and YZF-R models

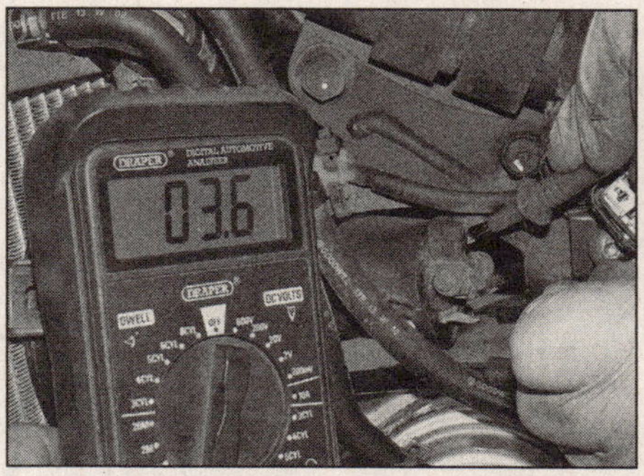

16.4 Testing the coil primary resistance

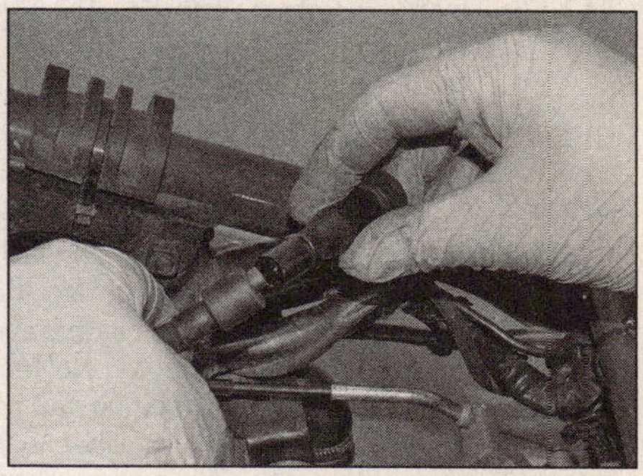

16.5a To test the coil secondary resistance unscrew the cap from the lead...

(see illustrations). Pull the cap off the spark plug (see illustration 15.3).

4 Set an ohmmeter or multimeter to the ohms x 1 scale and measure the resistance between the primary terminals on the coil **(see illustration)**. This will give a resistance reading of the primary windings of the coil and should be consistent with the value given in the Specifications at the beginning of the Chapter.

5 To check the condition of the secondary windings, unscrew the plug cap from the end of the HT lead **(see illustration)**. Set the meter to the K-ohm scale. Connect the positive (+) meter probe to the primary terminal for the orange wire on the coil, and insert the other probe in the end of the HT lead **(see illustration)**. If the reading obtained is not within the range shown in the Specifications, the coil is defective.

6 If the readings are as specified, measure the resistance of the spark plug cap by connecting the meter probes between the HT lead socket and the spark plug contact **(see illustration)**. If the reading obtained is not as specified, replace the spark plug cap with a new one.

Removal and installation

7 Remove the fuel tank (see Section 2).

8 Disconnect the primary wiring connectors from the coil **(see illustration 16.3a or b)**. Pull the cap off the spark plug **(see illustration 15.3)**.

9 Unscrew the bolts, noting the washers on WR models and the dampers on MT and YZF-R models, and remove the coil **(see illustration or 16.3b)**.

10 Installation is the reverse of removal.

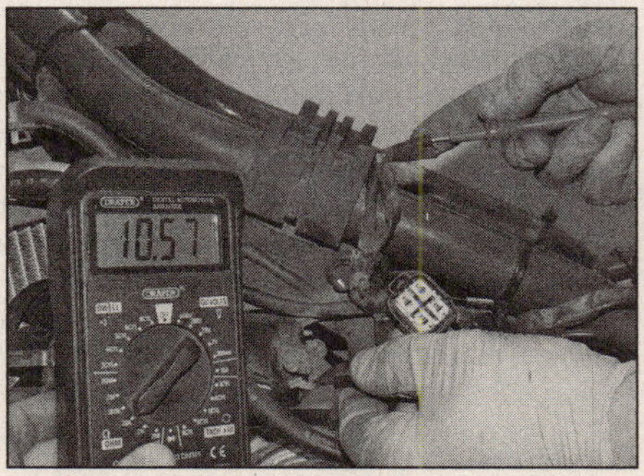

16.5b ...and connect the multimeter leads between the orange wire primary terminal and the spark plug lead end

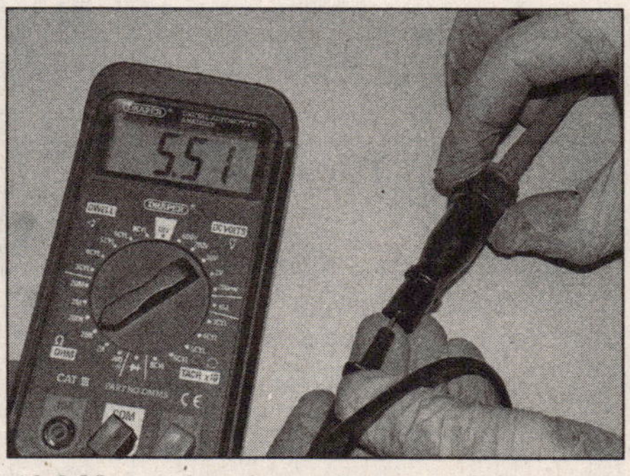

16.6 Measuring the resistance of the spark plug cap

16.9 Coil mounting bolts (arrowed) – WR models

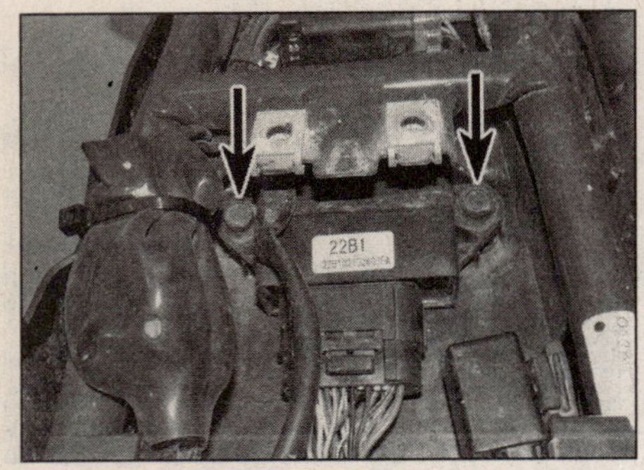

17.4 ECU mounting bolts (arrowed)

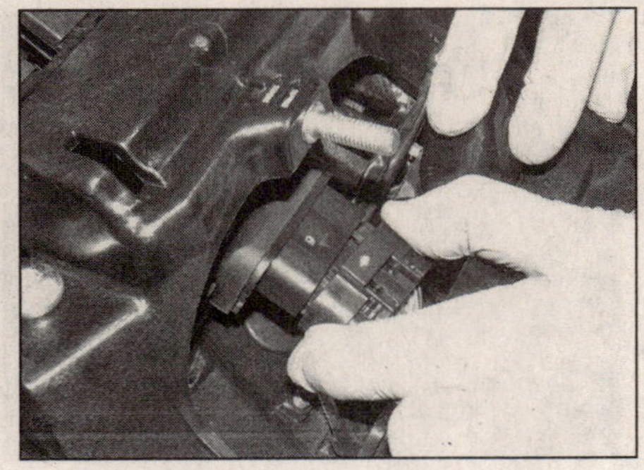

17.5a Disconnect the wiring...

17.5b ...then displace and remove the ECU

17 Electronic control unit (ECU)

Check

1 If the tests shown in the preceding or following Sections have failed to isolate the cause of an ignition fault, it is possible that the electronic control unit itself is faulty. No test details are available with which the unit can be tested. The best way to determine whether it is faulty is to substitute it with a known good one, if available. Otherwise, take the unit to a Yamaha dealer for assessment.

2 Before condemning the ECU make sure the wiring connector terminals are clean and none of the wires have broken **(see illustration 17.4 or 17.5)** – for access remove the seat on WR models and the seat cowls on MT and YZF-R models (see Chapter 7). Make sure the ignition is off before disconnecting the wiring connector.

Removal and installation

3 Make sure the ignition is off.

4 On WR models remove the seat and the tail cover (see Chapter 7). Unscrew the bolts, displace the ECU and disconnect the wiring connector **(see illustration)**.

5 On MT and YZF-R models remove the seats and seat cowls (see Chapter 7). Disconnect the wiring connector, then lift the ECU off its bracket and remove it **(see illustrations)**.

6 Installation is the reverse of removal. Make sure the wiring connector is securely connected.

18 Ignition timing

General information

1 Since no provision exists for adjusting the ignition timing and since no component is subject to mechanical wear, there is no need for regular checks: only if investigating a fault such as a loss of power or a misfire, should the ignition timing be checked.

2 The ignition timing is checked dynamically (engine running) using a stroboscopic lamp. The inexpensive neon lamps should be adequate in theory, but in practice may produce a pulse of such low intensity that the timing mark remains indistinct. If possible, one of the more precise xenon tube lamps should be used, powered by an external source of the appropriate voltage. Note: Do not use the machine's own battery, as an incorrect reading may result from stray impulses within the machine's electrical system.

Check

3 Warm the engine up to normal operating temperature, then stop it. Remove all sections of the fairing on the left-hand side and the centre section on the right-hand side (see Chapter 7).

4 Unscrew the timing inspection cap from the alternator cover on the left side of the engine **(see illustration)**.

5 The mark on the timing rotor which indicates the firing point at idle speed is an 'H' on its side **(see illustration)**. The static timing mark with which this should align is the pointer in the inspection hole.

> **HAYNES HiNT** *The timing marks can be highlighted with white paint to make them more visible under the stroboscope light.*

6 Connect the timing light to the HT lead as described in the manufacturer's instructions.

7 Start the engine and aim the light at the inspection hole.

8 With the machine idling, the mark on the rotor should align with the static timing mark.

9 Slowly increase the engine speed whilst observing the mark – it should appear to move clockwise, increasing in relation to the engine speed until it reaches full advance (no identification mark).

10 As already stated, there is no means of adjustment of the ignition timing on these machines. If the ignition timing is incorrect, or suspected of being incorrect, one of the ignition system components is at fault, and the system must be tested as described in the preceding Sections of this Chapter.

11 Fit the timing inspection cap using a new O-ring smeared with grease.

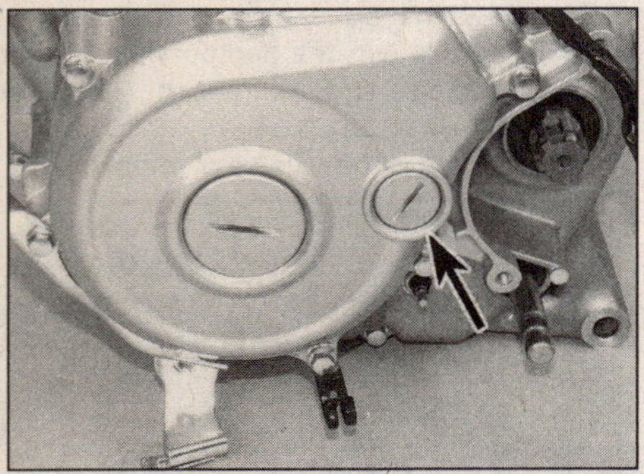

18.4 Unscrew the timing inspection cap (arrowed)

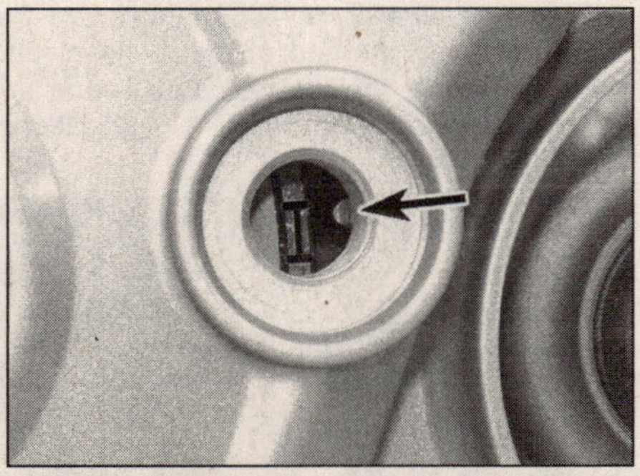

18.5 Ignition timing mark and the pointer (arrowed)

Chapter 5
Frame and suspension

Contents

Degrees of difficulty

Easy, suitable for novice with little experience	**Fairly easy,** suitable for beginner with some experience	**Fairly difficult,** suitable for competent DIY mechanic	**Difficult,** suitable for experienced DIY mechanic	**Very difficult,** suitable for expert DIY or professional

Specifications

Front forks

Fork oil type	10W fork oil
Fork oil capacity	
WR-R models	560 cc per fork
WR-X models	610 cc per fork
MT and YZF-R models	
Right-hand fork	434 cc
Left-hand fork	321 cc
Fork oil level (see text)	
WR-R models	165 mm
WR-X models	145 mm
MT and YZF-R models	
Right-hand fork	135 mm
Left-hand fork	not applicable
Fork spring free length (min)	
WR models	
Standard	520 mm
Service limit	468 mm
MT and YZF-R models	
Standard	333.5 mm
Service limit	311.5 mm
Fork tube runout limit	
WR models	0.3 mm
MT and YZF-R models	0.1 mm

Torque settings

Item	Torque
Clutch lever bracket clamp bolt(s)	9 Nm
Fork damper rod/cartridge bolt	
WR models with Paioli forks (see text)	28 Nm
WR models with Kayaba forks (see text)	30 Nm
MT and YZF-R models	23 Nm
Fork clamp bolts	
Top yoke	23 Nm
Bottom yoke	
WR models	22 Nm
MT and YZF-R models	23 Nm
Fork top bolt	
WR models	20 Nm
MT and YZF-R models	23 Nm
Front brake master cylinder clamp bolts	9 Nm
Gearchange linkage arm pinch bolt	10 Nm
Handlebars	
WR models	
Handlebar clamp bolts	23 Nm
Handlebar holder nuts	34 Nm
MT models	
Handlebar clamp bolts	23 Nm
Handlebar holder nuts	40 Nm
Handlebar end-weights	26 Nm
YZF-R models	
Handlebar positioning bolts	9 Nm
Handlebar clamp bolts	23 Nm
Handlebar end-weights	26 Nm
Rear shock absorber and suspension linkage	
WR models	
Shock absorber upper mounting bolt/nut	43 Nm
All other bolts/nuts	59 Nm
MT and YZF-R models – all bolts/nuts	44 Nm
Sidestand pivot bolt nut	55 Nm
Steering head bearing adjuster nut	
WR models	
Initial setting	38 Nm
Final setting	
2009 and 2010 models	4 Nm
2011-on models	9 Nm
MT and YZF-R models	
Initial setting	48 Nm
Final setting	13 Nm
Steering stem nut	
WR models	140 Nm
MT and YZF-R models	110 Nm
Swingarm pivot bolt nut	
WR models	80 Nm
MT and YZF-R models	79 Nm

1 General Information

1 On WR models the frame is a tubular steel cradle type. On MT and YZF-R model the frame is a steel Deltabox type that uses the engine as a stressed member.

2 Front suspension is by oil-damped 41 mm forks, and rear suspension is by a single shock absorber via a rising rate linkage, with a swingarm that pivots through the frame.

3 On WR models the front forks are not adjustable, and the rear shock absorber has adjustable spring pre-load. On MT and YZF-R models the suspension is not adjustable.

2 Frame inspection and repair

1 The frame should not require attention unless accident damage has occurred. In most cases, fitting a new frame is the only satisfactory remedy for such damage. Frame specialists have the jigs and other equipment necessary for straightening a frame to the required standard of accuracy, but even then there is no simple way of assessing to what extent it may have been over-stressed.

2 After a high mileage, examine the frame closely for signs of cracking or splitting at the welded joints. Loose engine mounting bolts can cause ovaling or fracturing of the mounting points. Minor damage can often be repaired by specialised welding, depending on the extent and nature of the damage.

3 Remember that a frame that is out of alignment will cause handling problems. If, as the result of an accident, misalignment is suspected, it will be necessary to strip the machine completely so the frame can be thoroughly checked.

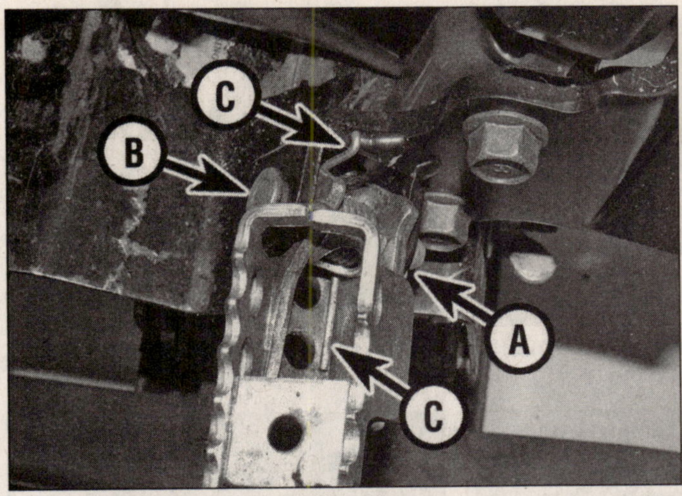

3.1a On WR models remove the split pin (A), then withdraw the pivot pin (B), noting how the spring ends (C) locate

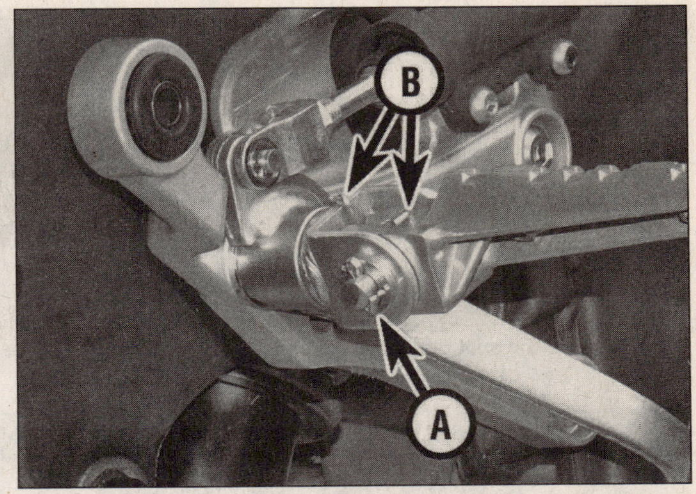

3.1b On MT and YZF-R models remove the split pin (A) and washer, then withdraw the pivot pin, noting how the spring ends (B) locate

3 Footrests, brake pedal and gearchange lever

Footrests

1 To remove a rider's footrest, straighten and remove the split pin, and on MT and YZF-R models remove the washer, from the bottom of the footrest pivot pin, then withdraw the pin and remove the footrest, noting how the return spring ends locate **(see illustrations)**. On MT and YZF-R models note the sleeve for the pivot pin in the footrest.

2 To remove a passenger footrest, straighten and remove the split pin from the bottom of the footrest pivot pin, then withdraw the pin and remove the footrest, collecting the detent ball and spring, and on MT and YZF-R models the detent plate, noting how they fit **(see illustration)**. On WR models note the sleeve for the pivot pin in the footrest.

3 Installation is the reverse of removal. Apply a small amount of multi-purpose grease to the pivot pin. Make sure the springs ends or detent plate, ball and spring locate correctly. Use new split pins on the pivot pins, and bend the ends around the pivot pin.

Brake pedal

WR models

4 Remove the split pin and washer from the clevis pin securing the brake pedal to the master cylinder pushrod, then withdraw the pin and detach the pushrod **(see illustration)**. A new split pin must be used.

5 Unhook the return spring from the pedal **(see illustration 3.4)**.

6 Unscrew the brake pedal bolt and remove the washer **(see illustration 3.4)**, then draw the pedal off.

7 Installation is the reverse of removal, noting the following:

- Clean all old grease off the pedal pivot and apply fresh grease.
- Clean the threads of the brake pedal bolt and apply some fresh threadlock.
- Replace the return spring with a new one if it has sagged or deformed.
- Clean all old grease off the clevis pin and apply fresh grease. Use a new split pin and bend the ends around to secure it.
- Check the operation of the rear brake (see Chapter 1).

MT and YZF-R models

8 Remove the split pin and washer from the clevis pin securing the brake pedal to the

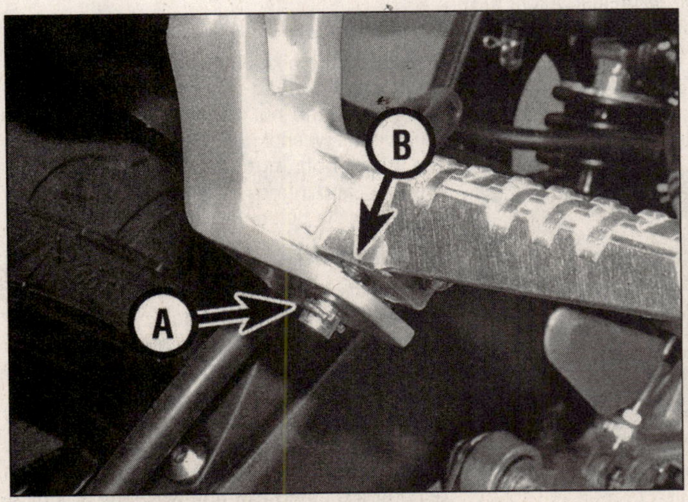

3.2 Remove the split pin (A), then withdraw the pivot pin, noting how the ball and spring (B) and detent plate (where fitted) locate

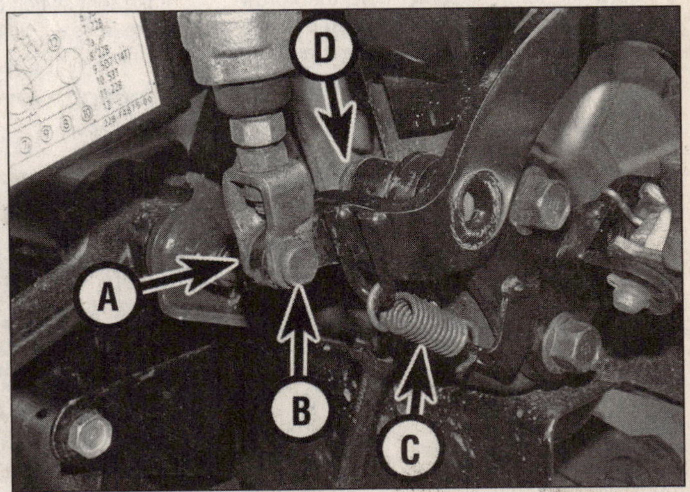

3.4 Remove the split pin (A) and washer, then withdraw the clevis pin (B). Return spring (C) and pedal bolt (D)

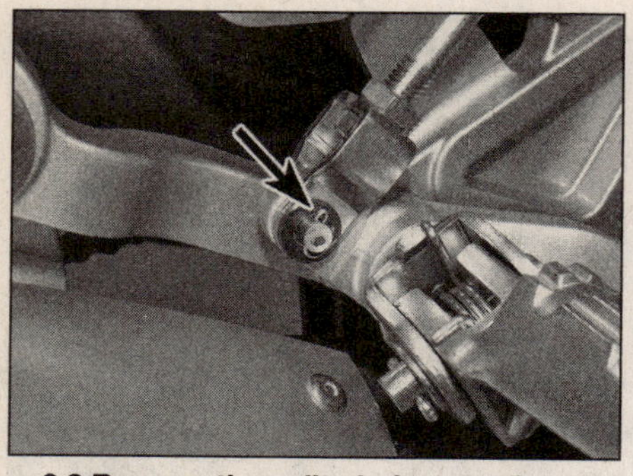
3.8 Remove the split pin (arrowed) and washer

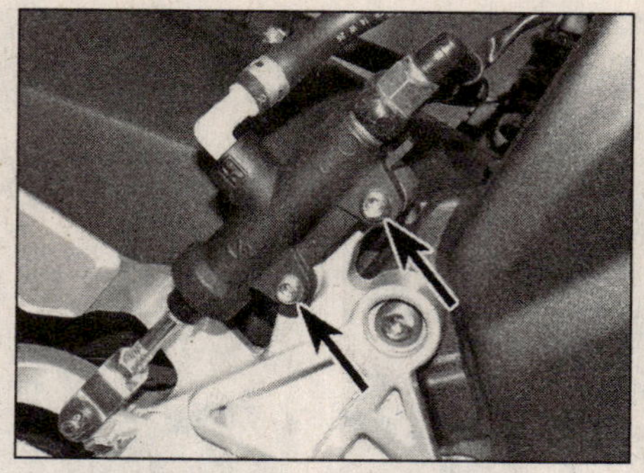
3.9a Unscrew the bolts (arrowed)...

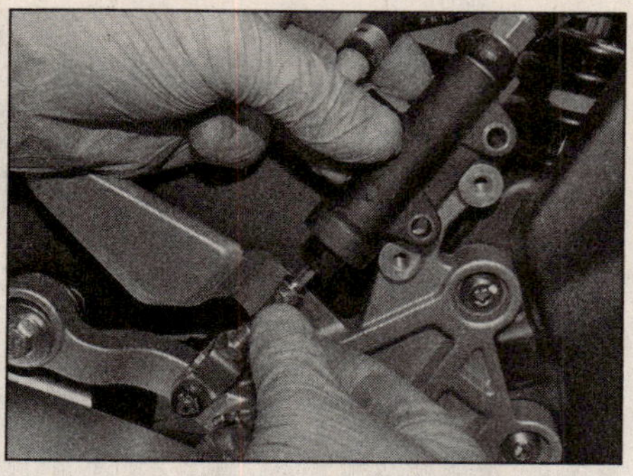
3.9b...and lift the master cylinder off the pushrod

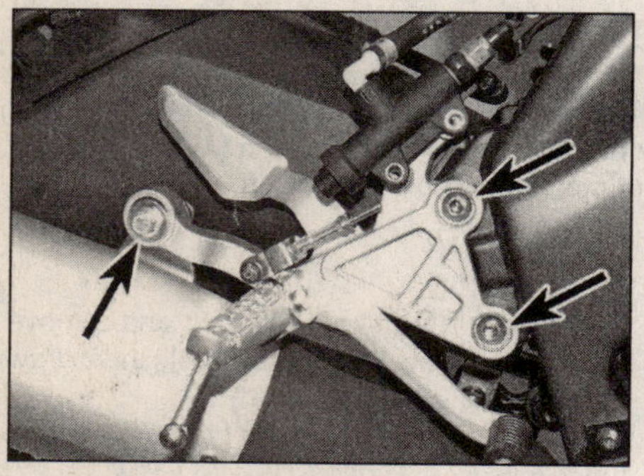
3.10 Unscrew the bolts (arrowed)

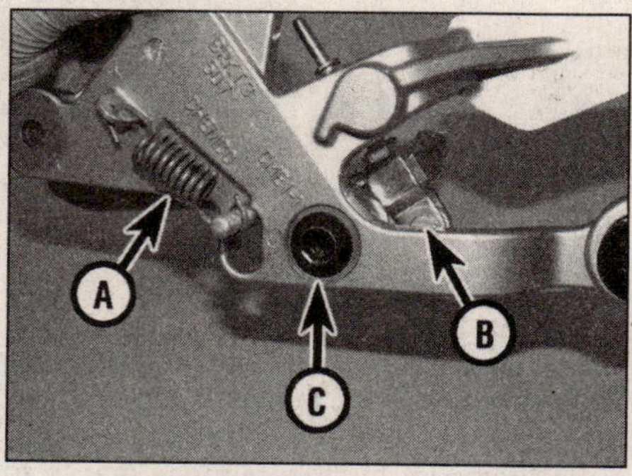

3.11 Pedal return spring (A), clevis (B), footrest holder bolt (C)

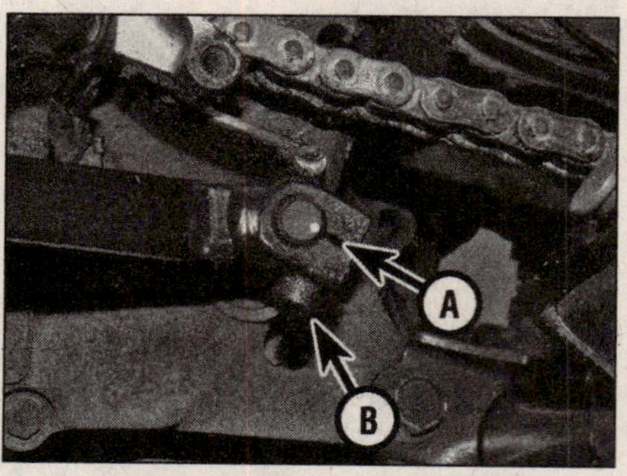

3.14 Mark the alignment (A), then unscrew the bolt (B) – WR model shown

master cylinder pushrod **(see illustration)**. A new split pin must be used.

9 Unscrew the master cylinder bolts and lift the mister cylinder off the pushrod, noting how the boot lip locates in the groove **(see illustration)**.

10 Unscrew the footrest bracket bolts and silencer mounting bolt and remove the bracket/pedal assembly **(see illustration)**.

11 Unhook the pedal return spring, and on models with ABS unhook the brake light switch spring **(see illustration)**. Move the pedal around so the clevis is clear of the bracket and withdraw it to free the pushrod. Unscrew the footrest holder bolt, then draw the footrest assembly off and remove the pedal, noting the washer between it and the bracket.

12 Installation is the reverse of removal, noting the following:

4.2 Unhook the springs (arrowed)

- Clean all old grease off the pedal pivot and apply fresh grease.
- Clean the threads of the footrest holder bolt and apply some fresh threadlock.
- Replace the return spring with a new one if it has sagged or deformed.
- When fitting the master cylinder onto the pushrod make sure the lip of the rubber boot seats in the groove in the pushrod.
- Clean all old grease off the clevis pin and apply fresh grease. Use a new split pin and bend the ends around to secure it.
- Check the operation of the rear brake (see Chapter 1). On models with ABS check the brake light switch comes on just before the brake does – if adjustment is required refer to Chapter 1).

Gearchange lever

13 On YZF-R model remove the lower section of the fairing on the left-hand side (see Chapter 7).

4.3 Unscrew the nut (arrowed) and remove the washer

14 Make an alignment mark where the gearchange shaft aligns with the slit in the lever clamp **(see illustration)**. Unscrew the pinch bolt and slide the lever off.

15 Installation is the reverse of removal. Make sure the lever is correctly aligned on the shaft.

4 Sidestand

Removal

1 Support the bike on an auxiliary stand.

2 Unhook the stand springs **(see illustration)**.

3 Unscrew the nut from the pivot bolt and remove the washer **(see illustration)**. Remove the pivot bolt, noting the washer on WR models, and remove the stand, noting the sleeve for the bolt on MT and YZF-R models.

Installation

4 Installation is the reverse of removal. Apply grease to the pivot bolt shank. Counter-hold the bolt while tightening the nut to the torque setting specified at the beginning of the Chapter.

5 Reconnect the springs, and check they hold the stand securely up when not in use **(see illustration 4.2)** – an accident could occur if the stand extends while the machine is in motion. Check the operation of the switch (see Chapter 1).

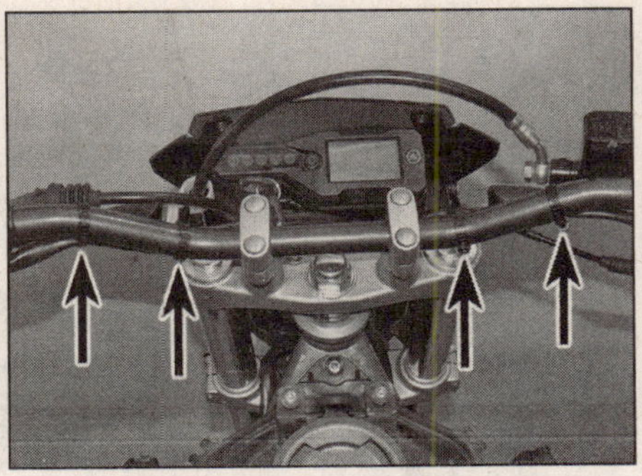

5.3a Release the ties (arrowed)

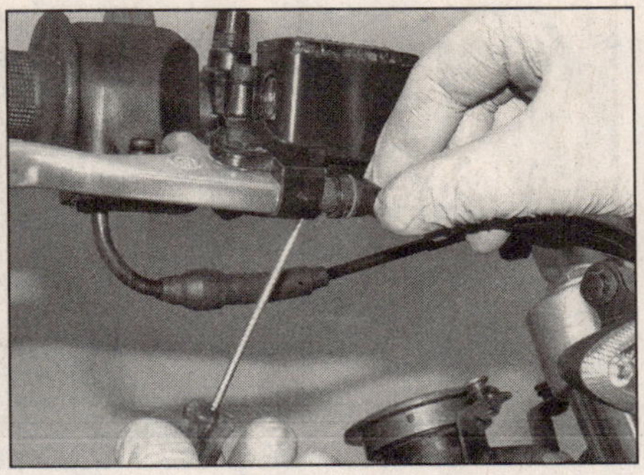

5.3b Push up on the release tab and draw the switch out

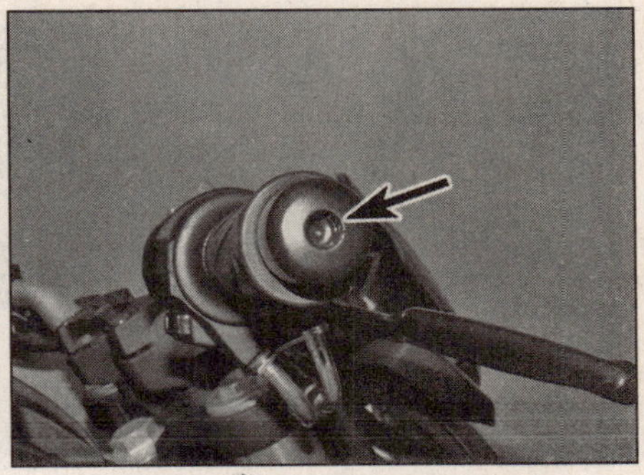

5.4a Use a hex key to unscrew the end-weight (arrow)

5 Handlebars and levers

Handlebar removal

1 Protect the fuel tank cover, and on YZF-R models the fairing panels, with plenty of rag, or remove them if required (see Chapter 7). Also cover the instruments with rag.

WR and MT models

2 Remove the mirrors (see Chapter 7).

3 On WR models release the cable-ties securing the switch wiring to the handlebar **(see illustration)**. Displace the front brake light switch from the lever bracket **(see illustration)**.

4 On MT models unscrew the end-weight from each end of the handlebar **(see illustration)**. Disconnect the brake light switch wiring connectors **(see illustration)**.

5 Unscrew the master cylinder clamp bolts, remove the clamp and displace the master cylinder **(see illustration)** – wrap it in some rag and secure it clear of the handlebar, keeping it upright.

5.4b Front brake light switch wiring connectors (arrowed)

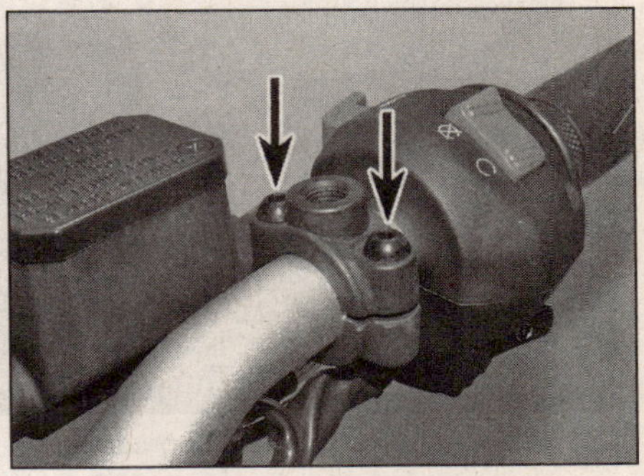

5.5 Master cylinder clamp bolts (arrowed)

6 Refer to Chapter 4 and disconnect the throttle cable(s) – this involves detaching the switch housing. Slide the twistgrip off.

7 Disconnect the clutch switch wiring connector **(see illustration)**. Undo the switch housing screws and displace the housing.

8 Remove the grip from the left-hand end of the handlebar – if it has been glued on or is stuck feed a wooden or plastic tool up the inside and move it round the bar to release it, or squirt some WD40 between the bar and grip but be careful to protect your eyes from spray back. At worst you will have to cut the grip off and fit a new one.

9 Disconnect the clutch cable (see Chapter 2). Slacken the clutch lever bracket clamp bolt and slide the lever bracket assembly off the handlebar **(see illustration)**.

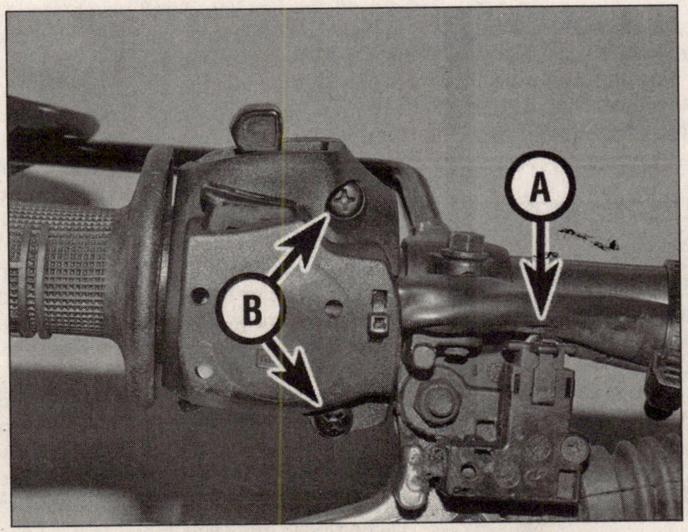

5.7 Clutch switch wiring connector (A), switch housing screws (B)

5.9 Clutch lever bracket clamp bolt (arrowed)

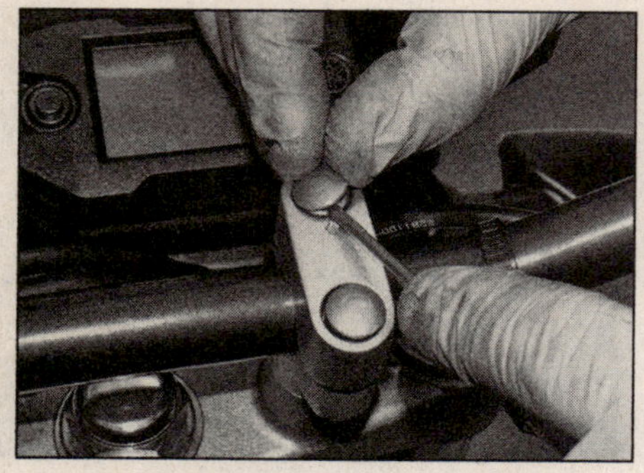

5.10a Remove the blanking caps

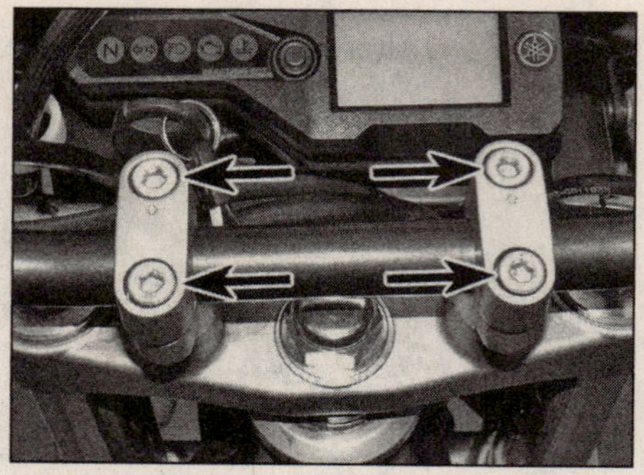

5.10b Handlebar clamp bolts (arrowed) – WR models

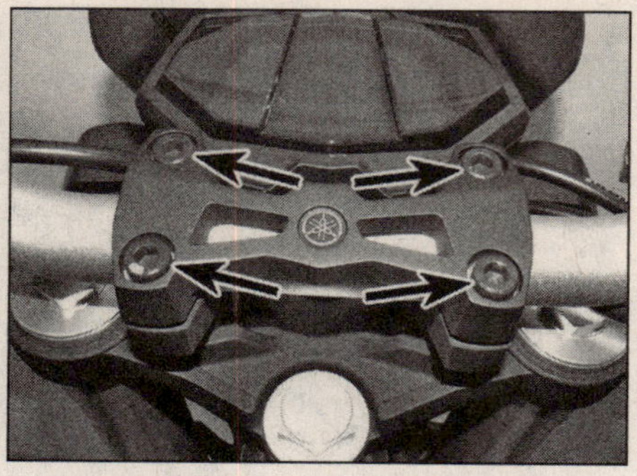

5.10c Handlebar clamp bolts (arrowed) – MT models

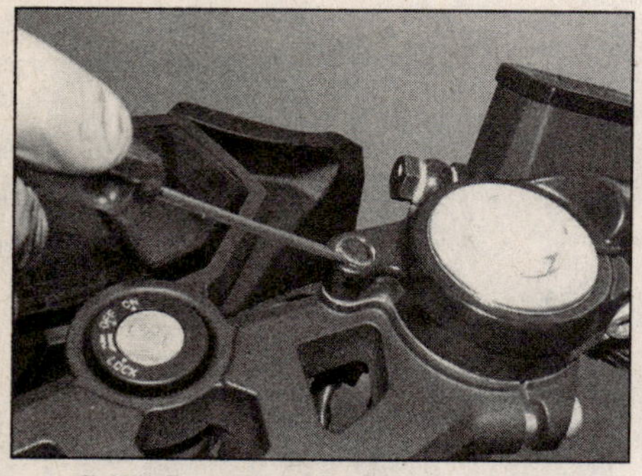

5.15a Remove the blanking cap...

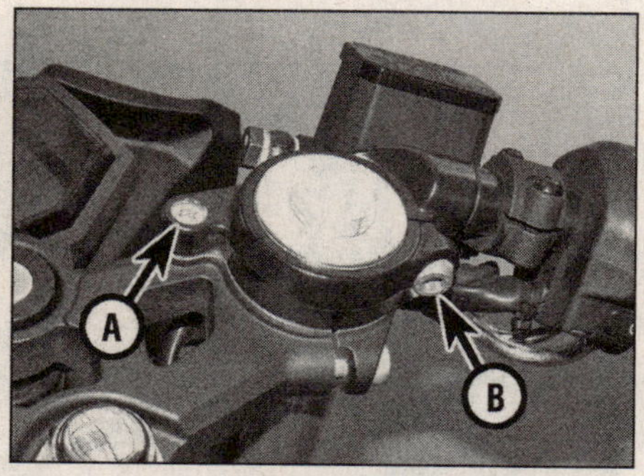

5.15b ...then unscrew the positioning bolt (A) and slacken the clamp bolt (B)

10 Carefully prise the blanking caps from the handlebar clamp bolts **(see illustration)**. Unscrew the bolts and remove the clamp(s) and the handlebar **(see illustrations)**.
11 If required, on the underside of the top yoke unscrew the nuts and remove the washers from the handlebar holders, then draw the holders out of the top yoke.

YZF-R models

Right handlebar

12 Use a hex key to unscrew the end-weight **(see illustration 5.4a)**.
13 Disconnect the front brake light switch wiring connectors **(see illustration 5.4b)**. Unscrew the brake master cylinder assembly clamp bolts and secure the assembly clear of the handlebar, wrapping it in some rag, keeping it upright, and making sure no strain is placed on the brake hose **(see illustration 5.5)**.
14 Refer to Chapter 4 and disconnect the throttle cables – this involves detaching the switch housing. Slide the twistgrip off.
15 Carefully prise the blanking cap out of the handlebar positioning bolt **(see illustration)**. Unscrew the positioning bolt and slacken the clamp bolt, then ease the handlebar up off the fork **(see illustration)**.

Left handlebar

16 Unscrew the end-weight **(see illustration 5.4a)**.
17 Disconnect the clutch switch wiring connector **(see illustration 5.7)**.
18 Undo the switch housing screws and displace the housing **(see illustration 5.7)**.
19 Disconnect the clutch cable (see Chapter 2).

5.23a Fit the clamps with the arrow pointing to the front

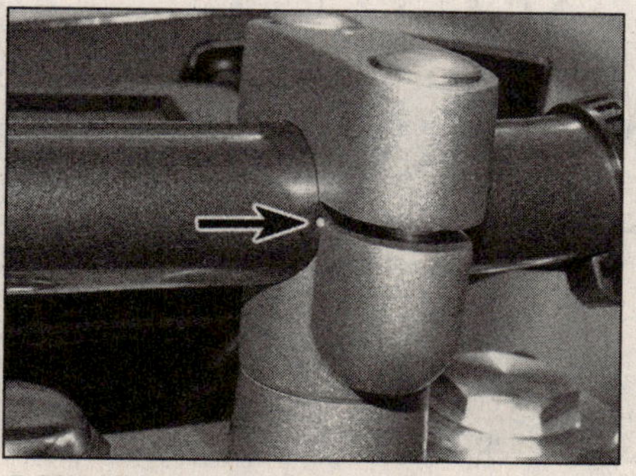

5.23b Align the punch mark (arrowed) with the upper surface of the right-hand holder

20 Remove the grip from the left-hand end of the handlebar – if it has been glued on or is stuck feed a wooden or plastic tool up the inside and move it round the bar to release it, or squirt some WD40 between the bar and grip but be careful to protect your eyes from spray back. At worst you will have to cut the grip off and fit a new one.
21 Unscrew the clutch lever bracket clamp bolt(s) and slide the assembly off the handlebar or displace it from the handlebar, according to clamp type fitted **(see illustration 5.9)**.
22 Carefully prise the blanking cap out of the handlebar positioning bolt **(see illustration 5.15a)**. Unscrew the positioning bolt and slacken the clamp bolt **(see illustration 5.15b)**. Ease the handlebar up off the fork.

Handlebar installation

23 Installation is the reverse of removal, noting the following.

- On WR and MT models, if removed fit the handlebar holders into the top yoke, with the arrow marks pointing forwards on MT models. Fit the washers and finger-tighten the nuts, allowing the clamps to be rotated for correct alignment.
- On WR models clean any corrosion and dirt off the handlebar and clamp mating surfaces. Position the handlebar centrally in the holders. Fit the clamps with the arrow marks facing forwards and finger-tighten the front bolts, then align the handlebar so the punch mark on the back aligns with the top surface of the right-hand holder, and finger-tighten the rear bolts **(see illustrations 5.23a and b)**. Now tighten the front bolts to the torque setting specified at the beginning of the Chapter, then tighten the rear bolts to the specified torque. Fit the blanking caps **(see illustration 5.10a)**. If the handlebar holders were removed now tighten the nuts to the specified torque.
- On MT models clean any corrosion and dirt off the handlebar and clamp mating surfaces. Position the handlebar centrally in the holders. Fit the clamp, making sure it is the correct way round as shown in illustration 5.10c, and finger-tighten the front bolts, then align the handlebar so the punch mark on the back aligns with the

top surface of the right-hand holder, and finger-tighten the rear bolts **(see illustration 5.23c)**. Now tighten the front bolts to the torque setting specified at the beginning of the Chapter, then tighten the rear bolts to the specified torque. Fit the blanking caps. If the handlebar holders were removed now tighten the nuts to the specified torque.

- On YZF-R models clean any corrosion or dirt off the handlebar, yoke and fork mating surfaces. Tighten the handlebar positioning bolt first, then the clamp bolt, tightening them both to the torque settings specified at the beginning of the Chapter **(see illustration 5.15b)**. Fit the blanking cap into the positioning bolt **(see illustration 5.15a)**.
- Fit the brake master cylinder clamp with the triangle pointing to the front and aligning the clamp joint with the punch mark on the handlebar, and tighten the front bolt first, then the rear, to the torque setting specified at the beginning of the Chapter **(see illustrations 5.23d and e)**.
- On all except YZF-RA models (with ABS) align the gap in the clutch lever bracket clamp with the punch mark, and tighten the bolt to the specified torque **(see illustration 5.23f)**. On YZF-RA models fit the clutch lever bracket after fitting the left switch housing, and align the mark on the face of the clamp with the mating surface surfaces of the switch housing halves, then tighten the upper bolt first, then the lower, to the specified torque setting.
- Refer to Chapter 4 to fit the throttle cable and Chapter 2 for the clutch cable.
- When fitting the switch housings, locate the peg in the hole in the handlebar.
- When fitting the handlebar end-weights on MT and YZF-R models, make sure there is a 1 to 3 mm gap between them and the grips. Tighten the end weights to the specified torque setting.
- Check and adjust clutch and throttle cable freeplay (see Chapter 1).

Levers

24 To remove the front brake lever, undo the lever pivot bolt locknut, then undo the pivot bolt and remove the lever **(see illustration)**.
25 To remove the clutch lever, loosen the

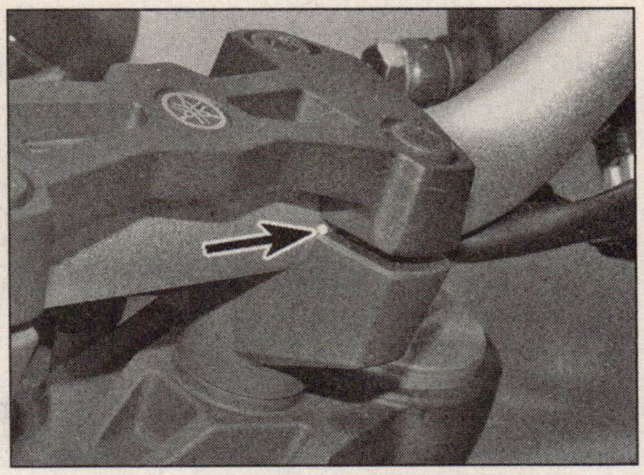

5.23c Align the punch mark (arrowed) with the upper surface of the right-hand holder

5.23e Align the clamp with the punch mark (arrowed)

cable adjuster lockring then thread the adjuster into the bracket to provide freeplay in the cable **(see illustration)**. Undo the lever pivot bolt locknut, then undo the pivot bolt and remove the lever, detaching the cable nipple as you do **(see illustration)**.
26 Installation is the reverse of removal, noting the following.

- Apply silicone grease to the front brake lever pivot bolt shaft, the contact area between the master cylinder pushrod tip and the lever, and to the contact areas between the lever and bracket.
- Apply lithium grease to the clutch cable end, the lever pivot bolt shaft and the contact areas between the lever and bracket.
- Make sure the levers move smoothly and freely.
- Adjust clutch cable freeplay (see Chapter 1).

5.23d Fit the clamp with the triangle (arrowed) at the front...

5.23f Align the gap in the clutch lever bracket clamp with the punch mark (arrowed)

6 Fork removal and installation

Removal

1 Work on one fork at a time. Note the routing of the cables, hose and wiring around the forks. Note the setting of the top of the fork in respect to the upper surface of the top yoke.
2 Remove the front wheel (see Chapter 6).
3 On WR-R models remove the fork protector, and on WR-X models remove the lower front mudguard (see Chapter 7). On all WR models release the speed sensor wiring from the right-hand fork and the brake hose from the left-hand fork as required.

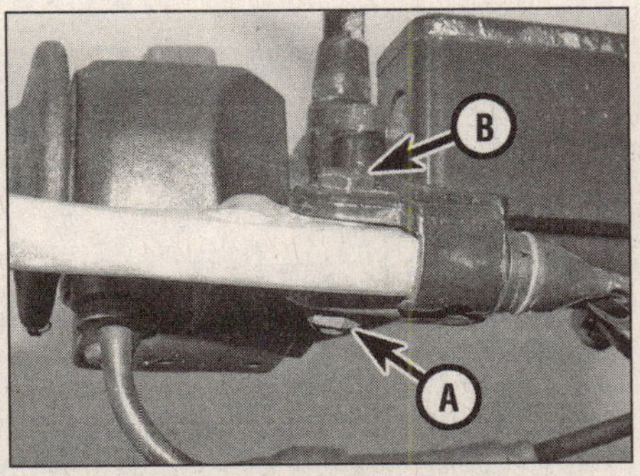

5.24 Unscrew the locknut (A) then undo the pivot bolt (B) and remove the brake lever

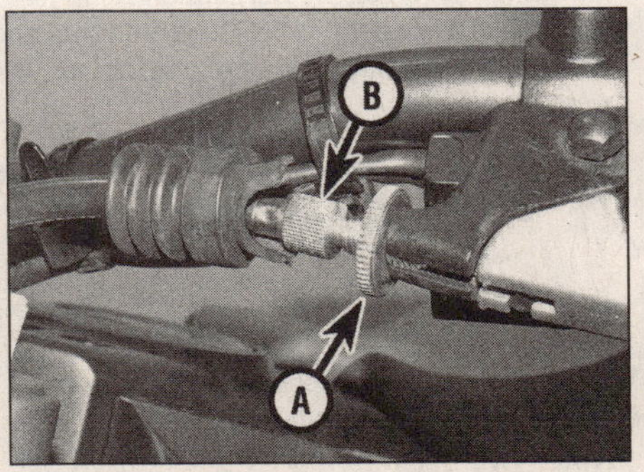

5.25a Pull back the boot then slacken the lockring (A) and thread the adjuster (B) in

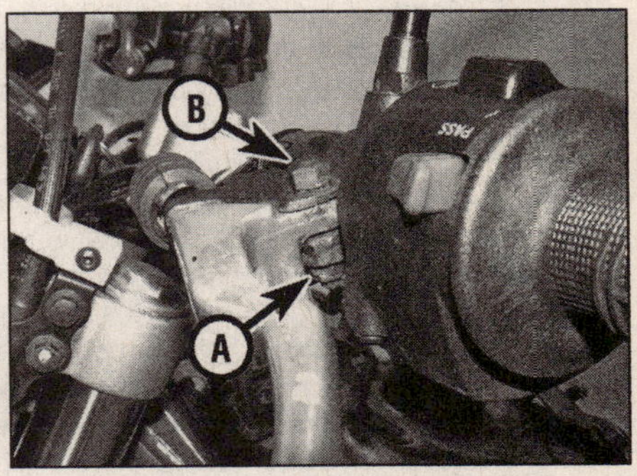

5.25b Unscrew the locknut (A) then undo the pivot bolt (B) and remove the clutch lever

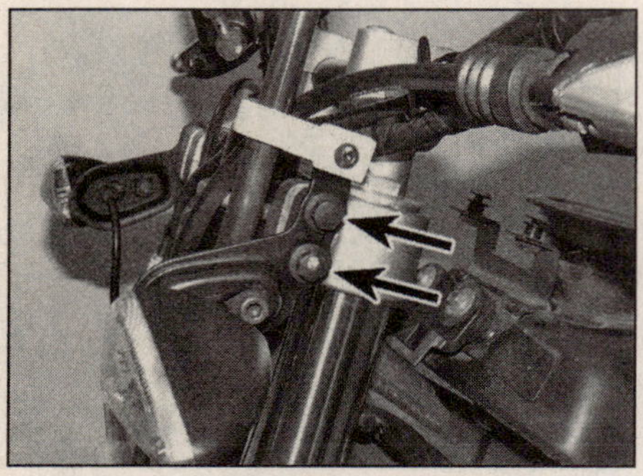

6.6a Top yoke fork clamp bolts (arrowed) – WR models

6.6b Top yoke fork clamp bolt (arrowed) – YZF-R models

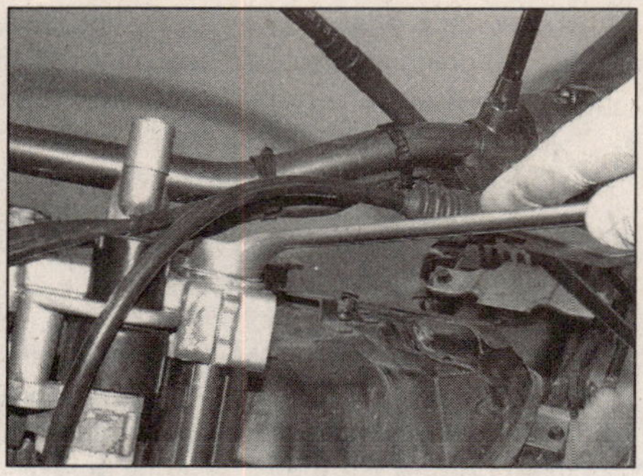

6.7 Slacken the top bolt if required

6.8a Slacken the fork clamp bolts (arrowed) in the bottom yoke...

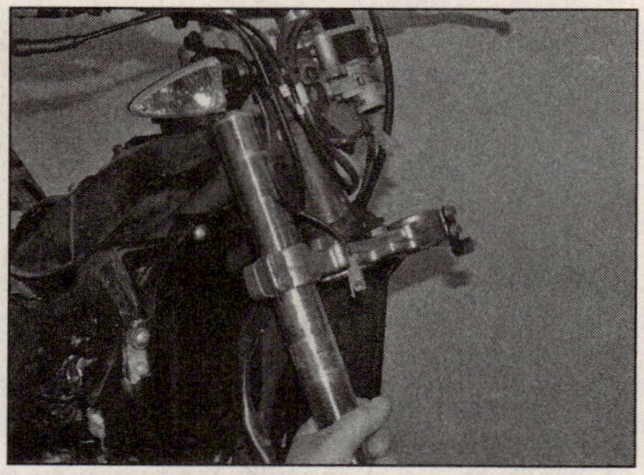

6.8b ...then draw the fork down and out of the yokes

6.10 Set the top of the tube level with the yoke or clamp so the bolt itself protrudes

4 On MT and YZF-R models remove the front mudguard (see Chapter 7).

5 On YZF-R models carefully prise the blanking cap from the handlebar positioning bolt, then slacken the positioning bolt and the handlebar clamp bolt **(see illustrations 5.15a and b)**.

6 Slacken the fork clamp bolt(s) in the top yoke **(see illustrations)**.

7 If the fork is to be disassembled, or if the fork oil is being changed, slacken the fork top bolt **(see illustration)**.

8 Slacken the fork clamp bolts in the bottom yoke **(see illustration)**. Remove the fork by twisting it and pulling it down **(see illustration)**.

HAYNES HINT ***If the fork legs are seized in the yokes, spray the area with penetrating oil and allow time for it to soak in before trying again.***

Installation

9 Remove all traces of corrosion from the fork tubes and the yokes. Make sure you fit the fork with the brake caliper lugs on the left-hand side.

10 Slide the fork up through the bottom yoke and into the top yoke, making sure the cables, hose and wiring are routed on the correct side of the fork **(see illustration 6.8b)**. Set the top of the fork inner tube (WR models) or outer tube (MT and YZF-R models) flush with the upper surface of the top yoke (WR and MT models) or handlebar clamp (YZF-R models), so the top bolt itself is above the surface **(see illustration)**. Tighten the clamp bolts in the bottom yoke to the torque setting specified at the beginning of the Chapter **(see illustration 6.8a)**.

11 If the fork has been dismantled or if the fork oil was changed, tighten the fork top bolt to the specified torque **(see illustration 6.7)**.

12 Tighten the fork clamp bolt(s) in the top yoke to its specified torque **(see illustration 6.6a or b)**.

13 On YZF-R models tighten the handlebar positioning bolt to the specified torque, then tighten the handlebar clamp bolt to the specified torque **(see illustration 5.15b)**. Fit the blanking cap into the positioning bolt **(see illustration 5.15a)**.

14 Install all remaining components.

15 Check the operation of the front forks and brake before taking the machine out on the road.

7 Fork oil change

WR models

Note: *Two different makes of fork have been fitted to WR models, Paioli and Kayaba. The only difference relevant to this procedure is that there is a washer fitted above and below the spacer on Paioli models, and only below the spacer on Kayaba models.*

1 After a high mileage the fork oil will deteriorate and its damping and lubrication qualities will be impaired. Always change the oil in both fork legs.

2 Remove the fork – make sure that the top bolt is loosened while the fork is still clamped in the bottom yoke (see Section 6).

3 Support the fork leg in an upright position and unscrew the top bolt from the top of the inner tube – the bolt is under pressure from the fork spring, so either use a ratchet tool so it does not need to be removed from the bolt as you unscrew it, and maintain some downward pressure on it, particularly as you come to the end of the threads, or alternatively hold the tool still and twist the fork tube to unthread it from the bolt **(see illustration)**. If the bolt

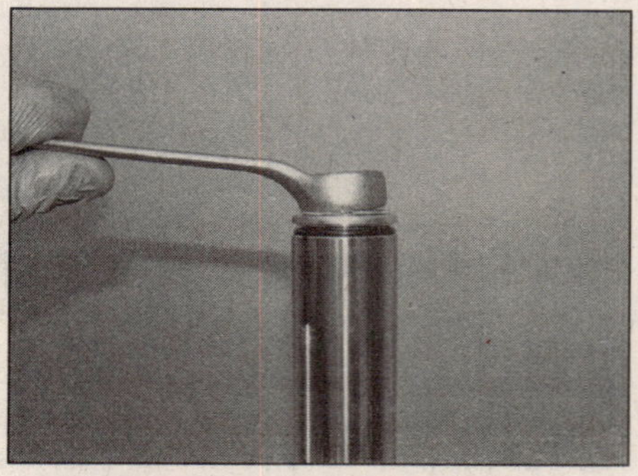

7.3 Unscrew the top bolt as described

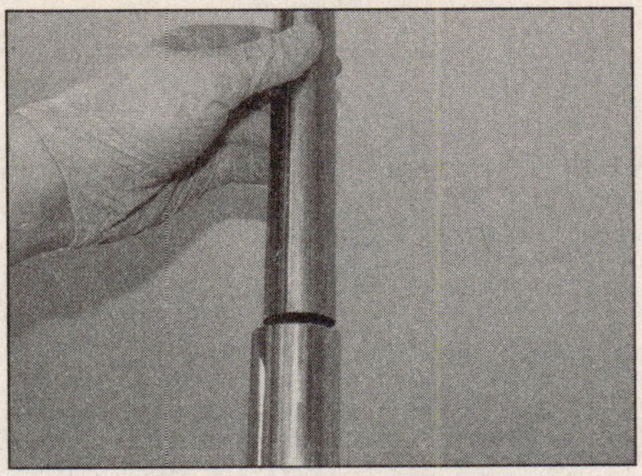

7.5a Remove the spacer...

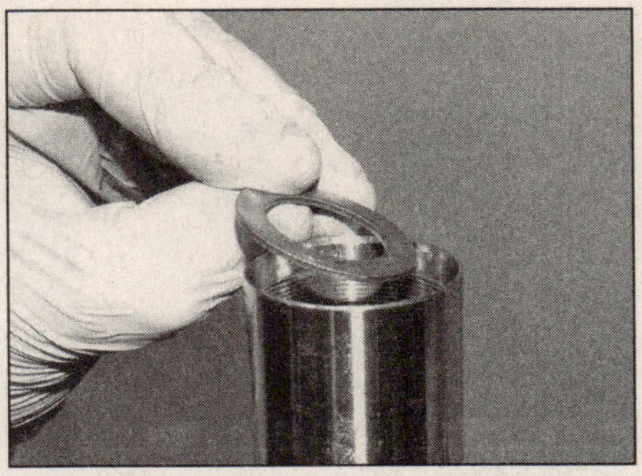

7.5b ...then slide the inner tube down and remove the washer...

7.5c ...and the spring

7.6 Invert the fork over a container and tip the oil out

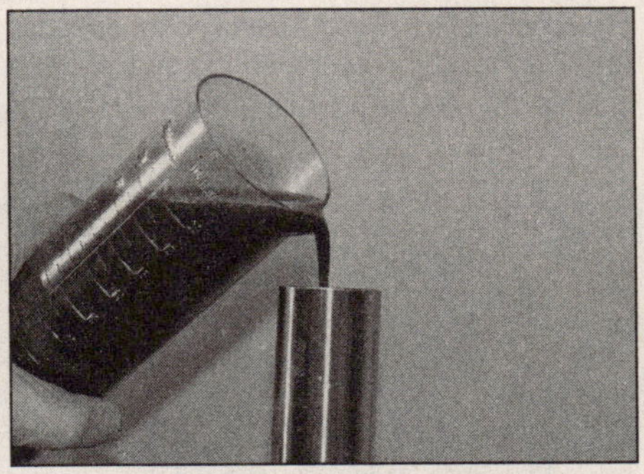

7.7a Pour the oil into the top of the tube and distribute and bleed it as described...

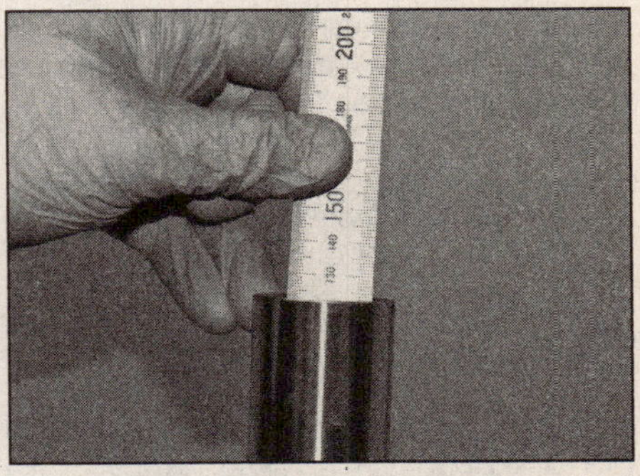

7.7b ...then measure the level as described using a ruler

O-ring is damaged or deteriorated replace it with a new one.

4 Where fitted remove the washer from the top of the spacer.

5 Remove the spacer **(see illustration)**. Slide the fork inner tube down and remove the washer and the spring **(see illustrations)**. Wipe any excess oil off the spring and spacer.

6 Invert the fork leg over a suitable container and pump the fork to expel as much oil as possible **(see illustration)**. Support the fork upside down in the container and allow it to drain for a few minutes. If the oil contains metal particles disassemble the fork and inspect the bushes for wear (see Section 8).

7 Slowly pour in the quantity and grade of fork oil specified at the beginning of the chapter, then pump the fork slowly ten times to distribute it evenly **(see illustration)**. Stand the fork upright for ten minutes to allow any air bubbles to rise. Slide the inner tube down until it seats then measure the oil level from the top of the tube **(see illustration)**. Add or subtract oil until it is at the level specified at the beginning of the Chapter.

8 Fit the spring into the fork **(see illustration 7.5c)**. Draw the inner tube up until it is flush with the top of the spring, then fit the washer **(see illustration 7.5b)**. Lift the tube some more and fit the spacer **(see illustration 7.5a)**.

9 Fit the washer on top of the spacer on Paioli forks.

10 Smear some fork oil onto the top bolt O-ring, using a new one if necessary **(see illustration)**. Fully extend the inner tube and fit the top bolt into it, compressing the spring as you do, and thread it in (making sure it does not cross-thread), keeping downward pressure on the spring, using a ratchet tool or by turning the tube while holding the bolt still as on removal. Lightly tighten the top bolt at this stage – tighten it further when the fork leg is being installed and is securely held in the bottom yoke (see Section 6).

11 Install the fork (see Section 6).

MT and YZF-R models

Note: *The right-hand fork is different internally to the left-hand fork – make sure you follow the correct procedure for the fork being worked on. For external identification the left-hand fork has the mountings for the brake caliper.*

12 After a high mileage the fork oil will deteriorate and its damping and lubrication qualities will be impaired. Always change the oil in both fork legs.

13 Remove the fork – make sure that the top bolt is loosened while the fork is still clamped in the bottom yoke (see Section 6).

Right-hand fork

14 Support the fork leg in an upright position and unscrew the top bolt from the top of the inner tube **(see illustration)**. If the bolt O-ring is damaged or deteriorated replace it with a new one.

15 Cut a 10 mm wide slot to the centre of

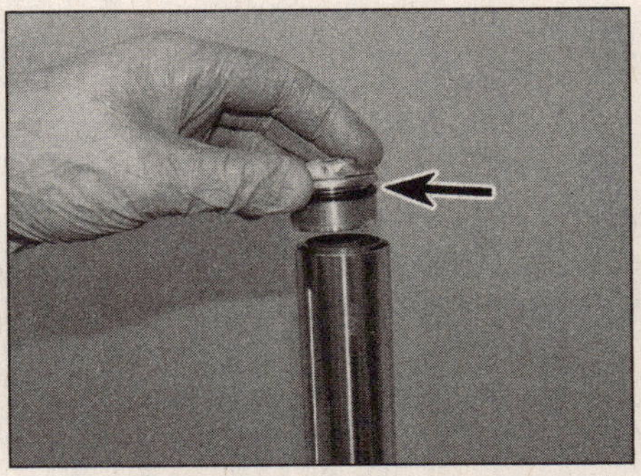

7.10 Lubricate the O-ring (arrowed) before threading the bolt in

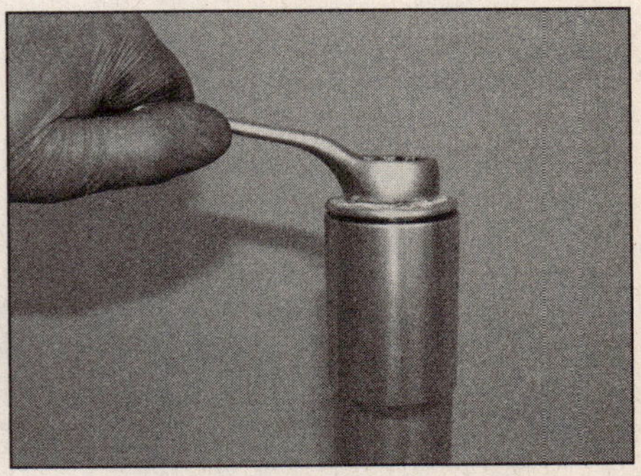

7.14 Unscrew the top bolt from the tube – it will remain threaded on the damper rod

7.15a Prepare a washer as described...

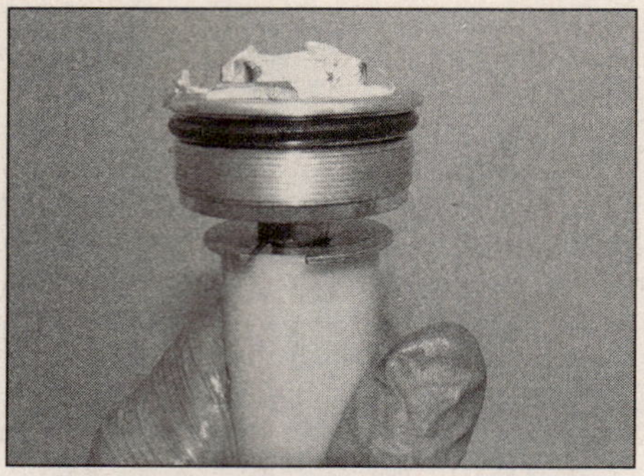
7.15b ...and slide it between the locknut and the spacer

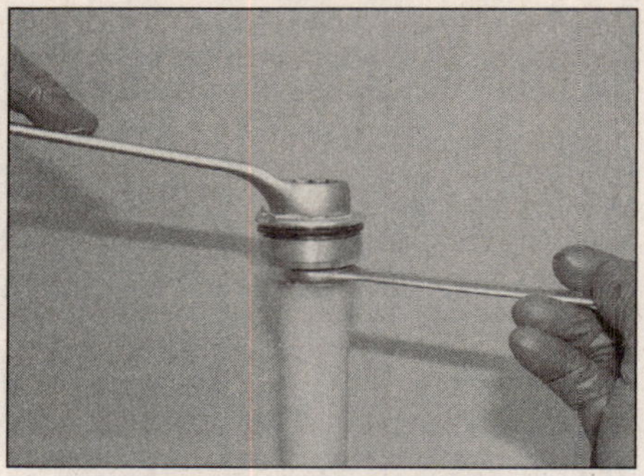
7.15c Release the locknut and thread the top bolt off

a 40 mm wide washer **(see illustration)**. Slide the outer tube down onto the base of the fork, then clean any oil off the spacer. Push the spacer down against the spring and fit the washer between the top of the spacer and the underside of the locknut, so the slot fits around the threaded rod, then relax the spring so the spacer seats against the washer **(see illustration)**. Hold the top bolt and slacken the locknut, then thread the top bolt off **(see illustration)**.

16 Remove the spacer **(see illustration)**. Remove the spring **(see illustration)**. Wipe any excess oil off the spring and spacer.

17 Invert the fork leg over a suitable container and pump the fork tubes and the damper rod to expel as much oil as possible **(see illustration 7.6)**. Support the fork upside down in the container and allow it to drain for a few minutes. If the oil contains metal particles disassemble the fork and inspect the bushes for wear (see Section 8).

18 Slowly pour in the quantity and grade of fork oil specified at the beginning of the chapter, then pump the damper rod slowly ten times to distribute it evenly **(see illustration 7.7a)**. Stand the fork upright for ten minutes to allow any air bubbles to rise. Slide the outer tube down until it is flush with the top of the inner tube, then measure the oil level from the top of the tube **(see illustration 7.7b)**. Add or subtract oil until it is at the level specified at the beginning of the Chapter.

19 Fit the spring over the rod and into the fork, with its closer-wound coils at the top **(see illustration 7.16b)**. Draw the damper rod out, then fit a piece of wire under the locknut to use as a handle to keep the rod extended **(see illustrations)**. Fit the spacer over the wire and rod and seat the narrower bottom section in the top of the spring **(see illustrations)**. Hold the rod and push down on the spacer to compress the spring, then remove the wire and fit the slotted washer between the spacer and locknut **(see illustration)**.

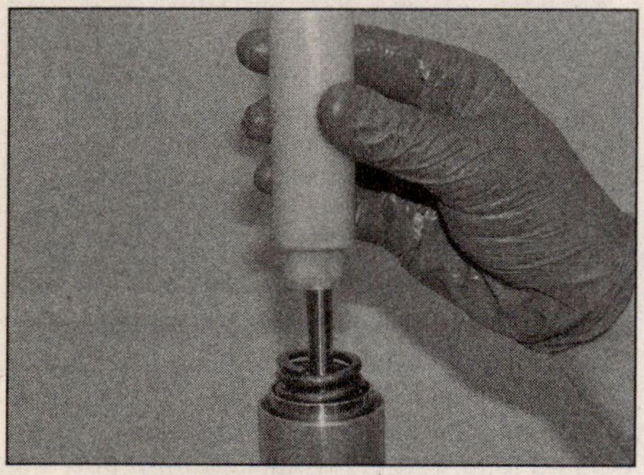
7.16a Remove the spacer...

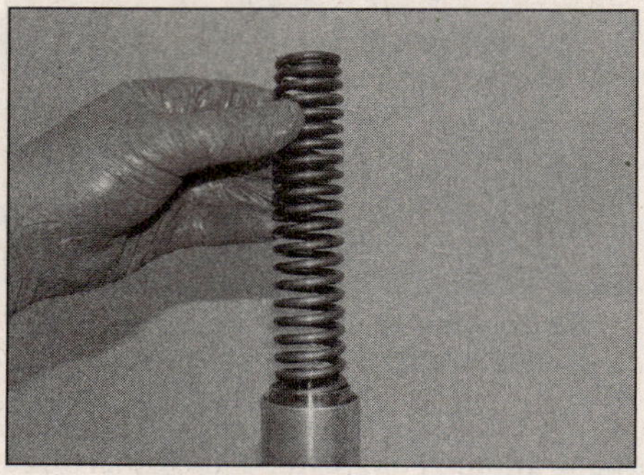
7.16b ...and the spring

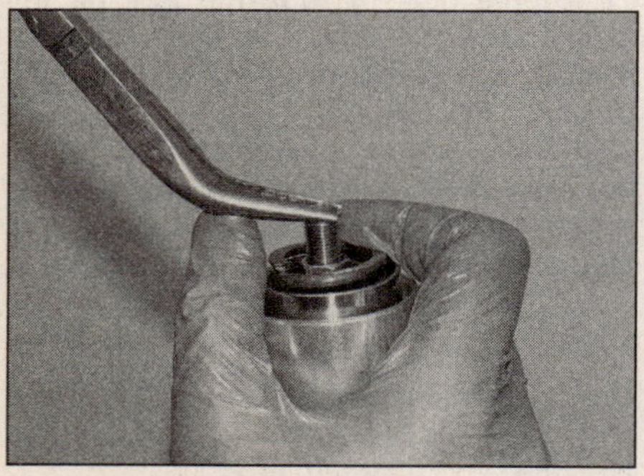
7.19a Draw the rod up...

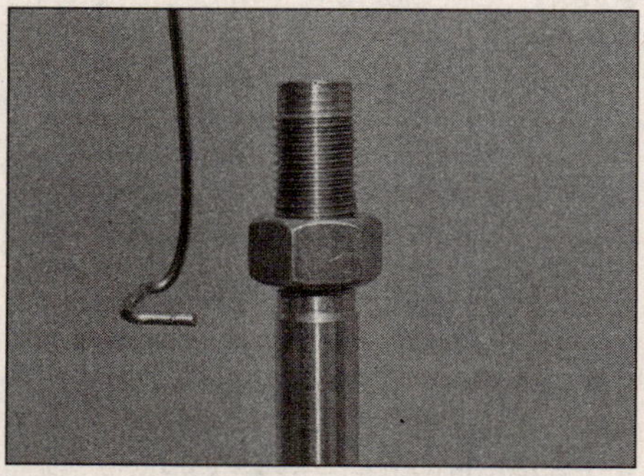
7.19b ...and hook a piece of wire under the locknut

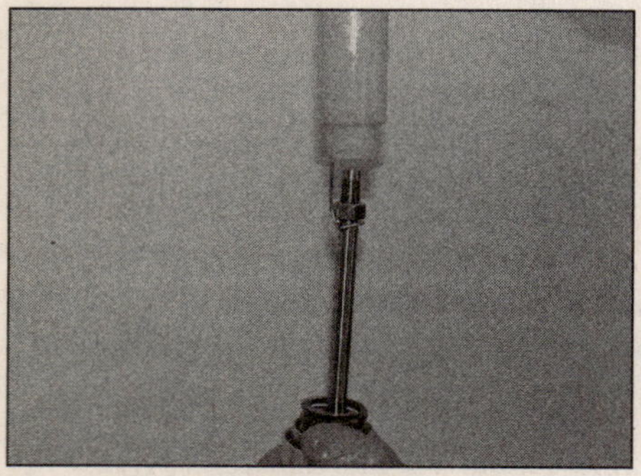
7.19c Slide the spacer down...

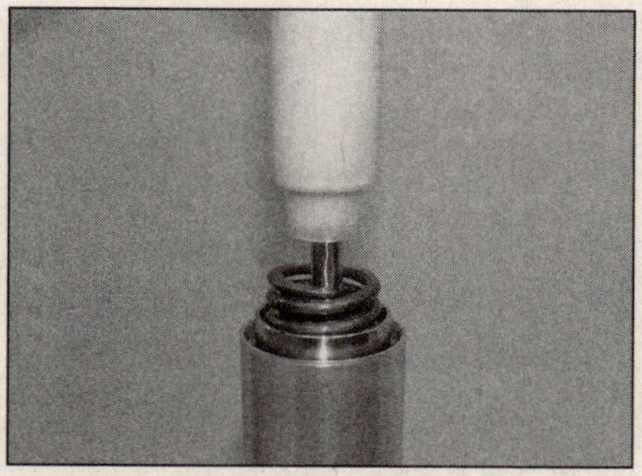
7.19d ...and seat the narrow end in the top of the spring

7.19e Fit the washer between the locknut and the spacer

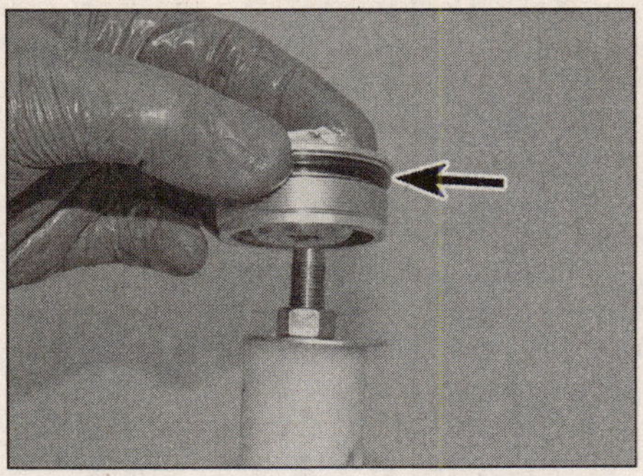

7.20 Lubricate the O-ring (arrowed) before threading the bolt on

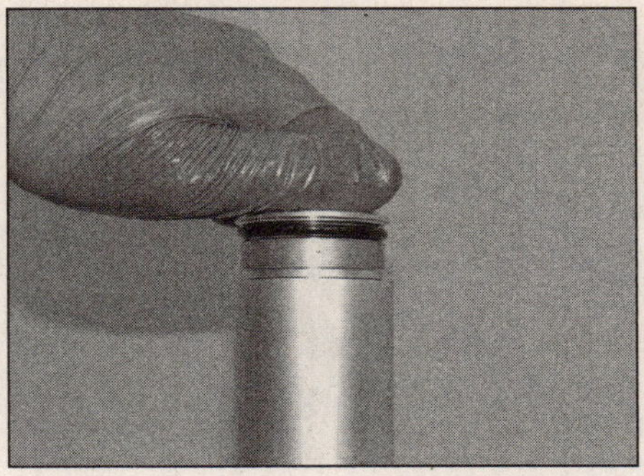

7.21 Thread the top bolt into the tube

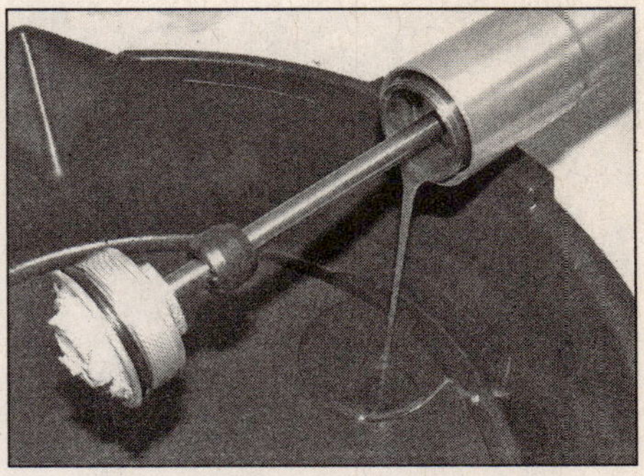

7.25 Invert the fork over a container and tip the oil out

20 Smear some fork oil onto the top bolt O-ring, using a new one if necessary **(see illustration)**. Thread the top bolt onto the damper rod until it seats, then hold it and tighten the locknut up against it **(see illustration 7.15c)**.

21 Fully extend the outer tube and thread the top bolt into it **(see illustration)**. Lightly tighten the top bolt at this stage – tighten it further when the fork leg is being installed and is securely held in the bottom yoke (see Section 6).

22 Install the fork (see Section 6).

Left-hand fork

23 Support the fork leg in an upright position and unscrew the top bolt from the top of the inner tube **(see illustration 7.14)**. If the bolt O-ring is damaged or deteriorated replace it with a new one.

24 Slide the outer tube down onto the base of the fork.

25 Invert the fork leg over a suitable container and drain the oil **(see illustration)**. Support the fork upside down in the container and allow it to drain for a few minutes. If the oil contains metal particles disassemble the fork and inspect the bushes for wear (see Section 8).

26 Slowly pour in the quantity and grade of fork oil specified at the beginning of the chapter**(see illustration)**. Stand the fork upright for ten minutes to allow any air bubbles to rise.

27 Smear some fork oil onto the top bolt O-ring, using a new one of necessary **(see illustration 7.21)**. Fully extend the outer tube and thread the top bolt into it. Lightly tighten the top bolt at this stage – tighten it further when the fork leg is being installed and is securely held in the bottom yoke (see Section 6).

28 Install the fork (see Section 6).

8 Fork overhaul

WR models

Disassembly

1 Remove the fork — make sure that the top bolt is loosened while the leg is still clamped in the bottom yoke (see Section 6). Always dismantle the fork legs separately to avoid interchanging parts. Store all components in separate, clearly marked containers.

2 Slacken the damper rod bolt in the base of the outer tube **(see illustration)**. If the damper rod turns with the bolt, turn the leg upside down and compress the fork so the pressure of the spring holds the damper while the bolt is loosened. Alternatively use an air impact wrench, if available. If the bolt cannot be loosened at this stage, Yamaha produce a service tool (Part No. 90890-01460) and T-bar (Part No. 90890-01326) which can be inserted down inside the inner tube once the spring has been removed – the tool has a tapered head that engages in the top end of the damper to hold it while the bolt is loosened. As an alternative we used a broom handle tapered at the end, and it did the job **(see illustration)**.

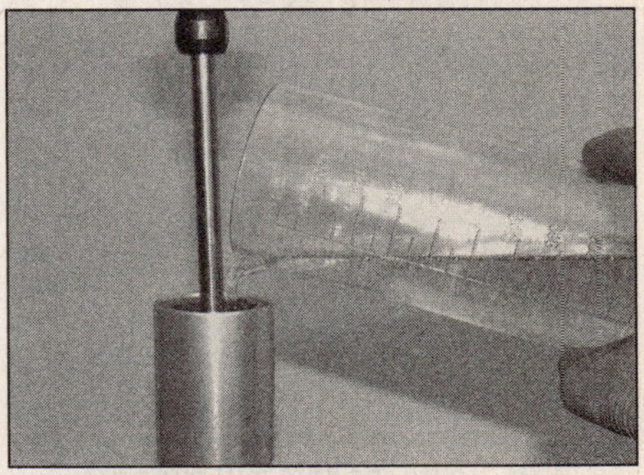

7.26 Pour the oil into the top of the tube

3 Refer to Steps 3 to 6 in Section 7 and drain the oil form the fork.

4 Remove the damper rod bolt and its copper sealing washer from the bottom of the outer tube, using a holding tool as described earlier if necessary **(see illustrations 8.2a and b)**. A new sealing washer must be used on reassembly. Tip the damper rod and rebound spring out **(see illustration)**.

5 Carefully prise out the dust seal from the

8.2a Slacken the damper rod bolt as described

8.2b Broom handle with end tapered to fit in the top of the damper rod

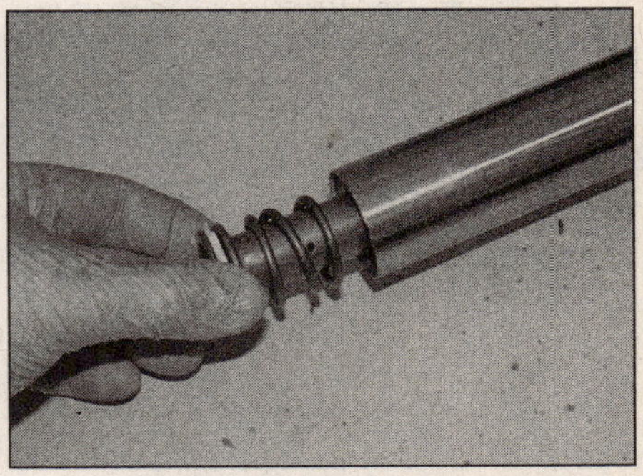

8.4 Tip the damper rod out

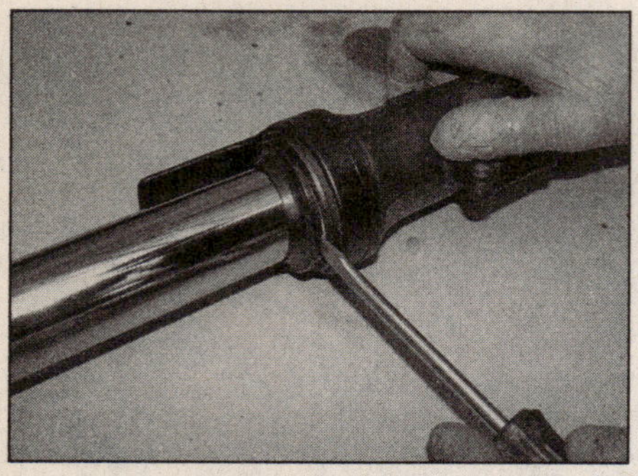
8.5 Prise out the dust seal using a flat-bladed screwdriver

8.6 Prise out the retaining clip using a flat-bladed screwdriver

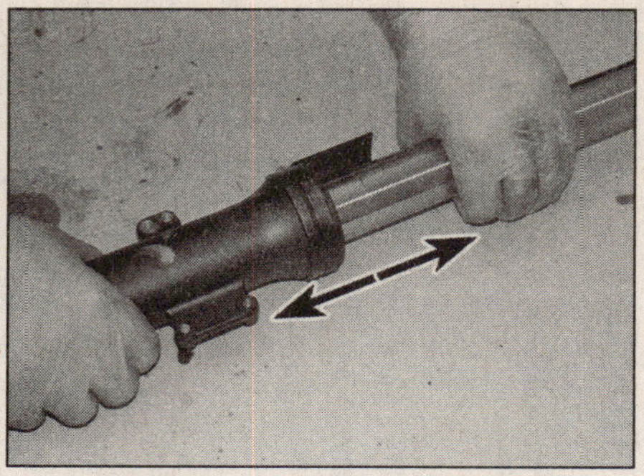
8.7a Repeatedly draw the tubes apart...

8.7b ... until the seal and bush are displaced

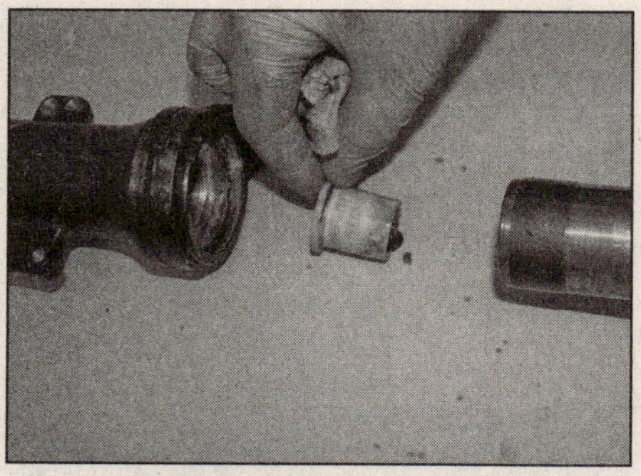
8.9a Retrieve the damper rod seat...

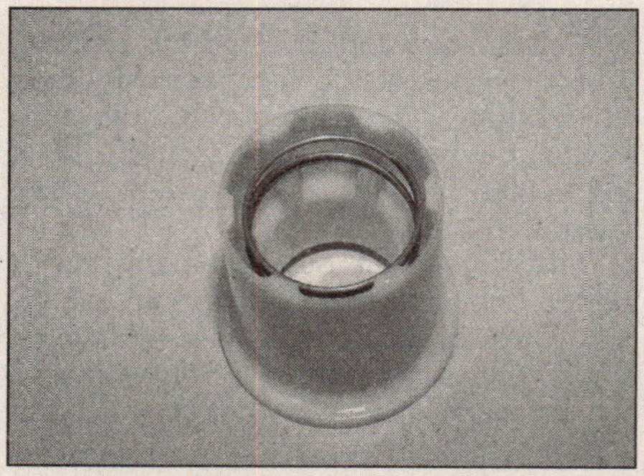
8.9b ... and note the spring fitted in it

top of the outer tube **(see illustration)**. A new seal must be used on installation.

6 Carefully remove the retaining clip, taking care not to scratch the surface of the tube **(see illustration)**.

7 To separate the inner tube from the outer tube it is necessary to displace the oil seal and top bush from the top of the outer tube. The bottom bush on the inner tube will not pass through the top bush in the outer tube, and this can be used to good effect. Slide the inner tube in, then pull it quickly out so the bottom bush strikes the top bush **(see illustration)**. Repeat this operation until the seal and top bush are tapped out of the outer tube and the inner tube can be fully withdrawn **(see illustration)**.

8 Slide the oil seal, washer and top bush off the inner tube, noting which way round they fit. A new oil seal must be used, but unless you have a dedicated seal installation tool keep the old one to use as an interface when driving the new seal in to prevent damage.

9 Remove the damper rod seat – if it is not in the bottom of the inner tube, tip it out of the outer tube **(see illustration)**. Note the spring inside the seat **(see illustration)**.

Inspection

10 Clean all parts in solvent and blow them dry with compressed air, if available. Check the inner fork tube for score marks, scratches, rust spots and flaking of the chrome finish. Any such damage will result in premature seal failure. Fork inner tubes can be re-chromed using hard chrome, or replace them with new ones. Check the fork seal seat for nicks, gouges and scratches. If damage is evident, leaks will occur.

11 Check the inner tube for runout using V-blocks and a dial gauge **(see illustration)**. If the amount of runout exceeds the service limit specified at the beginning of the chapter, the tube must be replaced with a new one.

⚠ ***Warning: If the tube is bent or exceeds the runout limit, it should not be straightened; replace it with a new one.***

12 Check the working surface of each bush for wear **(see illustration)** – the surface should be Teflon grey all over. If the Teflon has worn to expose the material below replace both bushes with new ones – Yamaha specify to use new ones as a matter of course, and as the expense is not great it is worth doing. To remove the bottom bush from the inner tube lever its ends apart using a screwdriver and slide it out of its seat **(see illustration)**.

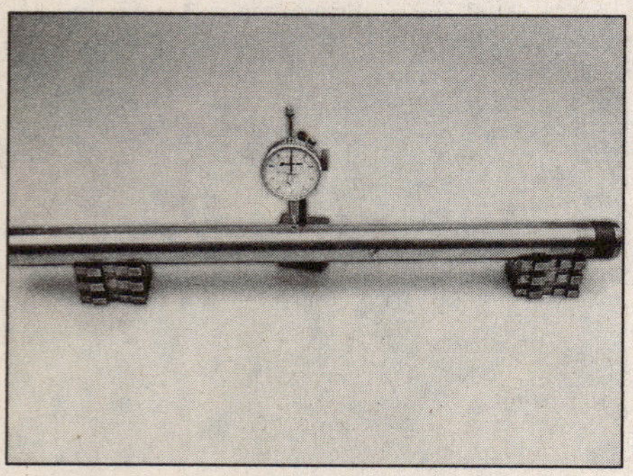
8.11 Checking the fork tube for runout

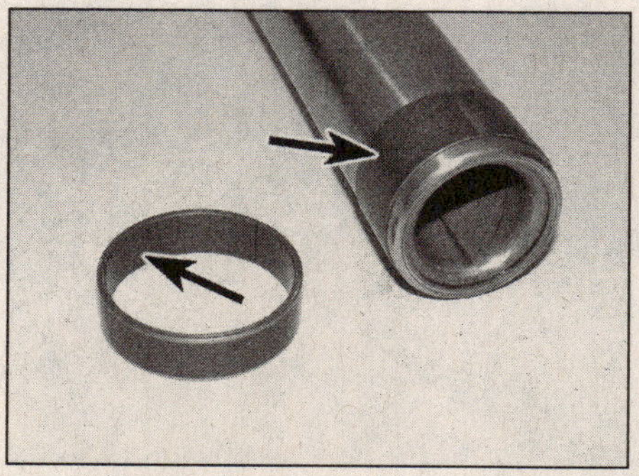
8.12a Check the working surface of each bush (arrowed) for wear

8.12b Lever the ends apart and slide the bush off

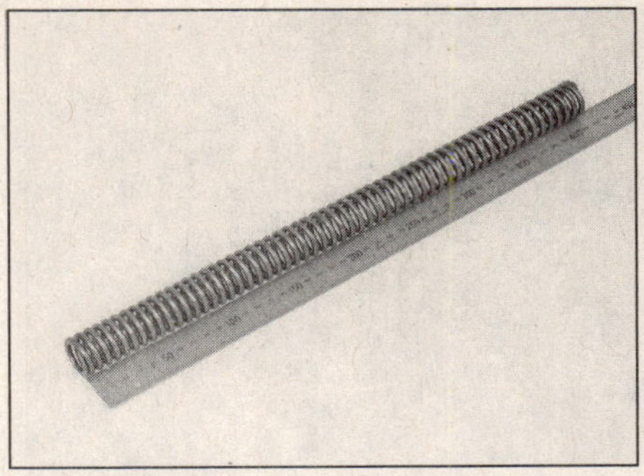

8.13 Measure the free length of the spring

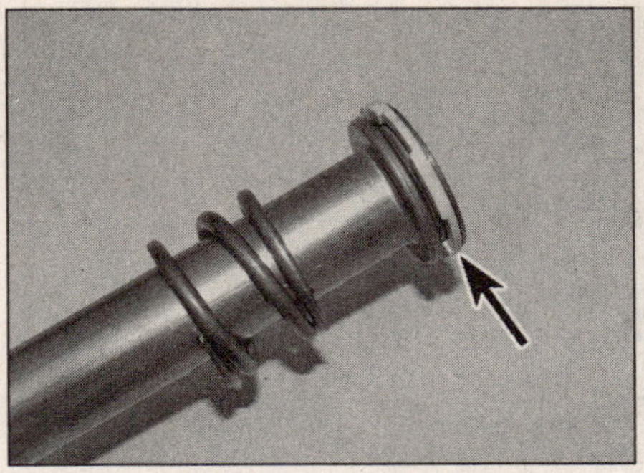

8.14 Check the rod, rebound spring and ring (arrowed) for wear

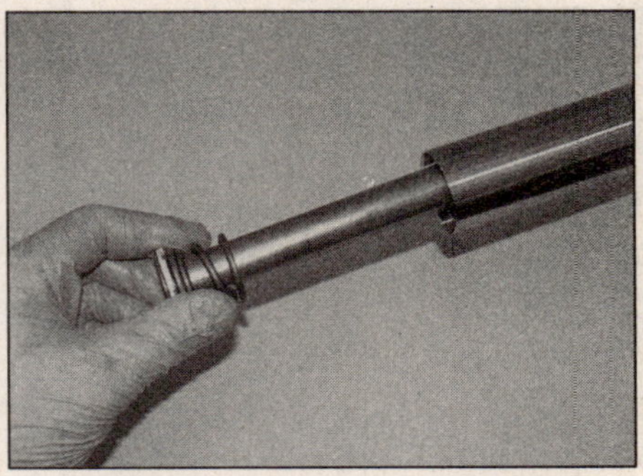

8.16a Slide the damper rod into the top of the tube...

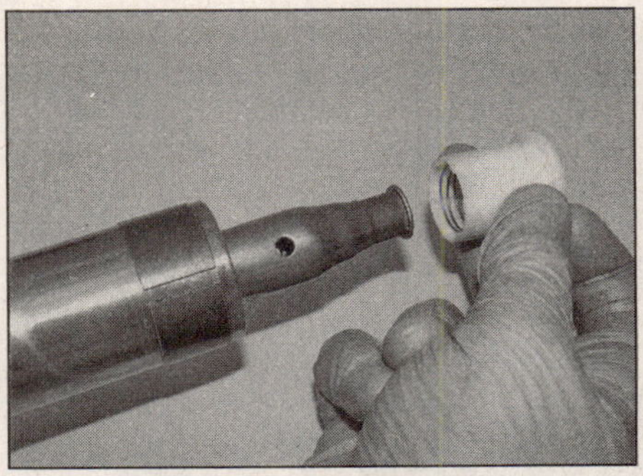

8.16b ... so it protrudes from the bottom, then fit the oil lock piece...

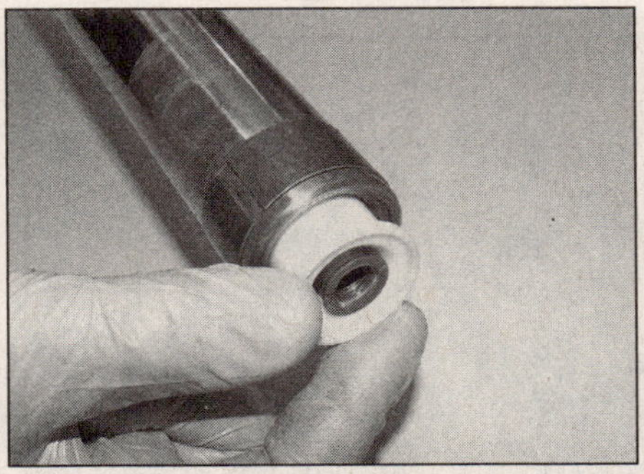

8.16c ... and push it into the bottom of the tube

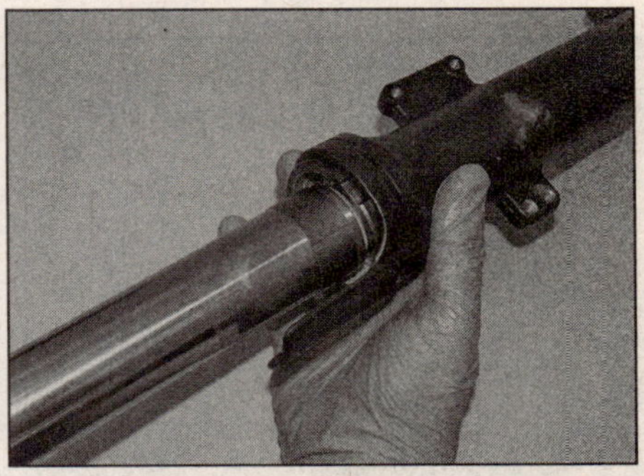

8.17 Fit the inner tube into the outer tube

13 Check the main spring for cracks and other damage. Measure the spring free length and compare the measurement to the specifications at the beginning of the Chapter **(see illustration)**. If it is defective or sagged below the service limit, replace the spring in each fork with a new one – never replace only one spring.

14 Check the damper rod, and in particular the ring in its head, and the rebound spring for damage and wear **(see illustration)**. Check the damper rod seat and its spring for damage.

Reassembly

15 If removed fit a new bottom bush into its seat on the inner tube – do not expand it any further than necessary to get it over the bottom of the tube **(see illustration 8.12b)**.

16 Fit the rebound spring onto the damper rod if removed **(see illustration 8.14)**. Slide the rod all the way down into the inner tube so it protrudes from the bottom **(see illustrations)**. Check the spring is correctly located in the damper rod seat **(see illustration 8.9b)**. Fit the seat onto the bottom of the rod, then push the seat up inside the tube **(see illustrations)**.

17 Lubricate the bottom bush on the inner tube with new 10W fork oil. Insert the tube into the outer tube and slide it fully down until it contacts the bottom **(see illustration)**.

18 Lay the fork flat on the bench. Fit a new copper sealing washer onto the damper bolt and apply a few drops of a suitable non-permanent thread locking compound **(see illustration)**. Fit the bolt into the bottom of the outer tube, thread it into the damper rod and tighten it to the torque setting specified at the beginning of the Chapter. If the damper rotates inside the tube as you tighten the bolt, use the same holding method as on disassembly.

19 Lubricate the top bush with fork oil and slide it down the inner tube and into the outer tube **(see illustration)**. Slide the washer down the tube and onto the bush **(see illustration)**. Carefully drive the bush onto its seat in the outer tube using a suitable drift against the washer (which acts as an interface to prevent

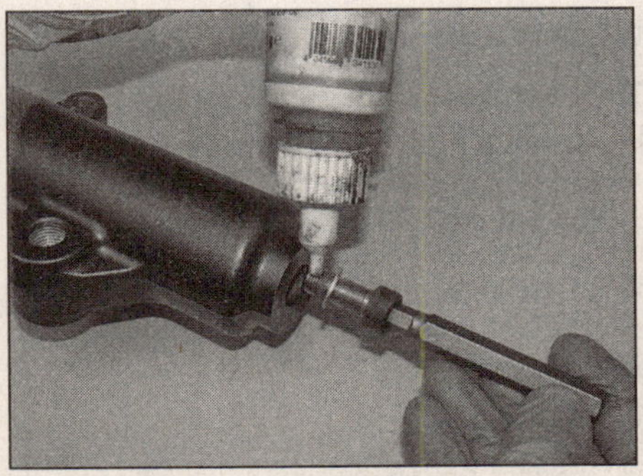

8.18 Fit a new sealing washer and apply threadlock

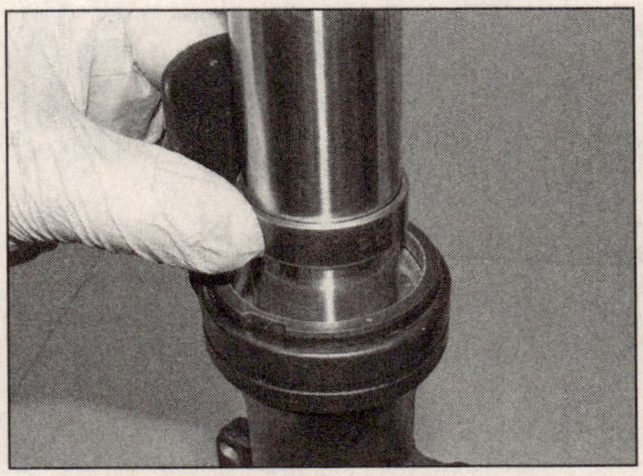

8.19a Slide the bush on...

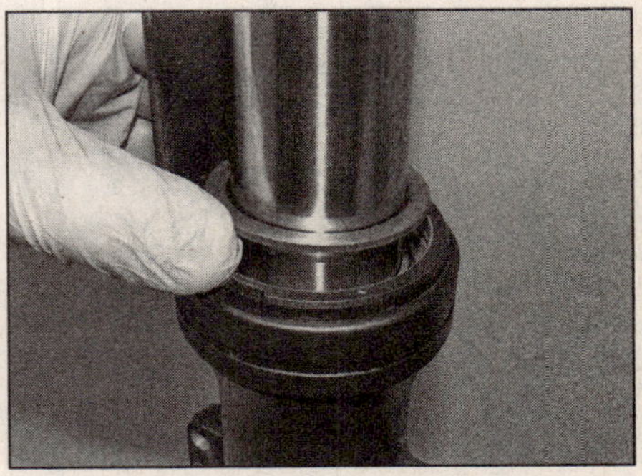

8.19b ... then seat the washer on it

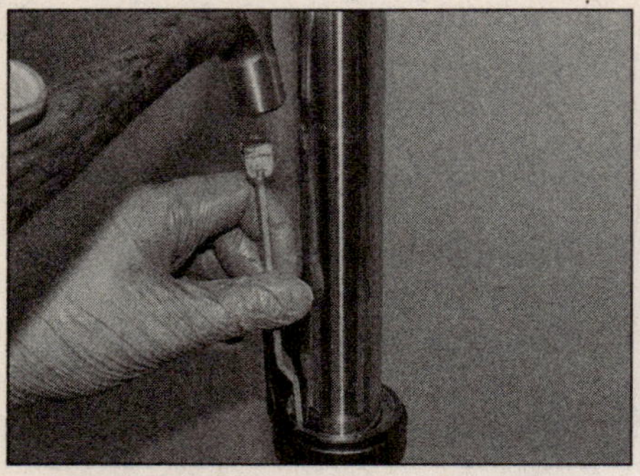

8.19c Drive the bush into place using a suitable drift – the one shown was specially shaped

8.19d Lift the washer to check the bush (arrowed) is fully recessed

8.20a Slide the oil seal on…

8.20b …and drive it in using a dedicated tool as shown…

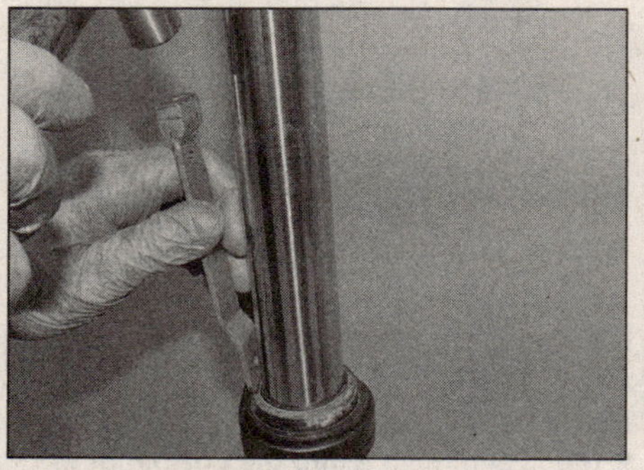

8.20c …or a drift with the old seal placed on top of the new one…

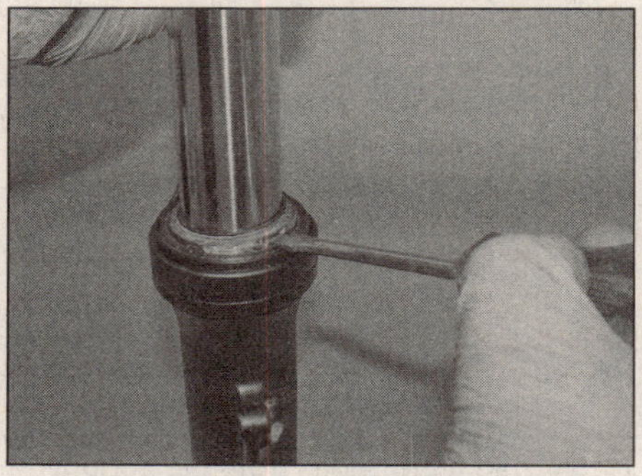

8.20d …in which case lever the old seal out when the new one is seated

8.20e Check the retaining ring groove (arrowed) is fully exposed

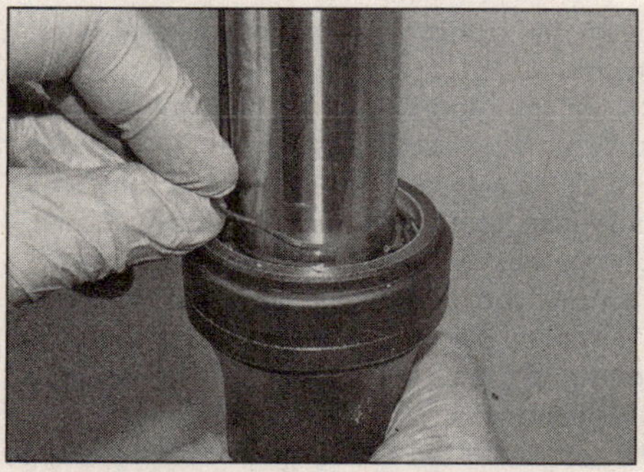

8.21 Make sure the ring seats fully in its groove

damage to the softer bush), turning the fork so the bush enters squarely **(see illustration)**. Take care not to let the drift slip against the inner tube. You will know when the bush is seated as the tone of the impact changes, but lift the washer off to check **(see illustration)**.

20 Lubricate the lips of the new oil seal with fork oil, then slide it down the inner tube and into the outer tube – make sure the marked side of the seal faces out **(see illustration)**. Carefully drive the seal in and onto its seat using the same drift, or a dedicated seal installation tool **(see illustration)** – if using a drift slide the old seal onto the new one to act as an interface to prevent damage, then use a screwdriver to lift the old seal out **(see illustrations)**. The new seal is seated when the retaining clip groove is fully exposed **(see illustration)**.

21 Fit the retaining ring into its groove **(see illustration)**.

22 Lubricate the lips of the new dust seal then slide it down the fork tube and press it into position **(see illustration)**.

23 Refer to Section 7, Steps 7 to 10 and fill the fork with oil and finish reassembly.

24 Install the fork (see Section 6).

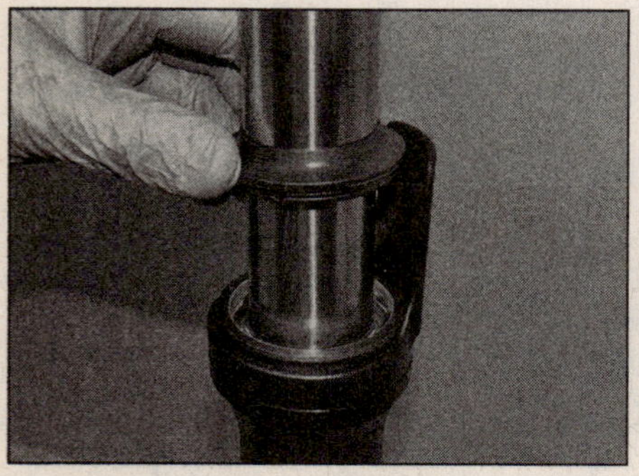

8.22 Slide the dust seal down and press it into the outer tube

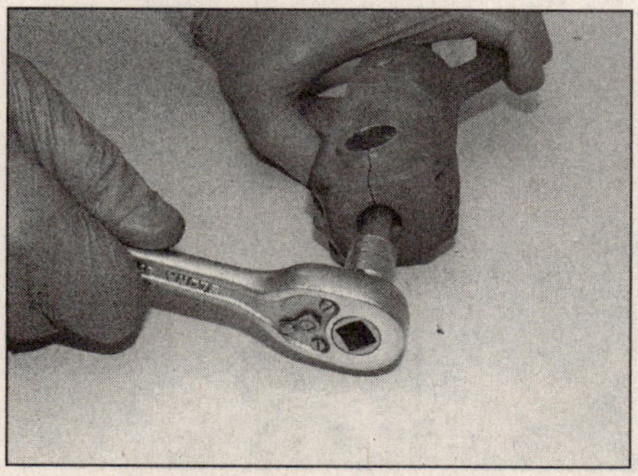

8.26 Slacken the damper cartridge bolt as described

MT and YZF-R models

Disassembly

25 Remove the fork — make sure that the top bolt is loosened while the leg is still clamped in the bottom yoke (see Section 6). Always dismantle the fork legs separately to avoid interchanging parts. Store all components in separate, clearly marked containers.

Right-hand fork

26 Slacken the damper cartridge bolt in the base of the inner tube **(see illustration)**. If the cartridge turns with the bolt, turn the leg

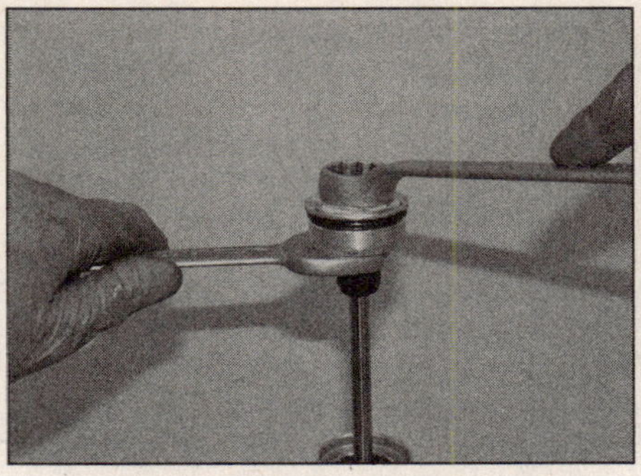

8.30 Release the locknut and thread the top bolt off

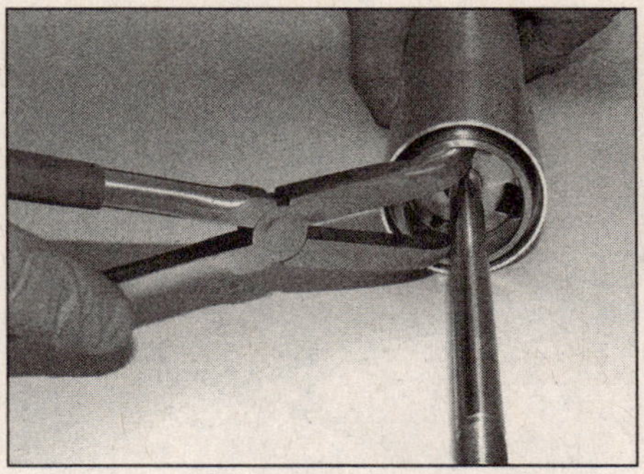

8.31a Using angled long-nosed pliers works well if they are a good fit and the holder is not overtight

8.31b You can make your own peg spanner out of a 26mm socket

8.31c This is the aftermarket 26/30 mm peg spanner...

8.31d ...the castellations locate in the holes in the holder...

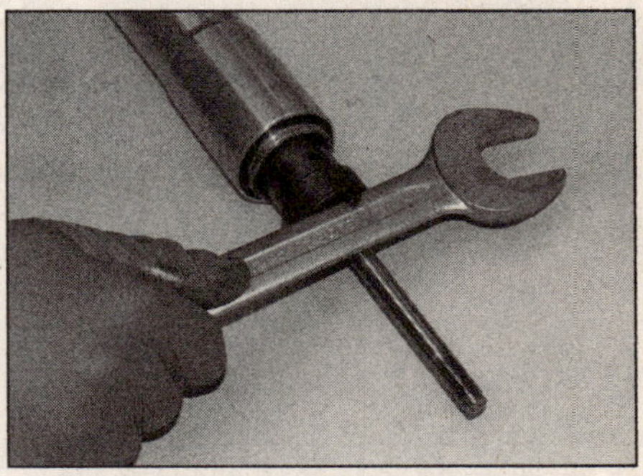

8.31e ...and the tool can be turned as shown

upside down and compress the fork so the pressure of the spring holds the cartridge while the bolt is loosened. If that doesn't work, and if available, use an air impact wrench. If the bolt cannot be loosened at this stage, Yamaha produces a service tool (Part No. 90890-11139) which can be inserted down inside the outer tube once the spring has been removed – the tool has a head that engages in the top of the damper cartridge to hold it while the bolt is loosened.

27 Refer to the relevant Steps in Section 7 and drain the oil form the fork.

28 Remove the damper cartridge bolt and its copper sealing washer from the bottom of the outer tube, using a holding tool as described earlier if necessary. A new sealing washer must be used on reassembly. Withdraw the damper cartridge from the fork.

Left-hand fork

29 Refer to the relevant Steps in Section 7 and drain the oil form the fork.

30 Hold the top bolt and slacken the locknut, then thread the top bolt off the damper rod **(see illustration)**. Thread the locknut off the rod and remove the rubber damper **(see illustrations 8.53b and a)**.

31 Using the Yamaha service tool (part No. 90890-11140) or a suitable alternative **(see Tool Tip)**, unscrew the damper rod holder inside the top of the outer tube **(see illustrations)**.

32 Remove the damper rod holder and the damper rod **(see illustrations 8.52d and c)**. Withdraw the spring, and tip the spacer out **(see illustrations)**.

Both forks

33 Carefully prise out the dust seal from the top of the outer tube **(see illustration)**. A new seal must be used on installation.

34 Carefully release the retaining clip, taking

TOOL TIP *As an alternative to buying the Yamaha tool the simplest thing is to try using a pair of long thin angled-nose pliers as shown. Alternatively cut some castellations into the rim of a 26 mm socket as shown, then grind some flats onto the top so a spanner can fit onto it. There is also a double-ended peg spanner (26 mm and 30 mm) sold by aftermarket motorcycle tool and accessory suppliers, that fits perfectly and can be turned using a spanner as shown.*

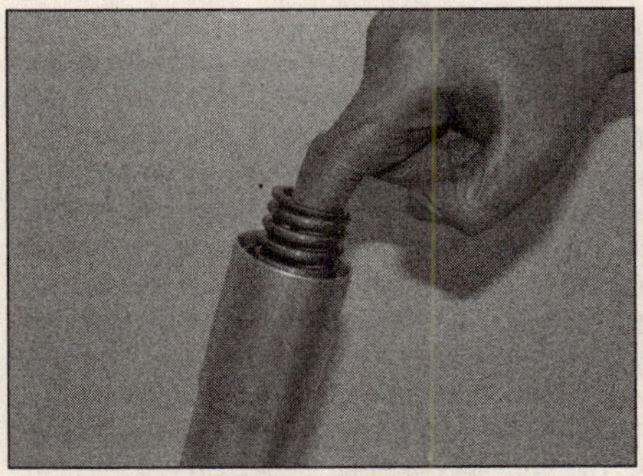

8.32a Pull the spring out...

8.32b ...then tip the spacer out

8.33 Prise out the dust seal using a flat-bladed screwdriver

8.34 Prise out the retaining clip using a flat-bladed screwdriver

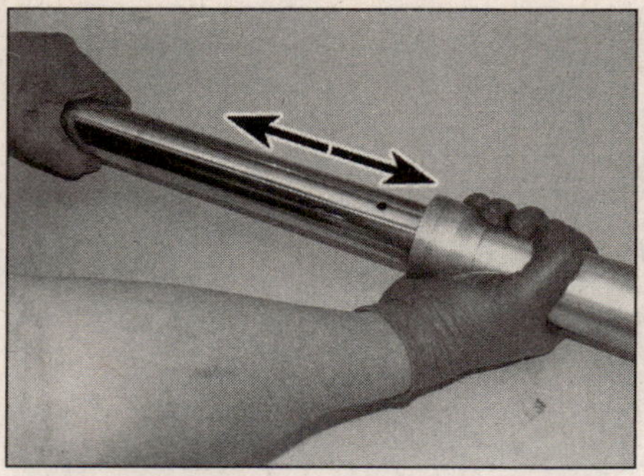

8.35a Repeatedly draw the tubes apart...

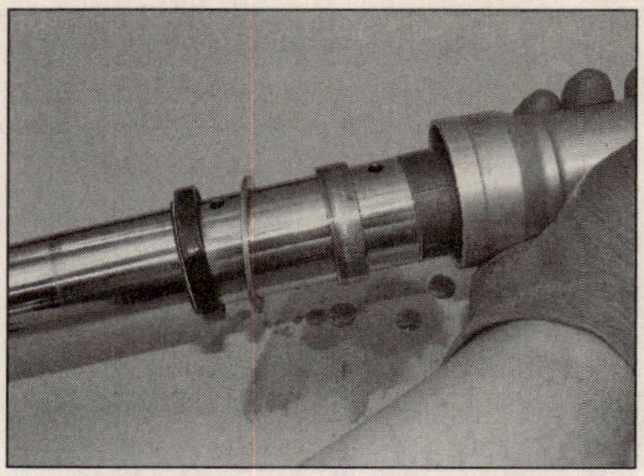

8.35b ... until the seal and bottom bush are displaced

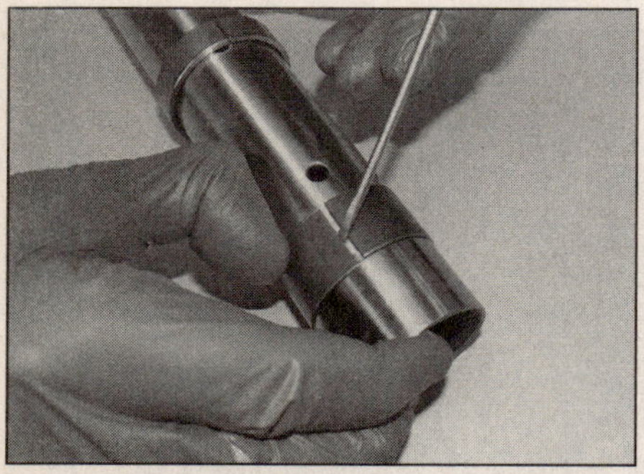

8.36 Lever the ends apart and slide the bush off

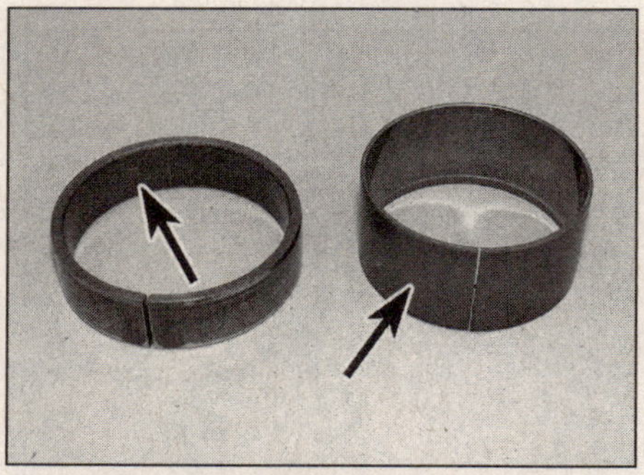

8.39 Check the working surface of each bush (arrowed) for wear

care not to scratch the surface of the tube **(see illustration)**.

35 To separate the inner tube from the outer tube it is necessary to displace the oil seal and bottom bush from the bottom of the outer tube. The top bush on the inner tube will not pass through the bottom bush in the outer tube, and this can be used to good effect. Slide the inner tube in, then pull it quickly out so the top bush strikes the bottom bush **(see illustration)**. Repeat this operation until the seal and bottom bush are tapped out of the outer tube and the inner tube can be fully withdrawn **(see illustration)**.

36 Lever the ends of the top bush apart and slide it out of its seat **(see illustration)**. Slide the bottom bush, washer, oil seal, retaining clip and dust seal off the inner tube, noting which way round they fit. A new oil seal and dust seal must be used, but unless you have a dedicated seal installation tool keep the old oil seal to use as an interface when driving the new seal in to prevent damage.

Inspection

37 Clean all parts in solvent and blow them dry with compressed air, if available. Check the inner fork tube for score marks, scratches, rust spots and flaking of the chrome finish. Any such damage will result in premature seal failure. Fork inner tubes can be re-chromed using hard chrome, or replace them with new ones. Check the fork seal seat for nicks, gouges and scratches. If damage is evident, leaks will occur.

38 Check the inner tube for runout using V-blocks and a dial gauge. If the amount of runout exceeds the service limit specified at the beginning of the chapter, the tube must be replaced with a new one **(see illustration 8.11)**.

Warning: If the tube is bent or exceeds the runout limit, it should not be straightened; replace it with a new one.

39 Check the working surface of each bush for wear **(see illustration)** – the surface should be Teflon grey all over. If the Teflon has worn to expose the material below replace both bushes with new ones – Yamaha specify to use new ones as a matter of course, and as the expense is not great it is worth doing.

40 Check the spring for cracks and other damage. Measure the spring free length and compare the measurement to the specifications at the beginning of the Chapter **(see illustration 8.13)**. If it is defective or sagged below the service limit, replace the spring in each fork with a new one – never replace only one spring.

41 On the right-hand fork check the damper cartridge for wear and damage. Check the oil passage holes are clear. Pump the rod in and out of the cartridge – it should move smoothly and freeely.

42 On the left-hand fork check the damper rod and the rebound spring for damage and wear. Check the damper rod holder and the rubber damper for damage.

Reassembly

Both forks

43 Wrap a single layer of insulating tape around the lower ridge of the seat for the top bush on the inner tube **(see illustration)**. Lubricate the surface of the inner tube (including the tape), the lips of the oil and dust seals, the inner surface of the bottom bush and the outer surface of the top bush with 10W fork oil. Slide the dust seal, the retaining clip, the oil seal (with the marked side facing the bottom of the fork), the washer and the bottom bush onto the inner tube and position them at the base of the fork **(see illustration)**. Remove the insulating tape. Fit the top bush into its seat on the inner tube – do not expand it any further than necessary to get it over the bottom of the tube **(see illustration 8.36)**.

8.43a The tape prevents damage to the lips of the new seal from the sharp edge

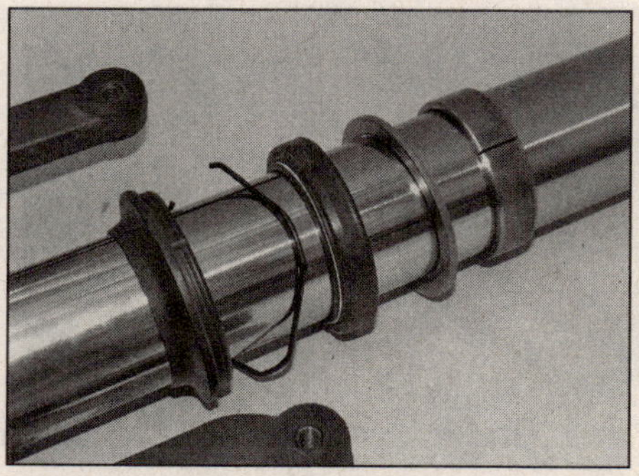

8.43b Slide the components onto the tube as shown

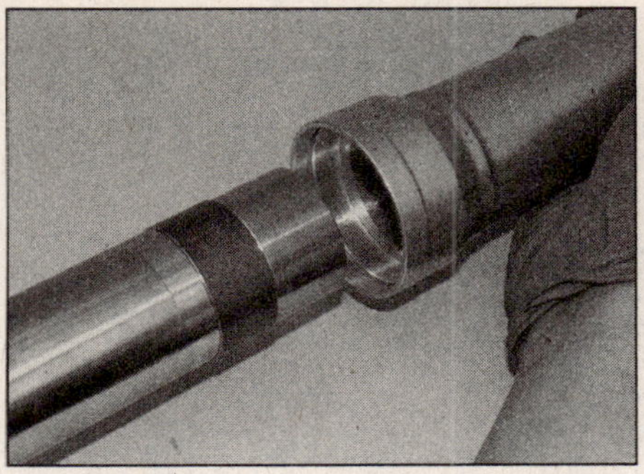
8.44 Fit the inner tube into the outer tube

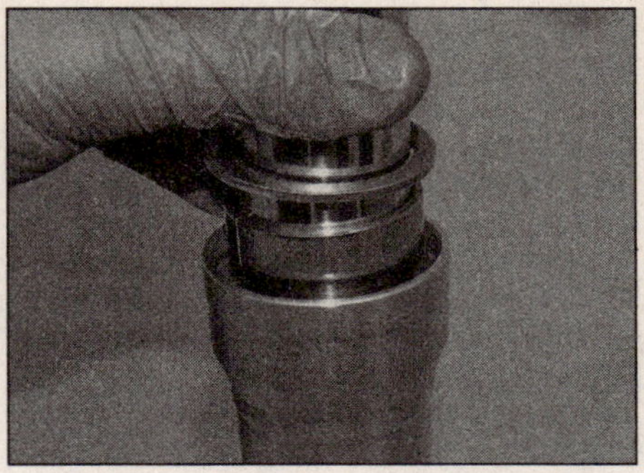
8.45a Slide the bush down and seat the washer on it

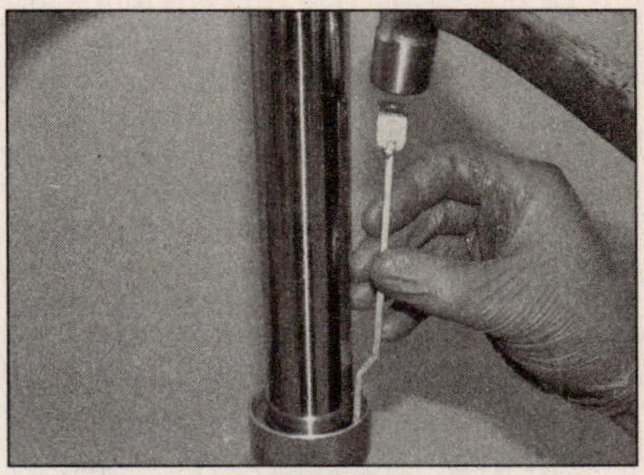
8.45b Drive the bush in using a suitable drift – this one was specially shaped

44 Insert the inner tube into the outer tube **(see illustration)**.

45 Stand the fork upside down and have an assistant keep the inner tube extended from the outer tube. Slide the bottom bush down the inner tube and into the outer tube, then seat the washer onto the bush **(see illustration)**. Carefully drive the bush onto its seat in the outer tube using a suitable drift against the washer (which acts as an interface to prevent damage to the softer bush), turning the fork so the bush enters squarely **(see illustration)**. Take care not to let the drift slip against the inner tube. You will know when the bush is seated as the tone of the impact changes, but lift the washer off to check **(see illustration)**.

46 Slide the oil seal down the inner tube and into the outer tube. Carefully drive the seal in and onto its seat using the same drift, or a dedicated seal installation tool **(see illustration 8.20b)** – if using a drift cut the old seal in half and fit it onto the new one to act as an interface to prevent damage, then use a screwdriver to lift the old seal out **(see illustrations)**. The new seal is seated when the retaining clip groove is fully exposed **(see illustration)**.

47 Fit the retaining ring into its groove **(see illustration)**.

48 Slide the dust seal down and press it into position **(see illustration)**.

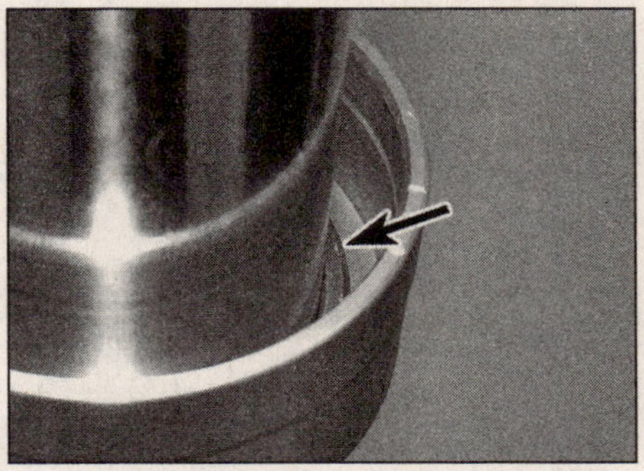
8.45c Lift the washer and check the bush (arrowed) is fully recessed

8.46a Cut the old seal in half...

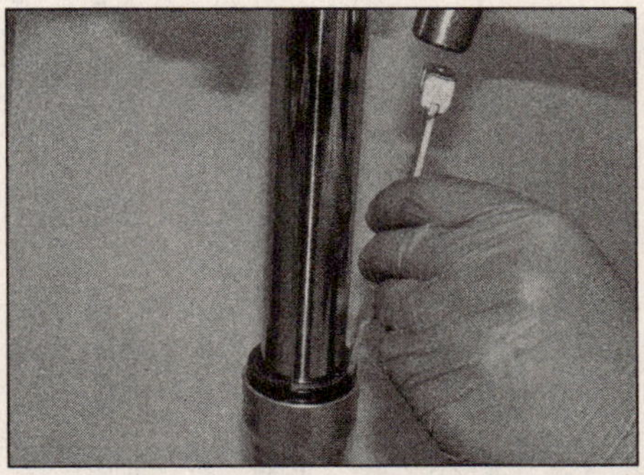
8.46b ...to act as an interface if using a drift...

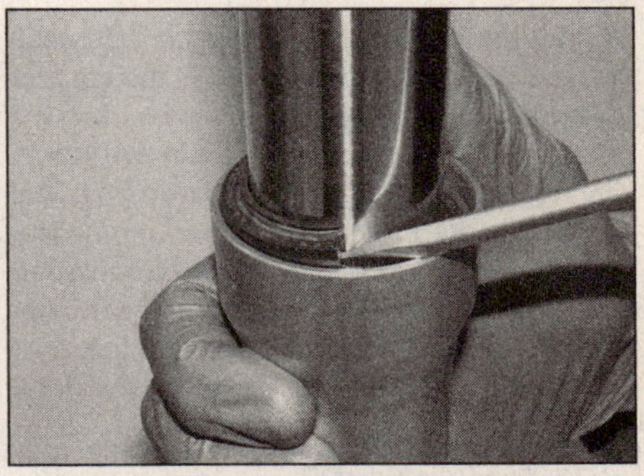
8.46c ...then lever it out using a screwdriver

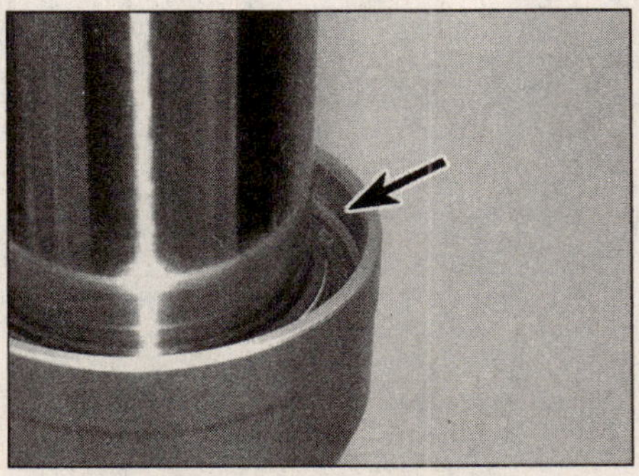
8.46d The new seal is seated when the retaining ring groove (arrowed) is fully exposed

8.47 Make sure the ring is seated fully in its groove

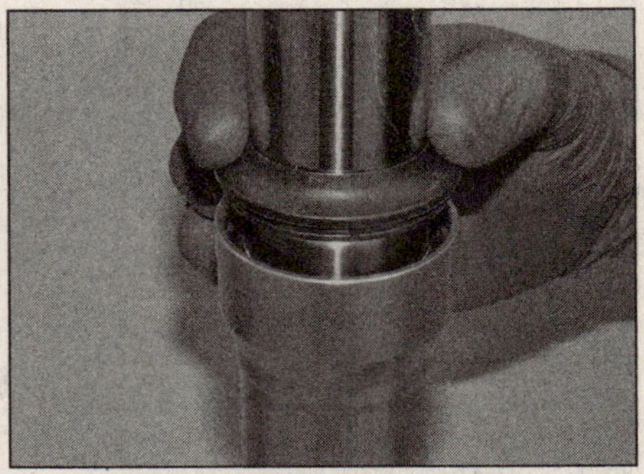
8.48 Slide the dust seal down and press it into the outer tube

8.52a Fit the spacer...

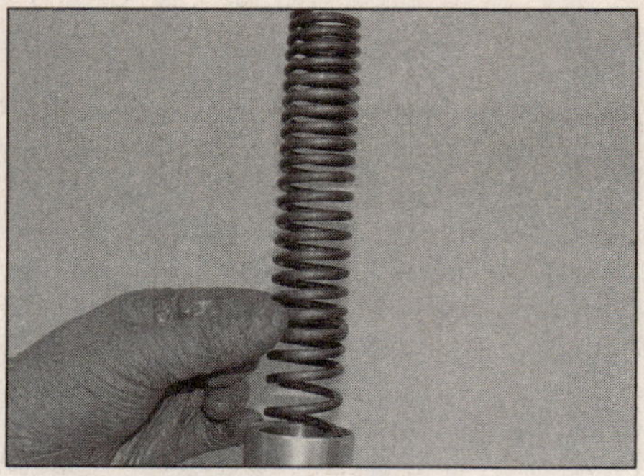

8.52b ...the spring...

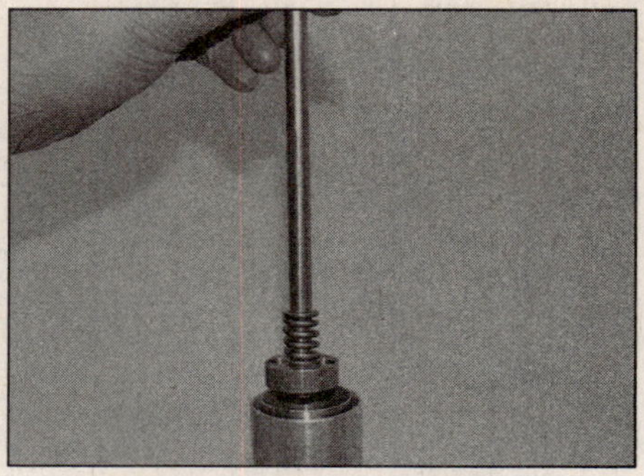

8.52c ...the damper rod...

8.52d ...and its holder

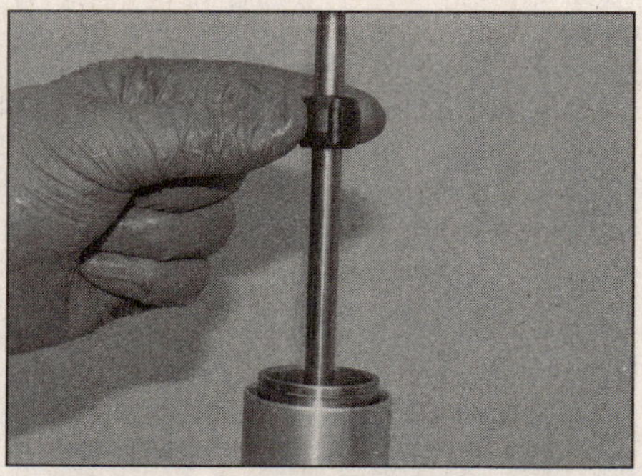

8.53a Slide the damper down the rod...

Right-hand fork

49 Lay the fork flat on the bench, and slide the inner tube all the way in. Slide the damper cartridge into the outer tube so it seats on the bottom of the inner tube. Fit a new copper sealing washer onto the damper bolt and apply a few drops of a suitable non-permanent thread locking compound **(see illustration 8.18)**. Fit the bolt into the bottom of the inner tube, thread it into the cartridge and tighten it to the torque setting specified at the beginning of the Chapter. If the cartridge rotates inside the tube as you tighten the bolt, use the same holding method as on disassembly.

50 Refer to Section 7 and fill the fork with oil and finish reassembly.

51 Install the fork (see Section 6).

Left-hand fork

52 Fit the spacer, then fit the spring with its closer wound coils at the top **(see illustrations)**. Fit the damper rod **(see illustration)**. Clean the threads of the damper rod holder then apply some fresh threadlock. Fit the holder and tighten it using the same tool as on removal **(see illustration)**.

53 Fit the rubber damper **(see illustration)**. Thread the locknut all the way onto the damper rod with the rounded side facing up **(see illustration)**. Thread the top bolt onto the damper rod until it seats **(see illustration)**. Hold the top bolt and tighten the locknut up against it **(see illustration 8.30)**.

54 Refer to Section 7 and fill the fork with oil and finish reassembly.

55 Install the fork (see Section 6).

9 Steering stem

Removal

1 On WR models remove the fuel tank cover (see Chapter 7). Remove the headlight (see Chapter 8). Cut the cable-tie from the

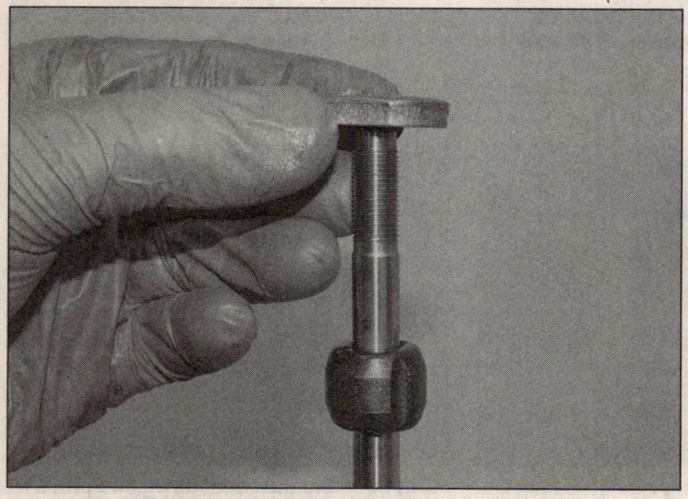

8.53b ...then thread the locknut on...

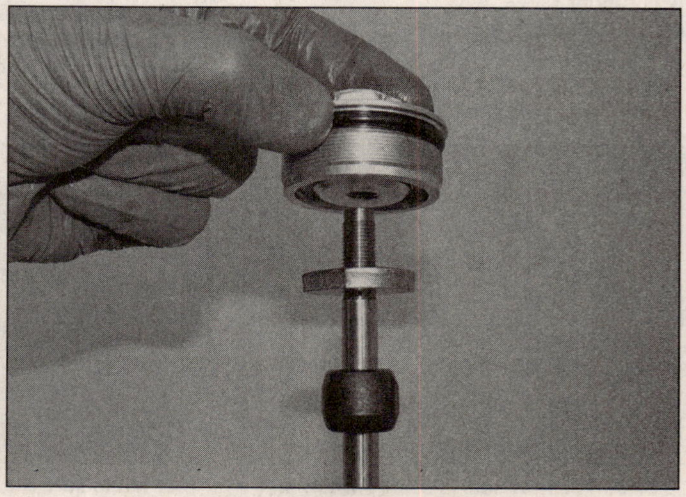

8.53c ...followed by the top bolt

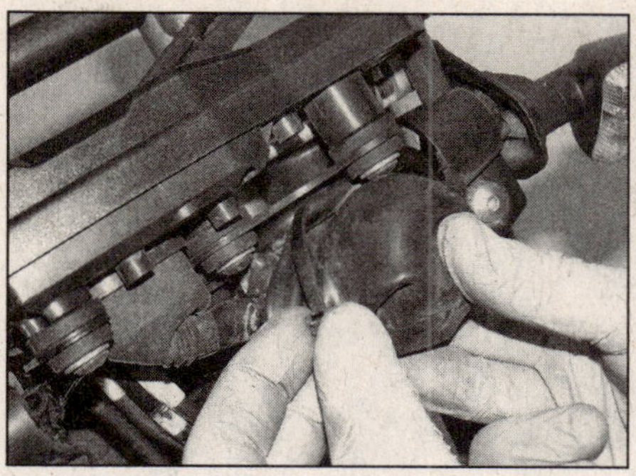
9.1a Cut the cable-tie

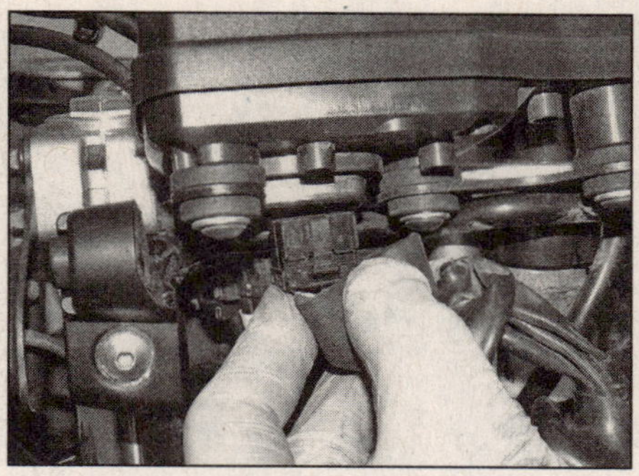
9.1b Disconnect the instrument wiring connector…

9.1c …and the connectors in the boot

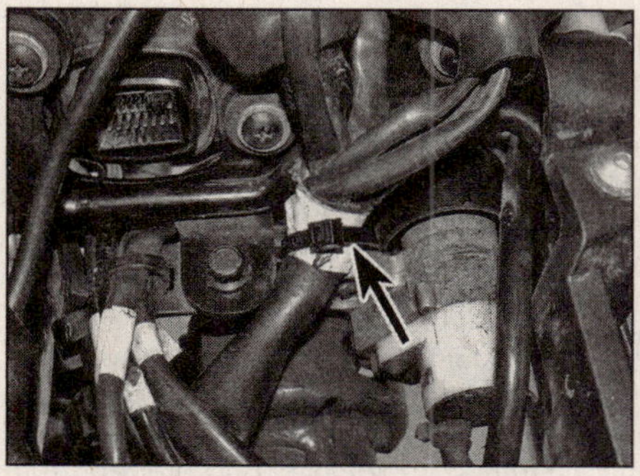
9.1d Cut the cable-tie (arrowed)

9.1e Undo the screws (arrowed)

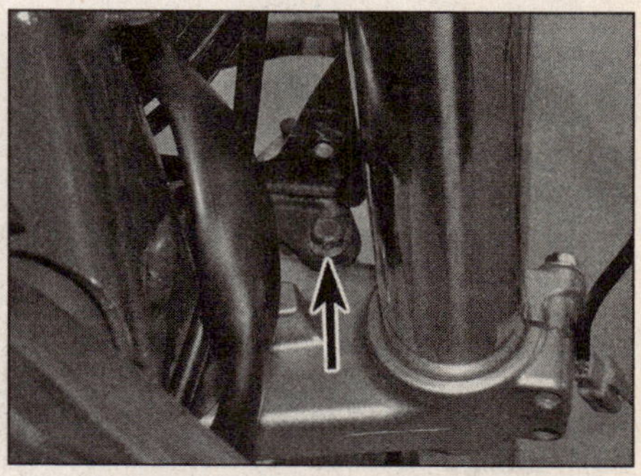
9.1f Unscrew the bolt (arrowed) on each side of the yoke…

9.1g …and the bolt (arrowed) at the top

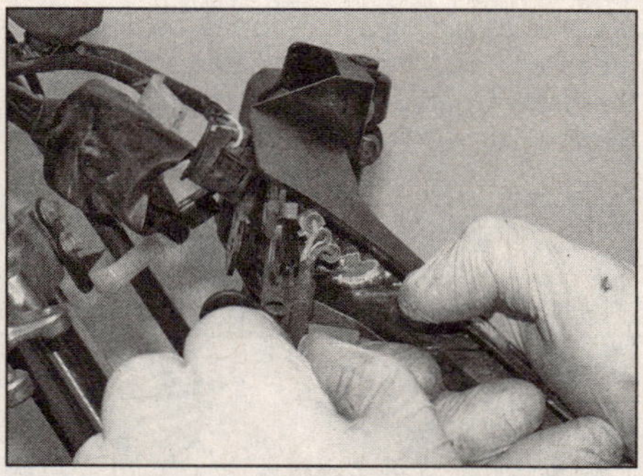
9.1h Displace the bracket and draw the wiring out

rubber boot **(see illustration)**. Disconnect the instrument wiring connector and all the wiring connectors inside the rubber boot **(see illustrations)**. Cut the cable-tie from the ignition switch **(see illustration)**. On R models remove the fork protectors and front mudguard, and on X models remove the front mudguards (see Chapter 7). Undo the bottom right-hand screw on the mudguard bracket and the wiring clamp screw next to it **(see illustration)**. Unscrew the three mudguard/instrument bracket bolts, displace the bracket/instrument assembly and feed the speed sensor wiring out, noting its routing **(see illustrations)**. Feed the wiring loom to the rubber boot and headlight connectors out from behind the handlebar wiring and cables **(see illustration)**. Undo the screw securing the brake hose guide to the bracket on the left-hand side of each yoke **(see illustration)**.

2 On MT models remove the fuel tank cover (see Chapter 7), and the headlight and instruments (see Chapter 8). Unscrew the headlight bracket bolt on each side and remove the bracket **(see illustration)**. Displace the brake pipe bracket from the bottom yoke **(see illustration 9.3)**.

3 On YZF-R models remove the fuel tank

9.1i Feed the loom out

9.1j Brake hose guide screw (arrowed) on bottom yoke

9.2 Unscrew the bolt (arrowed) on each side

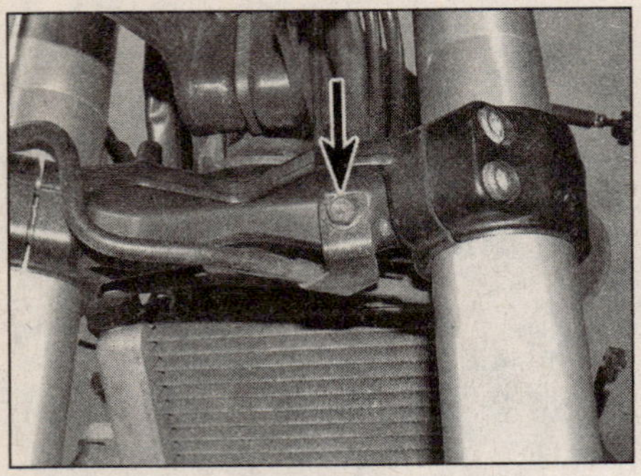

9.3 Unscrew the bolt (arrowed) and displace the bracket

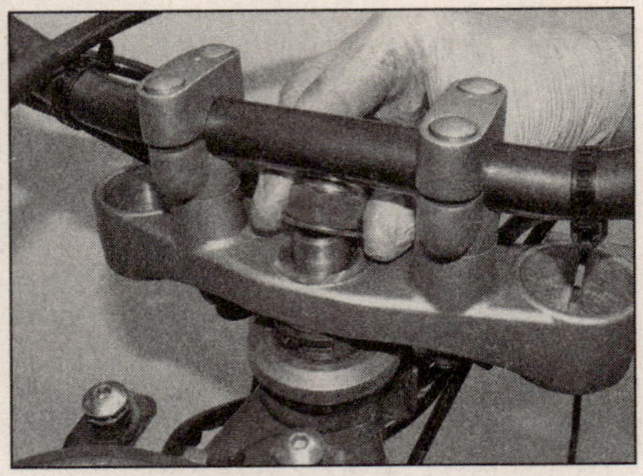

9.5a Unscrew the nut and remove the washer...

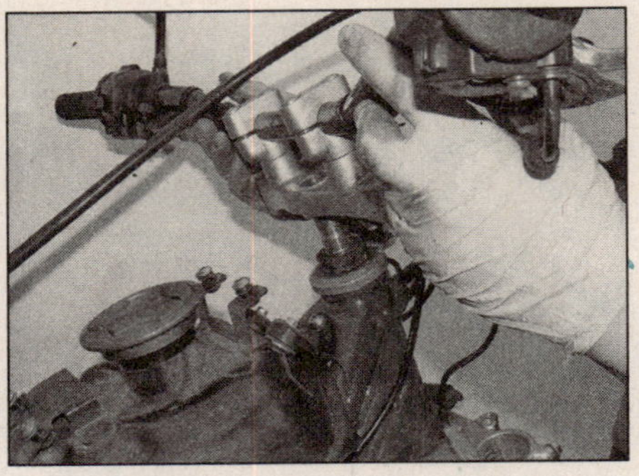

9.5b ... then lift the yoke up off the stem

cover, the front fairing and the centre and upper sections of the fairing on each side (see Chapter 7). Displace the brake pipe bracket from the bottom yoke **(see illustration)**.

4 Remove the front forks (see Chapter 7).

5 Unscrew the steering stem nut and remove the washer **(see illustration)**. Lift the top yoke/handlebar assembly up off the steering stem and rest it on some rag on the fuel tank, guiding the front brake caliper and hose around and supporting the caliper as well **(see illustration)**.

6 Remove the tabbed lock washer, noting how it fits **(see illustration 9.14c)**. Unscrew and remove the locknut, using either a C-spanner or a peg spanner – though it should only be finger-tight **(see illustration 9.14b)**. Remove the rubber washer **(see illustration 9.14a)**.

7 Support the bottom yoke and unscrew the bearing adjuster nut using a C-spanner **(see illustration)**. Remove the bearing cover, then gently lower the bottom yoke and steering stem out of the frame **(see illustrations)**.

8 Remove the upper bearing and its inner race from the top of the steering head **(see illustration)**. On MT and YZF-R models remove the lower bearing from the steering stem. Refer to Section 10 to remove the lower bearing on WR models and the lower bearing inner race on MT and YZF-R models, but only remove them if they are to be replaced with new ones – once removed they cannot be re-used. The same applies to the bearing outer races in the steering head.

9 Clean all old grease from the bearings and races using solvent or paraffin, then check them for wear or damage as described in Section 10.

Installation

10 Make sure the seal, the lower bearing on WR models and the lower bearing inner race on MT and YZF-R models are correctly in place **(see illustration)**. Smear a liberal quantity of lithium-based multi-purpose grease onto the races and bearings. On MT and YZF-R models fit the lower bearing onto the stem. On all models fit the upper bearing and its inner race into the head **(see illustrations 9.8)**.

11 Carefully lift the steering stem/bottom yoke up through the steering head and support it **(see illustration 9.7c)**. Fit the bearing cover onto the top of the steering head **(see illustration 9.7b)**. Thread the adjuster nut onto the steering stem and tighten it lightly **(see illustration)**.

12 To adjust the bearings as specified

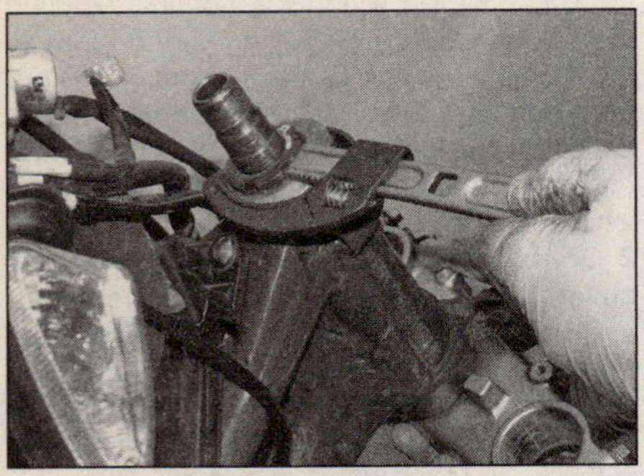

9.7a Unscrew the adjuster nut...

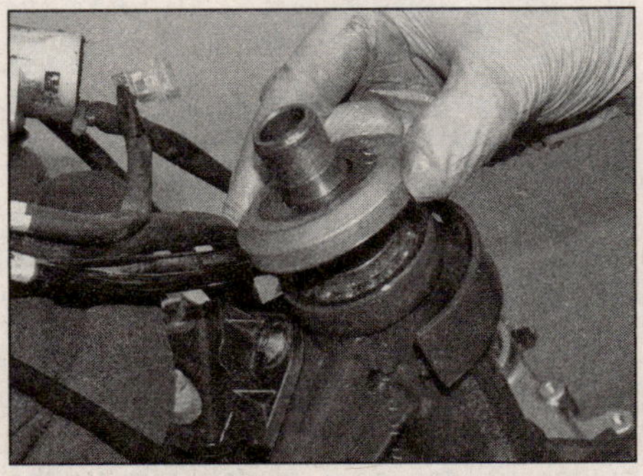

9.7b ... and remove the bearing cover...

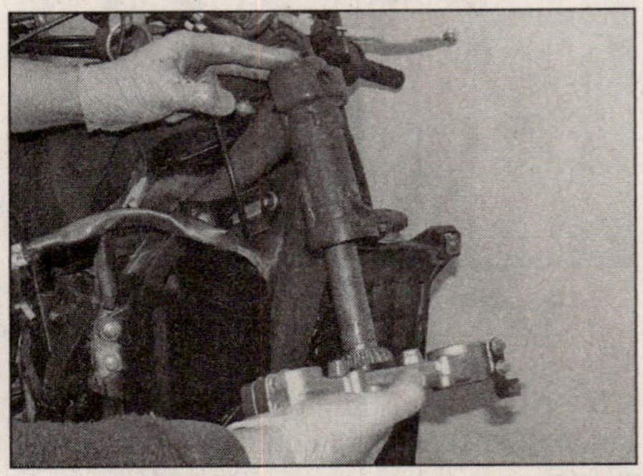

9.7c ... then draw the bottom yoke/steering stem out of the steering head

9.8 Remove the inner race and upper bearing from the top of the head

9.10 Lower bearing on WR models

9.11 Fit the adjuster nut and tighten lightly using a C-spanner

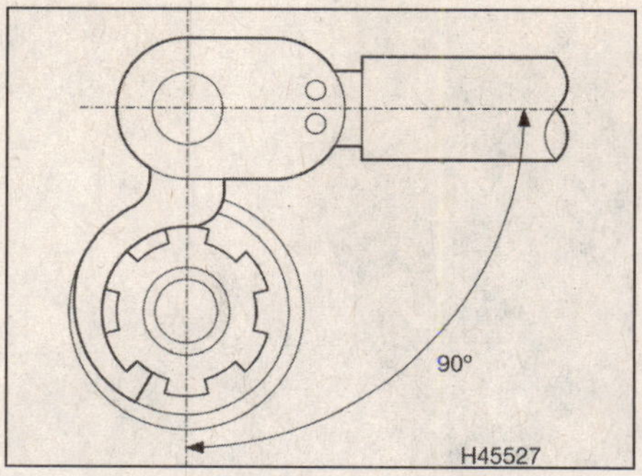

9.12 Using the Yamaha service tool to tighten the adjuster nut

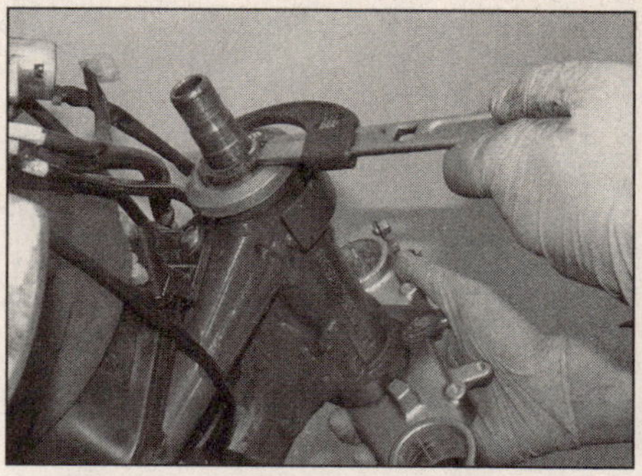

9.13 Using a C-spanner to tighten the adjuster nut

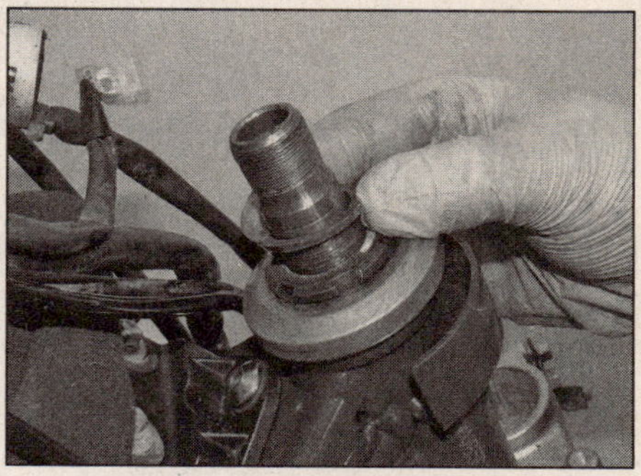

9.14a Fit the rubber washer...

by Yamaha, a special service tool (Pt. No. 90890-01403) and a torque wrench are required. If the tool is available, tighten the adjuster nut to the initial torque setting specified at the beginning of the Chapter, making sure the torque wrench arm is at 90° to the tool arm **(see illustration)**. Next fully slacken the nut, then tighten it to the final torque setting specified. Make sure that the steering stem is able to move freely from lock-to-lock, but that all freeplay is eliminated.

13 If the Yamaha tool is not available, using a C-spanner or peg spanner tighten the adjuster nut until all freeplay is removed, then tighten it a little more **(see illustration)**. This pre-loads the bearings. Now slacken the nut, then tighten it again, setting it so that all freeplay is just removed, yet the steering is able to move freely from side to side.

Caution: Take great care not to apply excessive pressure because this will cause premature failure of the bearings.

14 Fit the rubber washer, then the locknut **(see illustrations)**. Tighten the locknut finger-tight, then tighten it further until its notches align with those in the adjuster nut. If necessary, counter-hold the adjuster nut and tighten the locknut using a C-spanner until the notches align, but make sure the adjuster nut does not turn as well and note that the locknut should not be any tighter than necessary for alignment of the notches or the rubber washer will be damaged. Fit the tabbed lock washer so that the tabs fit into the notches in both the locknut and adjuster nut **(see illustration)**.

15 Fit the top yoke onto the steering stem **(see illustration 9.5b)**. Fit the washer and the steering stem nut and tighten the nut finger-tight **(see illustration 9.5a)**. Temporarily install one of the forks to align the top and bottom yokes, and secure it by tightening the bottom yoke clamp bolts only. Now tighten the steering stem nut to the torque setting specified at the beginning of the Chapter.

16 Install all remaining components in a reverse of the removal procedure, referring to the relevant Sections or Chapters where required, and to the torque settings specified at the beginning of the Chapter. Make sure the wiring, cables and hose are correctly routed.

17 Refer to the freeplay check procedure in Chapter 1 to make a final assessment of the bearings with the leverage and inertia of all components taken into account, and if necessary re-adjust.

10 Steering head bearings

Inspection

1 Remove the steering stem (see Section 9).

2 Clean all traces of old grease from the bearings and races using paraffin or solvent, and check them for wear or damage.

3 The races should be polished and free from indentations. Inspect the bearing rollers or balls and cages for signs of wear, damage or discoloration. If there are any signs of wear and damage on any of the above components both upper and lower bearing assemblies must be replaced with a new set. Only remove the outer races in the steering head and the lower bearing (WR models) or inner race (MT and YZF-R models) on the steering stem if they need to be replaced with new ones – do not reuse them once they have been removed.

Replacement

4 The outer races are an interference fit in the steering head – you should be able to tap them out using a suitable drift located in the

9.14b ...then tighten the locknut as described...

9.14c ...and fit the tabs on the washer into the aligned notches

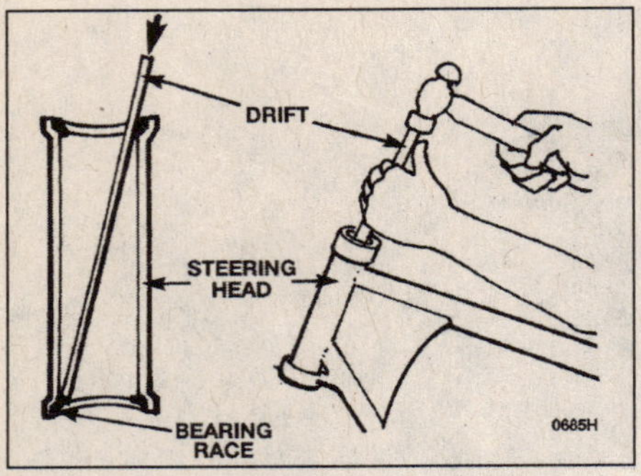

10.4 Locate the drift as shown to drive the races out

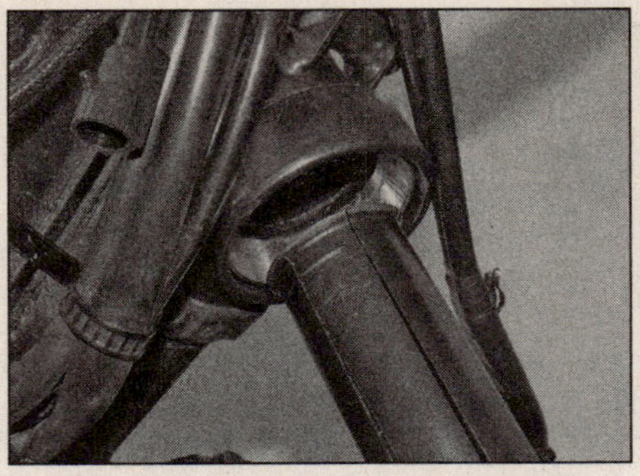

10.5a Locate the adapter behind the rim of the race and expand it to lock it...

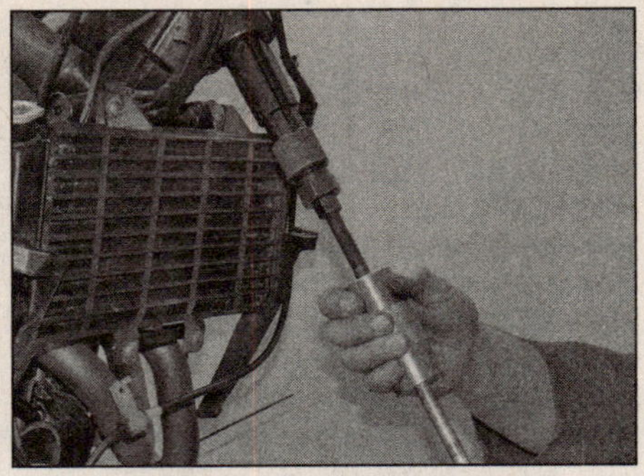

10.5b ...then fit the slide-hammer and jar the race out

cut-outs where present, or on the exposed inner lip of the race if there are no cut-outs **(see illustration)**. Tap firmly and evenly around each race to ensure that it is driven out squarely. Curve the end of the drift slightly to improve access if necessary.

5 Alternatively, remove the races using a slide-hammer type bearing extractor **(see illustrations)** – these can often be hired from tool shops.

6 Press the new outer races into the head using a drawbolt arrangement **(see illustration)**, or tap them in using a large diameter tubular drift (to do this the bike must be solidly supported as all the force needs to be transmitted to the race). Make sure that the drawbolt washer or drift (as applicable) bears only on the outer edge of the race and does not contact the working surface. Alternatively, have the races installed by a Yamaha dealer equipped with the bearing race installation tools.

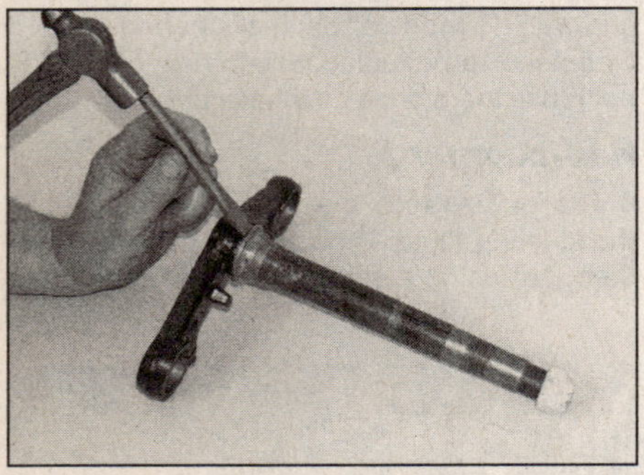

10.7a Remove the lower bearing race using a cold chisel...

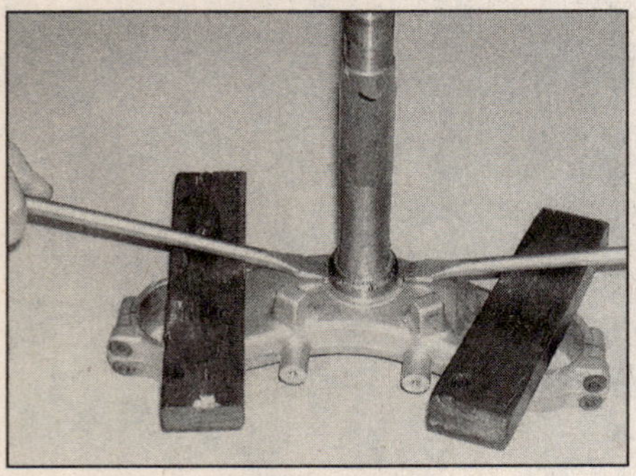

10.7b ...and screwdrivers...

HAYNES HiNT ***Installation of new bearing outer races is made much easier if the races are left overnight in the freezer. This causes them to contract slightly making them a looser fit. Alternatively, use a freeze spray on the races just before you install them.***

7 To remove the lower bearing or inner race from the steering stem, thread the steering stem nut onto the top of the stem to protect the threads, then position the yoke on its front for stability, and tap under the race using a cold chisel to dislodge it **(see illustration)**. Next use two screwdrivers placed on opposite sides to work the race free, using blocks of wood to improve leverage and protect the yoke **(see illustration)**. If the race is firmly in place it will be necessary to use a puller **(see illustration)**. Alternatively carefully cut the bearing/race off using a Dremel or angle grinder. Take the steering stem to a Yamaha dealer if required. Remove the seal from under the race and replace it with a new one.

8 Fit a new seal onto the steering stem. Tap the new bearing or race into position using a length of tubing with an internal diameter slightly larger than the steering stem so that it locates on the top of the race, and not on the bearing or the race's bearing surface (according to model) **(see illustration)**.

9 Install the steering stem (see Section 9).

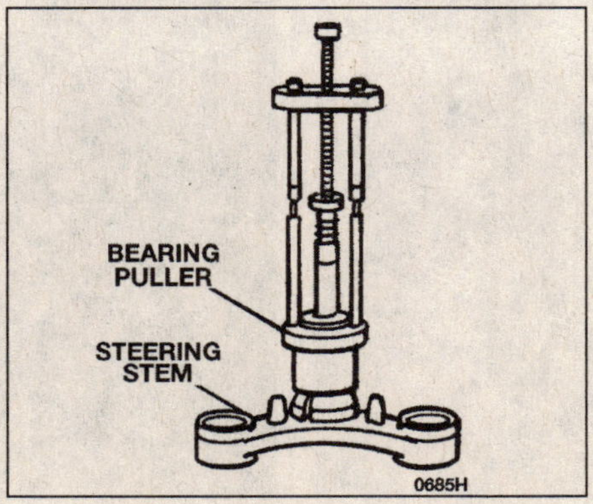

10.7c ...or a puller if necessary

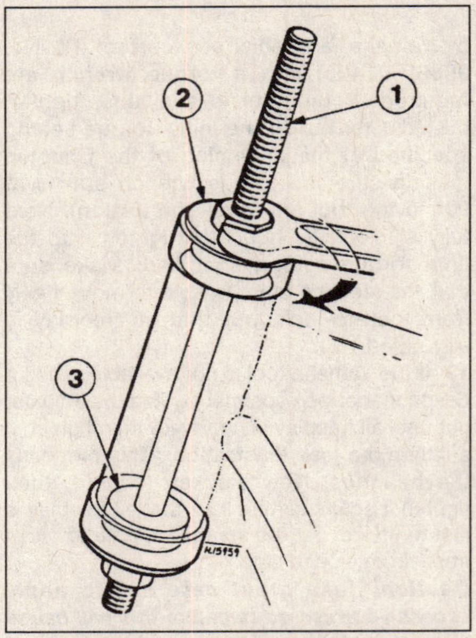

10.6 Drawbolt arrangement for fitting steering stem bearing races

1 Long bolt or threaded bar
2 Thick washer
3 Guide for lower race

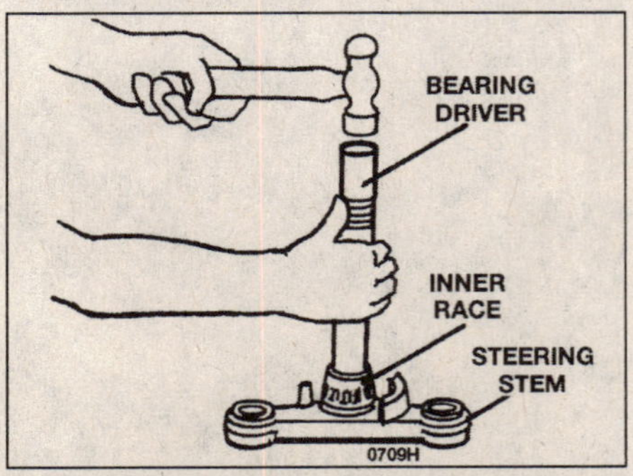

10.8 Drive the new bearing on using a suitable bearing driver or a length of pipe that bears only against the inner race and not against the balls or cage

11.1a Stand positioned under the frame on a WR model

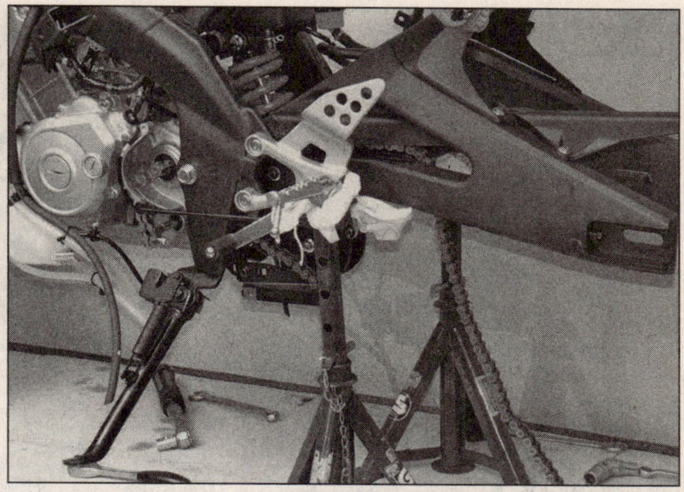

11.1b Axle stands positioned under the footrest brackets on a YZF-R model

11 Rear shock absorber

Warning: Do not attempt to disassemble the shock absorber. Improper disassembly could result in serious injury. No individual components are available for it.

Removal

1 Support the motorcycle using an auxiliary stand or stands so that no weight is transmitted through any part of the rear suspension **(see illustrations)** – tie the front brake lever to the handlebar to ensure the bike can't roll forward. Position a support under the rear wheel or swingarm so that it does not drop when the suspension is detached, but also making sure that the weight of the machine is off the rear suspension so that it is not compressed. Note the fitted direction of all bolts.

2 On WR models remove the right-hand side cover (see Chapter 7). Remove the toolkit. Release the air hose from its clip and move it aside, then unscrew the rear brake fluid reservoir bolt and displace the reservoir **(see illustration)**.

3 On YZF-R models remove the bottom section of the fairing (see Chapter 7). Unscrew the fairing bracket bolt on the left-hand side and remove the bracket, noting how it fits **(see illustration)**.

4 On MT and YZF-R models remove the rear wheel (see Chapter 6) – this allows the swingarm to be raised and lowered as required for best access and clearance.

5 On WR models unscrew the nut on the bolt securing the linkage plates to the linkage arm, then withdraw the bolt and swing the arm down **(see illustration)**. Unscrew the nut on the bolt securing the shock absorber to the linkage plates, then withdraw the bolt and swing the plates down **(see illustration)**.

6 On MT and YZF-R models unscrew the nut on the bolt securing the linkage plates to the linkage arm, then withdraw the bolt and swing the plates down **(see illustration)**. Unscrew the nut on the bolt securing the

11.2 Release the hose and displace the reservoir

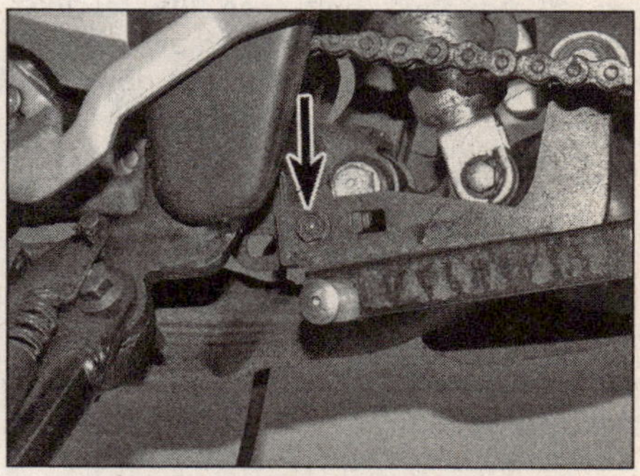

11.3 Fairing bracket bolt (arrowed)

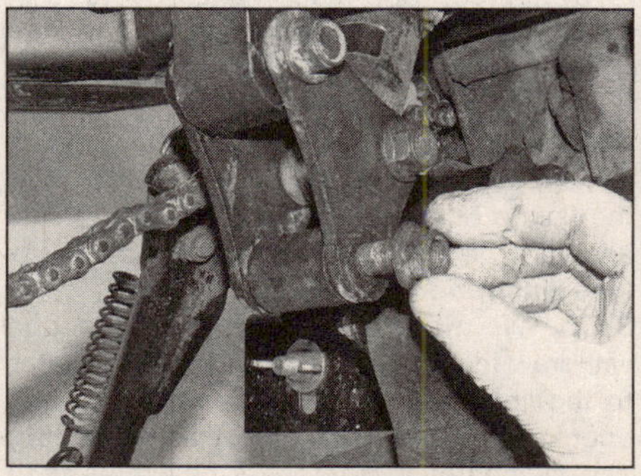

11.5a Unscrew the nut, withdraw the bolt and swing the arm down

11.5b Unscrew the nut, withdraw the bolt and swing the plates down

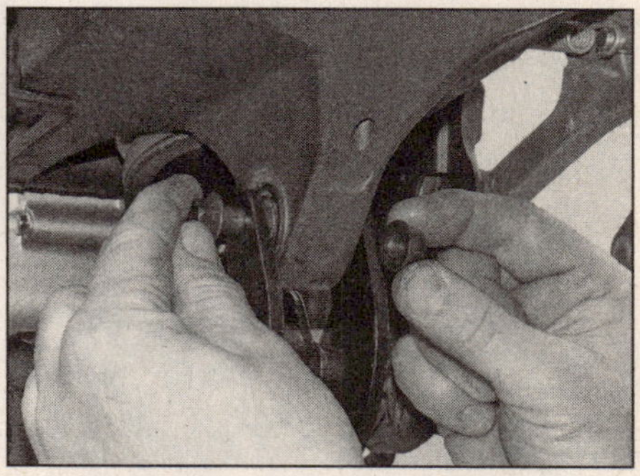

11.6a Unscrew the nut, withdraw the bolt and swing the plates down

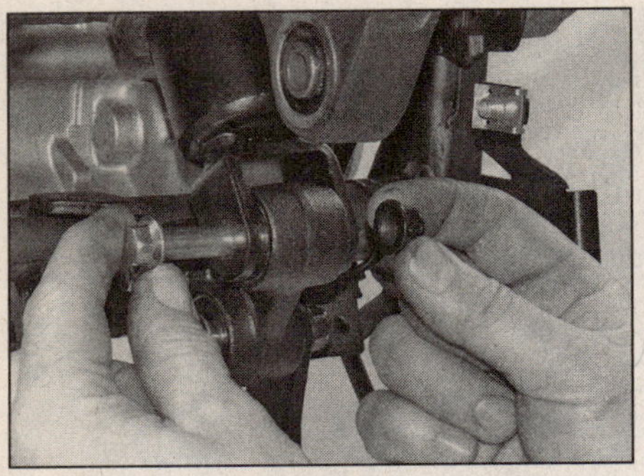

11.6b Unscrew the nut, withdraw the bolt and swing the arm down

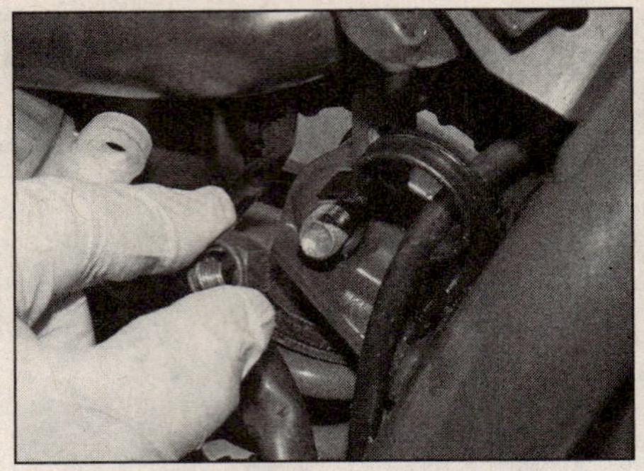

11.7a Unscrew the nut...

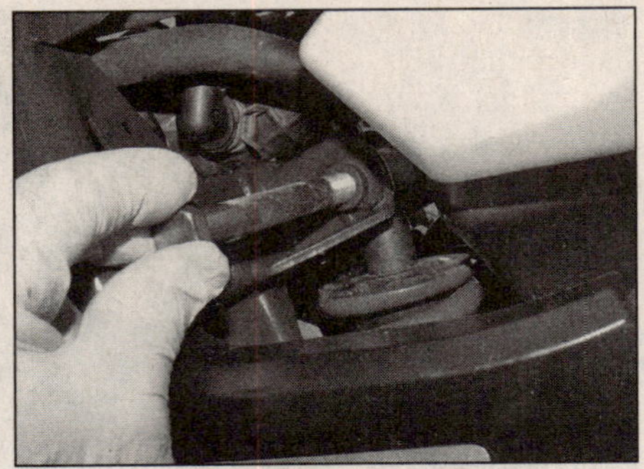

11.7b ...withdraw the bolt...

11.7c ...and remove the shock absorber

11.9 Check for signs of oil and pitting on the rod (arrowed)

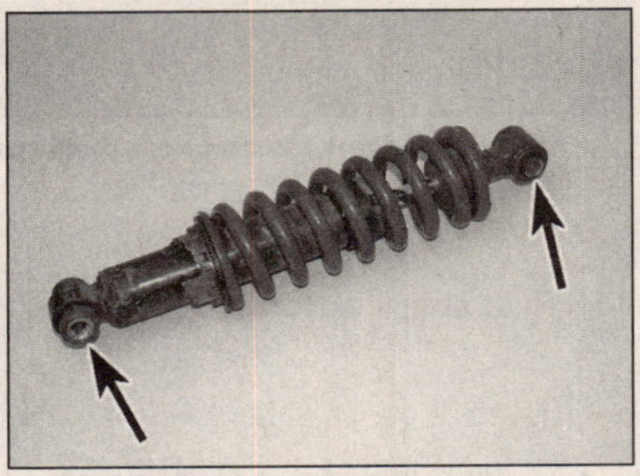

11.10 Check the bushes (arrowed) – WR shock shown

shock absorber to the linkage arm, then withdraw the bolt and swing the arm down **(see illustration)**.

7 Unscrew the nut on the shock absorber upper mounting bolt **(see illustration)**. Support the shock and withdraw the bolt, then draw the shock absorber down and manoeuvre it out **(see illustrations)**.

Inspection

8 Inspect the body of the shock absorber for obvious physical damage and the spring for looseness, cracks or signs of fatigue.

9 Inspect the damper rod for signs of pitting and oil leakage **(see illustration)**.

10 Inspect the pivot bush(es) in the mounting(s) for wear **(see illustration)** – if worn a new shock absorber must be fitted.

11 Refer to Section 12 and inspect the exposed seals and bushes (WR models) or bearings (MT and YZF-R models) in the linkage arm and swingarm. If there is evidence of wear, damage, dirt or corrosion remove the complete linkage assembly and remove the seals and sleeves, clean and check the bearings and either re-grease them or fit new ones as required, then fit new seals.

12 The shock cannot be dismantled for the replacement of parts. If it is worn or damaged, it must be replaced with a new one.

Installation

13 Installation is the reverse of removal, noting the following:

- Apply multi-purpose lithium grease (WR models) or molybdenum disulphide grease (MT and YZF-R models) to all pivot points and the mounting bolt shanks, and to the seal lips in the linkage arm and swingarm (if not already done).
- Insert all the bolts from the left. Install all bolts and nuts finger-tight only until all components are in position, then tighten the bolts to the torque setting(s) specified at the beginning of the Chapter for your model.

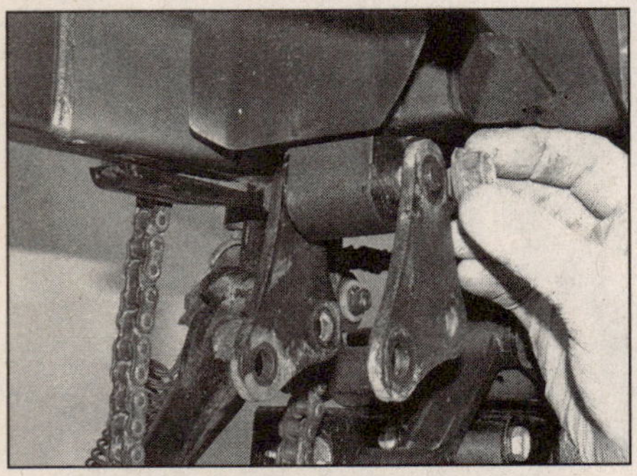

12.3a Unscrew the nut, withdraw the bolt and remove the plates

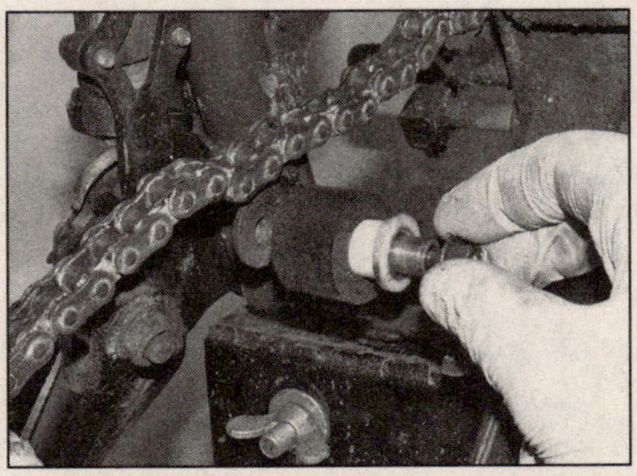

12.3b Note the collar and sleeve in the roller

12 Rear suspension linkage

Removal

1 Support the motorcycle using an auxiliary stand or stands so that no weight is transmitted through any part of the rear suspension **(see illustration 11.1a or b)** – tie the front brake lever to the handlebar to ensure the bike can't roll forward. Position a support under the rear wheel or swingarm so that it does not drop when the suspension is detached, but also making sure that the weight of the machine is off the rear suspension so that it is not compressed. Note the fitted direction of all bolts.

2 On YZF-R models remove the bottom section of the fairing (see Chapter 7). Unscrew the fairing bracket bolt on the left-hand side and remove the bracket, noting how it fits **(see illustration 11.3)**.

3 On WR models unscrew the nuts and withdraw the bolts securing the linkage plates to the linkage arm **(see illustration 11.5a)**, shock absorber **(see illustration 11.5b)** and swingarm and remove the plates **(see illustration)**. Remove the lower chain roller **(see illustration)**. Unscrew the nut on the bolt

securing the linkage arm to the frame, then withdraw the bolt and remove the arm **(see illustration)**.

4 On MT and YZF-R models unscrew the nut on the bolt securing the linkage plates to the swingarm, then withdraw the bolt and swing the plates down **(see illustration 11.6a)**. Unscrew the nut on the bolt securing the shock absorber to the linkage arm, then withdraw the bolt and swing the arm down **(see illustration 11.6b)**. Unscrew the nut on the bolt securing the linkage plates to the linkage arm, then withdraw the bolt and remove the plates **(see illustration)**. Unscrew the nut on the bolt securing the linkage arm to the frame, then withdraw the bolt and remove the arm **(see illustrations)**.

12.3c Unscrew the nut, withdraw the bolt and remove the arm

12.4a Unscrew the nut, withdraw the bolt and remove the plates

12.4b Unscrew the nut, withdraw the bolt...

12.4c ...and remove the linkage arm

Inspection

5 Withdraw the sleeve from each pivot of the linkage arm and from the linkage plate mount in the swingarm **(see illustrations)**. Thoroughly clean all components with a suitable solvent, removing all traces of dirt, corrosion and grease.

6 Inspect all components closely, looking for obvious signs of wear such as heavy scoring, or for damage such as cracks or distortion. Inspect the bolt holes in the linkage plates for elongation.

7 Check the condition of the bushes (WR models) or needle bearings (MT and YZF-R models) in the linkage arm and in the linkage plate mounting in the swingarm. Refer to Tools and Workshop Tips9,1 (Section 5) in the Reference section for more information on bearings. Slip each sleeve back into its bush or bearing and check that there is not an excessive amount of freeplay between them.

8 If the seals are obviously in bad condition, or if you are fitting new bushes or bearings, lever the seals out **(see illustration)**. Once removed they cannot be reused – new ones must be fitted.

9 Worn bushes and bearings can be driven or drawn out of their bores, but note that once removed they cannot be reused – new bearings must be fitted. The new bearings should be pressed or drawn into their bores rather than driven into position. In the absence of a press, a suitable drawbolt tool can be made up as described in *Tools and Workshop Tips* in the Reference section. When fitting the new bearings make sure they are central in their bores.

10 Lubricate the bushes or bearings, sleeves and seals with multi-purpose lithium grease on WR models, and molybdenum disulphide grease on MT and YZF-R models.

11 Press and/or drive the new seals squarely into place with the marked side facing out **(see illustration)**. Fit the sleeves **(see illustrations 12.5a, b and c)**.

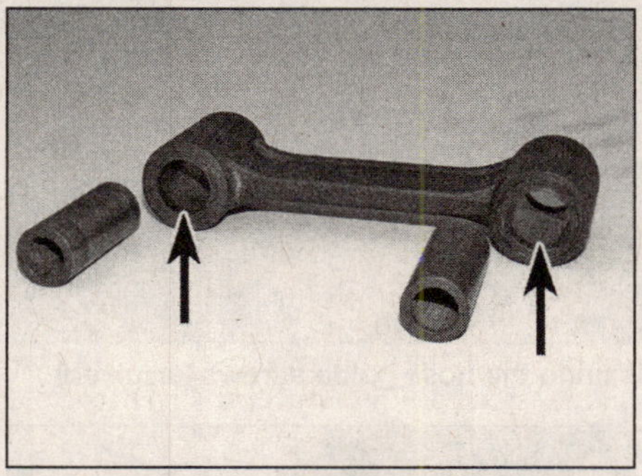

12.5a Linkage arm sleeves and bushes (arrowed) – WR models

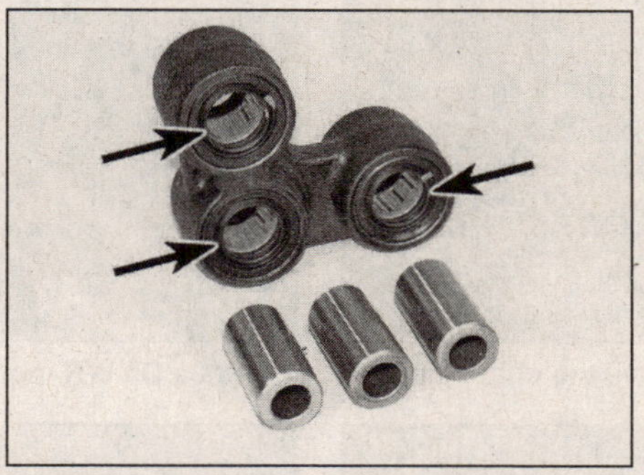

12.5b Linkage arm sleeves and bearings (arrowed) – MT and YZF-R models

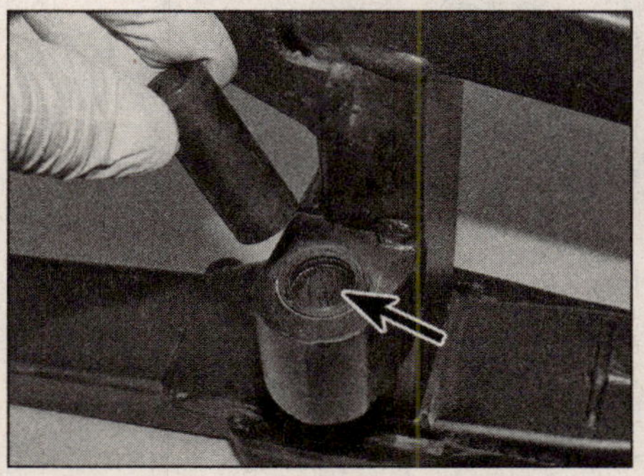

12.5c Swingarm sleeve and bearing or bush (arrowed)

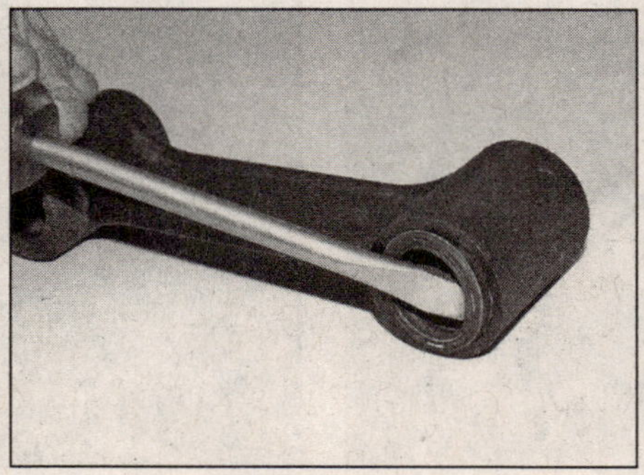

12.8 Lever the seals out

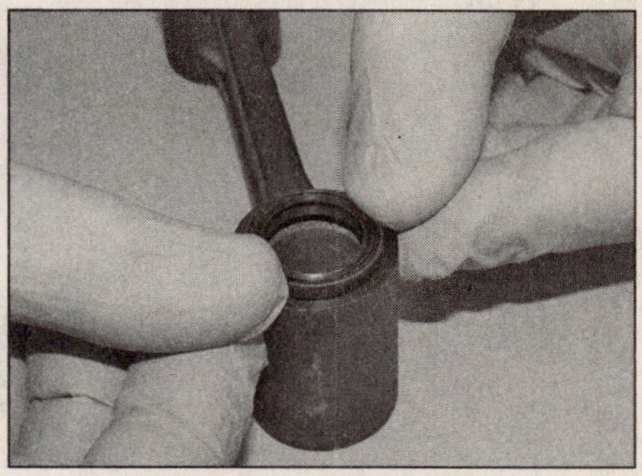

12.11 You should be able to press the new seals in with your thumbs

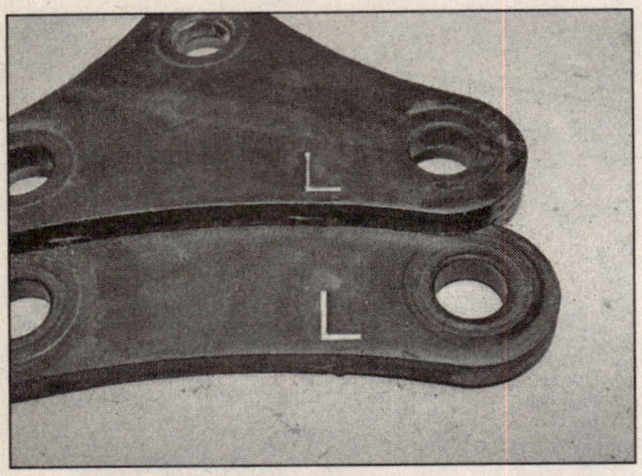

12.12 The L marks must be on the left

Installation

12 Installation is the reverse of removal, noting the following:

- If not already done, withdraw the sleeve from each pivot of the linkage arm and from the linkage plate mount in the swingarm, then clean the sleeves, seals and bushes or bearings, and apply multi-purpose lithium grease on WR models and molybdenum disulphide grease on MT and YZF-R models **(see illustrations 12.5a, b and c)**. Refit the sleeves.
- On WR models fit the linkage plates with the L mark facing to the left **(see illustration)**.
- On MT and YZF-R models fit the linkage arm with the two closer pivots to the front **(see illustration 12.4c)**. Fit the linkage plates with the longer arm to the rear.
- Insert all bolts from the left side. Fit all nuts and bolts finger-tight only until all components are in position, then tighten the nuts to the torque setting specified at the beginning of the Chapter for your model.

13 Swingarm

Removal

1 Support the motorcycle using an auxiliary stand or stands so that no weight is transmitted through any part of the rear suspension **(see illustration 11.1a or b)** – tie the front brake lever to the handlebar to ensure the bike can't roll forward. Note the fitted direction of all bolts.

2 On YZF-R models remove the bottom section of the fairing (see Chapter 7). Unscrew the fairing bracket bolt on the left-hand side and remove the bracket, noting how it fits **(see illustration 11.3)**.

3 On MT and YZF-R models remove the exhaust system (see Chapter 4).

4 Remove the rear wheel (see Chapter 6).

5 Remove the shock absorber and suspension linkage if required, or if not just detach the linkage plates and arm from the swingarm and shock absorber as required according to model — refer to Section 11, 12. Removing the shock absorber makes it easier to manoeuvre the swingarm out and back in.

6 On WR models remove the chainguard **(see illustration)**.

7 On MT and YZF-R models either remove the front sprocket and remove the swingarm with the chain looped through it, or split and remove the drive chain (see Chapter 6) – the method you choose will depend on your reason for removing the swingarm.

8 Free the brake hose from the swingarm, and from the hugger on MT and YZF-R models **(see illustrations)**. Secure the brake caliper clear.

9 On MT and YZF- R models, if required undo the screws securing the rear hugger, noting the sleeves, and remove the hugger **(see illustration)**.

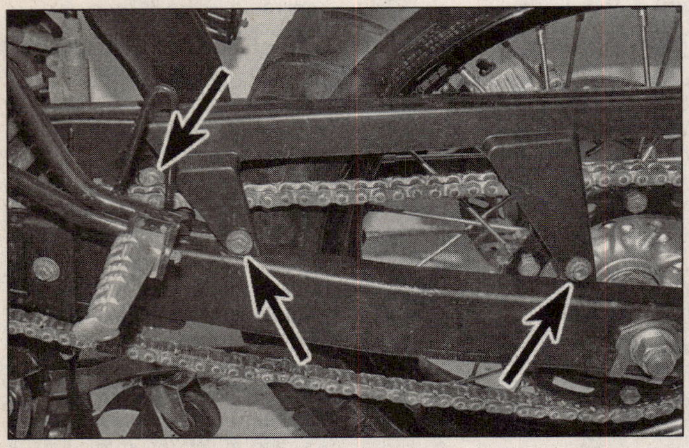

13.6 Unscrew the bolts (arrowed) and remove the chainguard

13.8a On WR models undo the hose guide screws (arrowed)

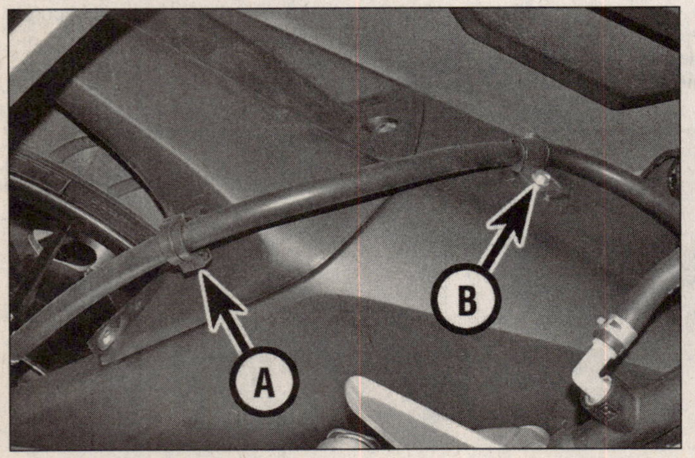

13.8b On MT and YZF-R models release the clip (A) and unscrew the bolt (B)

13.9 Rear hugger screws (arrowed) – there is one on each side

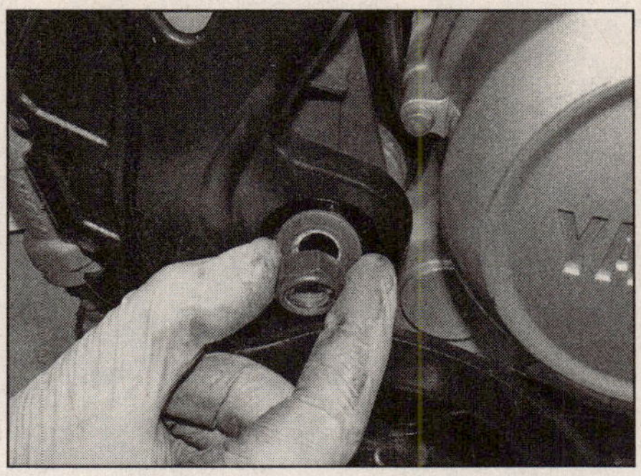

13.10a Unscrew the nut and remove the washer...

13.10b ... withdraw the bolt and remove the swingarm

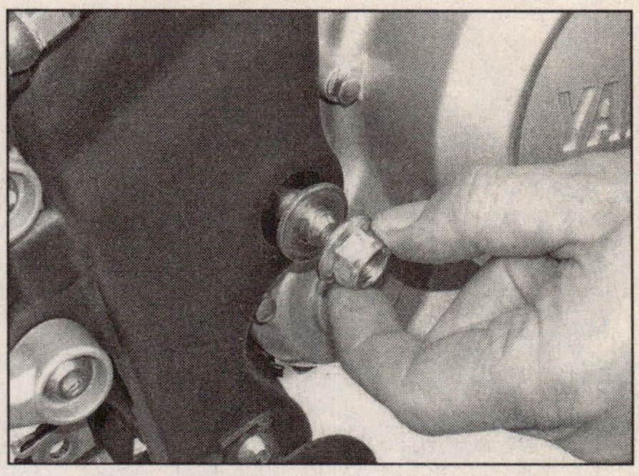

13.11a Unscrew the nut and remove the washer

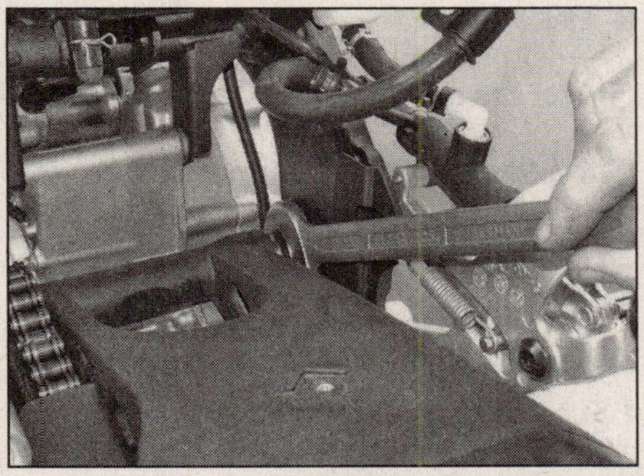

13.11b Turn the adjuster bolt in if required

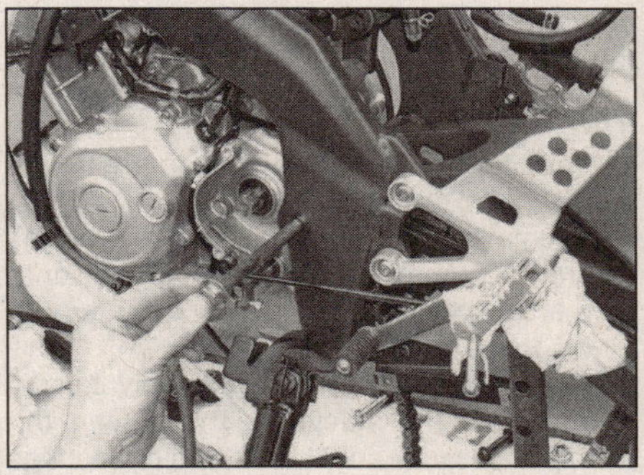

13.11c Withdraw the pivot bolt and remove the swingarm

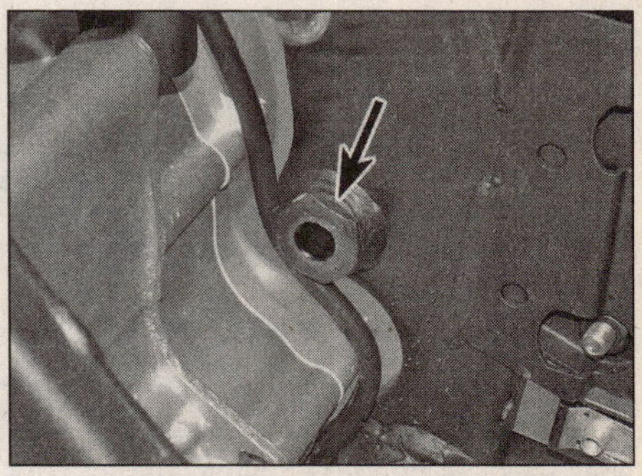

13.11d Unscrew and remove the adjusting bolt (arrowed) if required

10 On WR models unscrew the swingarm pivot bolt nut and remove the washer **(see illustration)**. Withdraw the pivot bolt and manoeuvre the swingarm out of the frame **(see illustration)**.

11 On MT and YZF-R models unscrew the swingarm pivot bolt nut and remove the washer **(see illustration)**. On the inside of the frame on the right-hand side there is a swingarm pivot adjusting bolt – there should be no need to disturb this when removing and installing the swingarm as it only just touches it (rather than being tight against it), and is probably best left alone to avoid disturbing its setting. However if you find that the swingarm is tight and difficult to remove after withdrawing the pivot bolt, you can turn the adjuster into the frame to give some clearance **(see illustration)**. Withdraw the pivot bolt, then manoeuvre the swingarm out of the frame **(see illustration)**. If required unscrew and remove the adjusting bolt from the frame **(see illustration)**.

12 If required, on MT and YZF-R models remove the chainguard and on all models remove the chain slider from the swingarm, noting how the collars fit with the bolts **(see illustration)**. Check the condition of the slider and replace it with a new one if necessary. On WR models check the condition of the chain rollers and replace them with new ones if necessary **(see illustration)**.

Inspection

13 Thoroughly clean the swingarm, removing all traces of dirt, corrosion and grease.

14 Inspect the swingarm closely, looking for obvious signs of wear such as heavy scoring, and cracks or distortion due to accident damage.

15 Remove the pivot cap from each side and withdraw the sleeve(s) **(see illustrations)**.

16 Thoroughly clean all pivot components with a suitable solvent, removing all traces of dirt, corrosion and grease.

13.12a Chain slider bolt (arrowed) – WR models

13.12b Check for wear and damage on the rollers (arrowed)

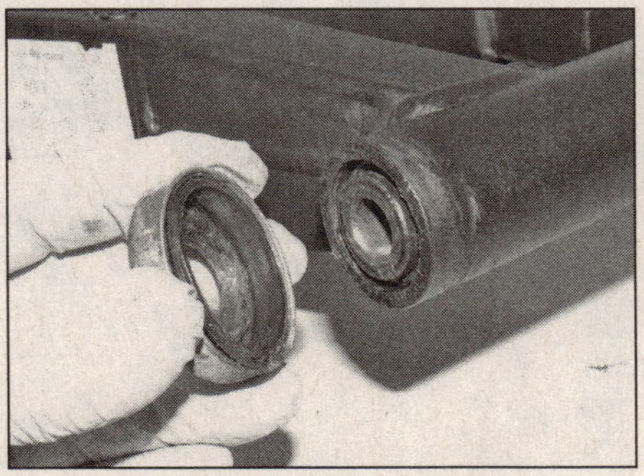

13.15a Remove the pivot caps...

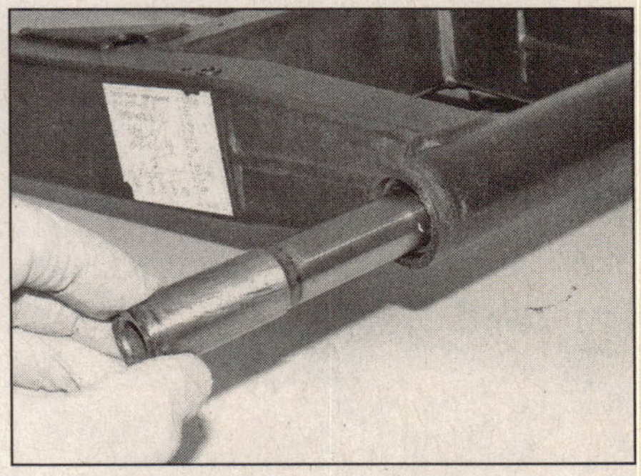

13.15b ... and withdraw the sleeve(s)

13.17 Check the bearings

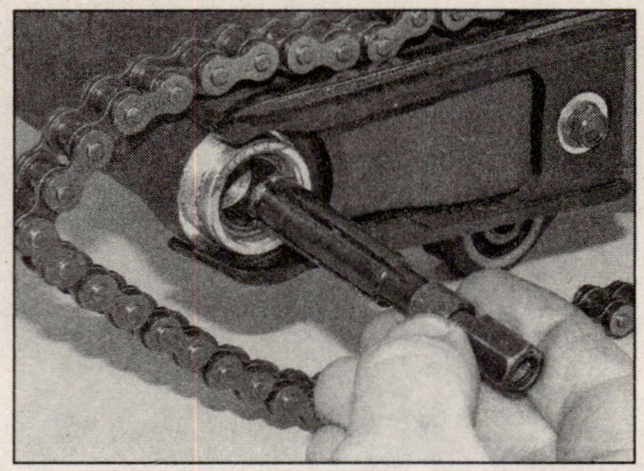

13.18a Fit the adapter behind the bearing and expand it...

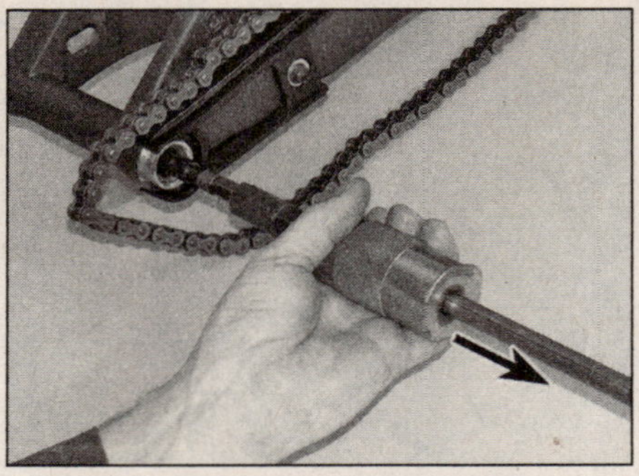

13.18b ...then attach the slide-hammer and jar the bearing out

17 Check the condition of the bushes (2009 WR models) or needle bearings (all other models) **(see illustration)**. Refer to Tools and Workshop Tips9,1 (Section 5) in the Reference section for more information on bearings. Slip the sleeve back into its bush or bearing and check that there is not an excessive amount of freeplay between them.

18 Worn bushes and bearings can be pulled out of their bores using an expanding puller with slide-hammer attachment, but note that once removed they cannot be reused – new ones must be fitted **(see illustrations)**. The new bushes or bearings should be pressed or drawn into their bores until they seat – do not drive them in. In the absence of a press, a suitable drawbolt tool can be made up as described in Tools and Workshop Tips9,1 in the Reference section.

19 Lubricate the bushes and sleeve on 2009 WR models with multi-purpose lithium grease, and the bearings and sleeve(s) on all other models with molybdenum disulphide grease. Insert the sleeve(s) **(see illustration 13.15b)**. Check the condition of the seal in each pivot cap and replace them with new ones if necessary – on 2010-on WR models they are listed separately from the caps, on all other models you may have to buy the complete cap. If fitting new seals fit the flat side of the seal into the cap so the lipped side faces the swingarm **(see illustration)**.

20 Check the swingarm pivot bolt is straight by rolling it on a flat surface such as a piece of plate glass (first wipe off all old grease and remove any corrosion using wire wool). Replace the bolt with a new one if it is bent.

Installation

21 Installation is the reverse of removal, noting the following:

- If removed, fit the chain slider, and on MT and YZF-R models the chainguard, onto the swingarm before installing the arm in the frame.
- If not already done, remove the pivot caps, withdraw the sleeve(s), then clean the caps, sleeve(s) and the bushes or bearings and apply multi-purpose lithium grease on 2009 WR models and molybdenum disulphide grease on all other models **(see illustrations 13.15a and b).** Refit the sleeve(s) and caps.
- On MT and YZF-R models, if removed thread the pivot adjusting bolt into the frame from the inside until it seats **(see illustration 13.11d).**
- Position the swingarm in the frame, making sure the pivot caps stay in place, then slide the pivot bolt in from the left **(see illustration 13.10b)**. Fit the washer and nut onto the pivot bolt and tighten the nut finger-tight **(see illustration 13.10a)**. On MT and YZF-R models, if disturbed turn the adjuster bolt out until it contacts the pivot cap, then turn it a little more but not so that it is tight – a torque of 8 Nm is specified **(see illustration 13.11b)**.
- Counter-hold the head of the pivot bolt and tighten nut to the torque setting specified at the beginning of the Chapter for your model.
- Install all remaining components in reverse order of removal, referring to the relevant Sections and Chapters (see Steps 8 to 2).

14 Suspension adjustment

Front forks

1 The front forks are not adjustable on any models.

Rear shock absorber

WR models

2 On WR models the rear shock has adjustable spring pre-load. Adjustment is made using the C-spanner and extension handle provided in the bike's toolkit. Remove the tools and fit the handle onto the C-spanner **(see illustration)**.

3 Fit the C-spanner ends into the notches in the adjuster ring on the bottom of the shock and turn it as required – to increase pre-load turn the adjuster ring anti-clockwise, and to decrease it turn it clockwise **(see illustration)**. There are seven settings, 1 to 7 from minimum to maximum, and the standard setting is number 3. After making any adjustment check the setting lug on the shock body is correctly seated in the detent in the ring.

MT and YZF-R models

4 On MT and YZF-R models the rear shock absorber is not adjustable.

13.19 The lipped side of the seal must face out of the cap

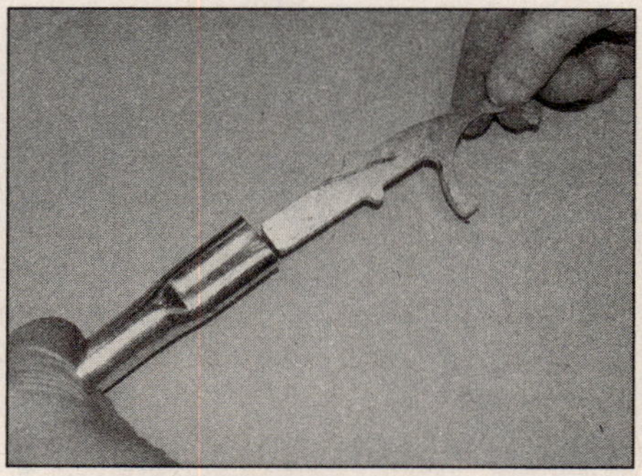

14.2 Fit the handle onto the spanner

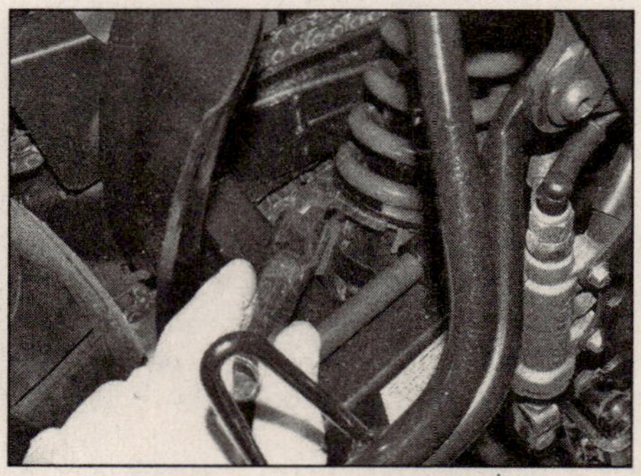

14.3 Locate the spanner in the notches and turn as required

Chapter 6
Brakes, wheels and final drive

Contents

Degrees of difficulty

Easy, suitable for novice with little experience	**Fairly easy,** suitable for beginner with some experience	**Fairly difficult,** suitable for competent DIY mechanic	**Difficult,** suitable for experienced DIY mechanic	**Very difficult,** suitable for expert DIY or professional

Specifications

Front brake

Brake fluid type	DOT 4
Brake pad friction material minimum thickness	
WR models	1.0 mm
MT and YZF-R models	2.0 mm
Caliper bore ID	
WR models	27 mm x 2
MT and YZF-R models	32 mm x 2, 27 mm x 2
Master cylinder bore ID	
WR models	13.0 mm
MT and YZF-R models	12.7 mm
Disc thickness	
WR-R models	
Standard	4.0 mm
Service limit	3.5 mm
WR-X, MT and YZF-R models	
Standard	4.5 mm
Service limit	4.0 mm
Disc maximum runout	0.15 mm

Rear brake

Brake fluid type	DOT 4
Brake pad friction material minimum thickness	1.0 mm
Caliper bore ID	
WR models	30.23 mm
MT and YZF-R models	32 mm
Master cylinder bore ID	12.7 mm
Disc thickness	
WR models	
Standard	4.5 mm
Service limit	4.0 mm
MT and YZF-R models	
Standard	4.0 mm
Service limit (min)	3.5 mm
Disc maximum runout	0.15 mm

Wheels

Maximum wheel runout (front and rear)	
WR models	
Axial (side-to-side)	2.0 mm
Radial (out-of-round)	2.0 mm
MT and YZF-R models	
Axial (side-to-side)	0.5 mm
Radial (out-of-round)	1.0 mm
Maximum axle runout	
Front – WR models	0.2 mm
Front – MT and YZF-R models, rear – all models	0.25 mm

Tyres

Tyre pressures	see *Pre-ride checks*
Tyre sizes*	
WR-R models	
Front	80/90-21 M/C 48P/S/R, tubed
Rear	110/80-18 M/C 58P/S/R, tubed
WR-X models	
Front	110/70-17 M/C 54H, tubed
Rear	140/70-17 M/C 66H, tubed
MT and YZF-R models	
Front	100/80-17 M/C 52H/S, tubeless
Rear	130/70-17 M/C 62H/S, tubeless

** Refer to the owners handbook or the tyre information label on the swingarm for approved tyre brands.*

Final drive

Drive chain slack, stretch limit and lubricant	see Chapter 1
Drive chain original equipment type	
WR models	428 ORM/REGINA 132 links
MT and YZF-R models	428 VI13/DAIDO 132 links
Sprocket sizes (No. of teeth)	
Front (engine) sprocket	14
Rear (wheel) sprocket	
WR models	53
MT and YZF-R models	48

Torque settings

ABS components	
Wheel speed sensor screw	8 Nm
Sensor rotor screws	8 Nm
Modulator brake pipe banjo bolts	
MT models	26 Nm
YZF-R models	30 Nm
Brake caliper bleed valves	6 Nm
Brake disc bolts	18 Nm
Front disc	
WR-R models	13 Nm
WR-X models	23 Nm
MT and YZF-R models	18 Nm
Rear disc	
WR models	12 Nm
MT and YZF-R models	18 Nm
Brake hose banjo bolts	
WR models	30 Nm
MT and YZF-R models	26 Nm
Front axle	
WR models	58 Nm
MT and YZF-R models	59 Nm
Front axle clamp bolts	
WR models	9 Nm
MT and YZF-R models	23 Nm
Front brake caliper mounting bolts	
WR models	30 Nm
MT and YZF-R models	38 Nm
Front brake master cylinder clamp bolts	9 Nm
Front brake pad retaining pin (WR models)	18 Nm
Front sprocket retainer bolts	10 Nm

Torque settings (continued)

Rear axle nut	
WR models	90 Nm
MT and YZF-R models	85 Nm
Rear brake light switch	
WR models	24 Nm
MT and YZF-R models (except ABS models)	26 Nm
Rear brake pad retaining pin(s)	
WR models	13 Nm
MT and YZF-R models	18 Nm
Rear brake caliper bolt (MT and YZF-R models)	18 Nm
Rear brake master cylinder bolts	10 Nm
Rear sprocket bolts – WR models	35 Nm
Rear sprocket nuts – MT and YZF-R models	39 Nm

1 General Information

1 All models have hydraulic brake systems front and rear, with a twin piston sliding caliper on WR models and a four-opposed piston caliper on MT and YZF-R models at the front, and a single piston sliding caliper on all models at the rear.

2 The drive to the rear wheel is by chain and sprockets.

3 WR models have steel spoked wheels with tubed tyres, and MT and YZF-R models have cast alloy wheels with tubeless tyres.

Caution: Disc brake components rarely require disassembly. Do not disassemble components unless absolutely necessary. If an hydraulic brake hose is loosened or disconnected, the union sealing washers must be replaced with new ones and the system bled upon reassembly. Do not use solvents on internal brake components. Solvents will cause the seals to swell and distort. Use only clean DOT 4 brake fluid for cleaning. Use care when working with brake fluid as it can injure your eyes and it will damage painted surfaces and plastic parts.

2 Front brake pads

Warning: The dust created by the brake system is harmful to your health. Never blow it out with compressed air and don't inhale any of it. An approved filtering mask should be worn when working on the brakes.

1 On WR models unscrew the pad retaining pin plug, then slacken the pin **(see illustration)**. Unscrew the caliper mounting bolts and slide the caliper off the disc **(see illustration)** – there is no need to disconnect the brake hose. Unscrew the pad pin and remove the pads **(see illustrations)**.

2 On MT and YZF-R models unscrew the caliper mounting bolts and slide the caliper

2.1a Remove the plug then slacken the pin (arrowed)

2.1b Caliper mounting bolts (arrowed)

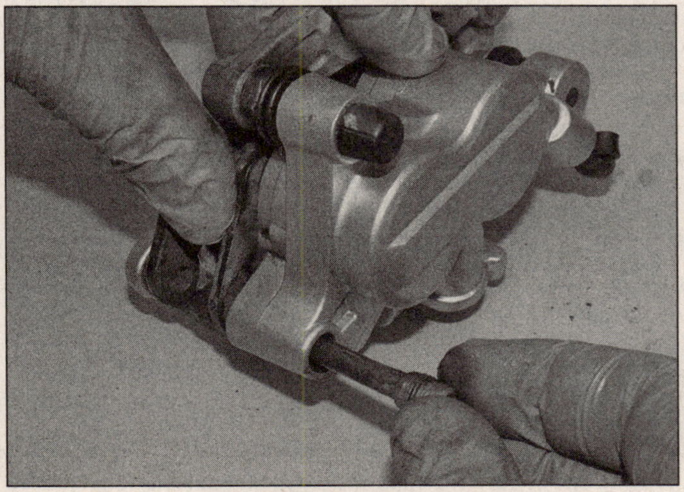

2.1c Unscrew the pin...

2.1d ...and remove the pads

2.2a Unscrew the bolts (arrowed) and slide the caliper off the disc

2.2b Remove the clips…

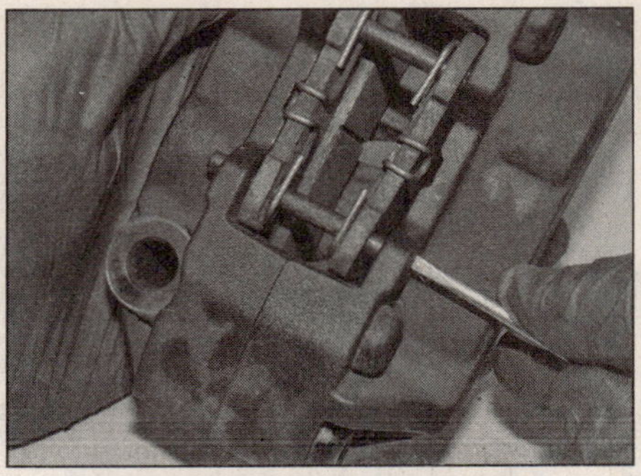

2.2c …then push out and withdraw the pins…

2.2d …and remove the pads

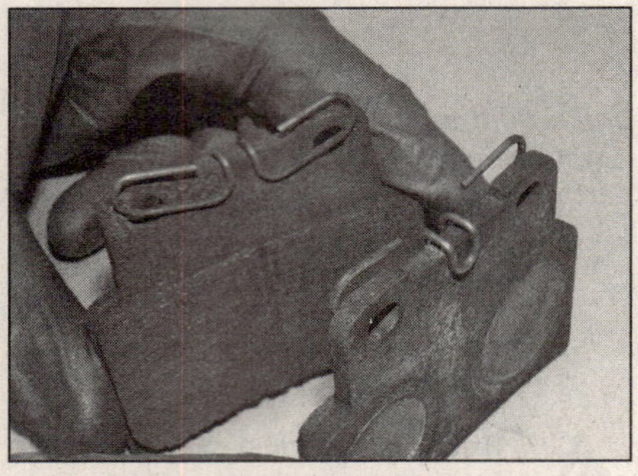

2.2e Remove the spring from the top of each pad if required

off the disc **(see illustration)** – on models with ABS note how the lower bolt secures the wheel speed sensor wiring guide **(see illustration 2.12a)**, and on YZF-RA models the upper bolt secures the hose guide. Remove the two R-clips from each pad pin, then withdraw the pins and remove the pads **(see illustrations)**. If new pads are being fitted remove the spring from the top of each pad **(see illustration)**.

3 Inspect the surface of each pad for contamination and check that the friction material has not worn beyond its service limit (see Chapter 1, Section 10). If either pad is worn down to, or beyond, the service limit wear indicator, is fouled with oil or grease, or heavily scored or damaged, fit a set of new pads. If required measure the thickness of the friction material to determine the extent of wear – the service limit is 1 mm on WR models and 2 mm on MT and YZF-R models. Note: It is not possible to degrease the friction material; if the pads are contaminated in any way they must be replaced with new ones. Also check that the pads are wearing evenly across the surface of the friction material – uneven wear is indicative of a sticking or seized piston.

4 If the pads are in good condition clean them carefully, using a fine wire brush that is completely free of oil and grease to remove all traces of road dirt and corrosion. Using a pointed instrument, dig out any embedded particles of foreign matter and clean out the grooves. If required, spray with a dedicated brake cleaner to remove any dust.

5 Check the condition of the brake disc (see Section 4).

6 Remove all traces of corrosion from the pad pin(s) and check for wear and damage. Fit a new pin or pins if necessary, along with new R-clips on MT and YZF-R models.

7 On WR models slide the caliper off the bracket **(see illustration)**. Clean off all traces of corrosion and hardened grease from the slider pins and their rubber boots. Replace the boots with new ones if they are damaged, deformed or deteriorated.

8 Clean around the exposed section of each piston to remove any dirt or debris that could cause the seals to be damaged. If new pads are being fitted, now push the pistons all the way back into the caliper to create room for them; if the old pads are still serviceable push the pistons in a little way. To push the pistons back use finger pressure or a piece of wood as leverage, or place the old pads back in the caliper and use a metal bar or a screwdriver inserted between them, or use grips and a piece of wood, with rag or card to protect the caliper body **(see illustration)**. Alternatively obtain a proper piston-pushing tool from a good tool supplier **(see illustration)**. If there is too much brake fluid in the reservoir it may be necessary to remove the master cylinder reservoir cover and diaphragm and siphon some out (see *Pre-ride checks*). If a piston is difficult to push back, remove the bleed valve cap, then attach a length of clear hose to the bleed valve and place the open end in a suitable container, then open the valve and try again (see Section 11). Take great care not to draw any air into the system. If in doubt, bleed the brake afterwards.

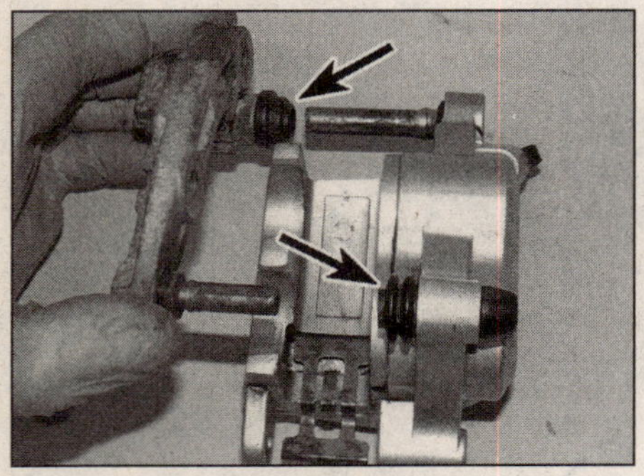

2.7 Slide the caliper off the bracket and clean and check the pins and boots (arrowed)

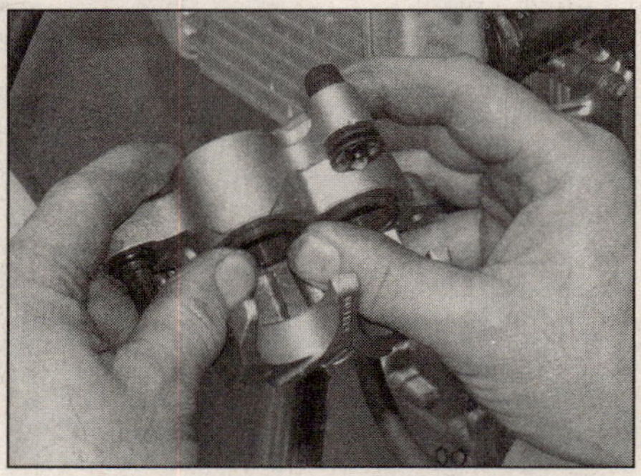

2.8a Push the pistons in using one of the methods described…

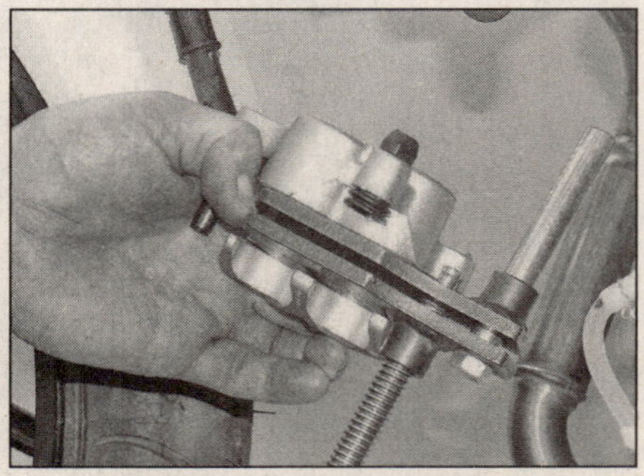

2.8b …or using a purpose built commercial tool

2.10a Make sure the pad guide (arrowed)...

2.10b ... and pad spring (arrowed) are correctly in place

2.11a Make sure the pads locate correctly against the guide

9 If a piston appears seized, apply the brake lever and check whether the piston in question moves at all – first block or hold the other piston(s) using wood or cable-ties. If the piston moves out but can't be pushed back in the chances are there is some hidden corrosion stopping it. If it doesn't move at all, overhaul the caliper (see Section 3).

10 On WR models make sure the pad guide and pad spring are correctly located **(see illustrations)**. Clean the face of the guide. If necessary replace the guide and spring with new ones. Apply a smear of silicone-based grease to the boots and slider pins. Slide the caliper onto the bracket, making sure each boot seats correctly around the base of its pin **(see illustration 2.7)**.

11 On WR models clean the threads of the pad retaining pin and caliper mounting bolts. Apply some fresh threadlock to the pin. Fit the pads **(see illustration 2.1d)**, making sure they locate correctly against the guide on the bracket **(see illustration)**. Press the pads up against the spring to align the holes and insert the pad pin, and tighten it finger-tight **(see illustration 2.1c)**. Apply some fresh threadlock to the bolts, then slide the caliper onto the disc, making sure the pads locate correctly on each side, and tighten the bolts to the torque setting specified at the beginning of the Chapter **(see illustration)**. Now tighten the pad pin to the specified torque. Fit the plug **(see illustration 2.1a)**.

12 On MT and YZF-R models clean the threads of the caliper mounting bolts. If removed fit the springs onto the pads as shown **(see illustration 2.2e)**. Fit the pads and slide the pins through, making sure they pass through the springs and locate correctly **(see illustration)**. Fit the R-clips to secure the pins **(see illustration 2.2b)**. Apply some fresh threadlock to the bolts, then slide the caliper onto the disc, making sure the pads locate correctly on each side, and fit the bolts, not forgetting to secure the wheel speed sensor wiring guide with the lower bolt on all models with ABS, and the hose guide with the upper bolt on YZF-RA models **(see illustrations)**. Tighten the bolts to the torque setting specified at the beginning of the Chapter.

13 Operate the brake lever until the pads contact with the disc. Check the level of fluid in the reservoir and top-up if necessary (see *Pre-ride checks*).

14 Check the operation of the brake before riding the motorcycle.

2.11b Slide the caliper onto the disc

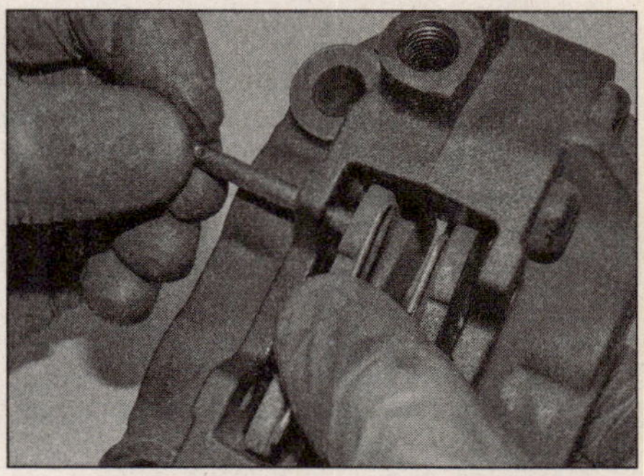
2.12a Align the holes and springs and insert the pins

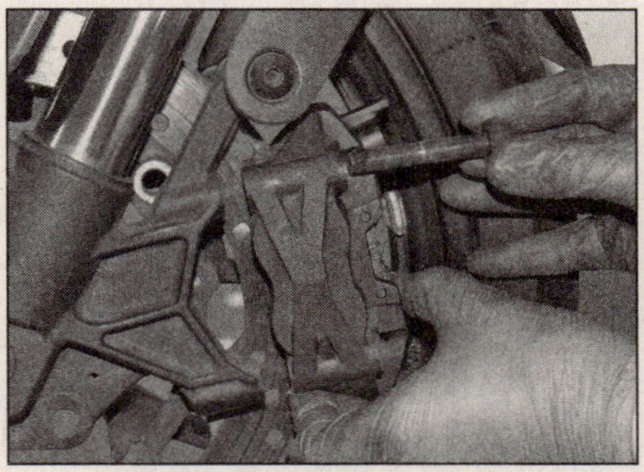
2.12b Slide the caliper onto the disc

2.12c Position the wiring guide as shown on ABS models

3 Front brake caliper

Note: *Brake caliper rebuild kits are available. On WR models there are different kits according to requirement – one kit has the seals and the rubber boots, another kit has the seals and pistons, and a third kit has just the rubber boots. Because you won't know which kit(s) you will need until the existing pistons and seals have been removed it is best to do this first before buying anything. On MT and YZF-R models there are two kits, one for each size of piston, and each kit contains two sets of seals and two pistons. On the kit we used for the WR model a sachet of silicone grease was included, but this may not be the case for all models. Check the kit when you buy it and if there is none you will need some.*

Warning: To prevent damage from spilled brake fluid, always cover paintwork when working on the braking system. Caliper overhaul must be done in a clean workspace to avoid the possibility of dirt entering the system. Do not use petroleum-based solvents to clean brake system components – use only clean DOT 4 brake fluid, a dedicated brake cleaner, or denatured alcohol.

Removal

Note: *Do not operate the brake lever while the caliper is off the disc.*

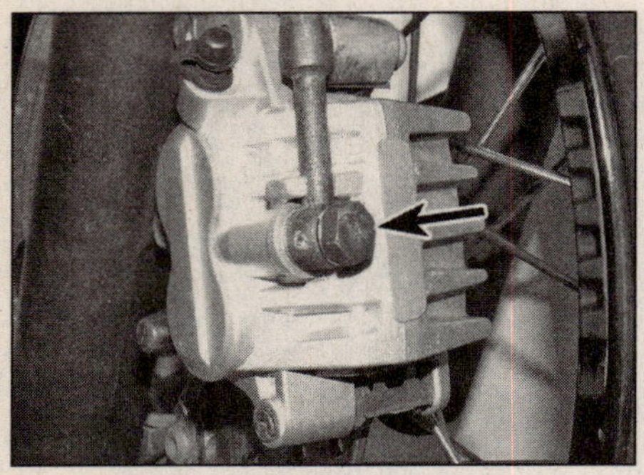

3.1a Brake hose banjo bolt (arrowed) – WR models

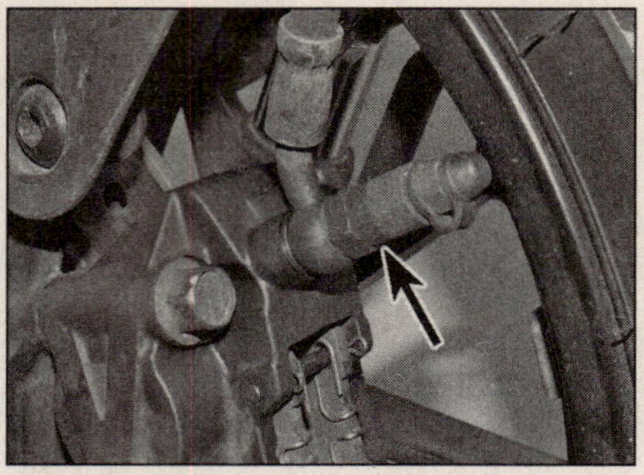

3.1b Brake hose banjo bolt (arrowed) – MT and YZF-R models. Note how the bleed valve threads into the top of the bolt

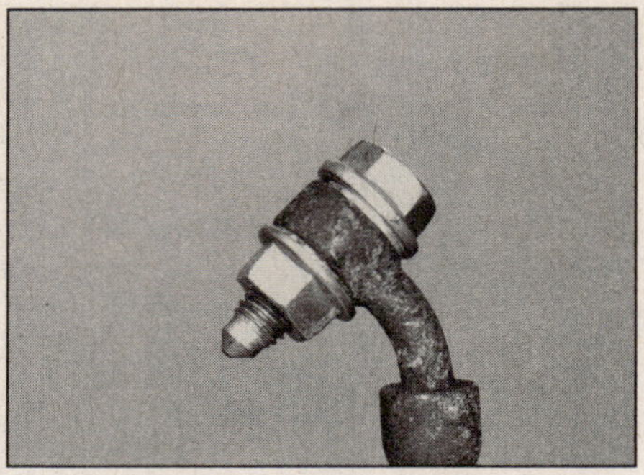

3.1c Using a nut and bolt and the sealing washers to seal the brake hose

1 Unscrew the brake hose banjo bolt and detach the banjo union, noting its alignment **(see illustrations)**. Tip the fluid in the caliper into a suitable container. Seal the banjo union using a nut and bolt and the two sealing washers **(see illustration)**, or wrap plastic foodwrap around it. Secure the hose in an upright position. New sealing washers must be fitted on reassembly.

2 Remove the caliper and brake pads as described in Section 2.

Overhaul

3 On WR models slide the caliper off the bracket **(see illustration 2.7)**. Clean off all traces of corrosion and hardened grease from the slider pins and their rubber boots. Replace the boots with new ones if they are damaged, deformed or deteriorated. Remove the pad spring, noting how it fits **(see illustration 2.10b)**.

4 Clean the caliper using brake system cleaner and an old toothbrush or similar. Mark the inside of each piston so it can be refitted into the bore it came from – on MT and YZF-R models two sizes of piston and seals are used in each caliper.

5 The pistons can usually be removed using a pair of external circlip pliers, straight on WR models and angled on MT and YZF-R models. There are also dedicated piston removal tools available from good suppliers, but make sure you choose one that is suitable for the caliper on your model. Grip the inner wall of the piston then twist and pull the piston out, keeping it square to the bore wall until it is free **(see illustrations)**.

Caution: Do not try to remove a piston by levering it out or buy using grips that bear on the outer wall – leverage will damage the caliper and grips will damage the surface of the piston.

6 If the pistons are difficult to remove using a hand tool use compressed air. On MT and YZF-R models cable-tie the pistons on one side to the caliper body so only the pistons from the opposite side can move, and complete the overhaul procedure on that side first before doing the other side, as there is not enough room for all four pistons to be removed at the same time **(see illustration)**. Place some rag between the pistons and the caliper on WR models and between the pistons on MT and YZF-R models, then apply the compressed air gradually and progressively to the fluid inlet and allow the pistons to ease most of the way out of their bores, controlling their movement so they are displaced evenly **(see illustrations)**. When they are almost out remove them by hand.

7 If a piston sticks in its bore and cannot be removed, replace the caliper with a new one.

8 Remove the dust seals and pistons seals

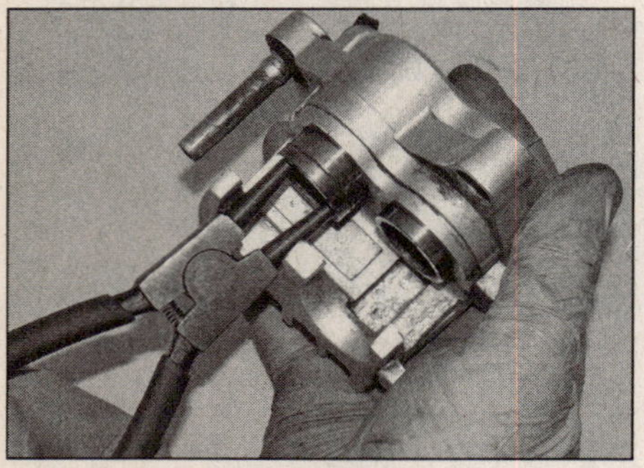

3.5a Using straight circlip pliers to draw a piston out on WR models

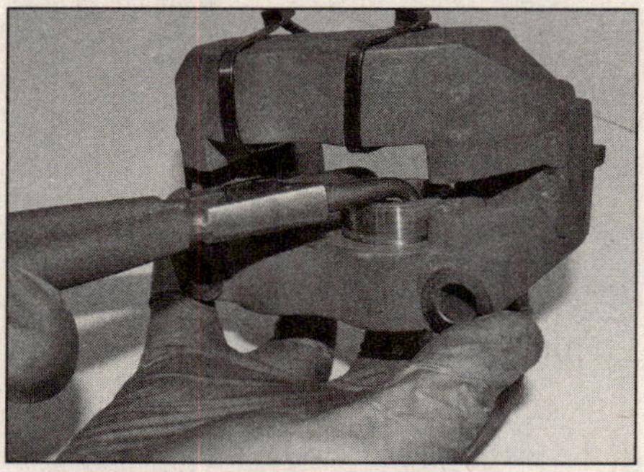

3.5b Using angled circlip pliers to draw a piston out on MT and YZF-R models

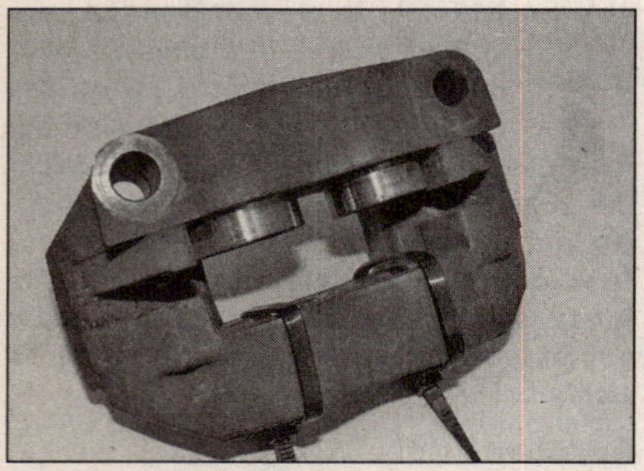

3.6a Cable-tie the pistons on one side to prevent them moving

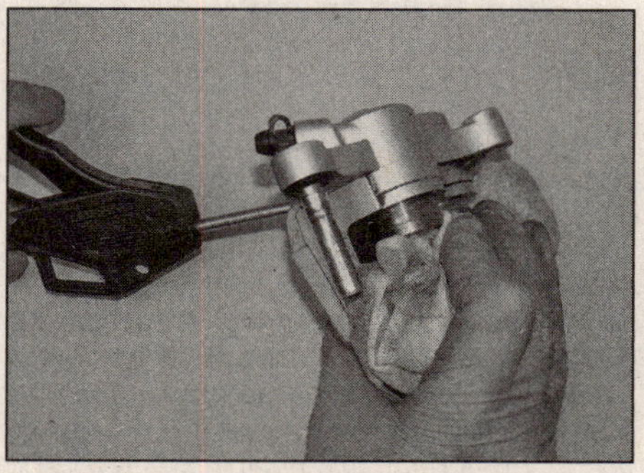

3.6b Using compressed air to expel the pistons on WR models

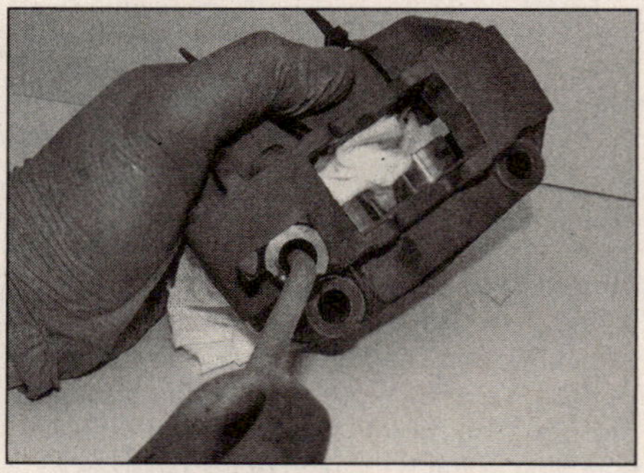

3.6c Using compressed air to expel the pistons on MT and YZF-R models

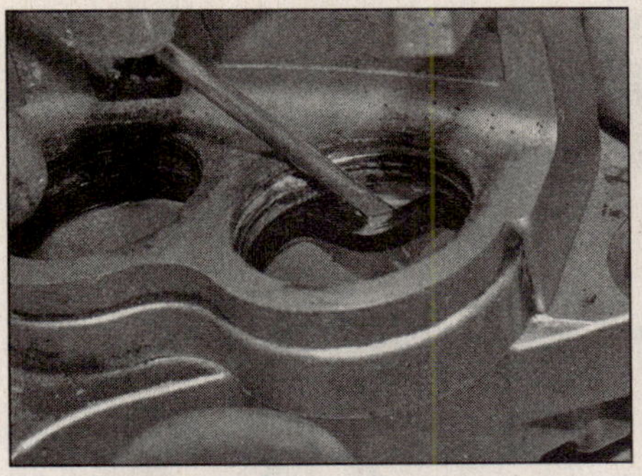
3.8 Extracting the piston seals from their grooves

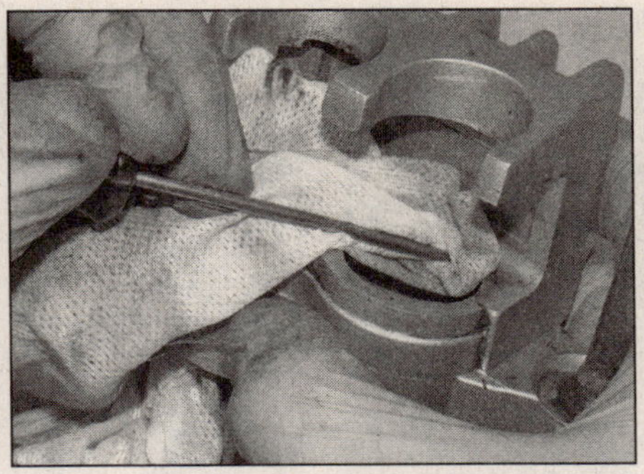
3.9 Clean the seal grooves, but take care not to scratch them

3.11a Lubricate the seals...

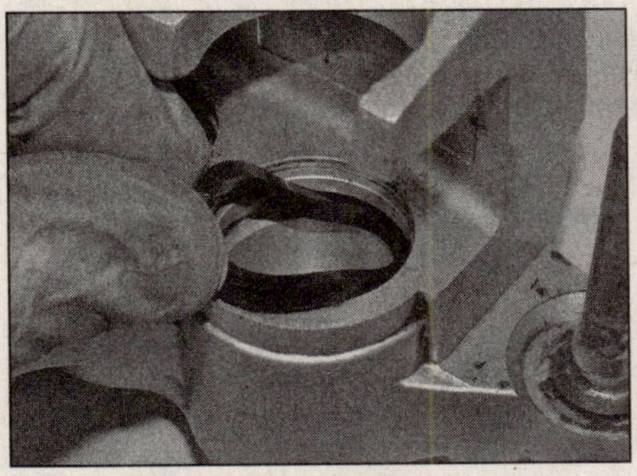
3.11b ...and fit them in the lower grooves

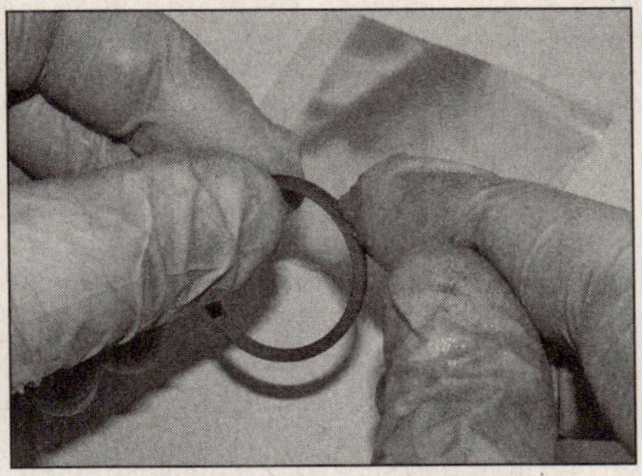
3.12a Lubricate the seals...

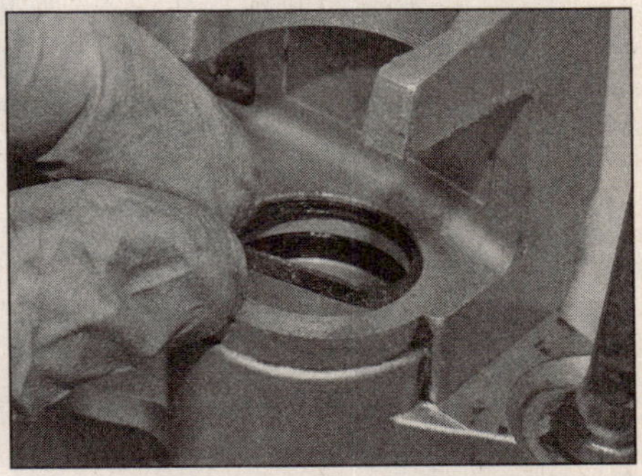
3.12b ...and fit them in the upper grooves

from their grooves **(see illustration)** – if you use a metal tool take care not to scratch the bore or groove. New seals must be used.

9 Clean the grooves and bores with clean brake fluid, then cover the caliper in rag and blow through the fluid passages with compresssed air **(see illustration)**. Check the caliper body for cracks and the bore walls for surface defects, and replace the caliper with a new one if necessary.

10 On WR models clean the pistons and check their outer surface for defects. Replace the pistons with new ones if necessary (see Note on rebuild kits above). On MT and YZF-R models new pistons come in the rebuild kit, so use them whatever the condition of the old ones.

11 Lubricate the new piston seals with new brake fluid, then carefully fit them into the lower grooves in the bores **(see illustrations)** – on MT and YZF-R models make sure the correct size seals and piston are fitted into the correct bore, though it should be obvious which fits where.

12 Lubricate the new dust seals with silicone grease and fit them into the upper grooves in the bores **(see illustrations)** – if you are lucky there may be a sachet of grease provided in the rebuild kit.

13 Lubricate the exterior of the pistons with new brake fluid **(see illustration)**. Fit the closed end of the pistons squarely into the bores and push them all the way in using your fingers, making sure the seals do not dislodge **(see illustration)**. Wipe off any excess grease or fluid as it will attract dirt.

Installation

14 Install the brake pads and caliper as described in Section 2.

15 Connect the brake hose to the caliper using new sealing washers on each side of the banjo union **(see illustration)**. Align the hose as noted on removal and tighten the banjo bolt to the torque setting specified at the beginning of the Chapter **(see illustration 3.1a or b)**.

16 Top up the reservoir with DOT 4 brake fluid and bleed the system as described in Section 11. Check that there are no fluid leaks and test the operation of the brake before riding the motorcycle.

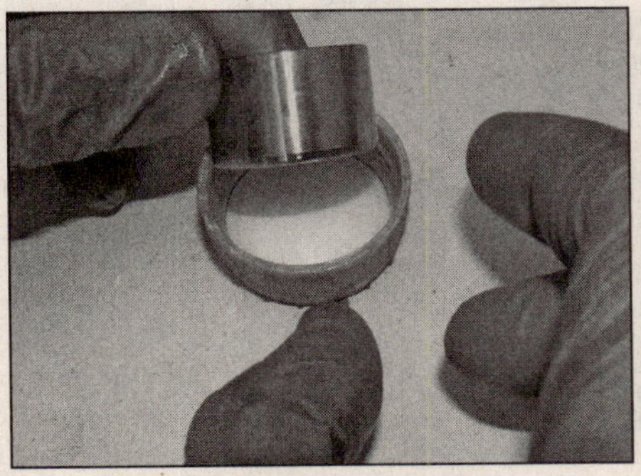
3.13a Lubricate the pistons...

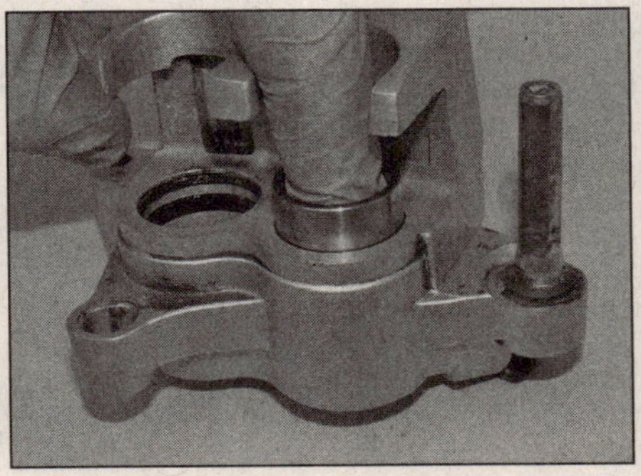
3.13b ...and push them all the way in

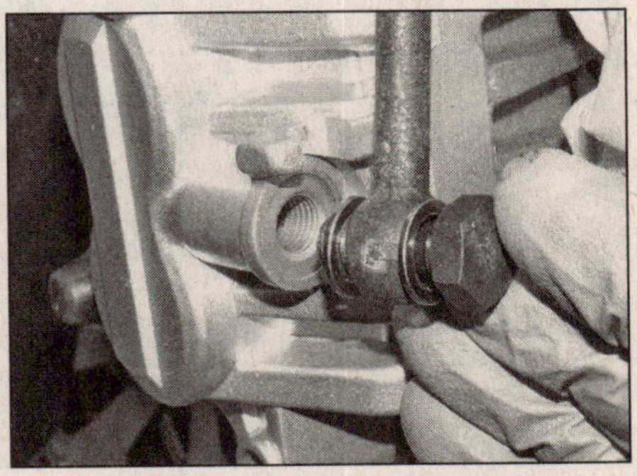
3.15 Always use new sealing washers

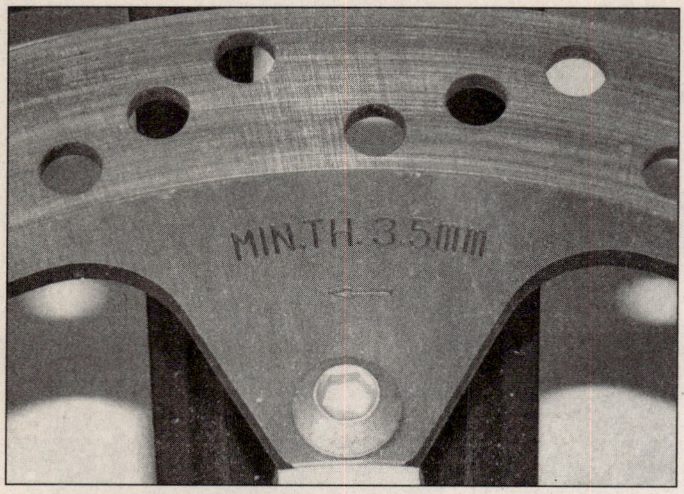

4.2a The minimum thickness is marked on the disc

4.2b Measure the thickness of the disc

4 Front brake disc

Inspection

1 Inspect the surface of the disc for score marks and other damage. Light scratches are normal after use and won't affect brake operation, but deep grooves and heavy score marks will reduce braking efficiency and accelerate pad wear. If a disc is badly grooved it must be replaced with a new one.

2 The disc must not be machined or allowed to wear down to a thickness less than the service limit listed in this Chapter's Specifications for your model (the minimum thickness is also usually marked on the disc) **(see illustration)**. Check the thickness of the disc in the middle of the pad contact area using a micrometer **(see illustration)** – do not measure across the rim of the disc with a ruler. Replace the disc with a new one if necessary.

3 To check if the disc is warped, position the bike on an auxiliary stand with the front wheel raised off the ground. Mount a dial gauge to the fork leg, with the gauge plunger touching the surface of the disc about 10 mm from the outer edge **(see illustration)**. Rotate the wheel and watch the gauge needle, comparing the reading with the limit listed in the Specifications at the beginning of this Chapter. If the runout is greater than the service limit, check the wheel bearings for play (see Chapter 1). If the bearings are worn, install new ones (see Section 16) and repeat this check. If the disc runout is still excessive, remove the disc (Steps 4 and 5) and check for corrosion where it seats on the hub and clean it up if necessary. You can also try moving the disc around the wheel one bolt hole at a time and after each movement rechecking for runout. In most cases a new disc will have to be fitted.

Removal

4 Remove the wheel (see Section 14).

Caution: Don't lay the wheel down and allow it to rest on the disc – the disc could become warped. Set the wheel on wood blocks so the wheel rim supports the weight of the wheel.

5 If you are not replacing the disc with a new one, mark the relationship of the disc to the wheel so it can be refitted in the same position. Unscrew the disc bolts, loosening them evenly and a little at a time in a criss-cross pattern to avoid distorting the disc, then remove the disc **(see illustration)**.

Installation

6 Before fitting the disc, make sure there is no dirt or corrosion where it seats on the hub. If the disc does not sit flat when it is bolted down, it will appear to be warped when checked or when the front brake is used.

7 Fit the disc onto the wheel with its marked

4.3 Checking disc runout with a dial gauge

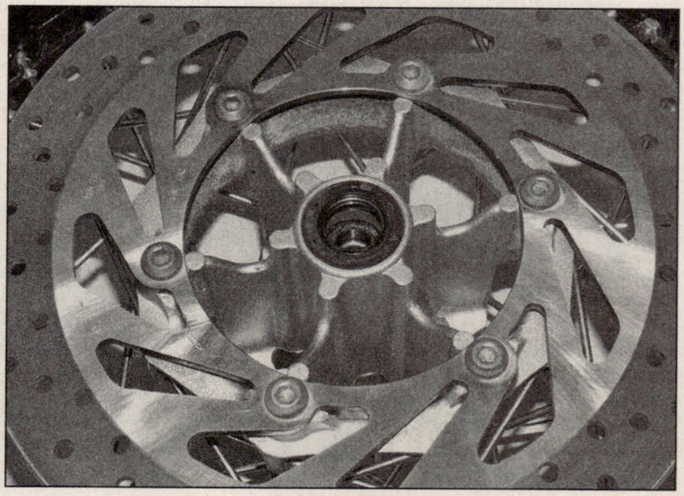
4.5 Brake disc bolts

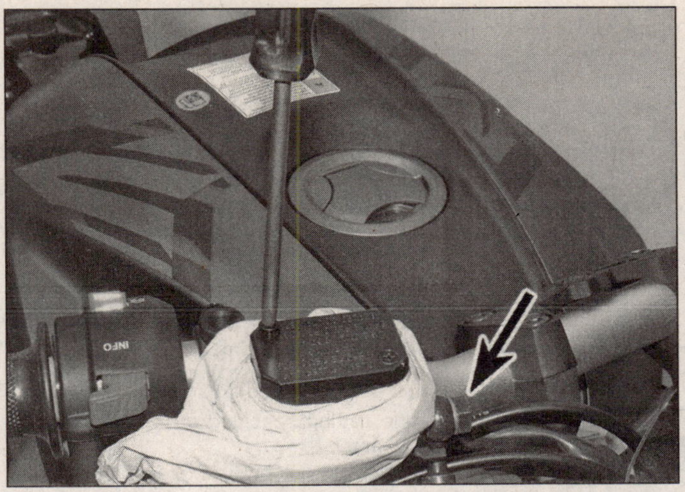

5.3a Slacken the cover screws. Brake hose banjo bolt (arrowed) – MT and YZF-R models

5.3b Brake hose banjo bolt (arrowed) – WR models

side facing out, aligning the previously applied matchmarks (if you're refitting the original disc) **(see illustration 4.2a)**.

8 Clean the threads of the disc mounting bolts, then apply a suitable non-permanent thread locking compound. Fit the bolts and tighten them evenly and a little at a time in a criss-cross pattern to the torque setting specified at the beginning of this Chapter for your model. Clean the disc using acetone or brake system cleaner. If a new disc has been fitted, remove any protective coating from its working surfaces and fit new brake pads.

9 Install the wheel (see Section 14).

10 Check the operation of the brake before riding the motorcycle.

5 Front brake master cylinder

Note: *Brake master cylinder rebuild kits are only available for MT and YZF-R models. On WR models, if the piston has seized or if there is fluid leaking past the seals a new master cylinder must be installed.*

Warning: To prevent damage from spilled brake fluid, always cover paintwork when working on the braking system. Caliper overhaul must be done in a clean workspace to avoid the possibility of dirt entering the system. Do not use petroleum-based solvents to clean brake system components – use only clean DOT 4 brake fluid, a dedicated brake cleaner, or denatured alcohol.

Removal

1 Remove the brake light switch (see Chapter 8).

2 Remove the brake lever (see Chapter 5).

3 Slacken the reservoir cover screws **(see illustration)**. Unscrew the brake hose banjo bolt and detach the banjo union, noting its alignment **(see illustration)**. Seal the banjo union using a nut and bolt and the two sealing washers, **(see illustration 3.1c)**,or wrap plastic foodwrap around it. Secure the hose in an upright position. New sealing washers must be fitted on reassembly.

4 Unscrew the master cylinder clamp bolts and remove the clamp, then lift the master cylinder away from the handlebar **(see illustration)**.

5 Remove the reservoir cover, diaphragm plate (MT and YZF-R models), and diaphragm and drain the fluid into a suitable container. Wipe any remaining fluid out of the reservoir with a clean rag.

Overhaul (MT and YZF-R models only)

6 Remove the pushrod and rubber boot **(see illustration)**.

7 The piston assembly is secured by a circlip – release it using internal circlip pliers

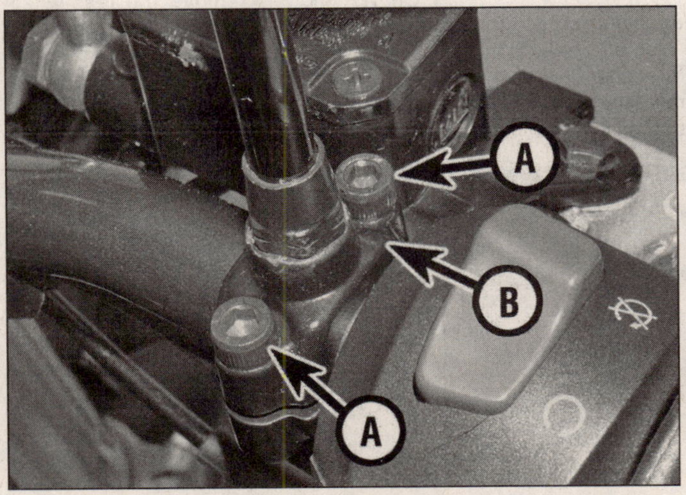

5.4 Unscrew the bolts (A) and remove the master cylinder. Note the triangle (B) that points to the front

5.6 Grasp the end of the pushrod and pull it out with the boot

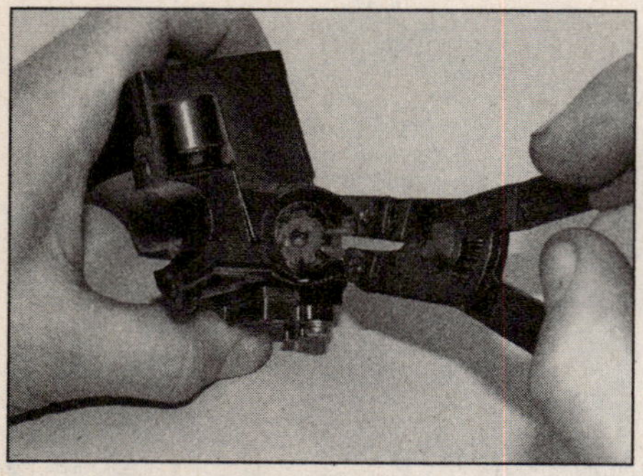
5.7a Release the circlip...

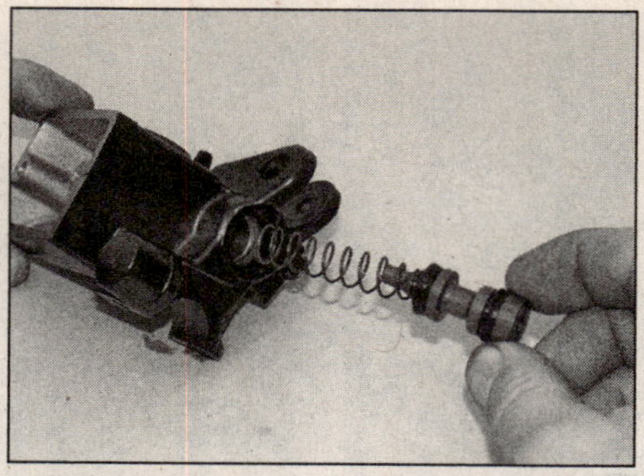
5.7b ...and remove the piston and spring

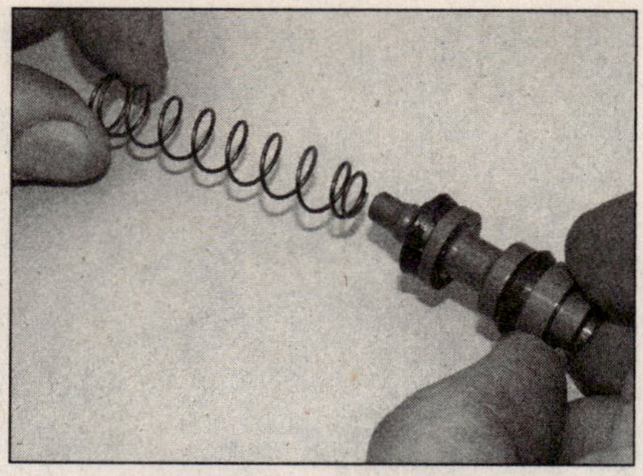
5.11 Fit the spring onto the piston

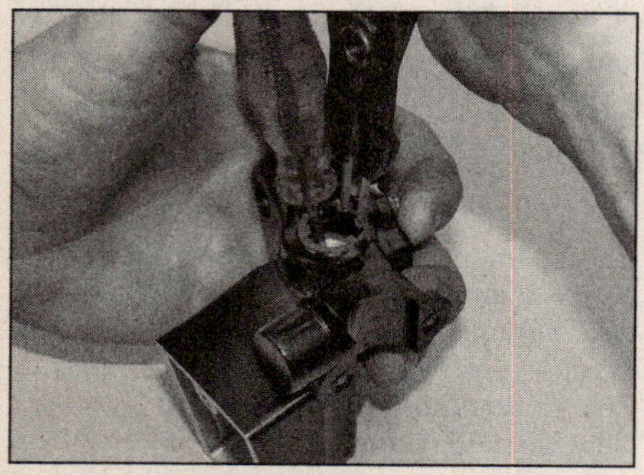
5.12 Push the piston beyond the groove then locate the circlip in the groove

and draw out the piston and spring **(see illustrations)**.

8 Clean inside the master cylinder with clean brake fluid. If filtered and un-lubricated compressed air is available blow it through the fluid passages.

9 Check the bore for surface defects and replace the master cylinder with a new one if any are evident.

10 All the internal components are supplied in the rebuild kit – use all of the new parts regardless of the apparent condition of the old ones.

11 If not already in place fit the narrow end of the spring onto the inner end of the piston **(see illustration)**. Lubricate the piston, cup and seal with new brake fluid, then slide the assembly into the master cylinder, spring first, making sure the lips of the cup and seal do not turn inside out **(see illustration 5.7b)**.

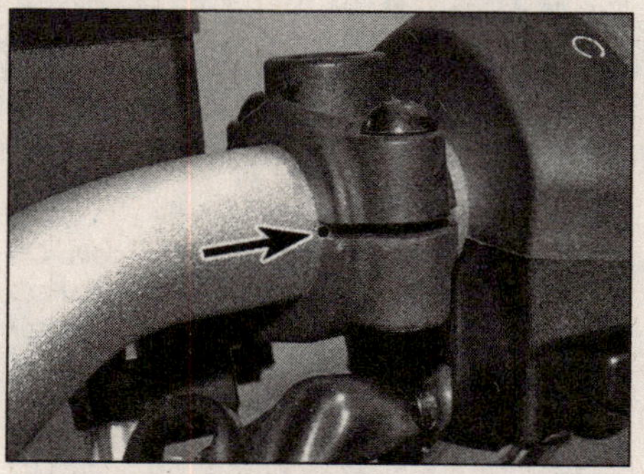
5.15 Align the gap in the clamp with the punch mark (arrowed)

12 Push the piston in and fit the new circlip into the groove **(see illustration)**. Release the piston and check the circlip is correctly seated.

13 If not already in place fit the pushrod into the narrow end of the boot, seating the boot lip in the groove **(see illustration 5.6)**. Seat the pushrod against the piston and push the wide end of the boot into the master cylinder.

14 Check the condition of the rubber diaphragm for the reservoir and replace with a new one if necessary.

Installation

15 Attach the master cylinder to the handlebar, aligning the clamp joint with the punch mark, then fit the clamp with the triangle pointing to the front **(see illustration)**. Tighten the front bolt first, then the rear, to the torque setting specified at the beginning of the Chapter.

16 Connect the brake hose to the master cylinder using new sealing washers on each side of the banjo union. Align the hose as noted on removal and tighten the banjo bolt to the torque setting specified at the beginning of the Chapter **(see illustration 5.3a or b)**.

17 Install the brake light switch (see Chapter 8).

18 Install the brake lever (see Chapter 5).

19 Fill the reservoir with DOT 4 brake fluid and bleed the system as described in Section 11.

20 Check that there are no fluid leaks and test the operation of the brake before riding the motorcycle.

6 Rear brake pads

Warning: The dust created by the brake system is harmful to your health. Never blow it out with compressed air and don't inhale any of it. An approved filtering mask should be worn when working on the brakes.

1 On WR models remove the rear wheel (see Section 15). Displace the caliper from the swingarm and hold it. Remove the pad retaining pin clip, then unscrew the pin, withdraw it and remove the pads **(see illustrations)**.

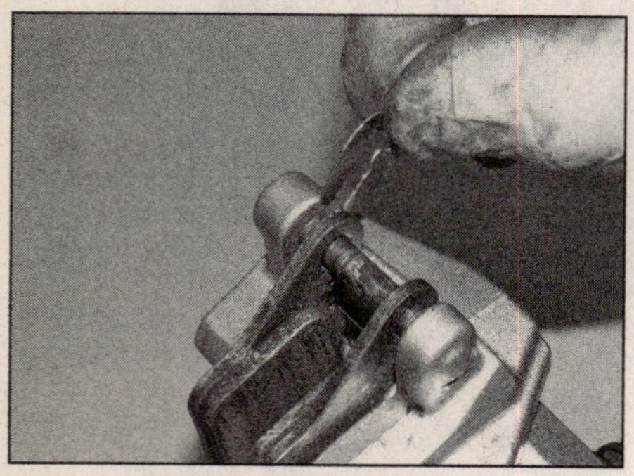
6.1a Remove the clip...

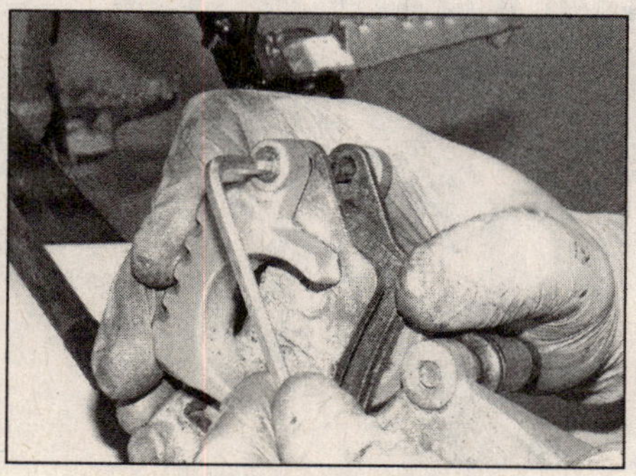
6.1b ...unscrew the pin...

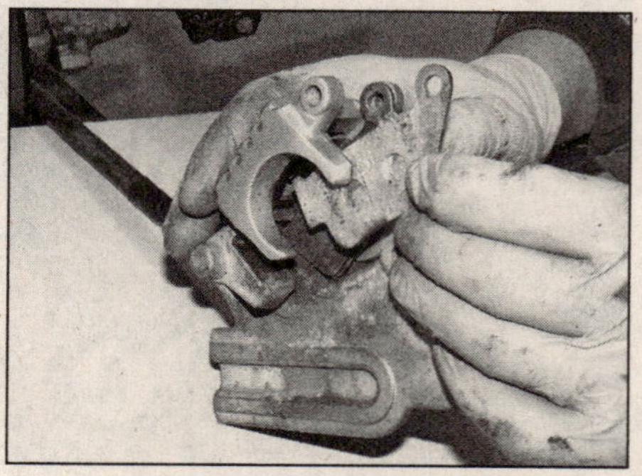
6.1c ...and remove the pads

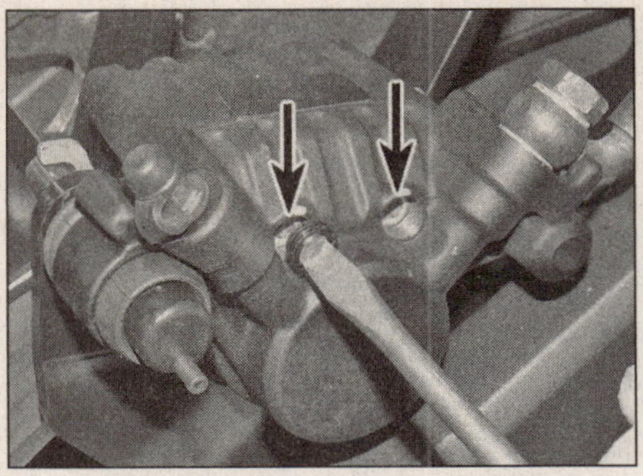

6.2a Remove the plugs then unscrew the pins (arrowed)

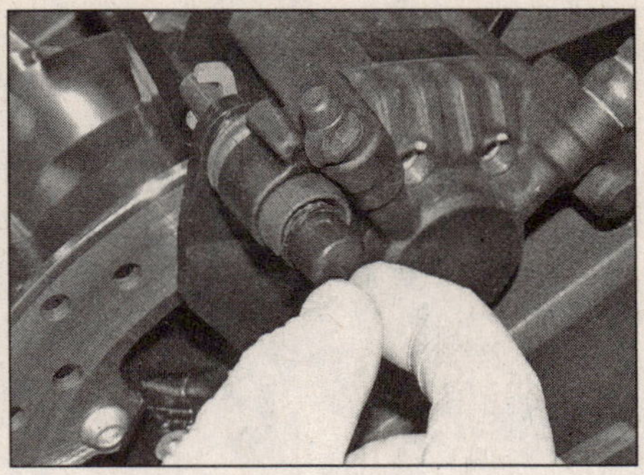

6.2b Remove the cap...

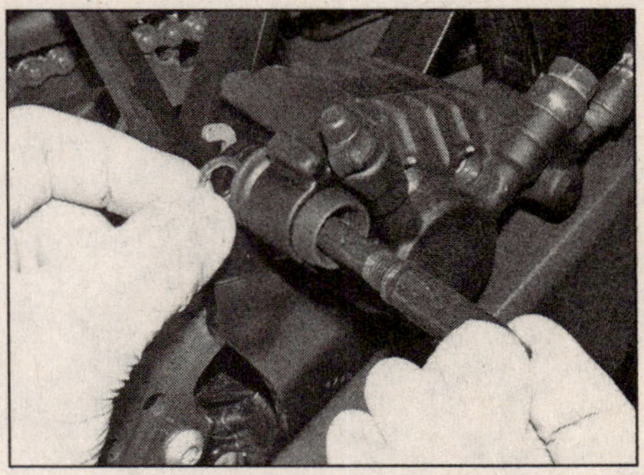

6.2c ...then unscrew the bolt and remove the washer

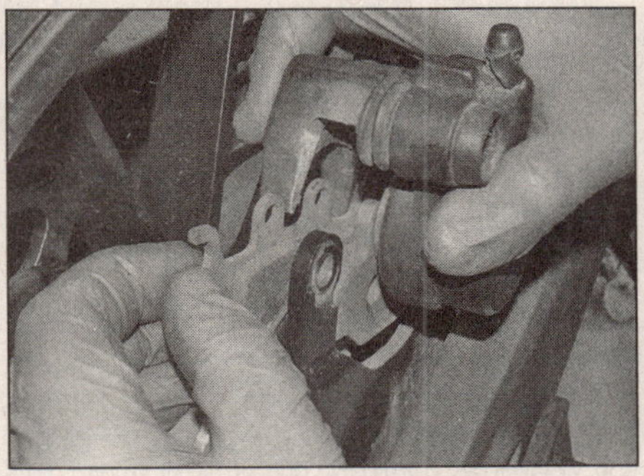

6.2d Remove the inner pad...

6.2e ...then the outer pad

6.2f Rear axle nut (arrowed)

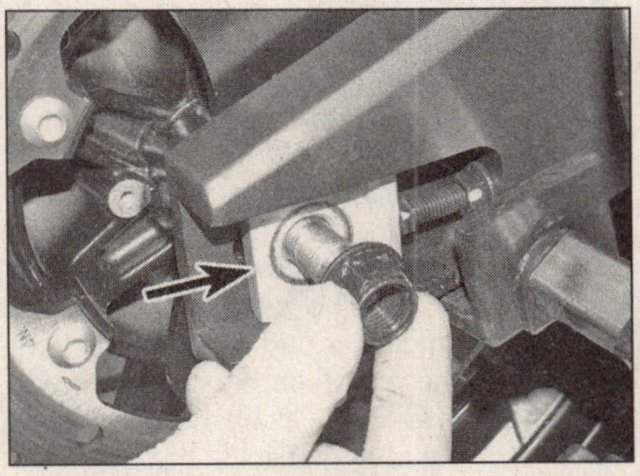

6.2g Unscrew the nut and remove the marker (arrowed)...

6.2h ...then withdraw the axle until it is clear of the caliper bracket

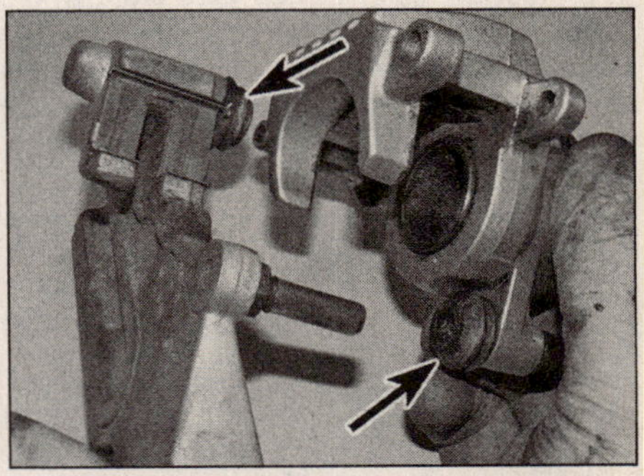

6.7 Slide the caliper off the bracket and clean and check the pins and boots (arrowed)

2 On MT and YZF-R models unscrew the pad pin plugs then unscrew and withdraw the pins **(see illustration)**. Remove the cap from the caliper bolt **(see illustration)**. Unscrew the bolt, withdraw it and retrieve the washer **(see illustration)**. Pivot the caliper up and remove the inner pad, then slide the caliper away from the wheel and remove the outer pad **(see illustrations)**. If the brake hose contacts the swingarm before you have enough clearance to remove the pads, place the bike on a rear paddock stand, then slacken the rear axle nut and pull the wheel back as far as it will go, and try again **(see illustration)**. If this does not work, unscrew the nut and remove the adjustment marker, then push the axle through and withdraw it enough so it is clear of the caliper bracket but still located in the swingarm **(see illustrations)**. Slide the caliper assembly to the rear, then pivot the caliper up and remove the pads.

3 Inspect the surface of each pad for contamination and check that the friction material has not worn beyond its service limit (see Chapter 1, Section 10). If either pad is worn down to, or beyond, the service limit wear indicator, is fouled with oil or grease, or heavily scored or damaged, fit a set of new pads. If required measure the thickness of the friction material to determine the extent of wear – the service limit is 1 mm. **Note:** *It is not possible to degrease the friction material; if the pads are contaminated in any way they must be replaced with new ones.*

4 If the pads are in good condition clean them carefully, using a fine wire brush that is completely free of oil and grease to remove all traces of road dirt and corrosion. Using a pointed instrument, dig out any embedded particles of foreign matter and clean out the grooves. If required, spray with a dedicated brake cleaner to remove any dust.

5 Check the condition of the brake disc (see Section 8).

6 Remove all traces of corrosion from the pad pin(s) and check for wear and damage. Fit a new pin or pins if necessary, along with a new clip on WR models.

7 On WR models slide the caliper off the bracket **(see illustration)**. Clean the slider pins and check the rubber boots. Replace the boots with new ones if they are damaged, deformed or deteriorated.

8 On MT and YZF-R models clean the caliper bolt and check the rubber boots. If new boots are needed remove the rear wheel (see Section 15), then displace the caliper bracket

6.11a Make sure the pad guide (arrowed) ...

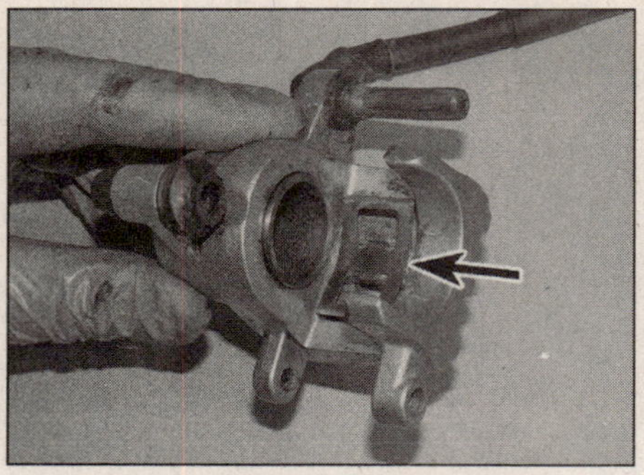

6.11b ... and pad spring (arrowed) are correctly in place

6.12 Make sure the pad spring (arrowed) is correctly in place

from the swingarm and slide the caliper off the bracket. Clean the slider pin on the bracket, and fit new boots.

9 Clean around the exposed section of the piston to remove any dirt or debris that could cause the seals to be damaged. If new pads are being fitted, push the piston all the way back into the caliper to create room for them; if the old pads are still serviceable push the piston in a little way. To push the piston back use finger pressure or a piece of wood as leverage, or place the old pads back in the caliper and use a metal bar or a screwdriver inserted between them, or use grips and a piece of wood, with rag or card to protect the caliper body **(see illustration 2.8a)**. Alternatively obtain a proper piston-pushing tool from a good tool supplier **(see illustration 2.8b)**. If there is too much brake fluid in the reservoir it may be necessary to remove the master cylinder reservoir cover and diaphragm and siphon some out (see *Pre-ride checks*). If the piston is difficult to push back, remove the bleed valve cap, then attach a length of clear hose to the bleed valve and place the open end in a suitable container, then open the valve and try again (see Section 11). Take great care not to draw any air into the system. If in doubt, bleed the brake afterwards.

10 If the piston appears seized, apply the brake pedal and check whether the piston moves at all. If the piston moves out but can't be pushed back in the chances are there is some hidden corrosion stopping it. If it doesn't move at all, overhaul the caliper (see Section 7).

11 On WR models make sure the pad guide and spring are correctly located **(see illustrations)**. Clean the face of the guide. If necessary replace the spring and guide with new ones. Apply a smear of silicone-based grease to the boots and slider pins. Slide the caliper onto the bracket, making sure each boot seats correctly around the base of its pin **(see illustration 6.7)**.

12 On MT and YZF-R models make sure the pad spring is correctly located **(see illustration)**. If necessary replace the spring with a new one.

13 On WR models fit the pads **(see illustration 6.1c)**, making sure they locate correctly against the guide on the bracket **(see illustration)**. Press the pads up against the spring to align the holes and insert the pad pin, and tighten it to the torque setting specified at the beginning of the Chapter **(see illustration 6.1b)**. Fit the clip into its groove **(see illustration 6.1a)**. Locate the caliper bracket on its lug on the swingarm **(see illustration)**. Install the wheel (see Section 15).

14 On MT and YZF-R models fit the outer pad into the bracket **(see illustration 6.2e)**, making sure it seats correctly **(see illustration)**. Slide the caliper towards the wheel and fit the inner pad, locating the front end around the post **(see illustration 6.2d)**. Pivot the caliper down over the pads, then slide the pins through, pushing the inner pad up against the spring to align the holes, and tighten them finger-tight **(see illustration)**. Fit the caliper bolt and its washer and tighten it finger-tight **(see illustration 6.2c)**. If the axle was withdrawn slide the caliper bracket forwards until it aligns then push the axle back in and fit the adjustment marker and the axle nut, then push the wheel against the adjuster bolts and tighten the nut to the torque setting specified at the beginning of the Chapter **(see illustrations 6.2h and g)**. If the wheel was pulled back push it forwards against the adjuster bolts and tighten the axle nut to the specified torque. Now tighten the caliper bolt and the pad pins to the specified torque. FIt the bolt cap and the pin plugs **(see illustrations 6.2b and a)**.

15 Operate the brake pedal until the pads contact with the disc. Check the level of fluid in the reservoir and top-up if necessary (see *Pre-ride checks*).

16 Check the operation of the brake before riding the motorcycle.

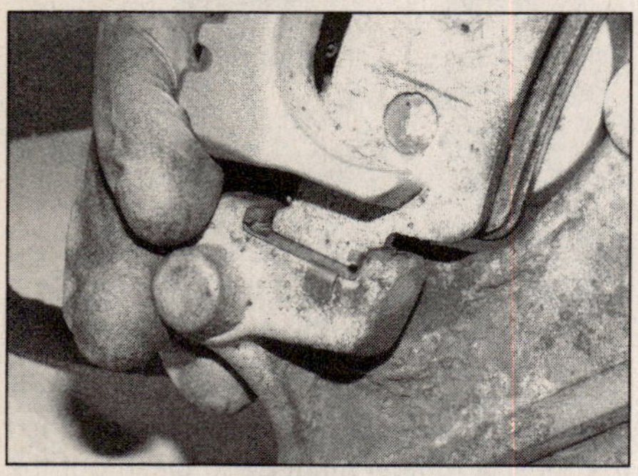

6.13a Make sure the pad ends seat against the guide

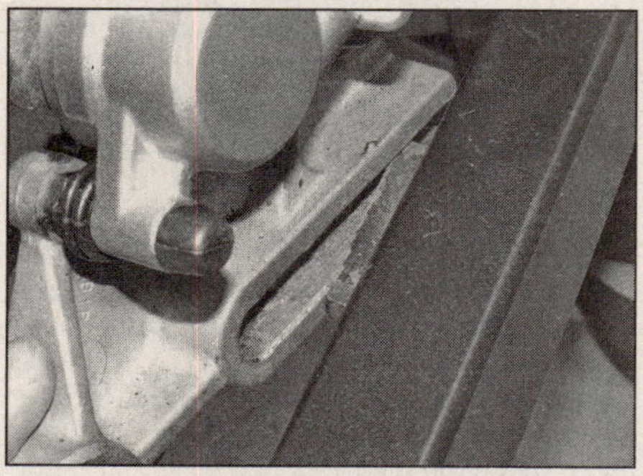

6.13b Seat the groove in the bracket over the lug on the swingarm

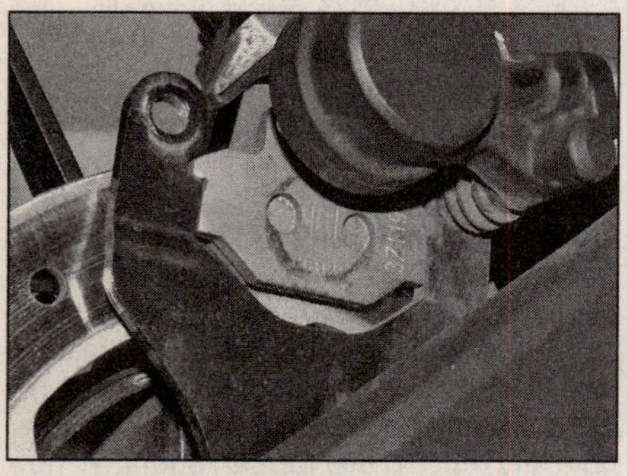

6.14a Make sure the pad ends located correctly on the bracket

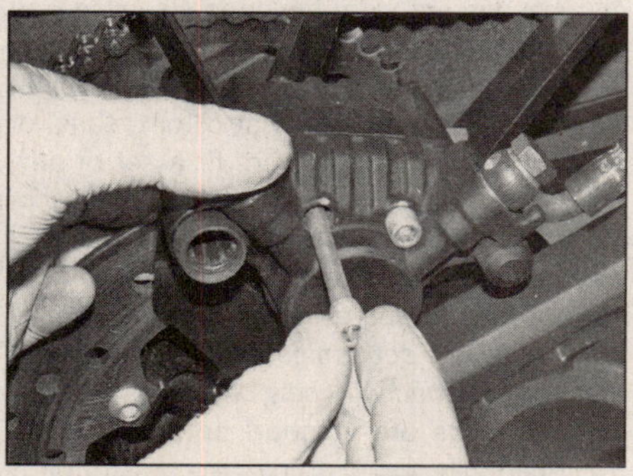

6.14b Align the holes and fit the pins

7.1 Brake hose banjo bolt (arrowed)

8.3 Rear brake disc bolts

7 Rear brake caliper

Note: *On WR models a rebuild kit containing the seals and piston is available, and the rubber boots are available separately. On MT and YZF-R models the rubber boots are available, but the brake caliper seals and piston are not available – if the piston has seized or if there is fluid leaking past the seals a new caliper must be installed.*

Warning: To prevent damage from spilled brake fluid, always cover paintwork when working on the braking system. Caliper overhaul must be done in a clean workspace to avoid the possibility of dirt entering the system. Do not use petroleum-based solvents to clean brake system components – use only clean DOT 4 brake fluid, a dedicated brake cleaner, or denatured alcohol.

Removal

Note: *Do not operate the brake pedal while the caliper is off the disc.*

1 Unscrew the brake hose banjo bolt and detach the banjo union, noting its alignment **(see illustration)**.Seal the banjo union using a nut and bolt and two sealing washers **(see illustration 3.1c)**, or wrap plastic foodwrap around it. Secure the hose in an upright position. New sealing washers must be used on reassembly.

2 On WR models remove the caliper and brake pads (see Section 6). Slide the caliper off the bracket **(see illustration 6.7)**.

3 On MT and YZF-R models remove the brake pads (see Section 6), then remove the rear wheel (see Section 15). Displace the caliper assembly from the swingarm, then slide the caliper off the bracket **(see illustration 6.7)**.

4 Clean off all traces of corrosion and hardened grease from the slider pin(s) and rubber boots **(see illustration 6.7)**. Replace the boots with new ones if they are damaged, deformed or deteriorated.

Overhaul (WR models only)

5 Remove the pad spring, noting how it fits **(see illustration 6.11b)**.

6 Clean the caliper using brake system cleaner and an old toothbrush or similar.

7 The piston can usually be removed using a pair of straight external circlip pliers. There are also dedicated piston removal tools available from good suppliers, but make sure you choose one that is suitable for the caliper. Grip the inner wall of the piston then twist and pull the piston out, keeping it square to the bore wall until it is free **(see illustration 3.5a)**. ***Caution: Do not try to remove a piston by levering it out or buy using grips that bear on the outer wall – leverage will damage the caliper and grips will damage the surface of the piston.***

8 If the piston is difficult to remove using a hand tool use compressed air. Place some rag between the piston and the caliper, then apply the compressed air gradually and progressively to the fluid inlet and allow the piston to ease most of the way out of the bore **(see illustration 3.6b)**. When it is almost out remove it by hand.

9 If the piston sticks in its bore and cannot be removed, replace the caliper with a new one.

10 Remove the dust seal and piston seal from their grooves using a tool that will not scratch the bores or grooves **(see illustration 3.8)**. New seals must be used.

11 Clean the grooves and bores with clean brake fluid, then cover the caliper in rag and blow through the fluid passages with compresssed air **(see illustration 3.9)**. Check the caliper body for cracks and the bore walls for surface defects, and replace the caliper with a new one if necessary.

12 Lubricate the new piston seal with new brake fluid, then carefully fit it into the inner groove in the bore **(see illustrations 3.11a and b)**.

13 Lubricate the new dust seal with silicone grease and fit it into the upper groove in the bore **(see illustrations 3.12a and b)**.

14 Lubricate the exterior of the pistons with new brake fluid **(see illustration 3.13a)**. Fit the closed end of the pistons squarely into the bores and push them all the way in using your fingers, making sure the seals do not dislodge **(see illustration 3.13b)**. Wipe off any excess grease or fluid as it will attract dirt.

Installation

15 Refer to the relevant Steps for your model in Section 6 to clean and check all components and to fit the brake pads and the caliper.

16 Connect the brake hose using new sealing washers on each side of the banjo union **(see illustration 3.15)**, and align it as noted on removal **(see illustration 7.1)**. Tighten the banjo bolt to the torque setting specified at the beginning of the Chapter.

17 Top up the fluid reservoir with DOT 4 brake fluid and bleed the system as described in Section 11. Check that there are no fluid leaks and test the operation of the rear brake before riding the motorcycle.

8 Rear brake disc

Inspection

1 Refer to Section 4 of this Chapter, noting that the dial gauge should be attached to the swingarm.

Removal

2 Remove the rear wheel (see Section 15). ***Caution: Don't lay the wheel down and allow it to rest on the disc or sprocket – they could become warped. Set the wheel on wood blocks so the wheel rim supports the weight of the wheel.***

3 If you are not replacing the disc with a new one, mark the relationship of the disc to the wheel so it can be refitted in the same position. Unscrew the disc bolts, loosening them evenly and a little at a time in a criss-cross pattern to avoid distorting the disc, then remove the disc **(see illustration)**.

Installation

4 Before fitting the disc, make sure there is no dirt or corrosion where it seats on the hub. If the disc does not sit flat when it is bolted down, it will appear to be warped when checked or when the rear brake is used.
5 Fit the disc on the wheel with its marked side facing out, aligning the previously applied matchmarks (if you're refitting the original disc).
6 Clean the threads of the disc bolts, then apply a suitable non-permanent thread locking compound. Fit the bolts and tighten them evenly and a little at a time in a criss-cross pattern to the torque setting specified at the beginning of this Chapter for your model. Clean the disc using acetone or brake system cleaner. If a new disc has been fitted, remove any protective coating from its working surfaces and fit new brake pads.
7 Install the rear wheel (see Section 15).
8 Check the operation of the rear brake before riding the motorcycle.

9 Rear brake master cylinder

Note: *On WR models a rebuild kit containing the rubber boot, circlip, pushrod, seals, piston and spring is available, and the reservoir hose joint and its O-ring are available separately. On MT and YZF-R models the reservoir hose joint and O-ring and the rubber boot and pushrod assembly are available, but there is no internal rebuild kit for the seals, piston and spring – if the piston has seized or if there is fluid leaking past the seals a new master cylinder must be installed.*

⚠ ***Warning: To prevent damage from spilled brake fluid, always cover paintwork when working on the braking system. Caliper overhaul must be done in a clean workspace to avoid the possibility of dirt entering the system. Do not use petroleum-based solvents to clean brake system components – use only clean DOT 4 brake fluid, a dedicated brake cleaner, or denatured alcohol.***

Removal

1 On WR models remove the toolkit **(see illustration)**. Unscrew the passenger footrest bracket bolts and remove the footrest bracket assembly. Remove the split pin and washer from the clevis pin securing the brake pedal to the master cylinder pushrod, then withdraw the pin and detach the pushrod **(see illustration)**. A new split pin must be used.
2 Unscrew the bolt securing the fluid reservoir to the frame, then undo the reservoir cap and remove the diaphragm plate and diaphragm **(see illustrations)**. Pour the brake fluid into a suitable container. Wipe any remaining fluid out of the reservoir with a clean rag. Check the diaphragm for damage and deformation and replace it with a new one if necessary.
3 On models with standard (non-ABS) brakes remove the brake light switch (see Chapter 8).
4 On models with ABS unscrew the brake hose banjo bolt and detach the banjo union, noting its alignment. Seal the banjo union using a nut and bolt and the two sealing washers **(see illustration 3.1c)**, or wrap plastic foodwrap around it. Secure the hose in an upright position. New sealing washers must be fitted on reassembly.
5 On WR models unscrew the master cylinder bolts and remove it along with the pushrod and reservoir **(see illustration)**.
6 On MT and YZF-R models unscrew the master cylinder bolts then draw the master cylinder off the pushrod, noting how the rubber boot lip locates in the groove, and remove it along with the reservoir **(see illustration)**. Check the condition of the boot and replace it with a new one if necessary.
7 If required release the clip securing the reservoir hose to the union on the master cylinder and detach the hose, being prepared to catch any residual fluid. Inspect the hose for cracks or splits and replace it with a new one if necessary. If required, release the circlip securing the union and detach it from the master cylinder. A new O-ring must be used. Check the hose clips for corrosion and deformation and replace them with new ones if necessary.

Overhaul (WR models only)

8 Slacken the locknut on the top of the clevis

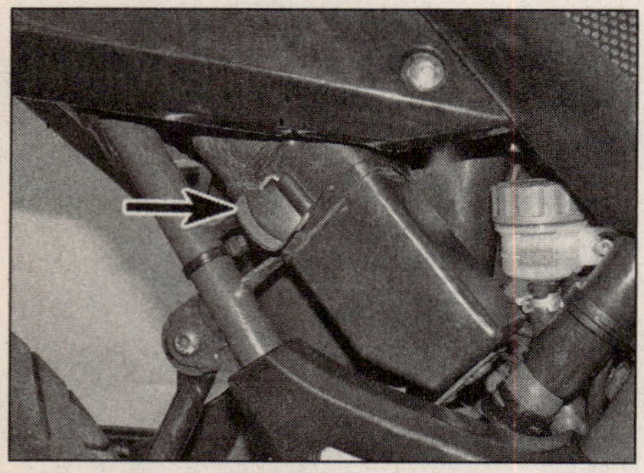

9.1a Unhook the strap (arrowed) and remove the toolkit

9.1b Remove the split pin (arrowed) and washer and withdraw the clevis pin

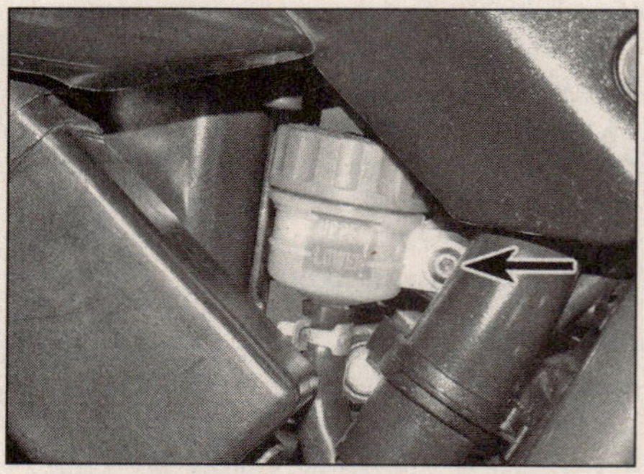

9.2a Fluid reservoir bolt (arrowed) – WR models

9.2b Fluid reservoir bolt (arrowed) – MT and YZF-R models

9.5 Unscrew the bolts (arrowed) and remove the master cylinder and reservoir assembly

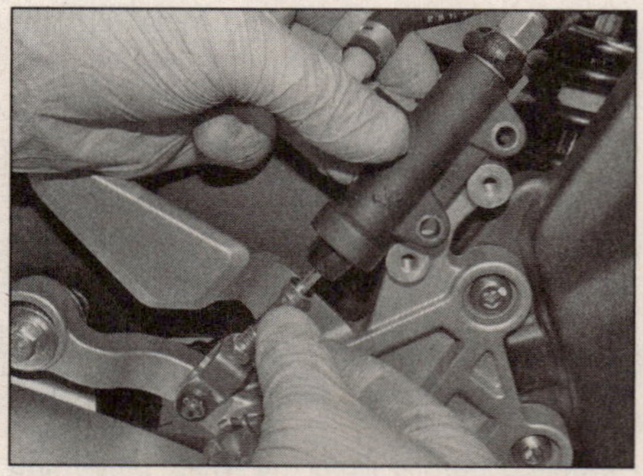

9.6 Lift the master cylinder off the pushrod

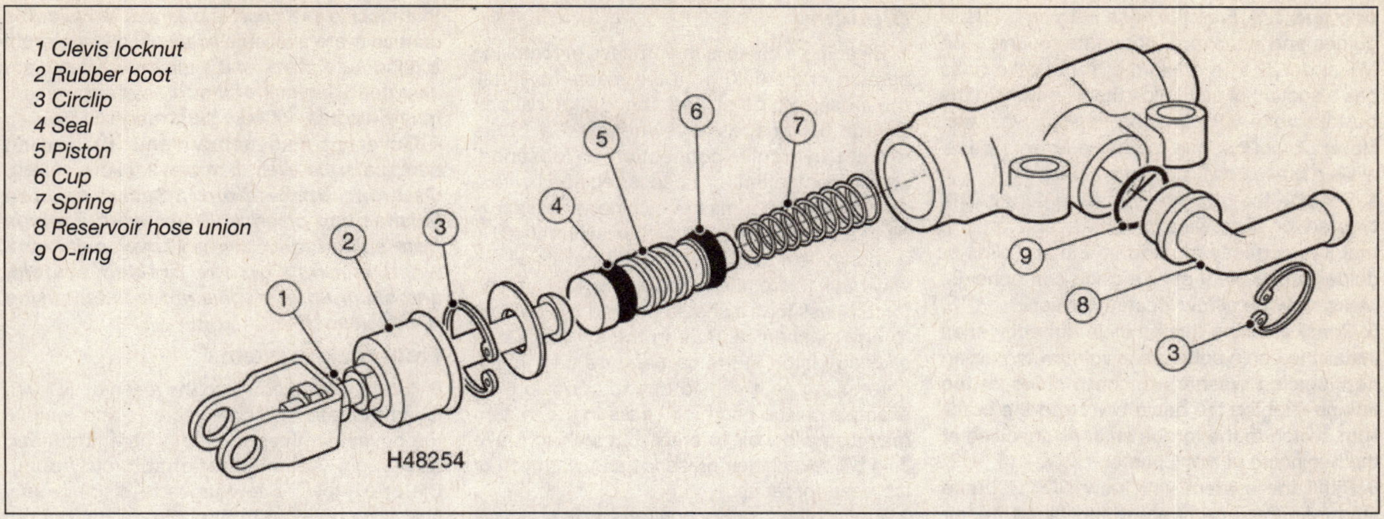

9.8 Rear brake master cylinder components

(see illustration). Note how far the clevis is threaded up the pushrod, then thread it off, followed by the locknut.

9 Pull the rubber boot out of the master cylinder and off the pushrod. Push the pushrod in and release the circlip using internal circlip pliers, and draw out the pushrod, piston assembly and spring.

10 Clean the inside of the master cylinder with fresh DOT 4 brake fluid. If compressed air is available blow it through the fluid passages. ***Caution: NEVER use a petroleum-based solvent to clean brake system components.***

11 Check the master cylinder bore for surface defects and replace the cylinder with a new one if necessary.

12 Use all of the parts contained in the rebuild kit regardless of the apparent condition of the old ones. If not already in place fit the narrow end of the spring onto the inner end of the piston. Lubricate the piston and seals with new brake fluid and fit the piston/spring assembly into the master cylinder, spring first, making sure the seal lips do not turn inside out.

13 Fit the rubber boot onto the pushrod, wide lip facing towards the washer, and seat the narrow lip in its groove. Fit the circlip onto the pushrod between the boot and the washer. Fit the rounded end of the pushrod against the end of the piston, push the piston in and seat the circlip in its groove in the master cylinder. Release the pushrod and check the circlip is securely located. Fit the upper lip of the boot into the master cylinder.

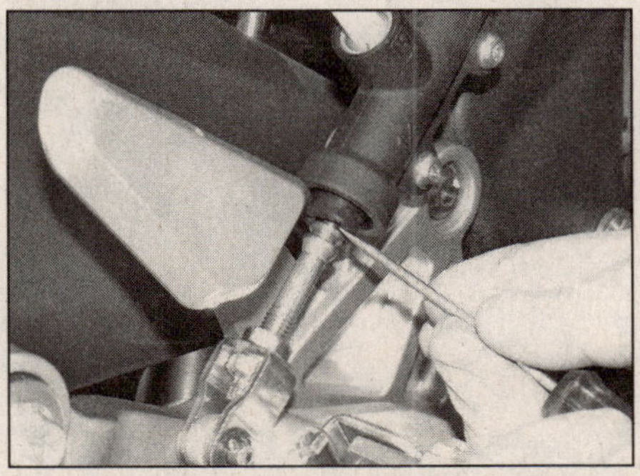

9.17 Seat the lip of the boot in the groove

14 Thread the locknut, clevis and nut onto the pushrod, position the clevis as noted on removal, and tighten the locknut against it.

Installation

15 If the reservoir hose union was removed fit a new O-ring smeared with brake fluid, then press the union into the master cylinder and secure it with a new circlip. Fit the hose and secure it with the clip. Check that the hose is secured with a clip at the reservoir end as well.

16 On WR models locate the master cylinder then fit the bolts and tighten them to the torque setting specified at the beginning of the Chapter **(see illustration 9.5)**.

17 On MT and YZF-R models, if the rubber boot was removed fit the wide lip of a new boot into the master cylinder. Position the master cylinder over the pushrod, fit the bolts and tighen them to the torque setting specified at the beginning of the Chapter **(see illustration 9.6)**. Carefully feed the lower lip of the boot into the groove in the pushrod **(see illustration)**.

18 Fit the fluid reservoir onto its mount and finger-tighten the bolt **(see illustration 9.2a or b)**.

19 On models with standard (non-ABS) brakes install the brake light switch (see Chapter 8).

20 On models with ABS connect the brake hose using new sealing washers on each side of the banjo union **(see illustration 3.15)**, and align it as noted on removal. Tighten the banjo bolt to the torque setting specified at the beginning of the Chapter.

21 On WR models align the clevis with the brake pedal, insert the clevis pin, then fit the washer and a new split pin, and bend its ends round to secure it **(see illustration 9.1b)**. Fit the passenger footrest bracket and the toolkit.

22 Fill the reservoir with DOT 4 brake fluid and bleed the system as described in Section 11.

23 Check that there are no fluid leaks and test the operation of the brake before riding the motorcycle.

10 Brake hoses and fittings

Inspection

1 Brake hose condition should be checked regularly and the hoses replaced with new ones every four years (see Chapter 1).

Removal and installation

2 Drain all old brake fluid from the system (see Section 11).

3 The brake hoses have banjo fittings on each end, with the exception that the rear master cylinder on models with standard (non-ABS) brakes have the brake light switch to secure the hose rather than a banjo bolt, so you must disconnect the wiring connector, release the wiring from any ties and feed it down to the switch before unscrewing it (see Chapter 8). Cover the surrounding area with plenty of rags and unscrew the banjo bolt (or the switch) at each end of the hose, noting the alignment of the fitting with the master cylinder or brake caliper **(see illustrations 3.1a or b, 5.3a**

or b and 7.1). Free the hose from any clips or guides and remove it, noting its routing – on MT and YZF-R models the front brake hose has a section of solid pipe that is bolted to the bottom yoke. Discard the sealing washers. **Note:** *Do not operate the brake lever or pedal while a brake hose is disconnected.*

4 Position the new hose, making sure it isn't twisted or otherwise strained, and ensure that it is correctly routed through any clips or guides and is clear of all moving components. Make sure the elbow locates correctly.

5 Check that the fittings align correctly, then install the banjo bolts/brake light switch, using new sealing washers on both sides of the fittings. Tighten the banjo bolts and the brake light switch to the torque settings specified at the beginning of this Chapter.

6 Refill the system with new DOT 4 brake fluid (see *Pre-ride checks*) and bleed the air from it (see Section 11).

7 Check the operation of the brakes before riding the motorcycle.

11 Brake system bleeding and fluid change

Note: *The brake bleeding equipment described in Step 3 will be required – ready-made bleeding kits are cheaply available from automotive stores. On models with ABS Yamaha specify the system should be pulse tested after any work, including bleeding the system. The pulse tests check for correct connection/routing of all the brake pipes/hoses, and for correct function of the solenoids and motor within the ABS modulator. To perform these tests it is advised the bike be taken to a Yamaha dealer for the system to be tested.*

Bleeding

1 Bleeding a brake is the process of removing aerated brake fluid from the master cylinder, the hose(s)/pipe(s) and the brake caliper. Bleeding is necessary whenever a brake system hydraulic connection is loosened, after a component or hose is replaced with a new one, when a master cylinder or caliper is overhauled (where possible), or when there is a spongy feel to the lever and it travels all the way back to the handlebar, and where braking force is less than it should be, and it is not due to any mechanical fault in the system (i.e. a sticking piston in the caliper, or a pad that is not moving as it should due to corrosion, for example on the pad pin). Leaks in the system may also allow air to enter, but leaking brake fluid will reveal their presence and warn you of the need for repair.

2 Brake bleeding is considered by some as a bit of a black art – seasoned professionals sometimes have trouble getting a good firm feel in the brake lever or pedal, while a first timer may have no trouble at all. One of the problems, particularly with the front brakes, is that you are working against natural principles – science dictates that air bubbles in a liquid will rise to the top, but the process entails pumping the brake fluid and any air bubbles it contains down, from the master cylinder at the top to the bleed valve in the caliper at the bottom, so while the fluid is moving down the air bubbles will want to rise. Air bubbles can also get trapped, particularly where there are high points in its path, and when there are extra components and pipes as on ABS models.

3 To bleed the brakes using the conventional method, you will need some new DOT 4 brake fluid, a length of clear flexible hose, a small container partially filled with clean brake fluid, some rags, and an 8 mm ring spanner to fit the brake caliper bleed valve. Bleeding kits that include the hose, a one-way valve and a container are available relatively cheaply from a good auto store, and simplify the task. You also need a block of wood as a support for the fluid container **(see illustration 11.6d)**.

4 Cover painted components to prevent damage in the event that brake fluid is spilled. ***Caution: Brake fluid attacks painted finishes and plastics – to prevent damage from spilled fluid, always cover paintwork when working on the braking system, and clean up any spills immediately using brake cleaner.***

Front brake system

5 Turn the handlebars so the reservoir is level. Undo the reservoir cover screws and remove the cover, diaphragm plate (where fitted) and diaphragm **(see illustrations)**. Slowly pump the brake lever a few times to dislodge any fine air bubbles from the holes in the bottom of the reservoir **(see illustration)**. Now hold the lever in to force any large air bubbles out – you can tie the lever to the handlebar and leave it pressurised for a while to prevent having to hold it, then release it and slowly pump it a few times.

6 Pull the dust cap off the bleed valve on

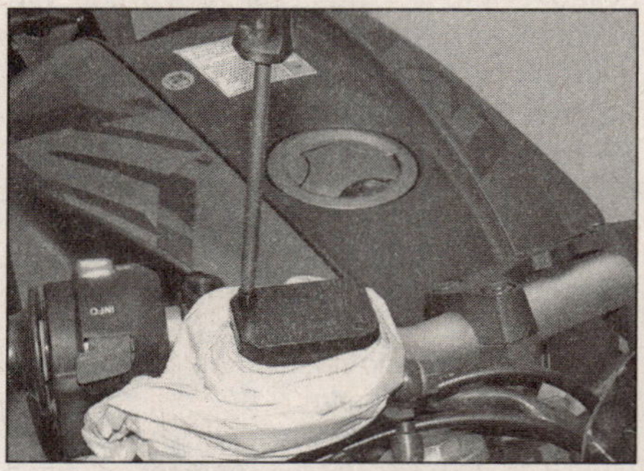

11.5a Undo the screws...

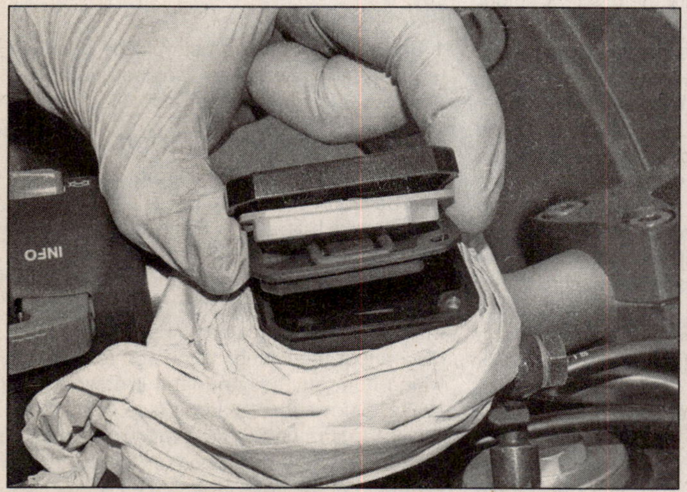

11.5b ... and remove the plate (MT and YZF-R models, shown) and rubber diaphragm

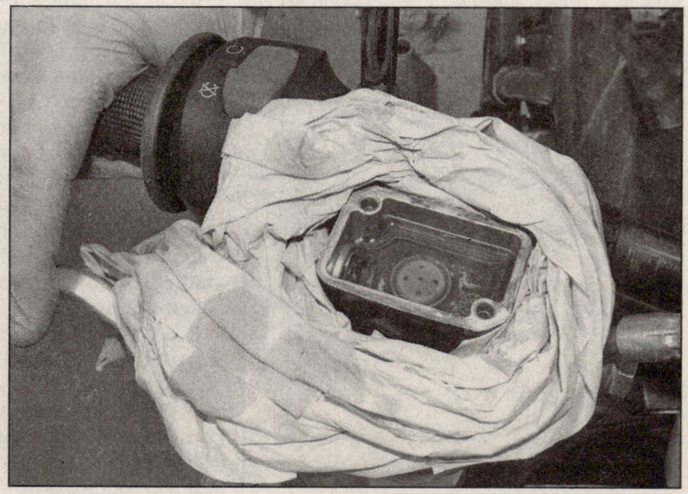

11.5c Slowly pump then hold the brake lever in to force any air out of the master cylinder

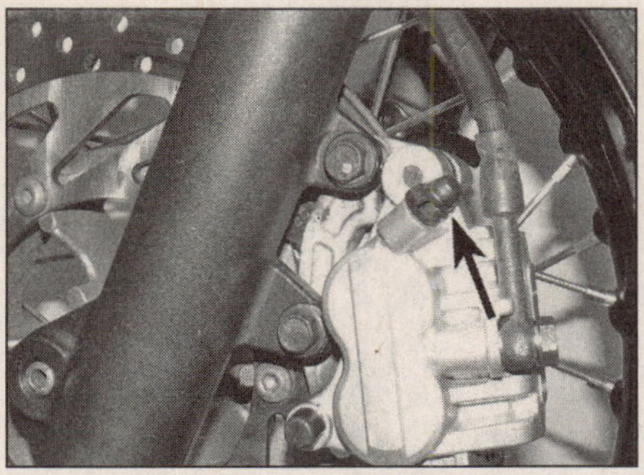
11.6a Front brake caliper bleed valve (arrowed) – WR models

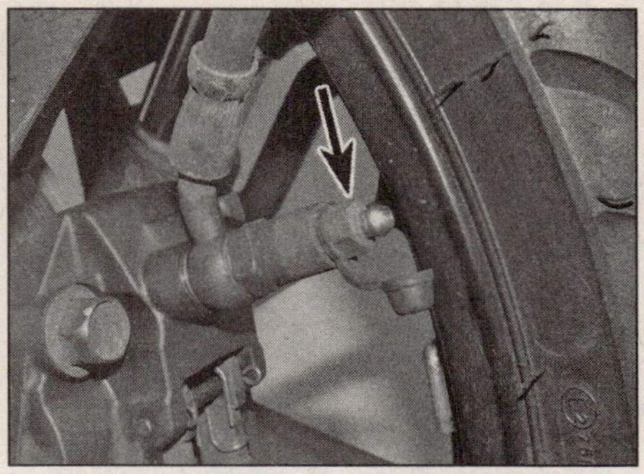
11.6b Front brake caliper bleed valve (arrowed) – MT and YZF-R models

11.6c Fit the spanner over the valve then fit the hose

the caliper **(see illustrations)**. If using a ring spanner (which is preferable to an open-ended one) fit it onto the valve. Attach one end of the bleeding hose to the bleed valve and, if not using a kit, submerge the other end in the clean brake fluid in the container **(see illustrations)**.

7 Check the fluid level in the reservoir – keep it topped up and do not allow the level to drop below the bottom of the window during the procedure **(see illustration)**.

8 Slowly squeeze the brake lever and open the bleed valve a quarter turn **(see illustration)**. When the valve is opened, brake fluid will flow out of the master cylinder into the clear tubing, and the lever will move to the handlebar. If there is air in the system there will be air bubbles in the brake fluid coming out of the caliper.

9 Tighten the bleed valve, then release the brake lever. Repeat the process until no air bubbles are visible in the brake fluid leaving the caliper, and the lever is firm when applied, topping the reservoir up when necessary. On completion tighten the bleed valve and remove the equipment, then fit the dust cap.

10 When the system has been successfully bled there should be a good and progressively firm feel as the lever is applied, and the lever should not be able to travel all the way back to the handlebar.

11.6d Set-up using a commercially available bleeding kit

11.7 Keep the reservoir topped up with new brake fluid

11 On ABS models the system should now be pulse tested (see Note at the beginning of this Section), then the bleeding procedure should be repeated.

12 Top-up the reservoir, then fit the diaphragm, diaphragm plate (where fitted), and cover. Check for spilled brake fluid and clean up as required.

13 Check there are no fluid leaks and test the operation of the brake before riding the motorcycle.

Rear brake system

14 Unscrew the bolt securing the fluid reservoir, then draw the reservoir out **(see illustration 9.2a or b)**.

15 Hold the reservoir and unscrew the cap, and remove the diaphragm plate and diaphragm **(see illustration)**. Slowly pump the brake pedal a few times to dislodge any air bubbles from the holes in the bottom of the reservoir.

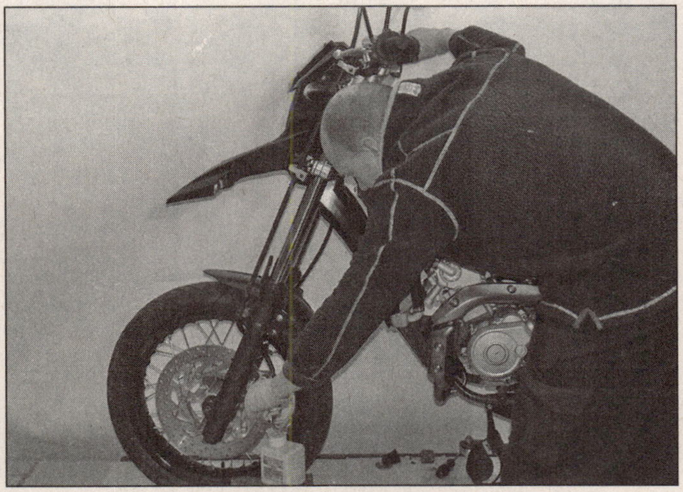
11.8 Bleeding the front brake

11.15 Unscrew the cap and remove the plate and rubber diaphragm

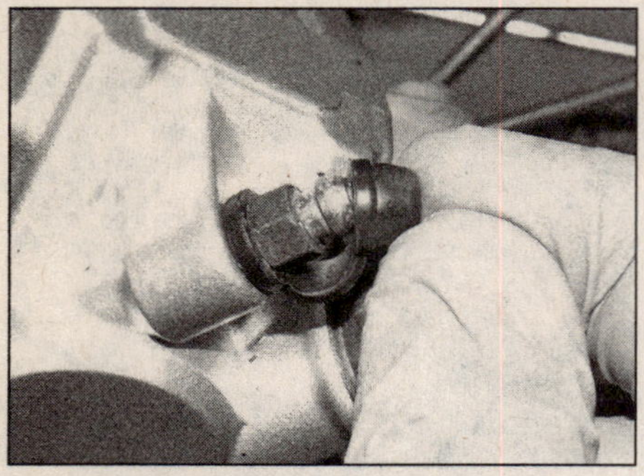

11.16a Pull the cap off the valve

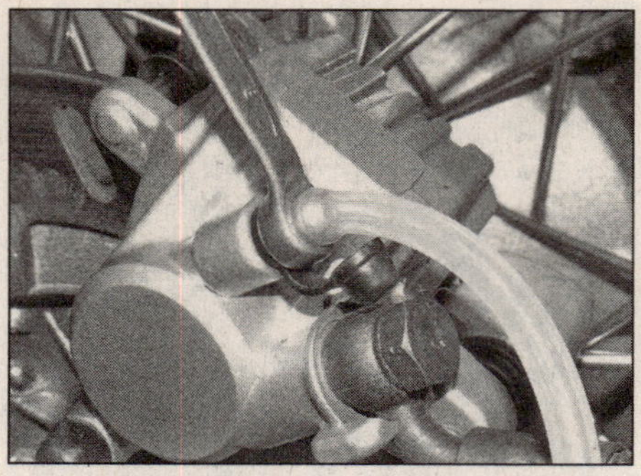

11.16b Fit the spanner onto the valve then fit the hose

11.16c Set-up using a commercially available bleeding kit

16 Pull the dust cap off the bleed valve on the caliper **(see illustration)**. If using a ring spanner (which is preferable to an open-ended one) fit it onto the valve. Attach one end of the bleeding hose to the bleed valve and, if not using a kit, submerge the other end in the clean brake fluid in the container **(see illustrations)**.

17 Check the fluid level in the reservoir – keep it topped up and do not allow the level to drop below the lower level line during the procedure **(see illustration)**.

18 Slowly press the brake pedal and open the bleed valve a quarter turn **(see illustration)**. When the valve is opened, brake fluid will flow out of the master cylinder into the clear tubing, and the pedal will move down. If there is air in the system there will be air bubbles in the brake fluid coming out of the caliper.

19 Tighten the bleed valve, then release the brake pedal. Repeat the process until no air bubbles are visible in the brake fluid leaving the caliper, and the pedal is firm when applied, topping the reservoir up when necessary.

20 When the system has been successfully bled there should be a good and progressively firm feel as the pedal is applied, and the pedal should not be able to travel all the way down to its stop.

21 On ABS models the system should now be pulse tested (see Note at the beginning of this Section), then the bleeding procedure should be repeated.

22 On completion tighten the bleed valve and remove the equipment, then fit the dust cap. Top-up the reservoir, then fit the diaphragm, diaphragm plate, and cap. Fit the reservoir **(see illustration 9.2a or b)**. Check for spilled brake fluid and clean up as required.

23 Check that there are no fluid leaks and test the operation of the brake before riding the motorcycle.

Both systems

24 If it is not possible to produce a firm feel to the lever or pedal, the fluid may be full of many tiny air bubbles rather than a few big ones. To remedy this apply some pressure to the system, for the front brake by tying the front brake lever lightly back to the handlebar, and for the rear by tying a weight to the brake pedal – do not apply too much pressure or the cup and seals in the master cylinder and caliper may fail. Let the fluid stabilise for a few hours, after which the tiny bubbles should either have risen to the top in the reservoir, or have formed into one or more big bubbles that can be more easily bled out by repeating the bleeding procedure.

25 If you are still having trouble look for any high point in the system in which a pocket of air may become trapped. Displace and agitate the hose or pipe so the bubble can be dislodged (but take care not to bend a pipe) – tapping it may help. If necessary displace the master cylinder and/or the caliper, and free the brake hose from any guides and move the parts around to dislodge the air and encourage it towards a bleed valve – refer to the relevant Sections as required to displace components. On models with ABS it is not practical to disturb the modulator as the pipes have to be detached, allowing more air to enter the system – if you cannot get the system to bleed correctly take the bike to a Yamaha dealer.

26 If bleeding the system using the conventional tools and methods stated does not give satisfactory results, or if otherwise preferred, you can use a commercially available vacuum-type brake bleeding tool, such as the mity-vac, following the

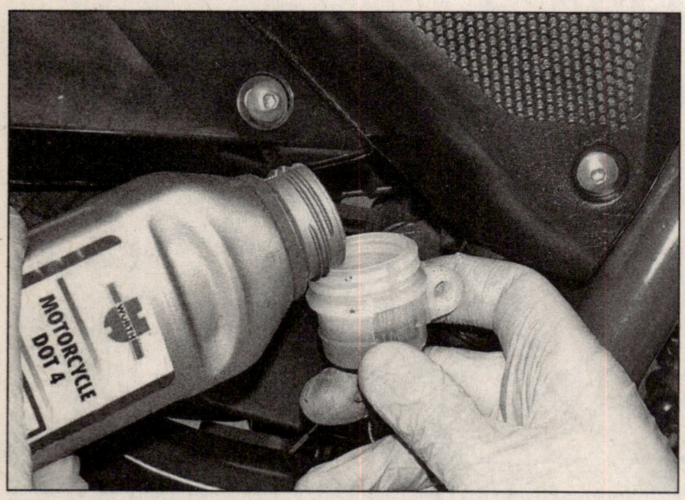

11.17 Keep the reservoir topped up with new brake fluid

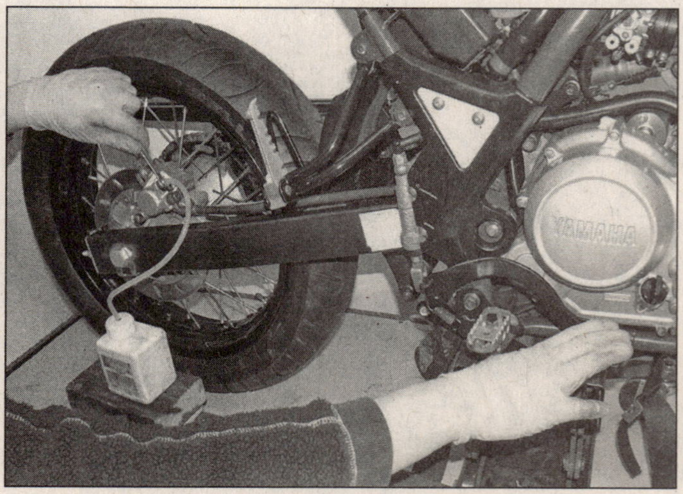

11.18 Bleeding the rear brake

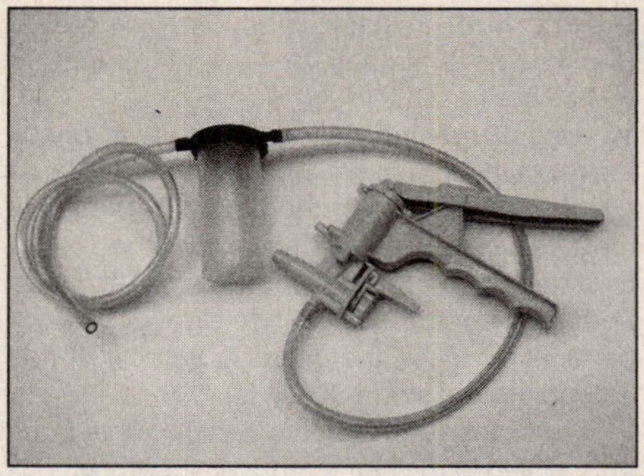

11.26 This tool creates a vacuum to suck the fluid out

manufacturer's instructions **(see illustration)**. This type of tool literally sucks the fluid out by creating a vacuum at the bleed valve. Users of such tools often get confused by the amount of air that appears to be in the brake fluid – more often than not this is caused by the vacuum sucking air past the bleed valve threads (air provides less resistance to the vacuum than the brake fluid) where it mixes with the fluid being drawn out. If this is the case the vacuum applied may be too great, or the bleed valve may have been loosened too much. One way to get round this is to remove the bleed valve and thread some PTFE tape around its threads, but note that doing so will be a bit messy, so have some rag to hand.

Fluid change

27 Changing the brake fluid is a similar process to bleeding the brakes and requires the same materials plus a suitable tool (such as a syringe, or alternatively lots of absorbent rag or paper) for siphoning the fluid out of the reservoir.

28 Cover painted components and fit the equipment to the relevant caliper following the appropriate Steps in the bleeding procedure given above. Remove the reservoir cover or cap, diaphragm plate (where fitted) and diaphragm **(see illustrations 11.5a and b, or 9.2a or b and 11.15)**. Remove the fluid from the reservoir into a suitable container, either by sucking it up using a tool as shown, drawing it out into a syringe, or soaking it up in some paper towel. Wipe the reservoir clean. Fill the reservoir with new brake fluid **(see illustration 11.7 or 11.17)**. Squeeze or press the brake lever or pedal and open the bleed valve **(see illustrations 11.8 and 11.18)**. When the valve is opened, brake fluid will flow out of the caliper into the clear tubing, and the lever will move toward the handlebar, or the pedal will move down.

29 Tighten the bleed valve, then slowly release the brake lever or pedal. Keep the reservoir topped-up with new fluid at all times or air may enter the system and greatly increase the length of the task. Repeat the process until new fluid can be seen emerging from the caliper bleed valve.

HAYNES HiNT ***Old brake fluid is invariably much darker in colour than new fluid, making it easy to see when all old fluid has been expelled from the system***

30 On completion tighten the bleed valve and remove the equipment, then fit the dust cap. Top-up the reservoir, then fit the diaphragm, diaphragm plate (where fitted), and cover or cap. Check for spilled brake fluid and clean up as required.

31 On ABS models the system should now be pulse tested (see Note at the beginning of this Section), then the bleeding procedure should be repeated.

32 Check that there are no fluid leaks and thoroughly test the operation of the brake before riding the motorcycle.

Draining the system for overhaul

33 Draining the brake fluid is again a similar process to bleeding the brakes. The quickest and easiest way is to use a commercially available vacuum-type brake bleeding tool (see Step 26) – follow the manufacturer's instructions. Otherwise follow the procedure described above for changing the fluid, but quite simply do not put any new fluid into the reservoir – the system fills itself with air instead.

34 When it comes to refilling the system start by adding new fluid from a sealed container to the reservoir, then perform the bleeding procedure as described above until the fluid comes out of the bleed valve, and keep at it until you are certain there is no more air left in the system.

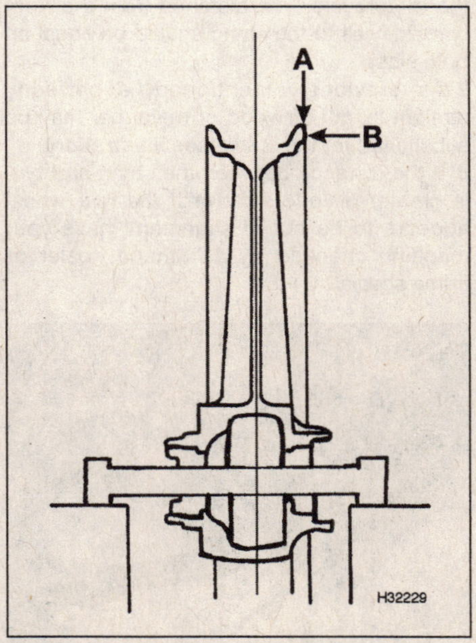

12.2 Check the wheel for radial (out-of-round) runout (A) and axial (side-to-side) runout (B)

12 Wheel inspection and repair

1 In order to carry out a proper inspection of the wheels, it is necessary to support the bike upright so that the wheel being inspected is raised off the ground. Position the motorcycle on an auxiliary stand. Clean the wheels thoroughly to remove mud and dirt that may interfere with the inspection procedure or mask defects. Make a general check of the wheels (see Chapter 1) and tyres (see *Pre-ride checks*).

2 Attach a dial gauge to the fork or the swingarm and position its tip against the side of the wheel rim. Spin the wheel slowly and check the axial (side-to-side) runout of the rim **(see illustration)**. The runout limits are given in the specifications at the beginning of the chapter.

3 In order to accurately check radial (out of round) runout with the dial gauge, remove the wheel from the machine, and the tyre from the wheel. With the axle clamped in a vice and the dial gauge positioned on the top of the rim, the wheel can be rotated to check the runout **(see illustration 12.2)**.

4 An easier, though slightly less accurate, method is to attach a stiff wire pointer to the fork or the swingarm and position the end a fraction of an inch from the wheel rim where the wheel and tyre join. If the wheel is true, the distance from the pointer to the rim will be constant as the wheel is rotated. Note: If wheel runout is excessive, check the wheel bearings very carefully before renewing the wheel.

5 Cast wheels should also be inspected for cracks, flat spots on the rim and other damage. Look very closely for dents in the area where the tyre bead contacts the rim. Dents in this area may prevent complete sealing of the tyre against the rim, which leads to deflation of the tyre over a period of time. If damage is evident, or if runout in either direction is excessive, the wheel will have to be renewed. Never attempt to repair a damaged cast alloy wheel.

6 Spoked wheels can be rebuilt and rims replaced, but it is a job for a wheel building specialist.

13 Wheel alignment check

1 Misalignment of the wheels due to a bent frame or forks can cause strange and possibly serious handling problems. If the frame or forks are at fault, repair by a frame specialist or renewal are the only options.

2 To check wheel alignment you will need an assistant, a length of string or a perfectly straight piece of wood and a ruler. A plumb

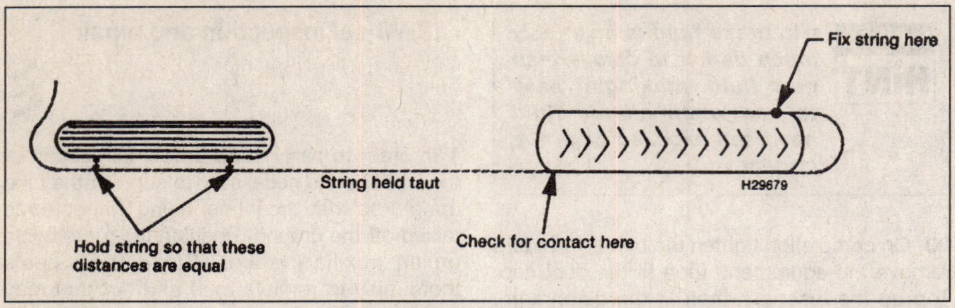

13.5 Wheel alignment check using string

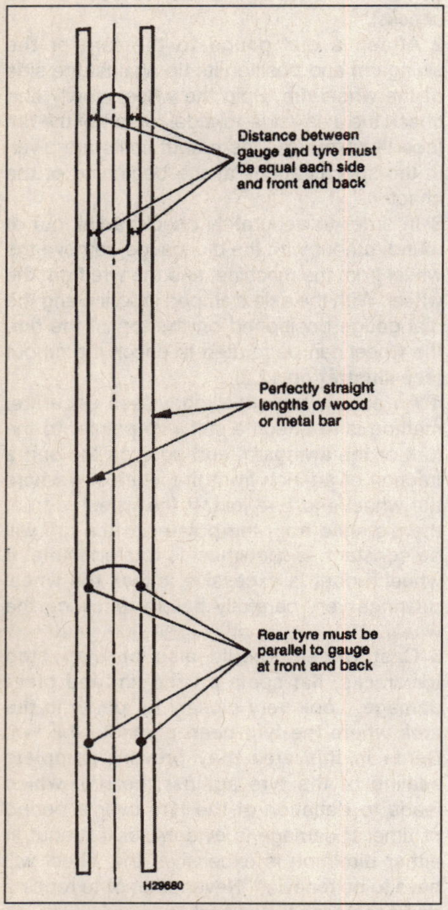

13.7 Wheel alignment check using a straight-edge

bob or spirit level for checking that the wheels are vertical will also be required.

3 In order to make a proper check of the wheels it is necessary to support the bike in an upright position, using an auxiliary stand. First ensure that the chain adjuster markings coincide on each side of the swingarm (see Chapter 1, Section 1). Next, measure the width of both tyres at their widest points. Subtract the smaller measurement from the larger measurement, then divide the difference by two. The result is the amount of offset that should exist between the front and rear tyres on both sides of the machine.

4 If a string is used, have your assistant hold one end of it about halfway between the floor and the rear axle, with the string touching the back edge of the rear tyre sidewall.

5 Run the other end of the string forward and pull it tight so that it is roughly parallel to the floor **(see illustration)**. Slowly bring the string into contact with the front edge of the rear tyre sidewall, then turn the front wheel until it is parallel with the string. Measure the distance from the front tyre sidewall to the string.

6 Repeat the procedure on the other side of the motorcycle. The distance from the front tyre sidewall to the string should be equal on both sides.

7 As previously mentioned, a perfectly straight length of wood or metal bar may be substituted for the string **(see illustration)**.

8 If the distance between the string and tyre is greater on one side, or if the rear wheel appears to be out of alignment, have your machine checked by a Yamaha dealer or frame specialist.

9 If the front-to-back alignment is correct, the wheels still may be out of alignment vertically.

10 Using a plumb bob or spirit level, check the rear wheel to make sure it is vertical. To do this, hold the string of the plumb bob against the tyre upper sidewall and allow the weight to settle just off the floor. If the string touches both the upper and lower tyre sidewalls and is perfectly straight, the wheel is vertical. If it is not, adjust the stand until it is.

11 Once the rear wheel is vertical, check the front wheel in the same manner. If both wheels are not perfectly vertical, the frame and/or major suspension components are bent.

14 Front wheel

Removal

1 Position the motorcycle on an auxiliary stand so that the front wheel is off the ground. If you are using a jack under the engine, on MT models remove the belly-pan and on YZF-R models remove the bottom and lower sections of the fairing (see Chapter 7). Always make sure the motorcycle is properly supported.

2 On models with ABS displace the wheel speed sensor (see Section 20) – there is no need to disconnect the wiring.

3 Unscrew the brake caliper mounting bolts and slide the caliper off the disc (see Section 3). Support the caliper with a cable-tie or a bungee cord so that no strain is placed on the hose – there is no need to disconnect the hose. **Note:** *Do not operate the front brake lever with the caliper removed.*

4 Slacken the axle clamp bolts on the bottom of the right-hand fork **(see illustration)**. On WR models remove the plug from the head of the axle. On all models unscrew the axle.

5 Take the weight of the wheel, then withdraw the axle from the right and lower the wheel **(see illustration)**. Draw the wheel forwards and remove it, on WR models displacing the speed sensor from the right-hand side **(see illustration)**.

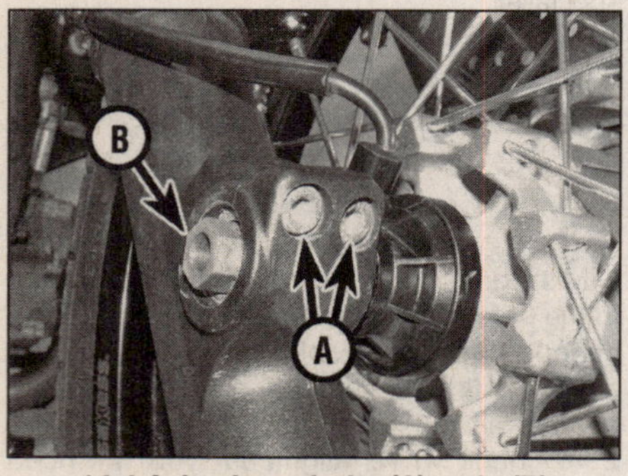

14.4 Axle clamp bolts (A), axle (B)

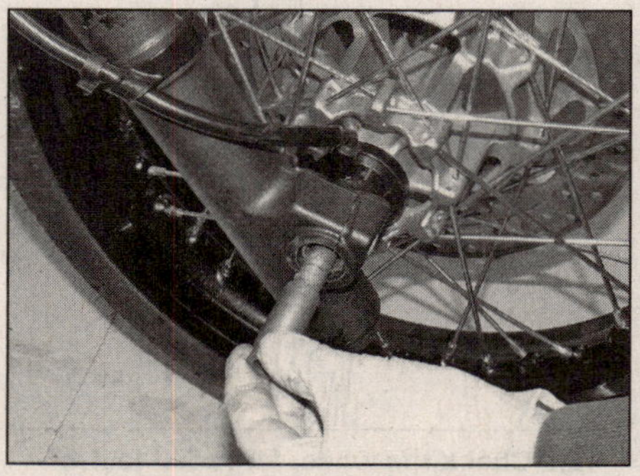

14.5a Withdraw the axle and lower the wheel

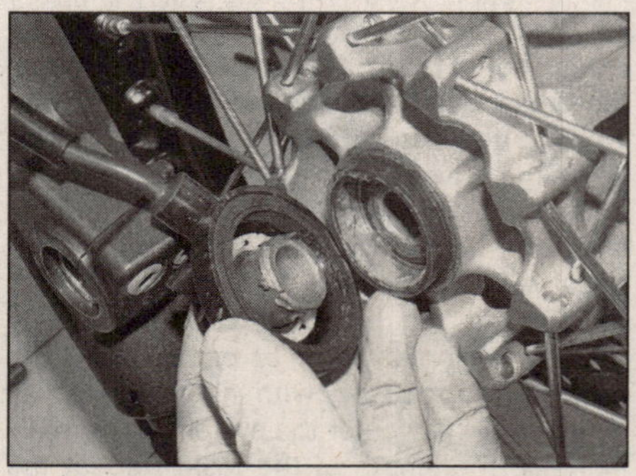

14.5b On WR models detach the sensor from the wheel

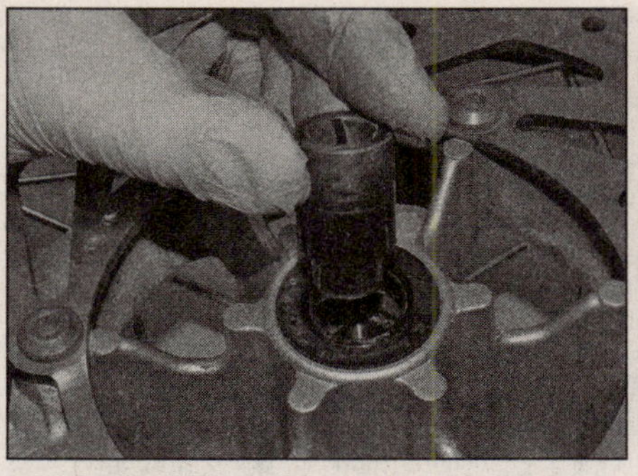

14.6a On WR models remove the spacer

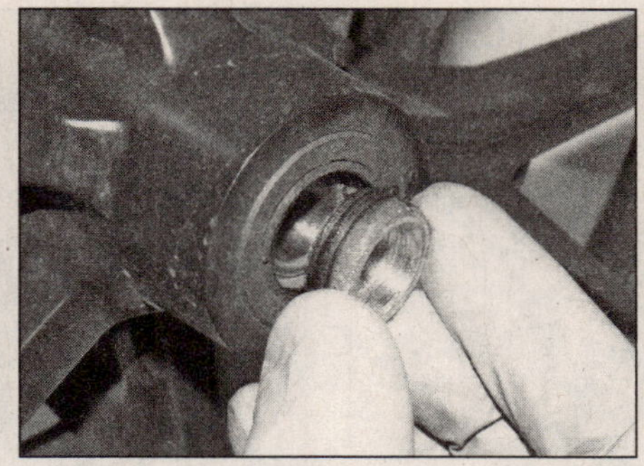

14.6b On MT and YZF-R models remove the plain spacer from the right side...

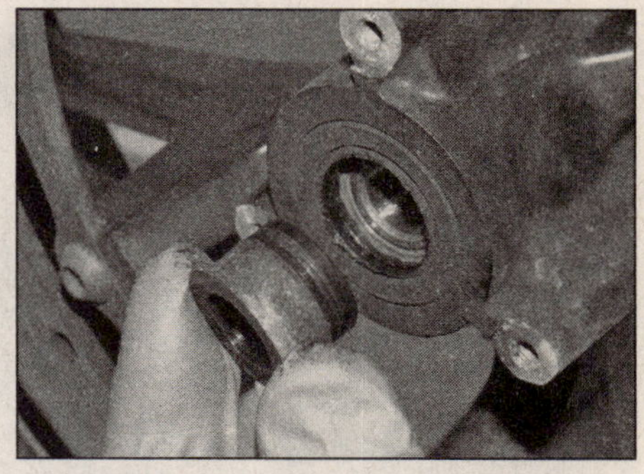

14.6c ...and the shouldered spacer from the left

6 On WR models remove the spacer from the left side of the wheel **(see illustration)** – on R models the spacer has a dust seal fitted on it. On MT and YZF-R models remove the plain spacer from the right-hand side of the wheel and the shouldered spacer from the left **(see illustrations)**. Clean all dirt and old grease from the spacer(s), axle and bearing seals, and on WR models from the speed sensor.

7 Check the axle is straight by rolling it on a flat surface such as a piece of plate glass (first remove any corrosion using wire wool or a suitable alternative). If the equipment is available, place the axle in V-blocks and measure the runout using a dial gauge. If the axle is bent or the runout exceeds the limit specified at the beginning of the Chapter, replace it with a new one.

8 Check the condition of the wheel bearings and seals (see Section 16).

Caution: Don't lay the wheel down and allow it to rest on the disc – it could become warped. Set the wheel on wood blocks so the disc doesn't support the weight of the wheel.

Installation

Note: *If a new tyre has been fitted, make sure the directional arrow on the tyre is pointing in the direction of normal rotation of the wheel.*

9 On WR-R models check that the dust seal is set on the spacer so the distance between the inner face of the seal and the inner end of the spacer is 8 mm. On all WR models smear some grease to the inside of the speed sensor, to the inside of the wheel spacer and to the lip of the bearing seal **(see illustration and 14.6a)**. Fit the spacer into the seal.

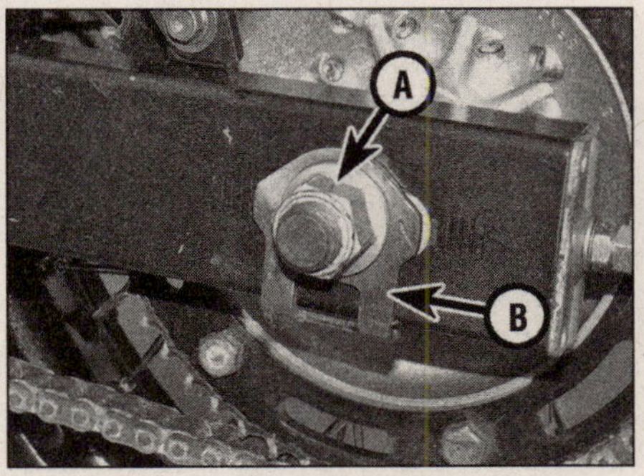

15.3a Axle nut (A) and adjustment marker (B) – WR models

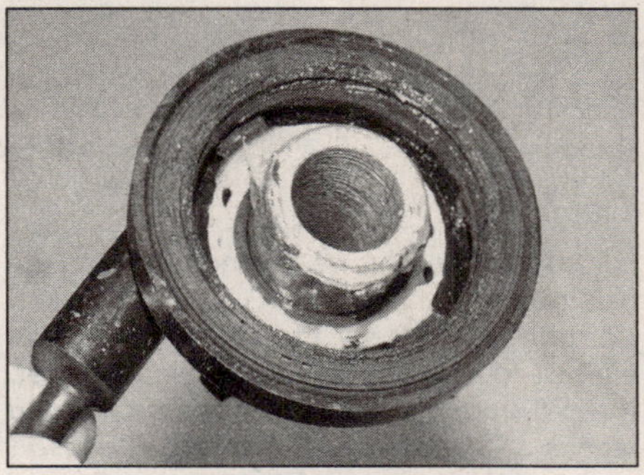

14.9 Smear some grease into the speed sensor

10 On MT and YZF-R models smear some grease onto the inside of each spacer and to the lip of each bearing seal **(see illustrations 14.6b and c)**. Fit the plain spacer into the seal on the right-hand side and the shouldered spacer into the seal on the left.

11 Manoeuvre the wheel into position between the forks, making sure the brake disc is on the left. On WR models fit the speed sensor onto the right side of the wheel, making sure the drive tab cast on the wheel locates in the gap between the tabs on the sensor **(see illustration 14.5b)**. Apply a thin coat of grease to the axle.

12 Lift the wheel into place, making sure the speed sensor and/or spacer(s) remain in position, and on WR models seat the tabs on the sensor around the lug on the fork **(see illustration)**. Slide the axle in from the right **(see illustration 14.5a)**.

13 Tighten the axle to the torque setting specified at the beginning of the Chapter.

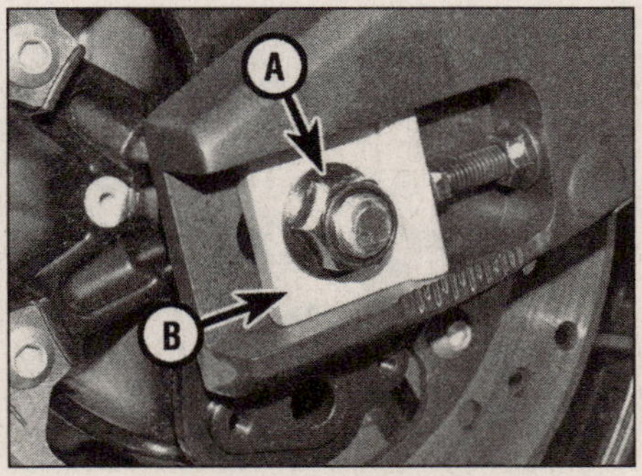

15.3b Axle nut (A) and adjustment marker (B) – MT and YZF-R models

14.12 On WR models make sure the lug (arrowed) seats between the tabs

14 Install the brake caliper (see Section 3). Apply the front brake a few times to bring the pads back into contact with the disc.

15 On models with ABS fit the wheel speed sensor (see Section 20).

16 Lower the bike so the wheel is on the ground, then hold the front brake on and push down on the handlebars to compress the forks several times to align the right-hand fork on the axle. Now tighten the axle clamp bolts to the specified torque **(see illustration 14.4)** – after tightening the second bolt, tighten the first bolt again as the tightening of the second bolt may make the first one a bit loose (the effect of off-centre tightening).

17 Check the front brake before riding the motorcycle.

15 Rear wheel

Removal

1 Position the motorcycle on an auxiliary stand so that the rear wheel is off the ground. Always make sure the motorcycle is properly supported. Create maximum slack in the chain (see Chapter 1, Section 3).

2 On models with ABS displace the wheel speed sensor (see Section 20) – there is no need to disconnect the wiring.

3 Unscrew the axle nut and remove the adjustment marker, noting how it fits **(see illustrations)**.

15.4 Slip the chain off the sprocket teeth

15.5a Withdraw the axle and lower the wheel...

15.5b ...then draw it back

4 Push the wheel forwards and slip the chain off the sprocket **(see illustration)**.

5 Take the weight of the wheel, then withdraw the axle, bringing the other adjustment marker with it, and lower the wheel to the ground **(see illustration)**. If the axle is difficult to withdraw, drive it through with a drift, making sure you don't damage the threads. Draw the wheel back from the swingarm **(see illustration)**.

6 Remove the spacer from each side of the wheel, on WR models noting the dust seals fitted on them, and which fits where as they are different **(see illustrations 15.10b and c)**. If required on WR models remove the adjuster from each side of the swingarm **(see illustration 15.10a)**.

Caution: Do not lay the wheel down and allow it to rest on the disc or the sprocket. Keep it upright, or set the wheel on wood blocks so the disc or the sprocket doesn't support the weight of the wheel. Do not operate the brake pedal with the wheel removed.

7 Clean all old grease off the spacers, bearing seals and axle.

8 Check the axle is straight by rolling it on a flat surface such as a piece of plate glass (first remove any corrosion with wire wool or a suitable alternative). If the equipment is available, place the axle in V-blocks and check the runout using a dial gauge. If the axle is bent or the runout exceeds the limit specified at the beginning of the Chapter, replace it with a new one.

9 Check the condition of the wheel bearings (see Section 16).

Installation

Note: *If a new tyre has been fitted, make sure the directional arrow on the tyre is pointing in the direction of normal rotation of the wheel.*

10 On WR models, if removed fit the adjuster into each end of the swingarm **(see illustration)**. Check that the dust seal is on each spacer. Smear some grease to the inside of each spacer and to the lip of each bearing seal. Fit the long spacer into the seal on the left-hand side of the wheel and the short spacer into the seal on the right **(see illustrations)**. Fit the right-hand chain adjustment marker onto the axle with the angled sections facing away from the axle head. Smear some grease onto the axle. The axle goes in from the right.

11 On MT and YZF-R models smear some grease onto the inside of each spacer and to the lip of each bearing seal. Fit the spacers into the seal on each side of the wheel. Fit the left-hand chain adjustment marker onto the axle with the raised side facing the axle head. Smear some grease onto the axle. The axle goes in from the left.

12 Make sure the caliper bracket is correctly located on the swingarm. Make sure there is enough room between the pads for the disc to locate between them **(see illustration 15.13a)**.

13 Manoeuvre the wheel into position between the ends of the swingarm with the sprocket to the left **(see illustration 15.5b)**. Align the brake disc between the brake pads

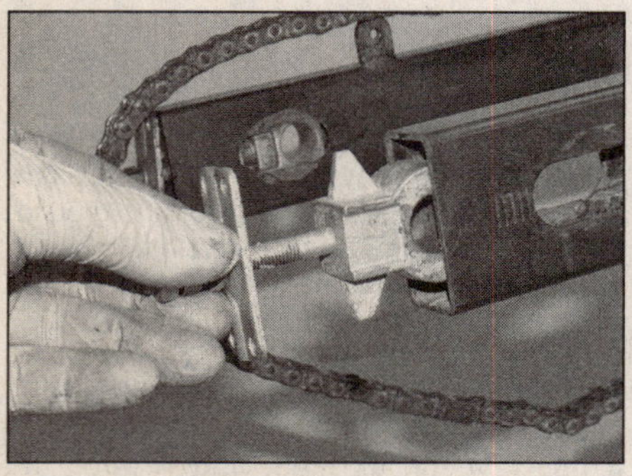

15.10a Fit the adjusters if removed

15.10b Fit the long spacer into the left side...

15.10c ...and the short spacer into the right

15.13a Align the disc between the pads

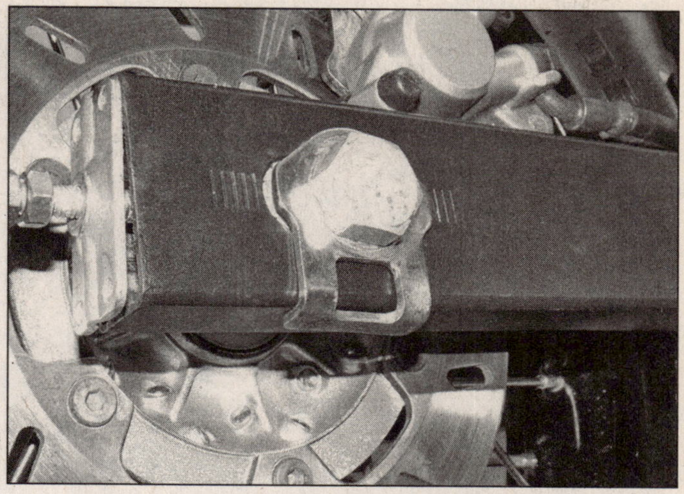

15.13b Correct fitted position of adjustment marker on WR models

(see illustration). Lift the wheel, making sure the spacers stay in place, the caliper bracket stays in place and the disc locates between the pads, and slide the axle in **(see illustration 15.5a)**. On WR models seat the angled sections of the adjustment marker under the swingarm **(see illustration)**. On MT and YZF-R models seat the thick end of the adjustment marker against the head of the adjuster bolt **(see illustration)**.

14 Fit the other adjustment marker in the same way, then fit the axle nut, but leave it loose **(see illustrations 15.3b and a)**.

15 Check and adjust the drive chain slack (see Chapter 1). On completion tighten the axle nut to the torque setting specified at the beginning of the Chapter.

16 On models with ABS fit the wheel speed sensor (see Section 20).

17 Operate the brake pedal several times to bring the pads into contact with the disc. Check the operation of the rear brake carefully before riding the bike.

16 Wheel bearings

Caution: Don't lay the wheel down and allow it to rest on the disc or the sprocket – they could become warped. Set the wheel on wood blocks so the wheel rim supports the weight of the wheel, or keep the wheel upright. Don't operate the brake lever/pedal with the wheel removed.

Note: *Always replace the wheel bearings in sets, never individually. Avoid using a high pressure cleaner on the wheel bearing area.*

Front wheel bearings

1 Remove the wheel (see Section 14). Lay the wheel rim on wood blocks. A caged ball bearing is fitted in each side of the wheel.

2 Inspect the seals and bearings – check that each bearing inner race turns smoothly and that the outer race is a tight fit in the hub (see *Tools and Workshop Tips* (Section 5) in the Reference Section). **Note:** *Do not remove the bearings unless they are going to be replaced with new ones.*

3 If new components are needed, it is best to remove the disc (see Section 4), and on models with ABS the sensor rotor (see Section 20), to prevent them being damaged or distorted during bearing removal.

4 Lever out the bearing seal from the left side of the hub on WR models and from each side on MT and YZF-R models using a flat-bladed screwdriver or a seal hook **(see illustration)**.

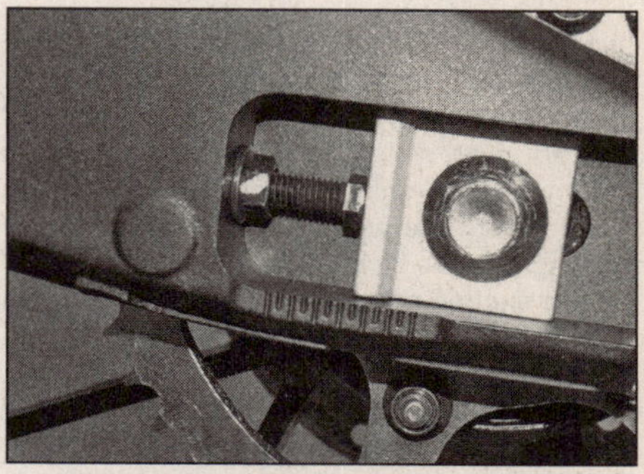

15.13c Correct fitted position of adjustment marker on MT and YZF-R models

Take care not to damage the hub. A new seal or seals must be used.

5 Move the bearing spacer aside to expose the inner race on the lower bearing **(see illustration)**. Using a suitable drift inserted through the centre of the upper bearing drive the lower bearing from the hub, moving the spacer around and relocating the drift so it's driven out squarely **(see illustration)**. The bearing spacer will also come out. Turn the wheel over so that the remaining bearing faces down. Drive the bearing out of the wheel using a socket on the inner race and an extension bar. If you can't move the

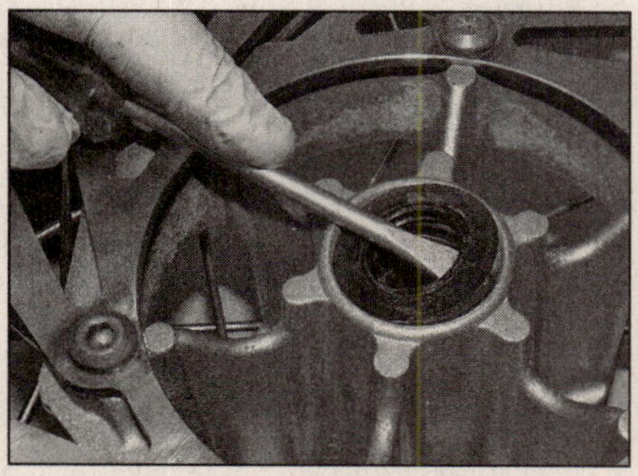

16.4 Lever out the bearing seal

16.5a Push the spacer aside to expose the bearing inner race (arrowed)...

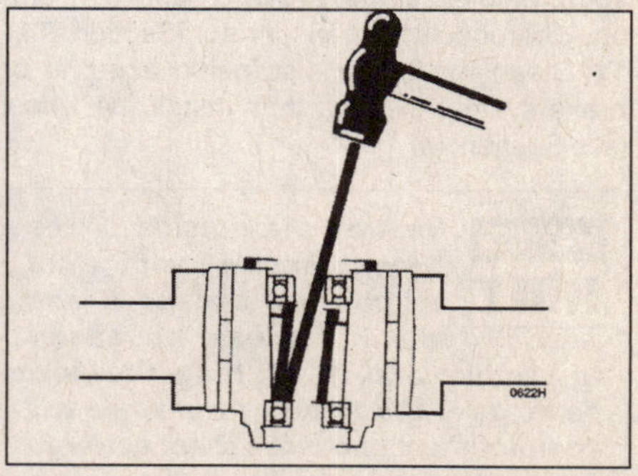

16.5b ... then locate the drift as shown and drive the bearing out

16.7 Using a socket to drive in the bearing

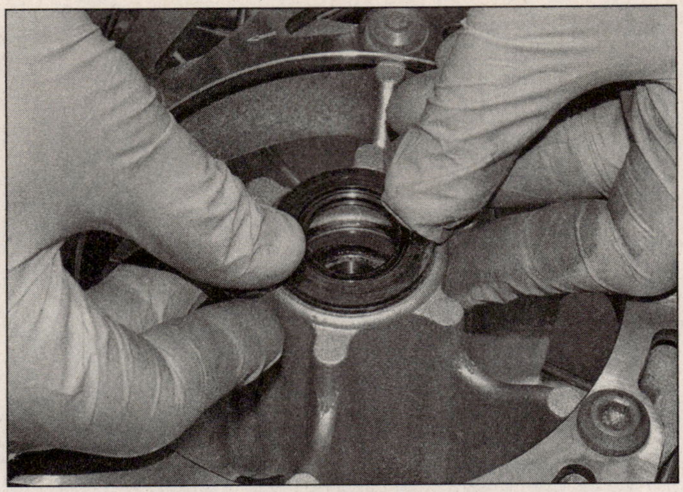

16.9 Press the new seal into place – using a piece of wood across the housing sets the seal flush

spacer, or if you can't get sufficient purchase with the drift, remove the bearings using an internal expanding puller with slide-hammer attachment, which can be obtained commercially – select the correct attachment and locate it between the inner race of the bearing and the spacer, then tighten the inner bolt to expand and lock the puller. Attach the slide-hammer, hold the wheel firmly down and jar the bearing out.

6 Thoroughly clean the hub area of the wheel with a suitable solvent and inspect the bearing housings for damage. If a housing is damaged, consult a Yamaha dealer before reassembling the wheel.

7 Fit the new bearings with the marked side facing out. Drive the first bearing in using a bearing driver or suitable socket that bears only on the outer race, and make sure the bearing fits squarely and all the way onto its seat **(see illustration)**. Alternatively draw it in using a drawbolt arrangement (see *Tools and Workshop Tips*).

8 Turn the wheel over then fit the bearing spacer and the other new bearing.

9 Fit a new seal into each side of the hub using finger pressure or a suitable driver that bears on the outer rim, setting them flush with the hub **(see illustration)**. Smear the seal lips with grease.

10 If removed fit the disc (see Section 4), and on ABS models the sensor rotor (Section 20).

11 Clean the brake disc using acetone or brake system cleaner, then install the wheel (see Section 14).

> **HAYNES HiNT** ***Heating the outside of the bearing housing with a hot air gun will expand it and make the bearing easier to remove and fit. Putting the new bearings in the freezer for a while will contract them and make them easier to fit.***

Rear wheel bearings

12 Remove the wheel (see Section 15). Set the wheel on wood blocks. A caged ball bearing is fitted in each side of the wheel on WR-R models. On WR-X, MT and YZF-R models a caged ball bearing is fitted in the right-hand side of the wheel, and two caged ball bearings are in the left side of the wheel.

13 Inspect the seals and bearings – check that each bearing inner race turns smoothly and that the outer race is a tight fit in the hub (see *Tools and Workshop Tips* (Section 5) in the Reference Section). Note: Do not remove the bearings unless they are going to be replaced with new ones.

14 If new components are needed it is best to remove the disc (see Section 8), and on models with ABS the sensor rotor (see Section 20), to prevent them being damaged or distorted during bearing removal.

15 Lever out the bearing seal from the each side of the hub using a flat-bladed screwdriver or a seal hook **(see illustration 16.4)**. Take care not to damage the hub. New seals must be fitted on reassembly.

16 Set the wheel with the right-hand (disc) side facing down. Move the bearing spacer aside to expose the inner race on the lower bearing **(see illustration 16.5a)**. Using a suitable drift inserted through the centre of the upper bearings drive the lower bearing from the hub, moving the spacer around and relocating the drift so it's driven out squarely **(see illustration 16.5b)**. The bearing spacer will also come out. Turn the wheel over so that the remaining bearing(s) face(s) down. Drive the bearing(s) out of the wheel using a socket on the inner race of the (inner) bearing and an extension bar, and drive the bearing(s) out. If you can't move the spacer, or if you can't get sufficient purchase with the drift, remove the bearings using an internal expanding puller with slide-hammer attachment, which can be obtained commercially – select the correct attachment and locate it between the inner race of the bearing and the spacer, then tighten the inner bolt to expand and lock the puller. Attach the slide-hammer, hold the wheel firmly down and jar the bearing out.

17 Thoroughly clean the hub area of the wheel and inspect the bearing housings for damage. If a housing is damaged, consult a Yamaha dealer or wheel specialist before reassembling the wheel.

18 Fit the new bearings with the marked side facing out. Drive the right-hand bearing in using a bearing driver or suitable socket that bears only on the outer race, and make sure the bearing fits squarely and all the way onto its seat **(see illustration 16.7)**. Alternatively draw it in using a drawbolt arrangement (see *Tools and Workshop Tips*).

19 Turn the wheel over then fit the bearing spacer and the other new bearing(s).

20 Fit a new seal into the each side of the hub using finger pressure or a suitable driver that bears on the outer rim, setting it flush with the hub **(see illustration 16.9)**. Smear the seal lips with grease.

21 If removed fit the disc (see Section 8), and on ABS models the sensor rotor (Section 20).

22 Clean the brake disc using acetone or brake system cleaner, then install the wheel (see Section 15).

17 Tyres

General information

1 The wheels fitted on all WR models are designed for tubed tyres only. The wheels on MT and YZF-R models are designed for tubeless tyres only. Tyre sizes are given in the Specifications at the beginning of this Chapter.

2 Refer to the *Pre-ride checks* listed at the beginning of this manual for tyre maintenance, and to Chapter 1 for wheel maintenance, particularly on the spoke wheels on WR models.

Fitting new tyres

3 When selecting new tyres, refer to the tyre information in the Owner's Handbook. Ensure that front and rear tyre types are compatible, the correct size and correct speed rating; if necessary seek advice from a Yamaha dealer or tyre fitting specialist **(see illustration)**.

4 It is recommended that tyres are fitted by a motorcycle tyre specialist rather than attempted in the home workshop, particularly on MT and YZF-R models – the beads on tubeless tyres are difficult to break from the rim, and are tight to fit, and you could end up damaging the wheel. Also a specialist will be able to balance the wheels after tyre fitting.

5 Note that punctured tubeless tyres can in some cases be repaired, but you should always seek the advice of, and if a repair is possible entrust the work to, a Yamaha dealer or tyre specialist.

18 Drive chain

Cleaning

1 Refer to Chapter 1 for details of routine cleaning with the chain installed on the sprockets.

2 If the chain is extremely dirty remove it from the motorcycle and soak it in paraffin (kerosene) for approximately five or six minutes, then clean it using a soft brush.

Caution: Don't use petrol, solvent or other cleaning fluids that might damage its internal sealing properties. Don't use high-pressure water. Remove the chain, wipe it off, then blow dry it with compressed air immediately. The entire process shouldn't take longer than ten minutes – if it does, the O-rings in the chain rollers could be damaged.

Removal and installation

Note: *The original equipment drive chain, endless on WR models and with a clip type master link on MT and YZF-R models, may have been replaced by a chain with riveted soft master link at some point. In this event refer to the section on chains in* 'Tools and Workshop Tips' *in the Reference Section at the end of this manual.*

WR models

3 Remove the front sprocket (see Section 19). Remove the swingarm (see Chapter 5). Remove the chain.

4 Installation is the reverse of removal.

MT and YZF-R models

5 Support the motorcycle so that the rear wheel is off the ground. Tie the front brake on. Remove the front sprocket cover **(see illustration 19.1a or b)**. Position the joining link at the back of the rear sprocket by rotating the back wheel.

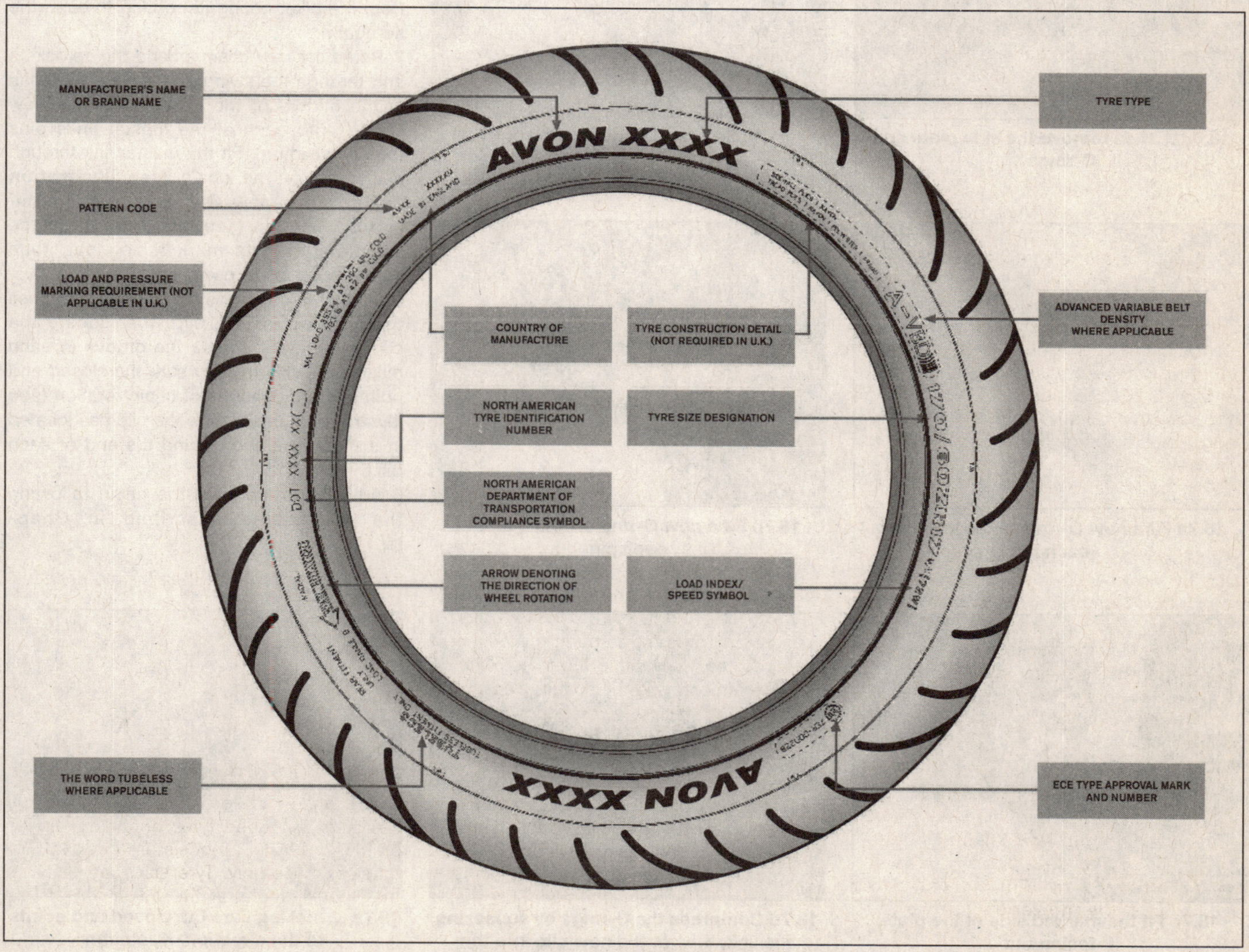

17.3 Common tyre sidewall markings

18.6a Release the open end of the master link with pliers...

18.6b ...and slide it off

18.6c If the side plate is tight use a punch to drive the master link pins out...

18.6d ...then remove the side plate and O-rings...

18.6e ...and draw the link out

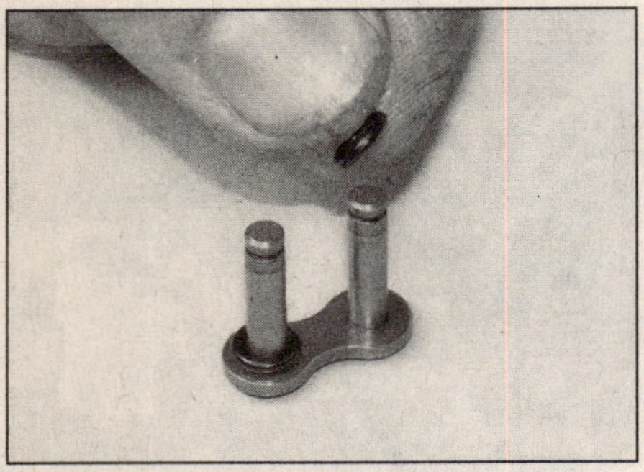

18.7a Fit a new O-ring all the way onto each pin

18.7b Fit a new O-ring onto the end of each pin

6 Release and remove the clip from the master link **(see illustration)**. Remove the sideplate and the O-rings **(see illustrations)**. Withdraw the master link from the inside and remove the O-rings **(see illustration)**. New O-rings must be fitted, along with a new clip, which all come in a kit. Remove the chain from the bike, noting its routing through the swingarm.

7 Route the new chain around the sprockets and through the swingarm, leaving the ends in the middle of the lower run. Fit a new O-ring onto each of the master links pins **(see illustration)**. Fit the master link through each end of the chain **(see illustration 18.6e)**. Fit a new O-ring onto the outer end of each pin **(see illustration)**. Fit the sideplate with its mark facing out, then squeeze the plate using grips and a socket as shown to compress the O-rings to expose the grooves for the clip, then locate the clip and slide it across the groove in each master link pin, making sure the closed end points in the direction of chain rotation **(see illustrations)**. Make sure the clip has located in the grooves and around the end of each pin.6

8 Adjust and lubricate the chain following the procedures described in Chapter 1.

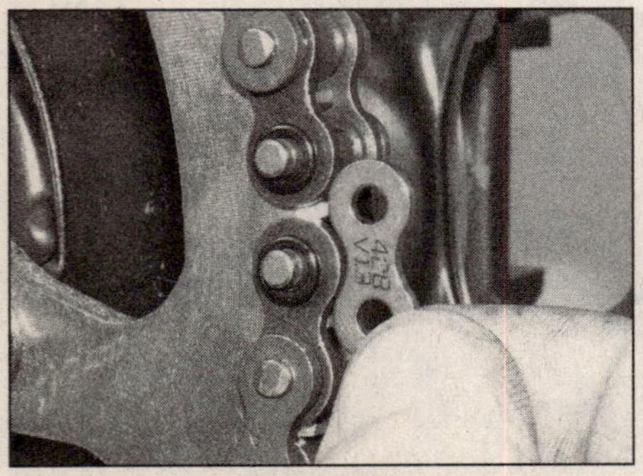

18.7c Fit the marked side of the plate facing out

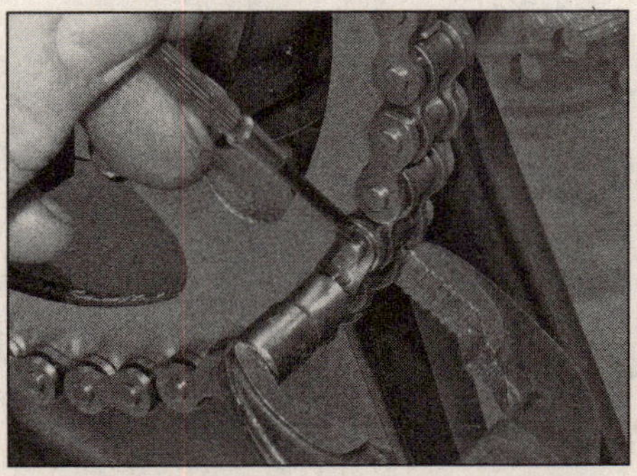

18.7d Compress the O-rings by squeezing the link, then fit the new clip into the grooves and push it on so it clicks round the pins...

18.7e ...making sure the closed end points to the direction of rotation

19.1a Front sprocket cover bolts (arrowed) – WR and MT models

19.1b Front sprocket cover bolts (arrowed) – YZF-R models

19 Sprockets

Front sprocket cover

1 Unscrew the bolts securing the front sprocket cover and remove it, on WR models releasing the sidestand switch wire from the its channel in the top of the cover **(see illustrations)**.

2 When fitting the cover, on WR models take care not to trap the neutral switch wire between the cover and the crankcase, and route the sidestand switch wire in its channel in the top of the cover. On MT and YZF-R models take care not to trap the sidestand switch wire between the cover and the crankcase.

Sprocket check

3 On YZF-R models remove the front sprocket cover **(see illustration 19.1a or b)**. Check the wear pattern on both sprockets (see Chapter 1, Section 1). If the sprocket teeth are worn excessively, replace the chain and both sprockets as a set – worn sprockets can ruin a new drive chain and vice versa. Whenever the sprockets are inspected, the drive chain should be inspected also (see Chapter 1).

4 Adjust and lubricate the chain following the procedures described in Chapter 1.

Sprocket removal and installation

Front sprocket

5 Remove the front sprocket cover (see Step 1). Tie the front brake on using a cable-tie or suitable alternative.

6 Unscrew the sprocket retainer plate bolts **(see illustration)**.

7 Fully slacken the drive chain as described in Chapter 1. If the rear sprocket is being removed as well, remove the rear wheel now to create full slack (see Section 15). Otherwise disengage the chain from the rear sprocket if required to provide more slack.

8 Turn the sprocket retainer plate to unlock it from the splines then slide it off the shaft **(see illustration)**. Slide the chain and sprocket off the input shaft then slip the sprocket out of the chain **(see illustration)**.

9 Engage the new sprocket with the chain, making sure the marked side is facing out, and slide it on the shaft **(see illustration 19.8b)**. Fit the retainer plate **(see illustration 19.8a)**, then turn it in the groove so it is locked in the splines and the bolt holes align **(see illustration)**.

10 If the rear wheel was removed, change

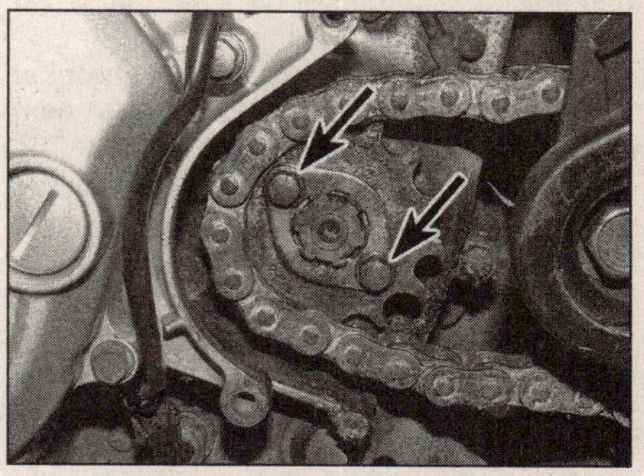

19.6 Unscrew the bolts (arrowed)

19.8a Release and remove the retainer...

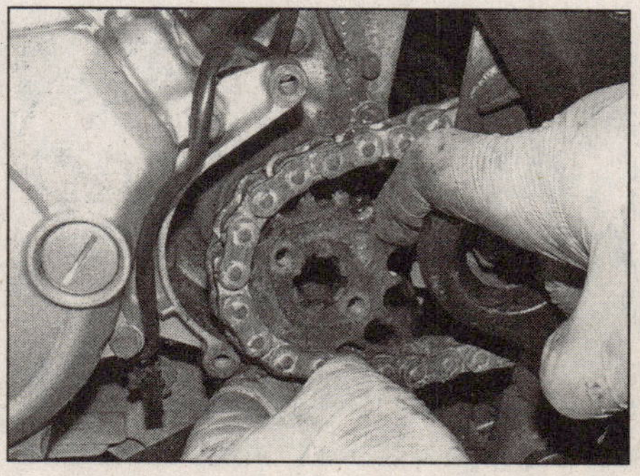

19.8b ...then draw the sprocket off the shaft and disengage the chain

19.9 Turn the plate in the groove so the splines and bolt holes align

19.14 Rear sprocket bolts – WR models

the sprocket now and install the wheel (see Section 15). If the chain was merely disengaged, fit it back onto the rear sprocket. Take up the slack in the chain.

11 Fit the retainer plate bolts and tighten them to the torque setting specified at the beginning of the Chapter **(see illustration 19.6)**.

12 Fit the sprocket cover (see Step 2). Adjust and lubricate the chain following the procedures described in Chapter 1.

Rear sprocket

13 Remove the rear wheel (see Section 15).

14 Unscrew the bolts (WR models) or nuts (MT and YZF-R models) securing the sprocket to the hub **(see illustration)**. Remove the sprocket. Note: If the sprocket is not being replaced with a new one, mark its outside face with a scratch, or dab of paint, so that it can be refitted the same way round.

15 Check the condition of the sprocket bolts or studs and nuts and replace them all with new ones if any are damaged. The studs on MT and YZF-R models can be removed using a stud tool, or by threading two nuts onto each stud and locking them together, then unscrewing the stud using the bottom nut. Apply a suitable thread locking compound to the threads of the new studs and tighten them into the sprocket coupling.

16 Fit the sprocket onto the hub with the stamped mark facing out. Fit the bolts or nuts and tighten them evenly and in a criss-cross sequence to the torque setting specified at the beginning of the Chapter for your model.

17 Install the rear wheel (see Section 15).

20 Anti-lock brake system (ABS) – MT125A and YZF-RA models

Note: *Special tool: To access and read ABS fault codes and for information on the fault represented the Yamaha diagnostic tool, part No. 90890-03231, is required. The tool is available from Yamaha, however it is very expensive – over four hundred pounds (in the UK) according to one Yamaha dealer. For this reason it is recommended that the bike is taken to a Yamaha dealer for the system to be tested, if necessary. If you decide to purchase the tool follow the instructions supplied with it.*

ABS operation

1 The anti-lock brake system (ABS) prevents the wheels from locking up under hard braking or on uneven road surfaces. A sensor on each wheel transmits information about the speed of rotation to the ABS control unit; if the unit senses that a wheel is about to lock, it releases brake pressure to that wheel momentarily, preventing a skid.

2 The anti-lock system is self-checking and is activated when the ignition switch is turned on – you may hear a clicking as the self-diagnosis routine is performed, or feel a pulse in the lever or pedal if applied. The ABS indicator light in the instrument cluster will come on when the ignition is turned on, and if the system is all good will go off when the bike is ridden above 6 mph (10 kph). Note: If the ABS indicator light does not come on initially there is a fault in the system – see below.

3 If the indicator light remains on or flashes, or comes on or flashes while the machine is being ridden, there is a fault in the system and the ABS function will be switched off – the brakes will still function but in normal mode. A fault code will be registered and stored in the ECU. If a fault is indicated stop the bike and turn the ignition off, then turn it back on again and ride the bike – if the light goes out the fault has cleared itself and can be considered a temporary glitch in the system. If the fault persists, next check the ABS fuses (see Chapter 8). If the fuses are good check the wheel speed sensor and modulator wiring connectors are securely connected and corrosion free **(see illustration 20.5a and b and 20.17)**, and check the wiring for any obvious breaks or damage – refer to Chapter 8 for information on electrical fault finding and for the wiring diagram for your model. Also check that the wheel speed sensor heads and rotors are clean and free of corrosion, and that there is no debris caught between the sensor rotor pulsers and that the rotor is not damaged or deformed in any way – see below for sensor and rotor removal and installation. If no problems can be found you need to retrieve the fault code.

4 To retrieve any stored fault codes, the diagnostic tool is required (see Special Tool above). If you purchase the tool follow the instructions supplied with it **(see illustration)**. Otherwise take the bike to a Yamaha dealer and get them to diagnose and repair the fault. **Note:** *The ABS indicator may diagnose a fault if tyre sizes other than those specified by Yamaha are fitted, if the tyre pressures are incorrect, if the machine has been run continuously over bumpy roads, if the front wheel comes off the ground whilst riding (wheelie) or if the machine is on an auxiliary stand with the engine running and the rear wheel turning.*

ABS components

Note: *Take great care not to damage the wheel sensor head or sensor rotor surface, or use magnetic tools near them, and take care not to subject them to any sort of impact. Replace the rotor screws with new ones if removed.*

Wheel speed sensors

5 Remove the right-hand side cover (see Chapter 7). Trace the wheel sensor wiring to the connector and disconnect it **(see illustrations)**. Feed the wiring down to the

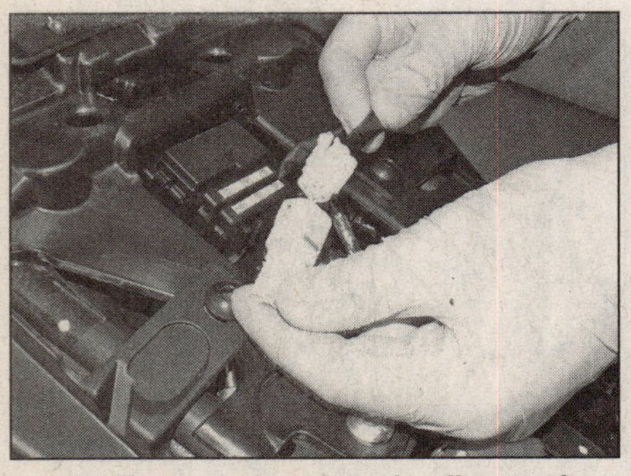

20.4 The tool plugs into the diagnostic wiring connector with a blanking cap

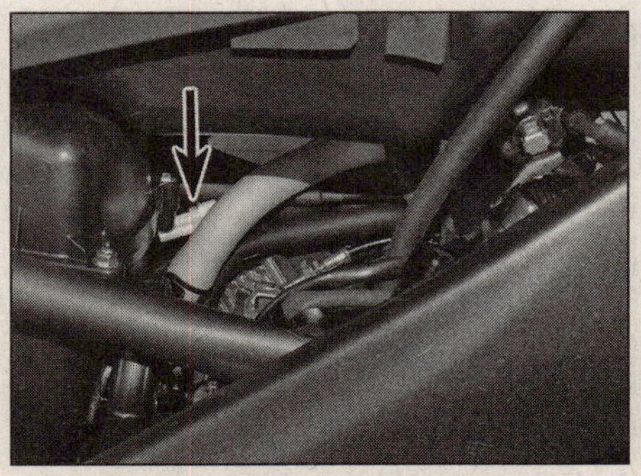

20.5a Front wheel speed sensor wiring connector (arrowed)

20.5b Rear wheel speed sensor wiring connector (arrowed)

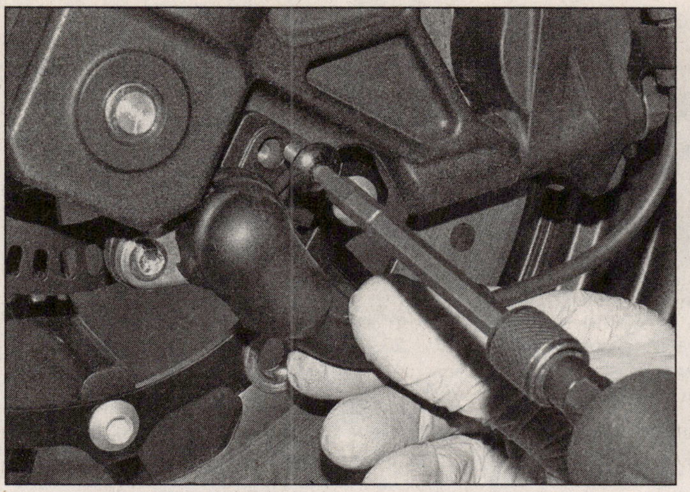

20.6 Remove the cover from the front wheel sensor

20.7 Removing the sensor

sensor, releasing any ties and guides, and noting its routing – front wheel sensor wire is held by a guide secured by the lower caliper mounting bolt, which must be unscrewed **(see illustration 2.12c)**.

6 When removing the front wheel sensor first undo the sensor cover screw and remove the cover **(see illustration)**.

7 Undo the sensor screw and remove the sensor **(see illustration)**.

8 Make sure the tip of the sensor and its mounting surfaces are clean and show no signs of damage or distortion **(see illustration 20.7)**. Clean the threads of the sensor screw and apply some fresh threadlock. Fit the sensor and tighten the screw to the torque setting specified at the beginning of the Chapter. Feed the wiring to the connector, routing and securing it as noted on removal – tighten the front caliper bolt to the specified torque after securing the guide **(see illustration 2.12c)**. Fit the cover over the front sensor **(see illustration 20.6)**.

Sensor rotors

9 Remove the relevant wheel (see Section 14 or Section 15).

10 Undo the rotor screws and lift the rotor off **(see illustration)**.

11 Make sure there is no dirt or corrosion where the rotor seats on the hub – if it does not sit flat the signals from the sensor could be distorted. Make sure the rotor is clean and shows no signs of damage or distortion. Fit the rotor with the A mark facing out **(see illustration)**. Fit new screws and apply a non-permanent thread locking compound, and tighten them to the torque setting specified at the beginning of the Chapter.

12 Install the wheel.

Modulator

13 Remove the seats and the seat cowls (see Chapter 7).

14 On MT models undo the eight tail cover screws **(see illustration)**.

20.10 Sensor rotor screws

20.11 The A must face out

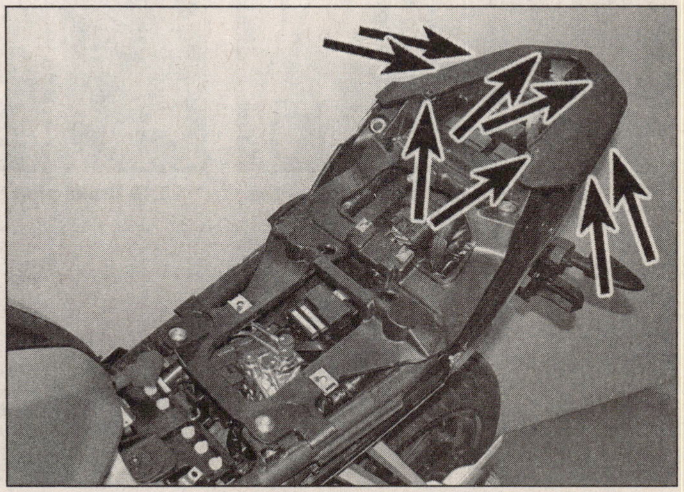

20.14 Undo the screws (arrowed) – the cover can stay in place

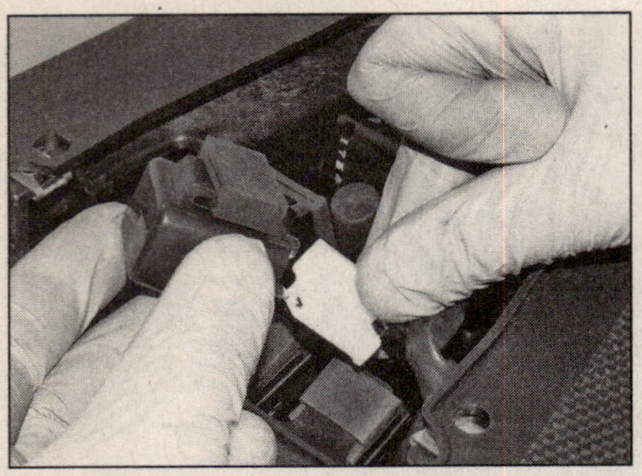

20.15a Displace, disconnect and remove the turn signal relay

20.15b TO sensor wiring connector (arrowed)

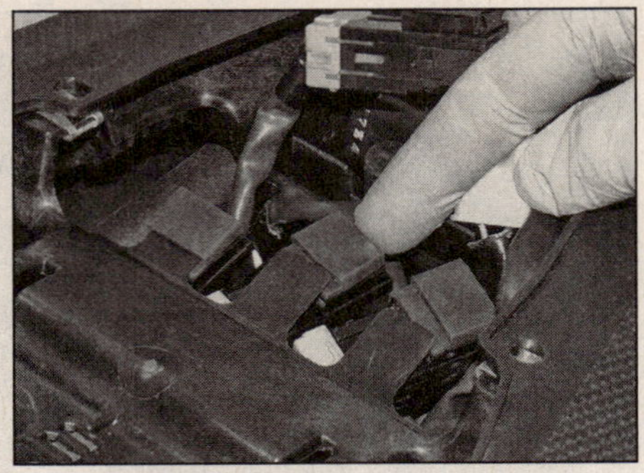

20.15c Displace the relays from their mounts

15 Disconnect the turn signal relay wiring connector and remove it **(see illustration)**. Disconnect the tip-over sensor wiring connector **(see illustration)**. Displace the remaining relays from their mounts **(see illustration)**.

16 Undo the five screws securing the tray and manoeuvre it out **(see illustrations)**.

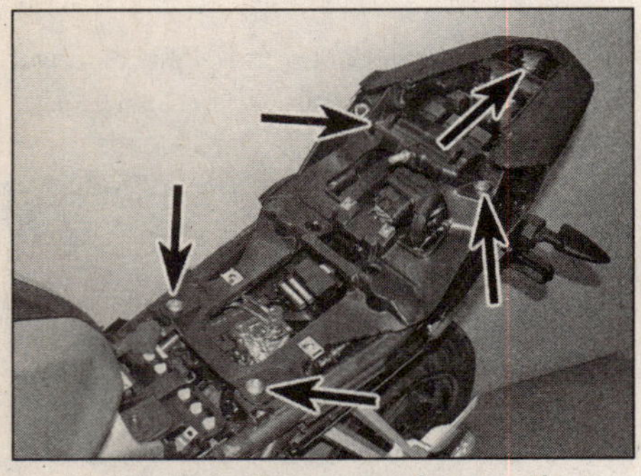

20.16a Undo the screws (arrowed)...

20.16b ...and remove the tray

17 Release the locking lever on the modulator wiring connector and disconnect it **(see illustration)**.

18 Cover the area around the modulator with clean rag to prevent damage to paintwork in the event that brake fluid is spilled.

19 Note the alignment of the brake pipes on the top of the modulator **(see illustration)**. Unscrew the brake pipe banjo bolts and detach the pipes. New sealing washers must be used.

20 Unscrew the modulator mounting bolts and remove the modulator, taking care not to snag it on the pipes **(see illustration)**. Note the collars fitted in the mounting rubbers. Replace the rubbers with new ones if necessary.

21 Seal the end of each pipe and plug the holes in the modulator to prevent dirt entering the system.

22 Installation is the reverse of removal, noting the following:

- Make sure the brake pipes are correctly aligned. Use a new sealing washer on each side of each pipe banjo union and tighten the banjo bolts to the torque setting specified at the beginning of the Chapter.
- Make sure the wiring connector is secure.
- Refer to Section 11 to fill and bleed the system. Check there are no fluid leaks and test the operation of the brakes before riding the bike.

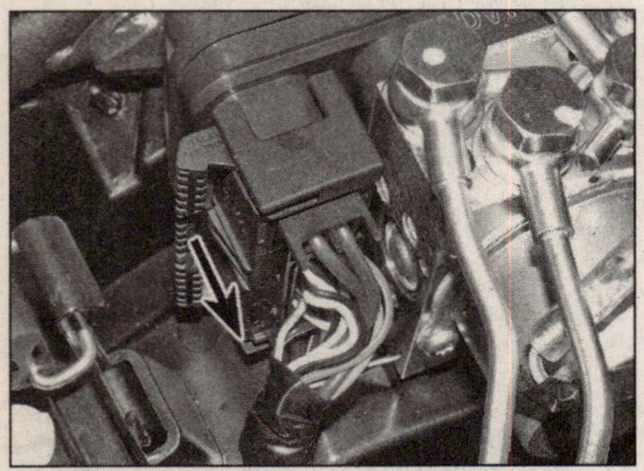

20.17 Pull the lever in the direction of the arrow to release the connector

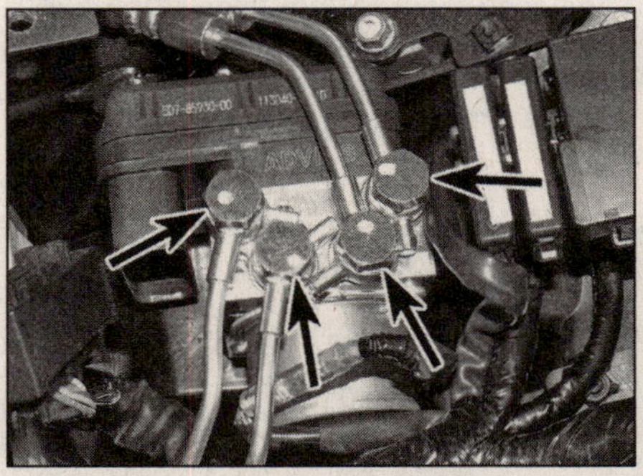

20.19 Brake pipe banjo bolts (arrowed)

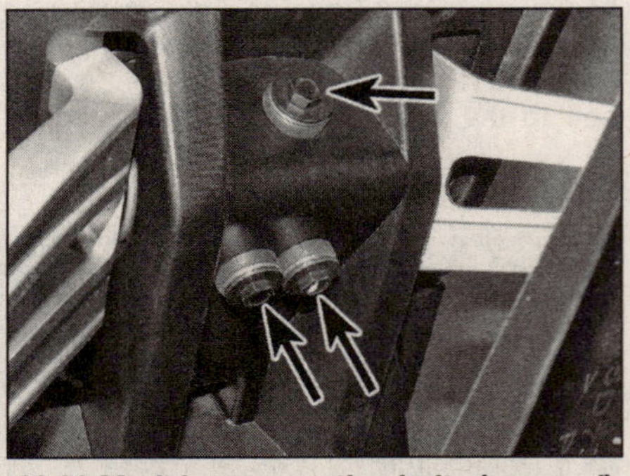

20.20 Modulator mounting bolts (arrowed)

Chapter 7
Bodywork

Contents

Degrees of difficulty

Easy, suitable for novice with little experience	**Fairly easy,** suitable for beginner with some experience	**Fairly difficult,** suitable for competent DIY mechanic	**Difficult,** suitable for experienced DIY mechanic	**Very difficult,** suitable for expert DIY or professional

1 General Information

1 This Chapter covers the procedures necessary to remove and install the body panels and related parts. Since many service and repair operations require the removal of the body panels, the procedures are grouped here and referred to from other Chapters.
2 In the case of damage to the body panels, it is usually necessary to remove the broken component and replace it with a new (or used) one. The material from which the panels are made does not lend itself to conventional repair techniques. There are, however, some shops that specialise in 'plastic welding', so it may be worthwhile seeking the advice of one of these specialists before consigning an expensive panel to the bin. There are also repair kits available for DIY use.
3 When attempting to remove any body panel, first study it closely, noting any fasteners and associated fittings, to be sure of returning everything to its correct place on installation. Once the evident fasteners have been removed, try to remove the panel as described but DO NOT FORCE IT – if it will not release, check that all fasteners have been removed and try again. Where a panel engages another by means of tabs, be careful not to break the tab or its mating slot or to damage the paintwork. Remember that a few moments of patience at this stage will save you a lot of money in replacing broken panels!
4 When installing a body panel, first study it closely, noting any fasteners and associated fittings removed with it, to be sure of returning everything to its correct place. Check that all fasteners are in good condition, including all trim clips and rubber mounts – any that are worn or damaged must be replaced with new ones. Check that all mounting brackets are straight, and repair them or replace them with new ones if necessary before installing the panel.
5 Be careful not to overtighten any of the fasteners or the panel may break (not always immediately).

Trim clips

6 The trim clips fitted have a centre pin which you push into the body of the clip, then you draw the clip out of the panel.
7 To install the clip, first expand the pawls of the clip body and push the centre pin back out. Now fit the clip body into its hole, then push the centre pin in so that it is flush with the clip head. The clip should now be locked in place.

2 WR models

Seat

1 Unscrew the bolt on each side **(see illustration)**. Lift the back of the seat and draw the seat back and off.

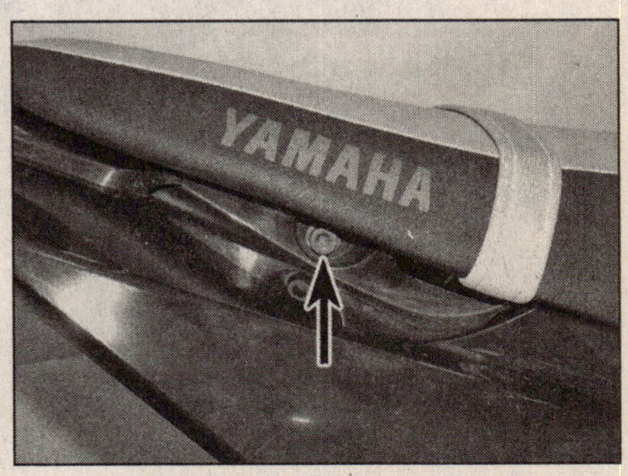

2.1 There is a bolt (arrowed) on each side

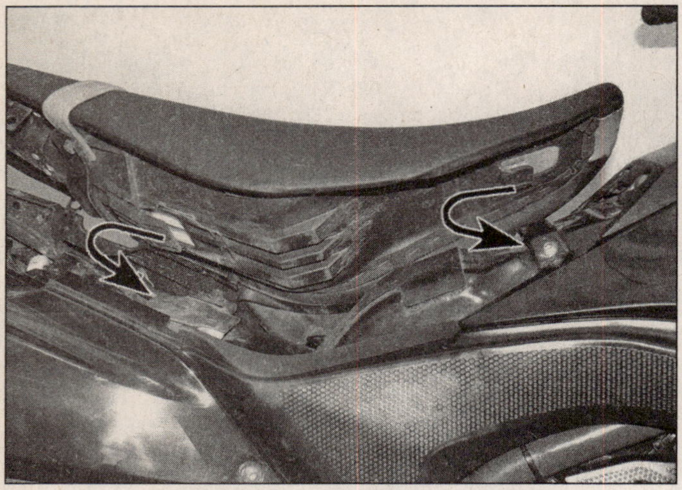

2.2 Slide the tabs under the brackets

2.4a Undo the screws (arrowed) ...

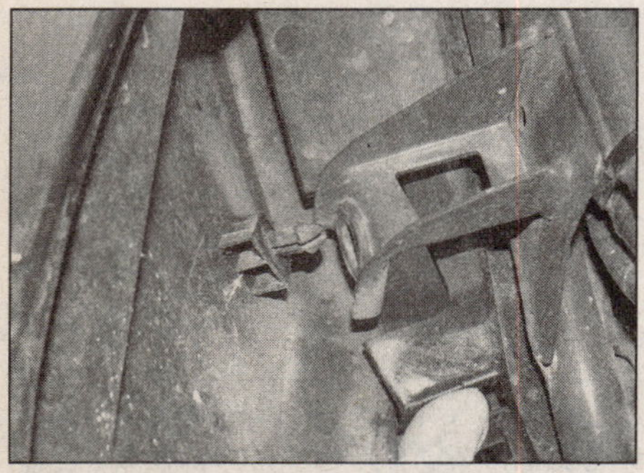

2.4b ... pull the peg out of the grommet ...

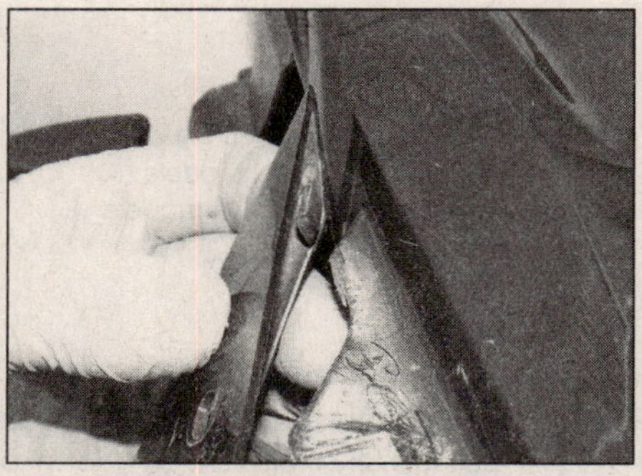

2.4c ... and release the tab

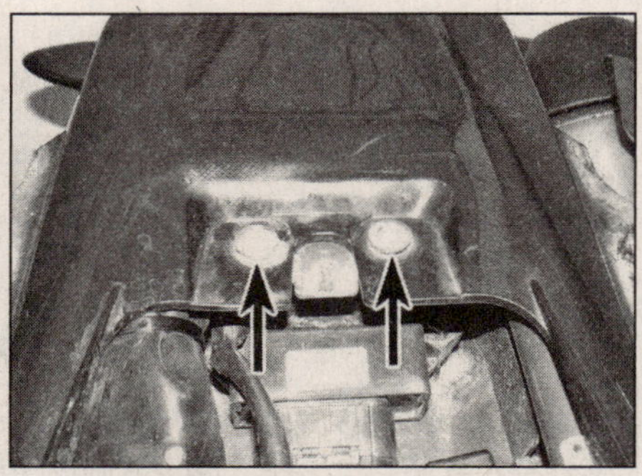

2.7 Tail cover screws (arrowed)

2 Installation is the reverse of removal – make sure the tabs locate correctly under the brackets **(see illustration)**.

Side covers

3 Remove the seat.

4 Undo the two screws **(see illustration)**. Carefully pull the panel away to release the peg from the grommet, then slide it to the rear to release the tab at the back **(see illustrations)**.

5 Installation is the reverse of removal. Make sure the grommet is in good condition.

Tail cover

6 Remove the side covers.

7 Undo the two screws, noting the collars **(see illustration)**. Draw the cover back to release the slot at the back from the tab **(see illustration 2.8)**.

8 Installation is the reverse of removal – slide the slot on the cover over the tab **(see illustration)**.

Frame covers

9 Undo the two screws and remove the cover **(see illustration)**.

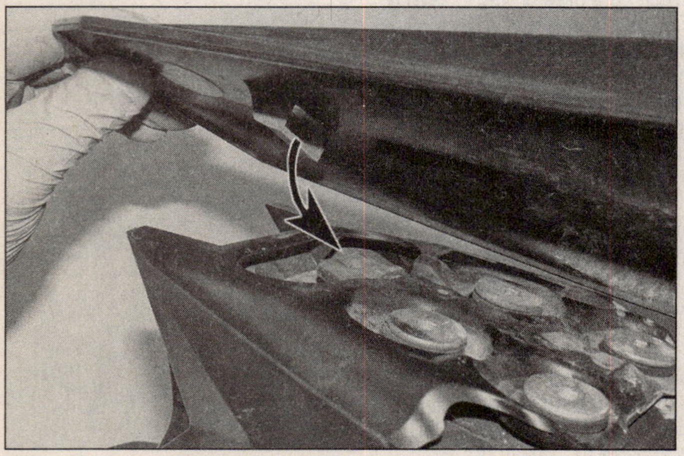

2.8 Locate the slot over the tab

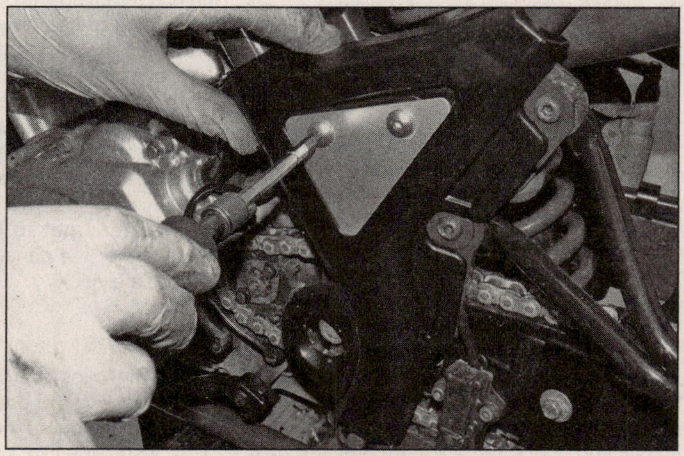

2.9 Removing the frame cover

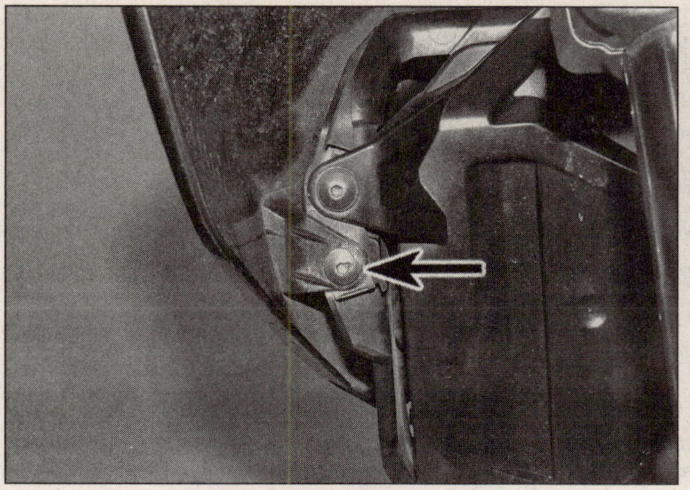

2.12a Front screw (arrowed)

2.12b Side screws (arrowed)

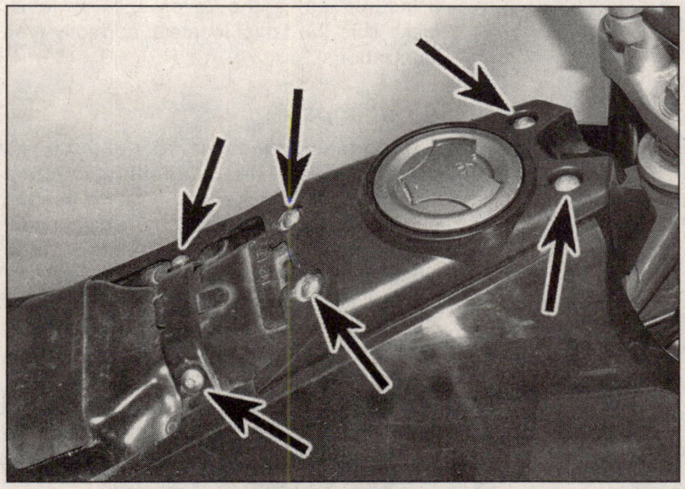

2.12c Top screws (arrowed)

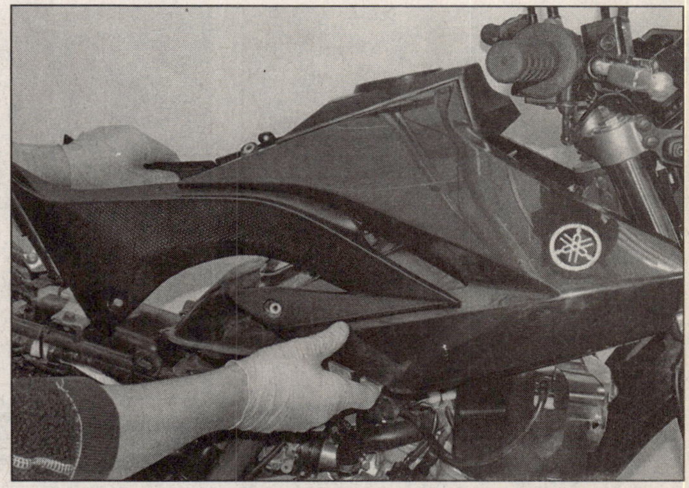

2.13 Remove the filler cap and lift the cover off

10 Installation is the reverse of removal.

Fuel tank cover

11 Remove the seat.

12 Undo the screw on each side at the front, the two screws on each side, and the six screws on the top **(see illustrations)**.

13 Remove the fuel filler cap, then carefully lift the tank cover off the tank **(see illustration)**. Refit the filler cap to the tank.

14 Installation is the reverse of removal.

Front mudguard(s)

15 To remove the main mudguard on all models, release the speed sensor wire from the right-hand side **(see illustration)**. Unscrew the nut and remove the front bolt **(see illustration)**. Unscrew the four bolts on the underside and remove the mudguard **(see illustration)**.

16 To remove the lower mudguard on WR-X

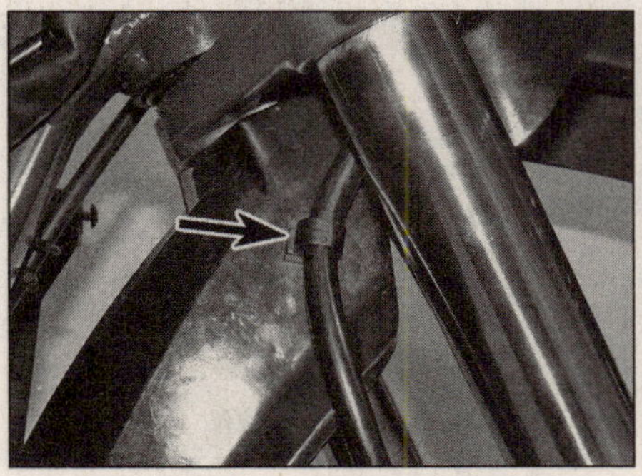

2.15a Release the guide (arrowed)

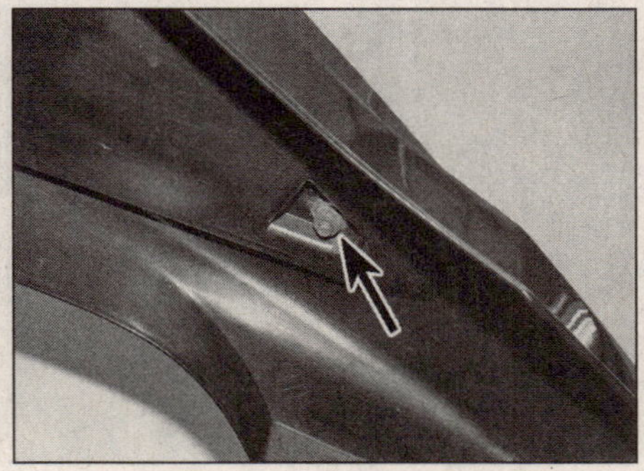

2.15b Unscrew the nut (arrowed) and remove the bolt

2.15c Unscrew the four bolts

2.16 Right-hand mudguard screws (arrowed) and speed sensor wiring guide

models undo the two screws on each side, noting the wiring guide on the right-hand side **(see illustration)**. Note the collars in the grommets.

17 Installation is the reverse of removal. Make sure the grommets are in good condition.

2.18 Mirror locknut (arrowed)

Mirrors

18 Slacken the locknut then turn the mirror to unscrew it **(see illustration)** – turn the right-hand mirror clockwise and the left-hand mirror anti-clockwise.

19 Installation is the reverse of removal – thread the mirror all the way in, then back it out to position it as required, and tighten the locknut.

3 MT models

Seats

1 To remove the rider's seat, unlock it using the ignition key, then lift the rear of the seat and remove it, noting how the tab at the front locates under the tank bracket **(see illustration)**.

2 To remove the passenger seat, remove the blanking cap at the front and unscrew the nut **(see illustration)**. Remove the seat, noting how the tab at the back locates in the hole.

3 Installation is the reverse of removal. make sure the tab(s) locate(s) correctly **(see illustrations)**.

Air scoops

4 Undo the screw at the front and the two screws on the side **(see illustrations)**. Carefully pull the air scoop away to free the pegs from the grommets, then disconnect the turn signal wiring connector **(see illustrations)**.

5 Installation is the reverse of removal. Make sure the grommets are in good condition.

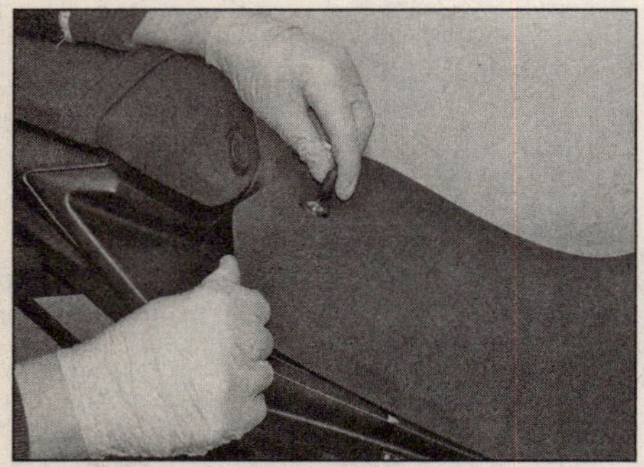

3.1 Release the lock then lift and remove the seat

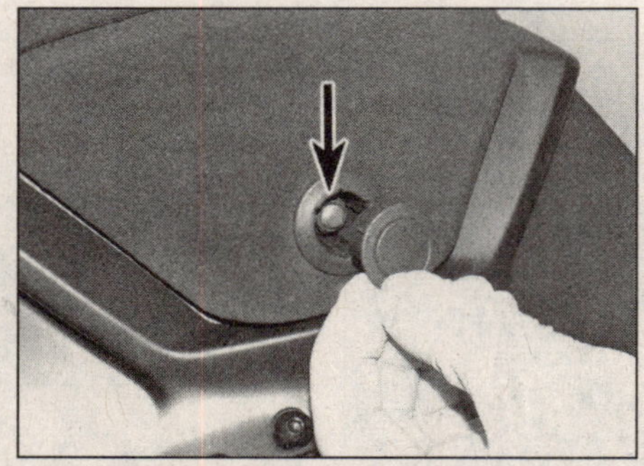

3.2 Remove the cap then unscrew the nut (arrowed)

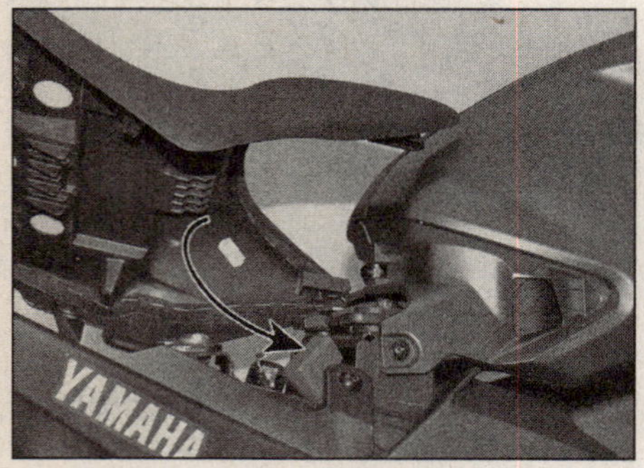

3.3a Slide the tab on the rider's seat under the fuel tank bracket

3.3b Slide the tab on the passenger seat into the hole

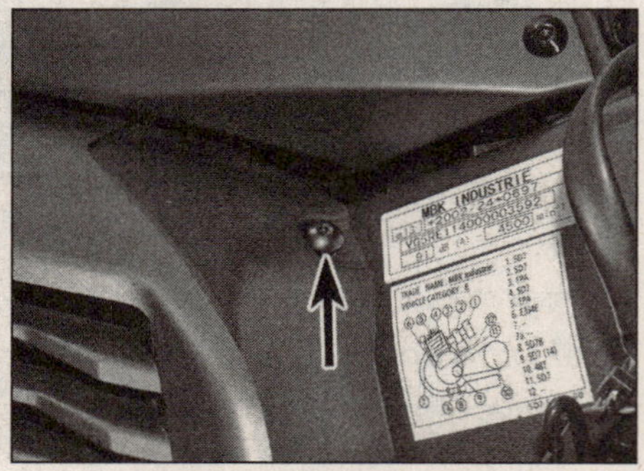

3.4a Front screw (arrowed)

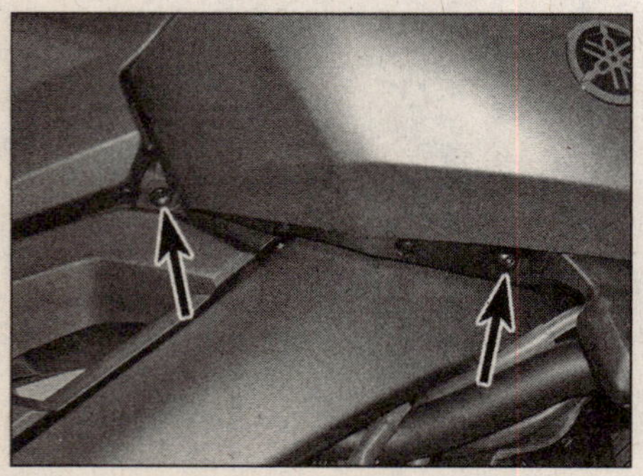

3.4b Side screws (arrowed)

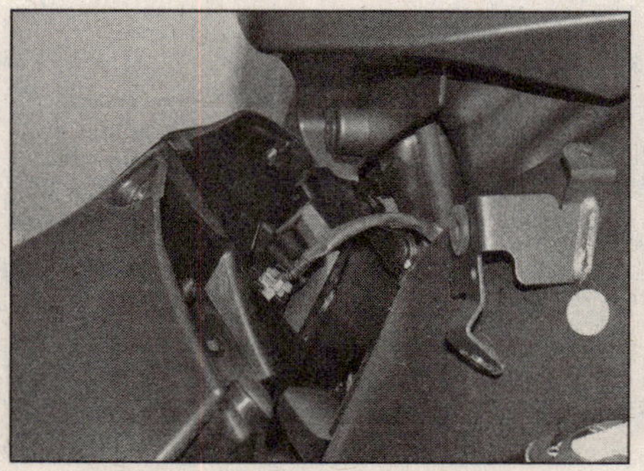

3.4c Release the pegs from the grommets...

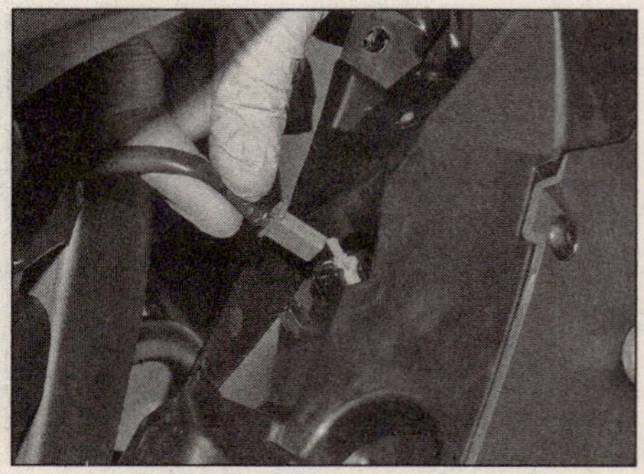

3.4d ...and disconnect the wiring connector

3.8 Undo the screws (arrowed)

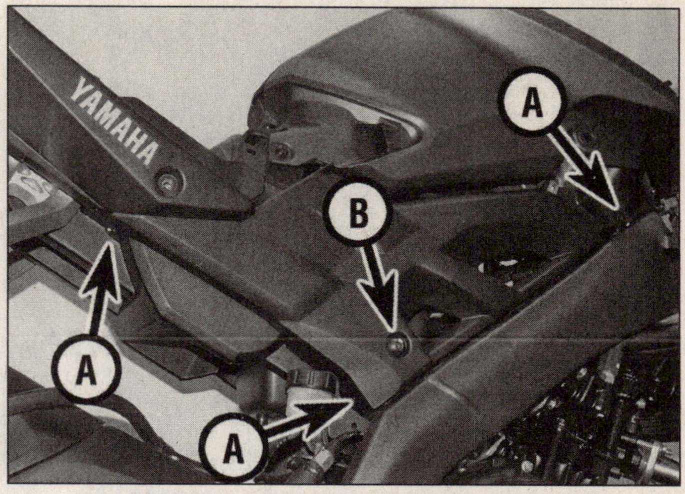

3.9a Side cover trim clips (A) and screw (B)

Side covers

6 Remove the rider's seat.
7 Remove the air scoop.
8 Undo the three screws securing the front of the seat cowl **(see illustration)**.
9 Release the three trim clips and undo the screw, then carefully pull the front of the seat cowl away and remove the side cover **(see illustrations)**.
10 Installation is the reverse of removal.

Fuel tank cover

11 Remove the rider's seat.
12 Remove the air scoops.
13 Remove the cap from the nut at the front, then unscrew the nut **(see illustration)**.
14 Undo the screw on each side **(see illustration)**.
15 Remove the fuel filler cap, then carefully lift the tank cover off the tank **(see illustration)**. Refit the filler cap to the tank.
16 Installation is the reverse of removal.

Seat cowls

17 Remove the seats.
18 Undo the five screws, then draw the cowl off to release the tabs on the underside **(see illustration)**.
19 Installation is the reverse of removal – make sure the tabs locate correctly.

3.9b Ease the cover out from behind the seat cowl

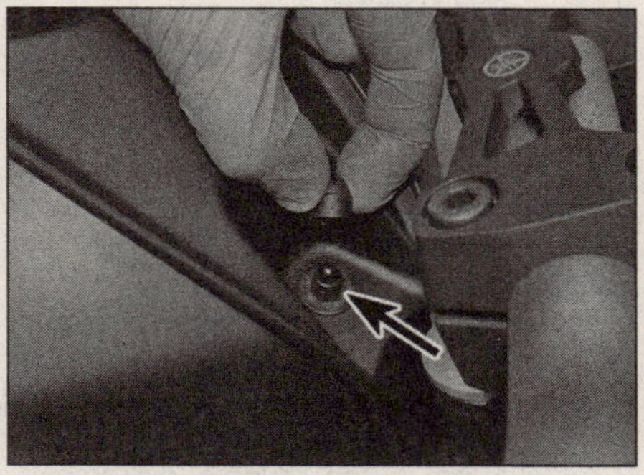

3.13 Unscrew the nut (arrowed)

3.14 Side screw (arrowed)

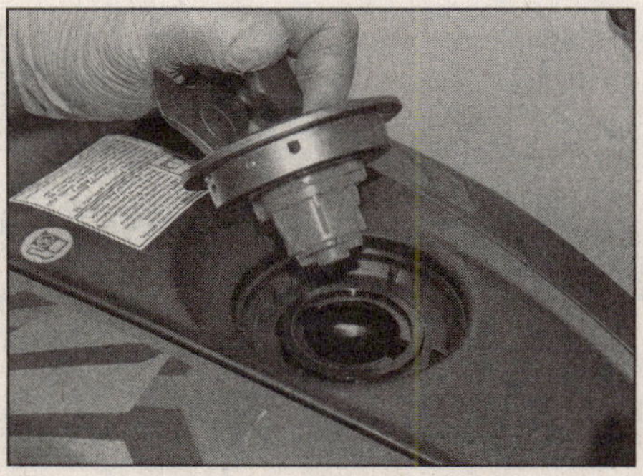

3.15 Remove the cap to release the cover

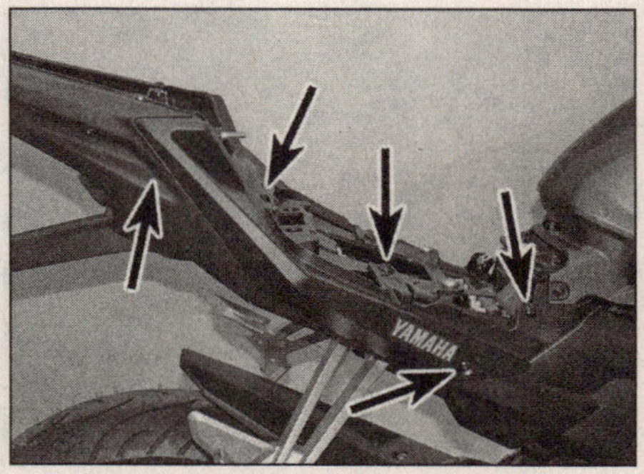

3.18a Seat cowl screws (arrowed)

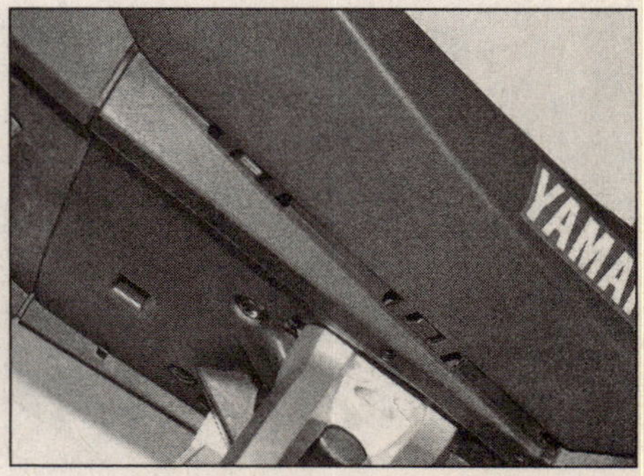

3.18b Draw the tabs out of the slots

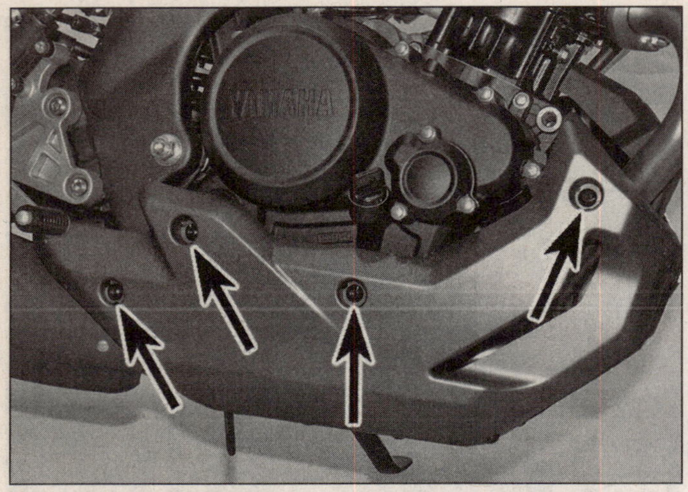
3.20a Belly-pan screws (arrowed) – right-hand side

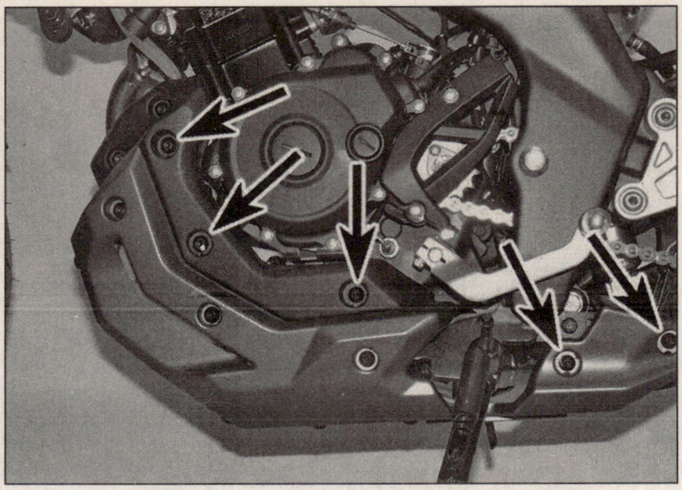
3.20b Belly-pan screws (arrowed) – left-hand side

3.22 Mudguard screws (arrowed)

Belly-pan

20 Undo the four screws on the right-hand side and the five on the left and remove the belly-pan **(see illustrations)**.
21 Installation is the reverse of removal.

Front mudguard

22 Undo the three screws on each side and remove the mudguard **(see illustration)**.
23 Installation is the reverse of removal.

Mirrors

24 Unscrew the mirror using the hex at the base **(see illustration 2.18)**.
25 Installation is the reverse of removal – thread the mirror all the way in, then back it out to position it as required, and tighten the locknut.

4 YZF-R models

Seats

1 To remove the rider's seat, unlock it using the ignition key, then lift the rear of the seat and remove it, noting how the tab at the front locates under the tank bracket **(see illustration 3.1)**.
2 To remove the passenger seat, remove the blanking cap at the front and unscrew the nut **(see illustration 3.2)**. Remove the seat, noting how the tab at the back locates in the hole.
3 Installation is the reverse of removal. Make sure the tab(s) locate(s) correctly **(see illustrations 3.3a and b)**.

Side covers

4 Remove the rider's seat (see Step 1).
5 Undo the three screws, noting the collars with the middle and rear screws, and remove the panel **(see illustrations)**.
6 Installation is the reverse of removal.

Fuel tank cover

7 Remove the rider's seat.
8 Remove the cap from the nut at the front, then unscrew the nut **(see illustration 3.13)**.
9 Undo the screw on each side **(see illustration 3.14)**.
10 Remove the fuel filler cap, then carefully lift the tank cover off the tank **(see illustration 3.15)**. Refit the filler cap to the tank.
11 Installation is the reverse of removal.

Seat cowls

12 Remove the seats (see Steps 1 and 2).
13 Remove the side covers.
14 Undo the two screws securing the top piece joining the halves at the back and remove it **(see illustration)**.
15 On the underside, release and remove the two trim clips on the side and the trim clip joining the sections in the middle, and undo

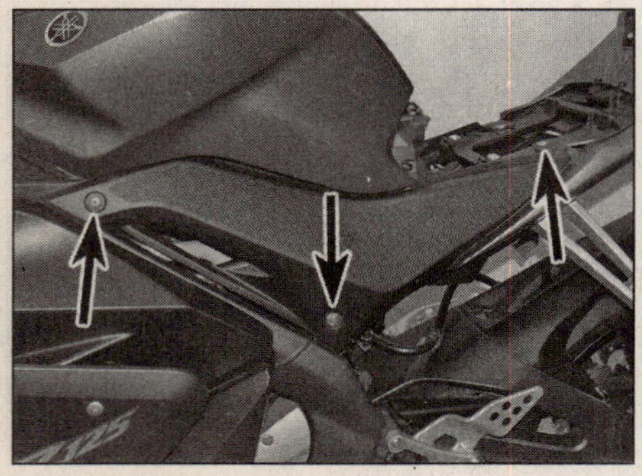
4.5a Undo the screws (arrowed)...

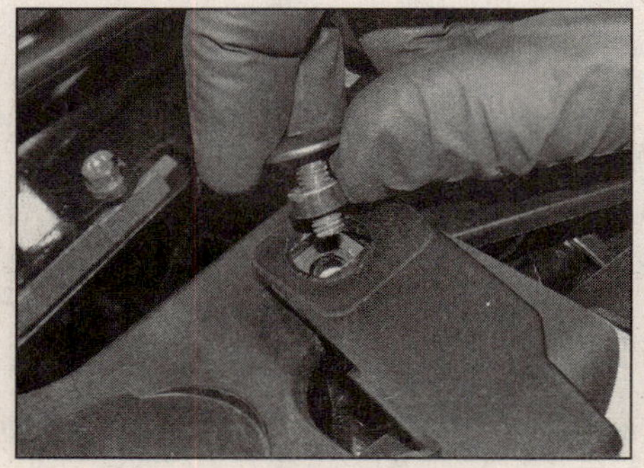
4.5b ...noting the collars

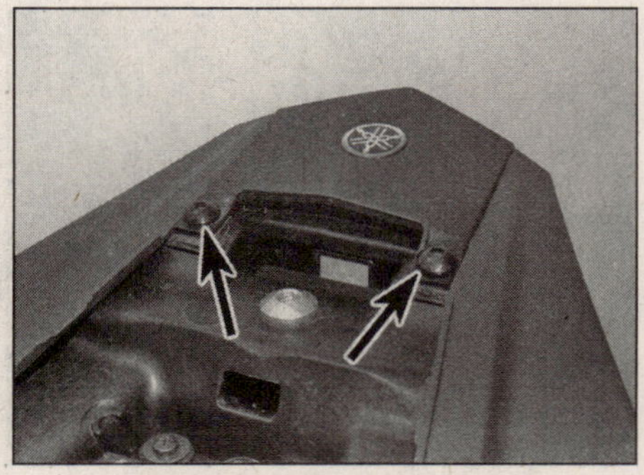
4.14 Top piece screws (arrowed)

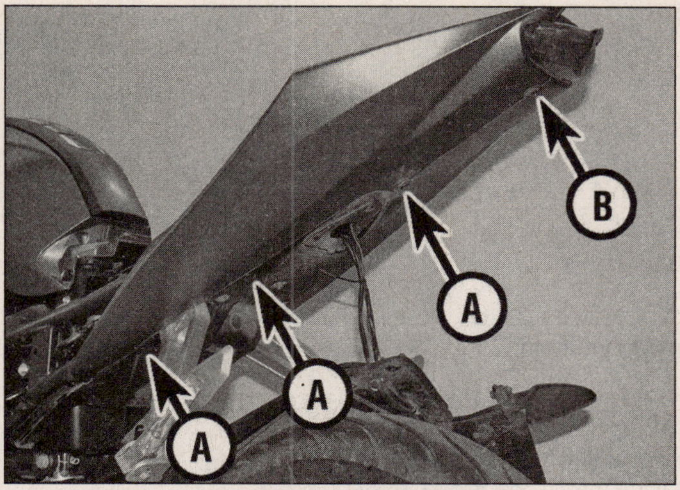

4.15 Release and remove the trim clips (A) and undo the screw (B)

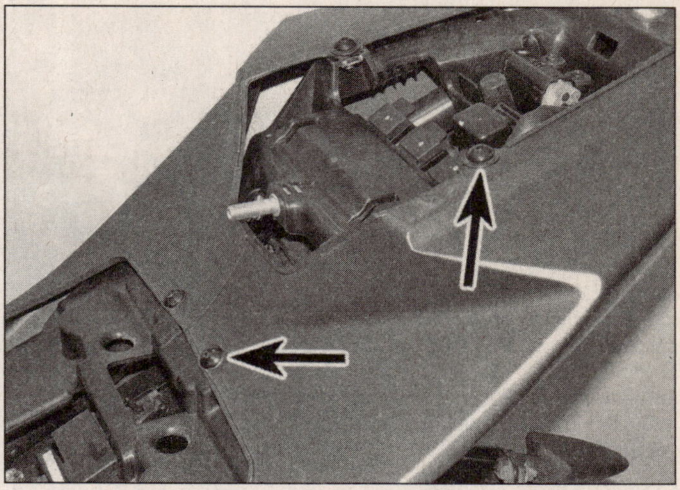
4.16 Undo the screws (arrowed), noting the collar and washer

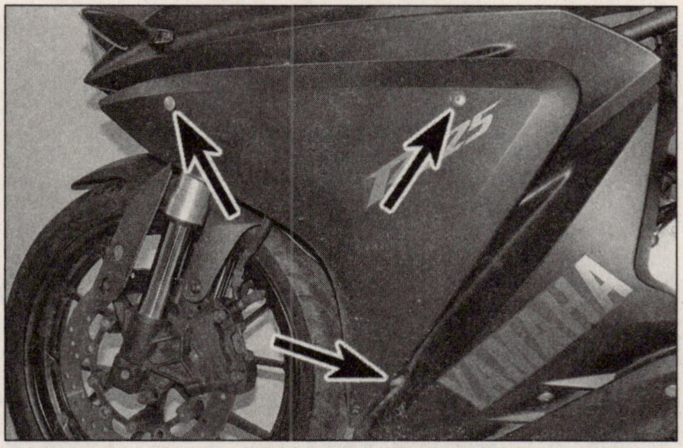
4.19 Centre section screws (arrowed)

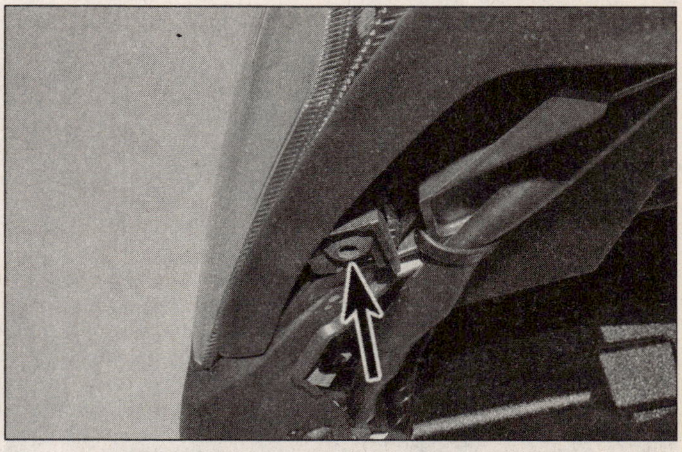
4.22a Undo the screw (arrowed) at the front...

the screw joining the sections at the back, noting the washer **(see illustration)**.

16 Undo the screws on the top of the cowling, noting the collar with the rear one and the washer with the front one **(see illustration)**. Remove the cowl.

17 After removing one side the other can be removed by releasing the two trim clips on the underside and undoing the two screws on the top.

18 Installation is the reverse of removal. Make sure the panels engage correctly with each other and the undertray.

Fairing sides

Centre sections

19 Undo the screws, noting the washers, and remove the centre section **(see illustration)**.

20 Installation is the reverse of removal.

Upper sections

21 Remove the centre section and the side cover.

22 Undo the screws and the bolts, noting the washers, then displace the upper section by sliding it forward to disengage the tab from the slot, and disconnect the turn signal wiring connector **(see illustrations)**.

23 Installation is the reverse of removal.

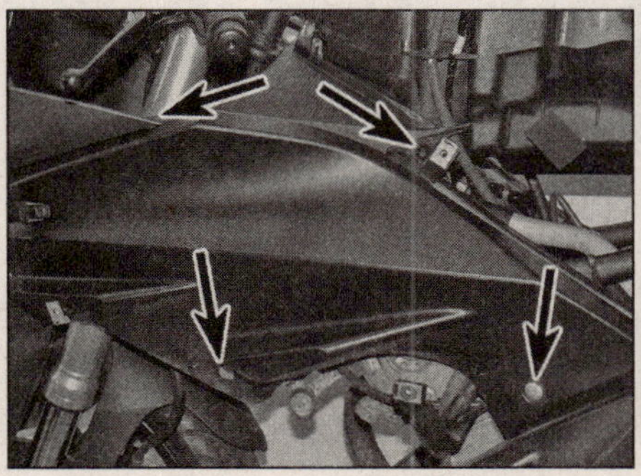
4.22b ...the screws on the top and side...

4.22c ...then displace the panel...

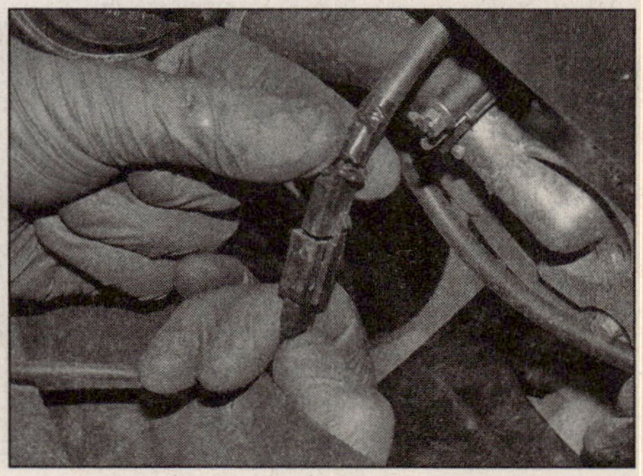
4.22d ...and disconnect the turn signal wiring connector

Check the operation of the turn signals afterwards.

Bottom and lower sections

24 Remove the centre section, the side panel, and the upper section.

25 Release and remove the trim clips and undo the screw joining the sections at the front **(see illustrations)**.

26 Release the trim clip and undo the screws on the side and remove the bottom and lower sections together **(see illustrations)**.

27 If required undo the two screws to separate the bottom section from the lower section.

28 Installation is the reverse of removal – make sure the drain hoses are routed as shown **(see illustration)**.

Cockpit trim panels

29 Remove the fuel tank cover and the centre and upper sections of the fairng.

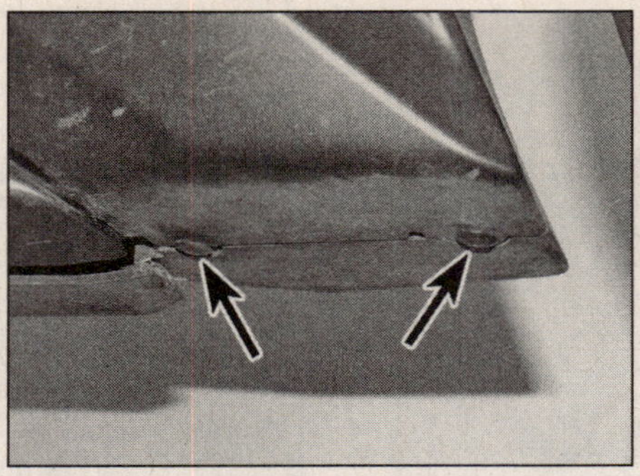

4.25a Release the trim clips (arrowed) ...

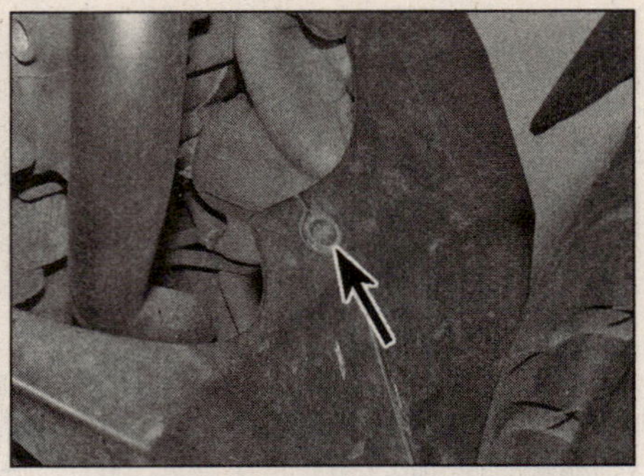

4.25b ... and undo the screw (arrowed)

30 Undo the two screws **(see illustration)**. Release and remove the panel, noting how it fits.

31 Installation is the reverse of removal.

Mirrors

32 Position the mirror as required to access the bolts, then unscrew them and remove the mirror and its rubber pad **(see illustrations)**.

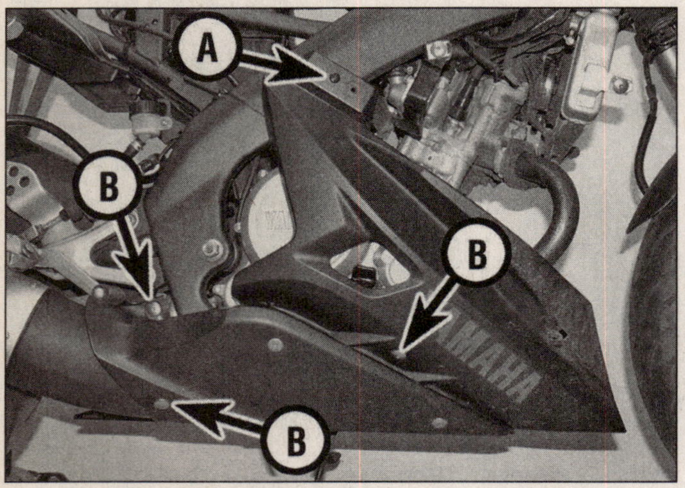

4.26a Trim clip (A) and screws (B) – right-hand sections

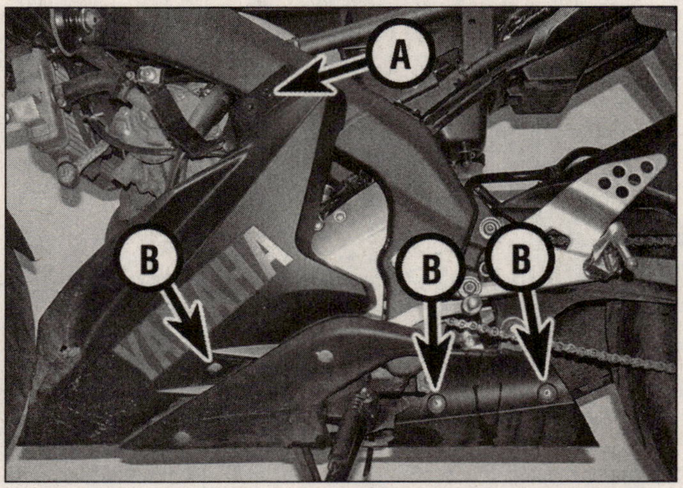

4.26b Trim clip (A) and screws (B) – left-hand sections

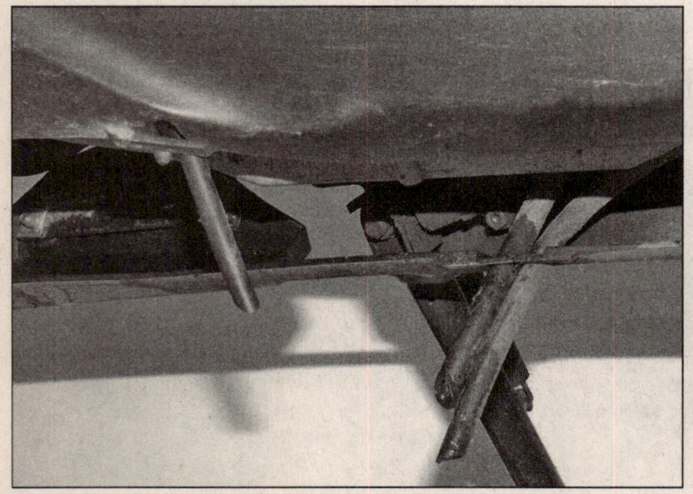

4.28 The hoses route through holes in the bottom section on each side

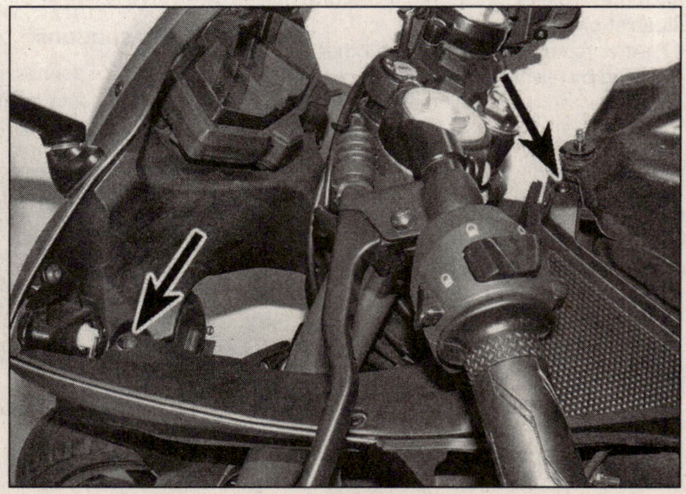

4.30 Cockpit trim panel screws (arrowed)

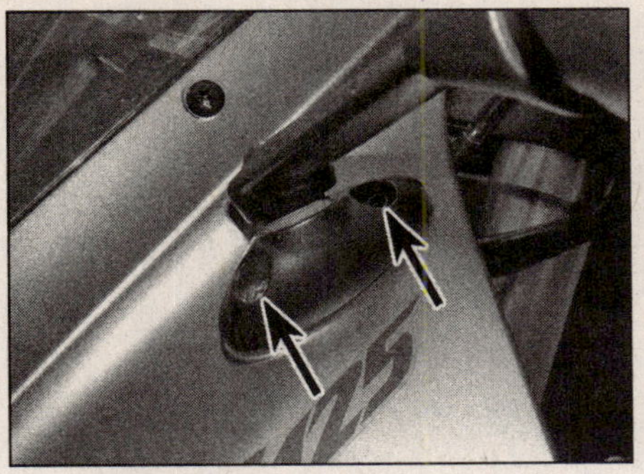

4.32a Mirror bolts (arrowed)

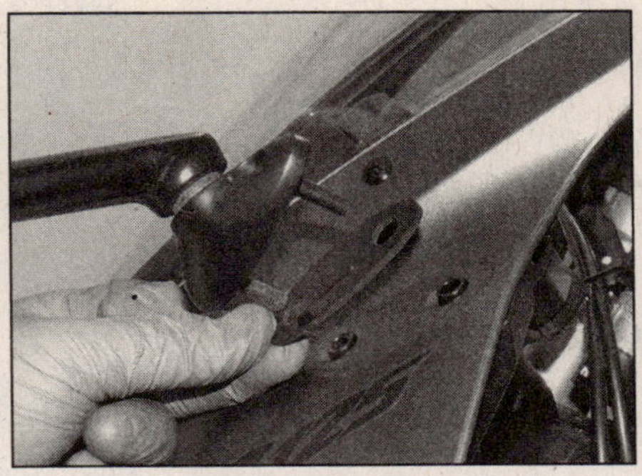

4.32b Note the rubber pad between the mirror and the fairing

4.37a Cut the cable-tie (arrowed) and draw the boot back...

33 Installation is the reverse of removal. Do not forget to fit the rubber pad.

Front fairing

34 Remove the centre sections and upper sections of the fairing on each side.
35 Remove the cockpit trim panels.
36 Remove the mirrors.
37 Disconnect the headlight loom wiring connectors **(see illustrations)**. Release the instrument wiring loom from the fairing and from the headlight wiring loom – working from the back of the fairing to the front, release (do not cut) the first two ties, then cut the third tie and release the fourth **(see illustration)**.
38 Undo the screws on the underside **(see illustration)**. Carefully lift the fairing off each mirror mount, draw it forwards and remove it **(see illustration)** – the headlights come away with the fairing.
39 Remove the rubber pads from the fairing stay if required **(see illustration)**.
40 If required, remove the headlights (see Chapter 8).
41 Installation is the reverse of removal. Make sure the rubber pads are in place.

Front mudguard

42 Undo the three screws on each side and remove the mudguard **(see illustration 3.22)**.
43 Installation is the reverse of removal.

Windshield

44 Undo the six screws and draw the windshield out of the fairing **(see illustration)**.
45 Installation is the reverse of removal.

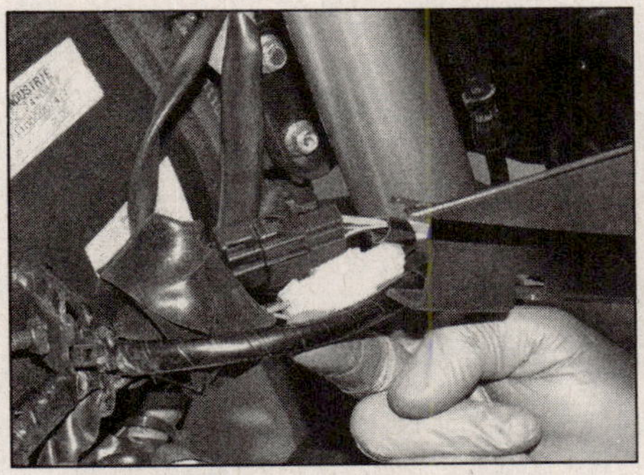

4.37b ... and disconnect the headlight wiring connectors

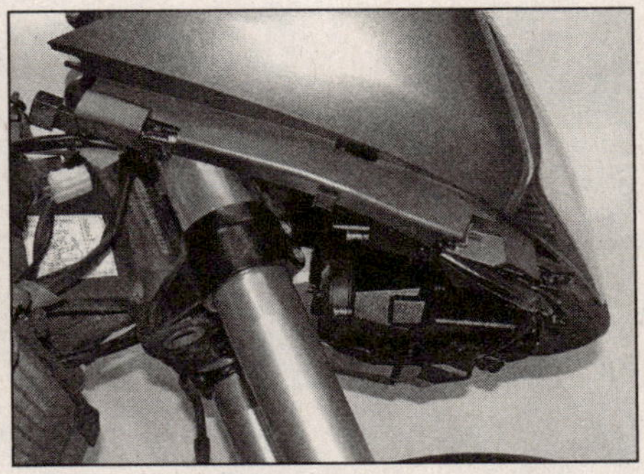

4.37c Release the wiring along the underside of the fairing as described

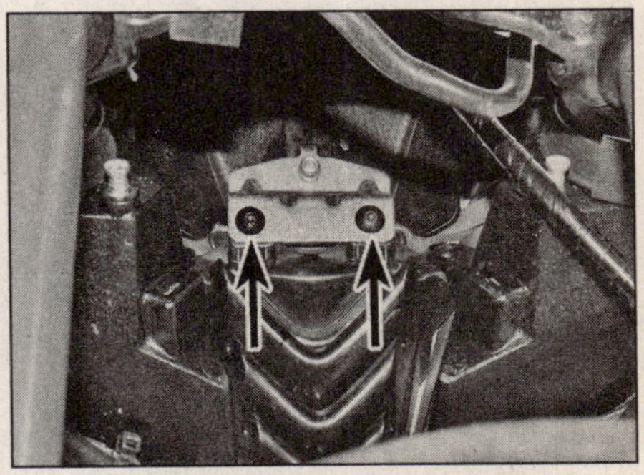

4.38a Undo the screws (arrowed)

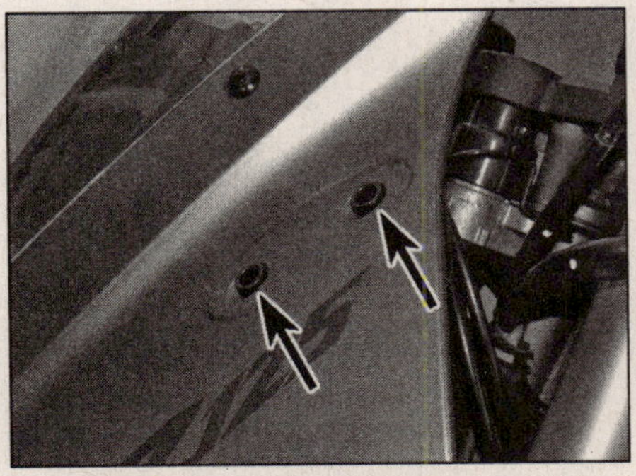

4.38b Lift each side of the fairing off the mirror mounts (arrowed)

4.39 Remove the rubber pads from the mirror mounts for safekeeping

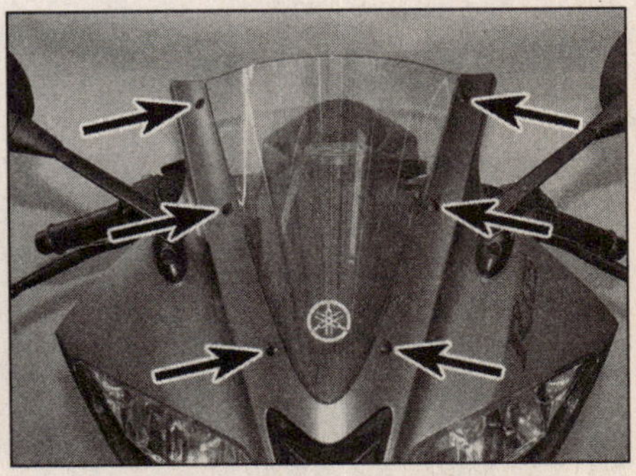

4.44 Windshield screws (arrowed)

Chapter 8
Electrical system

Contents

Degrees of difficulty

Easy, suitable for novice with little experience	**Fairly easy,** suitable for beginner with some experience	**Fairly difficult,** suitable for competent DIY mechanic	**Difficult,** suitable for experienced DIY mechanic	**Very difficult,** suitable for expert DIY or professional

Specifications

Battery

Type	Yuasa 12N5.5-4A
Capacity	12 V, 5.5 Ah
Voltage	
Fully-charged	above 12.8 V
Discharged	12.0 to 12.7 V
Charging rate	0.55 A for 5 to 10 hrs
Specific gravity	1.280 at 20°C

Charging system

Stator coil resistance	0.45 to 0.67 ohm
Nominal output	14.0 V, 20.8 A, 160 W, at 5000 rpm
Regulated voltage output	14.1 to 14.9 V at 5000 rpm
Current leakage	0.1 mA (max)

Bulbs

Headlight	
WR models	35/35 W x 1
MT models	55/60 W x 1
YZF-R models	55 W x 2
Sidelight	
WR models	5 W x 1
MT models	LED x 2
YZF-R models	5 W x 2
Brake/tail light	
WR models	21/5 W x 1
MT and YZF-R models	LED
Licence plate light	5 W
Turn signal lights	10 W x 4 amber
Instrument and warning lights	LED

Fuses

Main	20 A
Headlight	15 A
Signal (lighting, instruments, turn signals, horn)	7.5 A
Ignition	7.5 A
Fan	5 A
Back-up (MT and YZF-R models)	10 A
ABS (MT-A and YZF-RA models)	
Motor	30 A
Control unit	10 A
Solenoid	20 A

Fuel sender

Resistance	
WR models	
FULL position	19 to 21 ohms
EMPTY position	137 to 143 ohms
MT and YZF-R models	
FULL position	10 to 14 ohms
EMPTY position	267 to 273 ohms

Starter motor

Brush length	
Standard	7 mm
Service limit (min)	3.5 mm
Commutator diameter	
Standard	17.6 mm
Service limit (min)	16.6 mm
Mica undercut (depth)	1.35 mm
Armature coil resistance	0.0315 to 0.0385 ohm

Torque settings

Alternator cover bolts	10 Nm
Alternator rotor nut	70 Nm
Alternator stator and CKP sensor bolts	10 Nm
Neutral switch	20 Nm
Rear brake light switch (hydraulic type)	24 Nm
Starter motor mounting bolts	10 Nm

1 General Information

1 All models have a 12 volt electrical system charged by a three-phase alternator with separate regulator/rectifier.

2 The regulator maintains the charging system output within the specified range to prevent overcharging, and the rectifier converts the ac (alternating current) output of the alternator to dc (direct current) to power the lights and other components and to charge the battery. The alternator rotor is mounted on the left-hand end of the crankshaft.

3 The starter motor is mounted on the top of the crankcase. The starting system includes the motor, the battery, the relays (starter motor relay and starter circuit cut-off relay), and the various wires and switches. Some of the switches are part of a starter safety circuit – see Chapter 1 for further information and checks on the system.

Note: *Keep in mind that electrical parts, once purchased, often cannot be returned. To avoid unnecessary expense, make very sure the faulty component has been positively identified before buying a replacement part.*

2 Electrical system fault finding

1 A typical electrical circuit consists of an electrical component, the switches, relays, etc, related to that component and the wiring and connectors that link the component to the battery and the frame.

2 Before tackling any troublesome electrical circuit, first study the wiring diagram thoroughly to get a complete picture of what makes up that individual circuit. Trouble spots, for instance, can often be narrowed down by noting if other components related to that circuit are operating properly or not. If several components or circuits fail at one time, chances are the fault lies either in the fuse or in the common earth (ground) connection, as several circuits are often routed through the same fuse and earth (ground) connections.

3 Electrical problems often stem from simple causes, such as loose or corroded connections or a blown fuse. Prior to any electrical fault finding, always visually check the condition of the fuse, wires and connections in the problem circuit. Intermittent failures can be especially frustrating, since you can't always duplicate the failure when it's convenient to test. In such situations, a good practice is to clean all connections in the affected circuit, whether or not they appear to be good – where possible use a dedicated electrical cleaning spray along with sandpaper, wire wool or other abrasive material to remove corrosion, and a dedicated electrical protection spray to prevent further problems. All of the connections and wires should also be wiggled to check for looseness which can cause intermittent failure.

4 If you don't have a multimeter it is highly advisable to obtain one – they are not expensive and will enable a full range of electrical tests to be made. Go for a modern digital one with LCD display as they are easier to use. A continuity tester and/or test light are useful for certain electrical checks as an alternative, though are limited in their

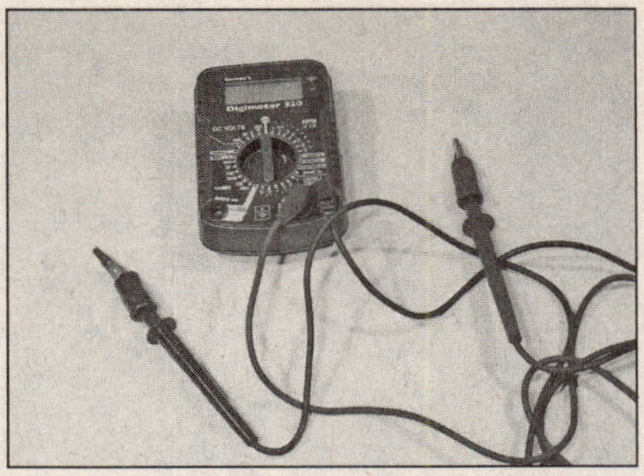

2.4a A digital multimeter can be used for all electrical tests

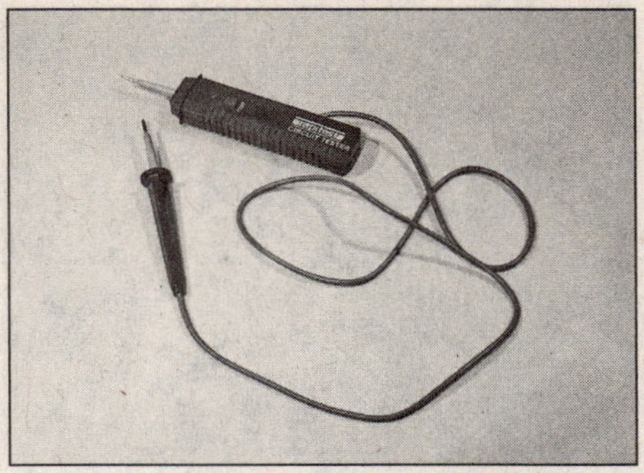

2.4b A battery-powered continuity tester

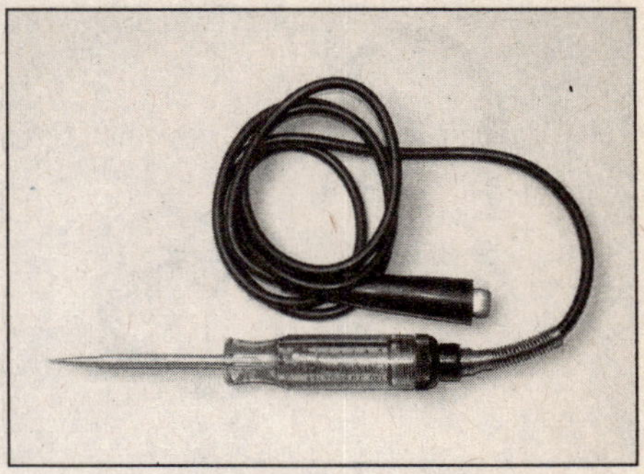

2.4c A simple test light is useful for voltage tests

usefulness compared to a multimeter **(see illustrations)**.

Continuity checks

5 The term continuity describes the uninterrupted flow of electricity through an electrical circuit. Continuity can be checked with a multimeter set either to its continuity function (a beep is emitted when continuity is found), or to the resistance (ohms / Ω) function, or with a dedicated continuity tester. Both instruments are powered by an internal battery, therefore the checks are made with the ignition OFF. As a safety precaution, always disconnect the battery negative (-) lead before making continuity checks, particularly if ignition switch checks are being made.

6 If using a multimeter, select the continuity function if it has one, or the resistance (ohms) function. Touch the meter probes together and check that a beep is emitted or the meter reads zero, which indicates continuity. If there is no continuity there will be no beep or the meter will show infinite resistance. After using the meter, always switch it OFF to conserve its battery.

7 A continuity tester can be used in the same way – its light should come on or it should beep to indicate continuity in the switch ON position, but should be off or silent in the OFF position.

8 Note that the polarity of the test probes doesn't matter for continuity checks, although care should be taken to follow specific test procedures if a diode or solid-state component is being checked.

Switch continuity checks

9 If a switch is at fault, trace its wiring to the wiring connectors. Separate the connectors and inspect them for security and condition. A build-up of dirt or corrosion here will most likely be the cause of the problem – clean up and apply a water dispersant such as WD40, or alternatively use a dedicated contact cleaner and protection spray.

10 If using a multimeter, select the continuity function if it has one, or the resistance (ohms) function, and connect its probes to the terminals in the connector **(see illustration)**. Simple ON/OFF type switches, such as brake light switches, only have two wires whereas combination switches, like the handlebar switches, have many wires. Study the wiring diagram to ensure that you are connecting to the correct pair of wires. Continuity should be indicated with the switch ON and no continuity with it OFF.

Wiring continuity checks

11 Many electrical faults are caused by damaged wiring, often due to incorrect routing or chaffing on frame components. Loose, wet or corroded wire connectors can also be the cause of electrical problems.

12 A continuity check can be made on a single length of wire by disconnecting it at each end and connecting the meter or continuity tester probes to each end of the wire **(see illustration)**. Continuity (low or no resistance – 0 ohms) should be indicated if the wire is good. If no continuity (high resistance) is shown, suspect a broken wire.

13 To check for continuity to earth in any earth wire connect one probe of your meter or tester to the earth wire terminal in the connector and the other to the frame, engine, or battery earth (-) terminal. Continuity (low or no resistance – 0 ohms) should be indicated if the wire is good. If no continuity (high resistance) is shown, suspect a broken wire or corroded or loose earth point (see below).

Voltage checks

14 A voltage check can determine whether power is reaching a component. Use a multimeter set to the dc voltage scale, or a test light. The test light is the cheaper component, but the meter has the advantage of being able to give a voltage reading.

15 Connect the meter or test light in parallel, i.e. across the load **(see illustration)**.

16 First identify the relevant wiring circuit by referring to the wiring diagram at the end of this manual. If other electrical components share the same power supply (i.e. are fed from the same fuse), take note whether they are working correctly – this is useful information in deciding where to start checking the circuit.

17 If using a meter, check first that the meter leads are plugged into the correct terminals on the meter (red to positive (+), black to

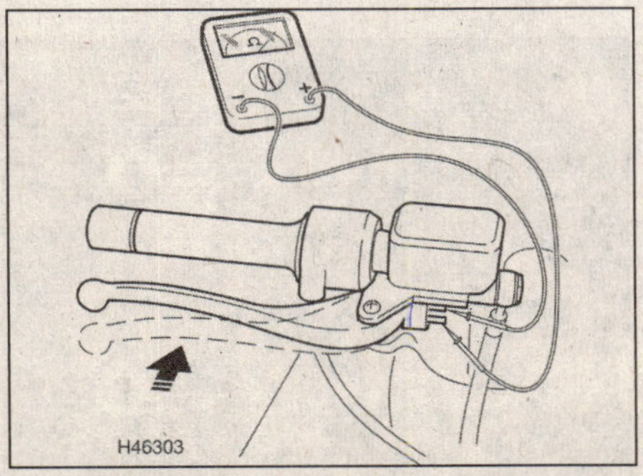

2.10 Continuity should be indicated across switch terminals when lever is operated

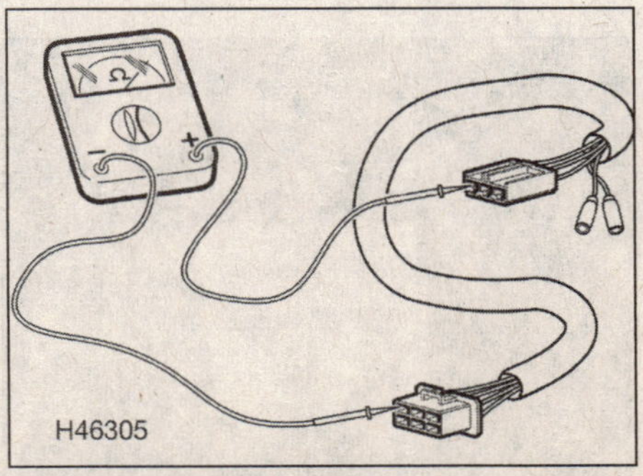

2.12 Wiring continuity check. Connect the meter probes across each end of the same wire

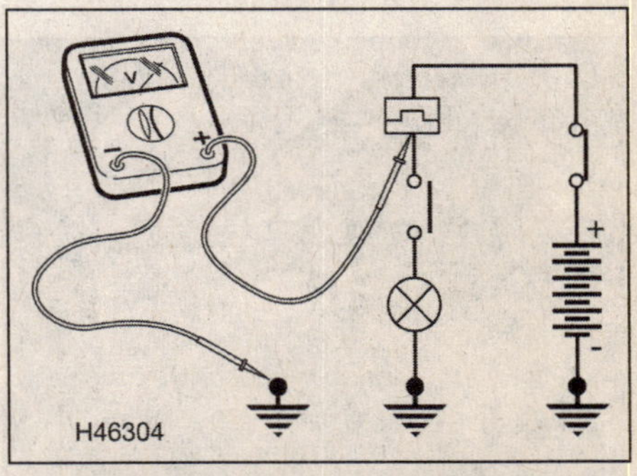

2.15 Voltage check. Connect the meter positive probe to the component and the negative probe to earth

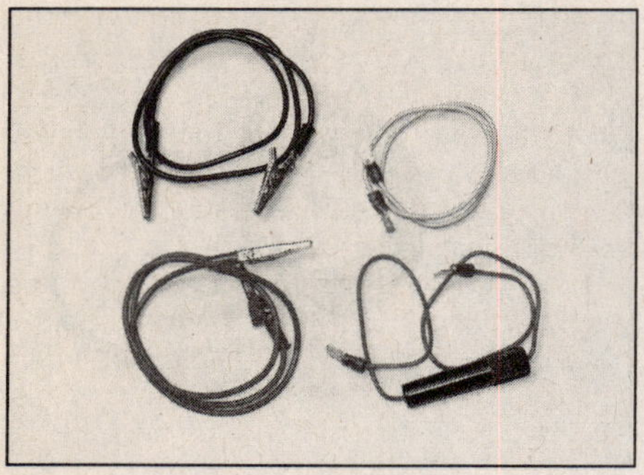

2.23 A selection of insulated jumper wires

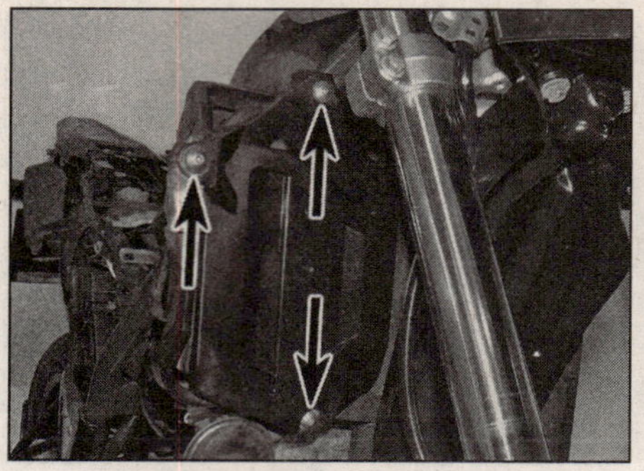

3.2 Battery cover screws (arrowed)

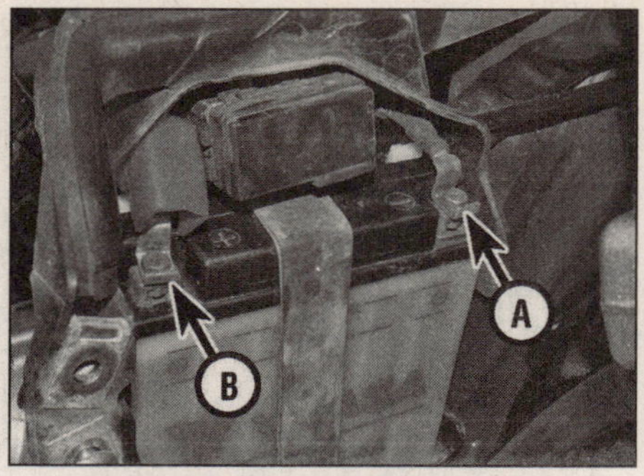

3.3 Negative terminal (A), positive terminal (B)

negative (-). Set the meter to the dc volts function, where necessary at a range suitable for the battery voltage – 0 to 20 vdc. Connect the meter red probe (+) to the power supply wire and the black probe to a good metal earth (ground) on the motorcycle's frame or directly to the battery negative terminal. Battery voltage should be shown on the meter with the ignition switch, and if necessary any other relevant switch, ON.

18 If using a test light, connect its positive (+) probe to the power supply terminal and its negative (-) probe to a good earth (ground) on the motorcycle's frame. With the switch, and if necessary any other relevant switch, ON, the test light should illuminate.

19 If no voltage is indicated, work back towards the fuse continuing to check for voltage. When you reach a point where there is voltage, you know the problem lies between that point and your last check point.

Earth (ground) checks

20 Earth connections are made either directly to the engine or frame (such as neutral switch, which only has a positive feed) or by a separate wire into the earth circuit of the wiring harness. Alternatively a short earth wire is sometimes run from the component directly to the motorcycle's frame.

21 Corrosion is a common cause of a poor earth connection, as is a loose earth terminal fastener.

22 If total or multiple component failure is experienced, check the security of the main earth lead from the negative (-) terminal of the battery, the earth lead bolted to the engine, and the main earth point(s) on the frame. If corroded, dismantle the connection and clean all surfaces back to bare metal. Remake the connection and prevent further corrosion from forming by smearing battery terminal grease over the connection.

23 To check the earth of a component, use an insulated jumper wire to temporarily bypass its earth connection **(see illustration)** – connect one end of the jumper wire to the earth terminal or metal body of the component and the other end to the motorcycle's frame. If the circuit works with the jumper wire installed, the earth circuit is faulty.

24 To check an earth wire first check for corroded or loose connections, then check the wiring for continuity (Step 13) between each connector in the circuit in turn, and then to its earth point, to locate the break.

3 Battery removal, installation and inspection

Caution: Be extremely careful when handling or working around the battery. The electrolyte is very caustic and an explosive gas (hydrogen) is given off when the battery is charging.

Removal and installation

WR models

1 Make sure the ignition is switched OFF. Remove the fuel tank cover (see Chapter 7).

2 Undo the battery cover screws and remove the cover **(see illustration)**.

3 Unscrew the negative (–) terminal bolt first and disconnect the lead from the battery **(see illustration)**. Lift up the insulating cover to access the positive (+) terminal, then unscrew the bolt and disconnect the lead.

4 Disconnect the breather hose from the side of the battery **(see illustration)**.

5 Unhook the battery strap and draw the battery out of its housing **(see illustration)**.

MT and YZF-R models

6 Make sure the ignition is switched OFF. Remove the rider's seat (see Chapter 7).

7 Unhook the battery strap **(see illustration)**. On models with ABS remove the toolkit and its tray.

8 Unscrew the negative (–) terminal bolt first and disconnect the lead from the battery **(see illustration 3.7)**. Lift up the insulating cover to access the positive (+) terminal, then unscrew the bolt and disconnect the lead.

9 Lift the battery from the bike and disconnect the breather hose.

All models

10 Installation is the reverse of removal. Clean the battery terminals and lead ends with a wire brush, fine sandpaper or steel wool.

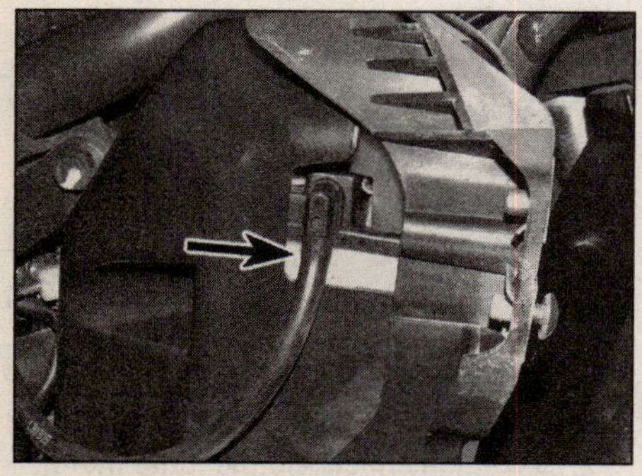

3.4 Pull the hose (arrowed) off its union

3.5 Release the strap (arrowed) and remove the battery

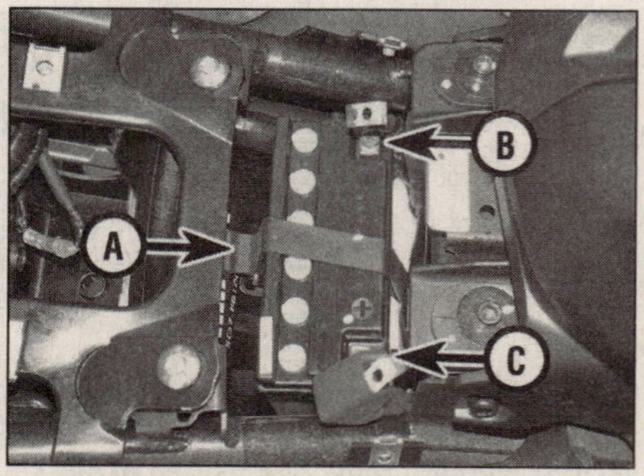

3.7 Unhook the strap (A). Negative terminal (B), positive terminal (C)

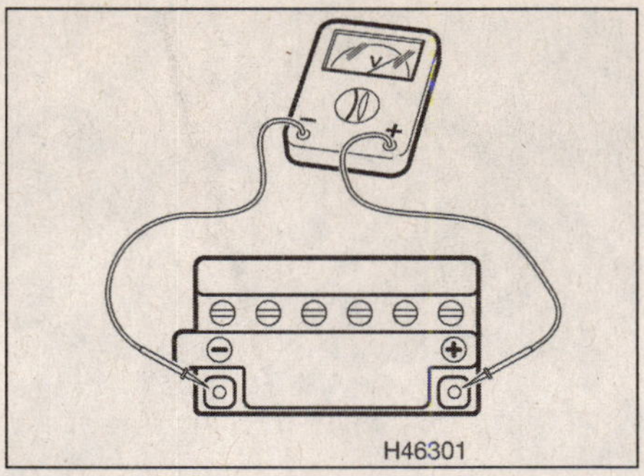

3.13 Checking battery voltage – connect the meter as shown

Do not forget to connect the breather hose. Reconnect the leads, connecting the positive (+) terminal first.

> **HAYNES HiNT** ***Battery corrosion can be kept to a minimum by applying a layer of battery terminal grease or petroleum jelly (Vaseline) to the terminals after the leads have been connected. DO NOT use a mineral-based grease.***

Inspection and maintenance

11 Special tool: To check the specific gravity of the battery you need a hydrometer.
12 For routine battery checks and maintenance see Chapter 1, Section 17.
13 Check the state of charge of the battery by measuring the voltage present at the battery terminals. Connect the voltmeter positive (+) probe to the battery positive (+) terminal, and the negative (–) probe to the battery negative (–) terminal **(see illustration)**. When fully-charged there should be more than 12.8 volts present. If the voltage falls much below this remove the battery (see above), and recharge it as described below in Section 4.
14 Next, unless you bike has been fitted with a maintenance-free (MF) battery (see Chapter 1), check the specific gravity of the electrolyte in each cell with a small hydrometer made especially for motorcycle batteries. These are available from most dealer parts departments or motorcycle accessory stores.
15 Remove all the cell caps **(see illustration 4.3a)**. Draw some electrolyte from the first cell into the hydrometer and note the specific gravity **(see illustration)**. Compare the reading to the Specifications at the beginning of the Chapter. Return the electrolyte to the appropriate cell and repeat the check for the remaining cells. When the check is complete, rinse the hydrometer thoroughly with clean water. Refit the cell caps.
16 If the specific gravity of the electrolyte in each cell is as specified, the battery is in good condition and is being charged by the machine's charging system.
17 If the specific gravity is low, the battery

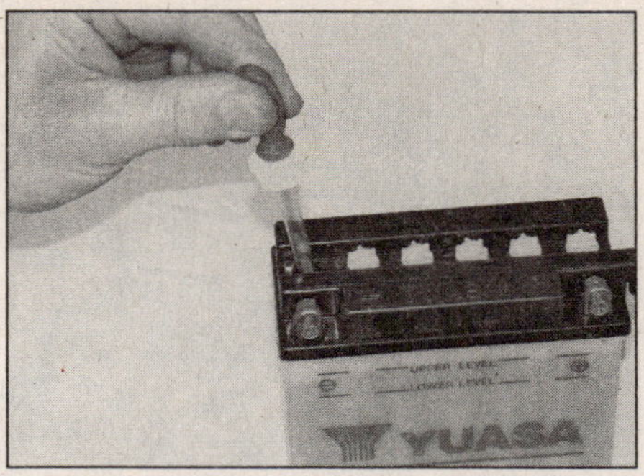

3.15 Checking the specific gravity of the electrolyte using a hydrometer

is not fully charged. This may be due to corroded battery terminals, a dirty battery case, a malfunctioning charging system, or loose or corroded wiring connections. On the other hand, it may be that the battery is worn out, especially if the machine is old, or that infrequent use of the motorcycle prevents normal charging from taking place.

4 Battery charging

Caution: Be extremely careful when handling or working around the battery. The electrolyte is very caustic and an explosive gas (hydrogen) is given off when the battery is charging.

1 Remove the battery (see Section 3). Check the electrolyte level before connecting the charger (see Chapter 1). If necessary add distilled water to any cells that are low.
2 The maximum charging rate for any battery is 1/10 of the rated amp/hour capacity. So the maximum charging rate for a 5.5 amp/hour battery would be 0.55 amps. If the battery is charged at a higher rate, it could be damaged. If a normal domestic charger is used check that after a possible initial peak, the charge rate falls to a safe level. If the battery becomes hot during charging stop. Further charging will cause damage. Note that there are many bike-specific chargers available from good suppliers that are designed for the maintenance and recovery of motorcycle batteries, in particular catering for the requirements of heavily discharged MF batteries. They are not too expensive, and are a worthwhile investment, especially if the bike is not used over winter. Follow the manufacturer's instructions.
3 If not already done loosen the cell caps **(see illustration)**. Connect the charger to the battery, making sure that the positive (+) lead on the charger is connected to the positive (+) terminal on the battery, and the negative (–) lead is connected to the negative (–) terminal **(see illustration)**.
4 Allow the battery to charge until the voltage is raised to the specified level, or until the specific gravity is as specified (see Section 3). If the battery overheats or gases excessively, the charging rate is too high. Either disconnect the charger or lower the charging rate to prevent damage to the battery. Before checking either the voltage or the specific gravity disconnect the charger and let the battery settle for about 30 minutes.
5 If one or more of the cells do not show an increase in specific gravity after a long slow charge, or if the battery as a whole does not seem to want to take a charge, it is time for a new battery.
6 If the recharged battery discharges rapidly if left disconnected it is likely that an internal short caused by physical damage or sulphation has occurred. A new battery is required. A sound item will tend to lose its charge at about 1% per day.
7 Check the electrolyte level and refit the cell caps before installing the battery (see Section 3).
8 If the motorcycle sits unused for long periods of time, charge the battery once every month to six weeks and leave it disconnected.

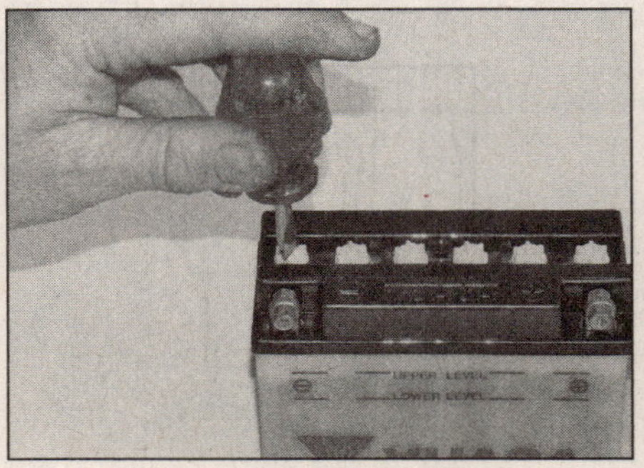

4.3a Loosen the cell caps

5 Fuses

1 The electrical system is protected by fuses of different ratings (see Specifications at the beginning of the Chapter). On WR models

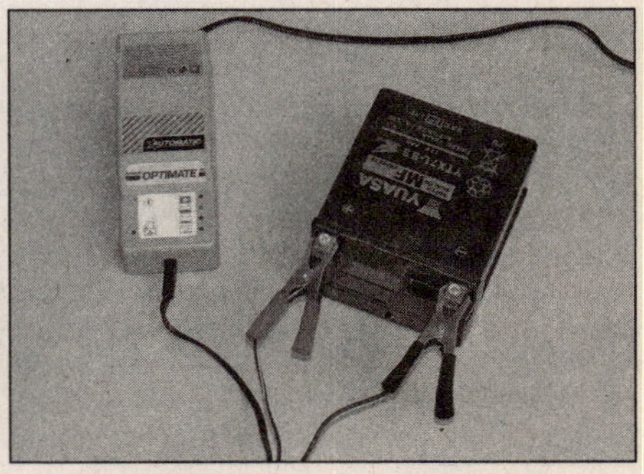

4.3b Battery connected to a charger

5.1a Fusebox (arrowed) – WR models

5.1b Fuseboxes (arrowed) – MT and YZF-R models

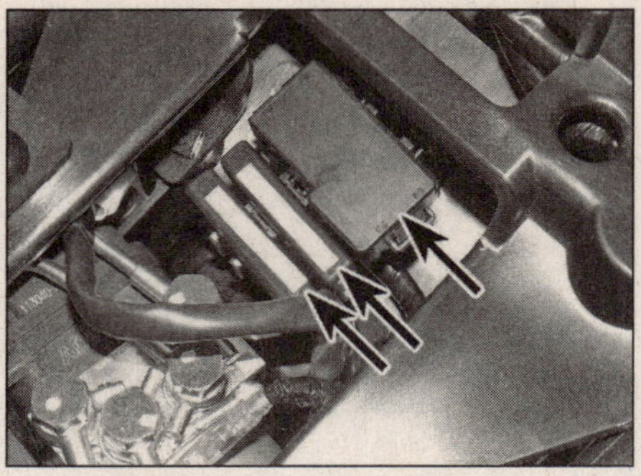

5.1c Fuseboxes (arrowed) – MT-A and YZF-RA models

all the fuses are in one box housed above the battery **(see illustration)**. On MT and YZF-R models all fuses are in two fuseboxes, and on MT-A and YZF-RA models in three fuseboxes, located under the rider's seat **(see illustrations)**. A spare fuse of each rating is housed in the fusebox. If a spare fuse is used, always replace it with a new one so that a spare of each rating is carried on the bike at all times.

2 On WR models remove the fuel tank cover (see Chapter 7). Undo the battery cover screws and remove the cover **(see illustration 3.2)**.

3 On MT and YZF-R models remove the rider's seat (see Chapter 7).

4 Unclip the fusebox lid to access the fuses **(see illustrations)**. The identity of each fuse is on a label in or on the lid – also refer to the Specifications at the beginning of the Chapter for the function and rating of each fuse.

5 The fuses can be removed and checked visually – if you can't pull the fuse out with your fingertips, use a fuse tool or a suitable pair of pliers **(see illustration)**. A blown fuse is easily identified by a break in the element **(see illustration)**. Each fuse is clearly marked with its rating and must only be replaced by a fuse of the correct rating.

Warning: Never put in a fuse of a higher rating or bridge the terminals with any other substitute, however temporary it may be. Serious damage may be done to the circuit, or a fire may start.

6 If the new fuse blows immediately check the wiring circuit very carefully for evidence of a short-circuit. Look for bare wires and chafed, melted or burned insulation.

7 Occasionally a fuse will blow or cause an open-circuit for no obvious reason. Corrosion of the fuse ends and fusebox terminals may occur and cause poor fuse contact. If this happens, remove the corrosion with a wire brush or emery paper, then spray the fuse end and terminals with electrical contact cleaner.

6 Lighting system check

Note: *Refer to Electrical System Fault Finding in Section 2 and to the wiring diagram at the end of this Chapter.*

1 If a light fitted with a standard bulb (as opposed to an LED) fails, first check the bulb (see relevant Section), the bulb terminals in the holder, and the wiring connector(s). If an LED fails first check the wiring connector for that LED. If none of the lights work, check the battery (see Section 3) – low voltage indicates either a faulty battery or a defective charging system. Refer to Section 3 for battery checks and Section 28 for charging system tests. Also, check the fuses (Section 5) – if there is more than one problem at the same time, it is likely to be a fault relating to a multi-function component, such as one of the fuses governing more than one circuit, or the ignition switch. When checking for a blown filament in a bulb, it is advisable to back up a visual check with a continuity test of the filament as it is not always apparent that a bulb has blown. When testing for continuity, remember that on single terminal bulbs it is the metal body of the bulb that is the earth (ground).

Headlight(s)

2 On WR and MT models the headlight has a twin filament bulb. On YZF-R models each headlight has a single filament bulb, the right-hand headlight for low beam and the left-hand for high beam. If one of the beams fails to work, first check the bulb (see Section 7). If both beams fail to work first check the headlight fuse (see Section 5). If all is good so far, the problem lies in the wiring or connectors, the headlight relay, or the dimmer switch. First make sure the wiring connectors are secure (see Section 7). Next check the relay (Step 3).

5.4a Accessing the fuses on WR models

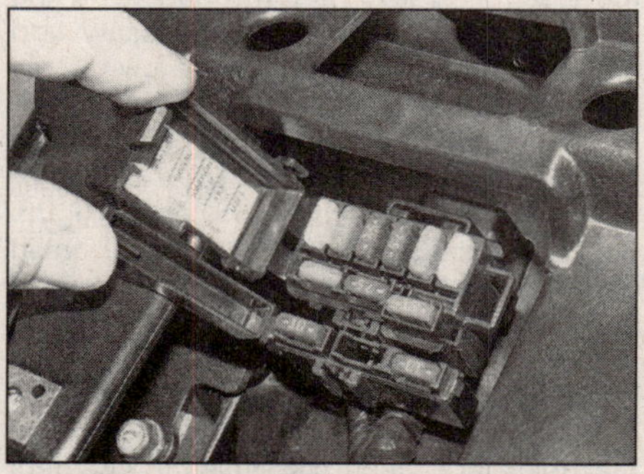

5.4b Accessing the fuses on MT and YZF-R models

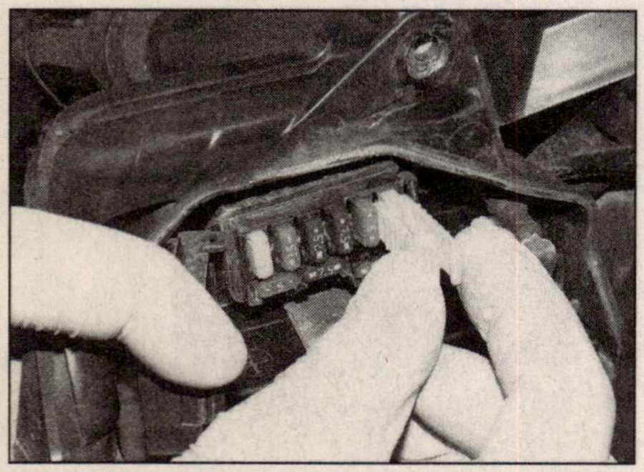

5.5a Removing the fuses using a fuse tool

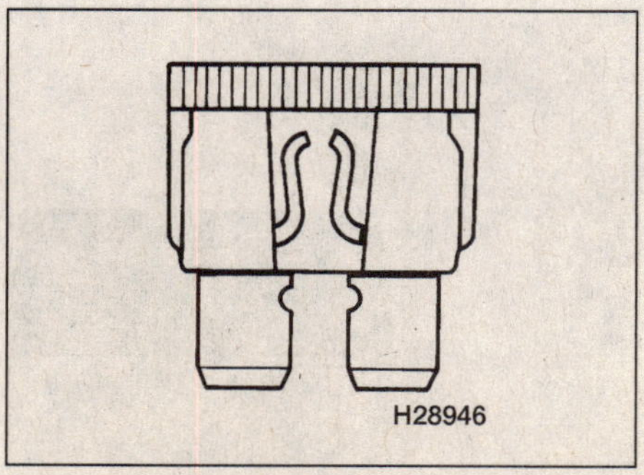

5.5b A blown fuse can be identified by a break in its element

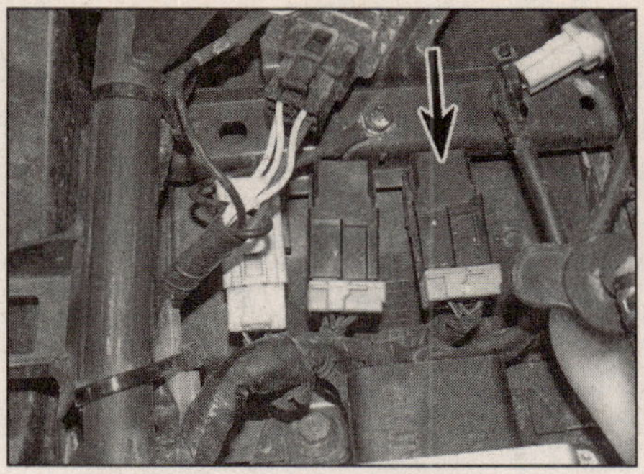

6.3a Headlight relay (arrowed) – WR models

6.3b Headlight relay (arrowed) – MT and YZF-R models

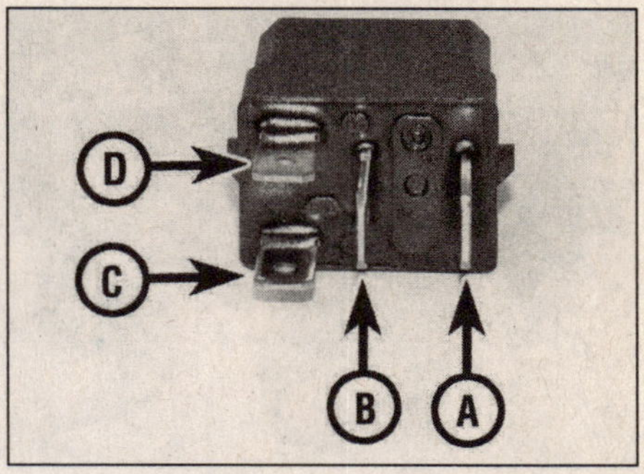

6.3c Red/yellow terminal (A), blue/black terminal (B), red/yellow terminal (C), white/black terminal (D)

3 To check the relay, on WR models remove the seat, and on MT and YZF-R models remove the passenger seat (see Chapter 7). Displace the relay and remove it from its holder **(see illustrations)**. Set a multimeter to the ohms x 1 scale and connect it across the relay's red/yellow and adjacent blue/black wire terminals **(see illustration)**. There should be no continuity (infinite resistance). Using a fully-charged 12 volt battery and two insulated jumper wires, connect the positive (+) terminal of the battery to the other red/yellow wire terminal, and the negative (–) terminal to the white/black wire terminal. At this point the relay should be heard to click and the meter read 0 ohms (continuity). If this is the case the relay is good. If the relay does not click when battery voltage is applied and indicates no continuity (infinite resistance) across its terminals, it is faulty and must be replaced with a new one.

4 If the relay is good, check for battery voltage at each red/yellow wire terminal in the relay wiring connector with the ignition ON. If there is no voltage check the wiring between the connector and the ignition switch via the fusebox. If the voltage is good check the blue/black wire between the relay and the dimmer switch, and then the yellow and green wires from the switch to the headlight for continuity, checking the switch at the same time by flicking it between LO and HI beam while checking for continuity from the blue/black wire through the switch to the green or yellow wire in the switch housing wiring connector according to the position of the switch, referring to Section 19 and the wiring diagram at the end of the Chapter. Next check the white/black wire from the relay to the ECU for continuity. Also make sure that all the terminals and connectors are clean and secure. Repair or renew the wiring or connectors as necessary.

5 If the LO beam does not work, and the bulb is good, check for battery voltage at the green wire terminal on the headlight wiring connector with the ignition ON and the dimmer switch set to LO. If the HI beam does not work, and the bulb is good, check for battery voltage at the yellow wire terminal on the headlight wiring connector with the ignition ON and the dimmer switch set to HI. If voltage is present, check for continuity to earth (ground) in the black wire from the wiring connector. Repair or renew the wiring or connectors as necessary.

Sidelights

6 On WR models there is a single sidelight bulb in the bottom of the headlight unit – if it fails to work first check the bulb. On MT models there is a sidelight LED in each top corner of the headlight – if one of them fails to work first check the wiring connector. On YZF-R models there is a sidelight bulb in each headlight – if one of them fails to work, first check the bulb. In each case refer to Section 7. If both sidelights fail on MT and YZF-R models, check the signal fuse (see Section 5). If all is good, check for battery voltage at the brown wire terminal in the loom side of the connector on MT models or the bulb holder on WR and YZF-R models, with the ignition switch ON. If no voltage is indicated, check the wiring and connectors in sidelight circuit, referring to the wiring diagrams at the end of this Chapter. If voltage is present, check for continuity to earth (ground) in the black wire. Repair or renew the wiring or connectors as necessary.

Tail light

7 On WR models the tail light has a conventional twin-filament bulb, the other filament being for the brake light – if the light fails to work first check the bulb (see Section 7), then check the signal fuse (see Section 5). On MT and YZF-R models the tail light has LEDs – if the light fails to work, first check the signal fuse (see Section 5). If all is good, on WR models remove the seat (see Chapter 7), and on MT and YZF-R models refer to Section 10, and disconnect the tail light unit wiring connector **(see illustrations)**. Check the connector terminals and the wiring to the light unit. On MT and YZF-R models check the tail light LEDs by connecting the positive (+) terminal of a 12 volt battery to the brown wire terminal in the light unit side of the connector, and the negative (-) terminal to the black wire terminal – the LEDs should come on. If they don't replace the tail light with a new one (see Section 10). If all is good so far check for battery voltage at the brown wire terminal on the loom side of the connector with the ignition switch ON. If no voltage is indicated, check the wiring and connectors in the tail light circuit, referring to the wiring diagram at the end of this Chapter. If voltage is present, check for continuity to earth (ground) in the black wire from the wiring connector. Repair or renew the wiring or connectors as necessary.

Brake light

8 On WR models the brake light has a conventional twin filament bulb, the other filament being for the tail light – if the light fails to work first check the bulb, then check the signal fuse. On MT and YZF-R models the brake light has LEDs – if the brake light fails to work, first check the signal fuse (see

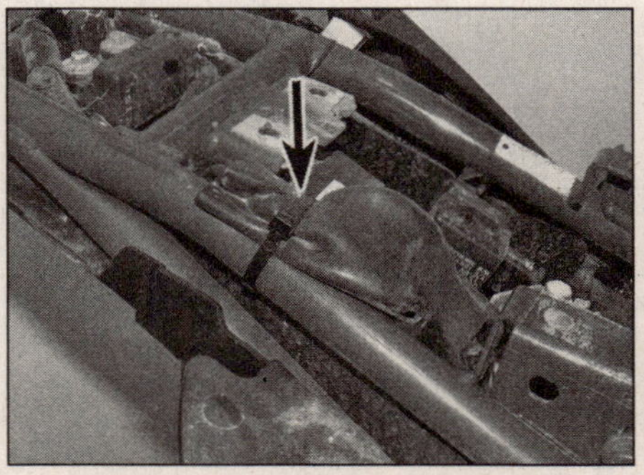

6.7a Cut the cable-tie (arrowed) and pull the boot back...

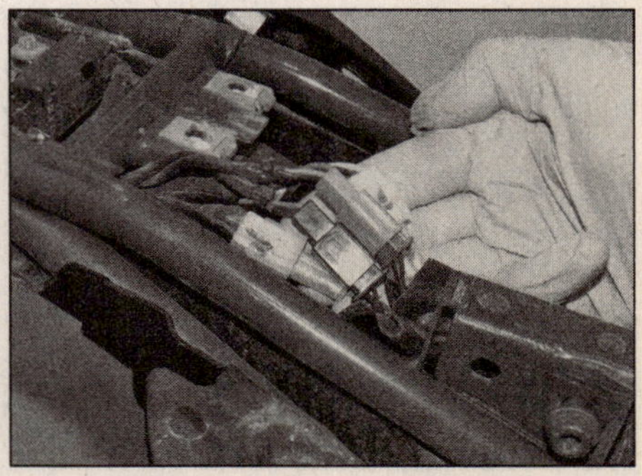

6.7b ...to access the connectors. Tail light connector is the one with three wires

7.2a Remove the cover...

7.2b ... release the retainer...

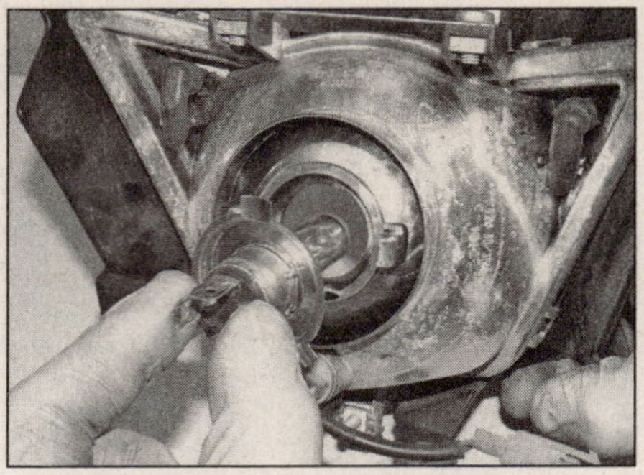

7.2c ... and remove the bulb

Section 5). If all is good, on WR models remove the seat (see Chapter 7), and on MT and YZF-R models refer to Section 10, and disconnect the tail light wiring connector **(see illustrations 6.7a and b)**. Check the connector terminals and the wiring to the light unit. On MT and YZF-R models check the LEDs by connecting the positive (+) terminal of a 12 volt battery to the green/yellow wire terminal in the light unit side of the connector, and the negative (-) terminal to the black wire terminal – the LEDs should come on. If they don't replace the tail light with a new one (see Section 10). If all is good so far, check for battery voltage at the green/yellow wire terminal on the loom side of the connector, first with the front brake lever pulled in, then with the rear brake pedal pressed down. If voltage is present with one brake on but not the other, then the switch or its wiring is faulty. If no voltage is indicated, check the wiring and connectors between the light unit and the switches, then check the switches themselves. Refer to Section 14 for the switch testing procedures, and also to the wiring diagram at the end of this Chapter. If voltage is present in both cases, check for continuity to earth (ground) in the black wire from the wiring connector. Repair or renew the wiring or connectors as necessary.

Licence plate light

9 If the licence plate light fails to work, first check whether the tail light is working – they run off the same circuit. If it isn't refer to Step 7. If the tail light functions ok, check the licence plate bulb (Section 9). If the bulb and tail light are both good check the wiring and connectors in the circuit, referring to the wiring diagram at the end of this Chapter.

Turn signals

10 See Section 11.

7 Headlight bulb(s) and sidelight bulb(s)

Note: *The headlight bulb is of the quartz-halogen type. Do not touch the bulb glass as skin acids will shorten the bulb's service life. If the bulb is accidentally touched, it should be wiped carefully when cold with a rag soaked in methylated spirit and dried before fitting.*

Headlight

WR models

1 Remove the headlight (see Section 8).
2 Remove the rubber cover, then release the bulb retainer by turning it anti-clockwise **(see illustrations)**. Withdraw the bulb **(see illustration)**.
3 Fit the new bulb in reverse order bearing in mind the information in the Note above.
4 Check the operation of the headlight.

MT models

5 Undo the headlight bracket bolt on each side **(see illustration)**. Displace the headlight forwards and hold it, then disconnect the wiring connector **(see illustration)**.
6 Remove the rubber cover, then release the bulb retainer by turning it anti-clockwise **(see illustrations)**. Withdraw the bulb **(see illustration)**.

7.5a Unscrew the bolt (arrowed) on each side

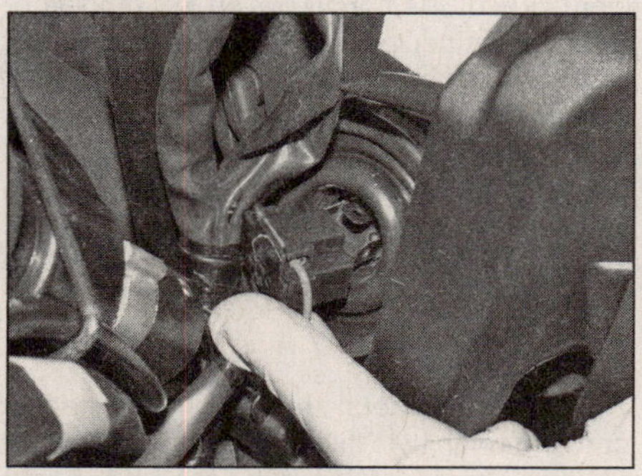

7.5b Tilt the headlight and disconnect the wiring

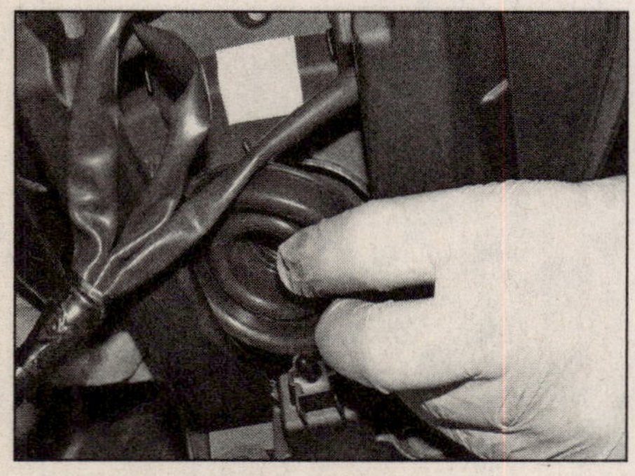

7.6a Remove the cover...

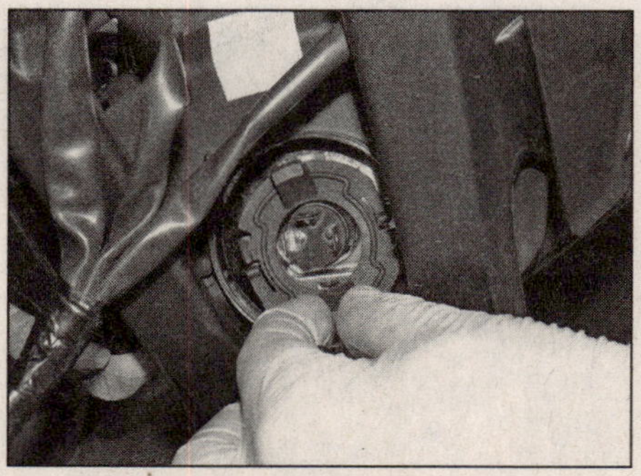

7.6b ... release the retainer...

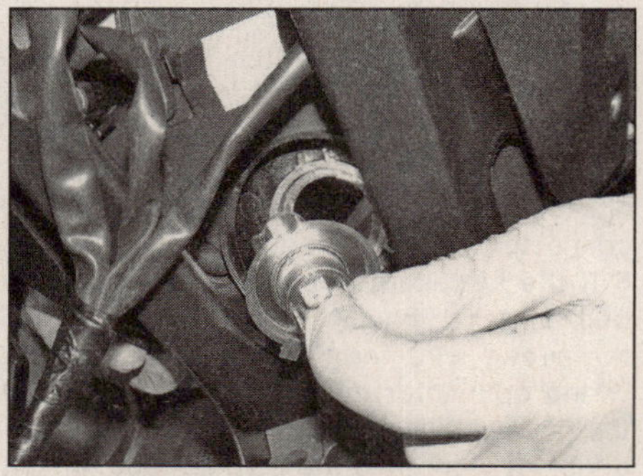

7.6c ... and remove the bulb

7.7 Seat the grommets over the pegs

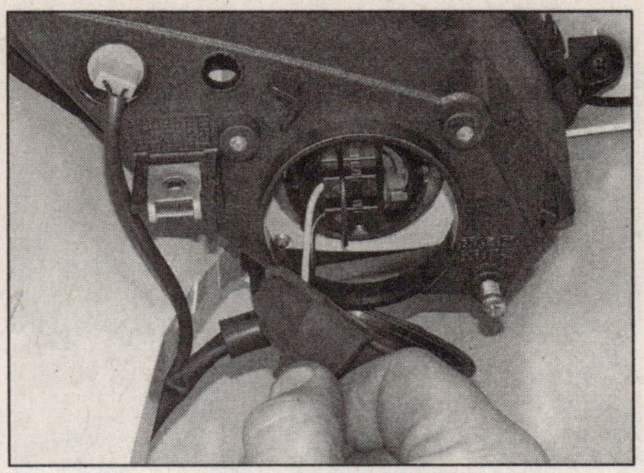

7.9a Remove the cover...

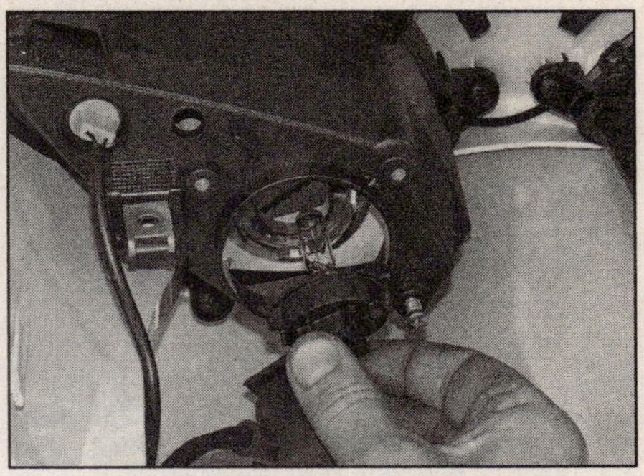

7.9b ...then turn the bulbholder anti-clockwise and draw it out

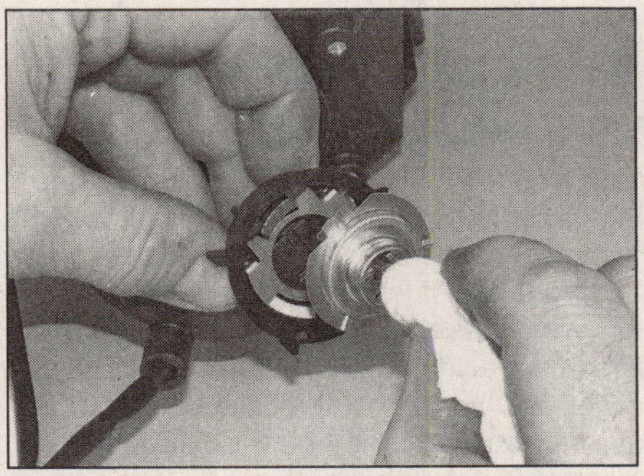

7.9c Remove the bulb from the holder

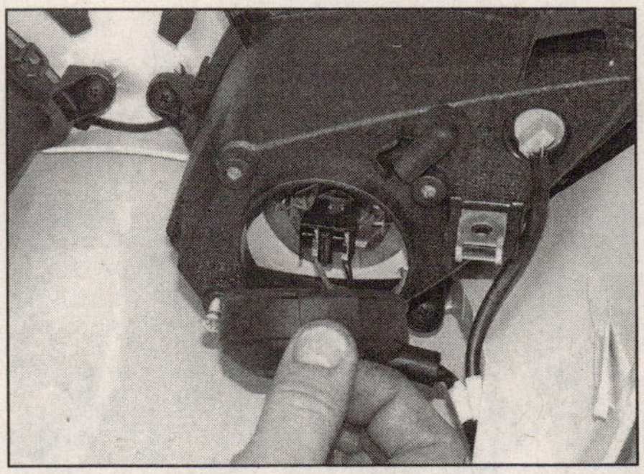

7.10a Remove the cover...

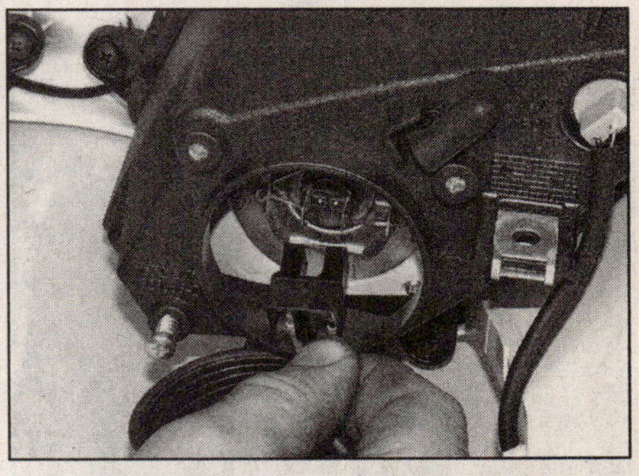

7.10b ...and disconnect the wiring connector...

7 Fit the new bulb in reverse order bearing in mind the information in the Note above. Make sure the headlight bracket grommets seat correctly over the pegs **(see illustration)**.
8 Check the operation of the headlight.

> **HAYNES HiNT** ***Always use a paper towel or dry cloth when handling new bulbs to prevent injury if the bulb should break and to increase bulb life.***

YZF-R models

9 The high beam bulb is in the left-hand headlight unit. Remove the cover, then turn the bulbholder anti-clockwise to release it **(see illustrations)**. Remove the bulb from the holder **(see illustration)**.
10 The low beam bulb is in the right-hand headlight unit. Remove the cover, then disconnect the wiring connector **(see illustration)**. Release the retaining clip and remove the bulb **(see illustration)**.
11 Fit the new bulb in reverse order, bearing in mind the information in the Note above.
12 Check the operation of the headlight.

Sidelight

WR models

13 Remove the headlight (see Section 8).
14 Carefully pull the sidelight bulbholder out, then carefully pull the bulb out of the holder **(see illustrations)**.

7.10c ...then release the clips...

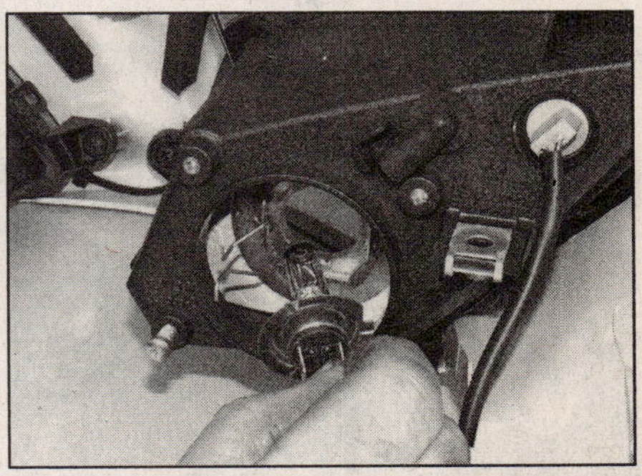

7.10d ...and remove the bulb

15 Fit the new bulb, then fit the holder into the headlight.
16 Check the operation of the sidelight.

MT models

17 The sidelights are LED that are integral components of the headlight – if either one

7.14a Pull the bulbholder out of the headlight...

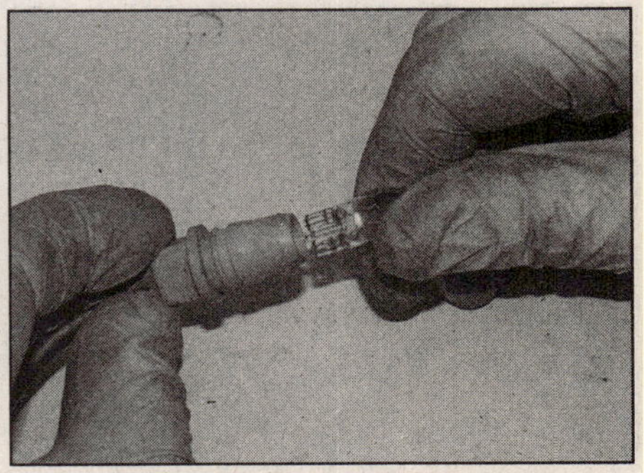

7.14b ...then pull the bulb out of the holder

fails replace the headlight with a new one (see Section 8).

YZF-R models

18 Carefully pull the sidelight bulbholder out, then carefully pull the bulb out of the holder **(see illustrations)**.
19 Fit the new bulb, then fit the holder into the headlight.
20 Check the operation of the sidelight.

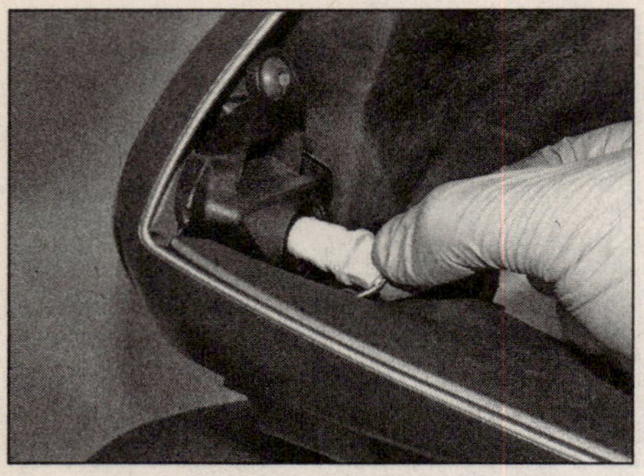

7.18a Pull the bulbholder out of the headlight...

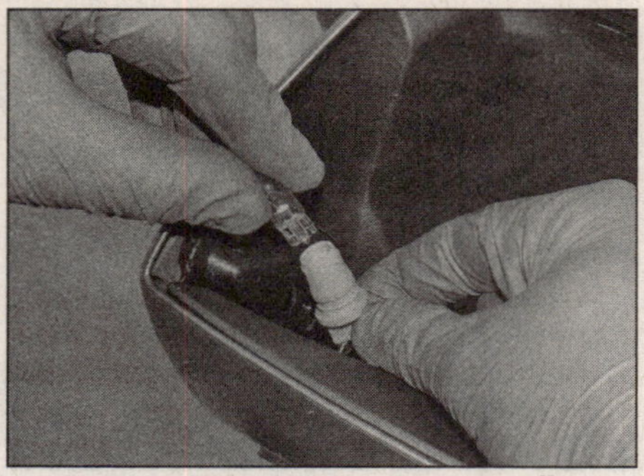

7.18b ... then pull the bulb out of the holder

8 Headlight

Removal and installation

WR models

1 Undo the screw on each side **(see illustration)**. Lift the headlight assembly off the pegs on the bracket, then disconnect the headlight and sidelight wiring connectors and remove the assembly **(see illustrations)**.
2 To separate the headlight from the cover, first make a note of the setting of the adjuster screw in the bottom by counting or measuring the exposed threads at the back **(see illustration 7.14a)**. Undo the screw and remove the washers and spring. Undo the two upper screws and remove the headlight from the cover (visible in illustration 7.2a). Remove the bulbs if required (see Section 7).
3 Installation is the reverse of removal. Make sure the four grommets are in place in the cover and are in good condition, the sleeves are fitted in the upper grommets, and the lower ones seat correctly over the pegs **(see illustration)**. Check the operation of the headlight and sidelight. Check the headlight aim.

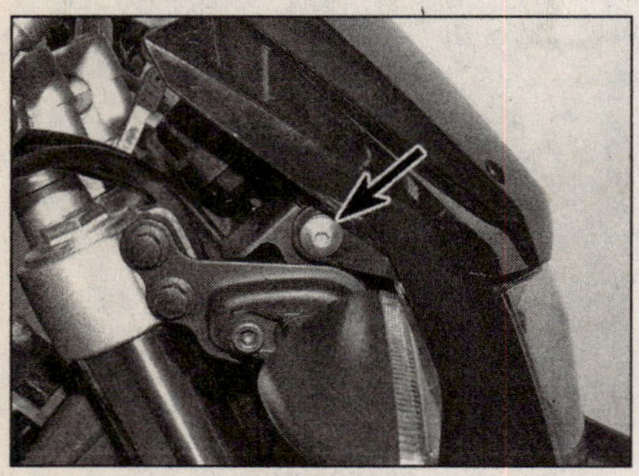

8.1a Undo the screw (arrowed) on each side

8.1b Disconnect the headlight connector...

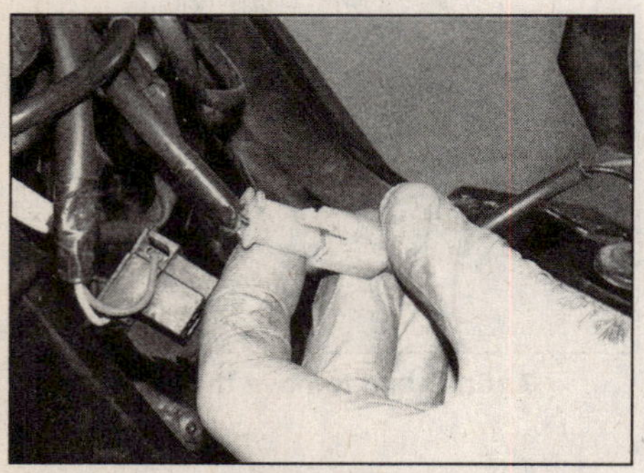

8.1c ... and the sidelight connector

8.3 Seat the grommets over the pegs

MT models

4 If fitted remove the front cowl **(see illustration)**. Undo the instrument cover screws and remove the cover **(see illustration)**. Undo the headlight cover screws and remove the cover **(see illustration)**.

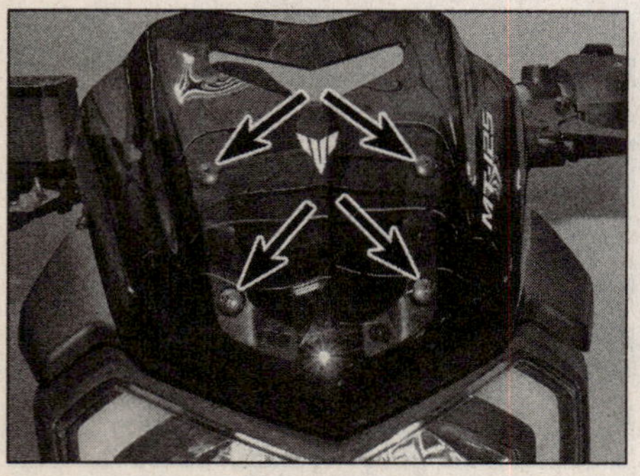

8.4a Front cowl screws (arrowed – if fitted)

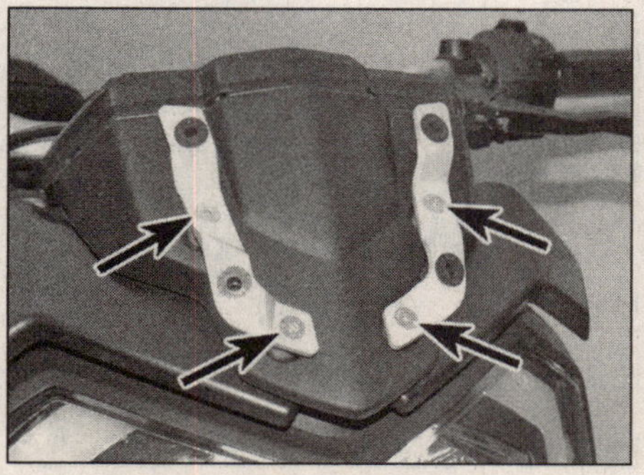

8.4b Instrument cover screws (arrowed – shown with front cowl brackets)

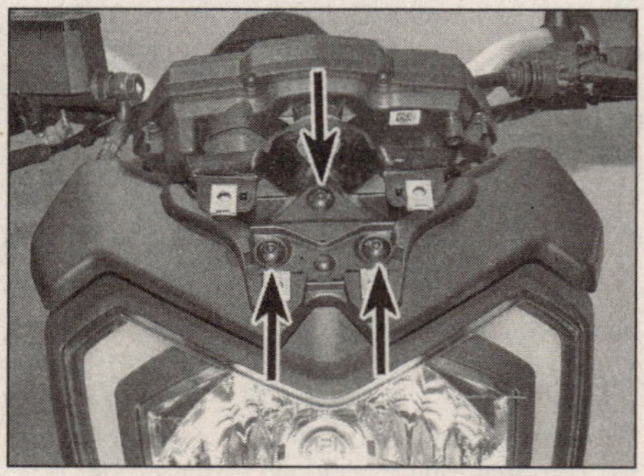

8.4c Headlight cover screws (arrowed)

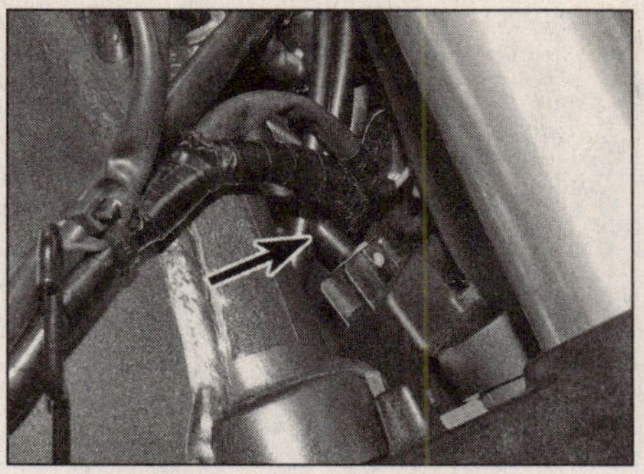
8.5a Remove the cap (arrowed) ...

8.5b ... and count or measure the exposed threads (arrowed) ...

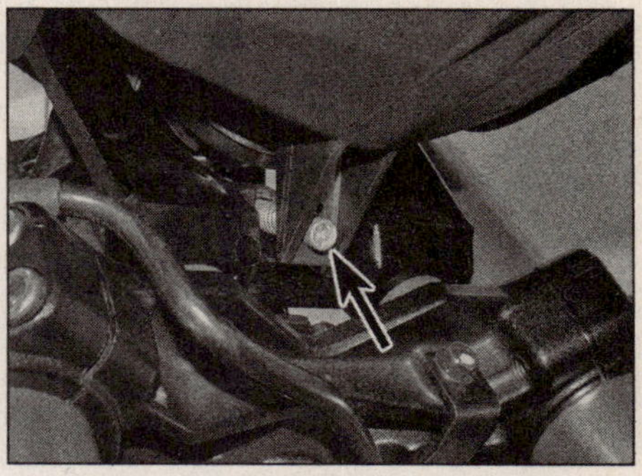
8.5c ... before undoing the screw (arrowed)

5 Remove the cap from the upper end of the headlight adjuster screw **(see illustration)**. Make a note of the setting of the screw by counting or measuring the exposed threads **(see illustration)**. Fully undo the screw and remove the washer and spring **(see illustration)**.

6 Undo the screw on each side **(see illustration)**. Displace the headlight forwards, then disconnect the headlight and sidelight wiring connectors and remove the headlight **(see illustration)**.

7 Installation is the reverse of removal. Make sure the grommets are in place in the bracket and are in good condition, and the collars are fitted in them. Check the operation of the headlight and sidelight. Check the headlight aim.

YZF-R models

8 Remove the front fairing (see Chapter 7).

9 Undo the screws and remove the headlight unit(s) from the fairing **(see illustration)**.

10 Remove the bulbs from the headlight if required (see Section 7).

11 Installation is the reverse of removal. Make sure all the wiring is correctly routed, connected and secured. Check the operation of the headlights and sidelights. Check the headlight aim if a new headlight unit has been fitted.

8.6a Undo the screw (arrowed) on each side

8.6b Disconnect the connectors (arrowed)

Headlight aim

Note: *An improperly adjusted headlight may cause problems for oncoming traffic or provide poor, unsafe illumination of the road ahead. Before adjusting the headlight aim, be sure to consult with local traffic laws and regulations – for UK models refer to MOT Test Checks in the Reference section.*

12 The headlight beam can adjusted vertically only. Before making any adjustment, check that the tyre pressures are correct and the suspension is adjusted as required. Make any adjustments to the headlight aim with the machine on level ground, with the fuel tank half full and with an assistant sitting on the seat. If the bike is usually ridden with a passenger on the back, have a second assistant to do this.

13 Adjustment is made by turning the adjuster screw at the base of the headlight on WR and MT models **(see illustration 8.5c)**, and next to each bulb cover on YZF-R models **(see illustration)**.

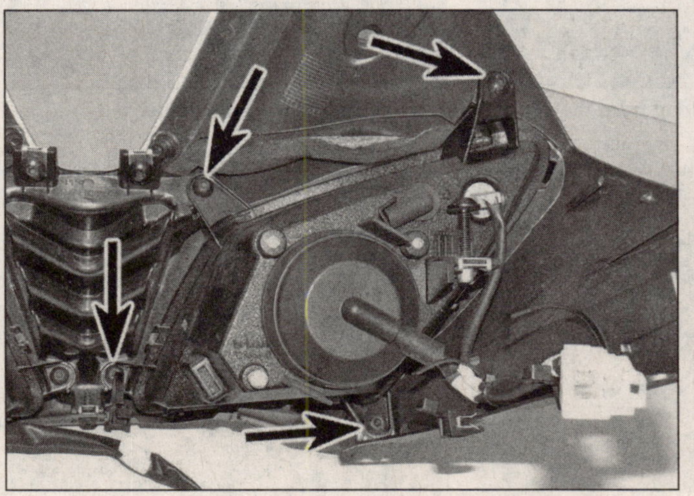
8.9 Four screws (arrowed) secure each headlight unit

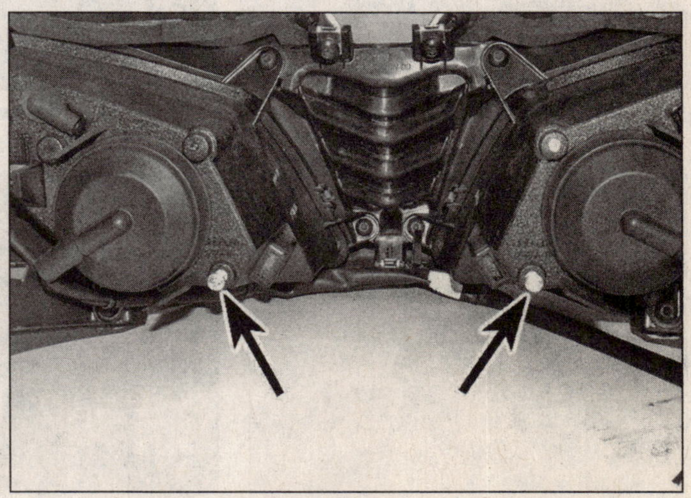
8.13 Headlight beam adjusters (arrowed) – YZF- R models

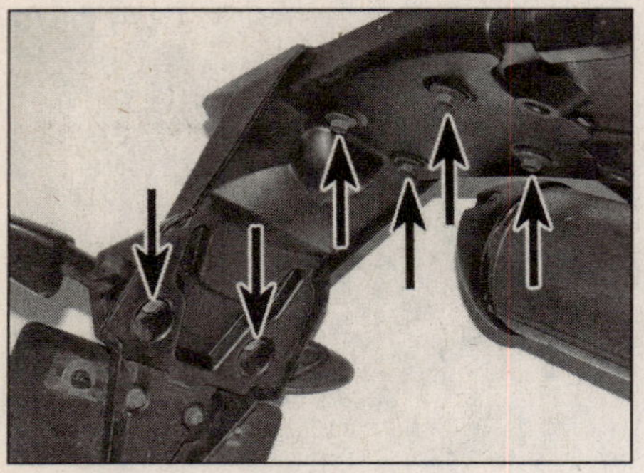
9.1a Unscrew the bolts (arrowed)…

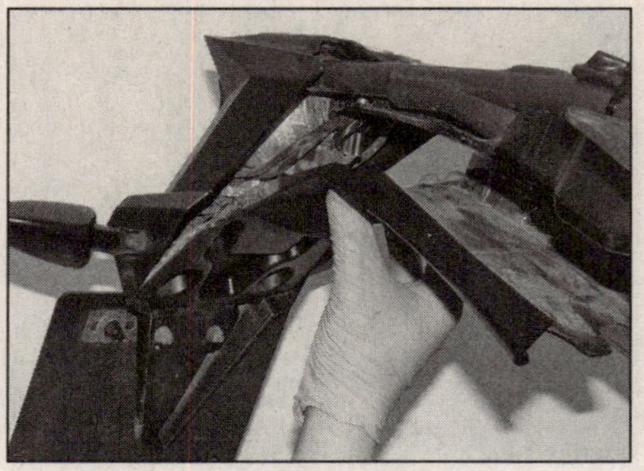
9.1b …and remove the cover

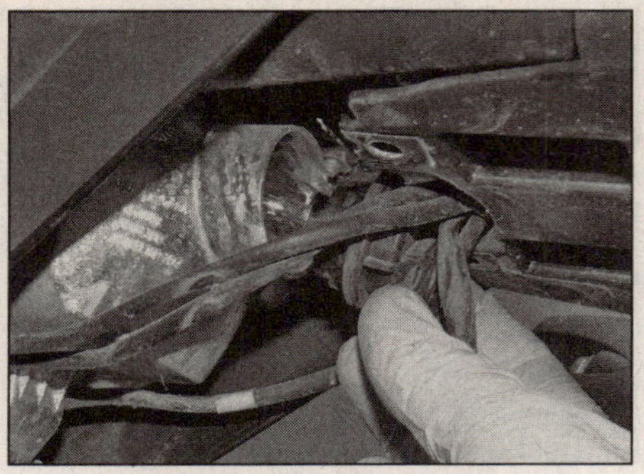
9.2 Release the bulb holder…

9 Brake/tail light bulb or LED, and licence plate bulb

Brake/tail light bulb – WR models

Note: *It is a good idea to use a paper towel or dry cloth when handling the new bulb to prevent injury if it breaks, and to increase bulb life.*

1 Remove the tail light cover **(see illustrations)**.

2 Turn the bulb holder anti-clockwise and draw it out of the tail light **(see illustration)**.

3 Carefully push the bulb into the holder then turn it anti-clockwise to release it **(see illustration)**.

4 Line up the pins of the new bulb with the slots in the socket, then push the bulb in and turn it clockwise until it locks into place.

5 Fit the bulb holder into the tail light and turn it clockwise to lock it.

6 Check the operation of the tail and brake lights. Fit the tail light cover.

Brake/tail light LED – MT and YZF-R models

7 The tail light contains LEDs which cannot be replaced with new ones. If the tests detailed in Section 6, prove that the LEDs are faulty replace the tail light unit with a new one (see Section 10).

Licence plate light bulb

Note: *It is a good idea to use a paper towel or dry cloth when handling the new bulb to prevent injury if it breaks, and to increase bulb life.*

WR models

8 Remove the tail light cover **(see illustrations 9.1a and b)**. Release the wiring clip **(see illustration)**.

9 Carefully pull the bulbholder out **(see illustration)**. Carefully pull the bulb out of its socket and replace it with a new one **(see illustrations)**.

10 Fit the bulb holder, then check the operation of the light. Fit the tail light cover.

MT and YZF-R models

11 Undo the licence plate light screw and displace the light, then carefully pull the bulbholder out **(see illustrations)**.

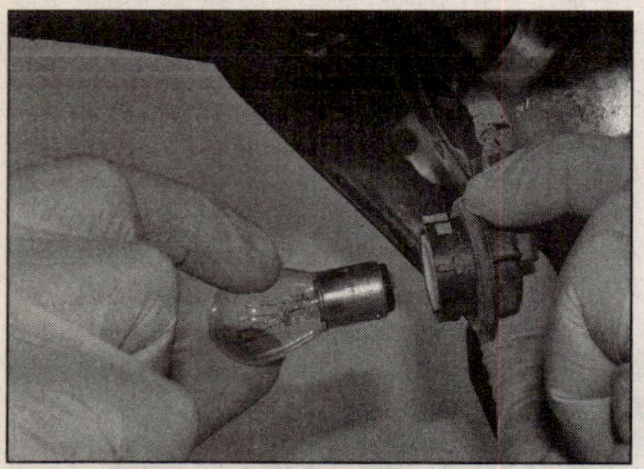
9.3 …and remove the bulb

9.8 Release the wiring from the clip

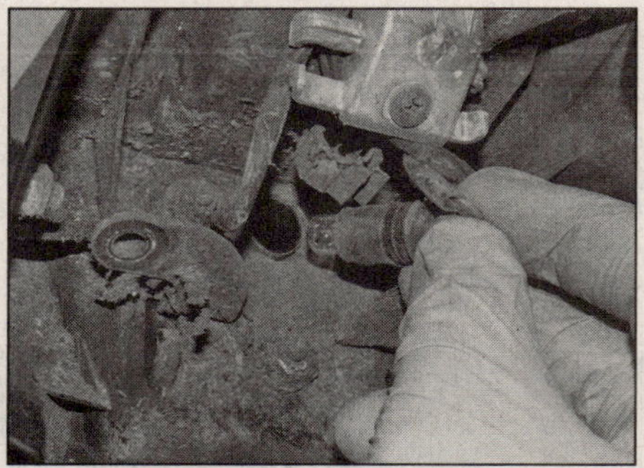
9.9a Pull the bulb holder out…

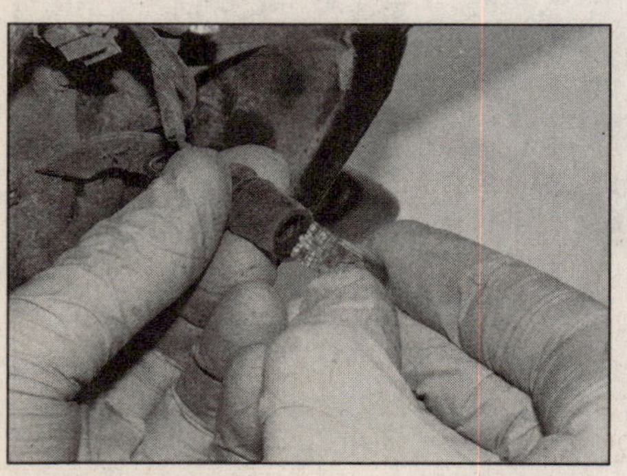
9.9b …then pull the bulb out of the holder

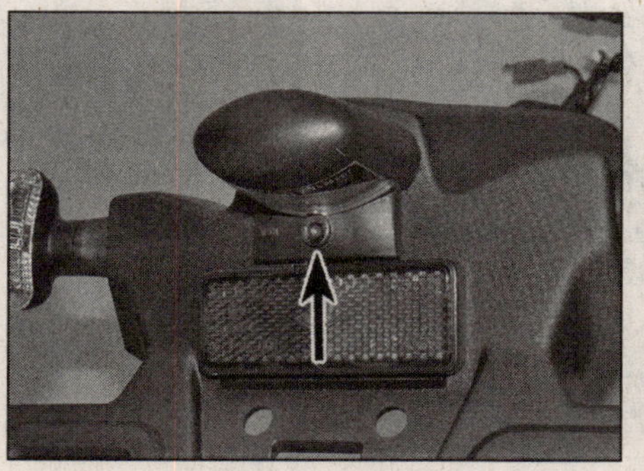
9.11a Licence plate light screw (arrowed)

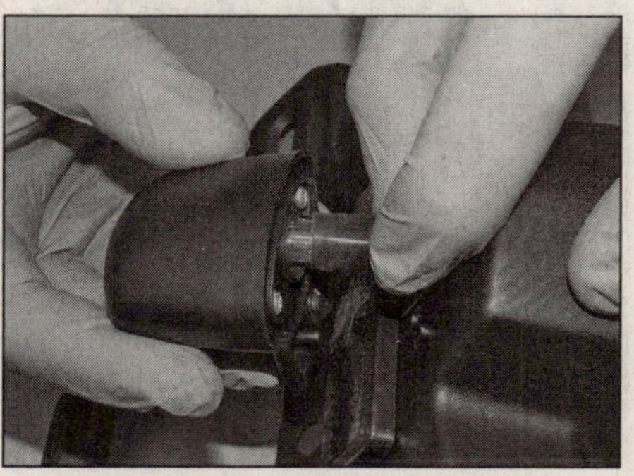
9.11b Pull the bulb holder out…

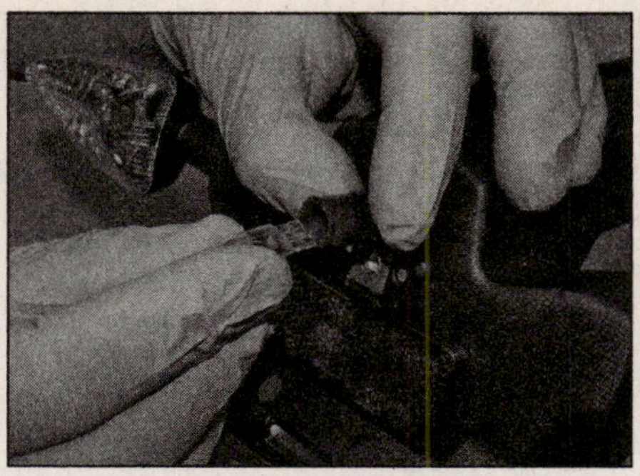

9.12 ... then pull the bulb out of the holder

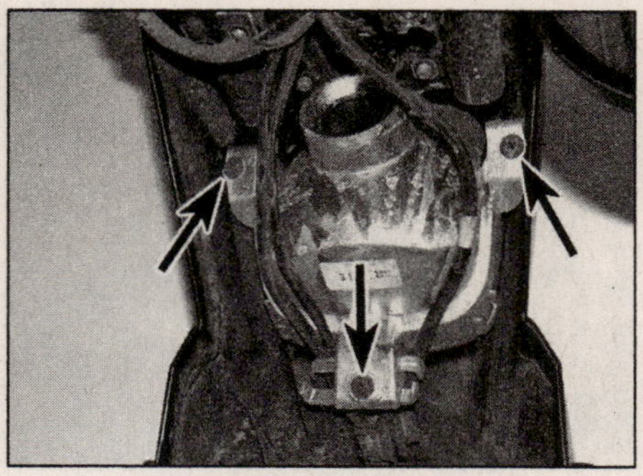

10.3 Tail light screws (arrowed)

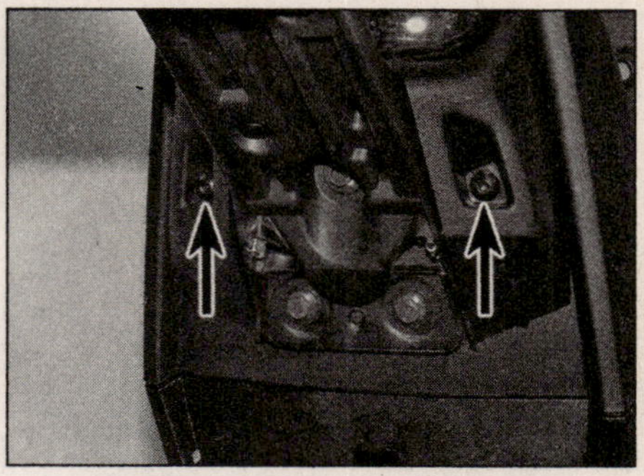

10.6a Undo the screws (arrowed) ...

12 Carefully pull the bulb out of its socket and replace it with a new one **(see illustration)**.

13 Fit the bulb holder into the light, then secure the light with its screw. Check the operation of the light.

10 Tail light

WR models

1 Remove the tail light cover **(see illustrations 9.1a and b)**.

2 Turn the bulb holder anti-clockwise and draw it out of the tail light **(see illustration 9.2)**.

3 Undo the screws and remove the tail light **(see illustration)**.

4 Installation is the reverse of removal – make sure the wiring is correctly routed around the light **(see illustration 10.3)**. Check the operation of the brake and tail lights.

MT models

5 Remove the ECU (see Chapter 4).

6 Remove the tail light cover **(see illustrations)**.

7 Disconnect the wiring connector **(see illustration)**.

8 Unscrew the nuts, remove the washers, and draw the tail light out. Note the collars in the grommets.

9 Installation is the reverse of removal. Check the operation of the tail and brake lights.

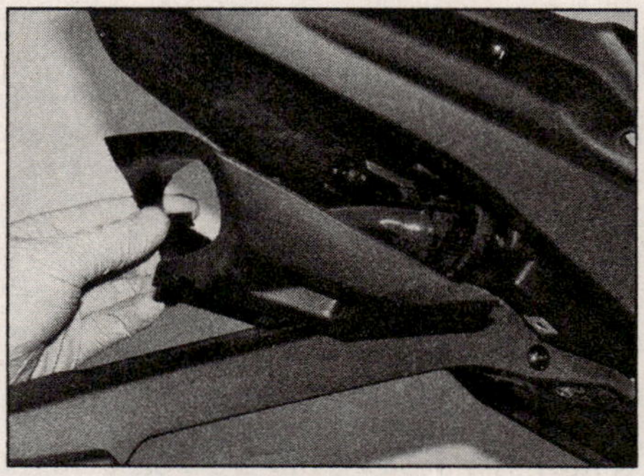

10.6b ... and remove the cover

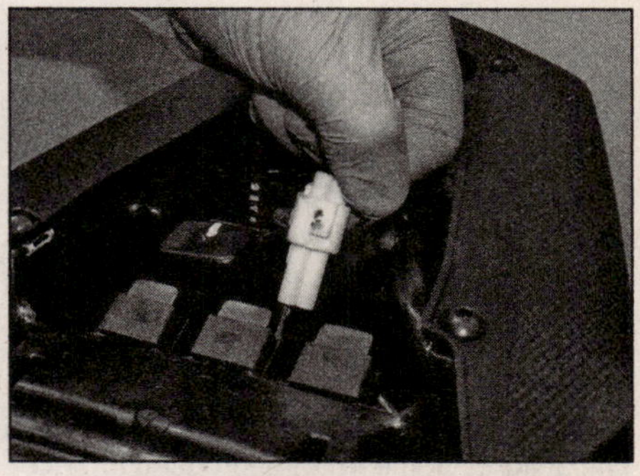

10.7 Tail light wiring connector

YZF-R models

10 Remove the seat cowls (see Chapter 7).

11 Disconnect the wiring connector and free the wiring from the tie **(see illustration)**.

12 Unscrew the nuts, remove the washers, and remove the tail light **(see illustration)**. Note the collars in the grommets.

13 Installation is the reverse of removal. Check the operation of the tail and brake lights.

11 Turn signal circuit check

Note: *Refer to Electrical System Fault Finding in Section 2 and to the wiring diagram at the end of this Chapter.*

1 Most turn signal problems are the result of a blown bulb or corroded socket. This is especially true when the turn signals function on one side (although possibly too quickly), but fail to work on the other side. If this is the case, first check the bulbs, the sockets and the wiring connectors. If all the turn signals fail to work, check the signal fuse (see Section 5), then the relay (see below). If all is good, the problem lies in the wiring or connectors, or the switch. Refer to Section 19 for the switch testing procedures, and also to the wiring diagram at the end of this Chapter.

2 On WR models remove the seat, and on MT and YZF-R models remove the passenger seat (see Chapter 7). Displace the relay

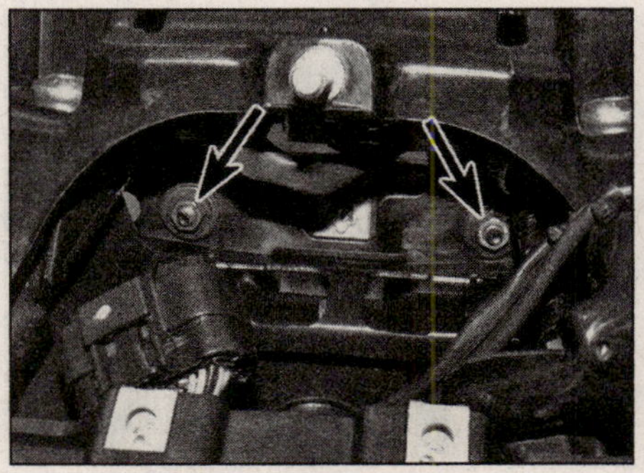

10.8 Tail light nuts (arrowed)

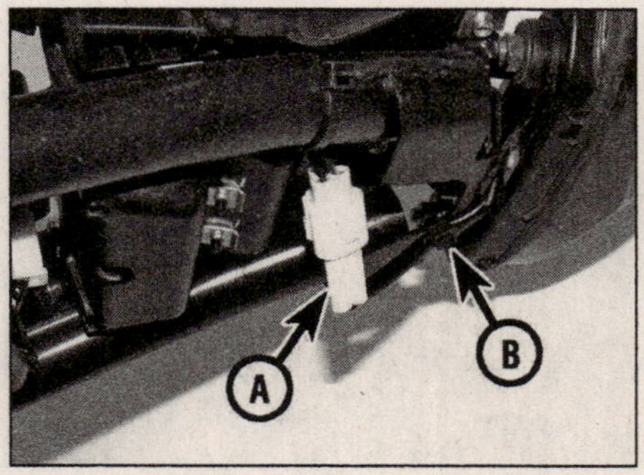

10.11 Tail light wiring connector (A) and cable-tie (B)

10.12 Unscrew the nut (arrowed) on each side

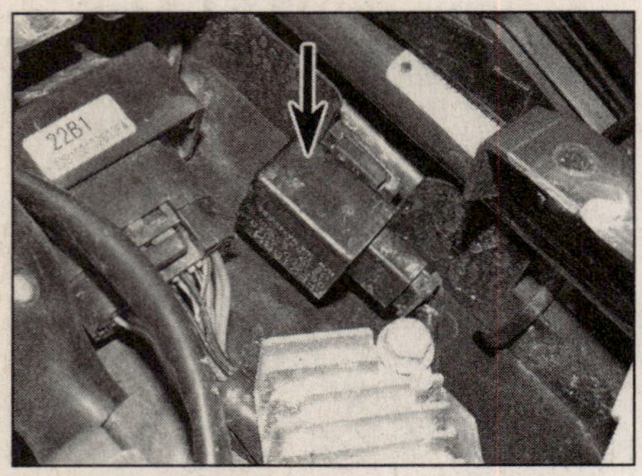

11.2a Turn signal relay (arrowed) – WR models

11.2b Turn signal relay (arrowed) – MT and YZF-R models

and disconnect the wiring connector **(see illustrations)**.

3 Check for battery voltage at the brown wire terminal on the loom side of the connector with the ignition ON. If no voltage is present, check the wiring from the relay to the ignition switch via the fusebox for continuity.

4 If voltage was present, short between the brown and brown/white wire terminals on the connector using a jumper wire. Turn the ignition ON and operate the turn signal switch, first in one direction, then the other. If the turn signal lights come on in each direction (they won't flash), the relay is confirmed faulty.

5 If none of the lights come on, check the brown/white wire for continuity to the left-hand switch housing, and repair or renew the wiring or connectors as required.

6 If all is good so far, or if some of the lights work but not all, check the wiring for the lights concerned between the left-hand switch housing and the turn signals themselves. Repair or renew the wiring or connectors as necessary.

12 Turn signal bulbs

Note: *It is a good idea to use a paper towel or dry cloth when handling the new bulb to prevent injury if the bulb should break and to increase bulb life.*

1 Undo the screw securing the lens and detach it from the housing, noting how it fits **(see illustrations)**.

2 Push the bulb into the holder and twist it anti-clockwise to remove it **(see illustration)**.

3 Line up the pins of the new bulb with the slots in the socket (it will only fit one way), then push the bulb in and turn it clockwise until it locks into place.

4 Fit the lens onto the housing, making sure it locates correctly, and secure it with the screw. Do not over-tighten the screw as it is easy to strip the threads or crack the lens.

13 Turn signal assemblies

Front

WR models

1 Remove the headlight (see Section 8).

2 Cut the cable-tie around the rubber boot, then draw out the wiring connectors **(see illustration)**. Disconnect the turn signal connector(s) as required **(see illustration)**.

3 Unscrew the bolt and remove the turn signal, taking care as you draw the wiring through **(see illustration)**.

4 Installation is the reverse of removal. Check the operation of the turn signals.

MT models

5 Remove the air scoop on the relevant side (see Chapter 7).

6 Release the wiring connector from its

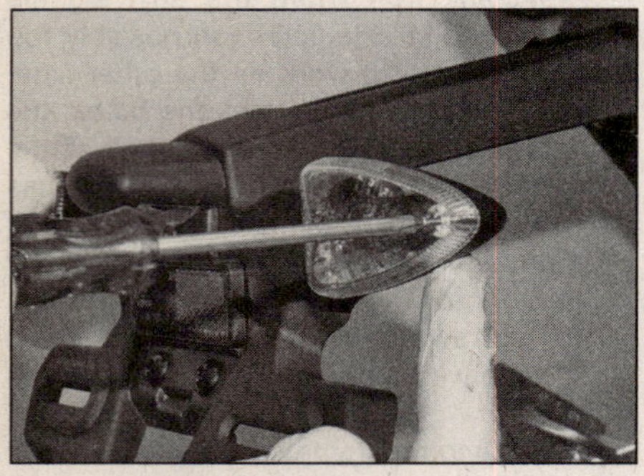

12.1a Undo the screw...

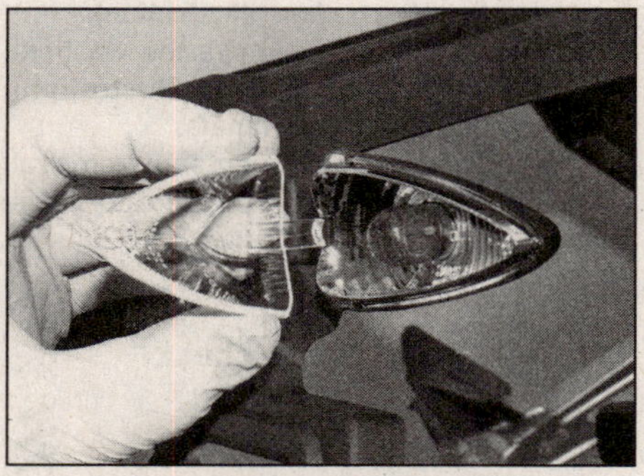

12.1b ... and detach the lens...

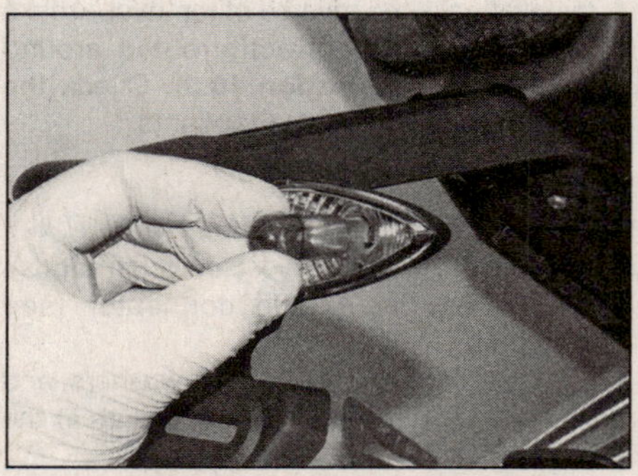

12.2 ... then remove the bulb

13.2a Cut the cable-tie (arrowed) and draw the boot back...

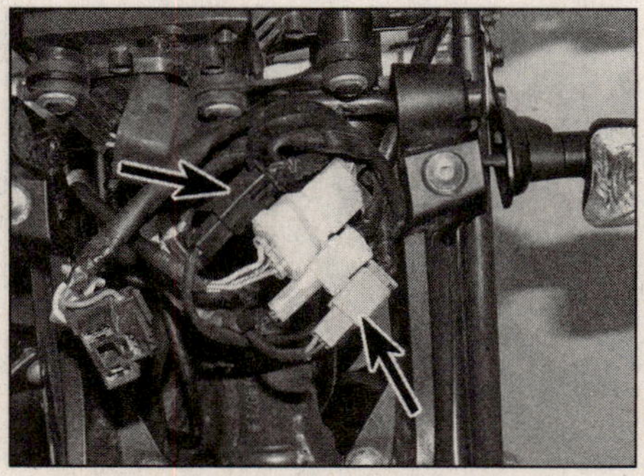

13.2b ... to access the connectors (arrowed)

13.3 Turn signal bolt (arrowed)

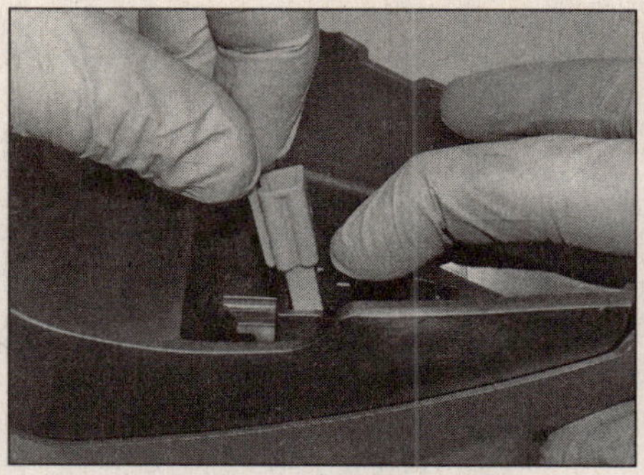
13.6a Release the clip and lift the connector out of its holder...

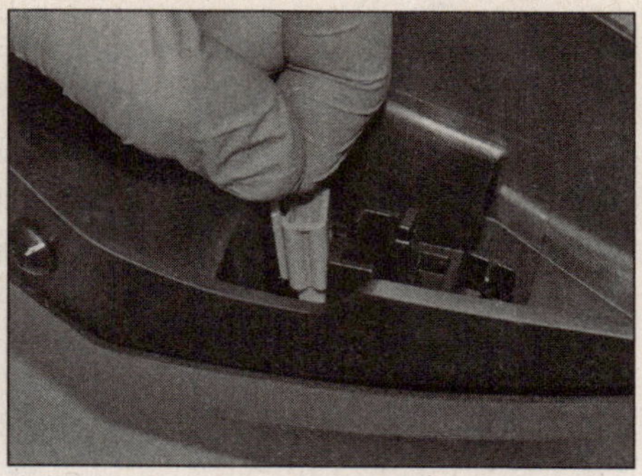
13.6b ...then push it through the hole

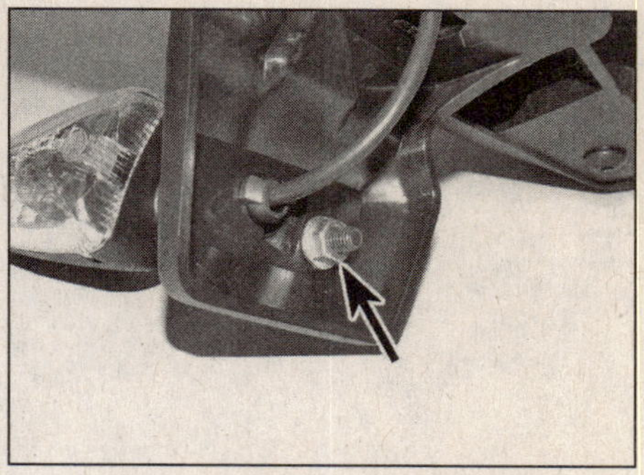
13.6c Unscrew the nut (arrowed) and remove the bolt

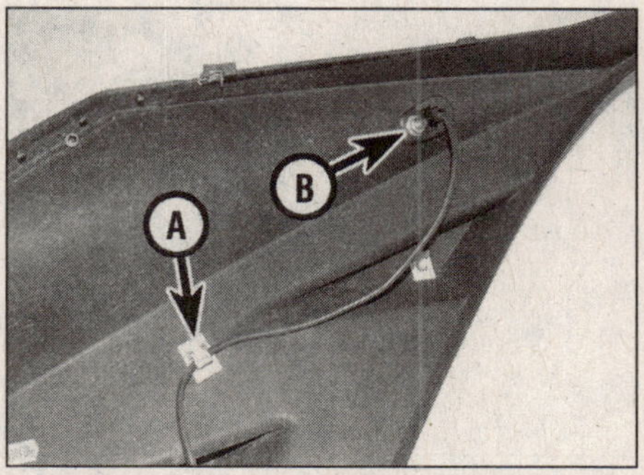

13.9 Release the clip (A), then unscrew the nut (B)

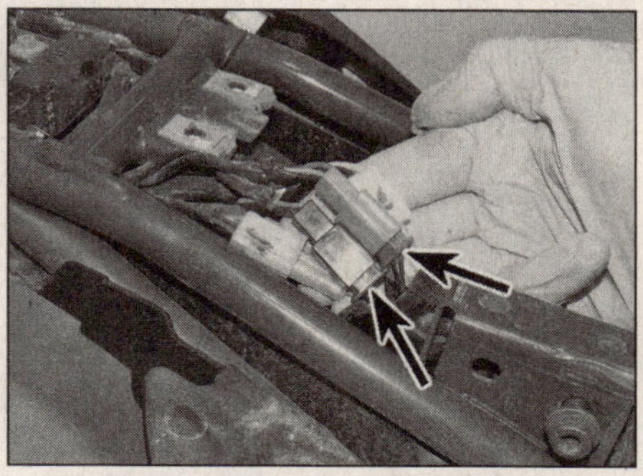
13.12 Turn signal wiring connectors (arrowed)

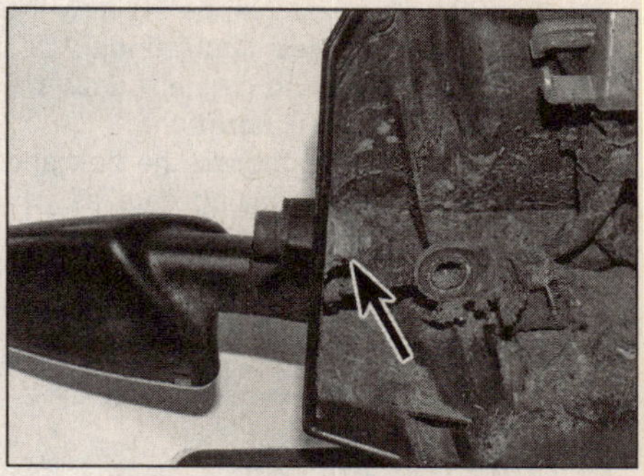
13.13 Turn signal nut (arrowed)

holder and feed it through the hole **(see illustrations)**. Unscrew the nut, withdraw the bolt and remove the turn signal, taking care as you draw the wiring through **(see illustration)**.
7 Installation is the reverse of removal. Check the operation of the turn signals.

YZF-R models

8 Remove the upper section of the fairing on the relevant side (see Chapter 7).
9 Release the wiring from its clip, then unscrew the nut, withdraw the bolt and remove the turn signal, taking care as you draw the wiring through **(see illustration)**.
10 Installation is the reverse of removal. Check the operation of the turn signals.

Rear

WR models

11 Remove the seat (see Chapter 7). Remove the tail light cover **(see illustrations 9.1a and b)**. Release the wiring clip **(see illustration 9.8)**.
12 Cut the cable-tie around the rubber boot, then draw out the wiring connectors **(see illustration 6.7a)**. Disconnect the turn signal connector(s) as required, then feed the connector(s) down to the turn signal(s), noting the routing **(see illustration)**.
13 Unscrew the nut, withdraw the bolt and remove the turn signal, taking care as you draw the wiring through **(see illustration)**.
14 Installation is the reverse of removal. Check the operation of the turn signals.

MT and YZF-R models

15 Remove the ECU (see Chapter 4).
16 Disconnect the turn signal and licence plate light wiring connectors **(see illustration)**.
17 On MT models remove the tail light cover **(see illustrations 10.6a and b)**.
18 Unscrew the tail hanger bolts, displace the hanger and carefully draw the wiring and connectors out **(see illustrations)**.
19 Undo the six screws and remove the

13.16 Disconnect the connectors (arrowed)

13.18a Tail hanger bolts (arrowed)

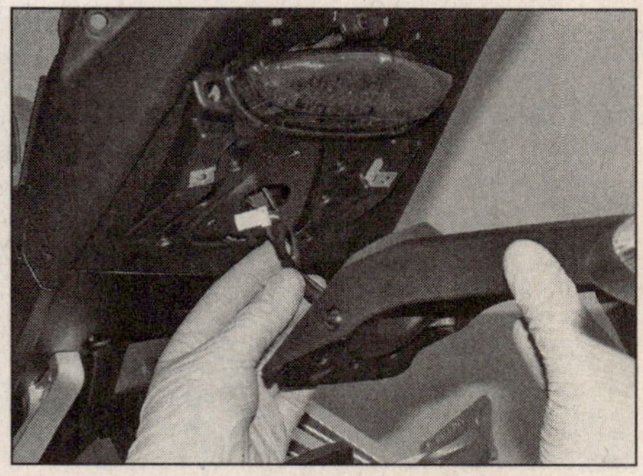
13.18b Draw the wiring out of the hole

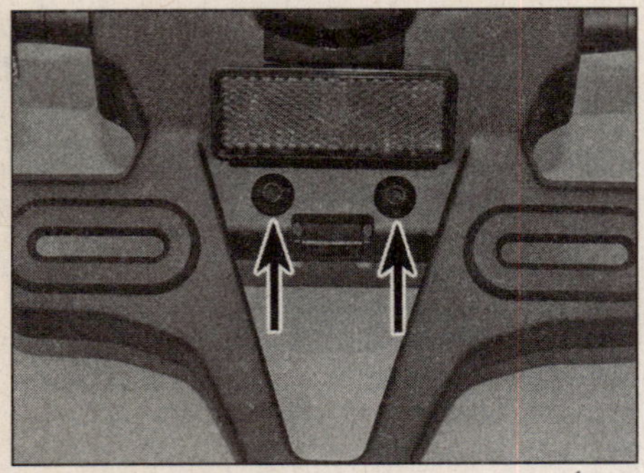

13.19a Undo the screws on the back (arrowed)...

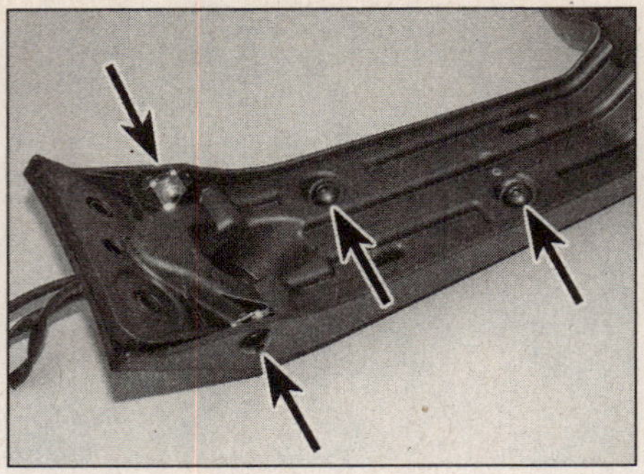

13.19b ...and the sides and underside...

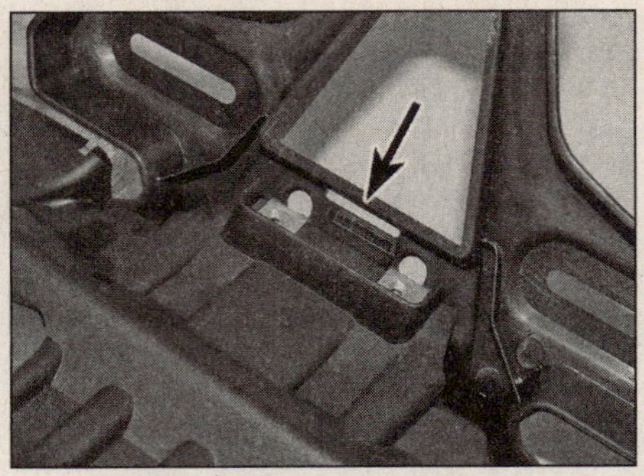

13.19c ...then release the tab from its slot (arrowed)

bottom section of the hanger, noting how the tab locates in the slot **(see illustrations)**.

20 Cut the cable-ties and carefully draw the relevant wiring out **(see illustration)**.

21 Unscrew the nut, withdraw the bolt and remove the turn signal, taking care as you draw the wiring through **(see illustration)**.

22 Installation is the reverse of removal. Check the operation of the turn signals and licence plate light.

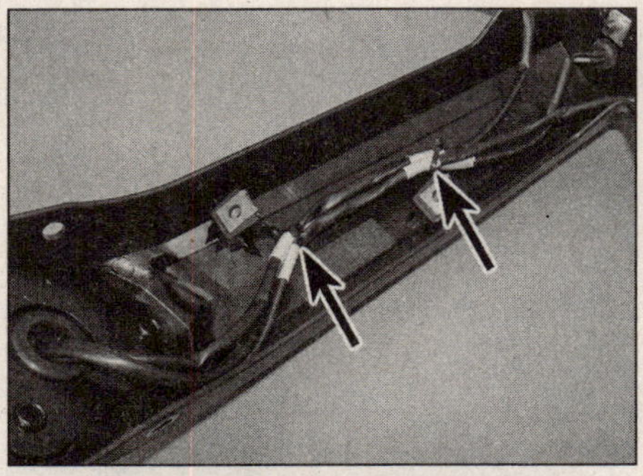

13.20 Cut the cable-ties (arrowed)

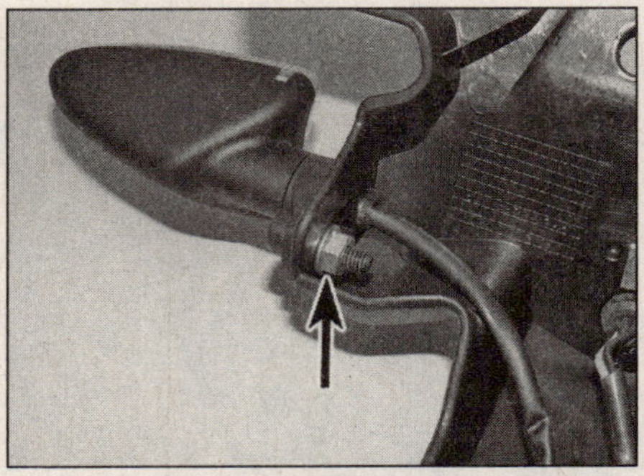

13.21 Turn signal nut (arrowed)

14 Brake light switches

Circuit check

Note: *Refer to Electrical System Fault Finding in Section 2 and to the wiring diagram at the end of this Chapter.*

1 Before checking the switches, and if not already done, check the brake light circuit (see Section 6).

Front brake lever switch

2 On WR models remove the fuel tank (see Chapter 4). Pull the rubber boot back and disconnect the 2-pin connector **(see illustration)**.

3 On MT and YZF-R models disconnect the wiring connectors from the switch **(see illustration)**.

4 Using a continuity tester, connect the probes to the terminals on the switch side of the connector on WR models, and to the terminals on the switch on MT and YZF-R models. With the brake lever at rest, there should be no continuity. With the lever applied, there should be continuity. If the results are not as stated remove the switch (see below) and check the plunger for damage **(see illustration)**. Replace the switch with a new one if necessary (see below).

5 If the switch is good, check for voltage at the brown wire terminal on the loom side of the connector, with the ignition switch ON – there should be battery voltage. If there's no voltage present, check the wiring between the connector and the ignition switch via the fusebox (see the wiring diagram at the end of this Chapter). If voltage is present, check the green/yellow wire for continuity to the tail light unit wiring connector, referring to the wiring diagram. Repair or renew the wiring as necessary.

Rear brake pedal switch

6 Models with a conventional (non-ABS) braking system have a hydraulic switch that is threaded into the top of the master cylinder. Models with ABS have a plunger typeswitch actuated by a spring connected to the brake pedal.

7 On WR models remove the seat, and on MT and YZF-R models remove the right-hand side cover (see Chapter 7). Trace the wiring from

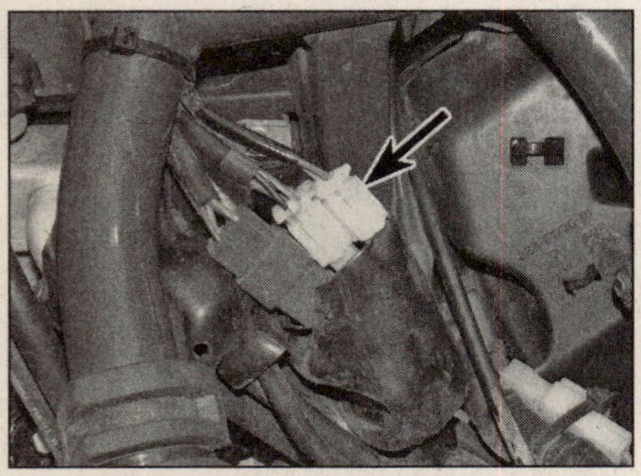

14.2 Front brake light switch connector (arrowed)

14.3 Front brake light switch wiring connectors (arrowed)

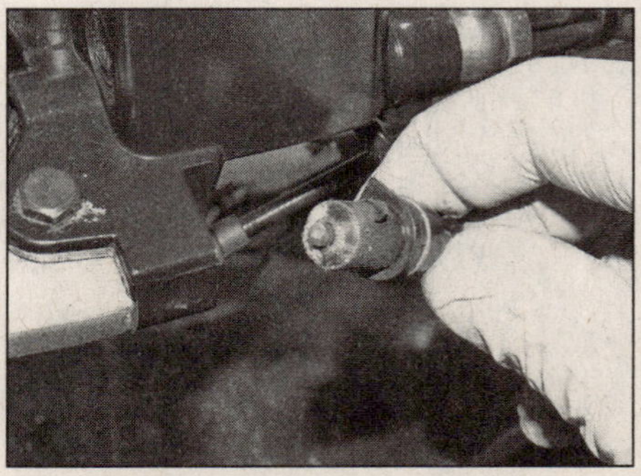

14.4 Check the switch plunger is not seized or broken (WR type shown)

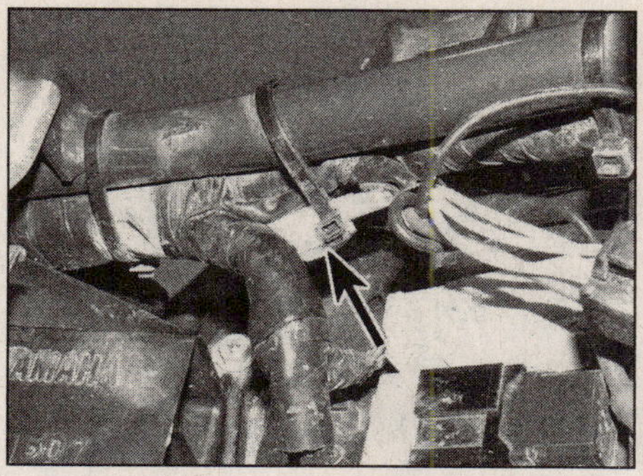

14.7a Rear brake light switch wiring connector (arrowed) – WR models

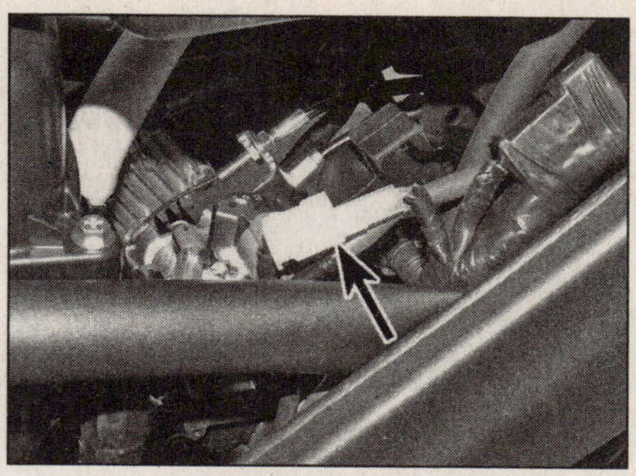

14.7b Rear brake light switch wiring connector (arrowed) – MT and YZF-R models

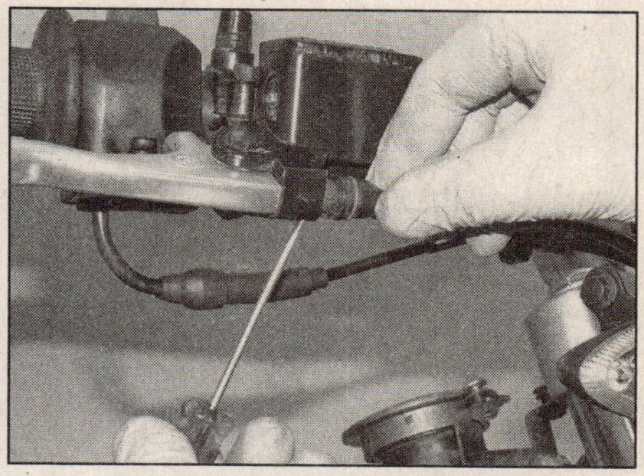

14.10 Release the catch and withdraw the switch

the switch and disconnect it at the connector **(see illustrations)**.

8 Using a continuity tester, connect the probes to the terminals on the switch side of the wiring connector. With the brake pedal at rest, there should be no continuity. With the pedal applied, there should be continuity. If the switch does not behave as described on models with a hydraulic switch, replace it with a new one. On models with a plunger switch first check the switch adjustment (see Chapter 1), and that the spring is connected to the pedal and the switch pushrod and is in good condition, then push the brake pedal down and check that that the pushrod is drawn out of the switch. Replace the switch with a new one if necessary.

9 If the switch is good, check for voltage at the brown wire terminal on the loom side of the connector, with the ignition switch ON – there should be battery voltage. If there's no voltage present, check the wiring between the connector and the ignition switch via the fusebox (see the wiring diagram at the end of this Chapter). If voltage is present, check the green/yellow wire for continuity to the tail light unit wiring connector, referring to the wiring diagram. Repair or renew the wiring as necessary.

Switch replacement

Front brake lever switch

10 On WR models remove the fuel tank (see Chapter 4). Trace the wiring from the switch and disconnect it at the 2-pin connector **(see illustration 14.2)**. Feed the wiring back to the switch, noting its routing and releasing it from any ties. Release the switch by pushing up on its catch via the hole using a small screwdriver, and pull the switch out of its socket **(see illustration)**.

11 On MT and YZF-R models disconnect the wiring connectors from the switch **(see illustration 14.3)**. Undo the screw and remove the switch.

12 Installation is the reverse of removal.

Rear brake pedal switch

Removal

13 Refer to Step 7 and disconnect the wiring connector. Feed the wiring down to the switch, releasing any ties and noting its routing.

14 On models with a hydraulic switch cover the switch and surrounding area with rag, then unscrew the switch and detach the banjo union, noting its alignment with the master cylinder **(see illustration)**. Once disconnected, seal the banjo union and secure the hose in an upright position to minimise fluid loss. New sealing washers must be fitted on reassembly.

15 On models with a conventional switch unhook the spring from the brake pedal then pull the switch out of its bracket **(see illustrations)**.

Installation

16 On models with a hydraulic switch connect the brake hose to the master cylinder, using new sealing washers on each side of the banjo fitting, and aligning it as noted on removal **(see illustration 14.14)**. Fit the brake light switch, hold the brake hose and tighten the switch to the torque setting specified at the beginning of the Chapter. Connect the wiring connector **(see illustration 14.7a or b)** – make sure the wiring is correctly routed and secured by any ties. Refer to Chapter 6 and bleed the rear brake.

17 On models with a conventional switch installation is the reverse of removal. Make sure the switch is correctly adjusted so the brake light comes on just before the brake does – refer to Chapter 1 for switch adjustment.

15 Instruments

Check

1 There are no test details for the individual instruments.

2 If there is a problem with the instruments, first check the signal fuse, and on MT and YZF-R models the back-up fuse (see Section 5), then check the wiring connector is secure and that all wires and terminals

14.14 Rear brake light switch (arrowed) – hydraulic type

14.15a Unhook the smaller of the two springs (arrowed)...

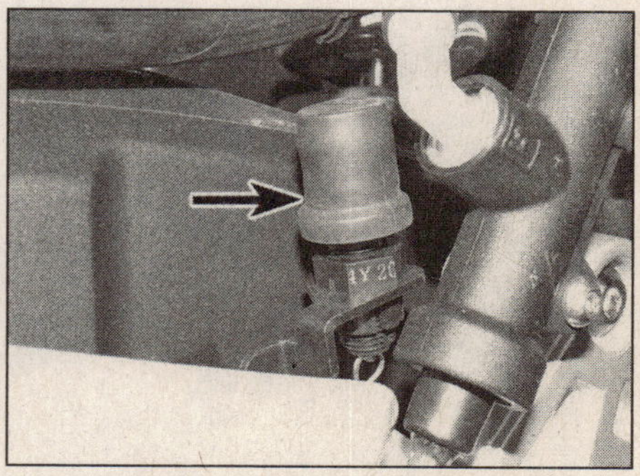

14.15b ...then release the switch from the bracket

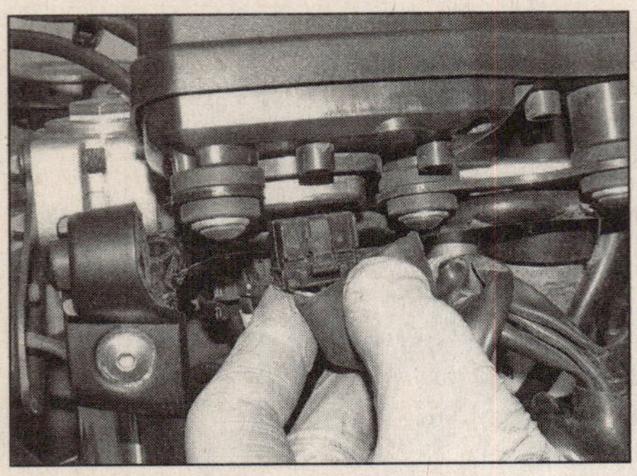

15.7 Disconnect the wiring...

15.8 ...then undo the screws

15.12a Undo the screws (arrowed) and lift the instruments...

are securely connected – refer below for access. Make sure the power supply is good by checking for battery voltage at the brown wire terminal with the ignition ON, and on MT and YZF-R models at the red wire terminal with the ignition ON or OFF. Also check for continuity to earth in the black wire on WR models and the black/white wire on MT and YZF-R models.

3 Next refer to Section 2 and to the Wiring Diagram at the end of the Chapter for your model and check the wiring and connectors in the relevant circuit. Also check the other components relevant to the circuit, e.g. neutral switch, dimmer switch, turn signals, fuel level sensor.

4 If there is a problem with the speedometer on WR and non-ABS MT and YZF models, check the sensor (see Chapter 4, Section 7).

Removal and installation

WR models

5 Remove the headlight (see Section 8).

6 Cut the cable-tie around the rubber boot and move the boot aside **(see illustration 13.2a)**.

7 Disconnect the instrument wiring connector **(see illustration)**.

8 Undo the three screws, noting the washers, and remove the instruments **(see illustration)**.

9 Installation is the reverse of removal. Make sure the grommets are in good condition.

MT models

10 If fitted remove the front cowl **(see illustration 8.4a)**. Undo the instrument cover screws and remove the cover **(see illustration 8.4b)**. Undo the headlight cover screws and remove the cover **(see illustration 8.4c)**.

11 Undo the headlight screw on each side and displace the light forwards **(see illustration 8.6a)**.

12 Undo the three screws, noting the washers, displace the instruments and disconnect the wiring connector **(see illustrations)**.

13 Installation is the reverse of removal. Make sure the grommets are in good condition.

YZF-R models

14 Remove the front fairing (see Chapter 7).

15 Undo the three screws, noting the washers, displace the instruments and disconnect the wiring connector **(see illustrations)**.

16 Installation is the reverse of removal.

16 Instrument and warning light LEDs

Note: *Refer to electrical system fault finding in Section 2 and to the wiring diagram for your model at the end of this Chapter.*

1 All instrument and warning lights are LEDs. If an LED does not work check the component and the circuit relevant to that LED, referring to Section 2 and to the wiring diagram for your model at the end of the Chapter. If the circuit is good and the LED has failed (you may be able to have this confirmed by a Yamaha dealer) a new instrument assembly must be fitted.

17 Fuel gauge and level sender

Note: *Refer to Electrical System Fault Finding in Section 2 and to the wiring diagram for your model at the end of this Chapter.*

Check

1 The circuit consists of the level sender that is an integral part of the fuel pump mounted inside the tank, and the gauge in the instruments. The gauge segments should all come on for a seconds when the ignition is switched ON, then go out – this serves as a check that the circuit is working correctly.

2 If the gauge does not work, remove the fuel pump (see Chapter 4).

3 Connect the positive (+) probe of a multimeter set to the ohms scale to the pink or red (according to model) wire terminal for the level sender and the negative (-) probe to the black wire terminal, and check the resistance is as specified at the beginning of the Chapter for your model with the float arm

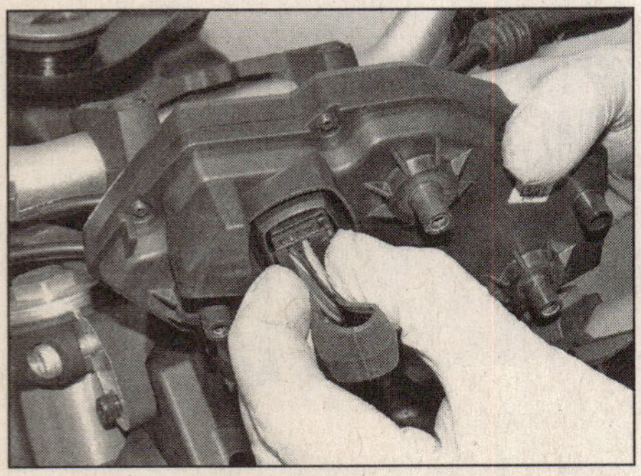

15.12b ...then disconnect the wiring

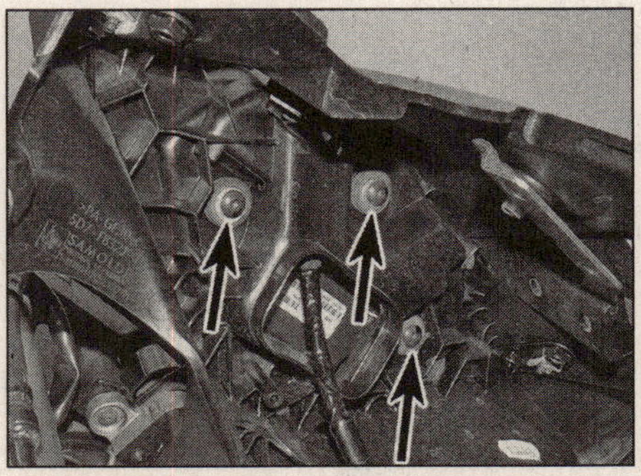

15.15a Undo the screws (arrowed) and lift the instruments...

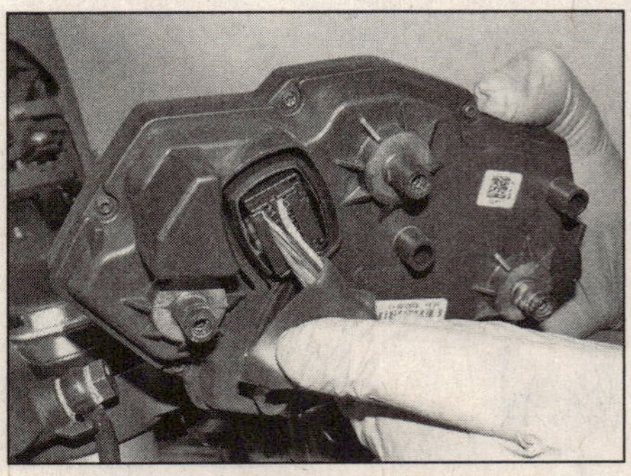

15.15b ...then disconnect the wiring

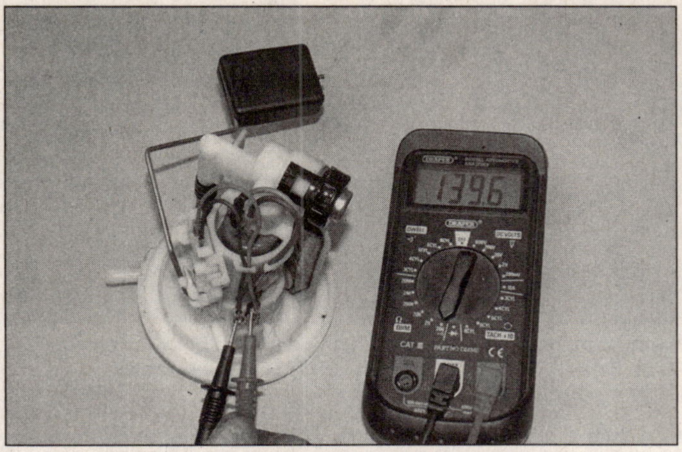

17.3a On WR models connect the probes as shown and measure the resistance with the float in the empty position...

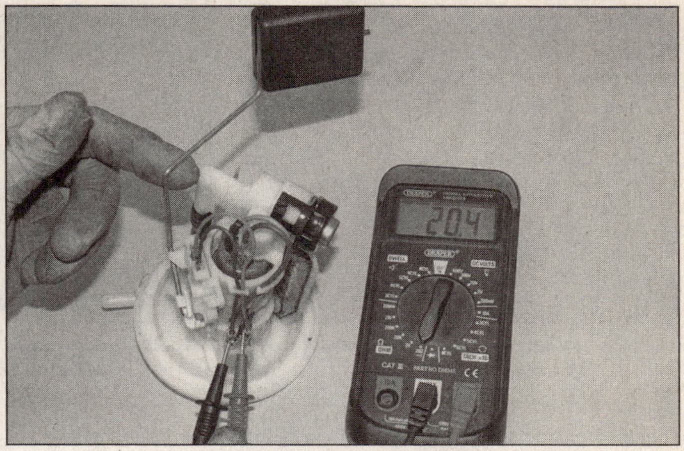

17.3b ...and in the full position

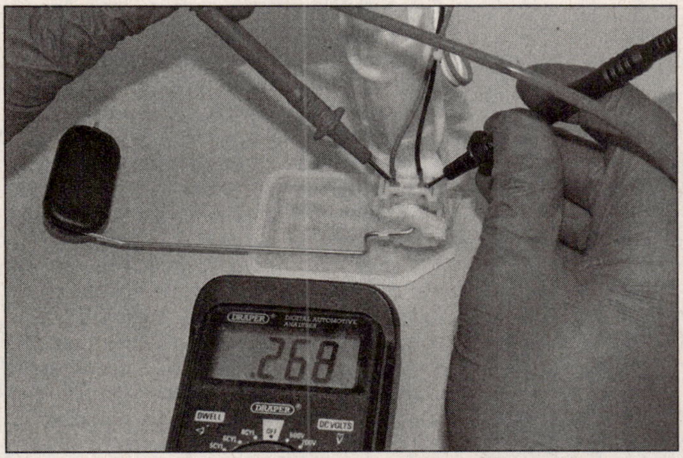

17.3c On MT and YZF-R models connect the probes as shown and measure the resistance with the float in the empty position...

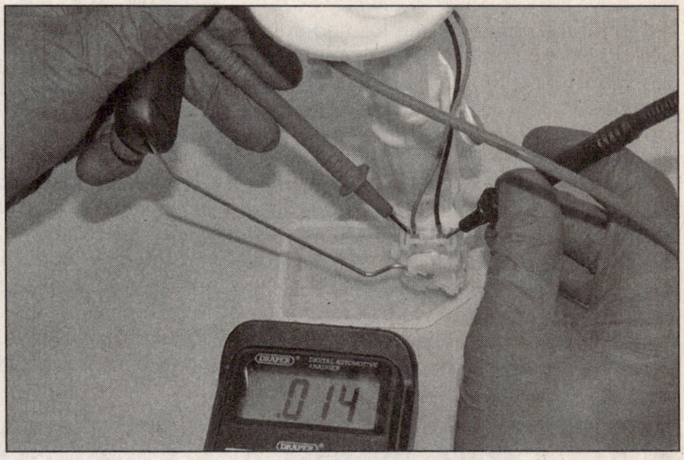

17.3d ...and in the full position

positioned firstly in the EMPTY position and then in the FULL position **(see illustrations)**. If the readings are not as specified the sender is faulty and a new fuel pump will have to be fitted (see Chapter 4) – the sender is not available separately.

4 If the sender is good, disconnect the instrument wiring connector (see Section 15), and check for continuity in the light blue and orange/white wires between the fuel pump wiring connector and the instrument connector on WR models, and in the green and orange/white wires between the sender and instrument connectors on MT and YZF-R models. If there is no continuity check the circuit and the connectors for faults.

5 If all is good have the instruments checked by a Yamaha dealer – if it is faulty a new one must be fitted (see Section 15).

Warning: Petrol (gasoline) is extremely flammable, so take extra precautions when you work on any part of the fuel system. Always remove the battery (see Section 3). Don't smoke or allow open flames or bare light bulbs near the work area, and don't work in a garage where a natural gas-type appliance is present. If you spill any fuel on your skin, rinse it off immediately with soap and water. When you perform any kind of work on the fuel system, wear safety glasses and have a fire extinguisher suitable for a class B type fire (flammable liquids) on hand.

Fuel level sender removal and installation

6 The sender is an integral part of the fuel pump assembly and is not available separately. If it is faulty a new pump must be fitted (see Chapter 4).

18 Ignition switch

Warning: To prevent the risk of short circuits, disconnect the battery negative (–) lead before making any ignition switch checks.

Check

Note: *Refer to Electrical System Fault Finding in Section 2 and to the wiring diagram for your model at the end of this Chapter.*

1 Remove the fuel tank (see Chapter 4).

2 Trace the wiring from the ignition switch and disconnect it at the red connector, pulling the rubber boot back to access it **(see illustrations)**.

3 Using an ohmmeter or a continuity tester, check the continuity of the connector terminal pairs (see the wiring diagram at the end of this Chapter). Continuity should exist between the terminals connected by a solid line on the diagram when the switch is in the indicated position.

4 If the switch fails the test, check for continuity in the wiring between the connector and the switch, and check the terminals on the switch. If necessary replace the switch with a new one.

5 If the switch is good, check for battery voltage at the red wire terminal on the loom side of the connector. If there is none, check the main fuse (Section 5), and if that is OK

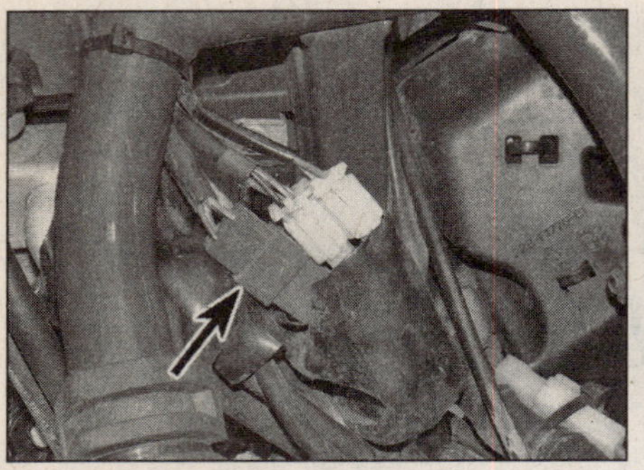

18.2a Ignition switch wiring connector (arrowed) – WR models

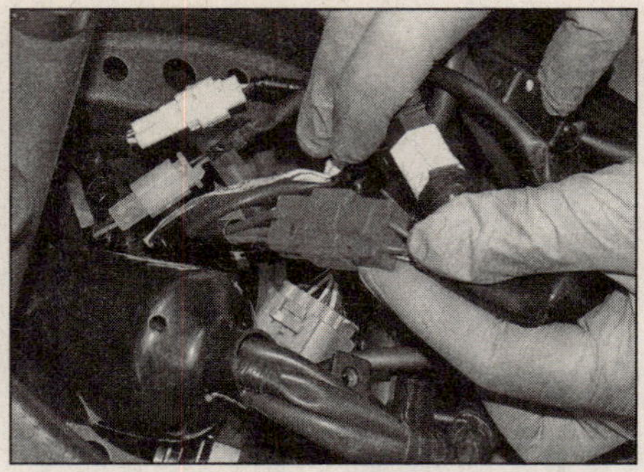

18.2b Ignition switch wiring connector – MT and YZF-R models

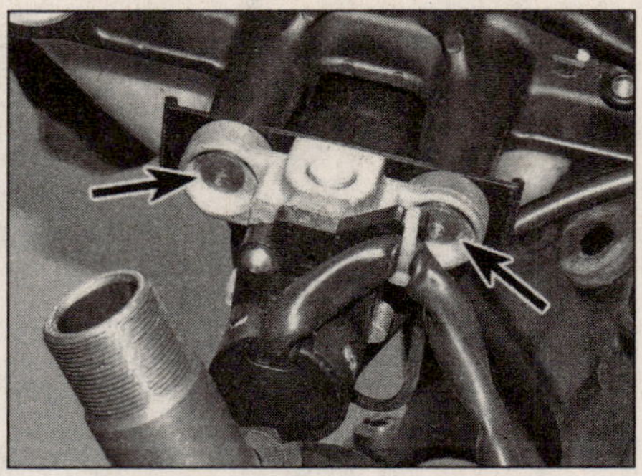

18.8 Ignition switch bolts (arrowed) – MT/YZF-R type shown

check for continuity in the wire between the switch and the battery via the fuse.

Removal and installation

6 Remove the fuel tank (see Chapter 4).
7 Trace the wiring from the ignition switch and disconnect it at the red connector, pulling the rubber boot back to access it **(see illustration 18.2a or b)**. Feed the wiring back to the switch, freeing it from any clips and ties and noting its routing.
8 The switch is secured by shear-head bolts, which have to be driven round until loose using a punch **(see illustration)**. Refer to Chapter 5 Section 5 and displace the handlebars, then to 5 Section 9 to remove the top yoke, following the relevant steps.
9 Installation is the reverse of removal. Fit new shear-head bolts and tighten them until the heads shear off. Make sure the wiring connector is correctly routed and securely connected.

19 Handlebar switches

Check

Note: *Refer to Electrical System Fault Finding in Section 2 and to the wiring diagram at the end of this Chapter.*
1 Generally speaking, the switches are reliable and trouble-free. Most troubles, when they do occur, are caused by dirty or corroded contacts, but wear and breakage of internal parts is a possibility that should not be overlooked. If breakage does occur, the entire switch and related wiring harness will have to be replaced with a new one, as individual parts are not available.
2 The switches can be checked for continuity using an ohmmeter or a continuity test light. Disconnect the battery negative (–) cable, which will prevent the possibility of a short circuit, before making the checks.
3 Remove the fuel tank (see Chapter 4).
4 Trace the wiring from the relevant switch and disconnect it at the connector(s), pulling the rubber boot back to access it/them **(see illustrations)**.
5 Check for continuity between the terminals of the switch connector with the switch in the various positions (i.e. switch off – no continuity, switch on – continuity) – see the wiring diagram at the end of this Chapter. Continuity should exist between the terminals connected by a solid line on the diagram when the switch is in the indicated position.
6 If the continuity check indicates a problem exists, displace the switch housing and check for any detached wires – if any are found, solder them back onto the switch. Spray the switch contacts with electrical contact cleaner (there is no need to remove the switch completely). If they are accessible, the contacts can be scraped clean with a knife or polished with crocus cloth. If switch components are damaged or broken, it should be obvious when the switch is disassembled.

Removal and installation

7 Remove the fuel tank (see Chapter 4).
8 Trace the wiring from the relevant switch and disconnect it at the connector(s), pulling the rubber boot back to access it/them **(see illustration 19.4a, b, c or d)**. Feed the wiring back to the switch, freeing it from any clips and ties and noting its routing. When removing the left-hand switch, disconnect the wiring connector from the clutch switch **(see illustration 22.2)**.
9 To remove the right-hand switch, refer to Chapter 4 and detach the throttle cable(s), which involves detaching the switch housing from the handlebars.
10 To remove the left-hand switch, undo the switch housing screws and free it from

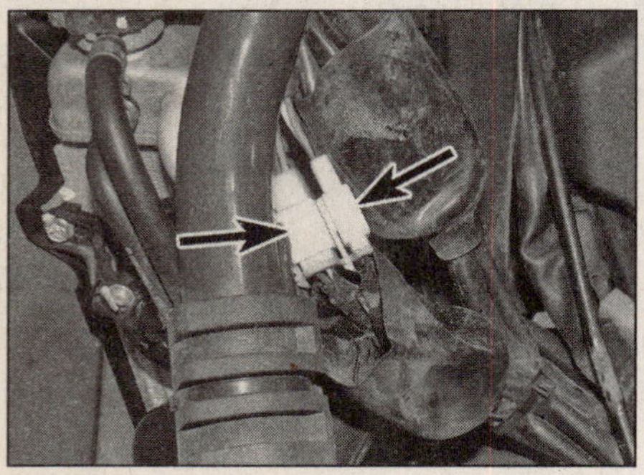

19.4a Left-hand switch wiring connectors (arrowed)...

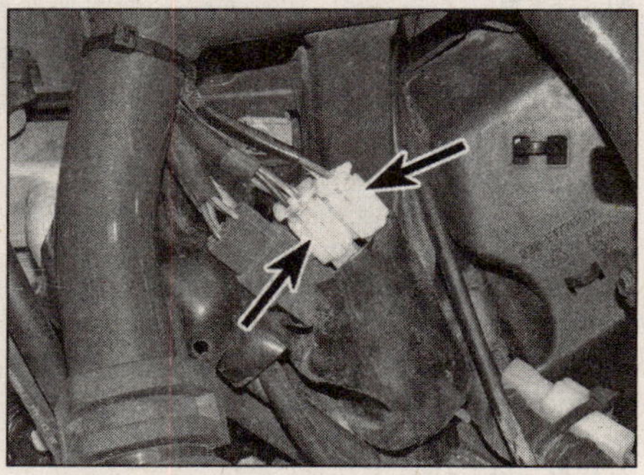

19.4b ... and right-hand switch connectors – WR models

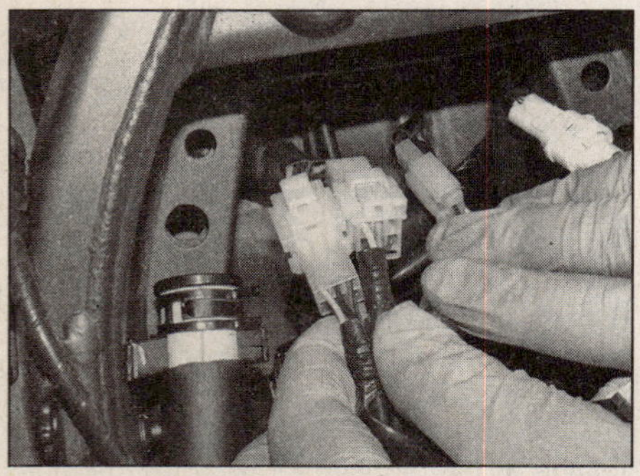

19.4c Left-hand switch wiring connectors (arrowed)...

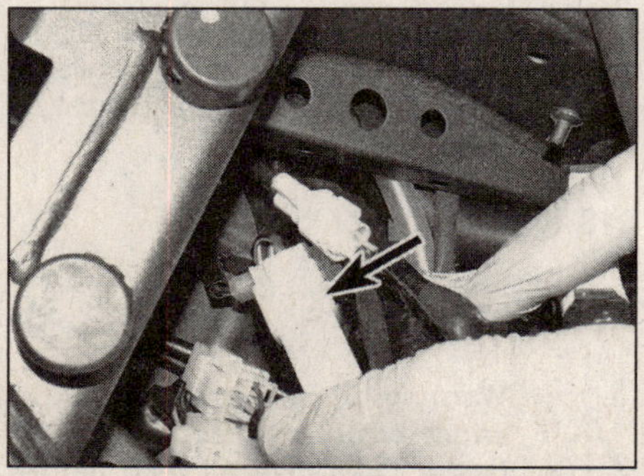

19.4d ... and right-hand switch connector (arrowed) – MT and YZF-R models

19.10 Left-hand switch housing screws (arrowed)

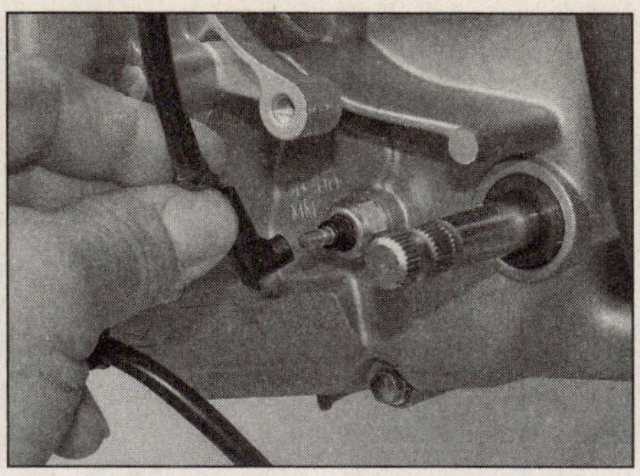

20.3 Pull the wiring connector off the switch

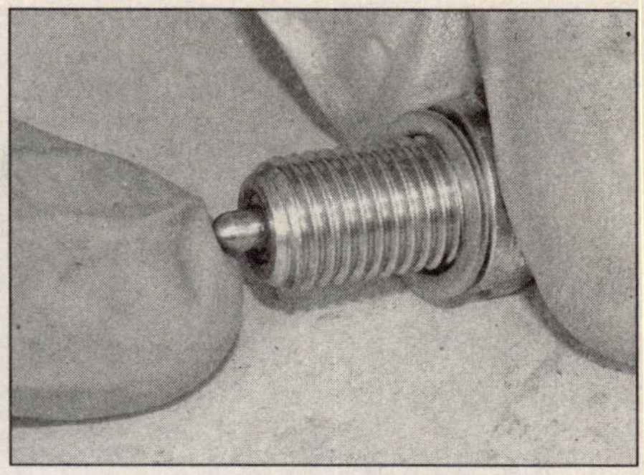

20.12 Check the plunger

the handlebar by separating the halves **(see illustration)**.

11 Installation is the reverse of removal. Make sure the locating pin in the switch housing locates in the hole in the handlebar. Refer to Chapter 4 for installation of the throttle cable(s) and right-hand switch housing.

20 Neutral switch

1 The neutral switch is part of the starter safety circuit (see Chapter 1, Section 16).

Check

Note: *Refer to Electrical System Fault Finding in Section 2 and to the wiring diagram at the end of this Chapter.*

2 Before checking the electrical circuit, check whether the neutral LED in the instrument cluster comes on when the ignition is switched on – if it does the LED is proved good; if it doesn't check it (Section 16).

3 The switch is located in the left-hand side of the transmission casing below the front sprocket cover – on YZF-R models remove the bottom and lower sections of the fairing on the left-hand side (see Chapter 7). Pull the wiring connector off the switch **(see illustration)**.

4 Make sure the transmission is in neutral. With the connector disconnected and the ignition switch ON, the neutral light should be out. If not, the wire between the connector and instrument cluster must be earthed (grounded) at some point.

5 Check for continuity between the switch terminal and the crankcase. With the transmission in neutral, there should be continuity. With the transmission in gear, there should be no continuity. If the tests prove otherwise, then remove the switch (see below) and check whether the plunger in the switch or its contact on the selector drum is bent or damaged.

6 If the continuity tests prove the switch is good, check for voltage at the wire terminal with the ignition on. If there's no voltage present, check the wire between the switch and the instrument cluster (see the wiring diagram at the end of this Chapter).

7 If the switch is good, check the other components (sidestand switch, clutch switch, starter circuit cut-off relay and diodes) and their wiring and connectors in the starter circuit as described in the relevant sections of this Chapter. If all components are good, check the wiring between the various components (see the wiring diagram at the end of this Chapter). Repair or renew the wiring as required.

Removal

8 The switch is located in the left-hand side of the transmission casing below the front sprocket cover – on MT models remove the belly-pan and on YZF-R models remove all sections of the fairing on each side (see Chapter 7).

9 Drain the engine oil (see Chapter 1).

10 Pull the wiring connector off the switch **(see illustration 20.3)**.

11 Unscrew and remove the switch. A new sealing washer must be used.

Inspection

12 Make sure the contact plunger moves in and out smoothly, and that the end is not broken **(see illustration)**.

Installation

13 Fit the switch using a new sealing washer and tighten to the torque setting specified at the beginning of the Chapter.

14 Connect the wiring **(see illustration 20.3)**. Check the operation of the switch.

15 Replenish the engine oil (see Chapter 1).

21 Sidestand switch

1 The sidestand switch is mounted on the sidestand bracket, above the sidestand on WR models and to the front of it on MT and YZF-R models. The switch is part of the starter safety circuit (see Chapter 1, Section 16).

2 To access the wiring connector, on WR models pull the rubber boot off the connectors on top of the crankcase, and on MT and YZF-R models remove the left-hand side cover (see Chapter 7) then cut the cable-tie and pull the boot off the connectors between the rear sub-frame and the air filter housing. To access the switch on MT models remove the belly-pan and on YZF-R models remove the bottom section of the fairing on the right-hand side (see Chapter 7).

Check

Note: *Refer to Electrical System Fault Finding in Section 2 and to the wiring diagram at the end of this Chapter.*

3 Trace the wiring from the switch and disconnect it at the blue connector **(see illustrations)**.

4 Check the operation of the switch using an ohmmeter or continuity tester. Connect the

21.3a Sidestand switch wiring connector (arrowed) – WR models

21.3b Sidestand switch wiring connector is inside the rubber boot (arrowed) on MT and YZF-R models

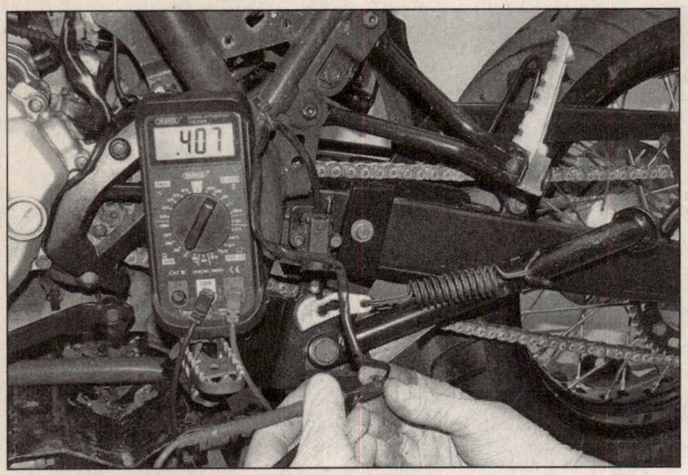

21.4a Check for continuity with the sidestand up...

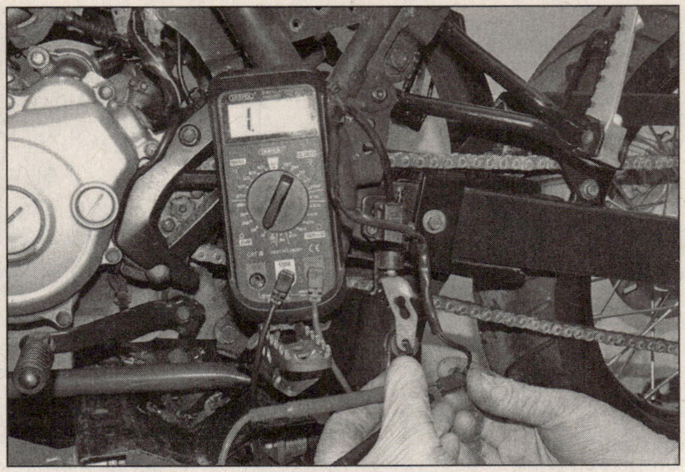

21.4b ...and for no continuity with it down

meter between the terminals on the switch side of the connector. With the sidestand up there should be continuity, and with it down there should be no continuity **(see illustrations)**. Make sure the switch plunger is clean, and that it moves freely and smoothly in and out of the switch under spring pressure.

5 If the switch does not perform as expected, it is faulty and must be replaced with a new one. If the switch is good, check the other components (clutch switch, neutral switch, starter circuit cut-off relay and diodes) and their wiring and connectors in the starter circuit as described in the relevant sections of this Chapter. If all components are good, check the wiring between the various components (see the wiring diagram at the end of this Chapter). Repair or renew the wiring as required.

Replacement

6 Trace the wiring from the switch and disconnect it at the connector **(see illustration 21.3a or b)**. On WR models remove the left-hand frame cover (see Chapter 7). Feed the wiring back to the switch, freeing it from any clips and ties and noting its routing.

7 On WR models unscrew the bolts and remove the switch **(see illustration)**.

8 On MT and YZF-R models hold the bolt heads, unscrew the nuts, withdraw the bolts and remove the switch and the mounting block **(see illustration)**.

21.7 Sidestand switch bolts (arrowed)

21.8 Sidestand switch mounting arrangement – MT and YZF-R models

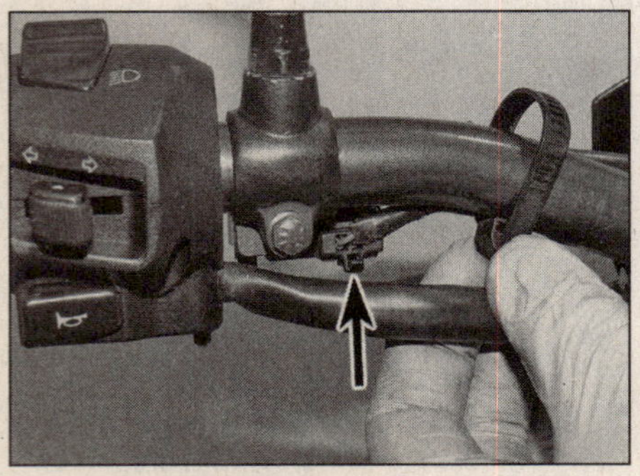

22.2 Clutch switch wiring connector (arrowed)

22.5 Clutch switch screw (arrowed)

9 Installation is the reverse of removal. Clean the threads of the bolts and apply a suitable non-permanent thread locking compound. Check the operation of the switch (see Chapter 1 Section 18).

22 Clutch switch

1 The clutch switch is mounted under the clutch lever bracket. The switch is part of the starter safety circuit (see Chapter 1, Section 16).

Check

Note: *Refer to Electrical System Fault Finding in Section 2 and to the wiring diagram at the end of this Chapter.*

2 Disconnect the wiring connector from the switch **(see illustration)**.

3 Using a continuity tester, connect the probes to the terminals on the switch. With the lever at rest, there should be no continuity. With the lever pulled in, there should be continuity. If the switch does not behave as described, replace it with a new one. If the results are not as stated remove the switch (see below) and check the plunger for damage. Replace the switch with a new one if necessary.

4 If the switch is good, check the other components (sidestand switch, neutral switch, starter circuit cut-off relay and diodes) and their wiring and connectors in the starter circuit as described in the relevant sections of this Chapter. If all components are good, check the wiring between the various components (see the wiring diagram at the end of this Chapter).

Replacement

5 Disconnect the wiring connector from the switch **(see illustration 22.2)**. Undo the screw and remove the switch **(see illustration)**.

6 Installation is the reverse of removal.

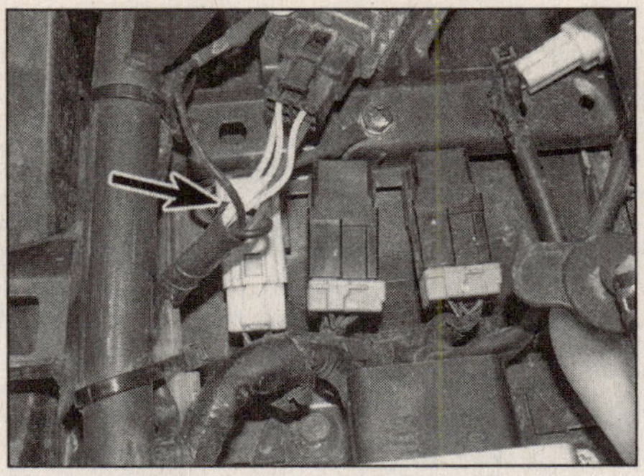

23.3a Starter circuit cut-off relay (arrowed) – WR models

23 Starter circuit cut-off relay and diodes

Note: *Refer to Electrical System Fault Finding in Section 2 and to the wiring diagram at the end of this Chapter.*

1 The starter circuit cut-off relay and its associated diodes are part of the starter safety circuit (see Chapter 1, Section 16).

Starter circuit cut-off relay

2 On WR model remove the seat, and on MT and YZF-R models remove the passenger seat (see Chapter 7).

3 Disconnect the battery negative (–) lead (see Section 3). Displace the relay and disconnect the wiring connector **(see illustrations)**.

4 To check the operation of the relay, using an ohmmeter or continuity tester, connect the positive (+) probe to the blue/black wire terminal on the relay unit and the negative (-) probe to the blue/white wire terminal. There should be no continuity. Using a fully-charged 12V battery and some jumper leads, connect the positive (+) terminal of the battery to the red/white wire terminal on the relay unit, and the negative (–) terminal to the red/black wire terminal. There should now be continuity between the blue/black and blue/white wire terminals. If the relay does not test as described, replace it with a new one. To test the diodes within the relay on 2010-on WR models, connect the positive probe of the multimeter (set to ohms) to the red/white wire terminal and the negative probe to the red/black wire terminal – there should be a resistance of 72 to 88 ohms. Now reverse the probes – there should be no continuity, or infinite resistance.

Diodes

5 All WR models have two diodes contained within a diode block, and 2010-on models also have two diodes in the starter circuit cut-off relay. MT and YZF-R models without ABS have three diodes contained within two blocks, and the models with ABS have four diodes contained within three blocks. The diode block(s) connect straight into and are taped to the wiring loom. Diodes allow current

23.3b Starter circuit cut-off relay (arrowed) – MT and YZF-R models

to flow through them in one direction only (in the direction of the pointed end of the triangle on a diode symbol), and can be checked by performing a continuity test – diodes should show continuity in the direction of current flow and no continuity in the other direction.

6 Locate the diode block, unwrap the insulating tape and disconnect the block **(see illustration)**.

7 Connect the multimeter (set to ohms) or continuity tester across the wire terminals for the diode being tested, and perform the following tests. If a diode shows the same condition in both directions it is faulty, and the block must be replaced with a new one.

Positive probe (+)	Negative probe (-)	Result
ALL MODELS		
Blue/black	Light blue/white	Continuity
Light blue/white	Blue/black	No Continuity
Red/black	Light blue/white	Continuity
Light blue/white	Red/black	No Continuity
All MT AND YZF-R MODELS		
Red/white	Red/white	Continuity
Red/white	Red/white	No continuity
MT AND YZF-R MODELS WITH ABS		
Brown	Blue/black	No continuity
Blue/black	Brown	Continuity

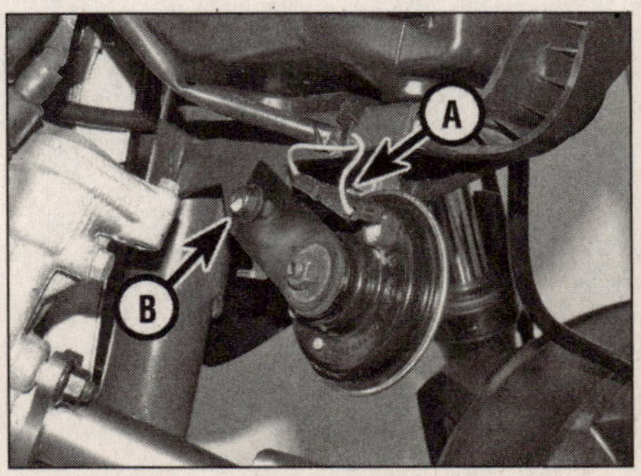

24.3a Horn wiring connectors (A) and mounting bolt (B) – WR models

23.6 Diode block (arrowed) – MT and YZF-R models

8 If the cut-off relay and diodes are good, but the starting system fault still exists, check all other components in the starting circuit (i.e. the neutral switch, sidestand switch, clutch switch, engine stop switch, starter button and starter relay) as described in the relevant Sections of this Chapter. If all components are good, check the wiring between the various components (see the wiring diagram at the end of this Chapter).

24 Horn

Check

Note: *Refer to Electrical System Fault Finding in Section 2 and to the wiring diagram at the end of this Chapter.*

1 The horn gets its power from the same circuit as the turn signals and tail and sidelights – if all these fail at the same time check the signal circuit fuse (see Section 5).

2 To check the horn, on YZF-R models remove the upper section of the fairing on the left side (see Chapter 7).

3 Disconnect the wiring connectors from the horn **(see illustrations)**. Check them for loose wires. Using two jumper wires, apply voltage from a fully-charged 12V battery directly to the terminals on the horn, positive (+) to the brown wire terminal, negative (-) to pink. If the horn doesn't sound, or if it sounds but the noise it produces is muted, turn the adjuster screw on the back of the horn to see if you

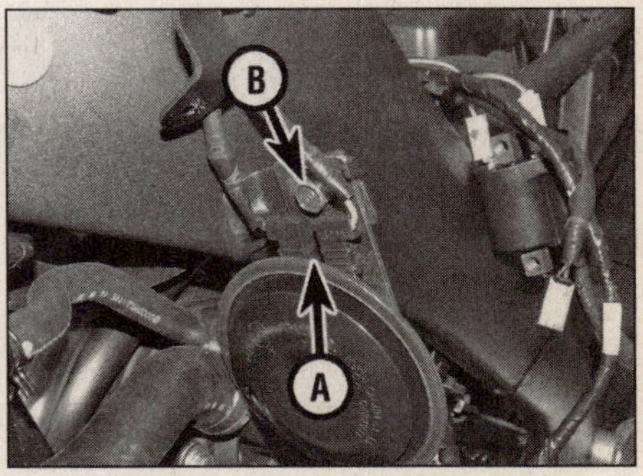

24.3b Horn wiring connectors (A) and mounting bolt (B) – MT and YZF-R models

25.2 Starter relay (arrowed) – MT and YZF-R models

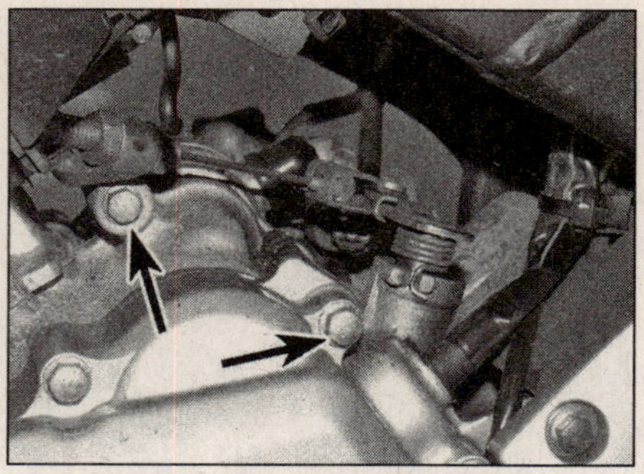

26.3a Unscrew the two bolts (arrowed)...

26.3b ...and displace the starter motor...

can get a (better) sound. If not, replace the horn with a new one.

4 If the horn works check for voltage at the brown wire connector with the ignition ON. If no voltage is present, check the brown wire for continuity to the fusebox.

5 If voltage is present, check the pink wire for continuity between the horn and the switch housing wiring connector, then check the horn button circuit (see Section 19).

6 If all the wiring and connectors are good, check the horn button contacts in the switch housing (see Section 19).

Replacement

7 On YZF-R models remove the upper section of the fairing on the left-hand side (see Chapter 7).

8 Disconnect the wiring connectors from the horn **(see illustration 24.3a or b)**. Unscrew the bolt and remove the horn.

9 Fit the horn, connect the wiring, and check that it works.

25 Starter relay

Note: *Refer to electrical system fault finding in Section 2 and to the wiring diagram for your model at the end of this Chapter.*

1 If the starter motor fails to work, first check the ignition fuse (see Section 5).

2 On WR models the starter relay is housed in the battery box, behind the battery – remove the battery to access it (see Section 3). On MT and YZF-R models the starter relay is in front of the battery under the rider's seat **(see illustration)** – remove the seat to access it (see Chapter 7). Remove the relay.

3 To check the operation of the relay, using an ohmmeter or continuity tester, connect the positive (+) probe to the red wire terminal on the relay and the negative (-) probe to the red/white wire terminal. There should be no continuity. Using a fully-charged 12V battery and some jumper leads, connect the positive (+) terminal of the battery to the red/black wire terminal on the relay unit, and the negative (–) terminal to the blue/black wire terminal. There should now be continuity between the red and red/white wire terminals. If the relay does not test as described, replace it with a new one.

4 If the relay is good, check the red wire from the battery to the relay, and the red/white wire from the relay to the starter motor – check that the terminals and connectors at each end are tight and corrosion-free.

5 Next check the red/black wire for continuity between the fusebox and the relay wiring connector, referring to Section 2 and to the Wiring Diagram at the end of the chapter, and then check the blue/black wire between the relay connector and the starter circuit cut-off relay.

6 If all appears good check the neutral switch, clutch switch, sidestand switch, starter circuit cut-off relay and diodes as described in the relevant sections of this Chapter. If all components are good, check the wiring between the various components (see the wiring diagram at the end of this Chapter).

26 Starter motor removal and installation

Removal

1 Disconnect the battery negative (–) lead (see Section 3). The starter motor is mounted on the top of the crankcase.

2 On YZF-R models remove the lower sections of the fairing on each side (see Chapter 7). For best access remove the throttle body (see Chapter 4).

3 Unscrew the two bolts securing the starter motor to the crankcase on the left-hand side **(see illustration)**. Slide the starter motor out **(see illustration)**.

4 Peel back the rubber terminal cover on the starter motor, then undo the screw securing the lead and detach it **(see illustration)** – if the terminal is corroded spray it with penetrating fluid and leave it for a while before attempting to undo it.

5 Remove the O-ring on the end of the starter motor – a new one must be used **(see illustration 26.6)**.

Installation

6 Fit a new O-ring onto the end of the starter motor **(see illustration)**. Apply a smear of grease to the O-ring.

7 Manoeuvre the motor into position and connect the lead **(see illustration 26.4)**. Fit the rubber cover over the terminal.

8 Slide the motor into the crankcase **(see illustration 26.3b)**. Make sure the starter motor shaft teeth mesh and the motor seats correctly. Fit the bolts and tighten them to the torque setting specified at the beginning of the chapter **(see illustration 26.3a)**.

9 Connect the battery negative (-) lead. Install the throttle body if removed, and on YZF-R models the fairing sections.

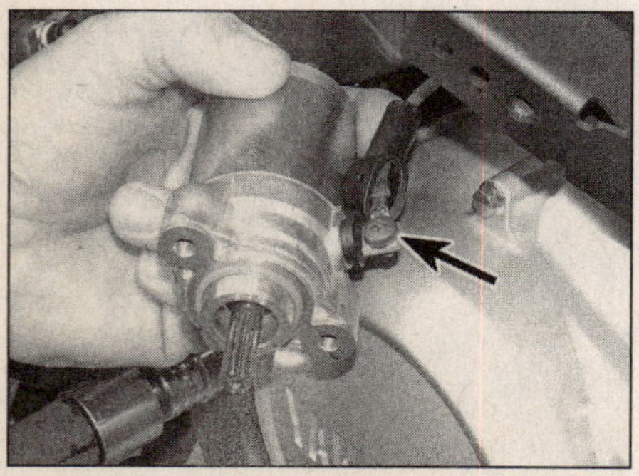

26.4 ...then pull back the terminal cover, undo the screw and detach the lead

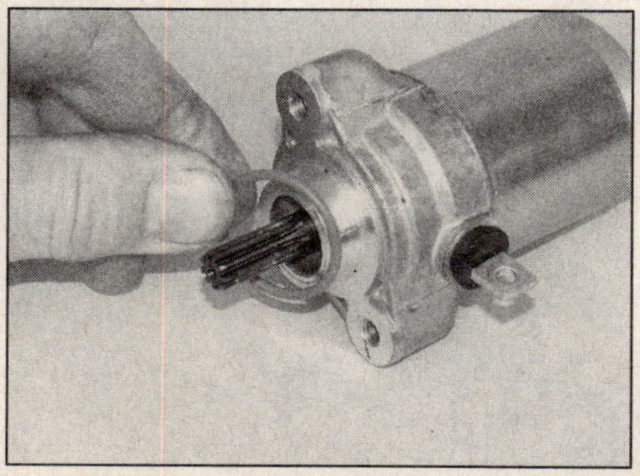

26.6 Fit a new O-ring and lubricate it

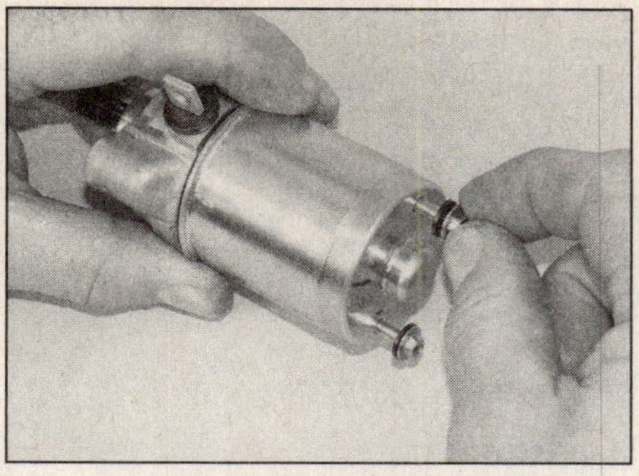

27.4a Unscrew the bolts...

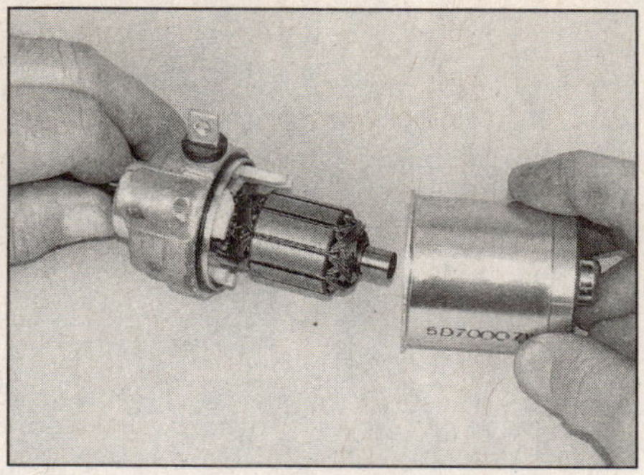

27.4b ... and draw the housing off

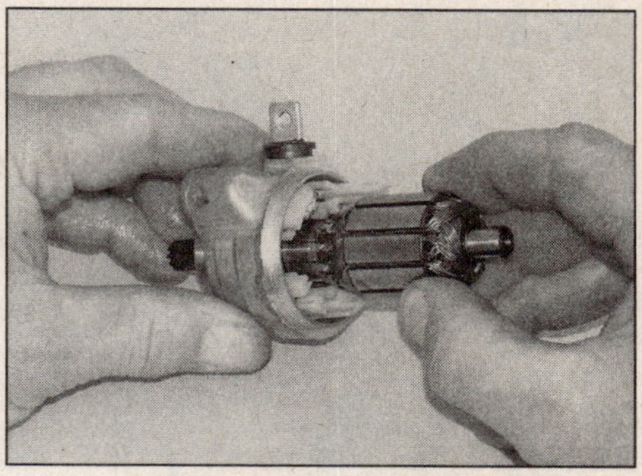

27.5 Draw the armature out

27 Starter motor overhaul

Check

1 Remove the starter motor (see Section 26). Cover its body in rag and clamp the motor in a soft-jawed vice – do not over-tighten it.

2 Using a fully-charged 12 volt battery and two insulated jumper wires, connect the positive (+) terminal of the battery to the protruding terminal on the starter motor, and the negative (–) terminal to one of the motor's mounting lugs. At this point the starter motor should spin. If this is the case the motor is proved good, though it is worth overhauling it if you suspect it of not working properly under load. If the motor does not spin, disassemble it for inspection.

Disassembly

3 Remove the starter motor (see Section 26).

4 Unscrew the two long bolts, noting the washers **(see illustration)**. Hold the shaft and draw the housing off the armature **(see illustration)**. Note the sealing ring **(see illustration 27.16)**.

5 Withdraw the armature from the front cover **(see illustration)**.

Inspection

6 Check for continuity between the terminal bolt and the positive brush **(see illustration)** – there should be continuity (zero resistance). Check for continuity between the terminal bolt and the housing – there should be no continuity (infinite resistance).

7 The parts of the starter motor that are most likely to require attention are the brushes. Measure the length of each brush and compare the results to the minimum given in the specifications at the beginning of the chapter **(see illustration)**. If either of the brushes are worn beyond the service limit, fit a new brush set – unsolder the positive brush from the terminal, then undo the two screws and remove the negative brush and brushplate, noting the springs **(see illustration)**. Fit the new set into the cover and solder the positive brush to the terminal. If the brushes are not worn excessively, nor cracked, chipped, or otherwise damaged, they may be reused.

8 Inspect the commutator bars on the armature for scoring, scratches and discoloration **(see illustration)**. Measure the diameter of the commutator and replace the starter motor with a new one if it is worn below the specified limit – the armature is not available separately. The commutator can be cleaned and polished with crocus cloth, but do not use sandpaper or emery paper. After cleaning, wipe away any residue with a cloth soaked in electrical system cleaner or denatured alcohol. Make sure the insulating mica between the bars is recessed by 1.35 mm **(see illustration)** – if it is less scrape it away using a suitable hacksaw blade or similar tool.

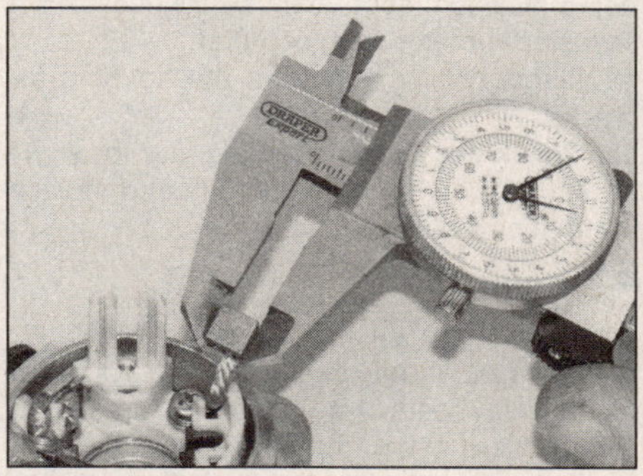

27.7a Measure the length of each brush

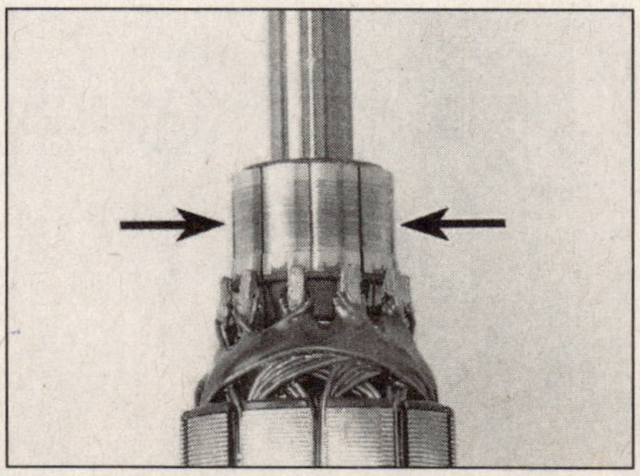

27.8a Check the bars for wear and damage...

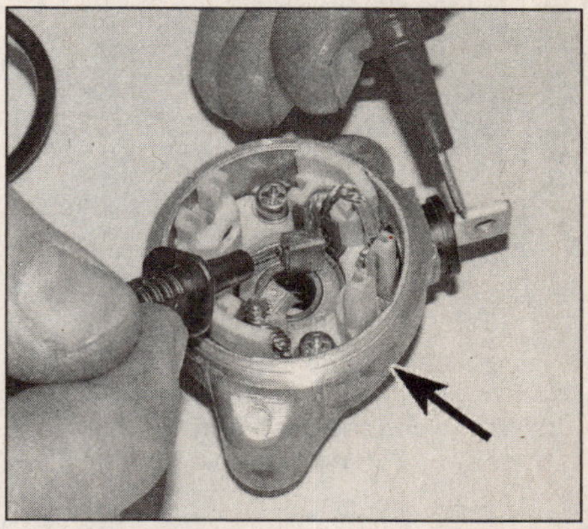

27.6 Check there is continuity between the brush and the terminal, and no continuity between the terminal and the cover (arrowed)

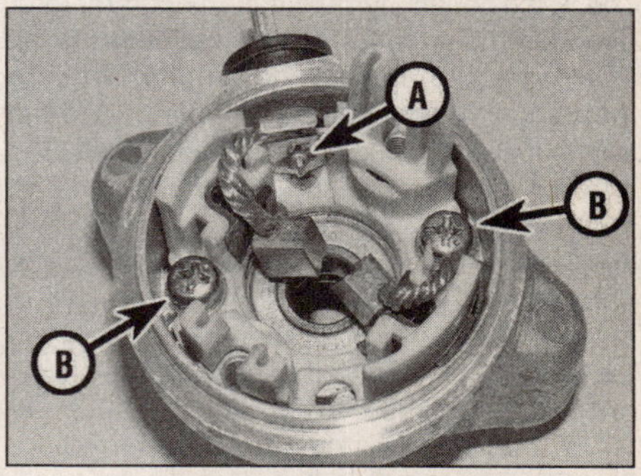

27.7b Unsolder the positive brush wire (A), then undo the brushplate screws (B)

27.8b ... and make sure the mica (arrowed) is below the surface of the bars

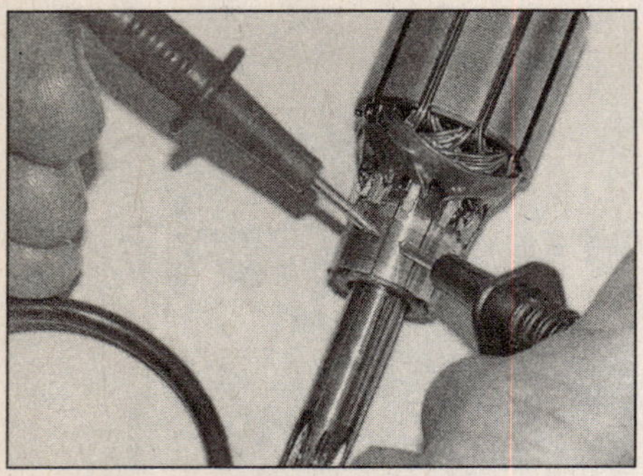

27.9a There should be continuity between the bars...

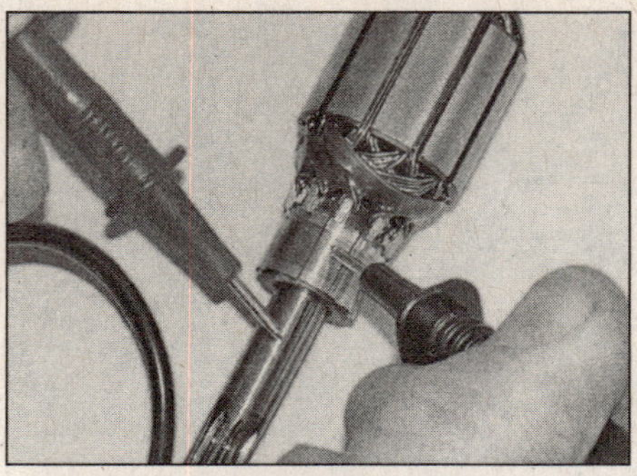

27.9b ...and no continuity between the bars and the shaft

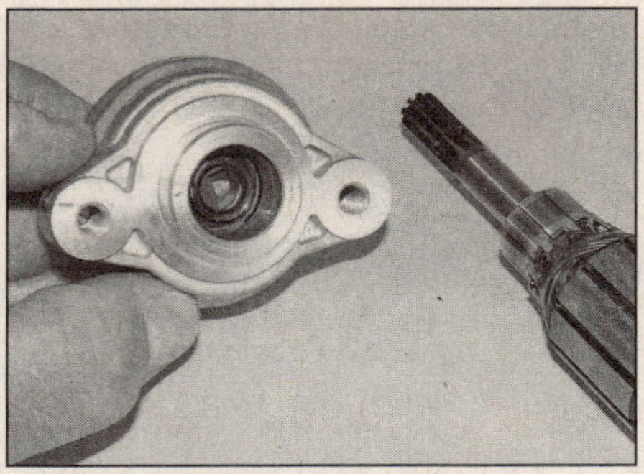

27.11a Check the bearing and seal in the front cover...

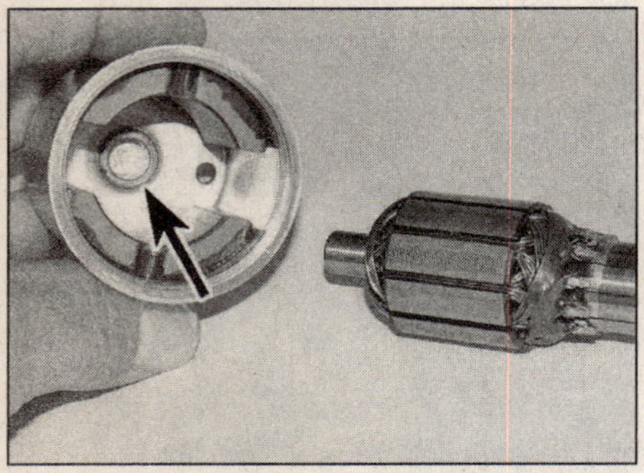

27.11b ...and the bush (arrowed) in the housing

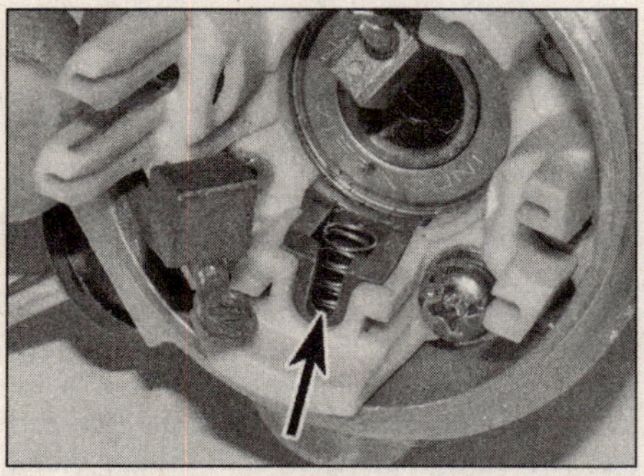

27.14a Make sure the springs (arrowed) are in place

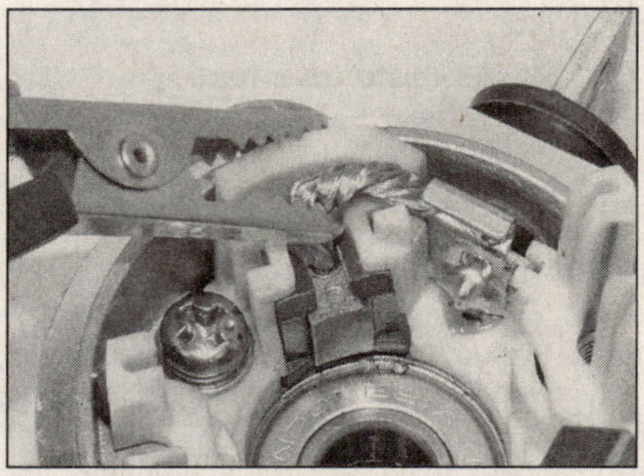

27.14b Push each brush into its housing and hold the wire as shown to keep them retracted

9 Using an ohmmeter or a continuity test light, check for continuity between the commutator bars **(see illustration)**. Continuity should exist between each bar and all of the others. Also, check for continuity between the commutator bars and the armature shaft **(see illustration)**. There should be no continuity (infinite resistance) between the commutator and the shaft. If the checks indicate otherwise, the armature is defective and a new starter motor must be fitted.

10 Check the shaft for worn, cracked, chipped and broken teeth. If any are found check the teeth of the idle/reduction gear via the starter orifice, and if necessary the starter driven gear in the starter clutch (see Chapter 2). If any gear is damaged or worn replace it with a new one.

11 Inspect the front cover and housing for signs of cracks or wear. Check the oil seal and the needle bearing in the front cover and the bush in the rear of the housing for wear and damage **(see illustrations)** – the seal, bearing, bush, cover and housing are not listed as being available separately so if necessary a new starter motor must be fitted.

12 Inspect the magnets in the housing for cracks.

13 Check the housing sealing ring for signs of deformation and deterioration and replace it with a new one if necessary.

Reassembly

14 Make sure the brush springs are correctly in place **(see illustration)**. Push the brushes all the way back into their housings and secure them using crocodile clips or similar so they are held retracted **(see illustration)**. Lubricate each end of the shaft with a smear of grease.

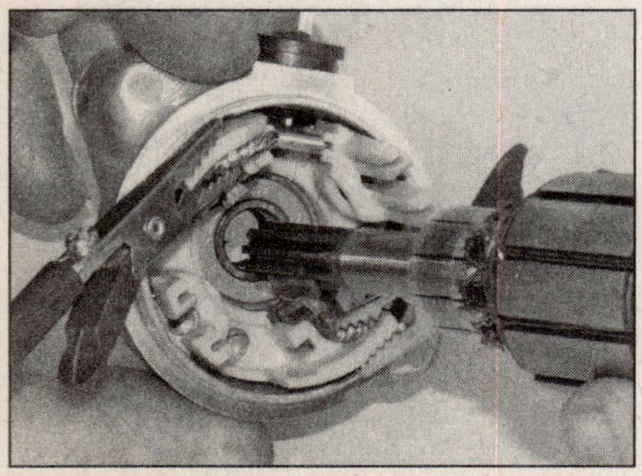

27.15 Insert the armature then release the brushes

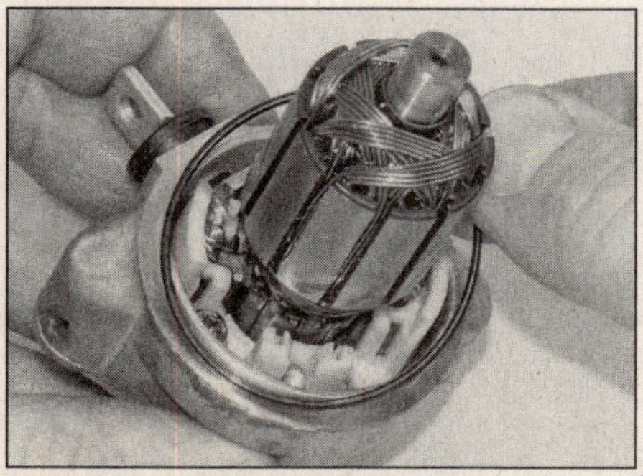

27.16 Fit the sealing ring, using a new one if necessary

15 Carefully insert the armature into the front cover, then release the brushes so they seat under spring pressure against the commutator **(see illustration)**. Check the armature turns.

16 Fit the sealing ring onto the front cover **(see illustration)**. Carefully fit the housing over the armature – it will be pulled on by the force of the magnets so keep a strong hold on the shaft and front cover **(see illustration 27.4b)**.

17 Fit the long bolts with their washers and tighten them **(see illustration 27.4a)**. Check the armature turns.

18 Install the starter motor (see Section 26).

28 Charging system testing

1 If the performance of the charging system is suspect, the system as a whole should be checked first, followed by testing of the individual components. Note: Before beginning the checks, make sure the battery is fully charged and that all system connections are clean and tight.

2 Checking the output of the charging system and the performance of the various components within the charging system requires the use of a multimeter (with voltage, current, and resistance functions). If a multimeter is not available, the job of checking the charging system should be left to a Yamaha dealer.

3 When making the checks, follow the procedures carefully to prevent incorrect connections or short circuits resulting in irreparable damage to electrical system components.

Regulated output test

4 On WR models remove the fuel tank cover (see Chapter 7), then undo the battery cover screws and remove the cover. On MT and YZF-R models remove the rider's seat (see Chapter 7). Start the engine and warm it up.

5 To check the regulated (DC) voltage output, allow the engine to idle. Connect a multimeter set to the 0-20 volts DC scale across the terminals of the battery with the positive (+) meter probe to battery positive (+) terminal and the negative (-) meter probe to battery negative (-) terminal **(see illustration)**. Note the reading obtained. Slowly increase engine speed to 5000 rpm and again note the reading obtained.

6 Compare the results with the Specifications at the beginning of this Chapter. If the regulated voltage output is outside the specifications, check the alternator and the regulator (see Sections 29 and 30).

Leakage test

HAYNES HiNT ***Clues to a faulty regulator are constantly blowing bulbs, with brightness varying considerably with engine speed, and battery overheating.***

Caution: Always connect an ammeter in series, never in parallel with the battery, otherwise it will be damaged. Do not turn the ignition ON or operate the starter motor when the ammeter is connected – a sudden surge in current will blow the meter's fuse.

7 Ensure the ignition is OFF, then disconnect the battery negative (-) lead (see Section 3).

8 Set the multimeter to the Amps function and connect its negative (-) probe to the battery negative (-) terminal, and positive (+) probe to the disconnected negative (-) lead **(see illustration)**. Always set the meter to a high amps range initially and then bring it down to the mA (milli Amps) range; if there is a high current flow in the circuit it may blow the meter's fuse.

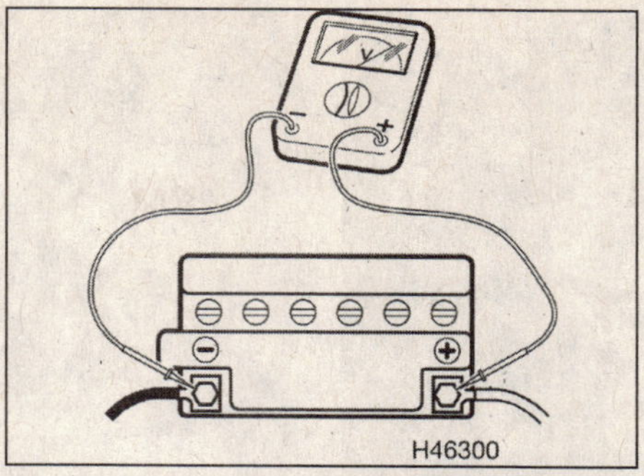

28.5 Checking regulated voltage output – connect the meter as shown

9 Current leakage should not exceed the maximum limit given in the specifications at the beginning of the chapter. If a higher leakage rate is shown there is a short circuit in the wiring, although if an after-market immobiliser or alarm is fitted, its current draw should be taken into account. Disconnect the meter and reconnect the battery negative (-) lead.

10 If leakage is indicated, refer to the wiring diagram at the end of this Chapter to systematically disconnect individual electrical components and repeat the test until the source is identified.

29 Alternator

Check

1 On MT and YZF-R models remove the left-hand side cover (see Chapter 7).

2 Trace the wiring from the alternator cover on the left side of the engine and disconnect it at the 3-pin connector with the white wires – it is housed inside a rubber boot, and on MT and YZF-R models you need to cut a cable-tie to get at it **(see illustration 21.3a or b)**. Check the connector terminals for corrosion and security.

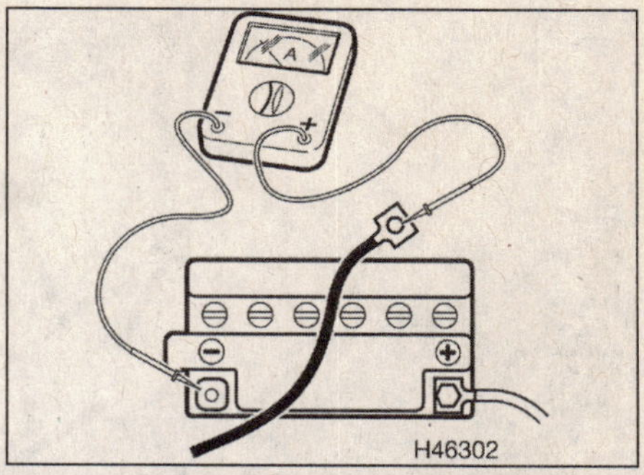

28.8 Checking the charging system leakage rate – connect the meter as shown

3 Using a multimeter set to the ohms x 1 (ohmmeter) scale measure the resistance of the stator coils between each pair of white wire terminals on the alternator side of the connector, taking a total of three readings, then check for continuity between each terminal and ground (earth).

4 If the coil windings are in good condition the reading(s) should be within the range given in the Specifications at the beginning of the chapter, and there should be no continuity (infinite resistance) between the terminals and ground (earth). If not, the alternator stator coil assembly is at fault and should be replaced with a new one. **Note:** *Before condemning the stator coils, check the fault is not due to damaged wiring between the connector and the coils.*

Removal

5 On MT models remove the left-hand side cover and the belly-pan, and on YZF-R models remove the left-hand side cover and the lower section of the fairing on each side (see Chapter 7).

6 Drain the engine oil (see Chapter 1).

7 Remove the front sprocket cover **(see illustrations)**.

29.7a Front sprocket cover bolts (arrowed) – WR and MT models

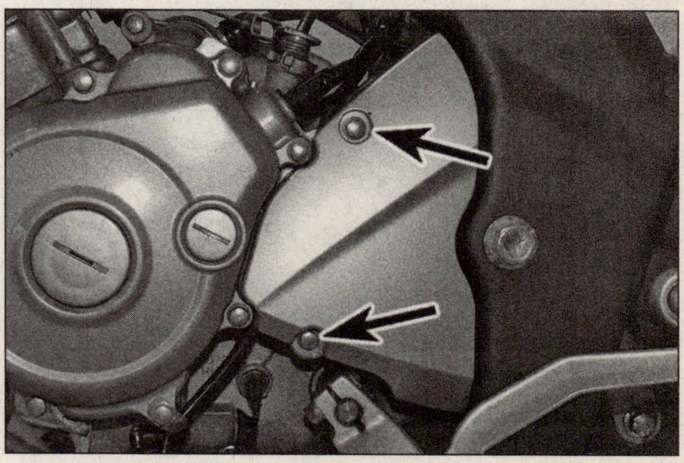

29.7b Front sprocket cover bolts (arrowed) – YZF-R models

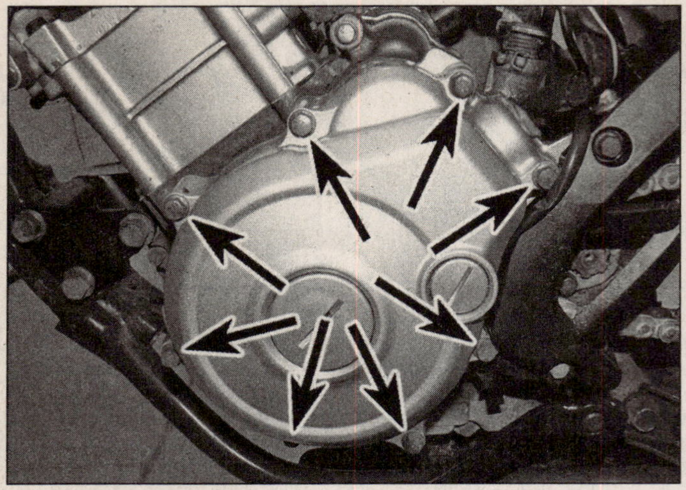

29.9a Alternator cover bolts (arrowed)

29.9b Belly-pan and reservoir bracket arrangement on MT models

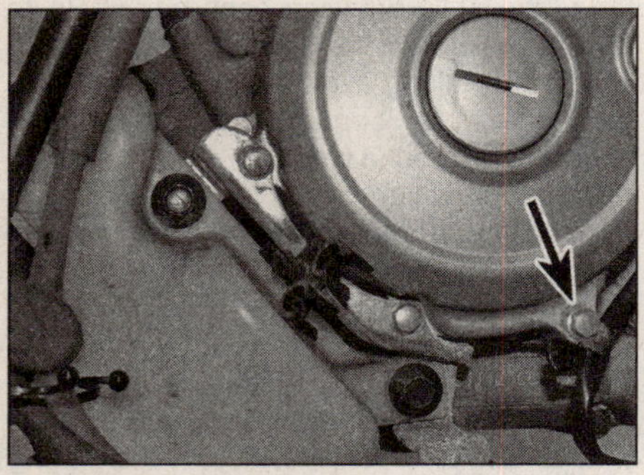

29.9c Fairing/reservoir bracket and wiring guide (arrowed) on YZF-R models

29.10 Using a rotor strap to hold the rotor while unscrewing the nut

8 Trace the wiring from the alternator cover on the left side of the engine and disconnect it at the connectors – they are housed inside a rubber boot, and on MT and YZF models you need to cut a cable-tie to get at them **(see illustration 21.3a or b)**. On YZF models release the hoses from the guides between the coolant reservoir and the alternator cover and move them aside.

9 Working in a criss-cross pattern, evenly slacken the alternator cover bolts **(see illustration)**. Remove the bolts, noting the belly-pan/reservoir brackets on MT models and the fairing/reservoir bracket and wiring guide on YZF-R models **(see illustrations)** – allow the reservoir to hang by its hoses, or tie it up if preferred. Draw the cover off the engine, noting that it will be restrained by the force of the rotor magnets, and be prepared to catch any residual oil. Remove and discard the gasket **(see illustration 29.19a)**. Remove the two dowels from either the cover or the crankcase if loose.

10 To slacken the rotor nut it is necessary to stop the rotor from turning. The best way is to use a commercially available rotor strap, taking care to avoid the raised triggers for the crankshaft position sensor on the outside of the rotor **(see illustration)**. If one is not available, try placing the transmission in gear and having an assistant apply the rear brake hard. Slacken and remove the nut and its washer.

11 To remove the rotor from the shaft it is necessary to use a rotor puller (Yamaha part No.90890-01362), or its commercially available equivalent – thread the puller bolts into the threaded holes in the rotor, then hold the rotor and tighten the puller bolt until the rotor is displaced from the shaft **(see illustrations)**. If the rotor is very tight use a hot air gun to heat the hub which will expand it off the shaft, and tap the puller bolt with a

29.11a Fit the puller as shown

29.11b Tighten the puller bolt until the rotor is displaced

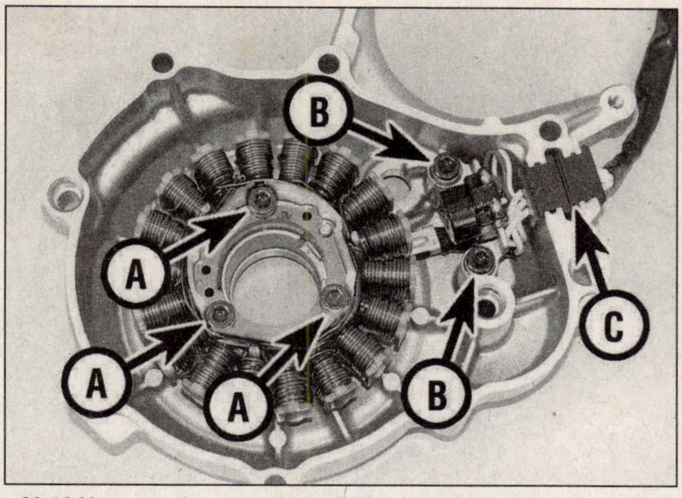

29.12 Unscrew the stator bolts (A) and the CKP sensor bolts (B) and free the grommet (C)

29.14a Lubricate the flat section of the end of the crankshaft (arrowed)

hammer, but not too hard. Remove the puller. Remove the Woodruff key from its slot in the crankshaft **(see illustration 29.16b)**. If the starter driven gear did not come away with the rotor, slide it off the end of the crankshaft along with the needle bearing, and the thrust washer **(see illustrations 29.14c and b)**. If required detach the starter clutch from the rotor (see Chapter 2).

12 To remove the stator from the cover, unscrew its bolts and the bolts securing the crankshaft position sensor, then remove the assembly, noting how the rubber wiring grommet fits **(see illustration)**.

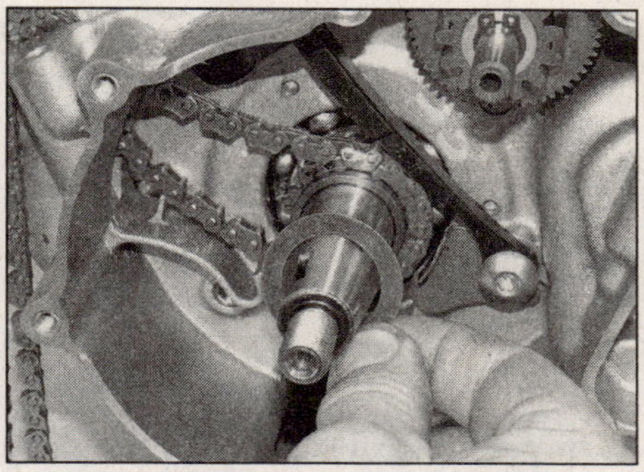

29.14b Slide the thrust washer...

29.14c ...then the needle bearing and driven gear onto the shaft

Installation

13 Clean the threads of the stator and CKP sensor bolts. Fit the stator and CKP sensor into the cover, aligning the rubber wiring grommet with the grooves **(see illustration 29.12)**. Apply a suitable non-permanent thread locking compound to the stator and sensor bolts, and tighten them to the torque setting specified at the beginning of the Chapter. Apply a suitable sealant to the wiring grommet, then press it into the cut-outs in the cover.

14 Smear some clean oil onto the inner un-tapered section of the crankshaft that the starter driven gear runs on **(see illustration)**. Slide the thrust washer onto the crankshaft **(see illustration)**. Fit the needle bearing and the driven gear onto the shaft **(see illustration)**.

15 If removed fit the starter clutch onto the rotor (see Chapter 2).

16 Clean the tapered end of the crankshaft and the corresponding mating surface on the inside of the rotor with a suitable solvent **(see illustration)**. Fit the Woodruff key into its slot in the crankshaft if removed **(see illustration)**.

17 Make sure that no metal objects have attached themselves to the magnet on the

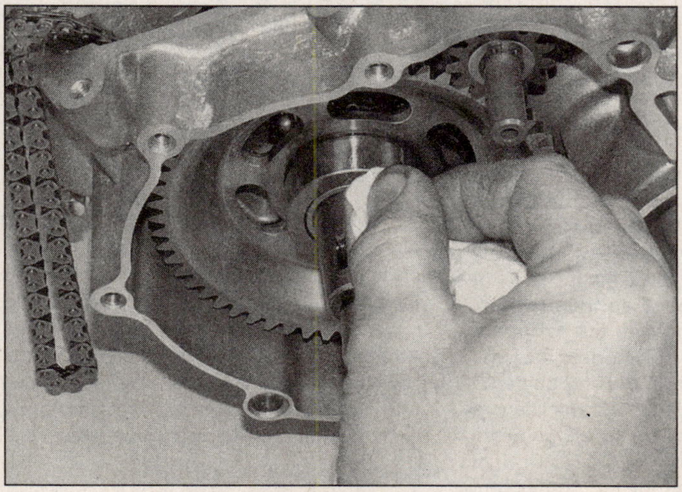

29.16a Clean the tapered section of the shaft...

29.16b ...then fit the key into its slot

29.17 Slide the rotor onto the shaft, turning the gear to ease entry

29.18a Fit the nut and washer...

29.18b ...and tighten the nut to the specified torque

29.19a Make sure the dowels (arrowed) are in place, then fit the new gasket...

inside of the rotor. Slide the rotor onto the shaft, making sure the groove on the inside is aligned with and fits over the Woodruff key, and turn the driven gear clockwise as you do so to spread the starter clutch sprags and allow the hub to enter **(see illustration)**. Make sure the Woodruff key does not become dislodged when installing the rotor.

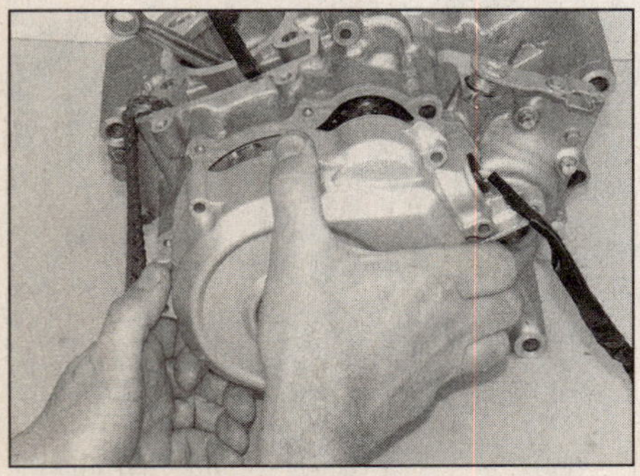

29.19b ...and the cover

18 Fit the nut with its washer and tighten it to the torque setting at the beginning of the chapter, using the method employed on removal to prevent the rotor from turning **(see illustrations)**.

19 Fit the two dowels into the crankcase if removed, then locate a new gasket onto them **(see illustration)**. Fit the alternator cover, noting that the rotor magnets will forcibly draw the cover/stator on, making sure it locates onto the dowels **(see illustration)**. Fit the cover bolts, along with the belly-pan/reservoir brackets on MT models and the fairing/reservoir bracket and wiring guide on YZF-R models, and tighten them evenly and a little at a time in a criss-cross sequence to the specified torque.

20 Reconnect the wiring at the connectors **(see illustration 21.3a or b)**.

21 Fit the front sprocket cover **(see illustration 29.7a or b)**.

22 Replenish the engine oil (see Chapter 1).

30 Regulator/rectifier

Check

1 No test details are given for the regulator/rectifier. If having checked the charging system and alternator as in Sections 28 and 29 there is obviously a problem, and the alternator stator and the wiring are good, the regulator/rectifier unit is probably faulty. Take it to a Yamaha dealer for confirmation of its condition before replacing it with a new one.

Removal and installation

2 On WR models remove the seat (see Chapter

30.2 Regulator/rectifier (arrowed) – WR models

30.3a Regulator/rectifier (arrowed) – MT and YZF-R models

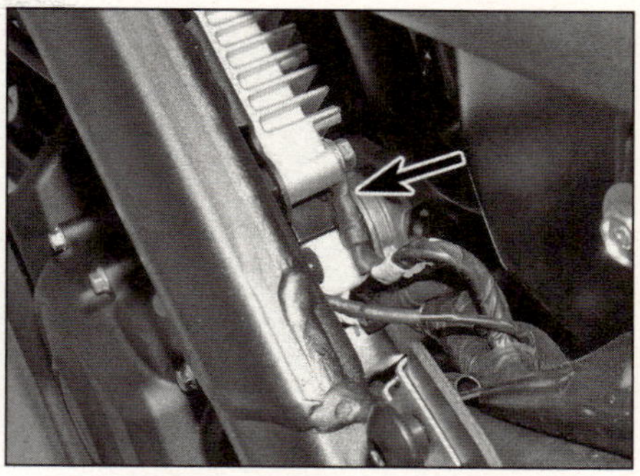

30.3b Note the earth lead (arrowed)

7). Disconnect the wiring connector **(see illustration)**. Unscrew the bolts, noting the earth lead, and remove the regulator/rectifier.

3 On MT and YZF-R models remove the fuel tank (see Chapter 4) – the regulator/rectifier is mounted on the inside of the left-hand frame beam **(see illustrations)**. Disconnect the wiring connector. Unscrew the bolts, noting the earth lead, and remove the regulator/rectifier.

4 Fit the new unit and tighten its bolts, not forgetting the earth lead **(see illustration 30.2 or 30.3b)**. Connect the wiring connector, making sure it is pushed fully into place.

5 Install the seat (WR models) or fuel tank (MT and YZF-R models).

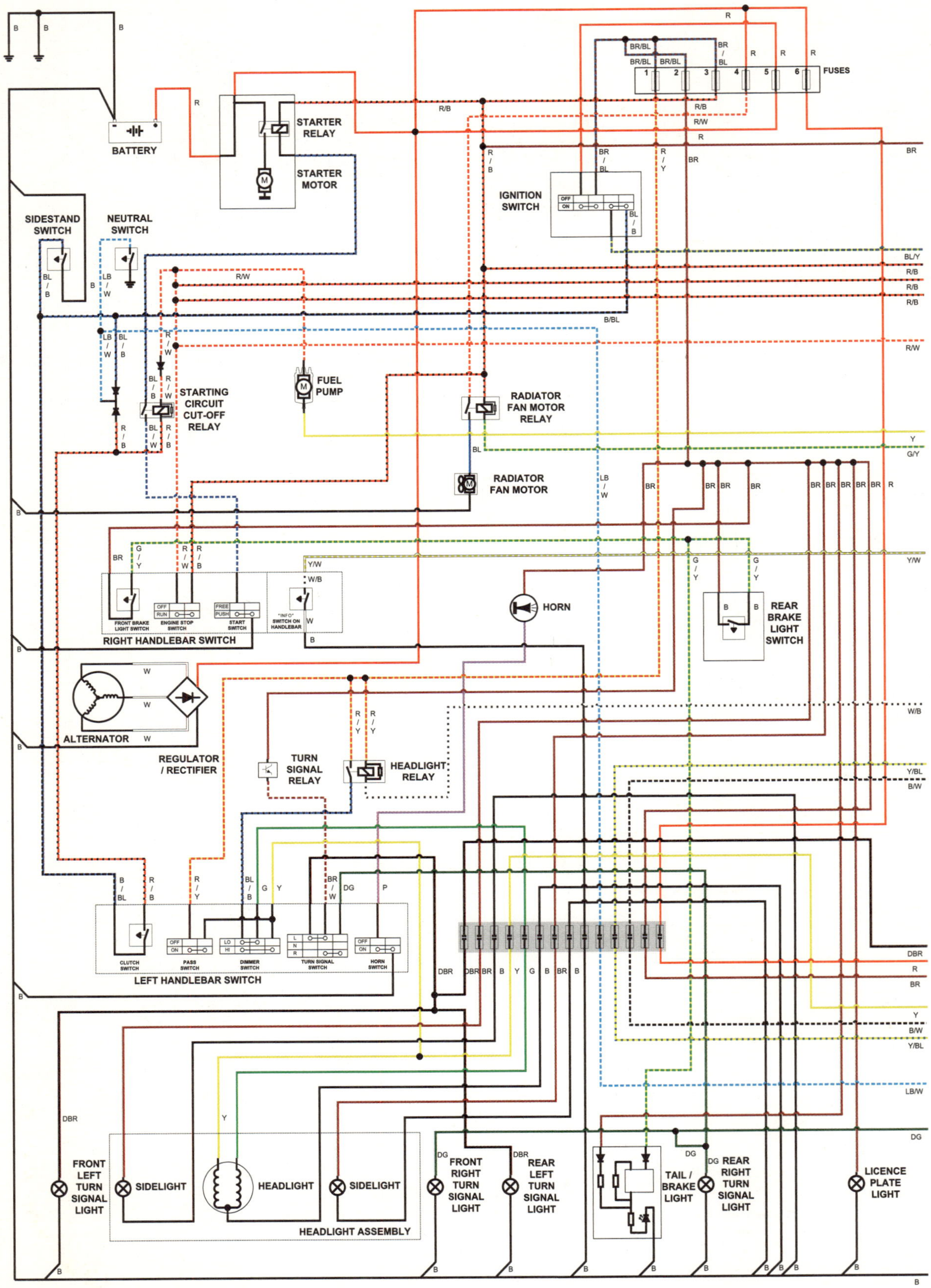
BATTERY
STARTER RELAY
STARTER MOTOR
FUSES
IGNITION SWITCH
SIDESTAND SWITCH
NEUTRAL SWITCH
STARTING CIRCUIT CUT-OFF RELAY
FUEL PUMP
RADIATOR FAN MOTOR RELAY
RADIATOR FAN MOTOR
FRONT BRAKE LIGHT SWITCH
ENGINE STOP SWITCH
START SWITCH
"INFO" SWITCH ON HANDLEBAR
RIGHT HANDLEBAR SWITCH
HORN
REAR BRAKE LIGHT SWITCH
ALTERNATOR
REGULATOR / RECTIFIER
TURN SIGNAL RELAY
HEADLIGHT RELAY
CLUTCH SWITCH
PASS SWITCH
DIMMER SWITCH
TURN SIGNAL SWITCH
HORN SWITCH
LEFT HANDLEBAR SWITCH
FRONT LEFT TURN SIGNAL LIGHT
SIDELIGHT
HEADLIGHT
SIDELIGHT
HEADLIGHT ASSEMBLY
FRONT RIGHT TURN SIGNAL LIGHT
REAR LEFT TURN SIGNAL LIGHT
TAIL / BRAKE LIGHT
REAR RIGHT TURN SIGNAL LIGHT
LICENCE PLATE LIGHT

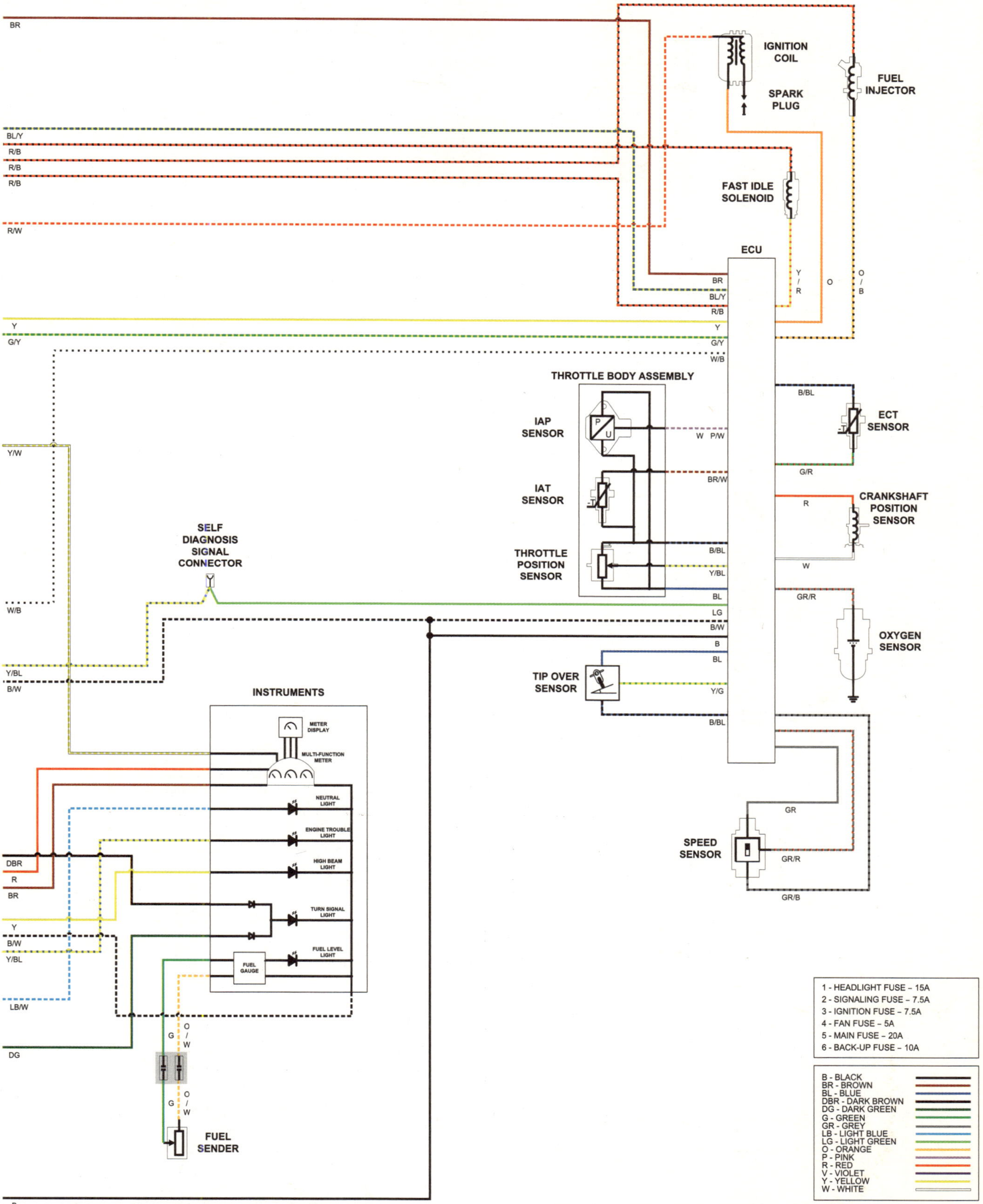
IGNITION COIL
SPARK PLUG
FUEL INJECTOR
FAST IDLE SOLENOID
ECU
THROTTLE BODY ASSEMBLY
IAP SENSOR
IAT SENSOR
THROTTLE POSITION SENSOR
ECT SENSOR
CRANKSHAFT POSITION SENSOR
OXYGEN SENSOR
SELF DIAGNOSIS SIGNAL CONNECTOR
TIP OVER SENSOR
SPEED SENSOR
INSTRUMENTS
METER DISPLAY
MULTI-FUNCTION METER
NEUTRAL LIGHT
ENGINE TROUBLE LIGHT
HIGH BEAM LIGHT
TURN SIGNAL LIGHT
FUEL LEVEL LIGHT
FUEL GAUGE
FUEL SENDER
1 - HEADLIGHT FUSE - 15A
2 - SIGNALING FUSE - 7.5A
3 - IGNITION FUSE - 7.5A
4 - FAN FUSE - 5A
5 - MAIN FUSE - 20A
6 - BACK-UP FUSE - 10A
B - BLACK
BR - BROWN
BL - BLUE
DBR - DARK BROWN
DG - DARK GREEN
G - GREEN
GR - GREY
LB - LIGHT BLUE
LG - LIGHT GREEN
O - ORANGE
P - PINK
R - RED
V - VIOLET
Y - YELLOW
W - WHITE

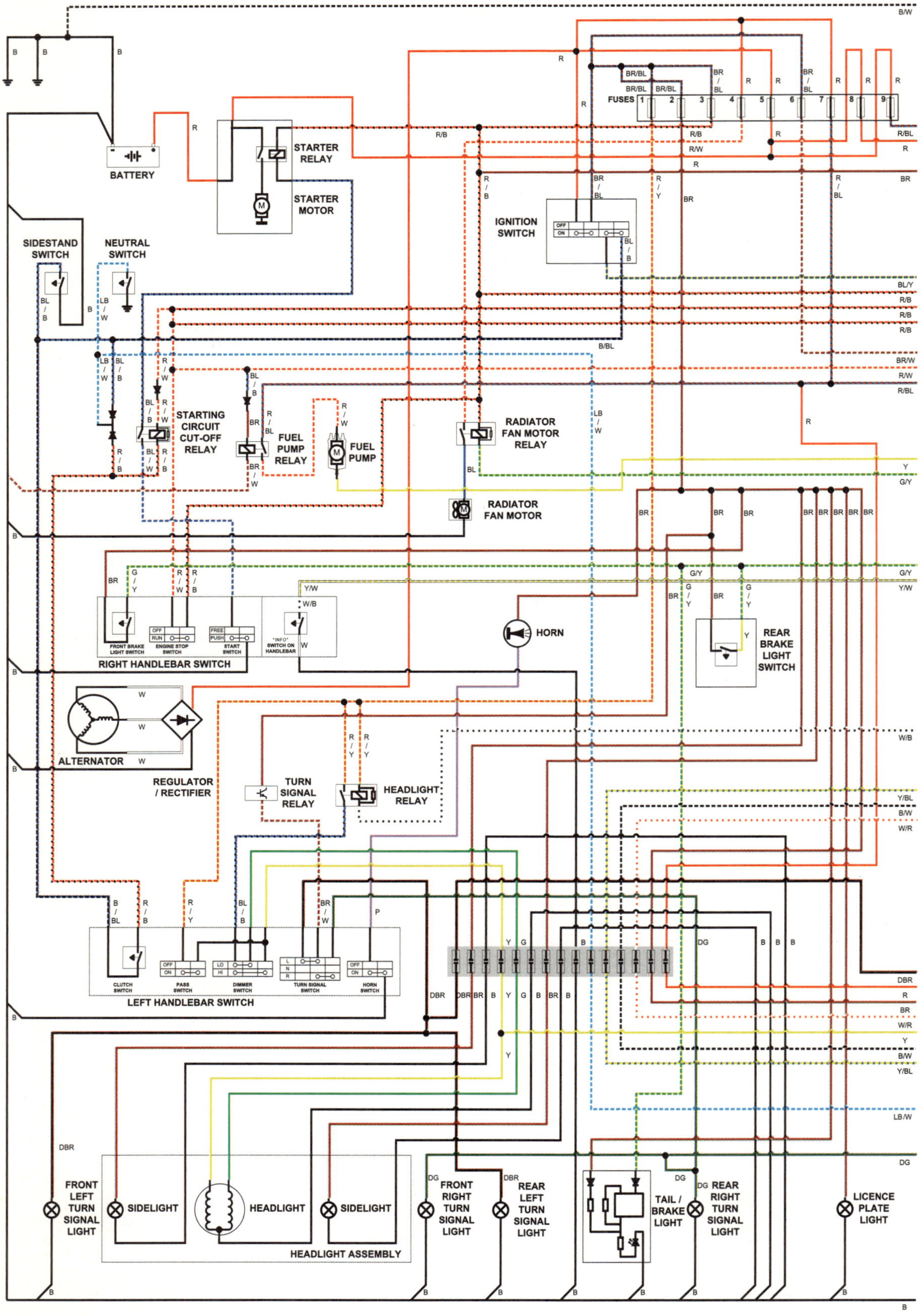

Yamaha MT125A

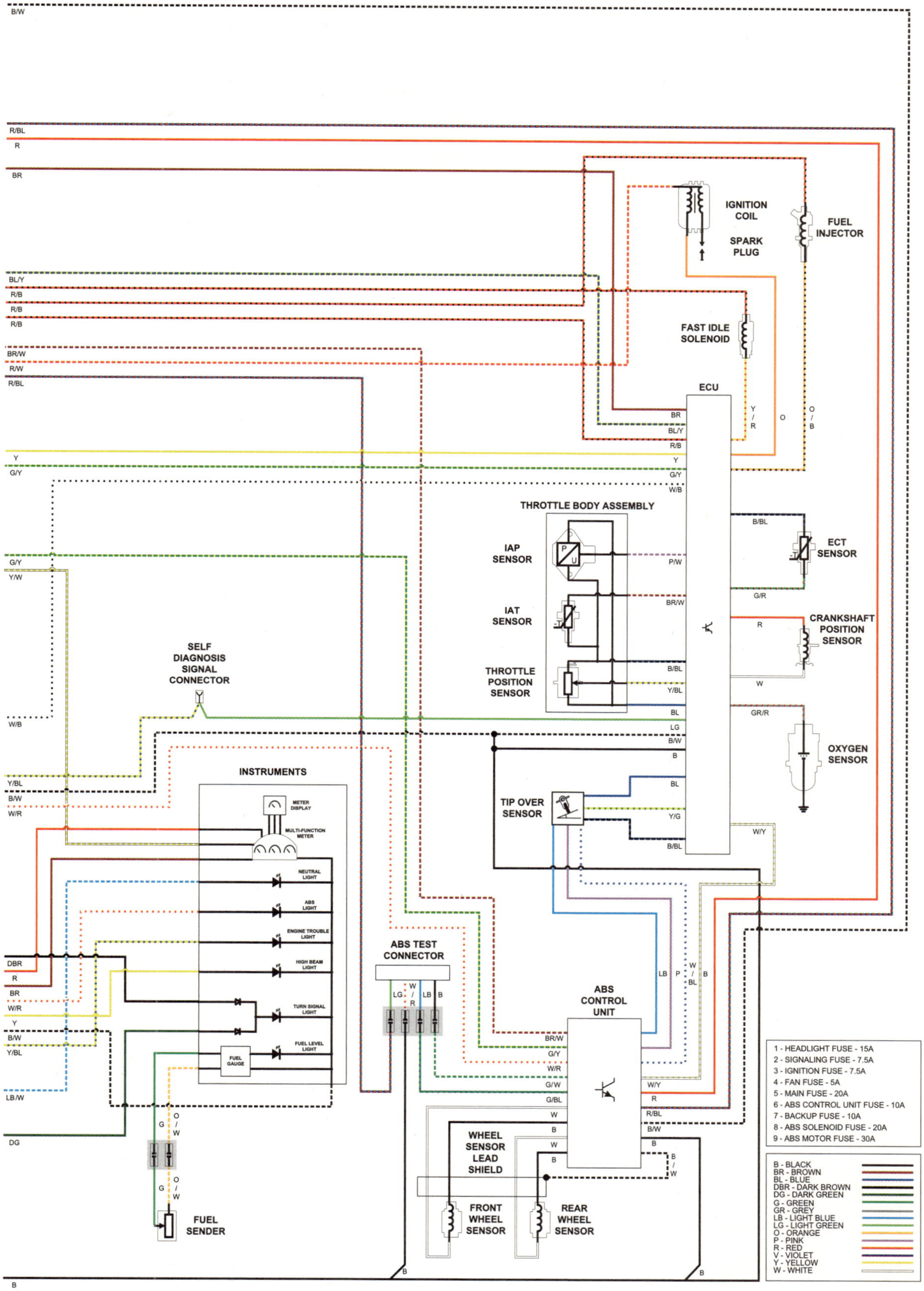

Yamaha MT125A

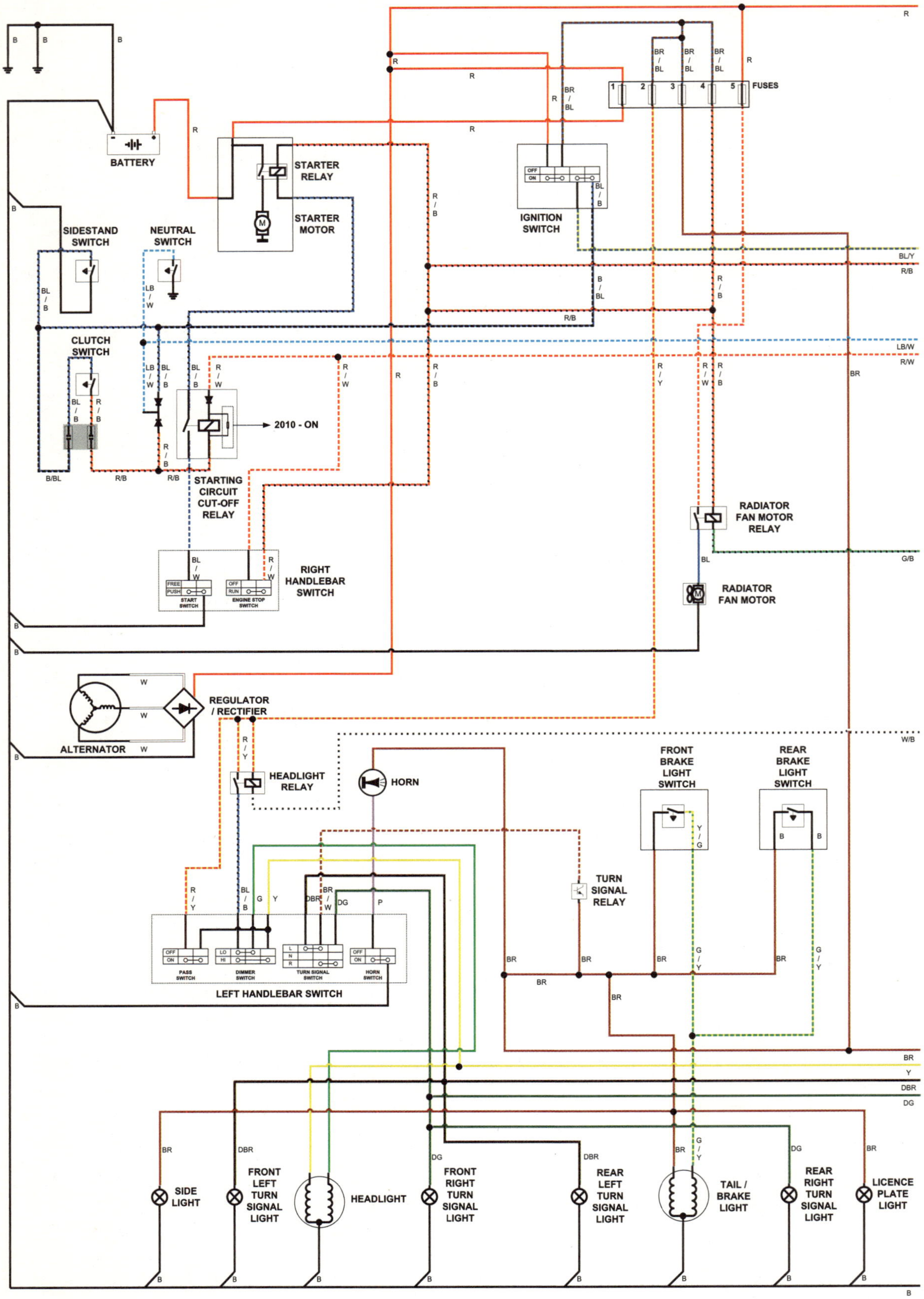

Yamaha WR125R and WR125X

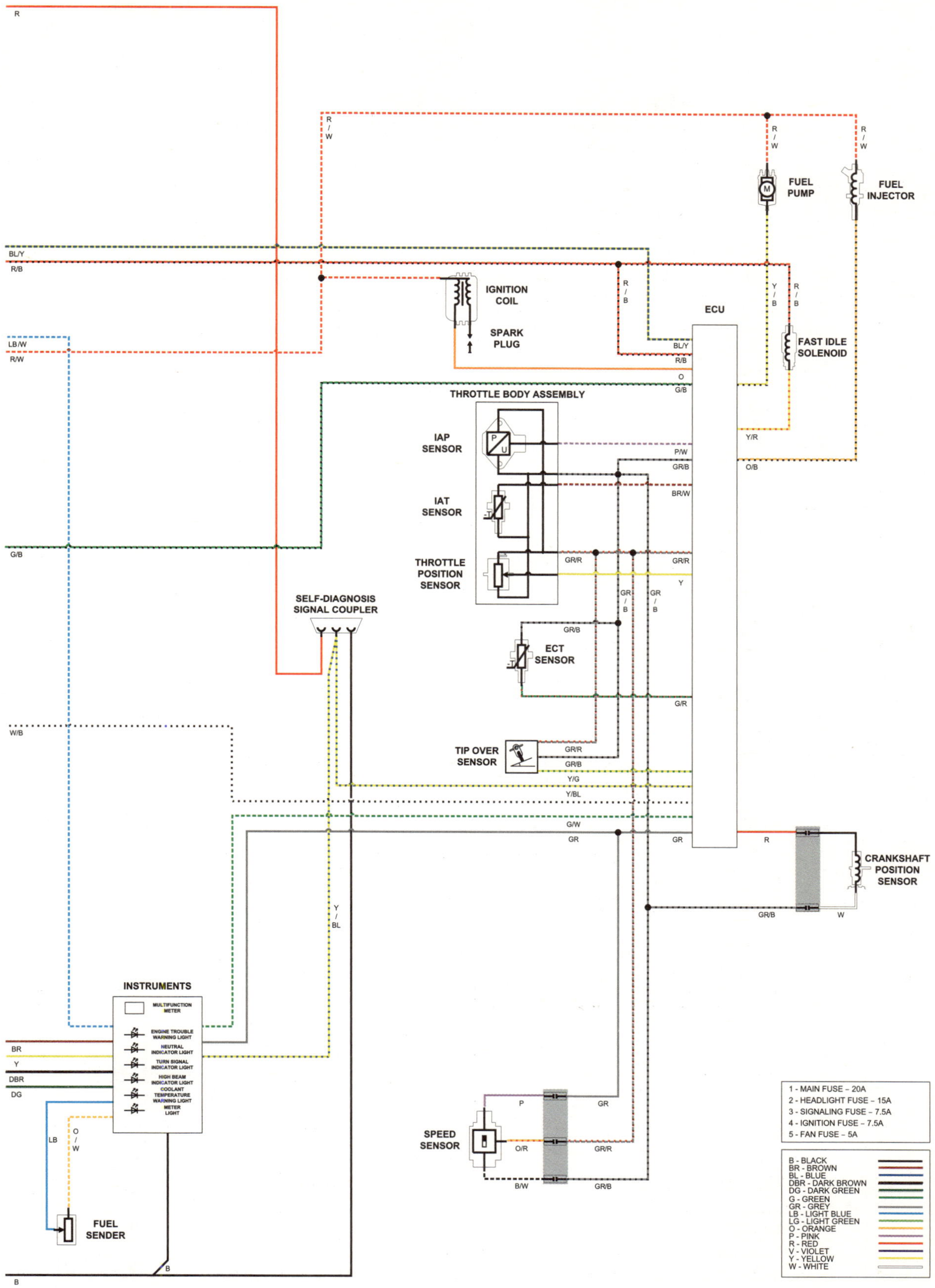

Yamaha WR125R and WR125X

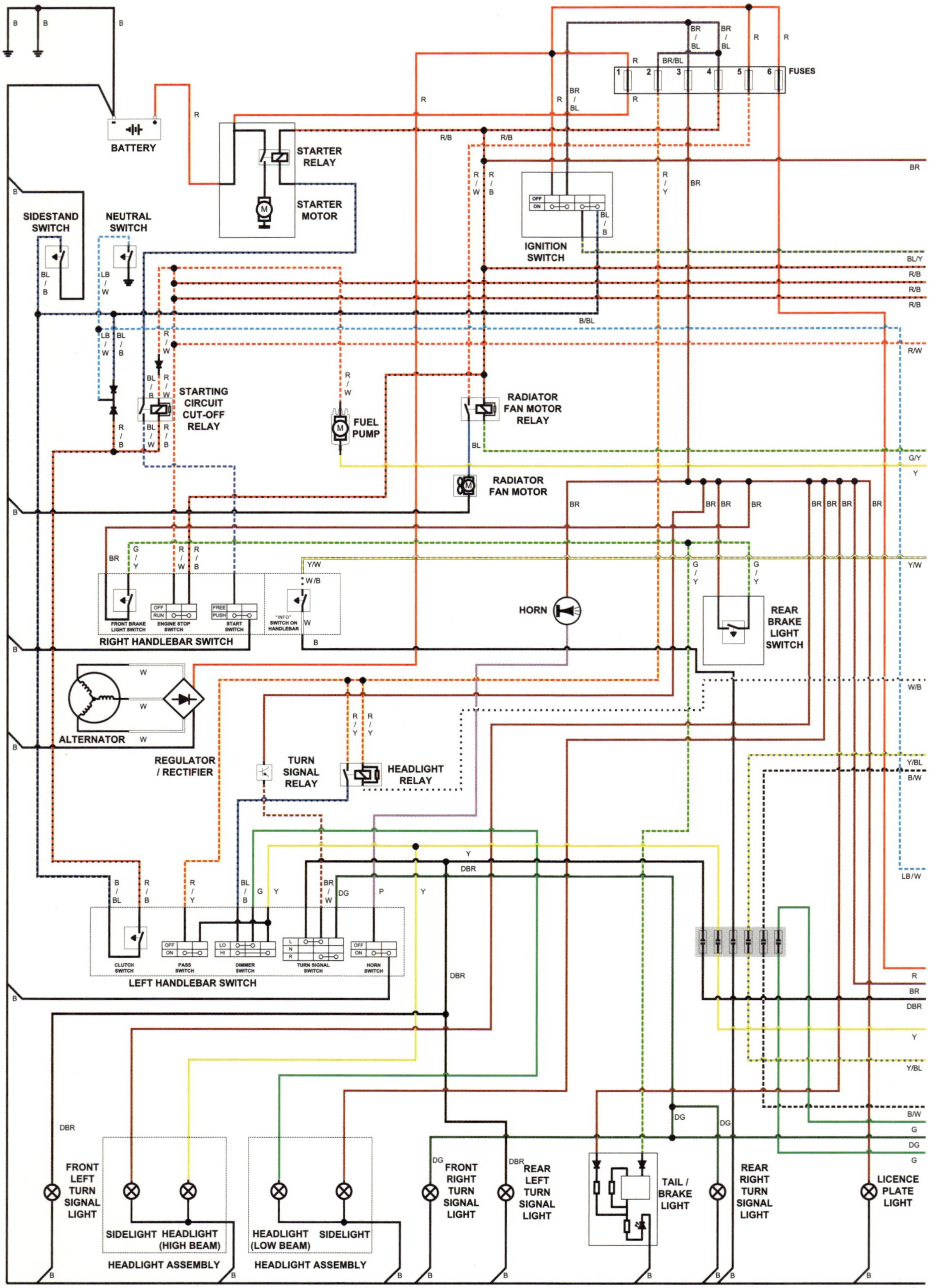
BATTERY
STARTER RELAY
STARTER MOTOR
FUSES
IGNITION SWITCH
SIDESTAND SWITCH
NEUTRAL SWITCH
STARTING CIRCUIT CUT-OFF RELAY
FUEL PUMP
RADIATOR FAN MOTOR RELAY
RADIATOR FAN MOTOR
FRONT BRAKE LIGHT SWITCH
ENGINE STOP SWITCH
START SWITCH
"INFO" SWITCH ON HANDLEBAR
RIGHT HANDLEBAR SWITCH
HORN
REAR BRAKE LIGHT SWITCH
ALTERNATOR
REGULATOR / RECTIFIER
TURN SIGNAL RELAY
HEADLIGHT RELAY
CLUTCH SWITCH
PASS SWITCH
DIMMER SWITCH
TURN SIGNAL SWITCH
HORN SWITCH
LEFT HANDLEBAR SWITCH
FRONT LEFT TURN SIGNAL LIGHT
SIDELIGHT
HEADLIGHT (HIGH BEAM)
HEADLIGHT ASSEMBLY
HEADLIGHT (LOW BEAM)
SIDELIGHT
HEADLIGHT ASSEMBLY
FRONT RIGHT TURN SIGNAL LIGHT
REAR LEFT TURN SIGNAL LIGHT
TAIL / BRAKE LIGHT
REAR RIGHT TURN SIGNAL LIGHT
LICENCE PLATE LIGHT

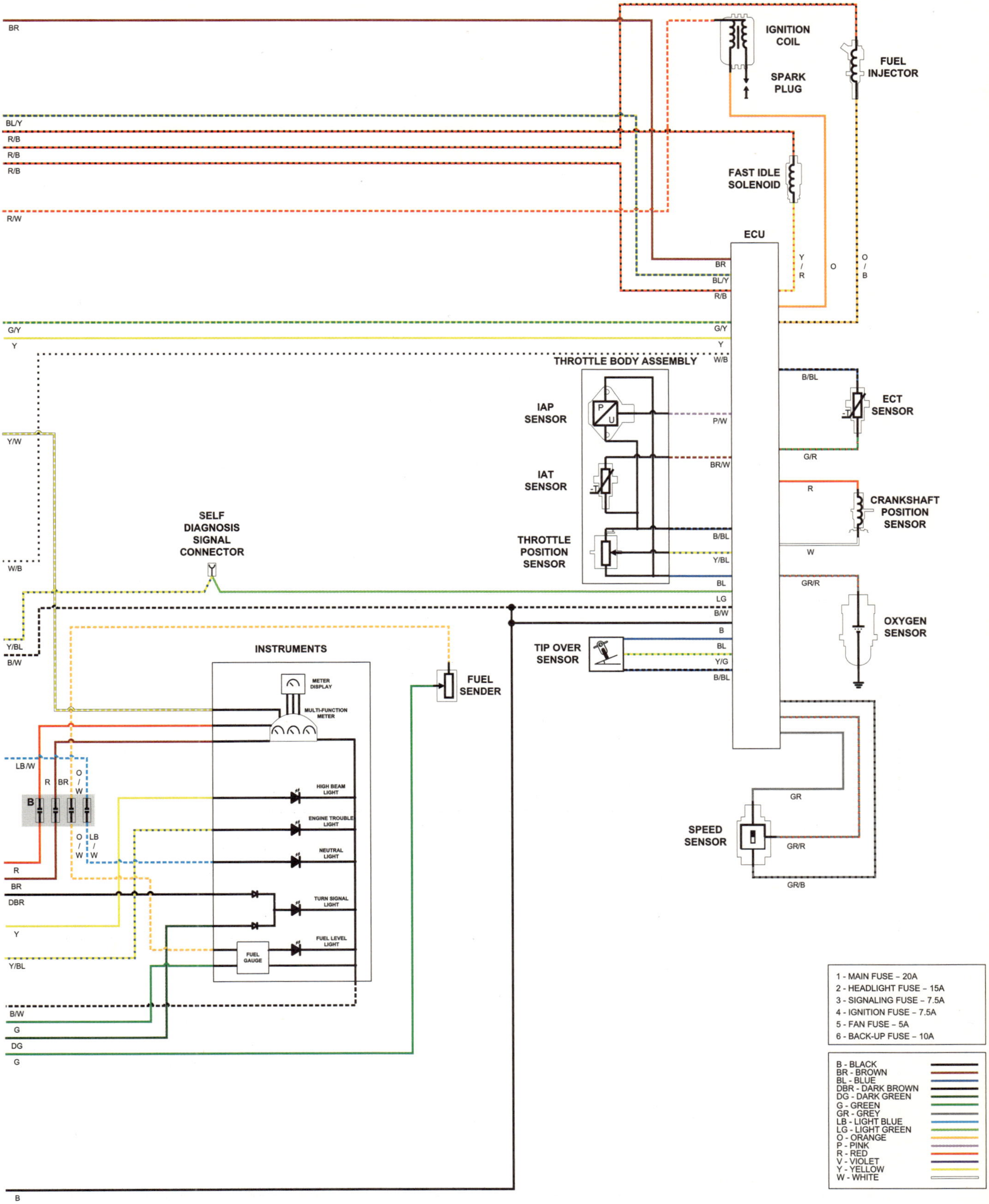
IGNITION COIL
SPARK PLUG
FUEL INJECTOR
FAST IDLE SOLENOID
ECU
THROTTLE BODY ASSEMBLY
IAP SENSOR
IAT SENSOR
THROTTLE POSITION SENSOR
ECT SENSOR
CRANKSHAFT POSITION SENSOR
OXYGEN SENSOR
TIP OVER SENSOR
SELF DIAGNOSIS SIGNAL CONNECTOR
FUEL SENDER
INSTRUMENTS
METER DISPLAY
MULTI-FUNCTION METER
HIGH BEAM LIGHT
ENGINE TROUBLE LIGHT
NEUTRAL LIGHT
TURN SIGNAL LIGHT
FUEL LEVEL LIGHT
FUEL GAUGE
SPEED SENSOR
1 - MAIN FUSE – 20A
2 - HEADLIGHT FUSE – 15A
3 - SIGNALING FUSE – 7.5A
4 - IGNITION FUSE – 7.5A
5 - FAN FUSE – 5A
6 - BACK-UP FUSE – 10A
B - BLACK
BR - BROWN
BL - BLUE
DBR - DARK BROWN
DG - DARK GREEN
G - GREEN
GR - GREY
LB - LIGHT BLUE
LG - LIGHT GREEN
O - ORANGE
P - PINK
R - RED
V - VIOLET
Y - YELLOW
W - WHITE

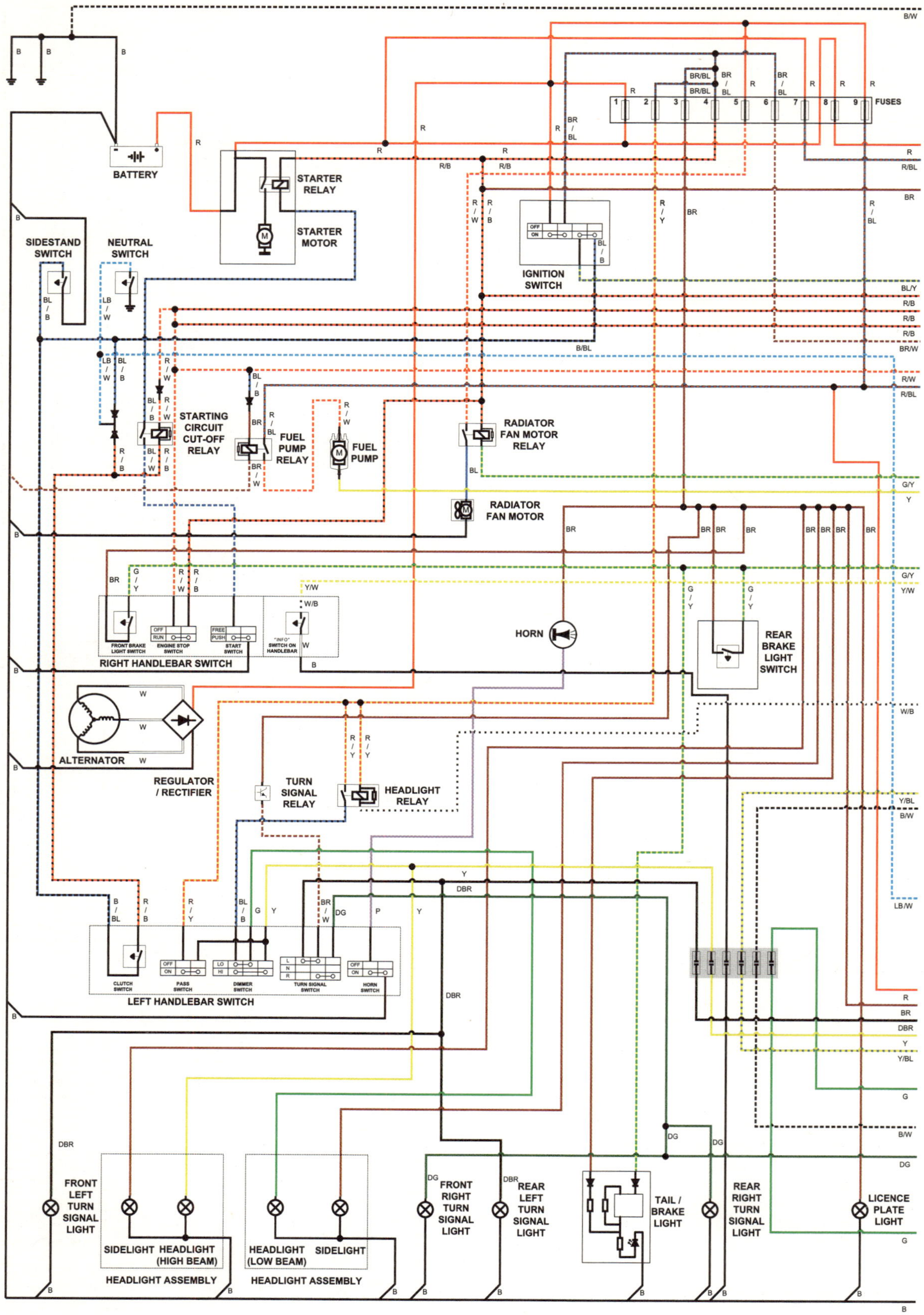

Yamaha YZF125A

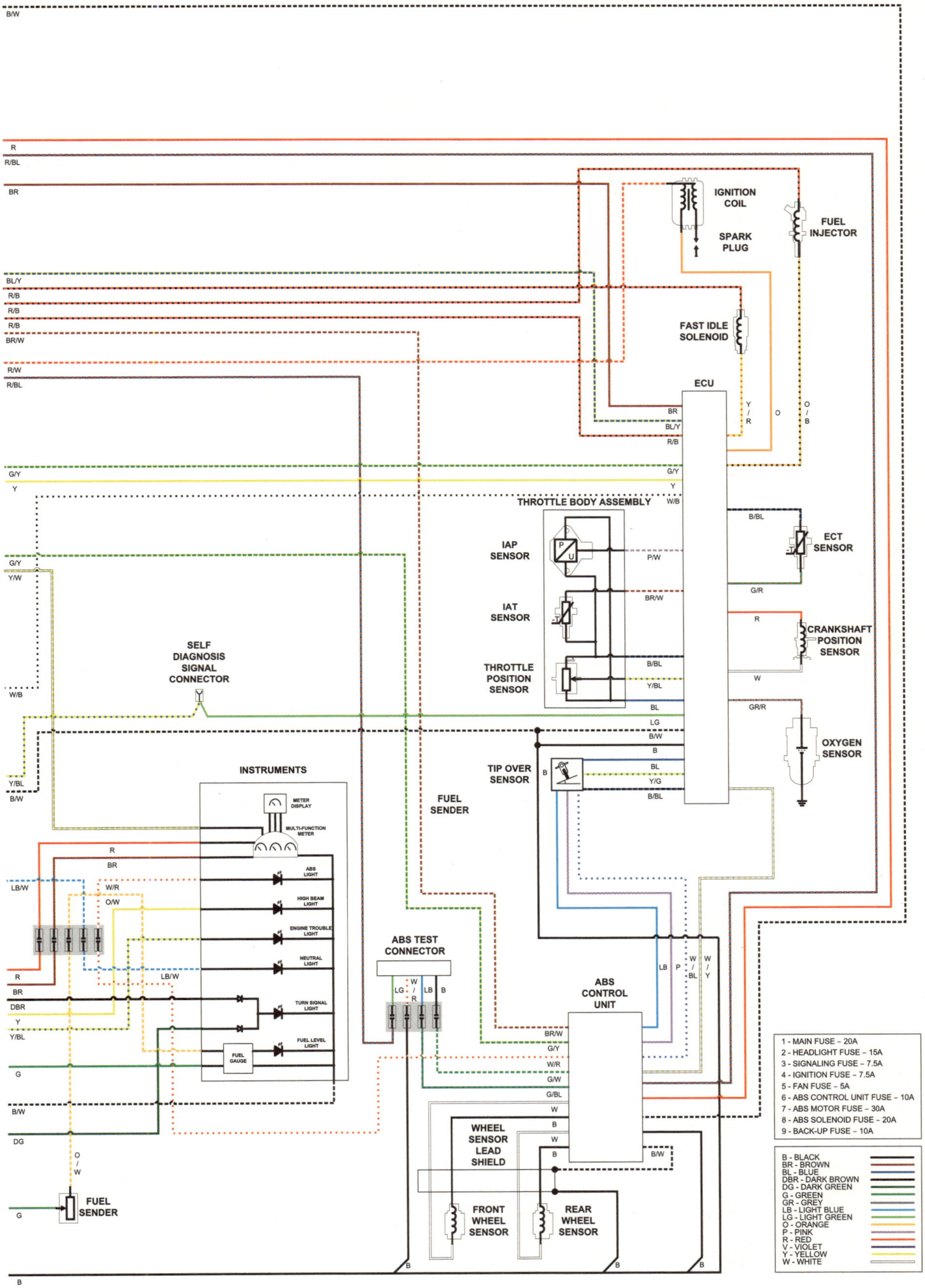
IGNITION COIL
SPARK PLUG
FUEL INJECTOR
FAST IDLE SOLENOID
ECU
THROTTLE BODY ASSEMBLY
IAP SENSOR
IAT SENSOR
THROTTLE POSITION SENSOR
ECT SENSOR
CRANKSHAFT POSITION SENSOR
OXYGEN SENSOR
SELF DIAGNOSIS SIGNAL CONNECTOR
TIP OVER SENSOR
FUEL SENDER
INSTRUMENTS
METER DISPLAY
MULTI-FUNCTION METER
ABS LIGHT
HIGH BEAM LIGHT
ENGINE TROUBLE LIGHT
NEUTRAL LIGHT
TURN SIGNAL LIGHT
FUEL LEVEL LIGHT
FUEL GAUGE
ABS TEST CONNECTOR
ABS CONTROL UNIT
WHEEL SENSOR LEAD SHIELD
FRONT WHEEL SENSOR
REAR WHEEL SENSOR
FUEL SENDER
1 - MAIN FUSE - 20A
2 - HEADLIGHT FUSE - 15A
3 - SIGNALING FUSE - 7.5A
4 - IGNITION FUSE - 7.5A
5 - FAN FUSE - 5A
6 - ABS CONTROL UNIT FUSE - 10A
7 - ABS MOTOR FUSE - 30A
8 - ABS SOLENOID FUSE - 20A
9 - BACK-UP FUSE - 10A
B - BLACK
BR - BROWN
BL - BLUE
DBR - DARK BROWN
DG - DARK GREEN
G - GREEN
GR - GREY
LB - LIGHT BLUE
LG - LIGHT GREEN
O - ORANGE
P - PINK
R - RED
V - VIOLET
Y - YELLOW
W - WHITE

Notes

Reference

Tools and Workshop Tips REF•2

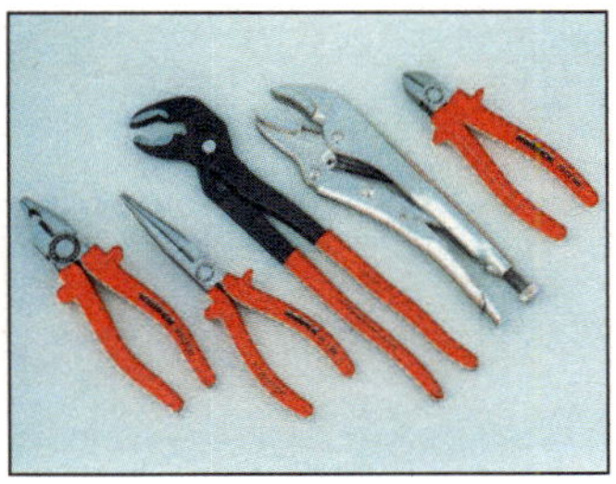

- Building up a tool kit and equipping your workshop
- Using tools
- Understanding bearing, seal, fastener and chain sizes and markings
- Repair techniques

Security REF•20

- Locks and chains
- U-locks
- Disc locks
- Alarms and immobilisers
- Security marking systems
- Tips on how to prevent bike theft

Lubricants and fluids REF•23

- Engine oils
- Transmission (gear) oils
- Coolant/anti-freeze
- Fork oils and suspension fluids
- Brake/clutch fluids
- Spray lubes, degreasers and solvents

MOT Test Checks REF•26

- A guide to the UK MOT test
- Which items are tested
- How to prepare your motorcycle for the test and perform a pre-test check

Storage REF•31

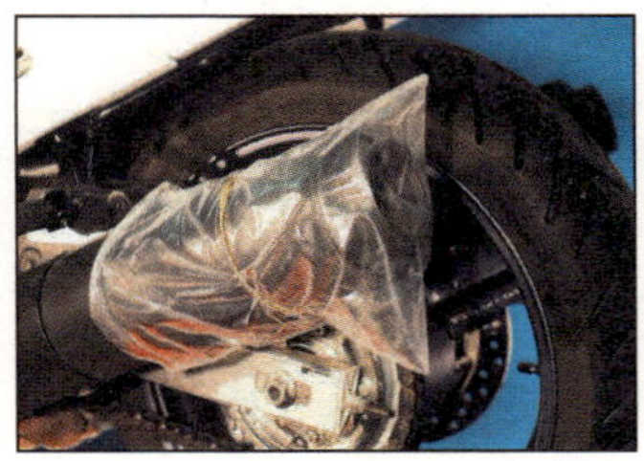

- How to prepare your motorcycle for going into storage and protect essential systems
- How to get the motorcycle back on the road

Conversion Factors REF•34

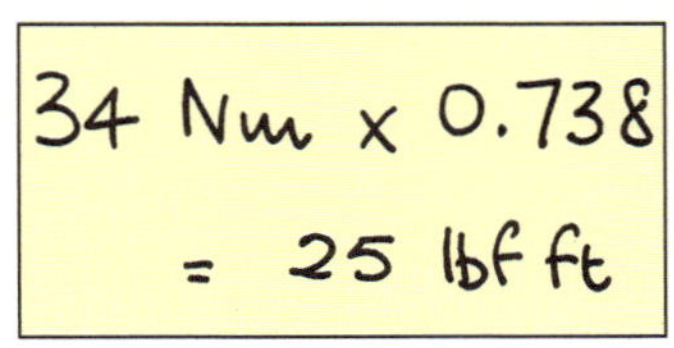

- Formulae for conversion of the metric (SI) units used throughout the manual into Imperial measures

Fault Finding REF•35

- Common faults and their likely causes
- Links to main chapters for testing and repair procedures

Technical Terms Explained REF•44

- Component names, technical terms and common abbreviations explained

Index REF•48

Buying tools

A toolkit is a fundamental requirement for servicing and repairing a motorcycle. Although there will be an initial expense in building up enough tools for servicing, this will soon be offset by the savings made by doing the job yourself. As experience and confidence grow, additional tools can be added to enable the repair and overhaul of the motorcycle. Many of the specialist tools are expensive and not often used so it may be preferable to hire them, or for a group of friends or motorcycle club to join in the purchase.

As a rule, it is better to buy more expensive, good quality tools. Cheaper tools are likely to wear out faster and need to be renewed more often, nullifying the original saving.

Warning: To avoid the risk of a poor quality tool breaking in use, causing injury or damage to the component being worked on, always aim to purchase tools which meet the relevant national safety standards.

The following lists of tools do not represent the manufacturer's service tools, but serve as a guide to help the owner decide which tools are needed for this level of work. In addition, items such as an electric drill, hacksaw, files, soldering iron and a workbench equipped with a vice, may be needed. Although not classed as tools, a selection of bolts, screws, nuts, washers and pieces of tubing always come in useful.

For more information about tools, refer to the Haynes *Motorcycle Workshop Practice Techbook* (Bk. No. 3470).

Manufacturer's service tools

Inevitably certain tasks require the use of a service tool. Where possible an alternative tool or method of approach is recommended, but sometimes there is no option if personal injury or damage to the component is to be avoided. Where required, service tools are referred to in the relevant procedure.

Service tools can usually only be purchased from a motorcycle dealer and are identified by a part number. Some of the commonly-used tools, such as rotor pullers, are available in aftermarket form from mail-order motorcycle tool and accessory suppliers.

Maintenance and minor repair tools

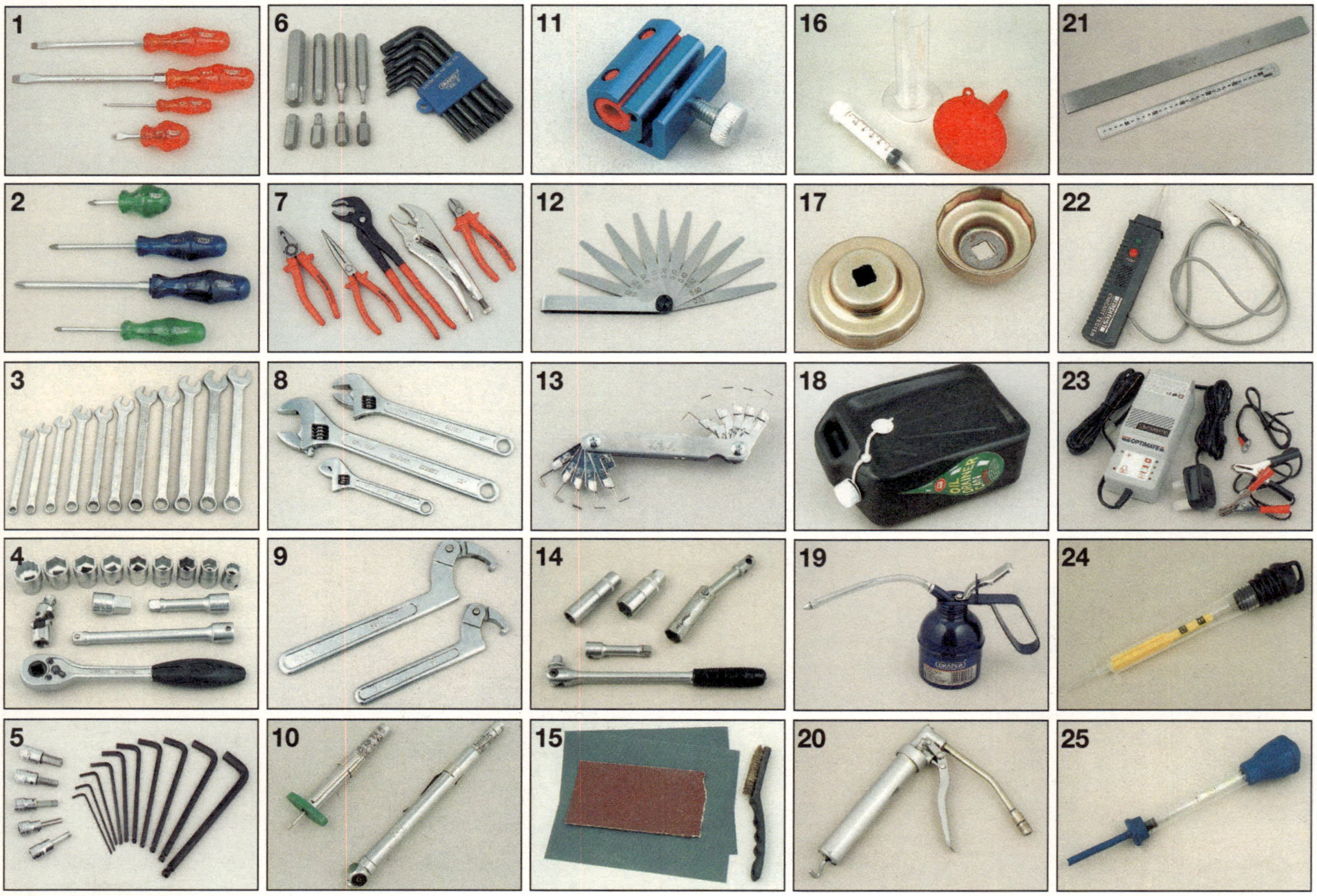

1 *Set of flat-bladed screwdrivers*
2 *Set of Phillips head screwdrivers*
3 *Combination open-end and ring spanners*
4 *Socket set (3/8 inch or 1/2 inch drive)*
5 *Set of Allen keys or bits*
6 *Set of Torx keys or bits*
7 *Pliers, cutters and self-locking grips (Mole grips)*
8 *Adjustable spanners*
9 *C-spanners*
10 *Tread depth gauge and tyre pressure gauge*
11 *Cable oiler clamp*
12 *Feeler gauges*
13 *Spark plug gap measuring tool*
14 *Spark plug spanner or deep plug sockets*
15 *Wire brush and emery paper*
16 *Calibrated syringe, measuring vessel and funnel*
17 *Oil filter adapters*
18 *Oil drainer can or tray*
19 *Pump type oil can*
20 *Grease gun*
21 *Straight-edge and steel rule*
22 *Continuity tester*
23 *Battery charger*
24 *Hydrometer (for battery specific gravity check)*
25 *Anti-freeze tester (for liquid-cooled engines)*

Repair and overhaul tools

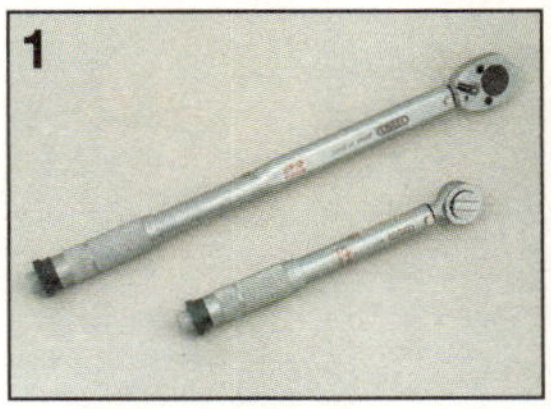

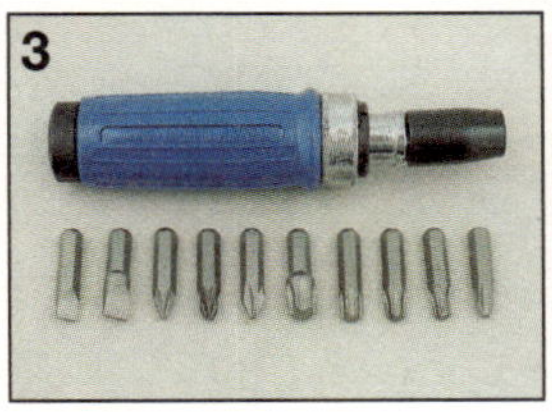

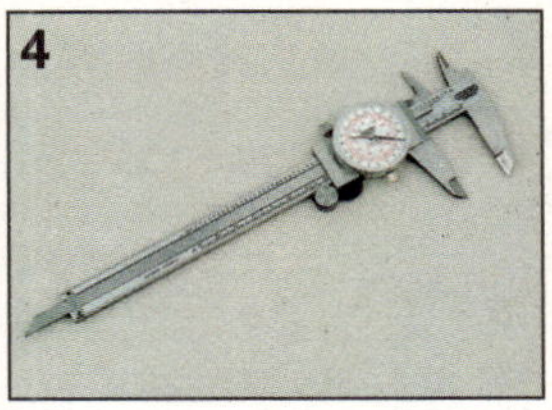

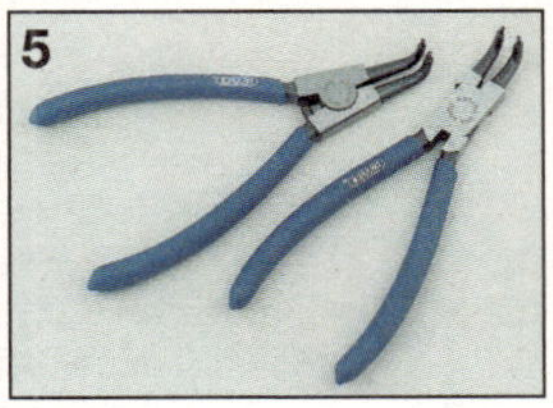

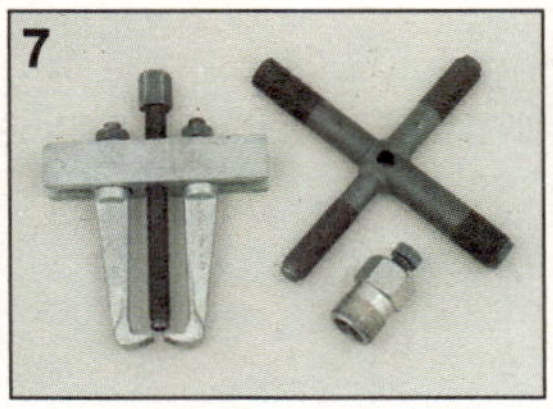

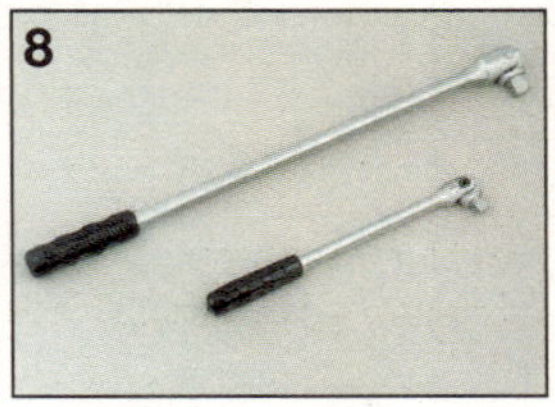

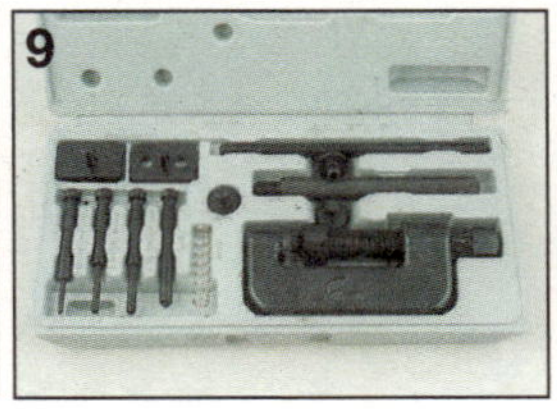

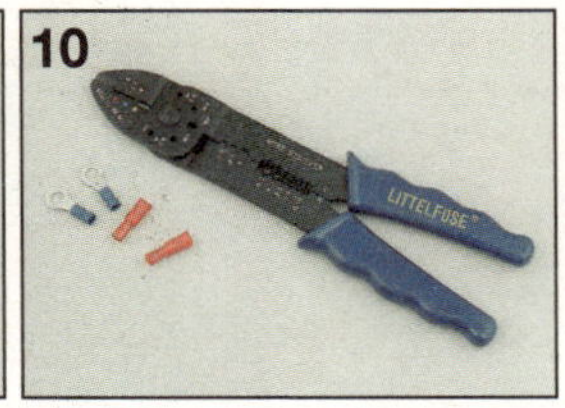

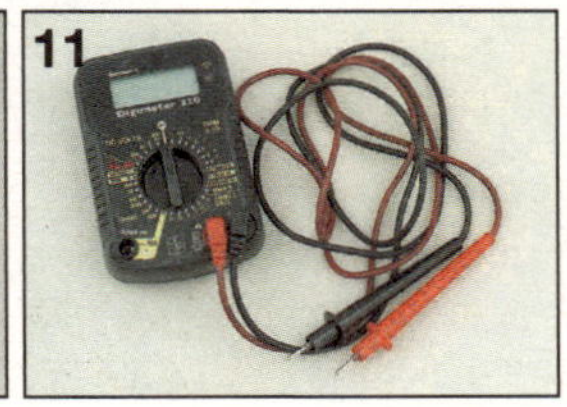

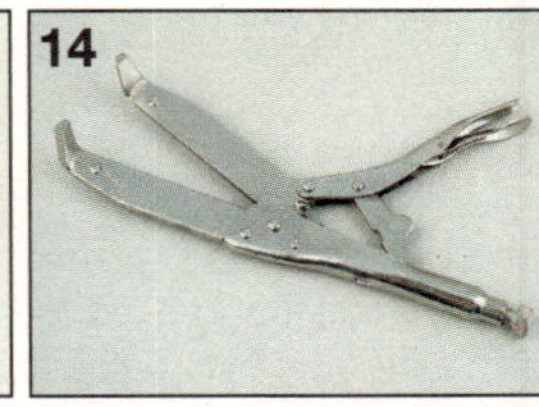

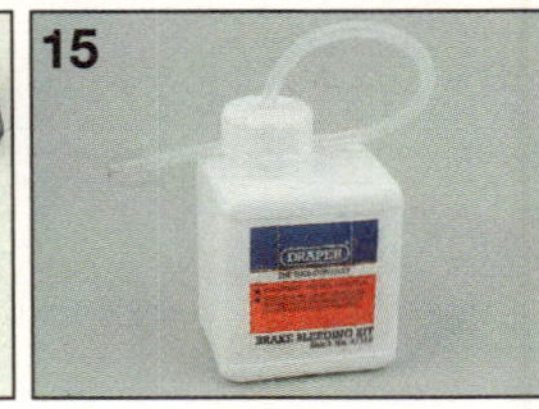

1 *Torque wrench (small and mid-ranges)*
2 *Conventional, plastic or soft-faced hammers*
3 *Impact driver set*
4 *Vernier gauge*
5 *Circlip pliers (internal and external, or combination)*
6 *Set of cold chisels and punches*
7 *Selection of pullers*
8 *Breaker bars*
9 *Chain breaking/ riveting tool set*
10 *Wire stripper and crimper tool*
11 *Multimeter (measures amps, volts and ohms)*
12 *Stroboscope (for dynamic timing checks)*
13 *Hose clamp (wingnut type shown)*
14 *Clutch holding tool*
15 *One-man brake/clutch bleeder kit*

Specialist tools

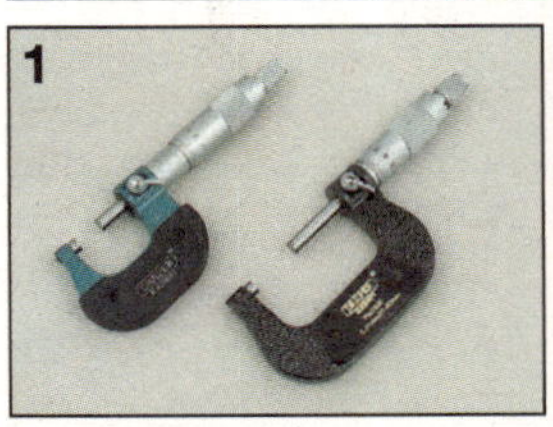

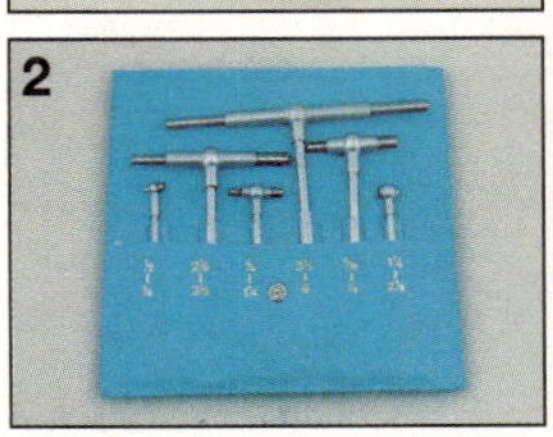

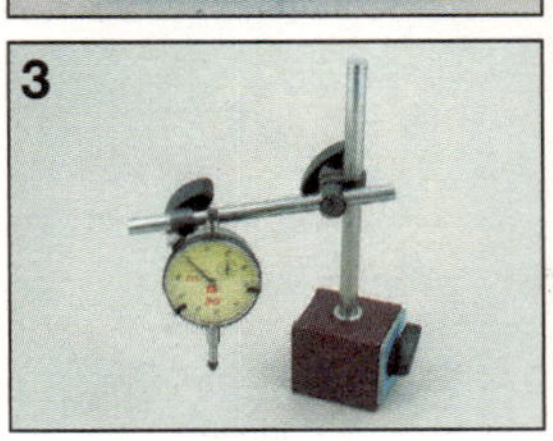

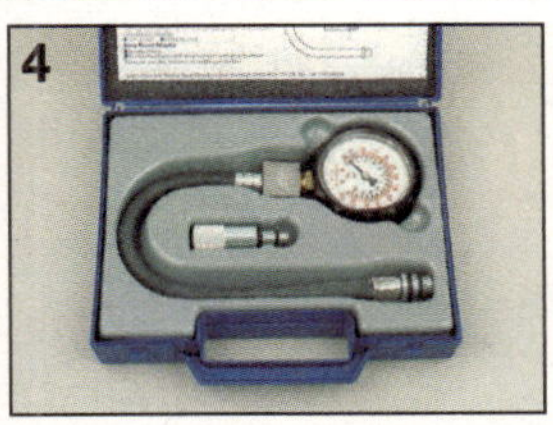

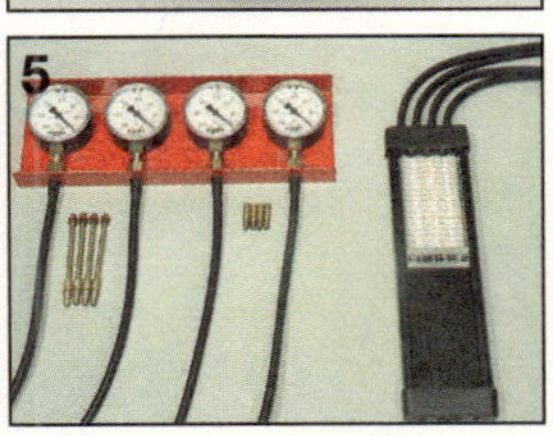

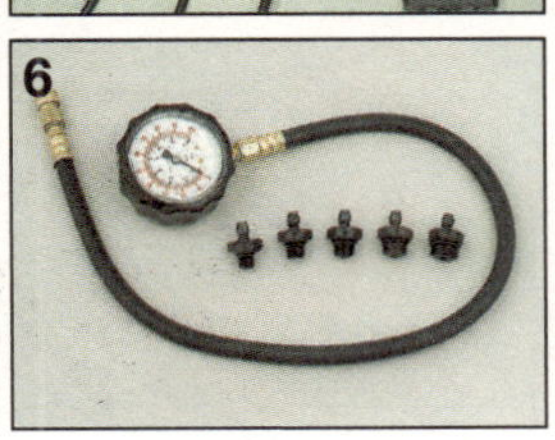

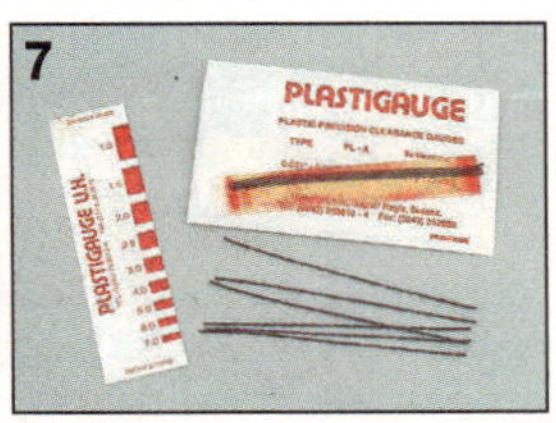

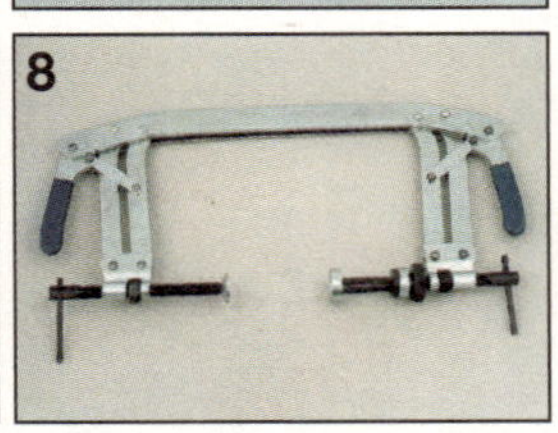

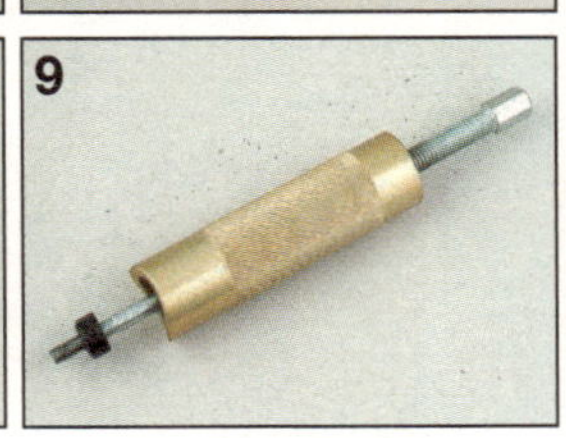

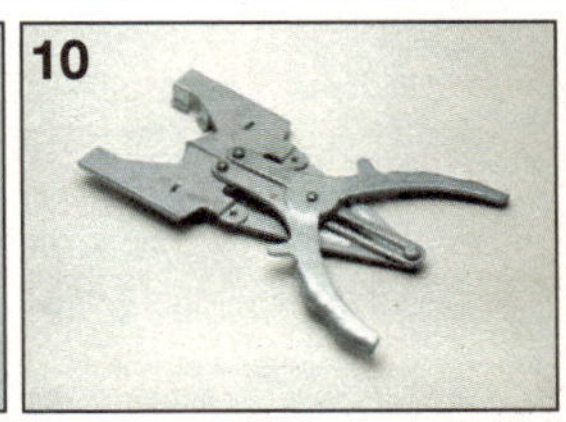

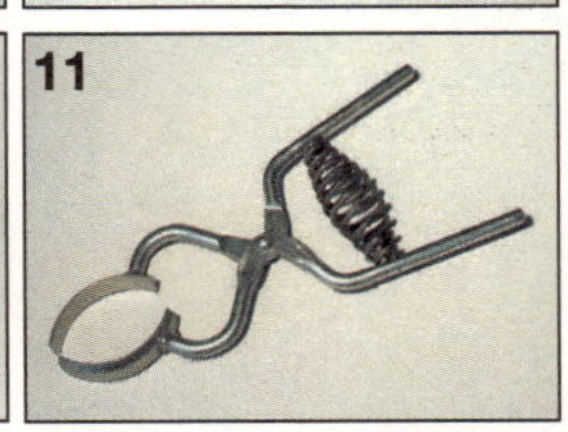

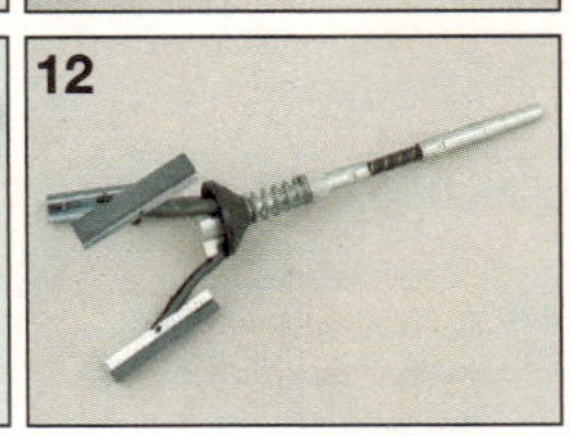

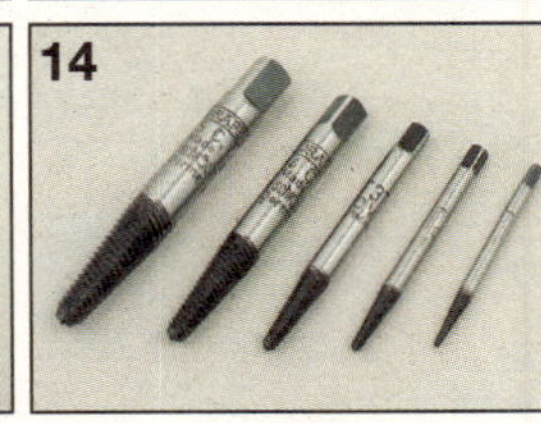

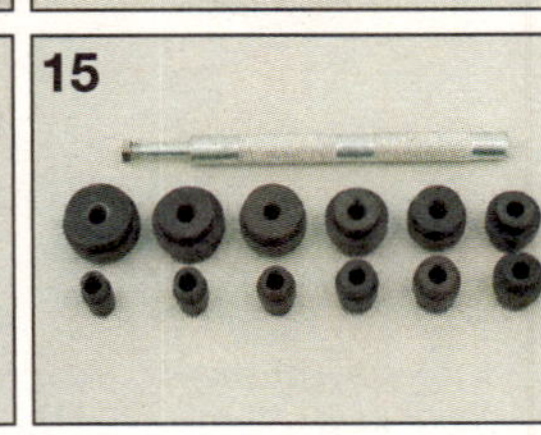

1 *Micrometers (external type)*
2 *Telescoping gauges*
3 *Dial gauge*
4 *Cylinder compression gauge*
5 *Vacuum gauges (left) or manometer (right)*
6 *Oil pressure gauge*
7 *Plastigauge kit*
8 *Valve spring compressor (4-stroke engines)*
9 *Piston pin drawbolt tool*
10 *Piston ring removal and installation tool*
11 *Piston ring clamp*
12 *Cylinder bore hone (stone type shown)*
13 *Stud extractor*
14 *Screw extractor set*
15 *Bearing driver set*

1 Workshop equipment and facilities

The workbench

● Work is made much easier by raising the bike up on a ramp - components are much more accessible if raised to waist level. The hydraulic or pneumatic types seen in the dealer's workshop are a sound investment if you undertake a lot of repairs or overhauls **(see illustration 1.1)**.

1.1 Hydraulic motorcycle ramp

● If raised off ground level, the bike must be supported on the ramp to avoid it falling. Most ramps incorporate a front wheel locating clamp which can be adjusted to suit different diameter wheels. When tightening the clamp, take care not to mark the wheel rim or damage the tyre - use wood blocks on each side to prevent this.

● Secure the bike to the ramp using tie-downs **(see illustration 1.2)**. If the bike has only a sidestand, and hence leans at a dangerous angle when raised, support the bike on an auxiliary stand.

1.2 Tie-downs are used around the passenger footrests to secure the bike

● Auxiliary (paddock) stands are widely available from mail order companies or motorcycle dealers and attach either to the wheel axle or swingarm pivot **(see illustration 1.3)**. If the motorcycle has a centrestand, you can support it under the crankcase to prevent it toppling whilst either wheel is removed **(see illustration 1.4)**.

1.3 This auxiliary stand attaches to the swingarm pivot

1.4 Always use a block of wood between the engine and jack head when supporting the engine in this way

Fumes and fire

● Refer to the Safety first! page at the beginning of the manual for full details. Make sure your workshop is equipped with a fire extinguisher suitable for fuel-related fires (Class B fire - flammable liquids) - it is not sufficient to have a water-filled extinguisher.

● Always ensure adequate ventilation is available. Unless an exhaust gas extraction system is available for use, ensure that the engine is run outside of the workshop.

● If working on the fuel system, make sure the workshop is ventilated to avoid a build-up of fumes. This applies equally to fume build-up when charging a battery. Do not smoke or allow anyone else to smoke in the workshop.

Fluids

● If you need to drain fuel from the tank, store it in an approved container marked as suitable for the storage of petrol (gasoline) **(see illustration 1.5)**. Do not store fuel in glass jars or bottles.

1.5 Use an approved can only for storing petrol (gasoline)

● Use proprietary engine degreasers or solvents which have a high flash-point, such as paraffin (kerosene), for cleaning off oil, grease and dirt - never use petrol (gasoline) for cleaning. Wear rubber gloves when handling solvent and engine degreaser. The fumes from certain solvents can be dangerous - always work in a well-ventilated area.

Dust, eye and hand protection

● Protect your lungs from inhalation of dust particles by wearing a filtering mask over the nose and mouth. Many frictional materials still contain asbestos which is dangerous to your health. Protect your eyes from spouts of liquid and sprung components by wearing a pair of protective goggles **(see illustration 1.6)**.

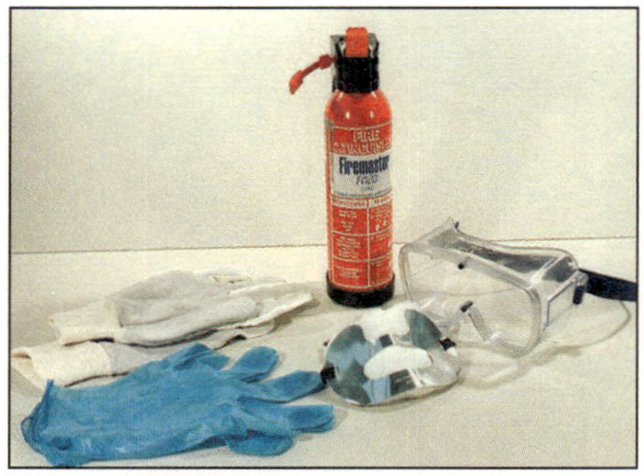

1.6 A fire extinguisher, goggles, mask and protective gloves should be at hand in the workshop

● Protect your hands from contact with solvents, fuel and oils by wearing rubber gloves. Alternatively apply a barrier cream to your hands before starting work. If handling hot components or fluids, wear suitable gloves to protect your hands from scalding and burns.

What to do with old fluids

● Old cleaning solvent, fuel, coolant and oils should not be poured down domestic drains or onto the ground. Package the fluid up in old oil containers, label it accordingly, and take it to a garage or disposal facility. Contact your local authority for location of such sites or ring the oil care hotline.

Note: It is antisocial and illegal to dump oil down the drain. To find the location of your local oil recycling bank in the UK, call 03708 506 506 or visit www.oilbankline.org.uk

In the USA, note that any oil supplier must accept used oil for recycling.

2 Fasteners - screws, bolts and nuts

Fastener types and applications

Bolts and screws

● Fastener head types are either of hexagonal, Torx or splined design, with internal and external versions of each type **(see illustrations 2.1 and 2.2)**; splined head fasteners are not in common use on motorcycles. The conventional slotted or Phillips head design is used for certain screws. Bolt or screw length is always measured from the underside of the head to the end of the item **(see illustration 2.11)**.

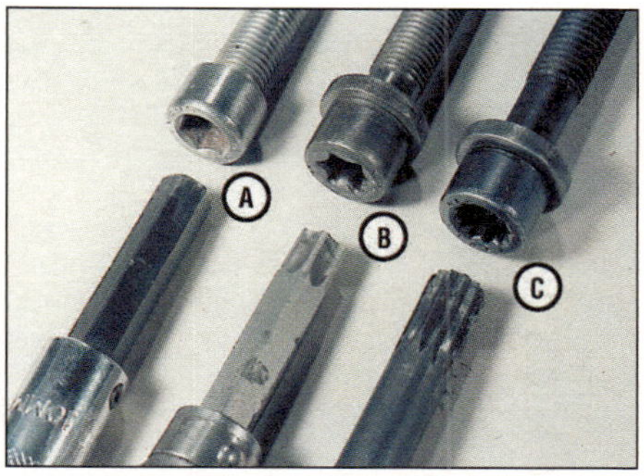

2.1 Internal hexagon/Allen (A), Torx (B) and splined (C) fasteners, with corresponding bits

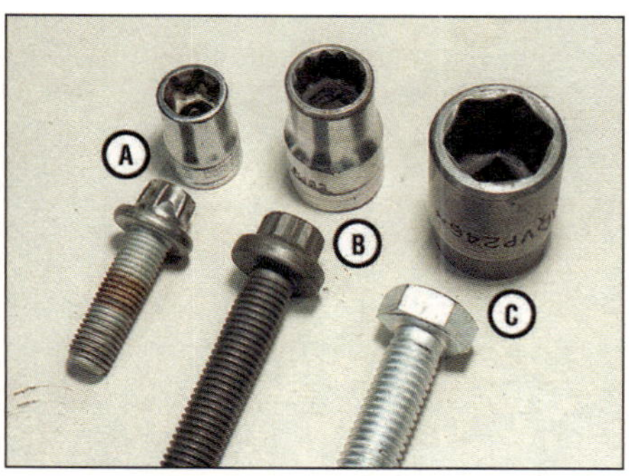

2.2 External Torx (A), splined (B) and hexagon (C) fasteners, with corresponding sockets

● Certain fasteners on the motorcycle have a tensile marking on their heads, the higher the marking the stronger the fastener. High tensile fasteners generally carry a 10 or higher marking. Never replace a high tensile fastener with one of a lower tensile strength.

Washers **(see illustration 2.3)**

● Plain washers are used between a fastener head and a component to prevent damage to the component or to spread the load when torque is applied. Plain washers can also be used as spacers or shims in certain assemblies. Copper or aluminium plain washers are often used as sealing washers on drain plugs.

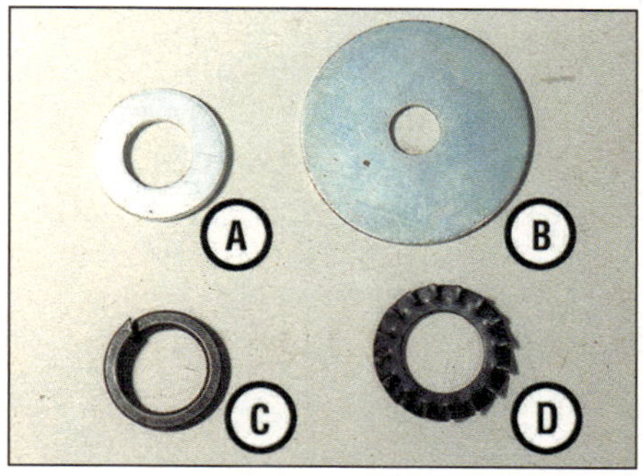

2.3 Plain washer (A), penny washer (B), spring washer (C) and serrated washer (D)

● The split-ring spring washer works by applying axial tension between the fastener head and component. If flattened, it is fatigued and must be renewed. If a plain (flat) washer is used on the fastener, position the spring washer between the fastener and the plain washer.

● Serrated star type washers dig into the fastener and component faces, preventing loosening. They are often used on electrical earth (ground) connections to the frame.

● Cone type washers (sometimes called Belleville) are conical and when tightened apply axial tension between the fastener head and component. They must be installed with the dished side against the component and often carry an OUTSIDE marking on their outer face. If flattened, they are fatigued and must be renewed.

● Tab washers are used to lock plain nuts or bolts on a shaft. A portion of the tab washer is bent up hard against one flat of the nut or bolt to prevent it loosening. Due to the tab washer being deformed in use, a new tab washer should be used every time it is disturbed.

● Wave washers are used to take up endfloat on a shaft. They provide light springing and prevent excessive side-to-side play of a component. Can be found on rocker arm shafts.

Nuts and split pins

● Conventional plain nuts are usually six-sided **(see illustration 2.4)**. They are sized by thread diameter and pitch. High tensile nuts carry a number on one end to denote their tensile strength.

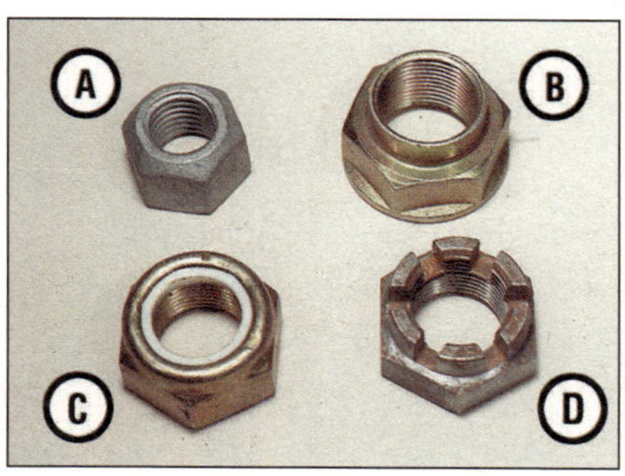

2.4 Plain nut (A), shouldered locknut (B), nylon insert nut (C) and castellated nut (D)

● Self-locking nuts either have a nylon insert, or two spring metal tabs, or a shoulder which is staked into a groove in the shaft - their advantage over conventional plain nuts is a resistance to loosening due to vibration. The nylon insert type can be used a number of times, but must be renewed when the friction of the nylon insert is reduced, ie when the nut spins freely on the shaft. The spring tab type can be reused unless the tabs are damaged. The shouldered type must be renewed every time it is disturbed.

● Split pins (cotter pins) are used to lock a castellated nut to a shaft or to prevent slackening of a plain nut. Common applications are wheel axles and brake torque arms. Because the split pin arms are deformed to lock around the nut a new split pin must always be used on installation - always fit the correct size split pin which will fit snugly in the shaft hole. Make sure the split pin arms are correctly located around the nut **(see illustrations 2.5 and 2.6)**.

2.5 Bend split pin (cotter pin) arms as shown (arrows) to secure a castellated nut

2.6 Bend split pin (cotter pin) arms as shown to secure a plain nut

> ***Caution: If the castellated nut slots do not align with the shaft hole after tightening to the torque setting, tighten the nut until the next slot aligns with the hole - never slacken the nut to align its slot.***

● R-pins (shaped like the letter R), or slip pins as they are sometimes called, are sprung and can be reused if they are otherwise in good condition. Always install R-pins with their closed end facing forwards **(see illustration 2.7)**.

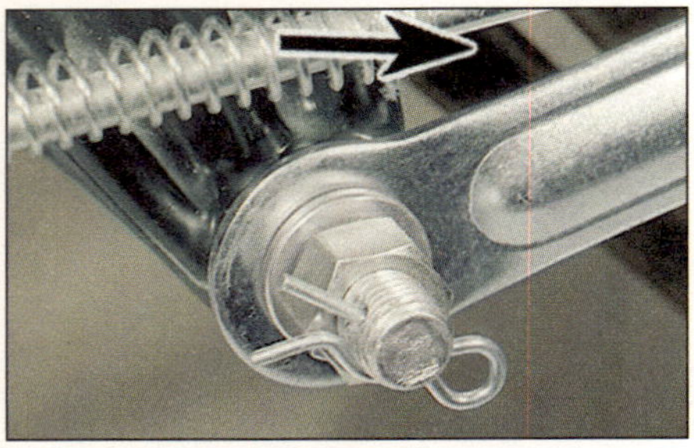

2.7 Correct fitting of R-pin. Arrow indicates forward direction

Circlips (see illustration 2.8)

● Circlips (sometimes called snap-rings) are used to retain components on a shaft or in a housing and have corresponding external or internal ears to permit removal. Parallel-sided (machined) circlips can be installed either way round in their groove, whereas stamped circlips (which have a chamfered edge on one face) must be installed with the chamfer facing away from the direction of thrust load **(see illustration 2.9)**.

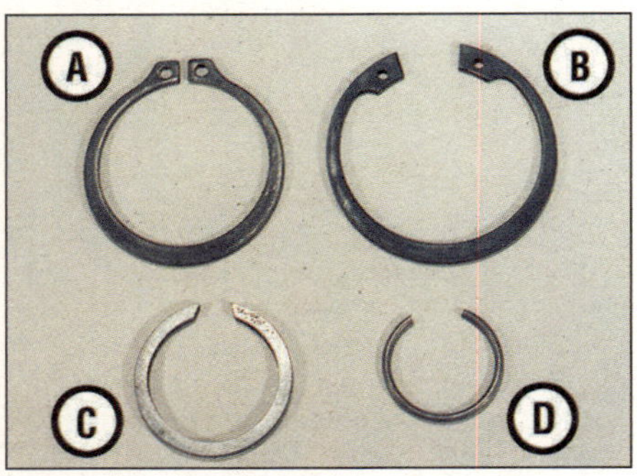

2.8 External stamped circlip (A), internal stamped circlip (B), machined circlip (C) and wire circlip (D)

● Always use circlip pliers to remove and install circlips; expand or compress them just enough to remove them. After installation, rotate the circlip in its groove to ensure it is securely seated. If installing a circlip on a splined shaft, always align its opening with a shaft channel to ensure the circlip ends are well supported and unlikely to catch **(see illustration 2.10)**.

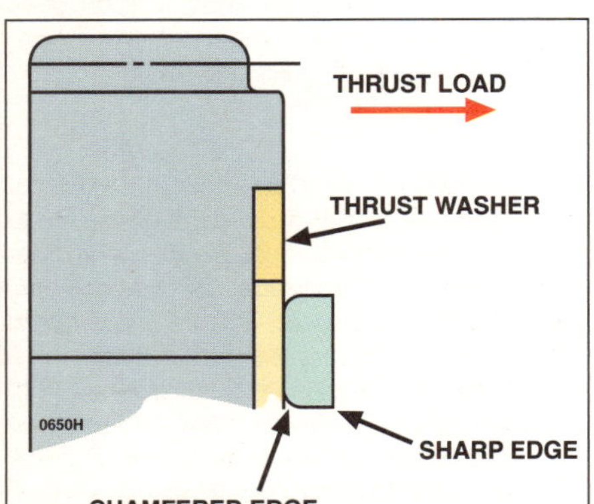

2.9 Correct fitting of a stamped circlip

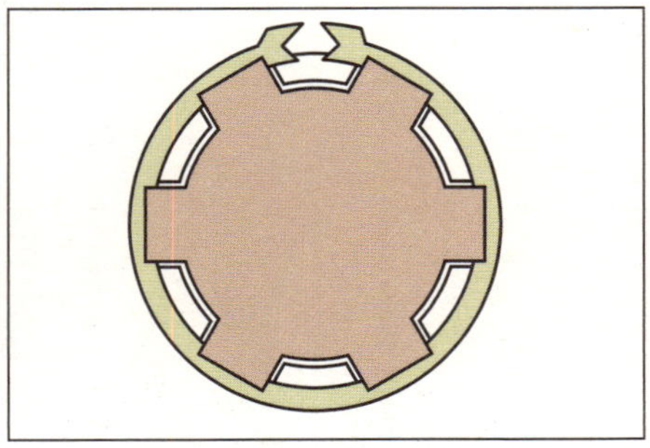

2.10 Align circlip opening with shaft channel

● Circlips can wear due to the thrust of components and become loose in their grooves, with the subsequent danger of becoming dislodged in operation. For this reason, renewal is advised every time a circlip is disturbed.

● Wire circlips are commonly used as piston pin retaining clips. If a removal tang is provided, long-nosed pliers can be used to dislodge them, otherwise careful use of a small flat-bladed screwdriver is necessary. Wire circlips should be renewed every time they are disturbed.

Thread diameter and pitch

● Diameter of a male thread (screw, bolt or stud) is the outside diameter of the threaded portion **(see illustration 2.11)**. Most motorcycle manufacturers use the ISO (International Standards Organisation) metric system expressed in millimetres, eg M6 refers to a 6 mm diameter thread. Sizing is the same for nuts, except that the thread diameter is measured across the valleys of the nut.

● Pitch is the distance between the peaks of the thread **(see illustration 2.11)**. It is expressed in millimetres, thus a common bolt size may be expressed as 6.0 x 1.0 mm (6 mm thread diameter and 1 mm pitch). Generally pitch increases in proportion to thread diameter, although there are always exceptions.

● Thread diameter and pitch are related for conventional fastener applications and the accompanying table can be used as a guide. Additionally, the AF (Across Flats), spanner or socket size dimension of the bolt or nut **(see illustration 2.11)** is linked to thread and pitch specification. Thread pitch can be measured with a thread gauge **(see illustration 2.12)**.

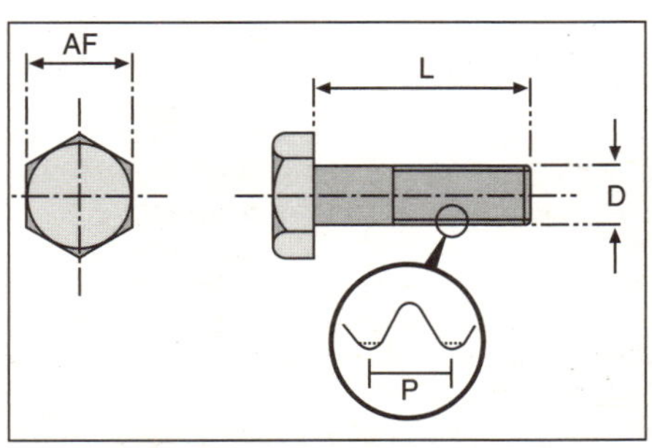

2.11 Fastener length (L), thread diameter (D), thread pitch (P) and head size (AF)

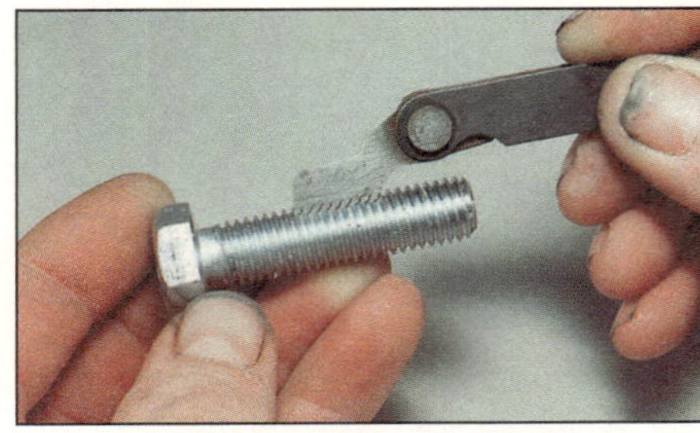

2.12 Using a thread gauge to measure pitch

AF size	Thread diameter x pitch (mm)
8 mm	M5 x 0.8
8 mm	M6 x 1.0
10 mm	M6 x 1.0
12 mm	M8 x 1.25
14 mm	M10 x 1.25
17 mm	M12 x 1.25

● The threads of most fasteners are of the right-hand type, ie they are turned clockwise to tighten and anti-clockwise to loosen. The reverse situation applies to left-hand thread fasteners, which are turned anti-clockwise to tighten and clockwise to loosen. Left-hand threads are used where rotation of a component might loosen a conventional right-hand thread fastener.

Seized fasteners

● Corrosion of external fasteners due to water or reaction between two dissimilar metals can occur over a period of time. It will build up sooner in wet conditions or in countries where salt is used on the roads during the winter. If a fastener is severely corroded it is likely that normal methods of removal will fail and result in its head being ruined. When you attempt removal, the fastener thread should be heard to crack free and unscrew easily - if it doesn't, stop there before damaging something.

● A smart tap on the head of the fastener will often succeed in breaking free corrosion which has occurred in the threads **(see illustration 2.13)**.

● An aerosol penetrating fluid (such as WD-40) applied the night beforehand may work its way down into the thread and ease removal. Depending on the location, you may be able to make up a Plasticine well around the fastener head and fill it with penetrating fluid.

2.13 A sharp tap on the head of a fastener will often break free a corroded thread

● If you are working on an engine internal component, corrosion will most likely not be a problem due to the well lubricated environment. However, components can be very tight and an impact driver is a useful tool in freeing them **(see illustration 2.14)**.

2.14 Using an impact driver to free a fastener

● Where corrosion has occurred between dissimilar metals (eg steel and aluminium alloy), the application of heat to the fastener head will create a disproportionate expansion rate between the two metals and break the seizure caused by the corrosion. Whether heat can be applied depends on the location of the fastener - any surrounding components likely to be damaged must first be removed **(see illustration 2.15)**. Heat can be applied using a paint stripper heat gun or clothes iron, or by immersing the component in boiling water - wear protective gloves to prevent scalding or burns to the hands.

2.15 Using heat to free a seized fastener

● As a last resort, it is possible to use a hammer and cold chisel to work the fastener head unscrewed **(see illustration 2.16)**. This will damage the fastener, but more importantly extreme care must be taken not to damage the surrounding component.

Caution: Remember that the component being secured is generally of more value than the bolt, nut or screw - when the fastener is freed, do not unscrew it with force, instead work the fastener back and forth when resistance is felt to prevent thread damage.

2.16 Using a hammer and chisel to free a seized fastener

Broken fasteners and damaged heads

● If the shank of a broken bolt or screw is accessible you can grip it with self-locking grips. The knurled wheel type stud extractor tool or self-gripping stud puller tool is particularly useful for removing the long studs which screw into the cylinder mouth surface of the crankcase or bolts and screws from which the head has broken off **(see illustration 2.17)**. Studs can also be removed by locking two nuts together on the threaded end of the stud and using a spanner on the lower nut **(see illustration 2.18)**.

2.17 Using a stud extractor tool to remove a broken crankcase stud

2.18 Two nuts can be locked together to unscrew a stud from a component

● A bolt or screw which has broken off below or level with the casing must be extracted using a screw extractor set. Centre punch the fastener to centralise the drill bit, then drill a hole in the fastener **(see illustration 2.19)**. Select a drill bit which is approximately half to three-quarters the diameter of the fastener and drill to a depth which will accommodate the extractor. Use the largest size extractor possible, but avoid leaving too small a wall thickness otherwise the extractor will merely force the fastener walls outwards wedging it in the casing thread.

2.19 When using a screw extractor, first drill a hole in the fastener . . .

● If a spiral type extractor is used, thread it anti-clockwise into the fastener. As it is screwed in, it will grip the fastener and unscrew it from the casing **(see illustration 2.20)**.

2.20 . . . then thread the extractor anti-clockwise into the fastener

● If a taper type extractor is used, tap it into the fastener so that it is firmly wedged in place. Unscrew the extractor (anti-clockwise) to draw the fastener out.

Warning: Stud extractors are very hard and may break off in the fastener if care is not taken - ask an engineer about spark erosion if this happens.

● Alternatively, the broken bolt/screw can be drilled out and the hole retapped for an oversize bolt/screw or a diamond-section thread insert. It is essential that the drilling is carried out squarely and to the correct depth, otherwise the casing may be ruined - if in doubt, entrust the work to an engineer.

● Bolts and nuts with rounded corners cause the correct size spanner or socket to slip when force is applied. Of the types of spanner/socket available always use a six-point type rather than an eight or twelve-point type - better grip

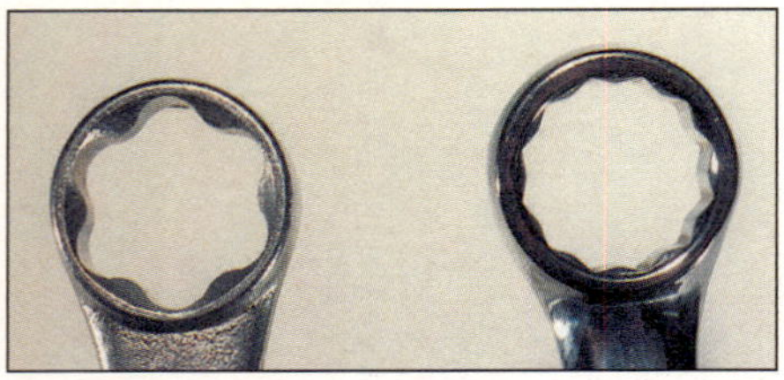

2.21 Comparison of surface drive ring spanner (left) with 12-point type (right)

is obtained. Surface drive spanners grip the middle of the hex flats, rather than the corners, and are thus good in cases of damaged heads **(see illustration 2.21)**.

- Slotted-head or Phillips-head screws are often damaged by the use of the wrong size screwdriver. Allen-head and Torx-head screws are much less likely to sustain damage. If enough of the screw head is exposed you can use a hacksaw to cut a slot in its head and then use a conventional flat-bladed screwdriver to remove it. Alternatively use a hammer and cold chisel to tap the head of the fastener around to slacken it. Always replace damaged fasteners with new ones, preferably Torx or Allen-head type.

A dab of valve grinding compound between the screw head and screw-driver tip will often give a good grip.

Thread repair

- Threads (particularly those in aluminium alloy components) can be damaged by overtightening, being assembled with dirt in the threads, or from a component working loose and vibrating. Eventually the thread will fail completely, and it will be impossible to tighten the fastener.
- If a thread is damaged or clogged with old locking compound it can be renovated with a thread repair tool (thread chaser) **(see illustrations 2.22 and 2.23)**; special thread

2.22 A thread repair tool being used to correct an internal thread

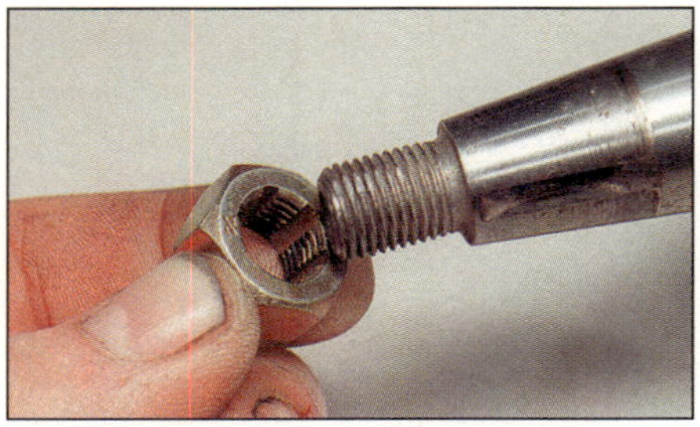

2.23 A thread repair tool being used to correct an external thread

chasers are available for spark plug hole threads. The tool will not cut a new thread, but clean and true the original thread. Make sure that you use the correct diameter and pitch tool. Similarly, external threads can be cleaned up with a die or a thread restorer file **(see illustration 2.24)**.

2.24 Using a thread restorer file

- It is possible to drill out the old thread and retap the component to the next thread size. This will work where there is enough surrounding material and a new bolt or screw can be obtained. Sometimes, however, this is not possible - such as where the bolt/screw passes through another component which must also be suitably modified, also in cases where a spark plug or oil drain plug cannot be obtained in a larger diameter thread size.
- The diamond-section thread insert (often known by its popular trade name of Heli-Coil) is a simple and effective method of renewing the thread and retaining the original size. A kit can be purchased which contains the tap, insert and installing tool **(see illustration 2.25)**. Drill out the damaged thread with the size drill specified **(see illustration 2.26)**. Carefully retap the thread **(see illustration 2.27)**. Install the

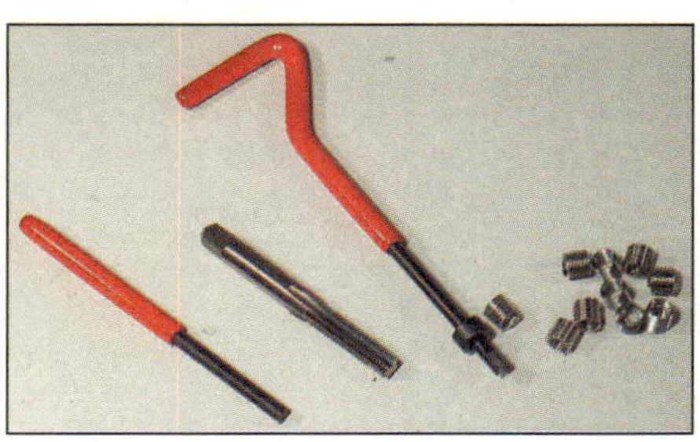

2.25 Obtain a thread insert kit to suit the thread diameter and pitch required

2.26 To install a thread insert, first drill out the original thread . . .

2.27 . . . tap a new thread . . .

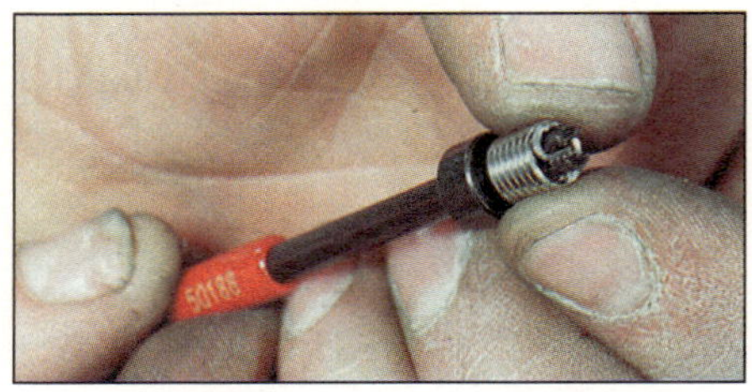

2.28 . . . fit insert on the installing tool . . .

2.29 . . . and thread into the component . . .

2.30 . . . break off the tang when complete

insert on the installing tool and thread it slowly into place using a light downward pressure **(see illustrations 2.28 and 2.29)**. When positioned between a 1/4 and 1/2 turn below the surface withdraw the installing tool and use the break-off tool to press down on the tang, breaking it off **(see illustration 2.30)**.

- There are epoxy thread repair kits on the market which can rebuild stripped internal threads, although this repair should not be used on high load-bearing components.

Thread locking and sealing compounds

- Locking compounds are used in locations where the fastener is prone to loosening due to vibration or on important safety-related items which might cause loss of control of the motorcycle if they fail. It is also used where important fasteners cannot be secured by other means such as lockwashers or split pins.
- Before applying locking compound, make sure that the threads (internal and external) are clean and dry with all old compound removed. Select a compound to suit the component being secured - a non-permanent general locking and sealing type is suitable for most applications, but a high strength type is needed for permanent fixing of studs in castings. Apply a drop or two of the compound to the first few threads of the fastener, then thread it into place and tighten to the specified torque. Do not apply excessive thread locking compound otherwise the thread may be damaged on subsequent removal.
- Certain fasteners are impregnated with a dry film type coating of locking compound on their threads. Always renew this type of fastener if disturbed.
- Anti-seize compounds, such as copper-based greases, can be applied to protect threads from seizure due to extreme heat and corrosion. A common instance is spark plug threads and exhaust system fasteners.

3 Measuring tools and gauges

Feeler gauges

- Feeler gauges (or blades) are used for measuring small gaps and clearances **(see illustration 3.1)**. They can also be used to measure endfloat (sideplay) of a component on a shaft where access is not possible with a dial gauge.
- Feeler gauge sets should be treated with care and not bent or damaged. They are etched with their size on one face. Keep them clean and very lightly oiled to prevent corrosion build-up.

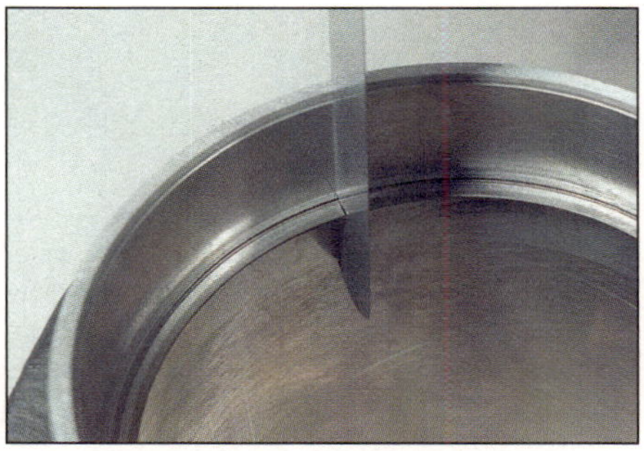

3.1 Feeler gauges are used for measuring small gaps and clearances - thickness is marked on one face of gauge

- When measuring a clearance, select a gauge which is a light sliding fit between the two components. You may need to use two gauges together to measure the clearance accurately.

Micrometers

- A micrometer is a precision tool capable of measuring to 0.01 or 0.001 of a millimetre. It should always be stored in its case and not in the general toolbox. It must be kept clean and never dropped, otherwise its frame or measuring anvils could be distorted resulting in inaccurate readings.
- External micrometers are used for measuring outside diameters of components and have many more applications than internal micrometers. Micrometers are available in different size ranges, eg 0 to 25 mm, 25 to 50 mm, and upwards in 25 mm steps; some large micrometers have interchangeable anvils to allow a range of measurements to be taken. Generally the largest precision measurement you are likely to take on a motorcycle is the piston diameter.
- Internal micrometers (or bore micrometers) are used for measuring inside diameters, such as valve guides and cylinder bores. Telescoping gauges and small hole gauges are used in conjunction with an external micrometer, whereas the more expensive internal micrometers have their own measuring device.

External micrometer

Note: *The conventional analogue type instrument is described. Although much easier to read, digital micrometers are considerably more expensive.*

- Always check the calibration of the micrometer before use. With the anvils closed (0 to 25 mm type) or set over a test gauge

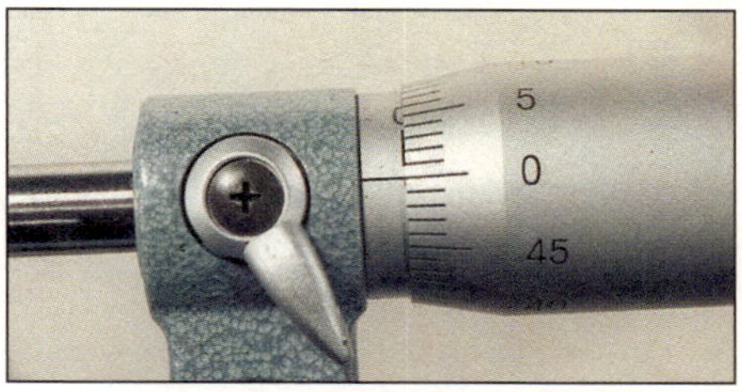

3.2 Check micrometer calibration before use

(for the larger types) the scale should read zero **(see illustration 3.2)**; make sure that the anvils (and test piece) are clean first. Any discrepancy can be adjusted by referring to the instructions supplied with the tool. Remember that the micrometer is a precision measuring tool - don't force the anvils closed, use the ratchet (4) on the end of the micrometer to close it. In this way, a measured force is always applied.

- To use, first make sure that the item being measured is clean. Place the anvil of the micrometer (1) against the item and use the thimble (2) to bring the spindle (3) lightly into contact with the other side of the item **(see illustration 3.3)**. Don't tighten the thimble down because this will damage the micrometer - instead use the ratchet (4) on the end of the micrometer. The ratchet mechanism applies a measured force preventing damage to the instrument.
- The micrometer is read by referring to the linear scale on the sleeve and the annular scale on the thimble. Read off the sleeve first to obtain the base measurement, then add the fine measurement from the thimble to obtain the overall reading. The linear scale on the sleeve represents the measuring range of the micrometer (eg 0 to 25 mm). The annular scale

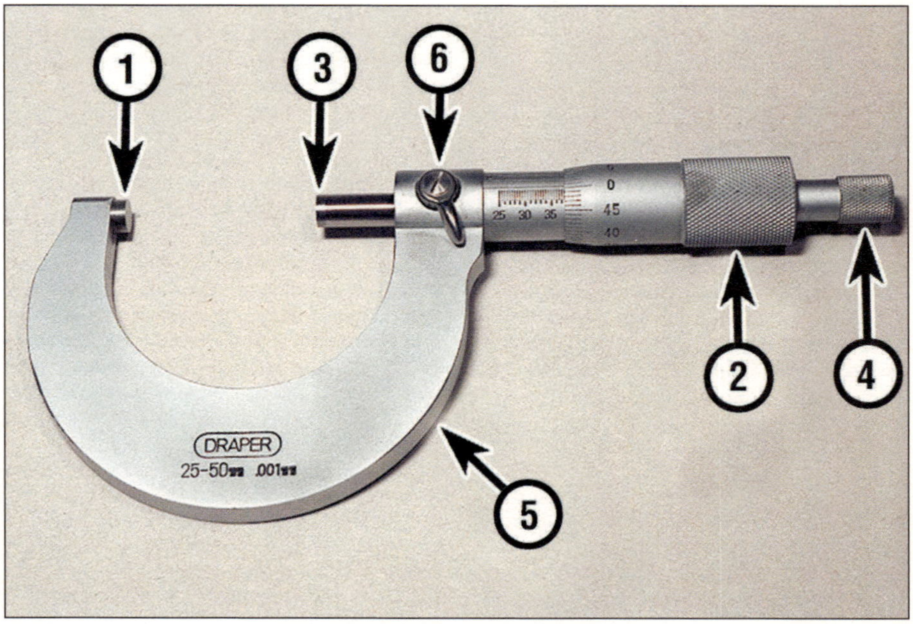

3.3 Micrometer component parts

1 Anvil
2 Thimble
3 Spindle
4 Ratchet
5 Frame
6 Locking lever

on the thimble will be in graduations of 0.01 mm (or as marked on the frame) - one full revolution of the thimble will move 0.5 mm on the linear scale. Take the reading where the datum line on the sleeve intersects the thimble's scale. Always position the eye directly above the scale otherwise an inaccurate reading will result.

In the example shown the item measures 2.95 mm **(see illustration 3.4)**:

Linear scale	2.00 mm
Linear scale	0.50 mm
Annular scale	0.45 mm
Total figure	2.95 mm

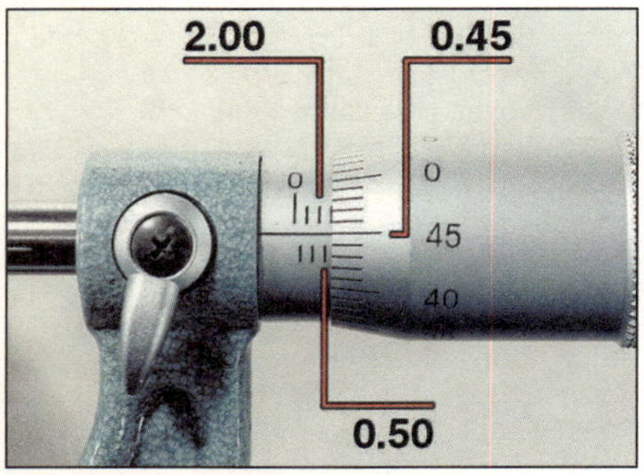

3.4 Micrometer reading of 2.95 mm

Most micrometers have a locking lever (6) on the frame to hold the setting in place, allowing the item to be removed from the micrometer.

● Some micrometers have a vernier scale on their sleeve, providing an even finer measurement to be taken, in 0.001 increments of a millimetre. Take the sleeve and thimble measurement as described above, then check which graduation on the vernier scale aligns with that of the annular scale on the thimble **Note:** *The eye must be perpendicular to the scale when taking the vernier reading - if necessary rotate the body of the micrometer to ensure this.* Multiply the vernier scale figure by 0.001 and add it to the base and fine measurement figures.

In the example shown the item measures 46.994 mm **(see illustrations 3.5 and 3.6)**:

Linear scale (base)	46.000 mm
Linear scale (base)	00.500 mm
Annular scale (fine)	00.490 mm
Vernier scale	00.004 mm
Total figure	46.994 mm

Internal micrometer

● Internal micrometers are available for measuring bore diameters, but are expensive and unlikely to be available for home use. It is suggested that a set of telescoping gauges and small hole gauges, both of which must be used with an external micrometer, will suffice for taking internal measurements on a motorcycle.

● Telescoping gauges can be used to measure internal diameters of components. Select a gauge with the correct size range, make sure its ends are clean and insert it into the bore. Expand the gauge, then lock its position and withdraw it from the bore **(see illustration 3.7)**. Measure across the gauge ends with a micrometer **(see illustration 3.8)**.

● Very small diameter bores (such as valve guides) are measured with a small hole gauge. Once adjusted to a slip-fit inside the component, its position is locked and the gauge withdrawn for measurement with a micrometer **(see illustrations 3.9 and 3.10)**.

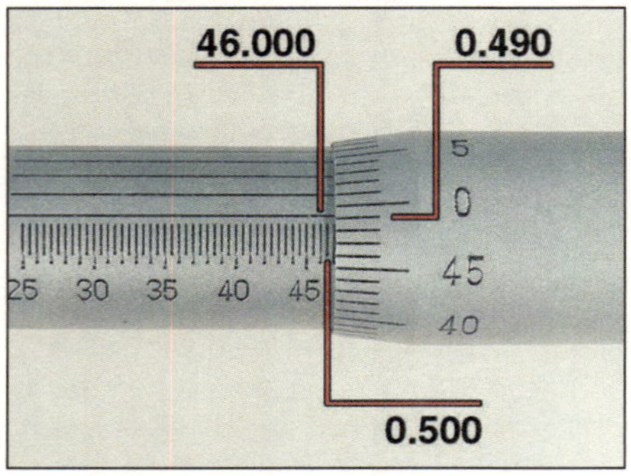

3.5 Micrometer reading of 46.99 mm on linear and annular scales . . .

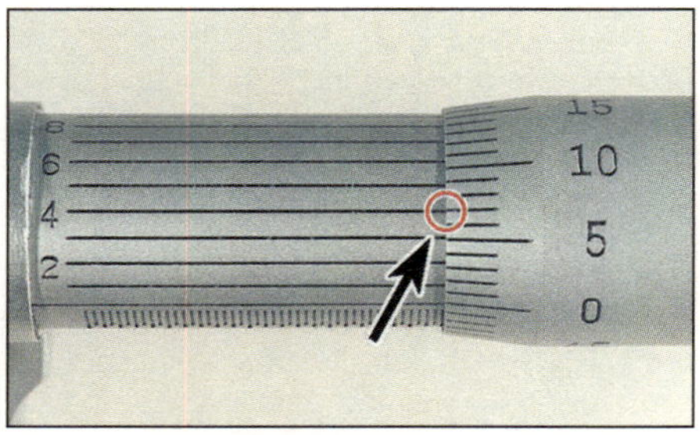

3.6 . . . and 0.004 mm on vernier scale

Vernier caliper

Note: *The conventional linear and dial gauge type instruments are described. Digital types are easier to read, but are far more expensive.*

● The vernier caliper does not provide the precision of a micrometer, but is versatile in being able to measure internal and external diameters. Some types also incorporate a depth gauge. It is ideal for measuring clutch plate friction material and spring free lengths.

● To use the conventional linear scale vernier, slacken off the vernier clamp screws (1) and set its jaws over (2), or inside (3), the item to be measured **(see illustration 3.11)**. Slide the jaw into contact, using the thumb-wheel (4) for fine movement of the sliding scale (5) then tighten the clamp screws (1). Read off the main scale (6) where the zero on the sliding scale (5) intersects it, taking the whole number to the left of the zero; this provides the base measurement. View along the sliding scale and select the division which lines up exactly with any of the divisions on the main scale, noting that the divisions usually represents 0.02 of a millimetre. Add this fine measurement to the base measurement to obtain the total reading.

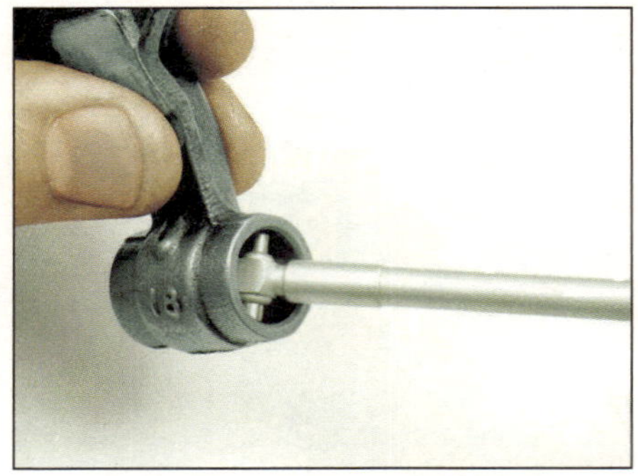

3.7 Expand the telescoping gauge in the bore, lock its position . . .

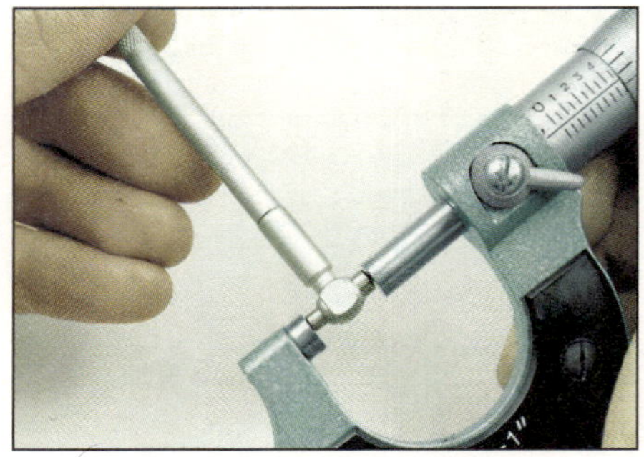

3.8 . . . then measure the gauge with a micrometer

3.9 Expand the small hole gauge in the bore, lock its position . . .

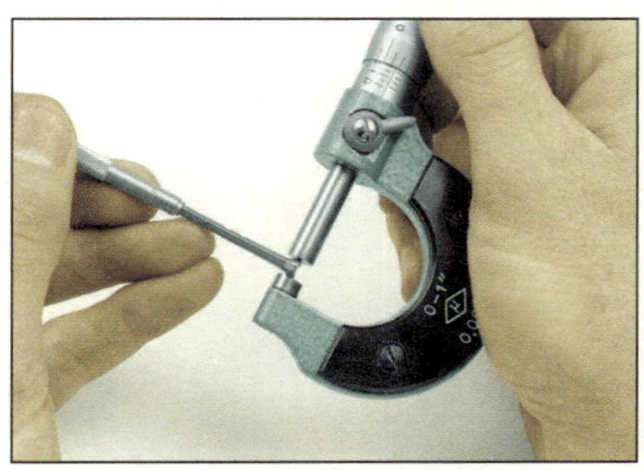

3.10 . . . then measure the gauge with a micrometer

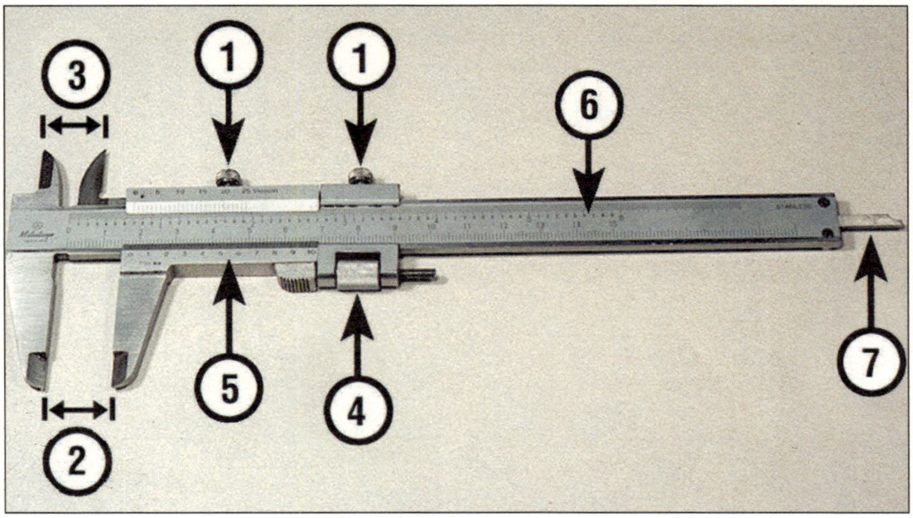

3.11 Vernier component parts (linear gauge)

1 *Clamp screws*
2 *External jaws*
3 *Internal jaws*
4 *Thumbwheel*
5 *Sliding scale*
6 *Main scale*
7 *Depth gauge*

In the example shown the item measures 55.92 mm **(see illustration 3.12)**:

Base measurement	55.00 mm
Fine measurement	00.92 mm
Total figure	55.92 mm

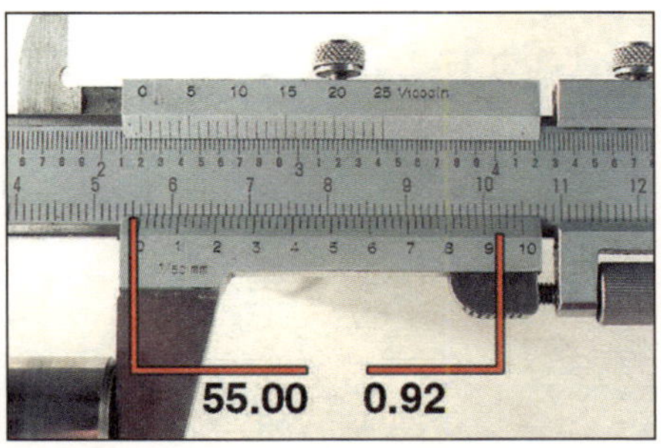

3.12 Vernier gauge reading of 55.92 mm

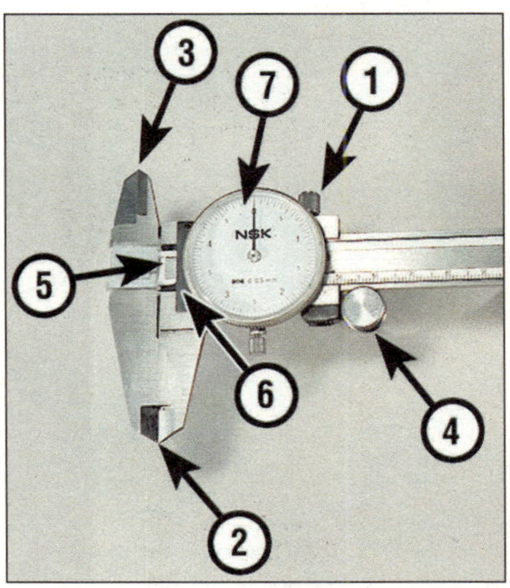

3.13 Vernier component parts (dial gauge)

1 *Clamp screw*
2 *External jaws*
3 *Internal jaws*
4 *Thumbwheel*
5 *Main scale*
6 *Sliding scale*
7 *Dial gauge*

- Some vernier calipers are equipped with a dial gauge for fine measurement. Before use, check that the jaws are clean, then close them fully and check that the dial gauge reads zero. If necessary adjust the gauge ring accordingly. Slacken the vernier clamp screw (1) and set its jaws over (2), or inside (3), the item to be measured **(see illustration 3.13)**. Slide the jaws into contact, using the thumbwheel (4) for fine movement. Read off the main scale (5) where the edge of the sliding scale (6) intersects it, taking the whole number to the left of the zero; this provides the base measurement. Read off the needle position on the dial gauge (7) scale to provide the fine measurement; each division represents 0.05 of a millimetre. Add this fine measurement to the base measurement to obtain the total reading.

In the example shown the item measures 55.95 mm **(see illustration 3.14)**:

Base measurement	55.00 mm
Fine measurement	00.95 mm
Total figure	55.95 mm

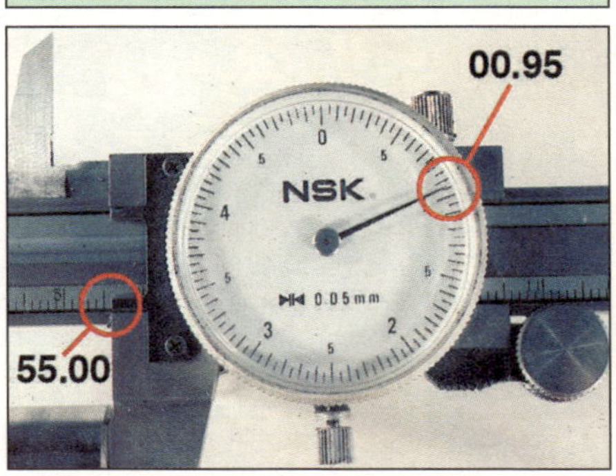

3.14 Vernier gauge reading of 55.95 mm

Plastigauge

- Plastigauge is a plastic material which can be compressed between two surfaces to measure the oil clearance between them. The width of the compressed Plastigauge is measured against a calibrated scale to determine the clearance.
- Common uses of Plastigauge are for measuring the clearance between crankshaft journal and main bearing inserts, between crankshaft journal and big-end bearing inserts, and between camshaft and bearing surfaces. The following example describes big-end oil clearance measurement.
- Handle the Plastigauge material carefully to prevent distortion. Using a sharp knife, cut a length which corresponds with the width of the bearing being measured and place it carefully across the journal so that it is parallel with the shaft **(see illustration 3.15)**. Carefully install both bearing shells and the connecting rod. Without rotating the rod on the journal tighten its bolts or nuts (as applicable) to the specified torque. The connecting rod and bearings are then disassembled and the crushed Plastigauge examined.

3.15 Plastigauge placed across shaft journal

- Using the scale provided in the Plastigauge kit, measure the width of the material to determine the oil clearance **(see illustration 3.16)**. Always remove all traces of Plastigauge after use using your fingernails.

Caution: Arriving at the correct clearance demands that the assembly is torqued correctly, according to the settings and sequence (where applicable) provided by the motorcycle manufacturer.

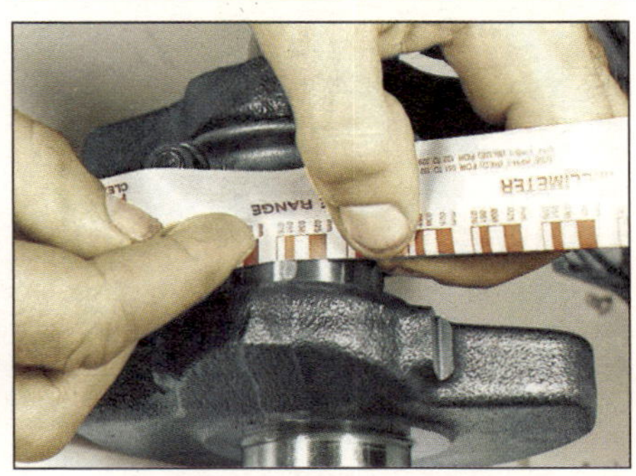

3.16 Measuring the width of the crushed Plastigauge

Dial gauge or DTI (Dial Test Indicator)

● A dial gauge can be used to accurately measure small amounts of movement. Typical uses are measuring shaft runout or shaft endfloat (sideplay) and setting piston position for ignition timing on two-strokes. A dial gauge set usually comes with a range of different probes and adapters and mounting equipment.

● The gauge needle must point to zero when at rest. Rotate the ring around its periphery to zero the gauge.

● Check that the gauge is capable of reading the extent of movement in the work. Most gauges have a small dial set in the face which records whole millimetres of movement as well as the fine scale around the face periphery which is calibrated in 0.01 mm divisions. Read off the small dial first to obtain the base measurement, then add the measurement from the fine scale to obtain the total reading.

In the example shown the gauge reads 1.48 mm **(see illustration 3.17)**:

Base measurement	1.00 mm
Fine measurement	0.48 mm
Total figure	1.48 mm

3.17 Dial gauge reading of 1.48 mm

● If measuring shaft runout, the shaft must be supported in vee-blocks and the gauge mounted on a stand perpendicular to the shaft. Rest the tip of the gauge against the centre of the shaft and rotate the shaft slowly whilst watching the gauge reading **(see illustration 3.18)**. Take several measurements along the length of the shaft and record the maximum gauge reading as the amount of runout in the shaft. **Note:** *The reading obtained will be total runout at that point - some manufacturers specify that the runout figure is halved to compare with their specified runout limit.*

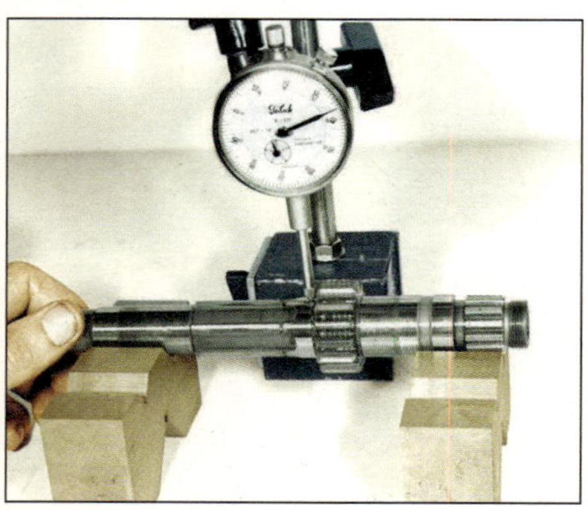

3.18 Using a dial gauge to measure shaft runout

● Endfloat (sideplay) measurement requires that the gauge is mounted securely to the surrounding component with its probe touching the end of the shaft. Using hand pressure, push and pull on the shaft noting the maximum endfloat recorded on the gauge **(see illustration 3.19)**.

3.19 Using a dial gauge to measure shaft endfloat

● A dial gauge with suitable adapters can be used to determine piston position BTDC on two-stroke engines for the purposes of ignition timing. The gauge, adapter and suitable length probe are installed in the place of the spark plug and the gauge zeroed at TDC. If the piston position is specified as 1.14 mm BTDC, rotate the engine back to 2.00 mm BTDC, then slowly forwards to 1.14 mm BTDC.

Cylinder compression gauges

● A compression gauge is used for measuring cylinder compression. Either the rubber-cone type or the threaded adapter type can be used. The latter is preferred to ensure a perfect seal against the cylinder head. A 0 to 300 psi (0 to 20 Bar) type gauge (for petrol/gasoline engines) will be suitable for motorcycles.

● The spark plug is removed and the gauge either held hard against the cylinder head (cone type) or the gauge adapter screwed into the cylinder head (threaded type) **(see illustration 3.20)**. Cylinder compression is measured with the engine turning over, but not running. The gauge will hold the reading until manually released.

3.20 Using a rubber-cone type cylinder compression gauge

Oil pressure gauge

● An oil pressure gauge is used for measuring engine oil pressure. Most gauges come with a set of adapters to fit the thread of the take-off point **(see illustration 3.21)**. If the take-off point specified by the motorcycle manufacturer is an external oil pipe union, make sure that the specified replacement union is used to prevent oil starvation.

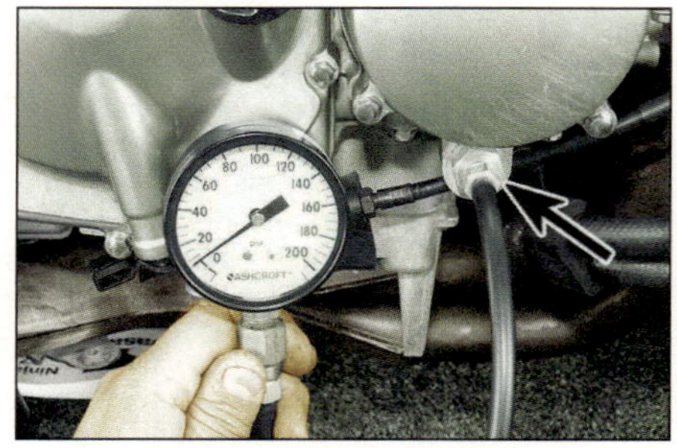

3.21 Oil pressure gauge and take-off point adapter (arrow)

● Oil pressure is measured with the engine running (at a specific rpm) and often the manufacturer will specify pressure limits for a cold and hot engine.

Straight-edge and surface plate

● If checking the gasket face of a component for warpage, place a steel rule or precision straight-edge across the gasket face and measure any gap between the straight-edge and component with feeler gauges **(see illustration 3.22)**. Check diagonally across the component and between mounting holes **(see illustration 3.23)**.

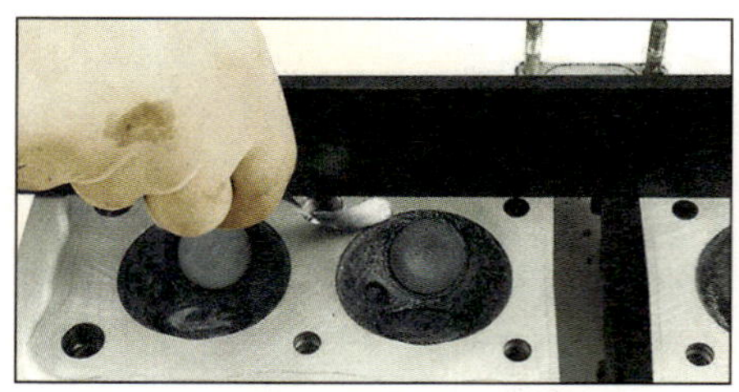

3.22 Use a straight-edge and feeler gauges to check for warpage

3.23 Check for warpage in these directions

- Checking individual components for warpage, such as clutch plain (metal) plates, requires a perfectly flat plate or piece or plate glass and feeler gauges.

4 Torque and leverage

What is torque?

- Torque describes the twisting force about a shaft. The amount of torque applied is determined by the distance from the centre of the shaft to the end of the lever and the amount of force being applied to the end of the lever; distance multiplied by force equals torque.
- The manufacturer applies a measured torque to a bolt or nut to ensure that it will not slacken in use and to hold two components securely together without movement in the joint. The actual torque setting depends on the thread size, bolt or nut material and the composition of the components being held.
- Too little torque may cause the fastener to loosen due to vibration, whereas too much torque will distort the joint faces of the component or cause the fastener to shear off. Always stick to the specified torque setting.

Using a torque wrench

- Check the calibration of the torque wrench and make sure it has a suitable range for the job. Torque wrenches are available in Nm (Newton-metres), kgf m (kilograms-force metre), lbf ft (pounds-feet), lbf in (inch-pounds). Do not confuse lbf ft with lbf in.
- Adjust the tool to the desired torque on the scale **(see illustration 4.1)**. If your torque wrench is not calibrated in the units specified, carefully convert the figure (see Conversion Factors). A manufacturer sometimes gives a torque setting as a range (8 to 10 Nm) rather than a single figure - in this case set the tool midway between the two settings. The same torque may be expressed as 9 Nm ± 1 Nm. Some torque wrenches have a method of locking the setting so that it isn't inadvertently altered during use.

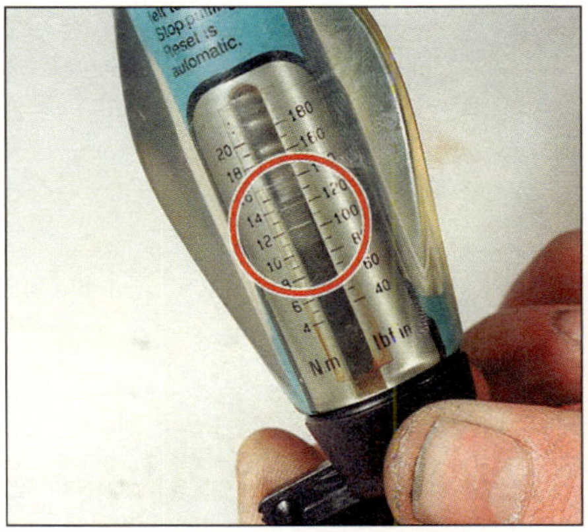

4.1 Set the torque wrench index mark to the setting required, in this case 12 Nm

- Install the bolts/nuts in their correct location and secure them lightly. Their threads must be clean and free of any old locking compound. Unless specified the threads and flange should be dry - oiled threads are necessary in certain circumstances and the manufacturer will take this into account in the specified torque figure. Similarly, the manufacturer may also specify the application of thread-locking compound.
- Tighten the fasteners in the specified sequence until the torque wrench clicks, indicating that the torque setting has been reached. Apply the torque again to double-check the setting. Where different thread diameter fasteners secure the component, as a rule tighten the larger diameter ones first.
- When the torque wrench has been finished with, release the lock (where applicable) and fully back off its setting to zero - do not leave the torque wrench tensioned. Also, do not use a torque wrench for slackening a fastener.

Angle-tightening

- Manufacturers often specify a figure in degrees for final tightening of a fastener. This usually follows tightening to a specific torque setting.
- A degree disc can be set and attached to the socket **(see illustration 4.2)** or a protractor can be used to mark the angle of movement on the bolt/nut head and the surrounding casting **(see illustration 4.3)**.

4.2 Angle tightening can be accomplished with a torque-angle gauge . . .

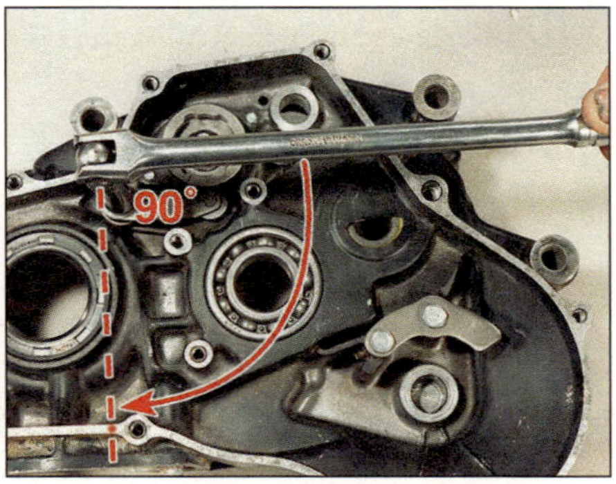

4.3 . . . or by marking the angle on the surrounding component

Loosening sequences

- Where more than one bolt/nut secures a component, loosen each fastener evenly a little at a time. In this way, not all the stress of the joint is held by one fastener and the components are not likely to distort.
- If a tightening sequence is provided, work in the REVERSE of this, but if not, work from the outside in, in a criss-cross sequence **(see illustration 4.4)**.

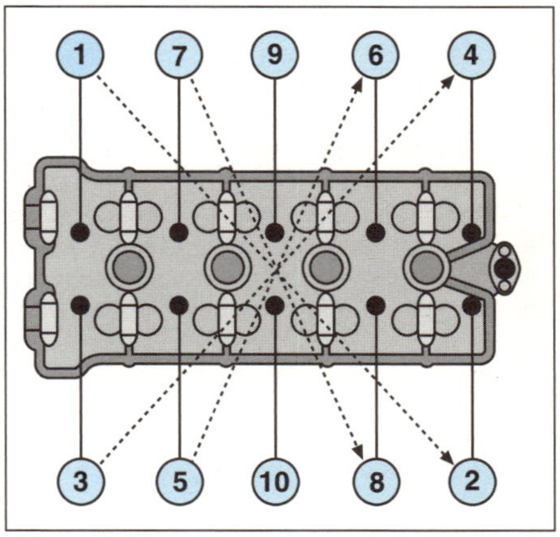

4.4 When slackening, work from the outside inwards

Tightening sequences

- If a component is held by more than one fastener it is important that the retaining bolts/nuts are tightened evenly to prevent uneven stress build-up and distortion of sealing faces. This is especially important on high-compression joints such as the cylinder head.
- A sequence is usually provided by the manufacturer, either in a diagram or actually marked in the casting. If not, always start in the centre and work outwards in a criss-cross pattern **(see illustration 4.5)**. Start off by securing all bolts/nuts finger-tight, then set the torque wrench and tighten each fastener by a small amount in sequence until the final torque is reached. By following this practice,

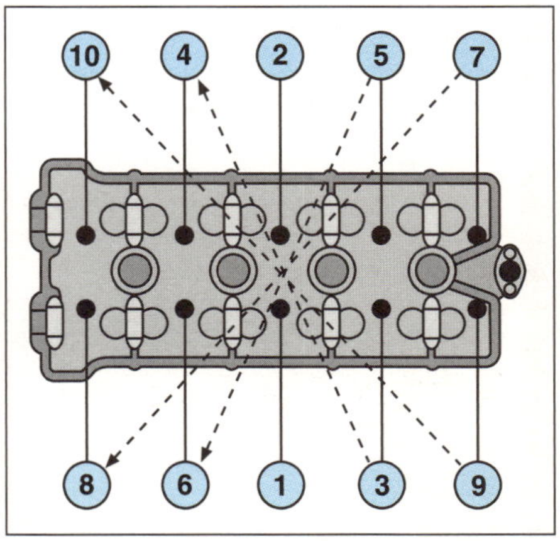

4.5 When tightening, work from the inside outwards

the joint will be held evenly and will not be distorted. Important joints, such as the cylinder head and big-end fasteners often have two- or three-stage torque settings.

Applying leverage

● Use tools at the correct angle. Position a socket wrench or spanner on the bolt/nut so that you pull it towards you when loosening. If this can't be done, push the spanner without curling your fingers around it **(see illustration 4.6)** - the spanner may slip or the fastener loosen suddenly, resulting in your fingers being crushed against a component.

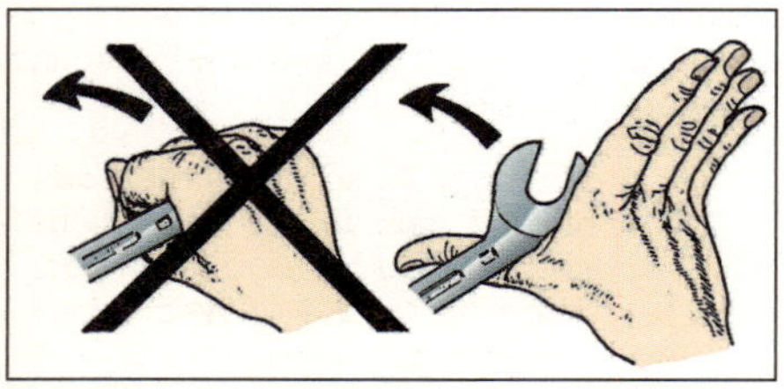

4.6 If you can't pull on the spanner to loosen a fastener, push with your hand open

● Additional leverage is gained by extending the length of the lever. The best way to do this is to use a breaker bar instead of the regular length tool, or to slip a length of tubing over the end of the spanner or socket wrench.

● If additional leverage will not work, the fastener head is either damaged or firmly corroded in place (see Fasteners).

5 Bearings

Bearing removal and installation

Drivers and sockets

● Before removing a bearing, always inspect the casing to see which way it must be driven out - some casings will have retaining plates or a cast step. Also check for any identifying markings on the bearing and if installed to a certain depth, measure this at this stage. Some roller bearings are sealed on one side - take note of the original fitted position.

● Bearings can be driven out of a casing using a bearing driver tool (with the correct size head) or a socket of the correct diameter. Select the driver head or socket so that it contacts the outer race of the bearing, not the balls/rollers or inner race. Always support the casing around the bearing housing with wood blocks, otherwise there is a risk of fracture. The bearing is driven out with a few blows on the driver or socket from a heavy mallet. Unless access is severely restricted (as with wheel bearings), a pin-punch is not recommended unless it is moved around the bearing to keep it square in its housing.

● The same equipment can be used to install bearings. Make sure the bearing housing is supported on wood blocks and line up the bearing in its housing. Fit the bearing as noted on removal - generally they are installed with their marked side facing outwards. Tap the bearing squarely into its housing using a driver or socket which bears only on the bearing's outer race - contact with the bearing balls/rollers or inner race will destroy it **(see illustrations 5.1 and 5.2)**.

● Check that the bearing inner race and balls/rollers rotate freely.

5.1 Using a bearing driver against the bearing's outer race

5.2 Using a large socket against the bearing's outer race

Pullers and slide-hammers

● Where a bearing is pressed on a shaft a puller will be required to extract it **(see illustration 5.3)**. Make sure that the puller clamp or legs fit securely behind the bearing and are unlikely to slip out. If pulling a bearing off a gear shaft for example, you may have to locate the puller behind a gear pinion if there is no access to the race and draw the gear pinion off the shaft as well **(see illustration 5.4)**.

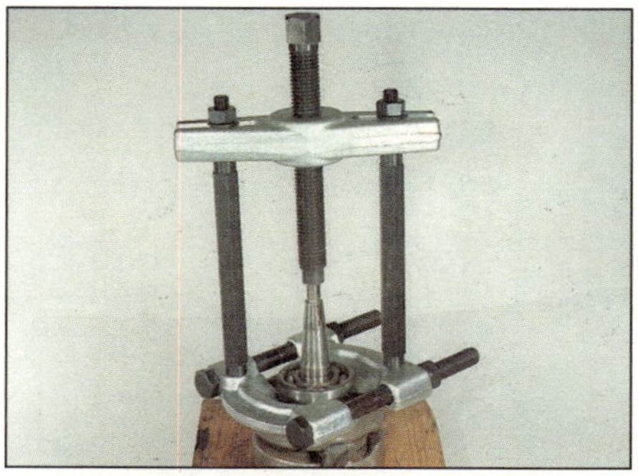

5.3 This bearing puller clamps behind the bearing and pressure is applied to the shaft end to draw the bearing off

Caution: Ensure that the puller's centre bolt locates securely against the end of the shaft and will not slip when pressure is applied. Also ensure that puller does not damage the shaft end.

5.4 Where no access is available to the rear of the bearing, it is sometimes possible to draw off the adjacent component

● Operate the puller so that its centre bolt exerts pressure on the shaft end and draws the bearing off the shaft.

● When installing the bearing on the shaft, tap only on the bearing's inner race - contact with the balls/rollers or outer race with destroy the bearing. Use a socket or length of tubing as a drift which fits over the shaft end **(see illustration 5.5)**.

5.5 When installing a bearing on a shaft use a piece of tubing which bears only on the bearing's inner race

● Where a bearing locates in a blind hole in a casing, it cannot be driven or pulled out as described above. A slide-hammer with knife-edged bearing puller attachment will be required. The puller attachment passes through the bearing and when tightened expands to fit firmly behind the bearing **(see illustration 5.6)**. By operating the slide-hammer part of the tool the bearing is jarred out of its housing **(see illustration 5.7)**.

● It is possible, if the bearing is of reasonable weight, for it to drop out of its housing if the casing is heated as described opposite.

5.6 Expand the bearing puller so that it locks behind the bearing . . .

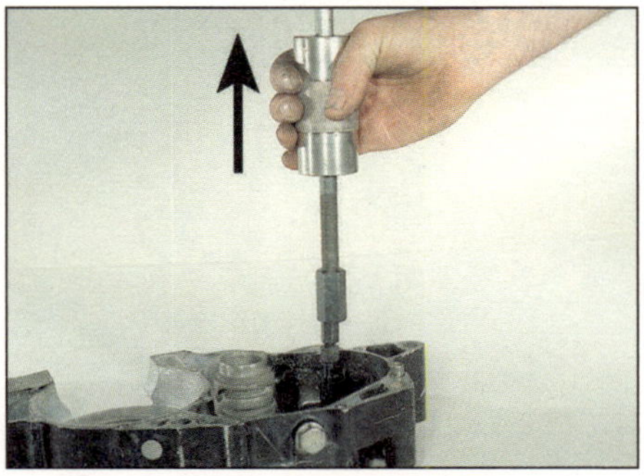

5.7 . . . attach the slide hammer to the bearing puller

If this method is attempted, first prepare a work surface which will enable the casing to be tapped face down to help dislodge the bearing - a wood surface is ideal since it will not damage the casing's gasket surface. Wearing protective gloves, tap the heated casing several times against the work surface to dislodge the bearing under its own weight **(see illustration 5.8)**.

5.8 Tapping a casing face down on wood blocks can often dislodge a bearing

- Bearings can be installed in blind holes using the driver or socket method described above.

Drawbolts

- Where a bearing or bush is set in the eye of a component, such as a suspension linkage arm or connecting rod small-end, removal by drift may damage the component. Furthermore, a rubber bushing in a shock absorber eye cannot successfully be driven out of position. If access is available to a engineering press, the task is straightforward. If not, a drawbolt can be fabricated to extract the bearing or bush.

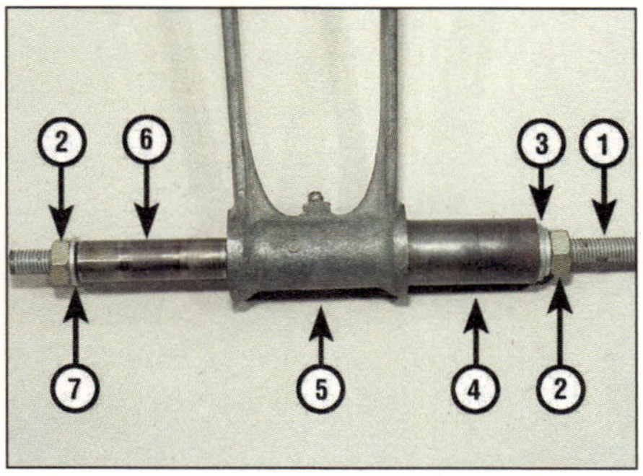

5.9 Drawbolt component parts assembled on a suspension arm

1. *Bolt or length of threaded bar*
2. *Nuts*
3. *Washer (external diameter greater than tubing internal diameter)*
4. *Tubing (internal diameter sufficient to accommodate bearing)*
5. *Suspension arm with bearing*
6. *Tubing (external diameter slightly smaller than bearing)*
7. *Washer (external diameter slightly smaller than bearing)*

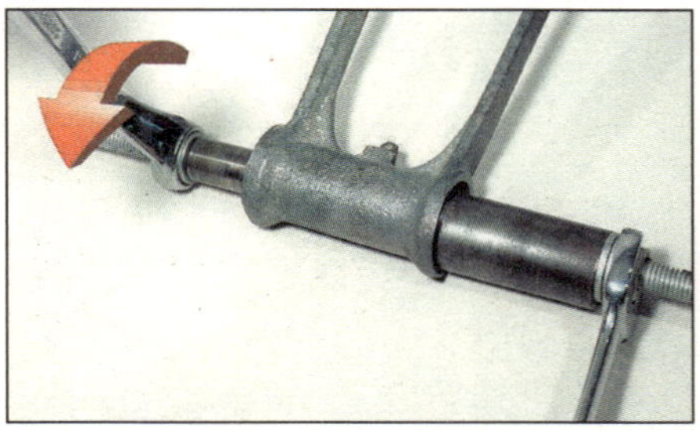

5.10 Drawing the bearing out of the suspension arm

- To extract the bearing/bush you will need a long bolt with nut (or piece of threaded bar with two nuts), a piece of tubing which has an internal diameter larger than the bearing/bush, another piece of tubing which has an external diameter slightly smaller than the bearing/bush, and a selection of washers **(see illustrations 5.9 and 5.10)**. Note that the pieces of tubing must be of the same length, or longer, than the bearing/bush.
- The same kit (without the pieces of tubing) can be used to draw the new bearing/bush back into place **(see illustration 5.11)**.

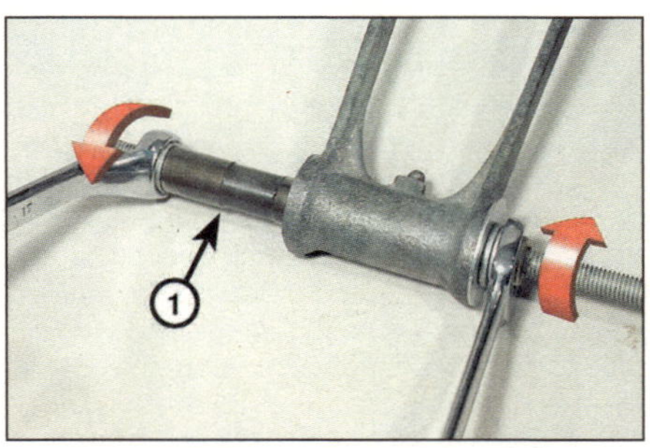

5.11 Installing a new bearing (1) in the suspension arm

Temperature change

- If the bearing's outer race is a tight fit in the casing, the aluminium casing can be heated to release its grip on the bearing. Aluminium will expand at a greater rate than the steel bearing outer race. There are several ways to do this, but avoid any localised extreme heat (such as a blow torch) - aluminium alloy has a low melting point.
- Approved methods of heating a casing are using a domestic oven (heated to 100°C) or immersing the casing in boiling water **(see illustration 5.12)**. Low temperature range localised heat sources such as a paint stripper heat gun or clothes iron can also be used **(see illustration 5.13)**. Alternatively, soak a rag in boiling water, wring it out and wrap it around the bearing housing.

Warning: All of these methods require care in use to prevent scalding and burns to the hands. Wear protective gloves when handling hot components.

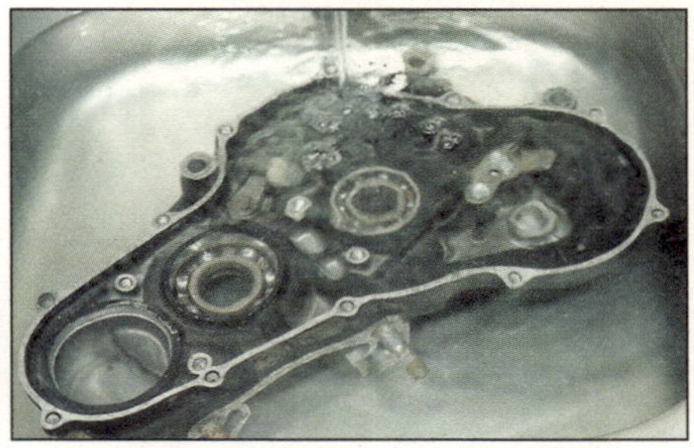

5.12 A casing can be immersed in a sink of boiling water to aid bearing removal

5.13 Using a localised heat source to aid bearing removal

- If heating the whole casing note that plastic components, such as the neutral switch, may suffer - remove them beforehand.
- After heating, remove the bearing as described above. You may find that the expansion is sufficient for the bearing to fall out of the casing under its own weight or with a light tap on the driver or socket.
- If necessary, the casing can be heated to aid bearing installation, and this is sometimes the recommended procedure if the motorcycle manufacturer has designed the housing and bearing fit with this intention.

● Installation of bearings can be eased by placing them in a freezer the night before installation. The steel bearing will contract slightly, allowing easy insertion in its housing. This is often useful when installing steering head outer races in the frame.

Bearing types and markings

● Plain shell bearings, ball bearings, needle roller bearings and tapered roller bearings will all be found on motorcycles **(see illustrations 5.14 and 5.15)**. The ball and roller types are usually caged between an inner and outer race, but uncaged variations may be found.

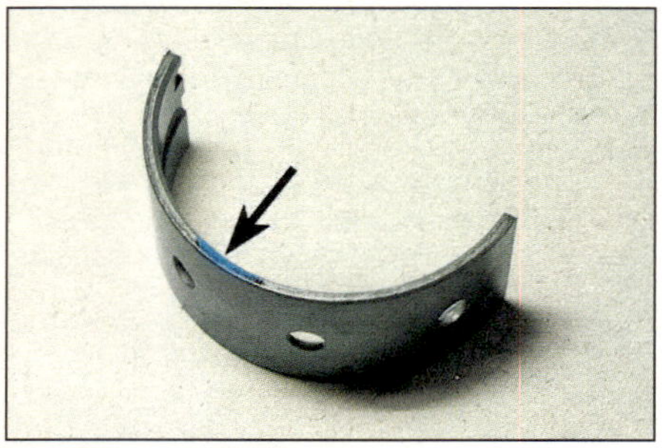

5.14 Shell bearings are either plain or grooved. They are usually identified by colour code (arrow)

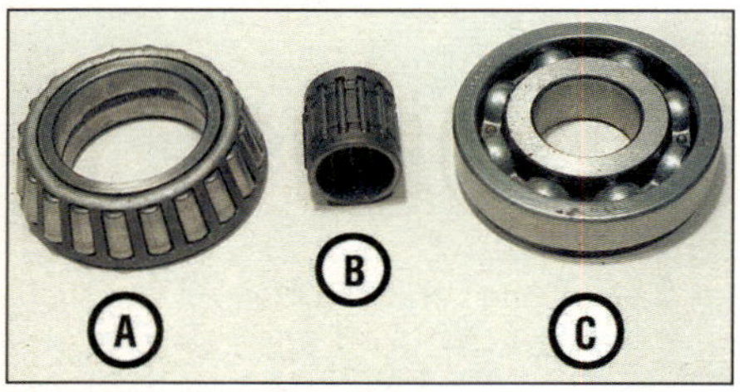

5.15 Tapered roller bearing (A), needle roller bearing (B) and ball journal bearing (C)

● Shell bearings (often called inserts) are usually found at the crankshaft main and connecting rod big-end where they are good at coping with high loads. They are made of a phosphor-bronze material and are impregnated with self-lubricating properties.

● Ball bearings and needle roller bearings consist of a steel inner and outer race with the balls or rollers between the races. They require constant lubrication by oil or grease and are good at coping with axial loads. Taper roller bearings consist of rollers set in a tapered cage set on the inner race; the outer race is separate. They are good at coping with axial loads and prevent movement along the shaft - a typical application is in the steering head.

● Bearing manufacturers produce bearings to ISO size standards and stamp one face of the bearing to indicate its internal and external diameter, load capacity and type **(see illustration 5.16)**.

● Metal bushes are usually of phosphor-bronze material. Rubber bushes are used in suspension mounting eyes. Fibre bushes have also been used in suspension pivots.

5.16 Typical bearing marking

Bearing fault finding

● If a bearing outer race has spun in its housing, the housing material will be damaged. You can use a bearing locking compound to bond the outer race in place if damage is not too severe.

● Shell bearings will fail due to damage of their working surface, as a result of lack of lubrication, corrosion or abrasive particles in the oil **(see illustration 5.17)**. Small particles of dirt in the oil may embed in the bearing material whereas larger particles will score the bearing and shaft journal. If a number of short journeys are made, insufficient heat will be generated to drive off condensation which has built up on the bearings.

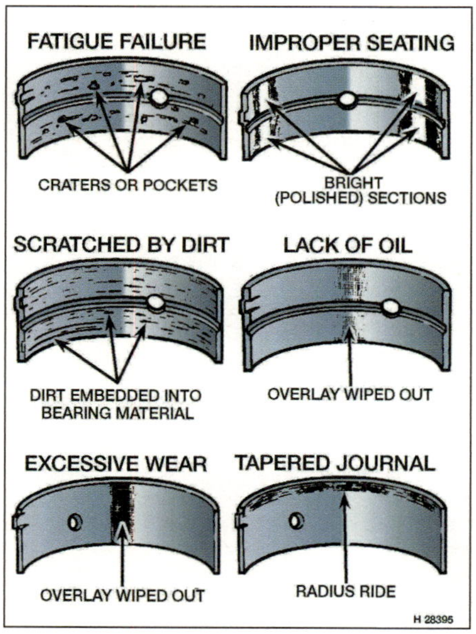

5.17 Typical bearing failures

● Ball and roller bearings will fail due to lack of lubrication or damage to the balls or rollers. Tapered-roller bearings can be damaged by overloading them. Unless the bearing is sealed on both sides, wash it in paraffin (kerosene) to remove all old grease then allow it to dry. Make a visual inspection looking to dented balls or rollers, damaged cages and worn or pitted races **(see illustration 5.18)**.

● A ball bearing can be checked for wear by listening to it when spun. Apply a film of light oil to the bearing and hold it close to the ear - hold the outer race with one hand and spin the inner race with the other hand **(see illustration 5.19)**. The bearing should be almost silent when spun; if it grates or rattles it is worn.

5.18 Example of ball journal bearing with damaged balls and cages

5.19 Hold outer race and listen to inner race when spun

6 Oil seals

Oil seal removal and installation

● Oil seals should be renewed every time a component is dismantled. This is because the seal lips will become set to the sealing surface and will not necessarily reseal.

● Oil seals can be prised out of position using a large flat-bladed screwdriver **(see illustration 6.1)**. In the case of crankcase seals, check first that the seal is not lipped on the inside, preventing its removal with the crankcases joined.

6.1 Prise out oil seals with a large flat-bladed screwdriver

● New seals are usually installed with their marked face (containing the seal reference code) outwards and the spring side towards the fluid being retained. In certain cases, such as a two-stroke engine crankshaft seal, a double lipped seal may be used due to there being fluid or gas on each side of the joint.

- Use a bearing driver or socket which bears only on the outer hard edge of the seal to install it in the casing - tapping on the inner edge will damage the sealing lip.

Oil seal types and markings

- Oil seals are usually of the single-lipped type. Double-lipped seals are found where a liquid or gas is on both sides of the joint.
- Oil seals can harden and lose their sealing ability if the motorcycle has been in storage for a long period - renewal is the only solution.
- Oil seal manufacturers also conform to the ISO markings for seal size - these are moulded into the outer face of the seal **(see illustration 6.2)**.

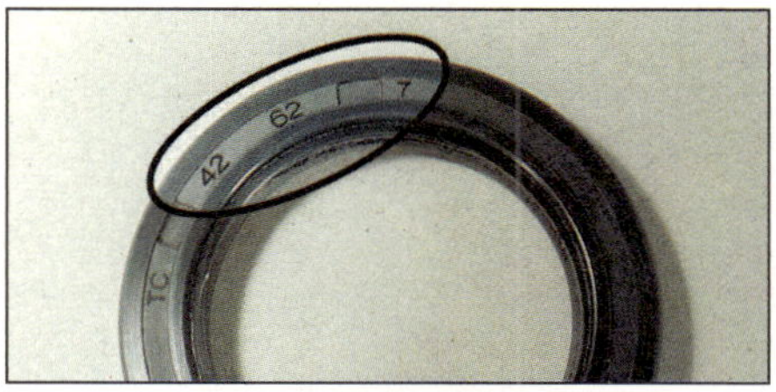

6.2 These oil seal markings indicate inside diameter, outside diameter and seal thickness

7 Gaskets and sealants

Types of gasket and sealant

- Gaskets are used to seal the mating surfaces between components and keep lubricants, fluids, vacuum or pressure contained within the assembly. Aluminium gaskets are sometimes found at the cylinder joints, but most gaskets are paper-based. If the mating surfaces of the components being joined are undamaged the gasket can be installed dry, although a dab of sealant or grease will be useful to hold it in place during assembly.
- RTV (Room Temperature Vulcanising) silicone rubber sealants cure when exposed to moisture in the atmosphere. These sealants are good at filling pits or irregular gasket faces, but will tend to be forced out of the joint under very high torque. They can be used to replace a paper gasket, but first make sure that the width of the paper gasket is not essential to the shimming of internal components. RTV sealants should not be used on components containing petrol (gasoline).
- Non-hardening, semi-hardening and hard setting liquid gasket compounds can be used with a gasket or between a metal-to-metal joint. Select the sealant to suit the application: universal non-hardening sealant can be used on virtually all joints; semi-hardening on joint faces which are rough or damaged; hard setting sealant on joints which require a permanent bond and are subjected to high temperature and pressure. **Note:** *Check first if the paper gasket has a bead of sealant impregnated in its surface before applying additional sealant.*
- When choosing a sealant, make sure it is suitable for the application, particularly if being applied in a high-temperature area or in the vicinity of fuel. Certain manufacturers produce sealants in either clear, silver or black colours to match the finish of the engine. This has a particular application on motorcycles where much of the engine is exposed.
- Do not over-apply sealant. That which is squeezed out on the outside of the joint can be wiped off, whereas an excess of sealant on the inside can break off and clog oilways.

Breaking a sealed joint

- Age, heat, pressure and the use of hard setting sealant can cause two components to stick together so tightly that they are difficult to separate using finger pressure alone. Do not resort to using levers unless there is a pry point provided for this purpose **(see illustration 7.1)** or else the gasket surfaces will be damaged.
- Use a soft-faced hammer **(see illustration 7.2)** or a wood block and conventional hammer to strike the component near the mating surface. Avoid hammering against cast extremities since they may break off. If this method fails, try using a wood wedge between the two components.

Caution: If the joint will not separate, double-check that you have removed all the fasteners.

7.1 If a pry point is provided, apply gently pressure with a flat-bladed screwdriver

7.2 Tap around the joint with a soft-faced mallet if necessary - don't strike cooling fins

Removal of old gasket and sealant

- Paper gaskets will most likely come away complete, leaving only a few traces stuck

HAYNES HiNT

Most components have one or two hollow locating dowels between the two gasket faces. If a dowel cannot be removed, do not resort to gripping it with pliers - it will almost certainly be distorted. Install a close-fitting socket or Phillips screwdriver into the dowel and then grip the outer edge of the dowel to free it.

on the sealing faces of the components. It is imperative that all traces are removed to ensure correct sealing of the new gasket.

- Very carefully scrape all traces of gasket away making sure that the sealing surfaces are not gouged or scored by the scraper **(see illustrations 7.3, 7.4 and 7.5)**. Stubborn deposits can be removed by spraying with an aerosol gasket remover. Final preparation of

7.3 Paper gaskets can be scraped off with a gasket scraper tool . . .

7.4 . . . a knife blade . . .

7.5 . . . or a household scraper

7.6 Fine abrasive paper is wrapped around a flat file to clean up the gasket face

7.7 A kitchen scourer can be used on stubborn deposits

the gasket surface can be made with very fine abrasive paper or a plastic kitchen scourer **(see illustrations 7.6 and 7.7)**.

- Old sealant can be scraped or peeled off components, depending on the type originally used. Note that gasket removal compounds are available to avoid scraping the components clean; make sure the gasket remover suits the type of sealant used.

8 Chains

Breaking and joining final drive chains

- Drive chains for all but small bikes are continuous and do not have a clip-type connecting link. The chain must be broken using a chain breaker tool and the new chain securely riveted together using a new soft rivet-type link. Never use a clip-type connecting link instead of a rivet-type link, except in an emergency. Various chain breaking and riveting tools are available, either as separate tools or combined as illustrated in the accompanying photographs - read the instructions supplied with the tool carefully.

> ***Warning: The need to rivet the new link pins correctly cannot be overstressed - loss of control of the motorcycle is very likely to result if the chain breaks in use.***

- Rotate the chain and look for the soft link. The soft link pins look like they have been

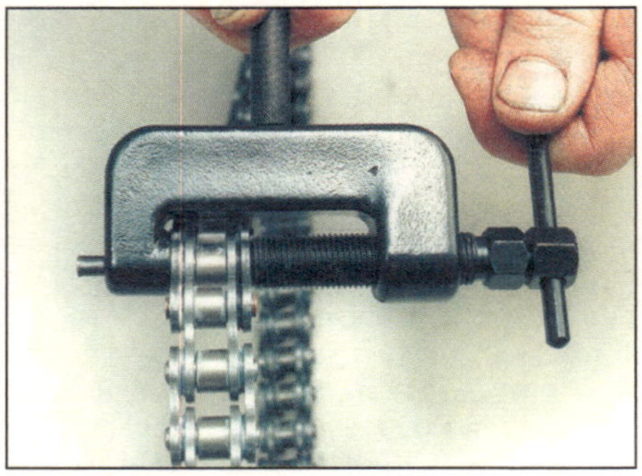

8.1 Tighten the chain breaker to push the pin out of the link . . .

8.2 . . . withdraw the pin, remove the tool . . .

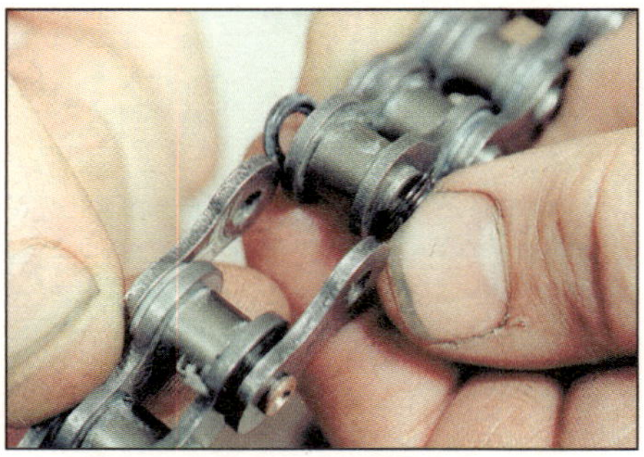

8.3 . . . and separate the chain link

deeply centre-punched instead of peened over like all the other pins **(see illustration 8.9)** and its sideplate may be a different colour. Position the soft link midway between the sprockets and assemble the chain breaker tool over one of the soft link pins **(see illustration 8.1)**. Operate the tool to push the pin out through the chain **(see illustration 8.2)**. On an O-ring chain, remove the O-rings **(see illustration 8.3)**. Carry out the same procedure on the other soft link pin.

> ***Caution: Certain soft link pins (particularly on the larger chains) may require their ends to be filed or ground off before they can be pressed out using the tool.***

- Check that you have the correct size and strength (standard or heavy duty) new soft link - do not reuse the old link. Look for the size marking on the chain sideplates **(see illustration 8.10)**.
- Position the chain ends so that they are engaged over the rear sprocket. On an O-ring

8.4 Insert the new soft link, with O-rings, through the chain ends . . .

8.5 . . . install the O-rings over the pin ends . . .

8.6 . . . followed by the sideplate

chain, install a new O-ring over each pin of the link and insert the link through the two chain ends **(see illustration 8.4)**. Install a new O-ring over the end of each pin, followed by the sideplate (with the chain manufacturer's marking facing outwards) **(see illustrations 8.5 and 8.6)**. On an unsealed chain, insert the link through the two chain ends, then install the sideplate with the chain manufacturer's marking facing outwards.

- Note that it may not be possible to install the sideplate using finger pressure alone. If using a joining tool, assemble it so that the plates of the tool clamp the link and press the sideplate over the pins **(see illustration 8.7)**. Otherwise, use two small sockets placed over

8.7 Push the sideplate into position using a clamp

8.8 Assemble the chain riveting tool over one pin at a time and tighten it fully

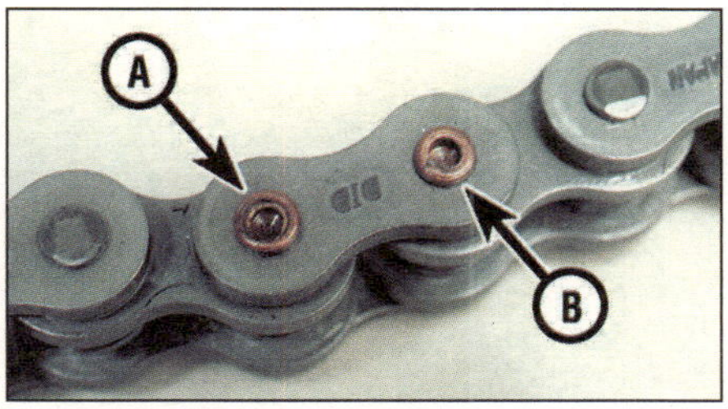

8.9 Pin end correctly riveted (A), pin end unriveted (B)

the rivet ends and two pieces of the wood between a G-clamp. Operate the clamp to press the sideplate over the pins.

- Assemble the joining tool over one pin (following the maker's instructions) and tighten the tool down to spread the pin end securely **(see illustrations 8.8 and 8.9)**. Do the same on the other pin.

> ***Warning: Check that the pin ends are secure and that there is no danger of the sideplate coming loose. If the pin ends are cracked the soft link must be renewed.***

Final drive chain sizing

- Chains are sized using a three digit number, followed by a suffix to denote the chain type **(see illustration 8.10)**. Chain type is either standard or heavy duty (thicker sideplates), and also unsealed or O-ring/X-ring type.
- The first digit of the number relates to the pitch of the chain, ie the distance from the centre of one pin to the centre of the next pin **(see illustration 8.11)**. Pitch is expressed in eighths of an inch, as follows:

8.10 Typical chain size and type marking

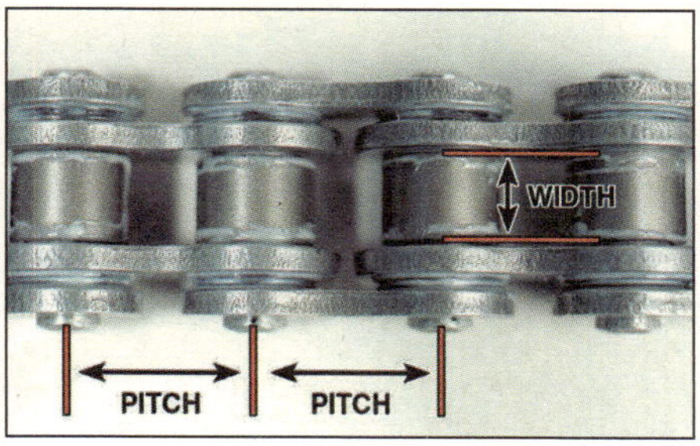

8.11 Chain dimensions

> Sizes commencing with a 4 (eg 428) have a pitch of 1/2 inch (12.7 mm)
>
> Sizes commencing with a 5 (eg 520) have a pitch of 5/8 inch (15.9 mm)
>
> Sizes commencing with a 6 (eg 630) have a pitch of 3/4 inch (19.1 mm)

- The second and third digits of the chain size relate to the width of the rollers, again in imperial units, eg the 525 shown has 5/16 inch (7.94 mm) rollers **(see illustration 8.11)**.

9 Hoses

Clamping to prevent flow

- Small-bore flexible hoses can be clamped to prevent fluid flow whilst a component is worked on. Whichever method is used, ensure that the hose material is not permanently distorted or damaged by the clamp.

a) A brake hose clamp available from auto accessory shops ***(see illustration 9.1)****.*

b) A wingnut type hose clamp ***(see illustration 9.2)****.*

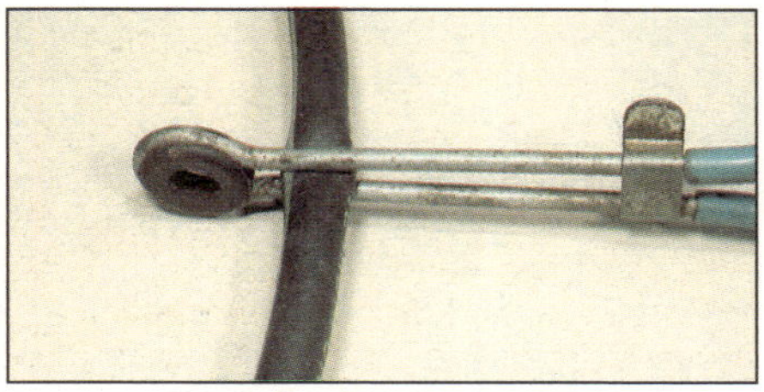

9.1 Hoses can be clamped with an automotive brake hose clamp . . .

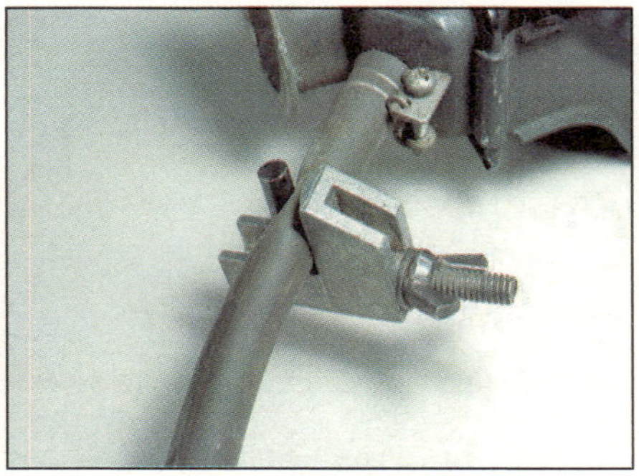

9.2 . . . a wingnut type hose clamp . . .

c) Two sockets placed each side of the hose and held with straight-jawed self-locking grips ***(see illustration 9.3)****.*

d) Thick card each side of the hose held between straight-jawed self-locking grips ***(see illustration 9.4)****.*

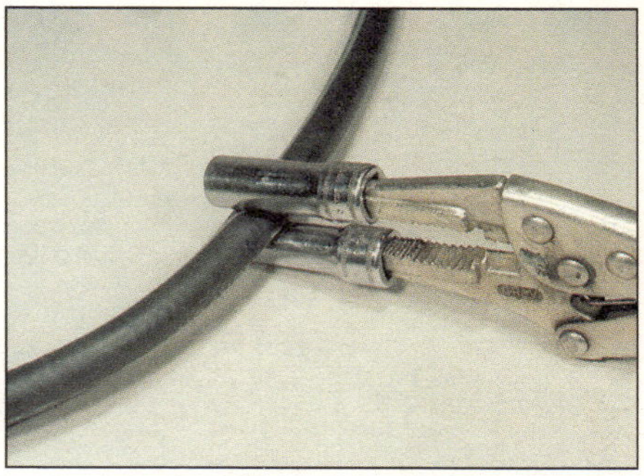

9.3 . . . two sockets and a pair of self-locking grips . . .

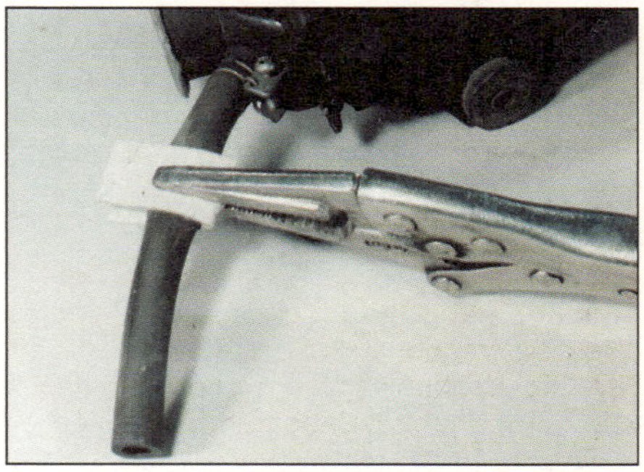

9.4 . . . or thick card and self-locking grips

Freeing and fitting hoses

- Always make sure the hose clamp is moved well clear of the hose end. Grip the hose with your hand and rotate it whilst pulling it off the union. If the hose has hardened due to age and will not move, slit it with a sharp knife and peel its ends off the union **(see illustration 9.5)**.
- Resist the temptation to use grease or soap on the unions to aid installation; although it helps the hose slip over the union it will equally aid the escape of fluid from the joint. It is preferable to soften the hose ends in hot water and wet the inside surface of the hose with water or a fluid which will evaporate.

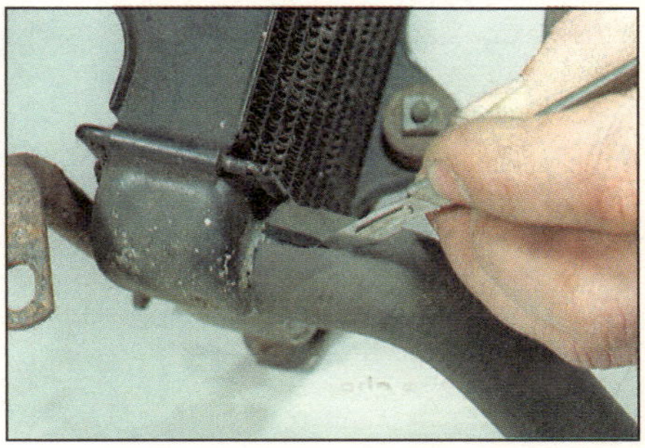

9.5 Cutting a coolant hose free with a sharp knife

Introduction

In less time than it takes to read this introduction, a thief could steal your motorcycle. Returning only to find your bike has gone is one of the worst feelings in the world. Even if the motorcycle is insured against theft, once you've got over the initial shock, you will have the inconvenience of dealing with the police and your insurance company.

The motorcycle is an easy target for the professional thief and the joyrider alike and the official figures on motorcycle theft make for depressing reading; on average a motor-cycle is stolen every 16 minutes in the UK!

Motorcycle thefts fall into two categories, those stolen 'to order' and those taken by opportunists. The thief stealing to order will be on the look out for a specific make and model and will go to extraordinary lengths to obtain that motorcycle. The opportunist thief on the other hand will look for easy targets which can be stolen with the minimum of effort and risk.

Whilst it is never going to be possible to make your machine 100% secure, it is estimated that around half of all stolen motorcycles are taken by opportunist thieves. Remember that the opportunist thief is always on the look out for the easy option: if there are two similar motorcycles parked side-by-side, they will target the one with the lowest level of security. By taking a few precautions, you can reduce the chances of your motorcycle being stolen.

Security equipment

There are many specialised motorcycle security devices available and the following text summarises their applications and their good and bad points.

Once you have decided on the type of security equipment which best suits your needs, we recommended that you read one of the many equipment tests regularly carried out by the motorcycle press. These tests compare the products from all the major manufacturers and give impartial ratings on their effectiveness, value-for-money and ease of use.

Ensure the lock and chain you buy is of good quality and long enough to shackle your bike to a solid object

No one item of security equipment can provide complete protection. It is highly recommended that two or more of the items described below are combined to increase the security of your motorcycle (a lock and chain plus an alarm system is just about ideal). The more security measures fitted to the bike, the less likely it is to be stolen.

Lock and chain

Pros: *Very flexible to use; can be used to secure the motorcycle to almost any immovable object. On some locks and chains, the lock can be used on its own as a disc lock (see below).*

Cons: *Can be very heavy and awkward to carry on the motorcycle, although some types will be supplied with a carry bag which can be strapped to the pillion seat.*

- Heavy-duty chains and locks are an excellent security measure **(see illustration 1).** Whenever the motorcycle is parked, use the lock and chain to secure the machine to a solid, immovable object such as a post or railings. This will prevent the machine from being ridden away or being lifted into the back of a van.

- When fitting the chain, always ensure the chain is routed around the motorcycle frame or swingarm **(see illustrations 2 and 3).** Never merely pass the chain around one of the wheel rims; a thief may unbolt the wheel and lift the rest of the machine into a van, leaving you with just the wheel! Try to avoid having excess chain free, thus making it difficult to use cutting tools, and keep the chain and lock off the ground to prevent thieves attacking it with a cold chisel. Position the lock so that its lock barrel is facing downwards; this will make it harder for the thief to attack the lock mechanism.

Pass the chain through the bike's frame, rather than just through a wheel . . .

. . . and loop it around a solid object

U-locks

Pros: *Highly effective deterrent which can be used to secure the bike to a post or railings. Most U-locks come with a carrier which allows the lock to be easily carried on the bike.*

Cons: *Not as flexible to use as a lock and chain.*

- These are solid locks which are similar in use to a lock and chain. U-locks are lighter than a lock and chain but not so flexible to use. The length and shape of the lock shackle limit the objects to which the bike can be secured **(see illustration 4)**.

4

U-locks can be used to secure the bike to a solid object – ensure you purchase one which is long enough

Disc locks

Pros: *Small, light and very easy to carry; most can be stored underneath the seat.*

Cons: *Does not prevent the motorcycle being lifted into a van. Can be very embarrassing if you forget to remove the lock before attempting to ride off!*

5

A typical disc lock attached through one of the holes in the disc

- Disc locks are designed to be attached to the front brake disc. The lock passes through one of the holes in the disc and prevents the wheel rotating by jamming against the fork/brake caliper **(see illustration 5)**. Some are equipped with an alarm siren which sounds if the disc lock is moved; this not only acts as a theft deterrent but also as a handy reminder if you try to move the bike with the lock still fitted.

- Combining the disc lock with a length of cable which can be looped around a post or railings provides an additional measure of security **(see illustration 6)**.

Alarms and immobilisers

Pros: *Once installed it is completely hassle-free to use. If the system is 'Thatcham' or 'Sold Secure-approved', insurance companies may give you a discount.*

Cons: *Can be expensive to buy and complex to install. No system will prevent the motorcycle from being lifted into a van and taken away.*

- Electronic alarms and immobilisers are available to suit a variety of budgets. There are three different types of system available: pure alarms, pure immobilisers, and the more expensive systems which are combined alarm/immobilisers **(see illustration 7)**.
- An alarm system is designed to emit an audible warning if the motorcycle is being tampered with.
- An immobiliser prevents the motorcycle being started and ridden away by disabling its electrical systems.
- When purchasing an alarm/immobiliser system, check the cost of installing the system unless you are able to do it yourself. If the motorcycle is not used regularly, another consideration is the current drain of the system. All alarm/immobiliser systems are powered by the motorcycle's battery; purchasing a system with a very low current drain could prevent the battery losing its charge whilst the motorcycle is not being used.

6

A disc lock combined with a security cable provides additional protection

7

A typical alarm/immobiliser system

8

Indelible markings can be applied to most areas of the bike – always apply the manufacturer's sticker to warn off thieves

9

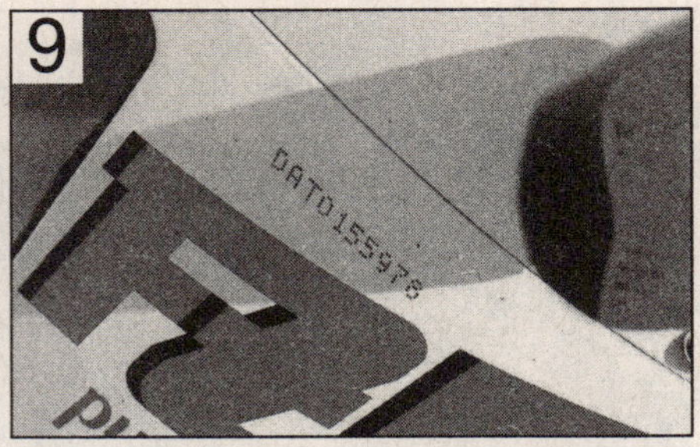

Chemically-etched code numbers can be applied to main body panels . . .

10

. . . again, always ensure that the kit manufacturer's sticker is applied in a prominent position

Security marking kits

Pros: *Very cheap and effective deterrent. Many insurance companies will give you a discount on your insurance premium if a recognised security marking kit is used on your motorcycle.*

Cons: *Does not prevent the motorcycle being stolen by joyriders.*

● There are many different types of security marking kits available. The idea is to mark as many parts of the motorcycle as possible with a unique security number **(see illustrations 8, 9 and 10)**. A form will be included with the kit to register your personal details and those of the motorcycle with the kit manufacturer. This register is made available to the police to help them trace the rightful owner of any motorcycle or components which they recover should all other forms of identification have been removed. Always apply the warning stickers provided with the kit to deter thieves.

Ground anchors, wheel clamps and security posts

Pros: *An excellent form of security which will deter all but the most determined of thieves.*

Cons: *Awkward to install and can be expensive.*

● Whilst the motorcycle is at home, it is a good idea to attach it securely to the floor or a solid wall, even if it is kept in a securely locked garage. Various types of ground anchors, security posts and wheel clamps are available for this purpose **(see illustration 11)**. These security devices are either bolted to a solid concrete or brick structure or can be cemented into the ground.

11

Permanent ground anchors provide an excellent level of security when the bike is at home

Security at home

A high percentage of motorcycle thefts are from the owner's home. Here are some things to consider whenever your motorcycle is at home:

● Where possible, always keep the motorcycle in a securely locked garage. Never rely solely on the standard lock on the garage door, these are usual hopelessly inadequate. Fit an additional locking mechanism to the door and consider having the garage alarmed. A security light, activated by a movement sensor, is also a good investment.

● Always secure the motorcycle to the ground or a wall, even if it is inside a securely locked garage.

● Do not regularly leave the motorcycle outside your home, try to keep it out of sight wherever possible. If a garage is not available, fit a motorcycle cover over the bike to disguise its true identity.

● It is not uncommon for thieves to follow a motorcyclist home to find out where the bike is kept. They will then return at a later date. Be aware of this whenever you are returning home on your motorcycle. If you suspect you are being followed, do not return home, instead ride to a garage or shop and stop as a precaution.

● When selling a motorcycle, do not provide your home address or the location where the bike is normally kept. Arrange to meet the buyer at a location away from your home. Thieves have been known to pose as potential buyers to find out where motorcycles are kept and then return later to steal them.

Security away from the home

As well as fitting security equipment to your motorcycle here are a few general rules to follow whenever you park your motorcycle.

● Park in a busy, public place.

● Use car parks which incorporate security features, such as CCTV.

● At night, park in a well-lit area, preferably directly underneath a street light.

● Engage the steering lock.

● Secure the motorcycle to a solid, immovable object such as a post or railings with an additional lock. If this is not possible, secure the bike to a friend's motorcycle. Some public parking places provide security loops for motorcycles.

● Never leave your helmet or luggage attached to the motorcycle. Take them with you at all times.

Lubricants and fluids

A wide range of lubricants, fluids and cleaning agents is available for motor-cycles. This is a guide as to what is available, its applications and properties.

Four-stroke engine oil

- Engine oil is without doubt the most important component of any four-stroke engine. Modern motorcycle engines place a lot of demands on their oil and choosing the right type is essential. Using an unsuitable oil will lead to an increased rate of engine wear and could result in serious engine damage. Before purchasing oil, always check the recommended oil specification given by the manufacturer. The manufacturer will state a recommended 'type or classification' and also a specific 'viscosity' range for engine oil.
- The oil 'type or classification' is identified by its API (American Petroleum Institute) rating. The API rating will be in the form of two letters, e.g. SG. The S identifies the oil as being suitable for use in a petrol (gasoline) engine (S stands for spark ignition) and the second letter, ranging from A to J, identifies the oil's performance rating. The later this letter, the higher the specification of the oil; for example API SG oil exceeds the requirements of API SF oil. **Note:** *On some oils there may also be a second rating consisting of another two letters, the first letter being C, e.g. API SF/CD. This rating indicates the oil is also suitable for use in a diesel engines (the C stands for compression ignition) and is thus of no relevance for motorcycle use.*
- The 'viscosity' of the oil is identified by its SAE (Society of Automotive Engineers) rating. All modern engines require multigrade oils and the SAE rating will consist of two numbers, the first followed by a W, e.g. 10W/40. The first number indicates the viscosity rating of the oil at low temperatures (W stands for winter – tested at –20°C) and the second number represents the viscosity of the oil at high temperatures (tested at 100°C). The lower the number, the thinner the oil. For example an oil with an SAE 10W/40 rating will give better cold starting and running than an SAE 15W/40 oil.
- As well as ensuring the 'type' and 'viscosity' of the oil match the recommendations, another consideration to make when buying engine oil is whether to purchase a standard mineral-based oil, a semi-synthetic oil (also known as a synthetic blend or synthetic-based oil) or a fully-synthetic oil. Although all oils will have a similar rating and viscosity, their cost will vary considerably; mineral-based oils are the cheapest, the fully-synthetic oils the most expensive with the semi-synthetic oils falling somewhere in-between. This decision is very much up to the owner, but it should be noted that modern synthetic oils have far better lubricating and cleaning qualities than traditional mineral-based oils and tend to retain these properties for far longer. Bearing in mind the operating conditions inside a modern, high-revving motorcycle engine it is highly recommended that a fully synthetic oil is used. The extra expense at each service could save you money in the long term by preventing premature engine wear.
- As a final note always ensure that the oil is specifically designed for use in motorcycle engines. Engine oils designed primarily for use in car engines sometimes contain additives or friction modifiers which could cause clutch slip on a motorcycle fitted with a wet-clutch.

Two-stroke engine oil

- Modern two-stroke engines, with their high power outputs, place high demands on their oil. If engine seizure is to be avoided it is essential that a high-quality oil is used. Two-stroke oils differ hugely from four-stroke oils. The oil lubricates only the crankshaft and piston(s) (the transmission has its own lubricating oil) and is used on a total-loss basis where it is burnt completely during the combustion process.
- The Japanese have recently introduced a classification system for two-stroke oils, the JASO rating. This rating is in the form of two letters, either FA, FB or FC – FA is the lowest classification and FC the highest. Ensure the oil being used meets or exceeds the recommended rating specified by the manufacturer.
- As well as ensuring the oil rating matches the recommendation, another consideration to make when buying engine oil is whether to purchase a standard mineral-based oil, a semi-synthetic oil (also known as a synthetic blend or synthetic-based oil) or a fully-synthetic oil. The cost of each type of oil varies considerably; mineral-based oils are the cheapest, the fully-synthetic oils the most expensive with the semi-synthetic oils falling somewhere in-between. This decision is very much up to the owner, but it should be noted that modern synthetic oils have far better lubricating properties and burn cleaner than traditional mineral-based oils. It is therefore recommended that a fully synthetic oil is used. The extra expense could save you money in the long term by preventing premature engine wear, engine performance will be improved, carbon deposits and exhaust smoke will be reduced.

- Always ensure that the oil is specifically designed for use in an injector system. Many high quality two-stroke oils are designed for competition use and need to be pre-mixed with fuel. These oils are of a much higher viscosity and are not designed to flow through the injector pumps used on road-going two-stroke motorcycles.

Transmission (gear) oil

- On a two-stroke engine, the transmission and clutch are lubricated by their own separate oil bath which must be changed in accordance with the Maintenance Schedule.
- Although the engine and transmission units of most four-strokes use a common lubrication supply, there are some exceptions where the engine and gearbox have separate oil reservoirs and a dry clutch is used.
- Motorcycle manufacturers will either recommend a monograde transmission oil or a four-stroke multigrade engine oil to lubricate the transmission.
- Transmission oils, or gear oils as they are often called, are designed specifically for use in transmission systems. The viscosity of these oils is represented by an SAE number, but the scale of measurement applied is different to that used to grade engine oils. As a rough guide a SAE90 gear oil will be of the same viscosity as an SAE50 engine oil.

Shaft drive oil

- On models equipped with shaft final drive, the shaft drive gears are will have their own oil supply. The manufacturer will state a recommended 'type or classification' and also a specific 'viscosity' range in the same manner as for four-stroke engine oil.
- Gear oil classification is given by the number which follows the API GL (GL standing for gear lubricant) rating, the higher the number, the higher the specification of the oil, e.g. API GL5 oil is a higher specification than API GL4 oil. Ensure the oil meets or exceeds the classification specified and is of the correct viscosity. The viscosity of gear oils is also represented by an SAE number but the scale of measurement used is different to that used to grade engine oils. As a rough guide an SAE90 gear oil will be of the same viscosity as an SAE50 engine oil.
- If the use of an EP (Extreme Pressure) gear oil is specified, ensure the oil purchased is suitable.

Fork oil and suspension fluid

- Conventional telescopic front forks are hydraulic and require fork oil to work. To ensure the forks function correctly, the fork oil must be changed in accordance with the Maintenance Schedule.
- Fork oil is available in a variety of viscosities, identified by their SAE rating; fork oil ratings vary from light (SAE 5) to heavy (SAE 30). When purchasing fork oil, ensure the viscosity rating matches that specified by the manufacturer.
- Some lubricant manufacturers also produce a range of high-quality suspension fluids which are very similar to fork oil but are designed mainly for competition use. These fluids may have a different viscosity rating system which is not to be confused with the SAE rating of normal fork oil. Refer to the manufacturer's instructions if in any doubt.

Brake and clutch fluid

- All disc brake systems and some clutch systems are hydraulically operated. To ensure correct operation, the hydraulic fluid must be changed in accordance with the Maintenance Schedule.
- Brake and clutch fluid is classified by its DOT rating with most motorcycle manufacturers specifying DOT 3 or 4 fluid. Both fluid types are glycol-based and can be mixed together without adverse effect; DOT 4 fluid exceeds the requirements of DOT 3 fluid. Although it is safe to use DOT 4 fluid in a system designed for use with DOT 3 fluid, never use DOT 3 fluid in a system which specifies the use of DOT 4 as this will adversely affect the system's performance. The type required for the system will be marked on the fluid reservoir cap.
- Some manufacturers also produce a DOT 5 hydraulic fluid. DOT 5 hydraulic fluid is silicone-based and is not compatible with the glycol-based DOT 3 and 4 fluids. Never mix DOT 5 fluid with DOT 3 or 4 fluid as this will seriously affect the performance of the hydraulic system.

Coolant/antifreeze

- When purchasing coolant/antifreeze, always ensure it is suitable for use in an aluminium engine and contains corrosion inhibitors to prevent possible blockages of the internal coolant passages of the system. As a general rule, most coolants are designed to be used neat and should not be diluted whereas antifreeze can be mixed with distilled water to provide a coolant solution of the required strength. Refer to the manufacturer's instructions on the bottle.
- Ensure the coolant is changed in accordance with the Maintenance Schedule.

Chain lube

- Chain lube is an aerosol-type spray lubricant specifically designed for use on motorcycle final drive chains. Chain lube has two functions, to minimise friction between the final drive chain and sprockets and to prevent corrosion of the chain. Regular use of a good-quality chain lube will extend the life of the drive chain and sprockets and thus maximise the power being transmitted from the transmission to the rear wheel.
- When using chain lube, always allow some time for the solvents in the lube to evaporate before riding the motorcycle. This will minimise the amount of lube which will

'fling' off from the chain when the motorcycle is used. If the motorcycle is equipped with an 'O-ring' chain, ensure the chain lube is labelled as being suitable for use on 'O-ring' chains.

Degreasers and solvents

- There are many different types of solvents and degreasers available to remove the grime and grease which accumulate around the motorcycle during normal use. Degreasers and solvents are usually available as an aerosol-type spray or as a liquid which you apply with a brush. Always closely follow the manufacturer's instructions and wear eye protection during use. Be aware that many solvents are flammable and may give off noxious fumes; take adequate precautions when using them *(see Safety First!)*.
- For general cleaning, use one of the many solvents or degreasers available from most motorcycle accessory shops. These solvents are usually applied then left for a certain time before being washed off with water.

Brake cleaner is a solvent specifically designed to remove all traces of oil, grease and dust from braking system components. Brake cleaner is designed to evaporate quickly and leaves behind no residue.

Carburettor cleaner is an aerosol-type solvent specifically designed to clear carburettor blockages and break down the hard deposits and gum often found inside carburettors during overhaul.

Contact cleaner is an aerosol-type solvent designed for cleaning electrical components. The cleaner will remove all traces of oil and dirt from components such as switch contacts or fouled spark plugs and then dry, leaving behind no residue.

Gasket remover is an aerosol-type solvent designed for removing stubborn gaskets from engine components during overhaul. Gasket remover will minimise the amount of scraping required to remove the gasket and therefore reduce the risk of damage to the mating surface.

Spray lubricants

- Aerosol-based spray lubricants are widely available and are excellent for lubricating lever pivots and exposed cables and switches. Try to use a lubricant which is of the dry-film type as the fluid evaporates, leaving behind a dry-film of lubricant. Lubricants which leave behind an oily residue will attract dust and dirt which will increase the rate of wear of the cable/ lever.
- Most lubricants also act as a moisture dispersant and a penetrating fluid. This means they can also be used to 'dry out' electrical components such as wiring connectors or switches as well as helping to free seized fasteners.

Greases

- Grease is used to lubricate many of the pivot-points. A good-quality multi-purpose grease is suitable for most applications but some manufacturers will specify the use of specialist greases for use on components such as swingarm and suspension linkage bushes. These specialist greases can be purchased from most motorcycle (or car) accessory shops; commonly specified types include molybdenum disulphide grease, lithium-based grease, graphite-based grease, silicone-based grease and high-temperature copper-based grease.

Gasket sealing compounds

- Gasket sealing compounds can be used in conjunction with gaskets, to improve their sealing capabilities, or on their own to seal metal-to-metal joints. Depending on their type, sealing compounds either set hard or stay relatively soft and pliable.

- When purchasing a gasket sealing compound, ensure that it is designed specifically for use on an internal combustion engine. General multi-purpose sealants available from DIY stores may appear visibly similar but they are not designed to withstand the extreme heat or contact with fuel and oil encountered when used on an engine *(see 'Tools and Workshop Tips' for further information)*:

Thread locking compound

- Thread locking compounds are used to secure certain threaded fasteners in position to prevent them from loosening due to vibration. Thread locking compounds can be purchased from most motorcycle (and car) accessory shops. Ensure the threads of the both components are completely clean and dry before sparingly applying the locking compound *(see 'Tools and Workshop Tips' for further information)*.

Fuel additives

- Fuel additives which protect and clean the fuel system components are widely available. These additives are designed to remove all traces of deposits that build up on the carburettors/injectors and prevent wear, helping the fuel system to operate more efficiently. If a fuel additive is being used, check that it is suitable for use with your motorcycle, especially if your motorcycle is equipped with a catalytic converter.
- Octane boosters are also available. These additives are designed to improve the performance of highly-tuned engines being run on normal pump-fuel and are of no real use on standard motorcycles.

About the MOT Test

In the UK, all vehicles more than three years old are subject to an annual test to ensure that they meet minimum safety requirements. A current test certificate must be issued before a machine can be used on public roads, and is required before a road fund licence can be issued. Riding without a current test certificate will also invalidate your insurance.

For most owners, the MOT test is an annual cause for anxiety, and this is largely due to owners not being sure what needs to be checked prior to submitting the motorcycle for testing. The simple answer is that a fully roadworthy motorcycle will have no difficulty in passing the test.

This is a guide to getting your motorcycle through the MOT test. Obviously it will not be possible to examine the motorcycle to the same standard as the professional MOT tester, particularly in view of the equipment required for some of the checks. However, working through the following procedures will enable you to identify any problem areas before submitting the motorcycle for the test.

It has only been possible to summarise the test requirements here, based on the regulations in force at the time of printing. Test standards are becoming increasingly stringent, although there are some exemptions for older vehicles. More information about the MOT test can be obtained from the TSO publications, *How Safe is your Motorcycle* and *The MOT Inspection Manual for Motorcycle Testing*.

Many of the checks require that one of the wheels is raised off the ground. If the motorcycle doesn't have a centre stand, note that an auxiliary stand will be required. Additionally, the help of an assistant may prove useful.

Certain exceptions apply to machines under 50 cc, machines without a lighting system, and Classic bikes - if in doubt about any of the requirements listed below seek confirmation from an MOT tester prior to submitting the motorcycle for the test.

Check that the frame number is clearly visible.

Electrical System

Lights, turn signals, horn and reflector

- With the ignition on, check the operation of the following electrical components. **Note:** *The electrical components on certain small-capacity machines are powered by the generator, requiring that the engine is run for this check.*
  - a) *Headlight and tail light. Check that both illuminate in the low and high beam switch positions.*
  - b) *Position lights. Check that the front position (or sidelight) and tail light illuminate in this switch position.*
  - c) *Turn signals. Check that all flash at the correct rate, and that the warning light(s) function correctly. Check that the turn signal switch works correctly.*
  - d) *Hazard warning system (where fitted). Check that all four turn signals flash in this switch position.*
  - e) *Brake stop light. Check that the light comes on when the front and rear brakes are independently applied. Models first used on or after 1st April 1986 must have a brake light switch on each brake.*
  - f) *Horn. Check that the sound is continuous and of reasonable volume.*
- Check that there is a red reflector on the rear of the machine, either mounted separately or as part of the tail light lens.
- Check the condition of the headlight, tail light and turn signal lenses.

Headlight beam height

- The MOT tester will perform a headlight beam height check using specialised beam setting equipment **(see illustration 1)**. This equipment will not be available to the home mechanic, but if you suspect that the headlight is incorrectly set or may have been maladjusted in the past, you can perform a rough test as follows.
- Position the bike in a straight line facing a brick wall. The bike must be off its stand, upright and with a rider seated. Measure the height from the ground to the centre of the headlight and mark a horizontal line on the wall at this height. Position the motorcycle 3.8 metres from the wall and draw a vertical line up the wall central to the centreline of the motorcycle. Switch to dipped beam and check that the beam pattern falls slightly lower than the horizontal line and to the left of the vertical line **(see illustration 2)**.

1

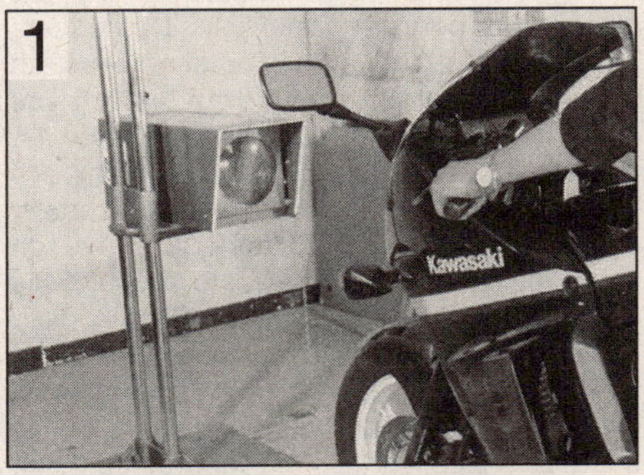

Headlight beam height checking equipment

2

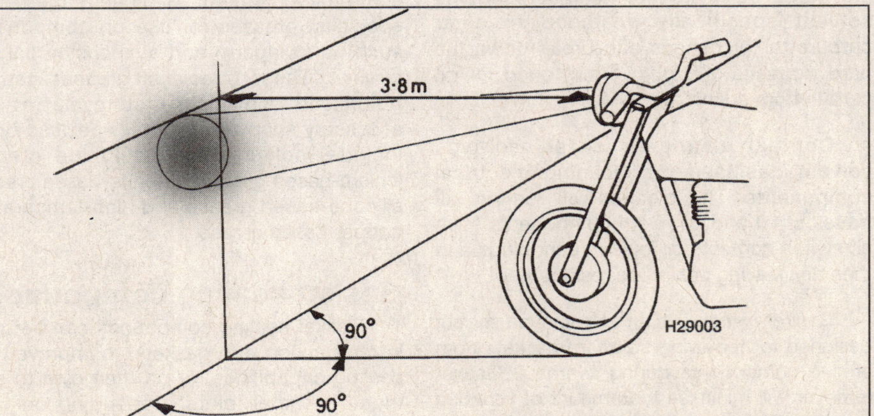

Home workshop beam alignment check

Exhaust System and Final Drive

Exhaust

- Check that the exhaust mountings are secure and that the system does not foul any of the rear suspension components.
- Start the motorcycle. When the revs are increased, check that the exhaust is neither holed nor leaking from any of its joints. On a linked system, check that the collector box is not leaking due to corrosion.
- Note that the exhaust decibel level ("loudness" of the exhaust) is assessed at the discretion of the tester. If the motorcycle was first used on or after 1st January 1985 the silencer must carry the BSAU 193 stamp, or a marking relating to its make and model, or be of OE (original equipment) manufacture. If the silencer is marked NOT FOR ROAD USE, RACING USE ONLY or similar, it will fail the MOT.

Final drive

- On chain or belt drive machines, check that the chain/belt is in good condition and does not have excessive slack. Also check that the sprocket is securely mounted on the rear wheel hub. Check that the chain/belt guard is in place.
- On shaft drive bikes, check for oil leaking from the drive unit and fouling the rear tyre.

Steering and Suspension

Steering

- With the front wheel raised off the ground, rotate the steering from lock to lock. The handlebar or switches must not contact the fuel tank or be close enough to trap the rider's hand. Problems can be caused by damaged lock stops on the lower yoke and frame, or by the fitting of non-standard handlebars.
- When performing the lock to lock check, also ensure that the steering moves freely without drag or notchiness. Steering movement can be impaired by poorly routed cables, or by overtight head bearings or worn bvearings. The tester will perform a check of the steering head bearing lower race by mounting the front wheel on a surface plate, then performing a lock to lock check with the weight of the machine on the lower bearing **(see illustration 3)**.
- Grasp the fork sliders (lower legs) and attempt to push and pull on the forks **(see illustration 4).** Any play in the steering head bearings will be felt. Note that in extreme cases, wear of the front fork bushes can be misinterpreted for head bearing play.
- Check that the handlebars are securely mounted.
- Check that the handlebar grip rubbers are secure. They should by bonded to the bar left end and to the throttle cable pulley on the right end.

3

Front wheel mounted on a surface plate for steering head bearing lower race check

Front suspension

- With the motorcycle off the stand, hold the front brake on and pump the front forks up and down **(see illustration 5)**. Check that they are adequately damped.

4

Checking the steering head bearings for freeplay

5
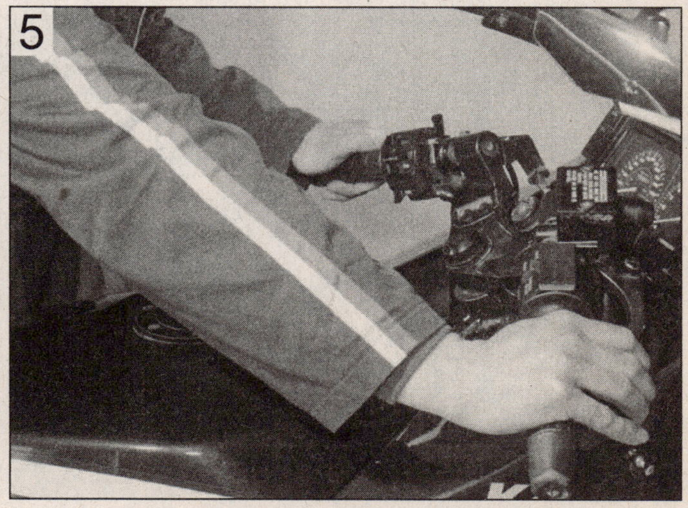

Hold the front brake on and pump the front forks up and down to check operation

6
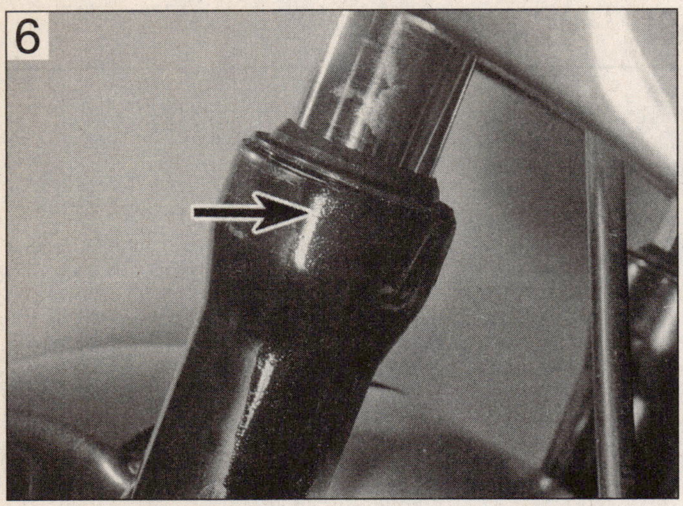

Inspect the area around the fork dust seal for oil leakage (arrow)

7
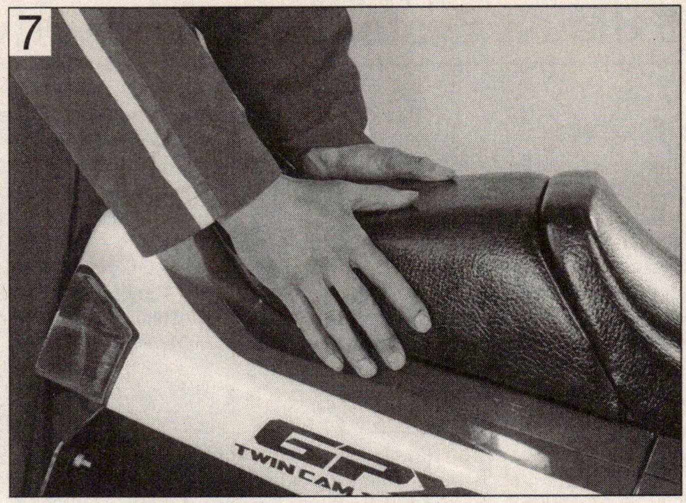

Bounce the rear of the motorcycle to check rear suspension operation

8
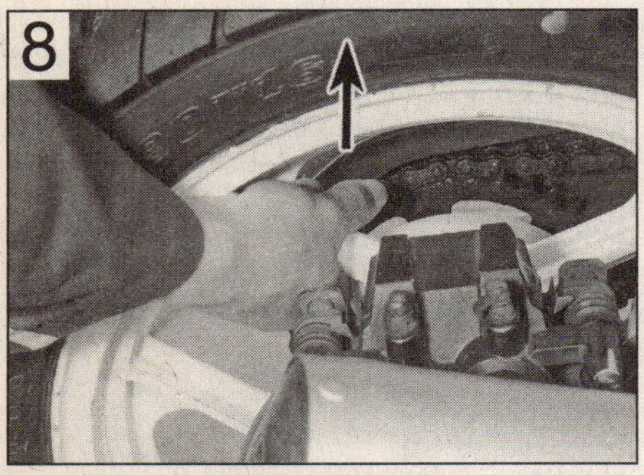

Checking for rear suspension linkage play

- Inspect the area above and around the front fork oil seals **(see illustration 6)**. There should be no sign of oil on the fork tube (stanchion) nor leaking down the slider (lower leg). On models so equipped, check that there is no oil leaking from the anti-dive units.
- On models with swingarm front suspension, check that there is no freeplay in the linkage when moved from side to side.

Rear suspension

- With the motorcycle off the stand and an assistant supporting the motorcycle by its handlebars, bounce the rear suspension **(see illustration 7)**. Check that the suspension components do not foul on any of the cycle parts and check that the shock absorber(s) provide adequate damping.
- Visually inspect the shock absorber(s) and check that there is no sign of oil leakage from its damper. This is somewhat restricted on certain single shock models due to the location of the shock absorber.
- With the rear wheel raised off the ground, grasp the wheel at the highest point and attempt to pull it up **(see illustration 8)**. Any play in the swingarm pivot or suspension linkage bearings will be felt as movement. **Note:** *Do not confuse play with actual suspension movement.* Failure to lubricate suspension linkage bearings can lead to bearing failure **(see illustration 9)**.
- With the rear wheel raised off the ground, grasp the swingarm ends and attempt to move the swingarm from side to side and forwards and backwards - any play indicates wear of the swingarm pivot bearings **(see illustration 10)**.

9

Worn suspension linkage pivots (arrows) are usually the cause of play in the rear suspension

10
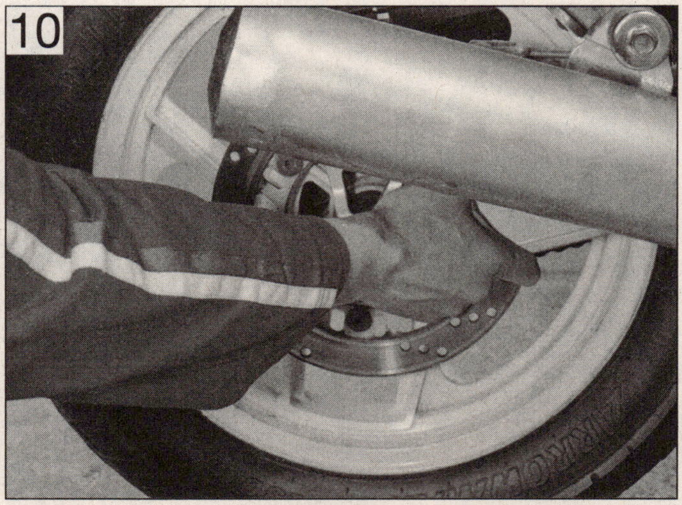

Grasp the swingarm at the ends to check for play in its pivot bearings

Brake pad wear can usually be viewed without removing the caliper. Most pads have wear indicator grooves (arrowed) and some also have indicator tangs or cut-outs.

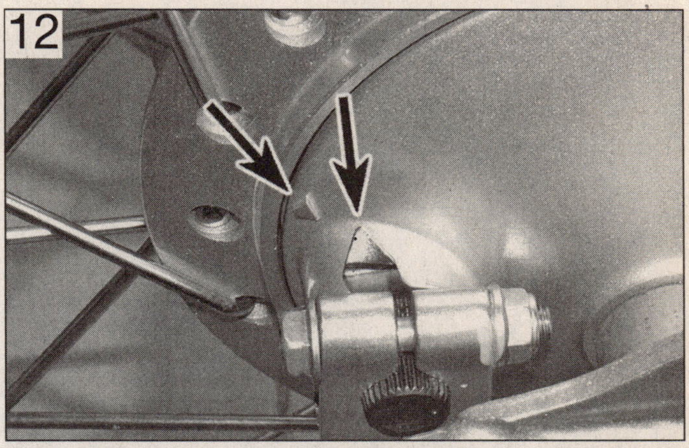

On drum brakes, check the angle of the operating lever with the brake fully applied. Most drum brakes have a wear indicator pointer or scale.

Brakes, Wheels and Tyres

Brakes

- With the wheel raised off the ground, apply the brake then free it off, and check that the wheel is about to revolve freely without brake drag.
- On disc brakes, examine the disc itself. Check that it is securely mounted and not cracked.
- On disc brakes, view the pad material through the caliper mouth and check that the pads are not worn down beyond the limit **(see illustration 11)**.
- On drum brakes, check that when the brake is applied the angle between the operating lever and cable or rod is not too great **(see illustration 12)**. Check also that the operating lever doesn't foul any other components.
- On disc brakes, examine the flexible hoses from top to bottom. Have an assistant hold the brake on so that the fluid in the hose is under pressure, and check that there is no sign of fluid leakage, bulges or cracking. If there are any metal brake pipes or unions, check that these are free from corrosion and damage. Where a brake-linked anti-dive system is fitted, check the hoses to the anti-dive in a similar manner.
- Check that the rear brake torque arm is secure and that its fasteners are secured by self-locking nuts or castellated nuts with split-pins or R-pins **(see illustration 13)**.
- On models with ABS, check that the self-check warning light in the instrument panel works.
- The MOT tester will perform a test of the motorcycle's braking efficiency based on a calculation of rider and motorcycle weight. Although this cannot be carried out at home, you can at least ensure that the braking systems are properly maintained. For hydraulic disc brakes, check the fluid level, lever/pedal feel (bleed of air if its spongy) and pad material. For drum brakes, check adjustment, cable or rod operation and shoe lining thickness.

Wheels and tyres

- Check the wheel condition. Cast wheels should be free from cracks and if of the built-up design, all fasteners should be secure. Spoked wheels should be checked for broken, corroded, loose or bent spokes.
- With the wheel raised off the ground, spin the wheel and visually check that the tyre and wheel run true. Check that the tyre does not foul the suspension or mudguards.
- With the wheel raised off the ground, grasp the wheel and attempt to move it about the axle (spindle) **(see illustration 14)**. Any play felt here indicates wheel bearing failure.

Brake torque arm must be properly secured at both ends

Check for wheel bearing play by trying to move the wheel about the axle (spindle)

Checking the tyre tread depth

Tyre direction of rotation arrow can be found on tyre sidewall

Castellated type wheel axle (spindle) nut must be secured by a split pin or R-pin

Two straightedges are used to check wheel alignment

- Check the tyre tread depth, tread condition and sidewall condition **(see illustration 15)**.
- Check the tyre type. Front and rear tyre types must be compatible and be suitable for road use. Tyres marked NOT FOR ROAD USE, COMPETITION USE ONLY or similar, will fail the MOT.
- If the tyre sidewall carries a direction of rotation arrow, this must be pointing in the direction of normal wheel rotation **(see illustration 16)**.
- Check that the wheel axle (spindle) nuts (where applicable) are properly secured. A self-locking nut or castellated nut with a split-pin or R-pin can be used **(see illustration 17)**.
- Wheel alignment is checked with the motorcycle off the stand and a rider seated. With the front wheel pointing straight ahead, two perfectly straight lengths of metal or wood and placed against the sidewalls of both tyres **(see illustration 18)**. The gap each side of the front tyre must be equidistant on both sides. Incorrect wheel alignment may be due to a cocked rear wheel (often as the result of poor chain adjustment) or in extreme cases, a bent frame.

General checks and condition

- Check the security of all major fasteners, bodypanels, seat, fairings (where fitted) and mudguards.
- Check that the rider and pillion footrests, handlebar levers and brake pedal are securely mounted.
- Check for corrosion on the frame or any load-bearing components. If severe, this may affect the structure, particularly under stress.

Sidecars

A motorcycle fitted with a sidecar requires additional checks relating to the stability of the machine and security of attachment and swivel joints, plus specific wheel alignment (toe-in) requirements. Additionally, tyre and lighting requirements differ from conventional motorcycle use. Owners are advised to check MOT test requirements with an official test centre.

Preparing for storage

Before you start

If repairs or an overhaul is needed, see that this is carried out now rather than left until you want to ride the bike again.

Give the bike a good wash and scrub all dirt from its underside. Make sure the bike dries completely before preparing for storage.

Engine

- Remove the spark plug(s) and lubricate the cylinder bores with approximately a teaspoon of motor oil using a spout-type oil can **(see illustration 1)**. Reinstall the spark plug(s). Crank the engine over a couple of times to coat the piston rings and bores with oil. If the bike has a kickstart, use this to turn the engine over. If not, flick the kill switch to the OFF position and crank the engine over on the starter **(see illustration 2)**. If the nature on the ignition system prevents the starter operating with the kill switch in the OFF position, remove the spark plugs and fit them back in their caps; ensure that the plugs are earthed (grounded) against the cylinder head when the starter is operated **(see illustration 3)**.

Warning: It is important that the plugs are earthed (grounded) away from the spark plug holes otherwise there is a risk of atomised fuel from the cylinders igniting.

> **HAYNES HiNT** *On a single cylinder four-stroke engine, you can seal the combustion chamber completely by positioning the piston at TDC on the compression stroke.*

- Drain the carburettor(s) otherwise there is a risk of jets becoming blocked by gum deposits from the fuel **(see illustration 4)**.
- If the bike is going into long-term storage, consider adding a fuel stabiliser to the fuel in the tank. If the tank is drained completely, corrosion of its internal surfaces may occur if left unprotected for a long period. The tank can be treated with a rust preventative especially for this purpose. Alternatively, remove the tank and pour half a litre of motor oil into it, install the filler cap and shake the tank to coat its internals with oil before draining off the excess. The same effect can also be achieved by spraying WD40 or a similar water-dispersant around the inside of the tank via its flexible nozzle.
- Make sure the cooling system contains the correct mix of antifreeze. Antifreeze also contains important corrosion inhibitors.
- The air intakes and exhaust can be sealed off by covering or plugging the openings. Ensure that you do not seal in any condensation; run the engine until it is hot,

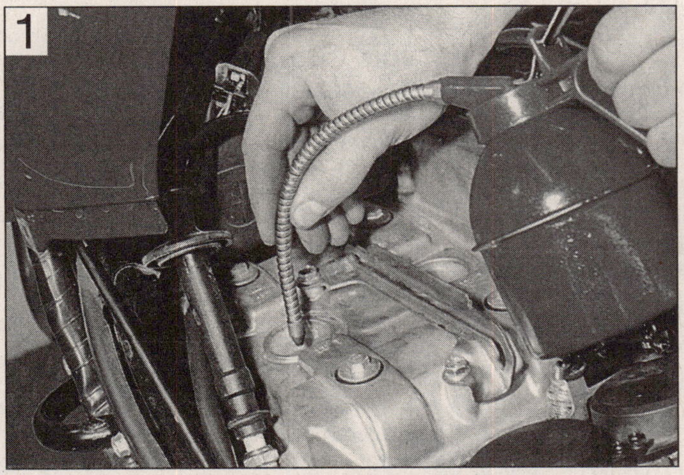

Squirt a drop of motor oil into each cylinder

Flick the kill switch to OFF . . .

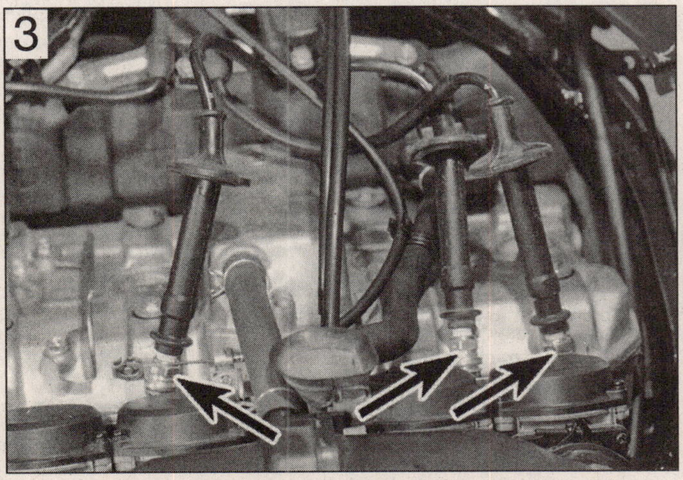

. . . and ensure that the metal bodies of the plugs (arrows) are earthed against the cylinder head

Connect a hose to the carburettor float chamber drain stub (arrow) and unscrew the drain screw

5

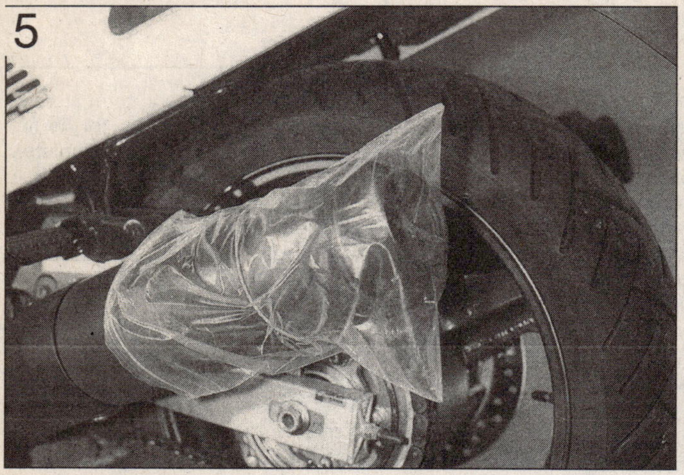

Exhausts can be sealed off with a plastic bag

6

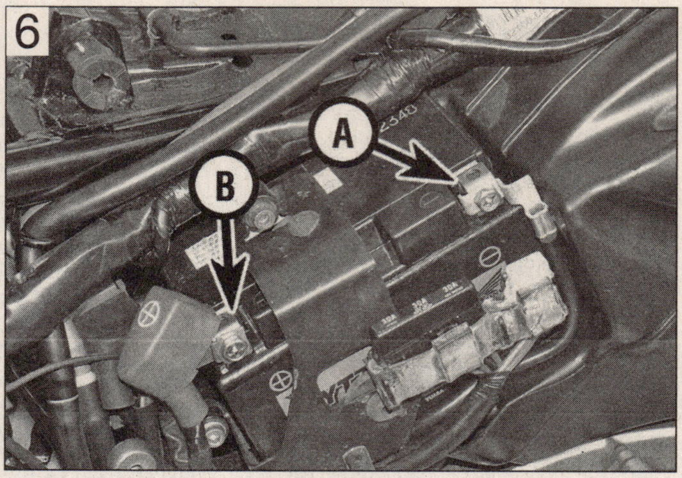

Disconnect the negative lead (A) first, followed by the positive lead (B)

7

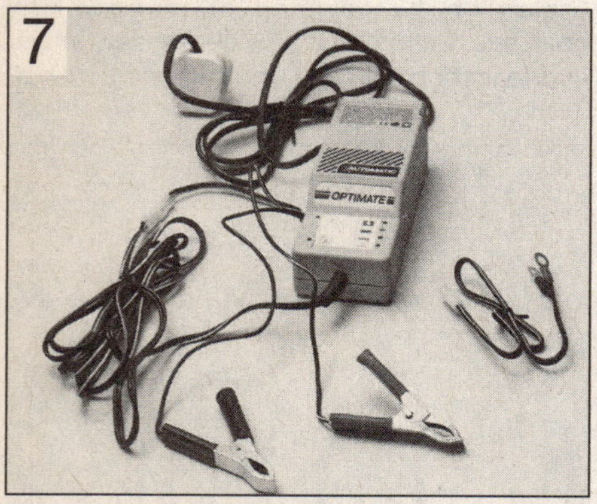

Use a suitable battery charger - this kit also assess battery condition

then switch off and allow to cool. Tape a piece of thick plastic over the silencer end(s) **(see illustration 5)**. Note that some advocate pouring a tablespoon of motor oil into the silencer(s) before sealing them off.

Battery

- Remove it from the bike - in extreme cases of cold the battery may freeze and crack its case **(see illustration 6)**.
- Check the electrolyte level and top up if necessary (conventional refillable batteries). Clean the terminals.
- Store the battery off the motorcycle and away from any sources of fire. Position a wooden block under the battery if it is to sit on the ground.
- Give the battery a trickle charge for a few hours every month **(see illustration 7)**.

Tyres

- Place the bike on its centrestand or an auxiliary stand which will support the motorcycle in an upright position. Position wood blocks under the tyres to keep them off the ground and to provide insulation from damp. If the bike is being put into long-term storage, ideally both tyres should be off the ground; not only will this protect the tyres, but will also ensure that no load is placed on the steering head or wheel bearings.
- Deflate each tyre by 5 to 10 psi, no more or the beads may unseat from the rim, making subsequent inflation difficult on tubeless tyres.

Pivots and controls

- Lubricate all lever, pedal, stand and footrest pivot points. If grease nipples are fitted to the rear suspension components, apply lubricant to the pivots.
- Lubricate all control cables.

Cycle components

- Apply a wax protectant to all painted and plastic components. Wipe off any excess, but don't polish to a shine. Where fitted, clean the screen with soap and water.
- Coat metal parts with Vaseline (petroleum jelly). When applying this to the fork tubes, do not compress the forks otherwise the seals will rot from contact with the Vaseline.
- Apply a vinyl cleaner to the seat.

Storage conditions

- Aim to store the bike in a shed or garage which does not leak and is free from damp.
- Drape an old blanket or bedspread over the bike to protect it from dust and direct contact with sunlight (which will fade paint). This also hides the bike from prying eyes. Beware of tight-fitting plastic covers which may allow condensation to form and settle on the bike.

Getting back on the road

Engine and transmission

- Change the oil and replace the oil filter. If this was done prior to storage, check that the oil hasn't emulsified - a thick whitish substance which occurs through condensation.
- Remove the spark plugs. Using a spout-type oil can, squirt a few drops of oil into the cylinder(s). This will provide initial lubrication as the piston rings and bores comes back into contact. Service the spark plugs, or fit new ones, and install them in the engine.
- Check that the clutch isn't stuck on. The plates can stick together if left standing for some time, preventing clutch operation. Engage a gear and try rocking the bike back and forth with the clutch lever held against the handlebar. If this doesn't work on cable-operated clutches, hold the clutch lever back against the handlebar with a strong elastic band or cable tie for a couple of hours **(see illustration 8)**.
- If the air intakes or silencer end(s) were blocked off, remove the bung or cover used.
- If the fuel tank was coated with a rust

8

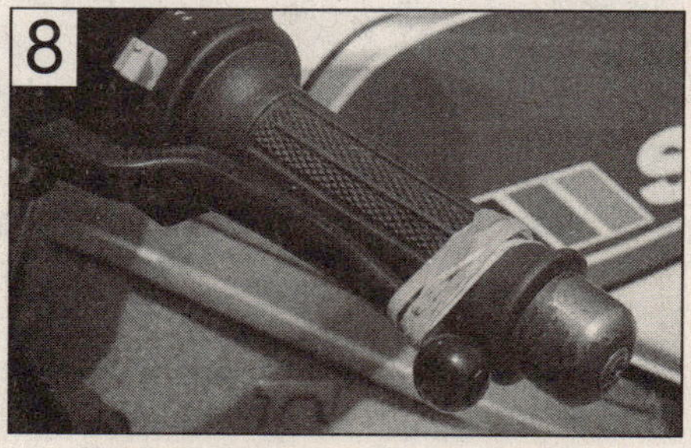

Hold clutch lever back against the handlebar with elastic bands or a cable tie

preventative, oil or a stabiliser added to the fuel, drain and flush the tank and dispose of the fuel sensibly. If no action was taken with the fuel tank prior to storage, it is advised that the old fuel is disposed of since it will go off over a period of time. Refill the fuel tank with fresh fuel.

Frame and running gear

- Oil all pivot points and cables.
- Check the tyre pressures. They will definitely need inflating if pressures were reduced for storage.
- Lubricate the final drive chain (where applicable).
- Remove any protective coating applied to the fork tubes (stanchions) since this may well destroy the fork seals. If the fork tubes weren't protected and have picked up rust spots, remove them with very fine abrasive paper and refinish with metal polish.
- Check that both brakes operate correctly. Apply each brake hard and check that it's not possible to move the motorcycle forwards, then check that the brake frees off again once released. Brake caliper pistons can stick due to corrosion around the piston head, or on the sliding caliper types, due to corrosion of the slider pins. If the brake doesn't free after repeated operation, take the caliper off for examination. Similarly drum brakes can stick due to a seized operating cam, cable or rod linkage.
- If the motorcycle has been in long-term storage, renew the brake fluid and clutch fluid (where applicable).
- Depending on where the bike has been stored, the wiring, cables and hoses may have been nibbled by rodents. Make a visual check and investigate disturbed wiring loom tape.

Battery

- If the battery has been previously removal and given top up charges it can simply be reconnected. Remember to connect the positive cable first and the negative cable last.
- On conventional refillable batteries, if the battery has not received any attention, remove it from the motorcycle and check its electrolyte level. Top up if necessary then charge the battery. If the battery fails to hold a charge and a visual checks show heavy white sulphation of the plates, the battery is probably defective and must be renewed. This is particularly likely if the battery is old. Confirm battery condition with a specific gravity check.
- On sealed (MF) batteries, if the battery has not received any attention, remove it from the motorcycle and charge it according to the information on the battery case - if the battery fails to hold a charge it must be renewed.

Starting procedure

- If a kickstart is fitted, turn the engine over a couple of times with the ignition OFF to distribute oil around the engine. If no kickstart is fitted, flick the engine kill switch OFF and the ignition ON and crank the engine over a couple of times to work oil around the upper cylinder components. If the nature of the ignition system is such that the starter won't work with the kill switch OFF, remove the spark plugs, fit them back into their caps and earth (ground) their bodies on the cylinder head. Reinstall the spark plugs afterwards.
- Switch the kill switch to RUN, operate the choke and start the engine. If the engine won't start don't continue cranking the engine - not only will this flatten the battery, but the starter motor will overheat. Switch the ignition off and try again later. If the engine refuses to start, go through the fault finding procedures in this manual. **Note:** *If the bike has been in storage for a long time, old fuel or a carburettor blockage may be the problem. Gum deposits in carburettors can block jets - if a carburettor cleaner doesn't prove successful the carburettors must be dismantled for cleaning.*
- Once the engine has started, check that the lights, turn signals and horn work properly.
- Treat the bike gently for the first ride and check all fluid levels on completion. Settle the bike back into the maintenance schedule.

Conversion factors

Length (distance)

Inches (in)	x 25.4	= Millimetres (mm)	x 0.0394	=	Inches (in)
Feet (ft)	x 0.305	= Metres (m)	x 3.281	=	Feet (ft)
Miles	x 1.609	= Kilometres (km)	x 0.621	=	Miles

Volume (capacity)

Cubic inches (cu in; in^3)	x 16.387	= Cubic centimetres (cc; cm^3)	x 0.061	=	Cubic inches (cu in; in^3)
Imperial pints (Imp pt)	x 0.568	= Litres (l)	x 1.76	=	Imperial pints (Imp pt)
Imperial quarts (Imp qt)	x 1.137	= Litres (l)	x 0.88	=	Imperial quarts (Imp qt)
Imperial quarts (Imp qt)	x 1.201	= US quarts (US qt)	x 0.833	=	Imperial quarts (Imp qt)
US quarts (US qt)	x 0.946	= Litres (l)	x 1.057	=	US quarts (US qt)
Imperial gallons (Imp gal)	x 4.546	= Litres (l)	x 0.22	=	Imperial gallons (Imp gal)
Imperial gallons (Imp gal)	x 1.201	= US gallons (US gal)	x 0.833	=	Imperial gallons (Imp gal)
US gallons (US gal)	x 3.785	= Litres (l)	x 0.264	=	US gallons (US gal)

Mass (weight)

Ounces (oz)	x 28.35	= Grams (g)	x 0.035	=	Ounces (oz)
Pounds (lb)	x 0.454	= Kilograms (kg)	x 2.205	=	Pounds (lb)

Force

Ounces-force (ozf; oz)	x 0.278	= Newtons (N)	x 3.6	=	Ounces-force (ozf; oz)
Pounds-force (lbf; lb)	x 4.448	= Newtons (N)	x 0.225	=	Pounds-force (lbf; lb)
Newtons (N)	x 0.1	= Kilograms-force (kgf; kg)	x 9.81	=	Newtons (N)

Pressure

Pounds-force per square inch (psi; lbf/in^2; lb/in^2)	x 0.070	= Kilograms-force per square centimetre (kgf/cm^2; kg/cm^2)	x 14.223	=	Pounds-force per square inch (psi; lbf/in^2; lb/in^2)
Pounds-force per square inch (psi; lbf/in^2; lb/in^2)	x 0.068	= Atmospheres (atm)	x 14.696	=	Pounds-force per square inch (psi; lbf/in^2; lb/in^2)
Pounds-force per square inch (psi; lbf/in^2; lb/in^2)	x 0.069	= Bars	x 14.5	=	Pounds-force per square inch (psi; lbf/in^2; lb/in^2)
Pounds-force per square inch (psi; lbf/in^2; lb/in^2)	x 6.895	= Kilopascals (kPa)	x 0.145	=	Pounds-force per square inch (psi; lbf/in^2; lb/in^2)
Kilopascals (kPa)	x 0.01	= Kilograms-force per square centimetre (kgf/cm^2; kg/cm^2)	x 98.1	=	Kilopascals (kPa)
Millibar (mbar)	x 100	= Pascals (Pa)	x 0.01	=	Millibar (mbar)
Millibar (mbar)	x 0.0145	= Pounds-force per square inch (psi; lbf/in^2; lb/in^2)	x 68.947	=	Millibar (mbar)
Millibar (mbar)	x 0.75	= Millimetres of mercury (mmHg)	x 1.333	=	Millibar (mbar)
Millibar (mbar)	x 0.401	= Inches of water (inH$_2$O)	x 2.491	=	Millibar (mbar)
Millimetres of mercury (mmHg)	x 0.535	= Inches of water (inH$_2$O)	x 1.868	=	Millimetres of mercury (mmHg)
Inches of water (inH$_2$O)	x 0.036	= Pounds-force per square inch (psi; lbf/in^2; lb/in^2)	x 27.68	=	Inches of water (inH$_2$O)

Torque (moment of force)

Pounds-force inches (lbf in; lb in)	x 1.152	= Kilograms-force centimetre (kgf cm; kg cm)	x 0.868	=	Pounds-force inches (lbf in; lb in)
Pounds-force inches (lbf in; lb in)	x 0.113	= Newton metres (Nm)	x 8.85	=	Pounds-force inches (lbf in; lb in)
Pounds-force inches (lbf in; lb in)	x 0.083	= Pounds-force feet (lbf ft; lb ft)	x 12	=	Pounds-force inches (lbf in; lb in)
Pounds-force feet (lbf ft; lb ft)	x 0.138	= Kilograms-force metres (kgf m; kg m)	x 7.233	=	Pounds-force feet (lbf ft; lb ft)
Pounds-force feet (lbf ft; lb ft)	x 1.356	= Newton metres (Nm)	x 0.738	=	Pounds-force feet (lbf ft; lb ft)
Newton metres (Nm)	x 0.102	= Kilograms-force metres (kgf m; kg m)	x 9.804	=	Newton metres (Nm)

Power

Horsepower (hp)	x 745.7	= Watts (W)	x 0.0013	=	Horsepower (hp)

Velocity (speed)

Miles per hour (miles/hr; mph)	x 1.609	= Kilometres per hour (km/hr; kph)	x 0.621	=	Miles per hour (miles/hr; mph)

Fuel consumption*

Miles per gallon, Imperial (mpg)	x 0.354	= Kilometres per litre (km/l)	x 2.825	=	Miles per gallon, Imperial (mpg)
Miles per gallon, US (mpg)	x 0.425	= Kilometres per litre (km/l)	x 2.352	=	Miles per gallon, US (mpg)

Temperature

Degrees Fahrenheit = (°C x 1.8) + 32

Degrees Celsius (Degrees Centigrade; °C) = (°F - 32) x 0.56

** It is common practice to convert from miles per gallon (mpg) to litres/100 kilometres (l/100km), where mpg x l/100 km = 282*

This Section provides an easy reference-guide to the more common faults that are likely to afflict your machine. Obviously, the opportunities are almost limitless for faults to occur as a result of obscure failures, and to try and cover all eventualities would require a book. Indeed, a number have been written on the subject.

Successful troubleshooting is not a mysterious 'black art' but the application of a bit of knowledge combined with a systematic and logical approach to the problem. Approach any troubleshooting by first accurately identifying the symptom and then checking through the list of possible causes, starting with the simplest or most obvious and progressing in stages to the most complex.

Take nothing for granted, but above all apply liberal quantities of common sense.

The main symptom of a fault is given in the text as a major heading below which are listed the various systems or areas which may contain the fault. Details of each possible cause for a fault and the remedial action to be taken are given, in brief, in the paragraphs below each heading. Further information should be sought in the relevant Chapter.

1 Engine doesn't start or is difficult to start

Starter motor doesn't rotate

- ☐ Engine kill switch OFF.
- ☐ Main fuse blown (Chapter 8).
- ☐ Battery voltage low. Check and recharge battery (Chapter 8).
- ☐ Starter motor defective. Make sure the wiring to the starter is secure. Make sure the starter relay clicks when the start button is pushed. If the relay clicks, then the fault is in the wiring or motor (see Chapter 8).
- ☐ Starter switch not contacting. The contacts could be wet, corroded or dirty. Disassemble and clean the switch (Chapter 8).
- ☐ Wiring open or shorted. Check all wiring connections and harnesses to make sure that they are dry, tight and not corroded. Also check for broken or frayed wires that can cause a short to ground (earth) (see Wiring diagram, Chapter 8).
- ☐ Ignition switch defective. Check the switch and replace with a new one if it is defective (see Chapter 8).
- ☐ Engine kill switch defective. Check for wet, dirty or corroded contacts. Clean or replace the switch with a new one as necessary (see Chapter 8).
- ☐ Faulty neutral switch, sidestand switch or clutch switch. Check the wiring to each switch and the switch itself (see Chapter 8).
- ☐ Faulty starter circuit cut-off relay or diodes (Chapter 8).
- ☐ Fuel injection system shutdown due to system fault (Chapter 4).

Starter motor rotates but engine does not turn over

- ☐ Starter clutch defective. Inspect and repair or replace with a new one (see Chapter 2).
- ☐ Damaged idle/reduction or starter gears. Inspect and replace the damaged parts (see Chapter 2).

Starter works but engine won't turn over (seized)

- ☐ Seized engine caused by one or more internally damaged components. Failure due to wear, abuse or lack of lubrication. Damage can include seized valves, rockers, camshaft, piston, crankshaft, connecting rod bearings, or transmission gears or bearings. Refer to Chapter 2 for engine disassembly.

No fuel flow

- ☐ No fuel in tank.
- ☐ Fuel tank breather hose obstructed.
- ☐ Fuel pump faulty (see Chapter 4).
- ☐ Fuel hose clogged. Remove the fuel hose and carefully blow through it.
- ☐ Fuel injector clogged. For the injector to be clogged, either a very bad batch of fuel with an unusual additive has been used, or some other foreign material has entered the tank. In some cases, if a machine has been unused for several months, the fuel turns to a varnish-like liquid which can cause an injector needle to stick to its seat. Drain the tank and clean the fuel system (Chapter 4).

Engine flooded

- ☐ Injector needle valve worn or stuck open, causing excess fuel to be admitted to the throttle body. In this case, the injector should be replaced with a new one.
- ☐ Starting technique incorrect. Under normal circumstances (i.e. if all the components of the fuel injection system are good) the machine should start with the throttle closed.

No spark or weak spark

- ☐ Ignition switch OFF.
- ☐ Engine kill switch turned to the OFF position.
- ☐ Ignition or kill switch shorted. This is usually caused by water, corrosion, damage or excessive wear. The switches can be disassembled and cleaned with electrical contact cleaner. If cleaning does not help, replace the switches (see Chapter 8).
- ☐ Battery voltage low. Check and recharge the battery as necessary (Chapter 8).
- ☐ Spark plug cap not making good contact. Make sure that the cap fits snugly over the plug.
- ☐ Spark plug dirty, defective or worn out. Identify reason for fouled plug using spark plug condition chart on the inside back cover and follow the plug maintenance procedures (see Chapter 1).
- ☐ Incorrect spark plug. Wrong type or heat range. Check and install correct plug (see Chapter 1).
- ☐ Ignition coil defective. Test and replace with new one if necessary (Chapter 4).
- ☐ Fuel injection system shutdown due to system fault (Chapter 4).
- ☐ Crankshaft position (CKP) sensor defective (see Chapter 4).
- ☐ Electronic control unit (ECU) defective (see Chapter 4).
- ☐ Wiring shorted or broken between:
  a) Ignition switch and engine kill switch (or blown fuse)
  b) ECU and engine kill switch
  c) ECU and ignition coil
  d) ECU and CKP sensor
  Make sure that all wiring connections are clean, dry and tight. Look for chafed and broken wires (see Chapters 4 and 8).

Compression low

- ☐ Spark plug loose. Remove the plug and inspect the threads. Reinstall and tighten securely (see Chapter 1).
- ☐ Cylinder head not sufficiently tightened down. If the cylinder head is suspected of being loose, then there's a chance that the gasket or head is damaged if the problem has persisted for any length of time. The head bolts should be tightened to the proper torque and in the correct sequence (Chapter 2).
- ☐ Improper valve clearance. This means that the valve is not closing completely and compression pressure is leaking past the valve. Check and adjust the valve clearances (Chapter 1).
- ☐ Cylinder and/or piston worn. Excessive wear will cause compression pressure to leak past the rings. This is usually accompanied by worn rings as well. A top-end overhaul is necessary (Chapter 2).
- ☐ Piston rings worn, weak, broken, or sticking. Broken or sticking piston rings usually indicate a lubrication or fuelling problem that causes excess carbon deposits to form on the piston and rings. Top-end overhaul is necessary (Chapter 2).
- ☐ Piston ring-to-groove clearance excessive. This is caused by excessive wear of the piston ring lands. Piston renewal is necessary (Chapter 2).
- ☐ Cylinder head gasket damaged. If the head is allowed to become loose, or if excessive carbon build-up on the piston crown and combustion chamber causes extremely high compression, the head gasket may leak. Retorquing the head is not always sufficient to restore the seal, so a new gasket is necessary (Chapter 2).
- ☐ Cylinder head warped. This is caused by overheating or improperly tightened head bolts. Machine shop resurfacing or head renewal is necessary (Chapter 2).
- ☐ Valve spring broken or weak. Caused by component failure or wear; the springs must be renewed (Chapter 2).
- ☐ Valve not seating properly. This is caused by a bent valve (from over-revving or improper valve adjustment), burned valve or seat (incorrect air/fuel mixture) or an accumulation of carbon deposits on the seat. The valves must be cleaned and/or renewed and the seats serviced (Chapter 2).

1 Engine doesn't start or is difficult to start (continued)

Stalls after starting

- ☐ Faulty fast idle system. Check the operation of the fast idle solenoid (see Chapter 4).
- ☐ Engine idle speed incorrect. Turn idle adjusting screw until the engine idles at the specified rpm (Chapter 1).
- ☐ Ignition malfunction (see Chapter 4).
- ☐ Fuel injection system malfunction (see Chapter 4).
- ☐ Fuel contaminated. The fuel can be contaminated with either dirt or water, or can change chemically if the machine has been unused for several months. Drain the tank and fuel system (Chapter 4).
- ☐ Intake air leak. Check for loose throttle body-to-intake duct joints (Chapter 4).

Rough idle

- ☐ Idle speed incorrect (see Chapter 1).
- ☐ Ignition fault (see Chapter 4).
- ☐ Fuel injection system malfunction (see Chapter 4).
- ☐ Fuel contaminated. The fuel can be contaminated with either dirt or water, or can change chemically if the machine has been unused for several months. Drain the tank and the fuel system (Chapter 4).
- ☐ Intake air leak. Check for loose throttle body-to-intake manifold connections, loose or damaged AIS vacuum hose (WR models) (Chapter 4).
- ☐ Air filter clogged. Clean the air filter element or replace it with a new one (Chapter 1).

2 Poor running at low speeds

Spark weak

- ☐ Battery voltage low. Check and recharge battery (see Chapter 8).
- ☐ Spark plug cap not making good contact. Make sure that the cap fits snugly over the plug.
- ☐ Spark plug dirty, defective or worn out. Locate reason for fouled plug using spark plug condition chart on the inside back cover and follow the plug maintenance procedures (see Chapter 1).
- ☐ Incorrect spark plug. Wrong type or heat range. Check and install correct plug (see Chapter 1).
- ☐ Ignition coil defective. Test and replace with new one if necessary (see Chapter 4).

Fuel/air mixture incorrect

- ☐ Fuel tank breather hose obstructed.
- ☐ Fuel pump faulty (see Chapter 4).
- ☐ Fuel hose squashed or restricted at some point. Remove the fuel hose and carefully blow through it.
- ☐ Fuel injector clogged. In some cases, if a machine has been unused for several months, the fuel turns to a varnish-like liquid which can cause the injector needle to stick to its seat. Drain the tank and fuel system (Chapter 4).
- ☐ Intake air leak. Check for loose throttle body-to-intake duct joints (Chapter 4).
- ☐ Air filter clogged. Clean the air filter element or replace it with a new one (Chapter 1).

Compression low

- ☐ Check by performing a compression test (see Chapter 2).
- ☐ Spark plug loose. Remove the plug and inspect the threads. Reinstall and tighten securely (see Chapter 1).
- ☐ Cylinder head not sufficiently tightened down. If the cylinder head is suspected of being loose, then there's a chance that the gasket or head is damaged if the problem has persisted for any length of time. The head bolts should be tightened to the proper torque and in the correct sequence (Chapter 2).
- ☐ Improper valve clearance. This means that the valve is not closing completely and compression pressure is leaking past the valve. Check and adjust the valve clearances (Chapter 1).
- ☐ Cylinder and/or piston worn. Excessive wear will cause compression pressure to leak past the rings. This is usually accompanied by worn rings as well. A top-end overhaul is necessary (Chapter 2).
- ☐ Piston rings worn, weak, broken, or sticking. Broken or sticking piston rings usually indicate a lubrication or fuelling problem that causes excess carbon deposits to form on the piston and rings. Top-end overhaul is necessary (Chapter 2).
- ☐ Piston ring-to-groove clearance excessive. This is caused by excessive wear of the piston ring lands. Piston renewal is necessary (Chapter 2).
- ☐ Cylinder head gasket damaged. If the head is allowed to become loose, or if excessive carbon build-up on the piston crown and combustion chamber causes extremely high compression, the head gasket may leak. Retorquing the head is not always sufficient to restore the seal, so a new gasket is necessary (Chapter 2).
- ☐ Cylinder head warped. This is caused by overheating or improperly tightened head bolts. Machine shop resurfacing or head renewal is necessary (Chapter 2).
- ☐ Valve spring broken or weak. Caused by component failure or wear; the springs must be renewed (Chapter 2).
- ☐ Valve not seating properly. This is caused by a bent valve (from over-revving or improper valve adjustment), burned valve or seat (improper fuelling) or an accumulation of carbon deposits on the seat (from fuelling or lubrication problems). The valves must be cleaned and/or renewed and the seats serviced (Chapter 2).

Poor acceleration

- ☐ Timing not advancing. The crankshaft position sensor (CKP) or the electronic control unit (ECU) may be defective (see Chapter 4). If so, they must be renewed.
- ☐ Engine oil viscosity too high. Using a heavier oil than that recommended in Chapter 1 can damage the oil pump or lubrication system and cause drag on the engine.
- ☐ Brakes dragging. Usually caused by debris which has entered the brake caliper piston seals, or from a warped disc or bent axle (see Chapter 6).

3 Poor running or no power at high speed

Firing incorrect

- ☐ Spark plug cap not making good contact. Make sure that the cap fits snugly over the plug and that the wiring is secure.
- ☐ Spark plug dirty, defective or worn out. Identify reason for fouled plug using spark plug condition chart on the inside back cover and follow the plug maintenance procedures (see Chapter 1).
- ☐ Incorrect spark plug. Wrong type or heat range. Check and install correct plug (see Chapter 1).
- ☐ Ignition coil defective. Test and replace with new one if necessary (see Chapter 4).
- ☐ Faulty ECU (electronic control unit) (see Chapter 4).

Fuel/air mixture incorrect

- ☐ Fuel tank breather hose obstructed.
- ☐ Fuel pump faulty (see Chapter 4).
- ☐ Fuel hose clogged. Remove the fuel hose and carefully blow through it.
- ☐ Fuel injector clogged. In some cases, if a machine has been unused for several months, the fuel turns to a varnish-like liquid which can cause the injector needle to stick to its seat. Drain the tank and fuel system (Chapter 4).
- ☐ Intake air leak. Check for loose throttle body-to-intake duct joints (Chapter 4).
- ☐ Air filter clogged. Clean the air filter element or replace it with a new one (Chapter 1).

Compression low

Note: *Check by performing a compression test (see Chapter 2).*

- ☐ Spark plug loose. Remove the plug and inspect the threads. Reinstall and tighten securely (see Chapter 1).
- ☐ Cylinder head not sufficiently tightened down. If the cylinder head is suspected of being loose, then there's a chance that the gasket or head is damaged if the problem has persisted for any length of time. The head bolts should be tightened to the proper torque and in the correct sequence (Chapter 2).
- ☐ Improper valve clearance. This means that the valve is not closing completely and compression pressure is leaking past the valve. Check and adjust the valve clearances (Chapter 1).
- ☐ Cylinder and/or piston worn. Excessive wear will cause compression pressure to leak past the rings. This is usually accompanied by worn rings as well. A top-end overhaul is necessary (Chapter 2).
- ☐ Piston rings worn, weak, broken, or sticking. Broken or sticking piston rings usually indicate a lubrication or fuelling problem that causes excess carbon deposits to form on the pistons and rings. Top-end overhaul is necessary (Chapter 2).
- ☐ Piston ring-to-groove clearance excessive. This is caused by excessive wear of the piston ring lands. Piston renewal is necessary (Chapter 2).
- ☐ Cylinder head gasket damaged. If a head is allowed to become loose, or if excessive carbon build-up on the piston crown and combustion chamber causes extremely high compression, the head gasket may leak. Retorquing the head is not always sufficient to restore the seal, so a new gasket is necessary (Chapter 2).
- ☐ Cylinder head warped. This is caused by overheating or improperly tightened head bolts. Machine shop resurfacing or head renewal is necessary (Chapter 2).
- ☐ Valve spring broken or weak. Caused by component failure or wear; the springs must be replaced with new ones (Chapter 2).
- ☐ Valve not seating properly. This is caused by a bent valve (from over-revving or improper valve adjustment), burned valve or seat (improper fuelling) or an accumulation of carbon deposits on the seat (from fuelling or lubrication problems). The valves must be cleaned and/or renewed and the seats serviced (Chapter 2).

Knocking or pinking

- ☐ Carbon build-up in combustion chamber. Use of a fuel additive that will dissolve the adhesive bonding the carbon particles to the piston crown and chamber is the easiest way to remove the build-up. Otherwise, the cylinder head will have to be removed and decarbonised (Chapter 2).
- ☐ Incorrect or poor quality fuel. Old or improper grades of fuel can cause detonation. This causes the piston to rattle, thus the knocking or pinking sound. Drain old fuel and always use the recommended fuel grade.
- ☐ Spark plug heat range incorrect. Uncontrolled detonation indicates the plug heat range is too hot. The plug in effect becomes a glow plug, raising cylinder temperatures. Install the proper heat range plug (Chapter 1).
- ☐ Improper air/fuel mixture. This will cause the cylinder to run hot, which leads to detonation. A blockage in the fuel system or an air leak can cause this imbalance (see Chapter 4).

Miscellaneous causes

- ☐ Throttle valve doesn't open fully. Adjust the throttle twistgrip freeplay (see Chapter 1).
- ☐ Clutch slipping due to loose or worn clutch components (see Chapter 2).
- ☐ Timing not advancing. The crankshaft position sensor (CKP) or the electronic control unit (ECU) may be defective (see Chapter 4). If so, they must be replaced with new ones.
- ☐ Engine oil viscosity too high. Using a heavier oil than the one recommended in Chapter 1 can damage the oil pump or lubrication system and cause drag on the engine.
- ☐ Brakes dragging. Usually caused by debris which has entered the brake caliper piston seals, or from a warped disc or bent axle (see Chapter 6).

4 Overheating

Engine overheats

- ☐ Coolant level low. Check and add coolant (see *Pre-ride checks*).
- ☐ Leak in cooling system. Check cooling system hoses and radiator for leaks and other damage. Repair or renew parts as necessary (see Chapter 3).
- ☐ Faulty thermostat. Check and renew as described in Chapter 3.
- ☐ Faulty radiator cap. Remove the cap and have it pressure tested.
- ☐ Coolant passages clogged. Drain, flush and refill with fresh coolant (Chapter 1).
- ☐ Water pump defective. Remove the pump and check the components (see Chapter 3).
- ☐ Clogged or damaged radiator fins (see Chapter 3).
- ☐ Faulty cooling fan, fan relay or ECT sensor (see Chapter 3).

Firing incorrect

- ☐ Spark plug dirty, defective or worn out. Identify reason for fouled plug using spark plug condition chart on the inside back cover and follow the plug maintenance procedures (see Chapter 1).
- ☐ Incorrect spark plug. Wrong type or heat range. Check and install correct plug (see Chapter 1).
- ☐ Ignition coil defective. Test and replace with a new one if necessary (see Chapter 4).
- ☐ Faulty ECU (electronic control unit) (see Chapter 4).

Fuel/air mixture incorrect

- ☐ Fuel tank breather hose obstructed.
- ☐ Fuel pump faulty (see Chapter 4).
- ☐ Fuel hose squashed or restricted at some point. Remove the fuel hose and carefully blow through it.
- ☐ Fuel injector clogged. In some cases, if a machine has been unused for several months, the fuel turns to a varnish-like liquid which can cause the injector needle to stick to its seat. Drain the tank and fuel system (Chapter 4).
- ☐ Intake air leak. Check for loose throttle body-to-intake manifold joints (Chapter 4).
- ☐ Air filter clogged. Clean the air filter element or replace it with a new one (Chapter 1).

Compression too high

Note: *Check by performing a compression test (see Chapter 2).*

- ☐ Carbon build-up in combustion chamber. Use of a fuel additive that will dissolve the adhesive bonding the carbon particles to the piston crown and chamber is the easiest way to remove the build-up. Otherwise, the cylinder head will have to be removed and decarbonised (Chapter 2).
- ☐ Improperly machined head surface or installation of incorrect gasket during engine assembly.

Engine load excessive

- ☐ Clutch slipping due to loose or worn clutch components (see Chapter 2).
- ☐ Engine oil level too high. Too much oil will cause pressurisation of the crankcase and inefficient engine operation. Check Specifications and drain to proper level (Chapter 1 and *Pre-ride checks*).
- ☐ Engine oil viscosity too high. Using a heavier oil than the one recommended in Chapter 1 can damage the oil pump or lubrication system as well as cause drag on the engine.
- ☐ Brakes dragging. Usually caused by debris which has entered the brake caliper piston seals, or from a warped disc or bent axle (see Chapter 6).

Lubrication inadequate

- ☐ Engine oil level too low. Friction caused by intermittent lack of lubrication or from oil that is overworked can cause overheating. The oil provides a definite cooling function in the engine. Check the oil level (see *Pre-ride checks*).
- ☐ Low engine oil pressure. Check the oil delivery (see Chapter 2).
- ☐ Blocked oil filter (see Chapter 1).

Miscellaneous causes

- ☐ Modification to exhaust system. Most aftermarket exhaust systems cause the engine to run leaner, which make them run hotter. When installing an accessory exhaust system, always check with the manufacturer/supplier as to whether the fuel system requires adjustment.

5 Clutch problems

Clutch slipping

- ☐ Insufficient clutch cable freeplay. Check and adjust (see Chapter 1).
- ☐ Clutch plates worn or warped. Overhaul the clutch assembly (see Chapter 2).
- ☐ Clutch springs broken or weak. Old or heat-damaged (from slipping clutch) springs should be renewed (Chapter 2).
- ☐ Faulty clutch release mechanism. Replace any defective parts with new ones (see Chapter 2).
- ☐ Clutch centre or housing unevenly worn. This causes improper engagement of the plates. Replace the damaged or worn parts (see Chapter 2).
- ☐ Incorrect oil used in engine. Oils designed for car engines often contain friction modifiers which if used in an engine with a wet clutch can promote clutch slip. Always use an oil designed for motorcycle engines (see *Pre-ride checks*).

Clutch not disengaging completely

- ☐ Excessive clutch cable freeplay. Check and adjust (see Chapter 1).
- ☐ Clutch plates warped or damaged. This will cause clutch drag, which in turn will cause the machine to creep. Overhaul the clutch assembly (see Chapter 2).
- ☐ Clutch springs fatigued or broken. Check and renew the springs (see Chapter 2).
- ☐ Engine oil deteriorated. Old, thin oil will not provide proper lubrication for the plates, causing the clutch to drag. Renew the oil and filter (see Chapter 1).
- ☐ Engine oil viscosity too high. Using a heavier oil than recommended in Chapter 1 can cause the plates to stick together. Change to the correct weight oil.
- ☐ Clutch housing seized on the transmission input shaft. Lack of lubrication, severe wear or damage can cause the bearing to seize. Overhaul of the clutch, and perhaps transmission, may be necessary to repair the damage (see Chapter 2).
- ☐ Faulty clutch release mechanism. Renew any defective parts (see Chapter 2).
- ☐ Loose clutch centre nut. Causes housing and centre misalignment putting a drag on the engine. Engagement adjustment continually varies. Overhaul the clutch assembly (see Chapter 2).

6 Gearchanging problems

Doesn't go into gear or lever doesn't return

- ☐ Clutch not disengaging (see above).
- ☐ Gearchange mechanism stopper arm spring weak or broken, or arm roller broken or worn. Replace the spring or arm with a new one (see Chapter 2).
- ☐ Wear of selector arm pawls and/or camplate pins (see Chapter 2).
- ☐ Selector fork(s) bent, worn or seized. Overhaul the transmission (see Chapter 2).
- ☐ Gear(s) stuck on shaft. Most often caused by a lack of lubrication or excessive wear in transmission bearings and bushes. Overhaul the transmission (see Chapter 2).
- ☐ Selector drum binding. Caused by lubrication failure or excessive wear. Replace the drum and/or its bearing with a new one (see Chapter 2).
- ☐ Gearchange mechanism centralising spring weak or broken (see Chapter 2).

Jumps out of gear

- ☐ Selector fork(s) worn (see Chapter 2).
- ☐ Selector fork groove(s) in selector drum worn (see Chapter 2).
- ☐ Gear pinion dogs or dog slots worn or damaged. The gear pinions should be inspected and renewed. No attempt should be made to repair the worn parts.

Overselects

- ☐ Gearchange mechanism stopper arm spring weak or broken, or arm roller broken or worn. Renew the spring or arm (see Chapter 2).
- ☐ Gearchange mechanism centralising spring weak or broken (see Chapter 2).

7 Abnormal engine noise

Knocking or pinking

- ☐ Carbon build-up in combustion chamber. Use of a fuel additive that will dissolve the adhesive bonding the carbon particles to the piston crown and chamber is the easiest way to remove the build-up. Otherwise, the cylinder head will have to be removed and decarbonised (Chapter 2).
- ☐ Incorrect or poor quality fuel. Old or improper grades of fuel can cause detonation. This causes the piston to rattle, thus the knocking or pinking sound. Drain old fuel and always use the recommended fuel grade.
- ☐ Spark plug heat range incorrect. Uncontrolled detonation indicates the plug heat range is too hot. The plug in effect becomes a glow plug, raising cylinder temperatures. Install the proper heat range plug (Chapter 1).
- ☐ Improper air/fuel mixture. This will cause the cylinder to run hot, which leads to detonation. A blockage in the fuel system or an air leak can cause this imbalance (see Chapter 4).

Piston slap or rattling

- ☐ Cylinder-to-piston clearance excessive. Cylinder and/or piston worn, usually accompanied by worn rings as well. A top-end overhaul is necessary (see Chapter 2).
- ☐ Piston ring(s) worn, broken or sticking. Overhaul the top-end (see Chapter 2).
- ☐ Piston pin, piston pin bore or connecting rod small-end worn from high mileage or seized due to lack of lubrication (see Chapter 2).
- ☐ Piston seizure damage. Usually from lack of lubrication or overheating. Replace the piston and block, as necessary (see Chapter 2).
- ☐ Connecting rod big-end clearance excessive. Caused by excessive wear or lack of lubrication. Replace worn parts.
- ☐ Connecting rod bent. Caused by over-revving, trying to start a badly flooded engine or from ingesting a foreign object into the combustion chamber. Replace the damaged parts (Chapter 2).

Valve noise

- ☐ Incorrect valve clearances – check and adjust (see Chapter 1).
- ☐ Valve spring broken or weak. Check and replace weak valve springs with new ones (see Chapter 2).
- ☐ Camshaft or camshaft bearings worn or damaged. Lubrication failure at high rpm is usually the cause of damage due to insufficient oil or failure to change the oil at the recommended intervals. Since there are no replaceable bearings in the head, the head itself will have to be replaced with a new one (see Chapter 2).

Other noise

- ☐ Cylinder head gasket leaking. Check around the joint for blowing with the engine running.
- ☐ Exhaust pipe leaking at cylinder head connection. Caused by incorrect fit of pipe(s), loose exhaust flange or damaged gasket. All exhaust system fasteners should be tightened evenly and carefully to avoid leaks (see Chapter 4).
- ☐ Crankshaft runout excessive. Caused by a bent crankshaft (from over-revving) or damage from an upper cylinder component failure. Can also be attributed to dropping the machine on either of the crankshaft ends.
- ☐ Engine mounting bolts loose – ensure all the bolts are tightened to the specified torque settings (see Chapter 2).
- ☐ Crankshaft bearings worn (see Chapter 2).
- ☐ Cam chain rattle, due to worn chain or defective tensioner. Also worn chain tensioner/guide blades (see Chapter 2).

8 Abnormal driveline noise

Clutch noise

- ☐ Clutch housing/friction plate clearance excessive (Chapter 2).
- ☐ Wear between the clutch housing splines and input shaft splines (Chapter 2).
- ☐ Worn release bearing (Chapter 2).

Transmission noise

- ☐ Bearings worn. Also includes the possibility that the shafts are worn. Overhaul the transmission (Chapter 2).
- ☐ Gears worn or chipped (Chapter 2).
- ☐ Metal chips jammed in gear teeth. Probably pieces from a broken clutch, gear or selector mechanism that were picked up by the gears. This will cause early bearing failure (Chapter 2).
- ☐ Engine oil level too low. Causes a howl from transmission. Also affects engine power and clutch operation (*Pre-ride checks*).

Final drive noise

- ☐ Chain not adjusted properly (Chapter 1).
- ☐ Front or rear sprocket loose. Tighten fasteners (Chapter 6).
- ☐ Sprockets and/or chain worn. Fit new sprockets and chain (Chapter 6).
- ☐ Rear sprocket warped. Fit a new sprocket (Chapter 6).

9 Abnormal frame and suspension noise

Front end noise

- ☐ Low fluid level or improper viscosity oil in forks. This can sound like spurting and is usually accompanied by irregular fork action (Chapter 5).
- ☐ Spring weak or broken. Makes a clicking or scraping sound. Fork oil, when drained, will have a lot of metal particles in it (Chapter 5).
- ☐ Steering head bearings loose or damaged. Clicks when braking. Check and adjust or replace with new ones as necessary (Chapters 1 and 5).
- ☐ Fork yoke clamp bolts loose – ensure all the bolts are tightened to the specified torque (Chapter 6).
- ☐ Forks bent. Good possibility if machine has been dropped. Replace the inner and outer tubes with new ones as required (Chapter 5).
- ☐ Front axle or axle clamp bolt loose. Tighten them to the specified torque (Chapter 6).
- ☐ Loose or worn wheel bearings. Check and replace with new ones as needed (Chapters 1 and 6).

Rear suspension noise

- ☐ Fluid level incorrect. Indicates a leak caused by defective seal. Shock will be covered with oil. Replace shock with a new one (Chapter 5).
- ☐ Defective shock absorber with internal damage. This is in the body of the shock and can't be remedied. The shock must be replaced with a new one or rebuilt (Chapter 5).
- ☐ Bent or damaged shock body or mounts. Check the mounts. If the shock absorber itself is damaged replace it with a new one (Chapter 5).
- ☐ Loose or worn suspension linkage components. Check and replace with new ones as necessary (Chapter 5).
- ☐ Loose or worn swingarm components. Check and replace with new ones as necessary (Chapter 5).

Brake noise

- ☐ Squeal caused by dust on brake pads. Usually found in combination with glazed pads. Clean using brake cleaning solvent (Chapter 6).
- ☐ Pads glazed. Caused by excessive heat from prolonged hard use or from contamination. DO NOT use sandpaper, emery cloth, carborundum cloth or any other abrasive to roughen the pad surfaces as abrasives will stay in the pad material and damage the disc. A very fine flat file can be used, but new pads is the best remedy (Chapter 6).
- ☐ Contamination of brake pads. Oil or brake fluid can cause the brake pads to chatter or squeal. Fit new pads. Identify the cause of the contamination, especially check the caliper piston seals for leaking fluid. Clean disc thoroughly with brake system cleaner (Chapter 6).
- ☐ Disc warped. Can cause a chattering, clicking or intermittent squeal. Usually accompanied by a pulsating lever and uneven braking. Replace the disc with new one (Chapter 6).
- ☐ Loose or worn wheel bearings. Check and replace with new ones as needed (Chapters 1 and 6).

10 Low oil level or pressure

- ☐ Engine oil level low. Inspect for leak or other problem causing low oil level and add recommended oil (see *Pre-ride checks*).
- ☐ Engine oil pump defective, blocked oil strainer gauze or filter. Carry out an oil delivery check (Chapter 2)
- ☐ Engine oil viscosity too low. Very old, thin oil or an improper weight of oil used in the engine. Change to correct oil (Chapter 1)
- ☐ Excessive engine wear causing drop in oil pressure. Abnormal wear could be caused by oil starvation at high rpm from low oil level or improper weight or type of oil (Chapter 1)

11 Excessive exhaust smoke

White smoke

- ☐ Piston rings worn or broken, causing oil from the crankcase to be pulled past the piston into the combustion chamber. Replace the rings with new ones (Chapter 2).
- ☐ Cylinder worn or scored. Caused by overheating or oil starvation. Install a new cylinder block and piston and rings (Chapter 2).
- ☐ Valve stem oil seal damaged or worn. Replace the oil seals with new ones (Chapter 2).
- ☐ Valve guide worn. Perform a complete valve job (Chapter 2).
- ☐ Engine oil level too high, which causes the oil to be forced past the rings. Drain oil to the proper level (see Chapter 1 and *Pre-ride checks*).
- ☐ Head gasket broken between oil return and cylinder. Causes oil to be pulled into the combustion chamber. Replace the head gasket with a new one and check the head for warpage (Chapter 2).
- ☐ Abnormal crankcase pressurisation which forces oil past the rings, usually caused by a clogged breather.

Black smoke

- ☐ Air filter clogged. Clean the air filter element or replace it with a new one (Chapter 1).
- ☐ Fuel injection system malfunction (Chapter 4).

Brown smoke

- ☐ Air filter poorly sealed or not installed (Chapter 1).
- ☐ Fuel injection system malfunction (Chapter 4).

12 Poor handling or stability

Handlebars hard to turn

- ☐ Steering head bearing adjuster nut too tight. Check adjustment as described in Chapter 1.
- ☐ Bearings damaged. Roughness can be felt as the bars are turned from side-to-side. Replace the bearings with new ones (Chapter 5).
- ☐ Races dented or worn. Denting results from wear in only one position (e.g., straight ahead), from a collision or hitting a pothole or from dropping the machine. Replace the bearings with new ones (Chapter 5).
- ☐ Steering stem lubrication inadequate. Causes are grease getting hard from age or being washed out by high pressure car washes. Disassemble steering head and repack bearings (Chapter 5).
- ☐ Steering stem bent. Caused by a collision, hitting a pothole or by dropping the machine. Replace damaged part. Don't try to straighten the steering stem (Chapter 5).
- ☐ Front tyre air pressure too low (*Pre-ride checks*).

Handlebar shakes or vibrates excessively

- ☐ Tyres worn or out of balance (Chapter 6).
- ☐ Swingarm bearings worn. Replace the bearings with new ones (Chapter 5).
- ☐ Wheel rim(s) warped or damaged. Inspect wheels for runout (Chapter 6).
- ☐ Wheel bearings worn. Worn front or rear wheel bearings can cause poor tracking. Worn front bearings will cause wobble (Chapters 1 and 6).
- ☐ Fork yoke clamp bolts or handlebar clamp bolts loose. Tighten them to the specified torque (Chapter 5).
- ☐ Engine mounting bolts loose. Will cause excessive vibration with increased engine rpm – ensure all the bolts are tightened to the specified torque settings (see Chapter 2).

Machine pulls to one side

- ☐ Frame bent. Definitely suspect this if the machine has been dropped. May or may not be accompanied by cracking near the steering head, swingarm mountings or engine mountings. Replace the frame with a new one (Chapter 5).
- ☐ Wheels out of alignment. Caused by improper location of axle spacers or from bent steering stem or frame (Chapter 5).
- ☐ Forks bent. Disassemble the forks and replace the damaged parts (Chapter 5).
- ☐ Swingarm bent or twisted. Replace the arm with a new one (Chapter 5).
- ☐ Fork oil level uneven. Check and add or drain as necessary (Chapter 5).

Poor shock absorbing qualities

- ☐ Too hard:
  - a) Fork oil level too high (Chapter 5).
  - b) Fork oil viscosity too high. Use a lighter oil (see the Specifications in Chapter 5).
  - c) Fork tube bent. Causes a harsh, sticking feeling (Chapter 5).
  - d) Fork internal damage (Chapter 5).
  - e) Shock shaft or body bent or damaged (Chapter 5).
  - f) Shock internal damage (Chapter 5).
  - g) Suspension linkage or swingarm bearings corroded or seized (Chapter 5).
  - h) Tyre pressure too high (*Pre-ride checks*).
- ☐ Too soft:
  - a) Fork oil level too low (Chapter 5).
  - b) Fork oil viscosity too light (Chapter 5).
  - c) Fork springs weak or broken (Chapter 5).
  - d) Fork or shock oil leaking (Chapter 5).
  - e) Shock internal damage (Chapter 5).

13 Braking problems

Brakes are spongy, don't hold

- ☐ Low brake fluid level (see *Pre-ride checks*).
- ☐ Air in hydraulic system. Caused by inattention to master cylinder fluid level or by leakage. Locate problem and bleed brakes (Chapter 6).
- ☐ Pad or disc worn (Chapters 1 and 6).
- ☐ Contaminated pads. Caused by contamination with oil, grease, brake fluid, etc. Fit new pads. Identify the cause of the contamination, especially check the caliper piston seals for leaking fluid. Clean disc thoroughly with brake system cleaner (Chapter 6).
- ☐ Brake fluid deteriorated. Fluid is old or contaminated. Drain system, replenish with new fluid and bleed the system (Chapter 6).
- ☐ Master cylinder internal seals worn or damaged causing fluid to bypass (Chapter 6).
- ☐ Master cylinder bore scratched by foreign material or broken spring. Fit a new master cylinder (Chapter 6).
- ☐ Disc warped. Replace disc with new one (Chapter 6).

Brake lever or pedal pulsates

- ☐ Disc warped. Replace disc with new one (Chapter 6).
- ☐ Axle bent. Replace axle with new one (Chapter 6).
- ☐ Brake caliper bolts loose – tighten the bolts to the specified torque (Chapter 6).
- ☐ Wheel warped or otherwise damaged (Chapter 6).
- ☐ Wheel bearings damaged or worn (Chapters 1 and 6).
- ☐ Fault in ABS, where fitted (Chapter 6).

Brakes drag

- ☐ Master cylinder piston seized. Caused by wear or damage to piston or cylinder bore (Chapter 6).
- ☐ Lever or pedal balky or stuck. Check pivot and lubricate (Chapter 5).
- ☐ Brake caliper piston seized in bore. Caused by corrosion or ingestion of dirt past deteriorated seal (Chapter 6).
- ☐ Caliper sticking on slider pins due to corrosion (front caliper on WR models, rear caliper on all models). Clean and lubricate pins and check dust boots (Chapter 6).
- ☐ Brake pad damaged. Pad material separated from backing plate. Usually caused by faulty manufacturing process or from contact with chemicals. Fit new pads (Chapter 6).
- ☐ Pads improperly installed (Chapter 6).
- ☐ Brake caliper incorrectly installed (Chapter 6).

14 Electrical problems

Battery dead or weak

- ☐ Battery faulty. Caused by sulphated plates which are shorted through sedimentation. Confirm by terminal voltage check (Chapter 8).
- ☐ Broken battery terminal making only occasional contact.
- ☐ Battery electrolyte level low. Top up (Chapter 1).
- ☐ Battery leads making poor contact (Chapter 8).
- ☐ Load excessive. Caused by addition of high wattage lights or other electrical accessories.
- ☐ Ignition switch defective. Switch either grounds (earths) internally or fails to shut off system. Renew the switch (Chapter 8).
- ☐ Regulator/rectifier defective (Chapter 8).
- ☐ Alternator stator coil open or shorted (Chapter 8).
- ☐ Charging system fault. Check for excessive current leakage (Chapter 8).
- ☐ Wiring faulty. Wiring grounded (earthed) or connections loose in ignition, charging or lighting circuits (Chapter 8).

Battery overcharged

- ☐ Regulator/rectifier defective. Overcharging is noticed when battery gets excessively warm (Chapter 8).
- ☐ Battery faulty. Confirm with battery terminal voltage check (Chapter 8).
- ☐ Battery amperage too low, wrong type or size of battery. Install manufacturer's specified amp-hour battery to handle charging load (Chapter 8).

A

ABS (Anti-lock braking system) A system, usually electronically controlled, that senses incipient wheel lockup during braking and relieves hydraulic pressure at wheel which is about to skid.
Aftermarket Components suitable for the motorcycle, but not produced by the motorcycle manufacturer.
Allen key A hexagonal wrench which fits into a recessed hexagonal hole.
Alternating current (ac) Current produced by an alternator. Requires converting to direct current by a rectifier for charging purposes.
Alternator Converts mechanical energy from the engine into electrical energy to charge the battery and power the electrical system.
Ampere (amp) A unit of measurement for the flow of electrical current. Current = Volts ÷ Ohms.
Ampere-hour (Ah) Measure of battery capacity.
Angle-tightening A torque expressed in degrees. Often follows a conventional tightening torque for cylinder head or main bearing fasteners **(see illustration)**.

Angle-tightening con-rod bolts

Antifreeze A substance (usually ethylene glycol) mixed with water, and added to the cooling system, to prevent freezing of the coolant in winter. Antifreeze also contains chemicals to inhibit corrosion and the formation of rust and other deposits that would tend to clog the radiator and coolant passages and reduce cooling efficiency.
Anti-dive System attached to the fork lower leg (slider) to prevent fork dive when braking hard.
Anti-seize compound A coating that reduces the risk of seizing on fasteners that are subjected to high temperatures, such as exhaust clamp bolts and nuts.
API American Petroleum Institute. A quality standard for 4-stroke motor oils.
Asbestos A natural fibrous mineral with great heat resistance, commonly used in the composition of brake friction materials. Asbestos is a health hazard and the dust created by brake systems should never be inhaled or ingested.
ATF Automatic Transmission Fluid. Often used in front forks.
ATU Automatic Timing Unit. Mechanical device for advancing the ignition timing on early engines.
ATV All Terrain Vehicle. Often called a Quad.
Axial play Side-to-side movement.
Axle A shaft on which a wheel revolves. Also known as a spindle.

B

Backlash The amount of movement between meshed components when one component is held still. Usually applies to gear teeth.
Ball bearing A bearing consisting of a hardened inner and outer race with hardened steel balls between the two races.
Bearings Used between two working surfaces to prevent wear of the components and a build-up of heat. Four types of bearing are commonly used on motorcycles: plain shell bearings, ball bearings, tapered roller bearings and needle roller bearings.
Bevel gears Used to turn the drive through 90°. Typical applications are shaft final drive and camshaft drive **(see illustration)**.

Bevel gears are used to turn the drive through 90°

BHP Brake Horsepower. The British measurement for engine power output. Power output is now usually expressed in kilowatts (kW).
Bias-belted tyre Similar construction to radial tyre, but with outer belt running at an angle to the wheel rim.
Big-end bearing The bearing in the end of the connecting rod that's attached to the crankshaft.
Bleeding The process of removing air from an hydraulic system via a bleed nipple or bleed screw.
Bottom-end A description of an engine's crankcase components and all components contained there-in.
BTDC Before Top Dead Centre in terms of piston position. Ignition timing is often expressed in terms of degrees or millimetres BTDC.
Bush A cylindrical metal or rubber component used between two moving parts.
Burr Rough edge left on a component after machining or as a result of excessive wear.

C

Cam chain The chain which takes drive from the crankshaft to the camshaft(s).
Canister The main component in an evaporative emission control system (California market only); contains activated charcoal granules to trap vapours from the fuel system rather than allowing them to vent to the atmosphere.
Castellated Resembling the parapets along the top of a castle wall. For example, a castellated wheel axle or spindle nut.
Catalytic converter A device in the exhaust system of some machines which converts certain pollutants in the exhaust gases into less harmful substances.
Charging system Description of the components which charge the battery, ie the alternator, rectifer and regulator.
Circlip A ring-shaped clip used to prevent endwise movement of cylindrical parts and shafts. An internal circlip is installed in a groove in a housing; an external circlip fits into a groove on the outside of a cylindrical piece such as a shaft. Also known as a snap-ring.
Clearance The amount of space between two parts. For example, between a piston and a cylinder, between a bearing and a journal, etc.
Coil spring A spiral of elastic steel found in various sizes throughout a vehicle, for example as a springing medium in the suspension and in the valve train.
Compression Reduction in volume, and increase in pressure and temperature, of a gas, caused by squeezing it into a smaller space.
Compression damping Controls the speed the suspension compresses when hitting a bump.
Compression ratio The relationship between cylinder volume when the piston is at top dead centre and cylinder volume when the piston is at bottom dead centre.
Continuity The uninterrupted path in the flow of electricity. Little or no measurable resistance.
Continuity tester Self-powered bleeper or test light which indicates continuity.
Cp Candlepower. Bulb rating commonly found on US motorcycles.
Crossply tyre Tyre plies arranged in a criss-cross pattern. Usually four or six plies used, hence 4PR or 6PR in tyre size codes.
Cush drive Rubber damper segments fitted between the rear wheel and final drive sprocket to absorb transmission shocks **(see illustration)**.

Cush drive rubbers dampen out transmission shocks

D

Decarbonisation The process of removing carbon deposits - typically from the combustion chamber, valves and exhaust port/system.
Degree disc Calibrated disc for measuring piston position. Expressed in degrees.
Detonation Destructive and damaging explosion of fuel/air mixture in combustion chamber instead of controlled burning.
Dial gauge Clock-type gauge with adapters for measuring runout and piston position. Expressed in mm or inches.

Diaphragm The rubber membrane in a master cylinder or carburettor which seals the upper chamber.

Diaphragm spring A single sprung plate often used in clutches.

Direct current (dc) Current produced by a dc generator.

Diode An electrical valve which only allows current to flow in one direction. Commonly used in rectifiers and starter interlock systems.

Disc valve (or rotary valve) A induction system used on some two-stroke engines.

Double-overhead camshaft (DOHC) An engine that uses two overhead camshafts, one for the intake valves and one for the exhaust valves.

Drivebelt A toothed belt used to transmit drive to the rear wheel on some motorcycles. A drivebelt has also been used to drive the camshafts. Drivebelts are usually made of Kevlar.

Driveshaft Any shaft used to transmit motion. Commonly used when referring to the final driveshaft on shaft drive motorcycles.

E

Earth return The return path of an electrical circuit, utilising the motorcycle's frame.

ECU (Electronic Control Unit) A computer which controls (for instance) an ignition system, or an anti-lock braking system.

EGO Exhaust Gas Oxygen sensor. Sometimes called a Lambda sensor.

Electrolyte The fluid in a lead-acid battery.

EMS (Engine Management System) A computer controlled system which manages the fuel injection and the ignition systems in an integrated fashion.

Endfloat The amount of lengthways movement between two parts. As applied to a crankshaft, the distance that the crankshaft can move side-to-side in the crankcase.

Endless chain A chain having no joining link. Common use for cam chains and final drive chains.

EP (Extreme Pressure) Oil type used in locations where high loads are applied, such as between gear teeth.

Evaporative emission control system Describes a charcoal filled canister which stores fuel vapours from the tank rather than allowing them to vent to the atmosphere. Usually only fitted to California models and referred to as an EVAP system.

Expansion chamber Section of two-stroke engine exhaust system so designed to improve engine efficiency and boost power.

F

Feeler blade or gauge A thin strip or blade of hardened steel, ground to an exact thickness, used to check or measure clearances between parts.

Final drive Description of the drive from the transmission to the rear wheel. Usually by chain or shaft, but sometimes by belt.

Firing order The order in which the engine cylinders fire, or deliver their power strokes, beginning with the number one cylinder.

Flooding Term used to describe a high fuel level in the carburettor float chambers, leading to fuel overflow. Also refers to excess fuel in the combustion chamber due to incorrect starting technique.

Free length The no-load state of a component when measured. Clutch, valve and fork spring lengths are measured at rest, without any preload.

Freeplay The amount of travel before any action takes place. The looseness in a linkage, or an assembly of parts, between the initial application of force and actual movement. For example, the distance the rear brake pedal moves before the rear brake is actuated.

Fuel injection The fuel/air mixture is metered electronically and directed into the engine intake ports (indirect injection) or into the cylinders (direct injection). Sensors supply information on engine speed and conditions.

Fuel/air mixture The charge of fuel and air going into the engine. See Stoichiometric ratio.

Fuse An electrical device which protects a circuit against accidental overload. The typical fuse contains a soft piece of metal which is calibrated to melt at a predetermined current flow (expressed as amps) and break the circuit.

G

Gap The distance the spark must travel in jumping from the centre electrode to the side electrode in a spark plug. Also refers to the distance between the ignition rotor and the pickup coil in an electronic ignition system.

Gasket Any thin, soft material - usually cork, cardboard, asbestos or soft metal - installed between two metal surfaces to ensure a good seal. For instance, the cylinder head gasket seals the joint between the block and the cylinder head.

Gauge An instrument panel display used to monitor engine conditions. A gauge with a movable pointer on a dial or a fixed scale is an analogue gauge. A gauge with a numerical readout is called a digital gauge.

Gear ratios The drive ratio of a pair of gears in a gearbox, calculated on their number of teeth.

Glaze-busting see **Honing**

Grinding Process for renovating the valve face and valve seat contact area in the cylinder head.

Gudgeon pin The shaft which connects the connecting rod small-end with the piston. Often called a piston pin or wrist pin.

H

Helical gears Gear teeth are slightly curved and produce less gear noise that straight-cut gears. Often used for primary drives.

Helicoil A thread insert repair system. Commonly used as a repair for stripped spark plug threads **(see illustration)**.

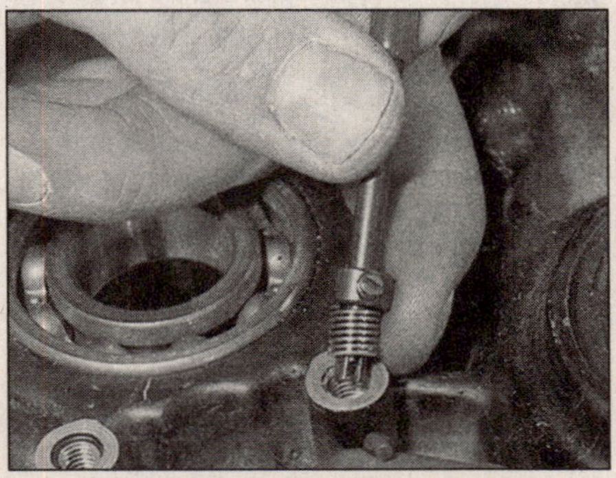

Installing a Helicoil thread insert

Honing A process used to break down the glaze on a cylinder bore (also called glaze-busting). Can also be carried out to roughen a rebored cylinder to aid ring bedding-in.

HT (High Tension) Description of the electrical circuit from the secondary winding of the ignition coil to the spark plug.

Hydraulic A liquid filled system used to transmit pressure from one component to another. Common uses on motorcycles are brakes and clutches.

Hydrometer An instrument for measuring the specific gravity of a lead-acid battery.

Hygroscopic Water absorbing. In motorcycle applications, braking efficiency will be reduced if DOT 3 or 4 hydraulic fluid absorbs water from the air - care must be taken to keep new brake fluid in tightly sealed containers.

I

lbf ft Pounds-force feet. An imperial unit of torque. Sometimes written as ft-lbs.

lbf in Pound-force inch. An imperial unit of torque, applied to components where a very low torque is required. Sometimes written as in-lbs.

IC Abbreviation for Integrated Circuit.

Ignition advance Means of increasing the timing of the spark at higher engine speeds. Done by mechanical means (ATU) on early engines or electronically by the ignition control unit on later engines.

Ignition timing The moment at which the spark plug fires, expressed in the number of crankshaft degrees before the piston reaches the top of its stroke, or in the number of millimetres before the piston reaches the top of its stroke.

Infinity (∞) Description of an open-circuit electrical state, where no continuity exists.

Inverted forks (upside down forks) The sliders or lower legs are held in the yokes and the fork tubes or stanchions are connected to the wheel axle (spindle). Less unsprung weight and stiffer construction than conventional forks.

J

JASO Quality standard for 2-stroke oils.

Joule The unit of electrical energy.

Journal The bearing surface of a shaft.

K

Kickstart Mechanical means of turning the engine over for starting purposes. Only usually fitted to mopeds, small capacity motorcycles and off-road motorcycles.

Kill switch Handebar-mounted switch for emergency ignition cut-out. Cuts the ignition circuit on all models, and additionally prevent starter motor operation on others.

km Symbol for kilometre.

kmh Abbreviation for kilometres per hour.

L

Lambda (λ) sensor A sensor fitted in the exhaust system to measure the exhaust gas oxygen content (excess air factor).

Lapping see Grinding.
LCD Abbreviation for Liquid Crystal Display.
LED Abbreviation for Light Emitting Diode.
Liner A steel cylinder liner inserted in a aluminium alloy cylinder block.
Locknut A nut used to lock an adjustment nut, or other threaded component, in place.
Lockstops The lugs on the lower triple clamp (yoke) which abut those on the frame, preventing handlebar-to-fuel tank contact.
Lockwasher A form of washer designed to prevent an attaching nut from working loose.
LT Low Tension Description of the electrical circuit from the power supply to the primary winding of the ignition coil.

M

Main bearings The bearings between the crankshaft and crankcase.
Maintenance-free (MF) battery A sealed battery which cannot be topped up.
Manometer Mercury-filled calibrated tubes used to measure intake tract vacuum. Used to synchronise carburettors on multi-cylinder engines.
Micrometer A precision measuring instrument that measures component outside diameters **(see illustration)**.

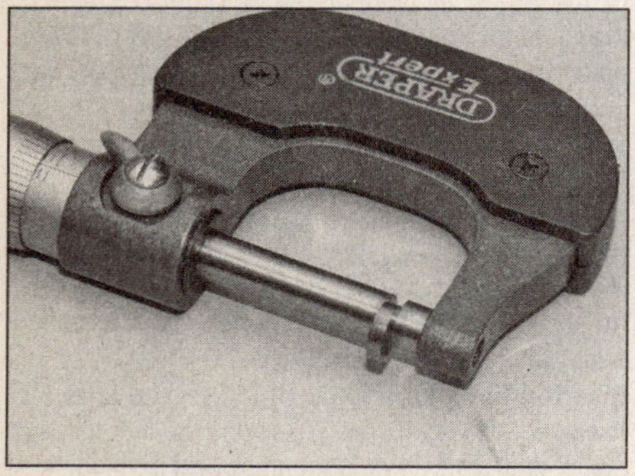

Tappet shims are measured with a micrometer

MON (Motor Octane Number) A measure of a fuel's resistance to knock.
Monograde oil An oil with a single viscosity, eg SAE80W.
Monoshock A single suspension unit linking the swingarm or suspension linkage to the frame.
mph Abbreviation for miles per hour.
Multigrade oil Having a wide viscosity range (eg 10W40). The W stands for Winter, thus the viscosity ranges from SAE10 when cold to SAE40 when hot.
Multimeter An electrical test instrument with the capability to measure voltage, current and resistance. Some meters also incorporate a continuity tester and buzzer.

N

Needle roller bearing Inner race of caged needle rollers and hardened outer race. Examples of uncaged needle rollers can be found on some engines. Commonly used in rear suspension applications and in two-stroke engines.
Nm Newton metres.
NOx Oxides of Nitrogen. A common toxic pollutant emitted by petrol engines at higher temperatures.

O

Octane The measure of a fuel's resistance to knock.
OE (Original Equipment) Relates to components fitted to a motorcycle as standard or replacement parts supplied by the motorcycle manufacturer.
Ohm The unit of electrical resistance. Ohms = Volts ÷ Current.
Ohmmeter An instrument for measuring electrical resistance.
Oil cooler System for diverting engine oil outside of the engine to a radiator for cooling purposes.
Oil injection A system of two-stroke engine lubrication where oil is pump-fed to the engine in accordance with throttle position.
Open-circuit An electrical condition where there is a break in the flow of electricity - no continuity (high resistance).
O-ring A type of sealing ring made of a special rubber-like material; in use, the O-ring is compressed into a groove to provide the sealing action.
Oversize (OS) Term used for piston and ring size options fitted to a rebored cylinder.
Overhead cam (sohc) engine An engine with single camshaft located on top of the cylinder head.
Overhead valve (ohv) engine An engine with the valves located in the cylinder head, but with the camshaft located in the engine block or crankcase.
Oxygen sensor A device installed in the exhaust system which senses the oxygen content in the exhaust and converts this information into an electric current. Also called a Lambda sensor.

P

Plastigauge A thin strip of plastic thread, available in different sizes, used for measuring clearances. For example, a strip of Plastigauge is laid across a bearing journal. The parts are assembled and dismantled; the width of the crushed strip indicates the clearance between journal and bearing.
Polarity Either negative or positive earth (ground), determined by which battery lead is connected to the frame (earth return). Modern motorcycles are usually negative earth.
Pre-ignition A situation where the fuel/air mixture ignites before the spark plug fires. Often due to a hot spot in the combustion chamber caused by carbon build-up. Engine has a tendency to 'run-on'.
Pre-load (suspension) The amount a spring is compressed when in the unloaded state. Preload can be applied by gas, spacer or mechanical adjuster.
Premix The method of engine lubrication on older two-stroke engines. Engine oil is mixed with the petrol in the fuel tank in a specific ratio. The fuel/oil mix is sometimes referred to as "petroil".
Primary drive Description of the drive from the crankshaft to the clutch. Usually by gear or chain.
PS Pfedestärke - a German interpretation of BHP.
PSI Pounds-force per square inch. Imperial measurement of tyre pressure and cylinder pressure measurement.
PTFE Polytetrafluroethylene. A low friction substance.
Pulse secondary air injection system A process of promoting the burning of excess fuel present in the exhaust gases by routing fresh air into the exhaust ports.

Q

Quartz halogen bulb Tungsten filament surrounded by a halogen gas. Typically used for the headlight **(see illustration)**.

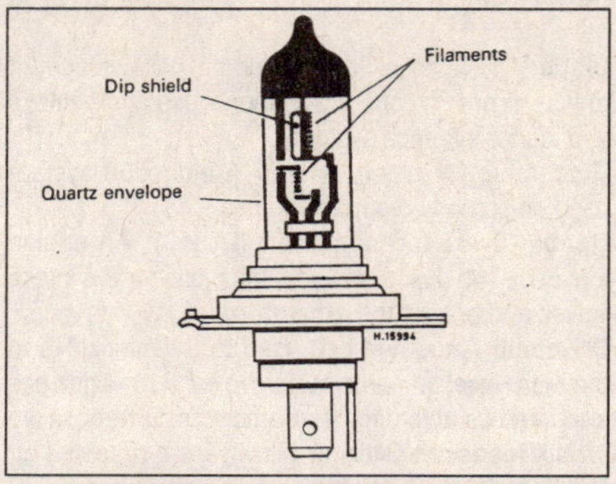

Quartz halogen headlight bulb construction

R

Rack-and-pinion A pinion gear on the end of a shaft that mates with a rack (think of a geared wheel opened up and laid flat). Sometimes used in clutch operating systems.
Radial play Up and down movement about a shaft.
Radial ply tyres Tyre plies run across the tyre (from bead to bead) and around the circumference of the tyre. Less resistant to tread distortion than other tyre types.
Radiator A liquid-to-air heat transfer device designed to reduce the temperature of the coolant in a liquid cooled engine.
Rake A feature of steering geometry - the angle of the steering head in relation to the vertical **(see illustration)**.

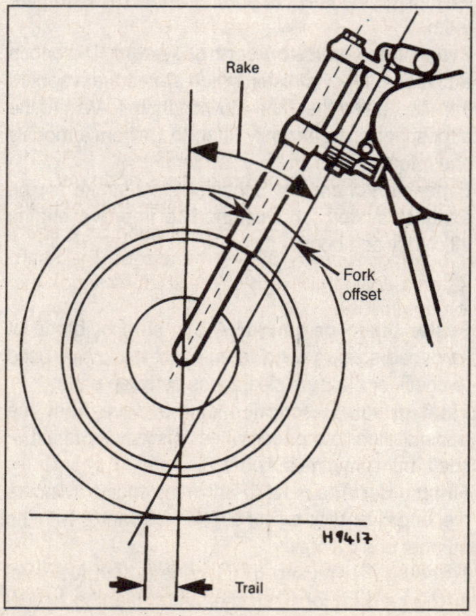

Steering geometry

Rebore Providing a new working surface to the cylinder bore by boring out the old surface. Necessitates the use of oversize piston and rings.

Rebound damping A means of controlling the oscillation of a suspension unit spring after it has been compressed. Resists the spring's natural tendency to bounce back after being compressed.

Rectifier Device for converting the ac output of an alternator into dc for battery charging.

Reed valve An induction system commonly used on two-stroke engines.

Regulator Device for maintaining the charging voltage from the generator or alternator within a specified range.

Relay A electrical device used to switch heavy current on and off by using a low current auxiliary circuit.

Resistance Measured in ohms. An electrical component's ability to pass electrical current.

RON (Research Octane Number) A measure of a fuel's resistance to knock.

rpm revolutions per minute.

Runout The amount of wobble (in-and-out movement) of a wheel or shaft as it's rotated. The amount a shaft rotates 'out-of-true'. The out-of-round condition of a rotating part.

S

SAE (Society of Automotive Engineers) A standard for the viscosity of a fluid.

Sealant A liquid or paste used to prevent leakage at a joint. Sometimes used in conjunction with a gasket.

Service limit Term for the point where a component is no longer useable and must be renewed.

Shaft drive A method of transmitting drive from the transmission to the rear wheel.

Shell bearings Plain bearings consisting of two shell halves. Most often used as big-end and main bearings in a four-stroke engine. Often called bearing inserts.

Shim Thin spacer, commonly used to adjust the clearance or relative positions between two parts. For example, shims inserted into or under tappets or followers to control valve clearances. Clearance is adjusted by changing the thickness of the shim.

Short-circuit An electrical condition where current shorts to earth (ground) bypassing the circuit components.

Skimming Process to correct warpage or repair a damaged surface, eg on brake discs or drums.

Slide-hammer A special puller that screws into or hooks onto a component such as a shaft or bearing; a heavy sliding handle on the shaft bottoms against the end of the shaft to knock the component free.

Small-end bearing The bearing in the upper end of the connecting rod at its joint with the gudgeon pin.

Spalling Damage to camshaft lobes or bearing journals shown as pitting of the working surface.

Specific gravity (SG) The state of charge of the electrolyte in a lead-acid battery. A measure of the electrolyte's density compared with water.

Straight-cut gears Common type gear used on gearbox shafts and for oil pump and water pump drives.

Stanchion The inner sliding part of the front forks, held by the yokes. Often called a fork tube.

Stoichiometric ratio The optimum chemical air/fuel ratio for a petrol engine, said to be 14.7 parts of air to 1 part of fuel.

Sulphuric acid The liquid (electrolyte) used in a lead-acid battery. Poisonous and extremely corrosive.

Surface grinding (lapping) Process to correct a warped gasket face, commonly used on cylinder heads.

T

Tapered-roller bearing Tapered inner race of caged needle rollers and separate tapered outer race. Examples of taper roller bearings can be found on steering heads.

Tappet A cylindrical component which transmits motion from the cam to the valve stem, either directly or via a pushrod and rocker arm. Also called a cam follower.

TCS Traction Control System. An electronically-controlled system which senses wheel spin and reduces engine speed accordingly.

TDC Top Dead Centre denotes that the piston is at its highest point in the cylinder.

Thread-locking compound Solution applied to fastener threads to prevent slackening. Select type to suit application.

Thrust washer A washer positioned between two moving components on a shaft. For example, between gear pinions on gearshaft.

Timing chain See **Cam Chain**.

Timing light Stroboscopic lamp for carrying out ignition timing checks with the engine running.

Top-end A description of an engine's cylinder block, head and valve gear components.

Torque Turning or twisting force about a shaft.

Torque setting A prescribed tightness specified by the motorcycle manufacturer to ensure that the bolt or nut is secured correctly. Undertightening can result in the bolt or nut coming loose or a surface not being sealed. Overtightening can result in stripped threads, distortion or damage to the component being retained.

Torx key A six-point wrench.

Tracer A stripe of a second colour applied to a wire insulator to distinguish that wire from another one with the same colour insulator. For example, Br/W is often used to denote a brown insulator with a white tracer.

Trail A feature of steering geometry. Distance from the steering head axis to the tyre's central contact point.

Triple clamps The cast components which extend from the steering head and support the fork stanchions or tubes. Often called fork yokes.

Turbocharger A centrifugal device, driven by exhaust gases, that pressurises the intake air. Normally used to increase the power output from a given engine displacement.

TWI Abbreviation for Tyre Wear Indicator. Indicates the location of the tread depth indicator bars on tyres.

U

Universal joint or U-joint (UJ) A double-pivoted connection for transmitting power from a driving to a driven shaft through an angle. Typically found in shaft drive assemblies.

Unsprung weight Anything not supported by the bike's suspension (ie the wheel, tyres, brakes, final drive and bottom (moving) part of the suspension).

V

Vacuum gauges Clock-type gauges for measuring intake tract vacuum. Used for carburettor synchronisation on multi-cylinder engines.

Valve A device through which the flow of liquid, gas or vacuum may be stopped, started or regulated by a moveable part that opens, shuts or partially obstructs one or more ports or passageways. The intake and exhaust valves in the cylinder head are of the poppet type.

Valve clearance The clearance between the valve tip (the end of the valve stem) and the rocker arm or tappet/follower. The valve clearance is measured when the valve is closed. The correct clearance is important - if too small the valve won't close fully and will burn out, whereas if too large noisy operation will result.

Valve lift The amount a valve is lifted off its seat by the camshaft lobe.

Valve timing The exact setting for the opening and closing of the valves in relation to piston position.

Vernier caliper A precision measuring instrument that measures inside and outside dimensions. Not quite as accurate as a micrometer, but more convenient.

Wet liner arrangement

VIN Vehicle Identification Number. Term for the bike's engine and frame numbers.

Viscosity The thickness of a liquid or its resistance to flow.

Volt A unit for expressing electrical "pressure" in a circuit. Volts = current x ohms.

W

Water pump A mechanically-driven device for moving coolant around the engine.

Watt A unit for expressing electrical power. Watts = volts x current.

Wear limit see **Service limit**

Wet liner A liquid-cooled engine design where the pistons run in liners which are directly surrounded by coolant **(see illustration)**.

Wheelbase Distance from the centre of the front wheel to the centre of the rear wheel.

Wiring harness or loom Describes the electrical wires running the length of the motorcycle and enclosed in tape or plastic sheathing. Wiring coming off the main harness is usually referred to as a sub harness.

Woodruff key A key of semi-circular or square section used to locate a gear to a shaft. Often used to locate the alternator rotor on the crankshaft.

Wrist pin Another name for gudgeon or piston pin.

Note: *References throughout this index are in the form - "Chapter number" • "Page number"*

Note: *References throughout this index are in the form - "Chapter number" • "Page number"*

Note: *References throughout this index are in the form - "Chapter number" • "Page number"*